History of the Town of Gloucester, Cape Ann

by John James Babson

Address:
HardPress
8345 NW 66TH ST #2561
MIAMI FL 33166-2626
USA
Email: info@hardpress.net

HISTORY

OF THE

TOWN OF GLOUCESTER,

Cape Ann,

INCLUDING THE TOWN OF ROCKPORT.

BY JOHN J. BABSON.

GLOUCESTER:
PUBLISHED BY PROCTER BROTHERS.
1860.

BOSTON:

PRINTED BY JOHN WILSON AND SON,

22, School Street.

PREFACE.

THE first suggestion that a HISTORY OF GLOUCESTER should be written came from the late Dr. Ebenezer Dale, in a lecture delivered before the Gloucester Lyceum about thirty years ago. In a contemporary notice of the lecture, he is reported to have urged the immediate attention of the Lyceum to the subject. His earnest appeal met with a quick response from one of the members of the institution, — the late Hon. William Ferson, — who engaged in the work with so much zeal and intelligence, that a speedy satisfaction of all reasonable wishes seemed about to be realized. But this citizen, who was not often driven by slight causes to abandon a work once begun, was somewhat appalled by the magnitude of the task he had undertaken, and finally felt himself compelled to relinquish this labor of love for employment that would yield a pecuniary reward. The collections he had made, consisting chiefly of extracts from the Town and Colony Records, were accordingly laid aside, and remained undisturbed, till, with his usual kindness, he submitted them to my inspection, to aid me in a genealogical research concerning the persons bearing my own family name. In looking over these papers, I first felt the force of Dr. Dale's appeal, and became convinced that it was the duty of some one to gather up such materials for a history of the town as the lapse of time had left accessible, and put our annals in print for the instruction and gratification of the present and future generations of the people of Cape Ann. The task seemed to me an inviting one, and I resolved to undertake it; not, however, without serious misgivings as to several disqualifying circumstances, not the least of which was the large demand of a laborious and responsible business occupation upon my time.

The result of my labor appears in the following pages; and nothing remains for me to add here but to express my warmest thanks to all who have rendered me assistance in the preparation of the work, and to offer it as a humble memorial of my interest in my native town.

J. J. B.

CONTENTS.

Chapter XXV.

Chapter XXVI.

Chapter XXVII.

Chapter XXVIII.

Chapter XXIX.

CHAPTER XXX.

CHAPTER XXXI.

CHAPTER XXXII.

CHAPTER XXXIII.

APPENDIX.

HISTORY OF GLOUCESTER.

CHAPTER I.

TOPOGRAPHICAL DESCRIPTION.

HARBORS. — COVES. — SOIL. — HILLS. — ROCKING STONES. — THE MAGNOLIA. — THE CUT. — PONDS. — ISLANDS. — NORMAN'S WOE.

THE territory of the original town of Gloucester occupies the whole northern promontory of Massachusetts Bay known as Cape Ann, and is bounded on the north by Ipswich Bay, on the east by the Atlantic Ocean, on the south by Massachusetts Bay, and on the west by the towns of Manchester and Essex. It is divided into two nearly equal parts by Annisquam River, an arm of the sea extending from Ipswich Bay, first in a south-westerly and then in a south-easterly direction, about four miles towards Gloucester Harbor, from which it is separated by a short and narrow neck of land. The territory varies but little in length, the greatest being about nine miles; which is from the corner bounds of Manchester and Essex, where these join each other, to Straitsmouth, on the easterly side of the Cape. Its greatest width is from Twopenny Loaf, near the mouth of Chebacco River, to Eastern Point; and is about six miles. The narrowest part, between Ipswich Bay and Massachusetts Bay, is a little less than four miles. The principal harbor is on the south side of the town, and is formed by Eastern Point, — a strip of unequal width, extending in a south-westerly direction about three miles, with a rock-bound coast that defies the violence of the surging waves dashing almost constantly against it, and affording within its friendly embrace safe shelter and anchorage for a large fleet. In the course of the year, many hundred vessels, mostly of the coasting and fishing classes, find here a refuge from the dangerous easterly gales and storms by which the coast is so often visited; and in autumn, when a favorable wind and clear weather follow an easterly blow, it is not an uncommon sight to see a fleet of two or three hundred sail working out of the harbor at the same time, and presenting a scene of surpassing interest and beauty.

Annisquam Harbor is a safe and snug haven at the mouth of Annisquam River, having a bar across its entrance, which renders it difficult of access. A current tradition among the people at Annisquam affirms that the name by which their section of the town has always been known is derived from Squam, an Indian word descriptive of the harbor; and Ann, the name of the cape within whose limits it is situated. The earliest mention of this name is on William Wood's Map of Massachusetts, drawn in 1633, where it is spelled Wonasquam. It also occurs in Winthrop's Journal, under the year 1635; and in Josselyn's "Account of Two Voyages to New England," the first of which was commenced in 1638. He spells it Wonasquam; and adds, "a dangerous place to Sail by in stormie weather, by reason of the many Rocks and foaming breakers."

There are several coves on the eastern extremity of the Cape, at some of which harbors have been made, by the construction, at a heavy cost, of massive stone piers and breakwaters. The shores of the town are indented by numerous other coves; but the only one deserving particular notice here is Trynall Cove, at which a ferry was established in 1694 for the conveyance of passengers over Annisquam River to Biskie Island, from which a causeway extended to the main land on the Chebacco side of the town. So important was this channel of communication, that, in 1759, the project of building a bridge at this place was discussed in town-meeting, but soon abandoned; and the ferry was made to serve the convenience of travellers till the latter part of the last century, when it was discontinued. The remains of the ancient causeway are still to be seen.

The surface of the town is uneven ; and its peculiar character strikes every beholder, at first sight, with astonishment. Bald, rocky hills, bold and precipitous ledges of rock, with acres of bowlders of various sizes, in many places scattered thickly over the surface, combine to present a rare scene of naked ruggedness and complete sterility. The small tracts and patches of clear land by which this view of barrenness is occasionally relieved are covered with a strong and fertile soil, suited to the growth of most of our New-England agricultural products. Much of their productiveness, however, is derived from the persevering industry which has removed the rocks from their surface, and converted the land into a state fit for cultivation.

The highest elevation of land in the town is a hill situated near its western border, called Tompson's Mountain. It is two hundred and fifty-five feet above the level of the sea, and its summit affords an extensive prospect of land and ocean. On a clear day, there are plainly discernible, at distances varying from twenty to eighty miles, Bunker-hill Monument ; Wachuset Mountain, in Worcester County ; Monadnock, Gunstock, and other mountain ranges, in New Hampshire ; and Agamenticus, in Maine.* The other hills deserving mention are Governor's,† commanding a fine view of the principal village, harbor, and the two bays whose waters are separated by the Cape ; Rail-cut, next in elevation to Tompson's ; and Pigeon Hill, on the north-easterly part of the Cape. The latter is the first land that salutes the eye of the mariner as he approaches the coast from the east ; and, in order to render it more conspicuous as a land-mark, the trees with which its summit was originally covered

* These several objects were pointed out to me by a member of a surveying party belonging to the United-States Coast Survey, which was stationed for several months on this hill.

† This name was given about the time of the first settlement of the town; but a use to which the hill was put in the Revolutionary War has caused the ancient appellation sometimes to yield to that of Beacon Pole. April 16, 1776, the General Court resolved that a beacon should be erected at Cape Ann, on Governor's Hill; another, at Marblehead; one at Boston, on the usual place; and one on the Blue Hills, in Milton. The selectmen and two commissioned officers nearest the beacons were to have charge of them, and, when an enemy's fleet was discovered, to fire their alarm-guns, set the bells ringing, and cause the beacons to be fired with all expedition.

received for many years the careful attention of the town. Here may be had a near, extensive, and sublime view of the "unbeginning, endless sea."

Besides these hills, there are some elevations that deserve notice on account of their structure and their striking and majestic forms. Of these, Poles * and Farm Ledge, two large masses of rock, whose precipitous sides and bold outline command the attention of every beholder, are the most conspicuous.

The rocks of Cape Ann are granite, of a beautiful, dark color; and are easily wrought into blocks of any needed size. Several quarries have been opened in different localities; but none are now extensively worked, except some valuable ones at the north-east part of the Cape. These are truly mines of wealth; for they yield a sure and ample return to the industry which turns out the useful material they furnish, and which finds every year an increased demand for its products. The time may come when the busy hand of labor will be seen plying its blows at the granite ledges in every part of the town, and extracting therefrom the means of a more substantial and permanent prosperity than was ever derived from the richest mines of the precious metals.

It is not only from a scenic or utilitarian point of view that the rocks of Cape Ann possess an interest: they afford a few natural curiosities, that amply repay the trouble and fatigue of a visit to their several localities. One of these, Rafe's Crack, which is said to have derived its name from a man named Ralph, who once resided in its vicinity, is a remarkable fissure in a ledge on the seacoast between Norman's Woe and Kettle Cove. Its length forms a right angle with the shore, from which it extends more than two hundred feet. Its width is irregular; but the greatest is about ten feet. The depth from the highest part of the rock, forming one of its sides to low-water mark, is computed at sixty feet. The ledge is one of the most remarkable on the Cape; being compact, of great size,

* I adapt the spelling of this word to its pronunciation. It is of early occurrence in the town-records; where its orthography is such as to authorize a conjecture that it was derived from the name of Powel, an early inhabitant.

and presenting, ocean-ward, an aspect of singular boldness and grandeur. The view of the spot, and the hollow, thundering noise of the sea, as it is dashed back from the rocks at the upper end of the chasm, cause every visitor to feel the presence of a sublime and majestic influence.

Another feature in the geological structure of the town is its rocking stones. The one most deserving of notice is that near Bass Rocks. It is situated at the end of a large and high ledge, jutting out into the sea; and is not perceived, without examination, to be a detached portion of it. It lies in such juxtaposition to the main rock as to strike against it at every oscillation. It is somewhat difficult of access, though the agile and adventurous may obtain a foothold upon it without difficulty. Its shape is so irregular, that its weight is rendered difficult of computation; but no estimate makes it less than five hundred tons. It has a rocking motion of about one inch; but as its vibrations are caused only by the sea, which leaves it at low water, the frequency and force of these depend upon the time of tide, and the violence with which it is struck by the waves. The best time to visit it is at or near half-tide; and, if a heavy sea should be then breaking upon the shore, it will exhibit a constant, tremulous motion, affording a rare illustration of hydro-dynamic power. This rock derives additional interest from the probability that it attracted the notice of a celebrated New-England divine many years since, who thus mentions it in a letter* to a foreign correspondent: —

"You may Judge me akin to Johannes de Rupe Scissa by my obtruding upon you another Story of a Rock, after my having transcribed unto our (Alas! deceased) Friend an Account of the Rockuing Stone to be seen at the town of Gloucester, in this American Colony. But tho' the thing be Little above the Quality of a trifle, yett, because there is a little curiousity in it, and some other Things as Trivial have been commemorated among observable Rarities, I will now give you a

* This letter, written by Rev. Cotton Mather, is dated "Sept. 24, 1724," and is addressed to Dr. James Jurin. It is in possession of the Massachusetts Historical Society. Such an exaggerated account of the motion of this rock would hardly be expected, even from such a source.

Relation of another Large Rock in the very same Town of Gloucester, the circumstances whereof are a little singular.

"There stands on the Shore there, between Low and High Water Mark, a Rock upon a Rock, where it would require many Team of Oxen to draw it from its Basis. The Rock is about 19 or 20 foot long, about 9 or 10 foot wide, but Sidewise, that it faces the Sea. But when a Storm arises, and the Sea beats tempestuously upon this Rock, the spectators have a sight that a Little Surprises them. They see the Rock, notwithstanding the vast Bulk and Weight of it, move backwards and forwards three or four feet, and, in less than a Minute or two, perform its motion with Continual Repetitions. The Rock whereon it stands is worn into a most Regular Smoothness as far as this motion extends, and a Rock on which ye Back of it is is also thereby worn considerably."

The Rocking Stone, of which he had previously written, was probably that situated in a pasture on the north side of the Cape. It is a bowlder, weighing about seventy tons, resting on a rock on a level with the surface of the ground, and may be set in motion by one person; so that, after the withdrawal of the force, about fifteen vibrations may be counted.

The rocky surface of the town, which now presents many large tracts, offering scarcely a tree or bush to relieve the eye, was once covered with a fine growth of various kinds of wood: but the work of levelling it began when the town was first settled, and has been continued with unfaltering perseverance; till, at length, only in a few places are there any trees to be found. In addition to the wood cut for fuel for domestic consumption, and the timber felled for ship-building and for the construction of tenements in town, quite a brisk business was early carried on in the exportation of the article to Boston. A stray leaf of an old account-book reveals the fact, that in about three weeks, in 1711, over five hundred cords of wharf-wood were shipped to one firm in that place.

The botany of Cape Ann is rich in the possession of a rare plant called the *Magnolia glauca*, whose only native place in Massachusetts is a swamp in the westerly part of the town. It belongs to a genus named after Magnol, a distinguished French botanist; and is of a family comprehending many beautiful trees and shrubs very common in the Southern and South-western States. The *M. glauca* grows to the height of about ten feet, and yields a beautiful, fragrant flower through nearly the whole of the warm season. These are in such request, that large numbers of them are annually carried out of town for sale. Many of the shrubs are taken up every year for transplanting; and, as little care is exercised for the preservation of the plant in its original locality, it is to be feared that it will soon be completely extirpated. Of those that have been transplanted, few have thrived; owing in most cases, perhaps, to the change from a wet soil to a dry one. This plant possesses valuable medicinal properties, and is said to have been used with great success in chronic rheumatism and intermittent fever.

The project of a cut, or passage, through the narrow neck of land that separated the waters of Massachusetts Bay from those of Ipswich Bay, received the early attention of the Colonial Government; for, as early as 1638, the records of the General Court say, "Mr. Endicott was willed to send three men to view Cape Ann, whether it may be cut through, and how they find it." But it was not probably deemed of sufficient public advantage to be undertaken by the government; and its execution was left to the individual enterprise of Rev. Richard Blynman, the first minister of the town, who, by a vote of the town, "26th 5 mo. 1643," was to "cut the beach through, and to maintain it, and to have the benefit of it to himself and his for ever; giving the inhabitants of the town free passage." The masonry of this ancient canal was of the lightest and most simple kind; consisting merely of two parallel walls of small rocks, which approached near each other at the bottom, and thence sloped to the top, where the width was just sufficient to allow the passage of small shallops. The bridge was so constructed, that, by raising one end slightly from the wall on which it rested, it could be swung round on a pivot fixed into the other. This channel was of great convenience to the early settlers of the town; but it was cut, undoubtedly, with reference to the accommodation of the coastwise navigation between Massachusetts Bay and the eastern shores, which was carried on in small vessels that, by means of this passage, could avoid the risk and delay of an outside voyage around the Cape. Nothing is preserved on record to show the extent to which it was used. It was kept open without obstruction till the winter of 1704; when, by the combined action of a violent storm and remarkably high tide, it was so filled with sand and gravel as to become useless.

Just before this event occurred, the town had taken its first action in relation to the Cut since the original grant. At a meeting, May 15, 1704, a vote was passed, "that whatever person or persons that passeth through the Cut, and shall leave the bridge open, and shall not turn the bridge over the Cut again, — every such person or persons shall pay, as a fine to ye proprietors of said Cut, six shillings in money for every time they shall leave the said bridge and do not turn it over the Cut again." The ownership of it had passed from Mr. Blynman to William Stevens; but it was now the property of Capt. Nathaniel Coit. On his refusal or neglect to clear it, a memorial was presented to the General Court in behalf of the town, setting forth the inconvenience suffered in consequence of its useless condition, and praying the interference of that body to compel Capt. Coit to put it again in navigable order. The court ordered him to have it cleared; and, for his compensation, allowed him to tax every vessel, not belonging to the town, that passed through, two shillings each time; and those belonging to Gloucester, seven shillings yearly. After some delay, he commenced work upon it; but progressed so slowly, that he was at last hurried on by the General Court to complete it in twelve days, or submit to have it done by the town at his expense. No further action appears on record in relation to it at this time; and it was, without doubt, soon made passable: but only a few years elapsed before it again became the subject of controversy, and of frequent and lengthy debate in town-meetings.

In February, 1723, a remarkably high tide, attended with a storm of unusual violence, again filled this channel with sand. Ineffectual attempts were made by the town, by petition to the General Court and complaints to the Court of Sessions, to compel Samuel Stevens, jun., the owner of the Cut at that time, to open it again. The last effort to this end, Feb. 1, 1727, was the choice of an agent, Elder James Sayward, with appropriation of ten pounds for his expenses, to prosecute Mr. Stevens in a court of law. Against this vote, John Sargent, John Parsons, and Eliezer Parsons, entered their dissent, "because it was spending the town's money without prospect of benefit, or gaining the supposed end for which said agent is chosen." A few months afterwards, a town-meeting was held to consider a proposition to open the Cut at the town's charge; which, after much debate, was negatived: and finally, Feb. 8, 1728, the town gave "liberty to any person, so far as they are concerned, to open and clear" it. The unwillingness of the town to assume the management of this channel, and to open it and keep it in navigable order, shows that it was not of much public utility.

After the lapse of nearly a century, the minds of the people were again aroused to the convenience and advantages of the ancient union of the two bays. At this period, the maritime intercourse between the commercial capital of New England and all the ports and havens from Ipswich Bay to Penobscot River employed a great number of small craft, which, it was supposed, would seek this passage if it were navigable; and the recent application of steam as a motive power for propelling vessels through the water gave rise to extravagant expectations as to the extent to which it might be used by vessels so propelled. In the most sanguine belief that the enterprise would yield a fair return for the capital needed to carry it forward, about six thousand dollars were subscribed towards it by individuals, who were incorporated by the State, under the name of the Gloucester Canal Corporation. The Commonwealth became a stockholder to the amount of fifteen hundred dollars; and an appropriation of six thousand dollars was obtained from the General Government, on the representation of the great public benefit the channel would undoubtedly prove to be in case of war, as shown by the constant danger of capture and annoyance by the enemy's cruisers, to which the outside navigation was exposed in the conflict with England a few years before. The Act of Incorporation bears date Feb. 16, 1822. The work was immediately commenced, and finished during the next year; but, to the great disappointment of its projectors, it was so little used at first as to yield an insufficient sum for repairs, and finally ceased to be resorted to at all. A drawbridge was maintained for a few years, which finally gave place to a permanent one, and that has now yielded to the solid road. During the time the passage was open, one steam-vessel only made use of it. She was one of the smallest boats * of her class, which, with a party of pleasure, made the circumnavigation of the Cape in August, 1829.

There are but two ponds of considerable magnitude within the limits of Gloucester. The largest (Cape Pond) is situated near the easterly end of the Cape; and is a beautiful sheet of water, covering about seventy acres. It is nearly environed by high and rocky hills, which on one side recede with abruptness from the shore. Perch and pickerel are occasionally caught there; but it is seldom visited for the purpose of fishing. The brook by which it has its outlet takes a westerly direction; and after flowing about two miles, in part through a swamp filled with the high blueberry and other shrubs, mingles its waters with those of the sea, at Mill River. Trout have been taken from this stream; but it is not so plentifully supplied with them as to make it a resort for anglers. The other pond, a sheet of water of smaller size than Cape Pond, is on Eastern Point, and covers a considerable portion of the width of this strip of land at the place where it is situated. A narrow ridge, composed of sand and pebbles, separates it from the waters of the ocean, which, at times of its unusual height and violent agitation, have been known to throw their briny spray over the barrier, and mingle with those of the pond.

The islands near the Cape and in its harbors are few in number, and of but little importance, except for the historical

* On that account, named the "Tom Thumb." The dimensions of the canal barely admitted her passage.

interest connected with the three that attracted the notice of the early and celebrated navigator, who associated them with one of the marvellous exploits of his own wonderful career. One of these three islands lies off the head of the Cape, and is separated from it by a channel of only a few rods in width. Its surface is rocky, and covers not more than forty or fifty acres. Its present name (Straitsmouth) was given before 1699, when the island was granted by the General Court to Capt. James Davis, in consideration that he had "been at much charge and expense in the late wars with the French and Indian enemy, and spent much time in said service." Its value, in the depreciated currency of 1732, was two hundred and twenty-five pounds. A light-house was erected on it a few years since, for the accommodation of the in-shore navigation of the Cape. The other islands of this group are situated on the south-east side of the Cape, within a mile of its shores. Thatcher's, the larger of the two, is estimated to contain about eighty acres, most of which consists of good soil, affording rich pasturage for a few cattle. In 1714, it was purchased by Rev. John White for a hundred pounds. He sold it in 1727 to Joseph Allen, for a hundred and seventy-five pounds. In 1771, the Colonial Government became its owner, at a cost of five hundred pounds, and proceeded in the same year to erect two light-houses and a dwelling-house on it. The lights were lighted for the first time, Dec. 21, 1771. At the commencement of the Revolutionary War, the keeper of the lights (Kirkwood) was forcibly removed from the island by Capt. Rogers's company of minute-men, as a person inimical to the patriotic sentiments generally held by the people of the town. After a lapse of time, the lights were relighted, and have ever since thrown forth their friendly beams to greet the anxious mariner, and, in the darkness of night, direct his way over the pathless sea. Milk Island, lying a short distance south of Thatcher's, rises but little above the level of the sea. Its soil is sufficient for the pasturage of a few sheep; for which purpose only has it ever been used. In 1718, it was sold by Petter Bennet, of Georgetown, Me., to his brother Anthony, of Gloucester, for forty-seven pounds.

Near the entrance of the principal harbor, on the westerly side, is Kettle Island, which is high and rocky, and of no importance as to size or use. It may have received its name from the family of John Kettle, an early settler; though it was known by its present name as early as 1634, when five men, belonging to Salem, were drowned from a canoe, near it. In the waters of the harbor lie Ten-pound Island and Five-pound Island, both very small, but mentioned by their present names in the early records of the town; a vote of which, in 1644, indicates the use then made of the former:—

"Ten Pound Island shall be reserved for Rams onlie; and whoever shall put on anie but great Ramms shall forfeit 2s. 6d. per head."

Among the grants to William Vinson, an early settler, was "an Island that lyes in the coave before his house, called ffive-pound Island."

Other islands, of sufficient importance to receive names in the early settlement of the town, but deserving no further notice here, are Obadiah Bruen's, Cow, Norawaie, Cormorant, and Hemlock.

On the westerly side of the harbor is Norman's Oh, or Woe; a large rock, lying a few rods from the shore, and connected with it by a reef of rocks, which the sea leaves bare at low water. The tradition, that a man named Norman was shipwrecked and lost there, has no other confirmation than that derived from the name itself. A William Norman was an early settler of Manchester; and a Richard Norman is shown, by the probate records of Essex County, to have sailed on a voyage from which he never returned home, some time before 1682. The doleful name applied to this spot may commemorate a misfortune to one of those individuals. It will recall to the minds of the readers of American poetry, if it did not suggest to the author, a pathetic ballad of one of our most popular poets.

CHAPTER II.

EARLY VOYAGES TO NORTH AMERICA.

GOSNOLD'S VOYAGE. — PRING'S. — ATTEMPT TO PLANT A COLONY AT SAGADAHOC. — VOYAGE OF CAPT. JOHN SMITH IN 1614: HE NAMES NEW ENGLAND. — OTHER VOYAGES TO THE COAST. — PLYMOUTH SETTLED. — PLYMOUTH COMPANY IN ENGLAND. — FURTHER ATTEMPTS AT SETTLEMENT.

ALTHOUGH the continent of America was first discovered within a few degrees of the prominent headland upon which Gloucester is situated, and although the century following that event was, for the most part, distinguished for maritime adventure and discovery, there is no account of a visit to any part of the shores of New England, from Cape Cod to the eastern coast of Maine, for more than one hundred years after the voyage of Cabot in 1497. During that time, some portions of the shores of North America were repeatedly visited by vessels belonging to the chief maritime nations of Europe. Within the first ten years of the sixteenth century, French navigators had found the great fishing-ground of Newfoundland, and had sailed into the river St. Lawrence. In 1524, Verazzani, in the service of France, ranged along the American coast several hundred miles, and entered some of its harbors. About this time, too, several French vessels were engaged in the fisheries at Newfoundland; and, not long after, the memorable voyage of Cartier prepared the way for the ultimate permanent settlement of the French in North America. English fishermen, also, made voyages to Newfoundland at this early period; and the number of vessels of different nations resorting to that fishing-ground continued to increase from year to year, till, at the end of the century, it amounted to no less than four hundred. In the reign of Queen Elizabeth, the zeal for maritime adventure and discovery was the most conspicuous national characteristic. English ships circumnavigated the globe, and visited distant parts of the earth hitherto unknown. Many voyages were also made in the attempt to found colonies in Newfoundland and Virginia; but the intervening coast does not seem to have attracted attention, nor does history relate that any navigator had sailed near the shores of Cape Ann, or come to anchor in its vicinity, before 1602. There can be scarcely a doubt, however, as will immediately appear, that a European vessel had visited some part of the neighboring coast at the eastward just before that time.

On Friday, the 14th of May, 1602, Capt. Bartholomew Gosnold, in a small ship called the "Concord," — carrying, besides the ship's crew, a company designed for settlement in the country, — fell in with the land somewhere on the coast of Maine, after a passage of forty-nine days from Falmouth, England. Standing along by the shore till about noon of the same day, he then came to anchor, and soon descried approaching his ship a Biscay shallop, in which were eight Indians, two of whom were dressed partly in European costume. These Indians came from a rock, which, from this circumstance, was called Savage Rock; the first spot on the shores of New England that received an English name. The accounts of this day's navigation, by the journalists of the voyage, are not sufficiently clear to enable us to determine with certainty the location of Savage Rock; but it is nearly certain that it was not the ledge off our Cape now known as the Salvages.* From a comparison of the accounts, the most probable conclusion is, that the first land made by Gosnold was Cape Elizabeth; and that Savage Rock was the

* The Salvages are two ledges, situated about two miles east of Straitsmouth Island. One of them is covered by the sea at high water. Tradition has preserved no account of the origin of their name, and mention of it in any printed account could only be expected on the occurrence of disaster or shipwreck on or near them. In such connection they are mentioned in December, 1768, when a schooner was cast upon them in a heavy sea; involving, as an inevitable consequence, the loss of all on board.

Nubble, — a large, high rock, near the shore, on the east side of York Harbor, Me.* Gosnold anchored near Savage Rock; and

* So at least it is in the opinion of Mr. Ebenezer Pool of Rockport, who is well acquainted with the entire line of seacoast from Cape Ann to the Kennebec, and who, after reading the narratives, came at once to this conclusion, and kindly communicated the same to me. These narratives — one by Archer, and the other by Brereton — are in Massachusetts Historical Collections, vol. xxviii. The first says, "The fourteenth, about six in the morning, we descried land that lay north, &c. The northerly part we called the north land, which to another rock upon the same, lying twelve leagues west: that we called Savage Rock (because the savages first showed themselves there). Five leagues towards the said rock is an out-point of woody ground, the trees thereof very high and straight, from the rock east-north-east. From the said rock came towards us a Biscay shallop," &c. He then relates the visit of the Indians to his ship, and mentions "leaving them and their coast." Next he says, "About sixteen leagues south-west from thence, we perceived in that course two small islands, — the one lying eastward from Savage Rock, the other to the southward of it." Brereton says, "We made the land, being full of fair trees; the land somewhat low; certain hummocks, or hills, lying into the land; the shore full of white sand, but very stony or rocky. And standing fair along by the shore, about twelve of the clock the same day, we came to an anchor." He then gives an account of the visit of the Indians, and proceeds: "It seemed, by some words and signs they made, that some Basques, or of St. John de Luz, have fished or traded in this place, being in the latitude of forty-three degrees. But riding here in no very good harbor, and, withal, doubting the weather, about three of the clock the same day, in the afternoon, we weighed; and, standing southerly off into sea the rest of that day and the night following, with a fresh gale of wind, in the morning we found ourselves embayed with a mighty headland." This "headland" was, of course, Cape Cod. The "north land," Mr. Pool thinks, was Cape Elizabeth; and the "out-point of woody ground," five leagues towards Savage Rock, Cape Porpoise. The expression, "about sixteen leagues from thence," refers, in his opinion, to the place where they made the land in the morning, and not to Savage Rock. And this seems reasonable; because, after sailing that distance southerly from the rock, it is hardly possible that they should have "perceived" a small island eastward from it. Besides, the time spent in sailing sixteen leagues from Savage Rock, where they weighed anchor about three o'clock, must have expired in the night; and that distance from Savage Rock, wherever the rock was, must have carried them more than half-way from that place to Cape Cod. Savage Rock, then, was about sixteen leagues south-west from the "north land;" "the shore full of white sand," along which they sailed before reaching the rock, was the long beach between Wood Island and Cape Porpoise, and the beach in Well's Bay; the small island eastward from it was Boon Island; and those south of it, the Isles of Shoals, mistaken perhaps, at the distance of ten miles, for a single island. Brereton says that the place of their anchorage was in the latitude of 43°. York lies in 43° 16′. The distance thence to Cape Cod is about seventy miles; and as Gosnold was about fourteen hours in sailing from Savage Rock to that place, and considering that his bark was "weak," and that he was "loth" to press her with much sail," and, further, that he was on an unknown coast, which he would so cautiously navigate as not to sail, "with a fresh gale of wind," more than five miles an hour, there is much probability for the supposition that the place of his first anchorage was near York, and that Mr. Pool, from these and the other facts in the case, has correctly located Savage Rock. It is pretty evident that it was not a very prominent locality: for it is not, to my knowledge, mentioned in any subsequent voyage, except that of Pring in 1603.

after a few hours' intercourse with the natives, finding himself "short of his purposed place," he weighed anchor, and proceeded. Getting a sight, perhaps, of our Cape before dark, and passing the entrance of Massachusetts Bay in the night, on the morning of the 15th he was off the mighty headland, which, on account of the great number of codfish with which the voyagers "pestered their ships" there, then received the name of Cape Cod. Gosnold sailed thence along the coast, and discovered the islands forming what is now called the Vineyard Sound. On one of these islands — that now known as Cuttyhunk * — he erected a storehouse, and made preparations for the men who were to stay in the country: but, upon some disagreement, these concluded not to remain; and, after stopping at this place several days, during which the ship's company had considerable intercourse with the Indians, he departed on the 18th of June for England, where, on the 23d of July, he safely arrived.

Thus terminated a voyage which was not only the first attempt of the English to make a settlement within the limits of New England, but also the first voyage of discovery to its shores. At that time, not a single European family had a home in any part of North America, north of Mexico.† Three years later, the French made the first permanent settlement in this part of the country, at Nova Scotia; from which the leaders of the enterprise desired in a short time to remove the colony to a milder climate. With this end in view, they explored the coast southerly as far as Cape Cod; but the hostility of the Indians, and other adverse circumstances, discouraged their attempts, and caused an abandonment of their design.

New England — or North Virginia, as it was then called — was, by the voyage of Gosnold, brought prominently before the English people as a promising field for further discovery. The favorable reports carried home by that captain and his companions undoubtedly influenced the merchants and others, of Bristol; who, in the next year, despatched a second expedition to our coasts. Martin Pring, in a ship of fifty tons called the

---

* Belknap; American Biography, art. "Gosnold."

† Holmes's Annals, vol. i. p. 123.

"Speedwell," accompanied by a bark of twenty-six tons called the "Discoverer," sailed from England in April, 1603. They made the land at the mouth of Penobscot Bay, and ranged along the coast to the south-west, entering several inlets as they proceeded; from the most westerly of which they shaped their course for Savage Rock. Here they tarried long enough to land on the main, in pursuit of sassáfras; to procure which article, then highly esteemed as a sovereign remedy for various diseases,* was one object of their voyage. Where they landed they found inhabitants, but no sassafras. They succeeded, however, in finding an abundance of it in another part of the coast, to which they went from Savage Rock, and from which, after a stay of a few weeks, they sailed for England.

There is reason to suppose that Capt. Pring sailed along in view of our Cape: and perhaps he landed on its shores; for, according to the journal of the voyage, after leaving Savage Rock, the ships "bare into that great gulf which Capt. Gosnold overshot the year before, coasting, and finding people, on the north side thereof."

The next English navigator who visited the coast of New England was Capt. George Weymouth, who, in May, 1605, made the land somewhere about Nantucket, and then sailed off northerly till he came to an island — which, it is supposed, was Monhegan — near the entrance to Penobscot Bay. In this vicinity he remained about a month, and then departed for home; first sowing the seeds of an abundant harvest of future trouble, by basely stealing, for transportation to England, five of the natives. This act, the journalist of the voyage declares, "was a matter of great importance for the full accomplishment of our voyage;" which had, according to the same authority, for its "sole intent," a "true zeal of promulgating God's holy church, by planting Christianity." † The natural rights of men

* Gosnold carried home a considerable quantity of it; and Archer, one of his company, testifies to its medicinal effect: "The powder of sassafras, in twelve hours, cured one of our company that had taken a great surfeit by eating the bellies of dogfish, — a very delicious meat."

† See Weymouth's Voyage in Massachusetts Historical Collections, vol. xxviii.

were then little respected; and the enslaving of Indians was, long before this date and many years subsequent to it, considered a lawful act.*

The accounts carried to England by these discoverers and explorers of the coast of North Virginia were favorable to projects for colonization on its shores. The bays and harbors were numerous, spacious, and safe; the climate healthy, and the disposition of the natives peaceable. The means of subsistence were abundant, and industry might reasonably expect a sufficient reward for its labors. The waters abounded with cod larger than those of Newfoundland; and the hills and valleys of the land were full of animals, furnishing valuable skins and furs, in which a profitable trade was already commenced. Under such inducements, though permanent settlement was long delayed, the watery track between the two countries was regularly navigated; and, from this time, one or more English ships came annually to the coast.

The period for vigorous attempts at colonization had arrived. Possessing such right to dispose of the territory as Cabot's discovery could give to the crown of England, King James I., in 1606, granted to certain persons of Bristol, Plymouth, and other parts of the west of England, a strip of land along the Atlantic coast of America, lying between the thirty-eighth and forty-fifth degrees of north latitude, for the purpose of planting a colony there. In furtherance of their design, some of the company despatched two ships; one of which, of fifty tons, commanded by Henry Challons, having two of Weymouth's stolen men on board, was taken by a Spanish fleet, and carried with her crew to Spain. The other ship, of which Martin Pring was master, proceeded to the coast, and, after making "a perfect discovery of all those rivers and harbors he was informed of by his instructions," returned to England.

Not discouraged, those zealous friends of colonization in America sent out the next year, in two ships, "one hundred and twenty persons for planters," well prepared to lay the foun-

---

* Bancroft; History of the United States, vol. i. p. 168.

dation of a permanent settlement. Under the presidency of George Popham, on the 20th of August, 1607, this company began to build a fort and erect their buildings on a peninsula at the west side of the mouth of the Sagadahoc, now the Kennebec River: but the rigor of a severe winter and other discouragements caused the abandonment of the plantation the next year; some of the colonists returning in a pinnace of thirty tons, which they had built, and called the "Virginia;" * the first vessel built in New England. Sagadahoc and Jamestown were planted at the same time. The latter survived its early disasters, and was the first permanent abode of the English in America. The former, under no very dispiriting circumstances, was abandoned in a year. The settlement was projected and planted by men of rank and wealth, in whose thoughts, without doubt, the few humble families, then fleeing across the German Ocean from religious persecution in their native land, were the last to be the founders of the first permanent Colony in New England.

The Sagadahoc colonists, on their return to England, branded the country they had left as "over-cold," and not habitable by English people. The chief movers of the enterprise were therefore disheartened; but a zeal for making further attempts was kept alive in the breast of one of them (Sir Ferdinando Gorges), whose career from this time is intimately connected with the history of New England. He became the owner of a ship himself, he says; and sent her here for trade and discovery, under Richard Vines as leader of the enterprise. He does not say, in his account of his proceedings, when the first voyage was made; † but he held this course "some years together:" and Vines and his men are said to have been in the country in the winter of the great "plague," which, according to all the early historians of New England, destroyed many of the natives, and which is supposed to have made its ravages in 1616 and 1617. ‡ The place to which Vines resorted, and

* Massachusetts Historical Collections, vol. xxi. p. 246.

† Williamson (History of Maine, vol. i. p. 227) says it was in 1609.

‡ Massachusetts Historical Collections, vol. xxvi. p. 57.

where he spent the winter, was probably at the mouth of the Saco River. Another of the Sagadahoc adventurers (Sir Francis Popham) sent a ship for several years, on his own account, for fishing and trade, to the coast about Monhegan. He followed this business as late as 1614, certainly.*

The only voyage to the coast during the six years preceding the date last named, besides that annually made by Popham's ship, was one under the charge of Capt. Edward Harlow, who is said to have been sent to "discover an island supposed to be about Cape Cod." He fell in with the land at "Monahigan," and thence sailed to the place of his destination. On the coast he encountered hostility from the natives, and three of his men were wounded by their arrows; but he succeeded in making captives of five of them, with whom he returned to England. The voyage was fruitful in bad results only; for one of the savages, named Epenow, thus ruthlessly torn away from his home, subsequently retaliated the injury inflicted upon himself and his countrymen.

It is not known that any English foot had, previous to 1614, yet pressed our soil; and our Cape still remained without a name. But it was destined this year to be associated with that of a remarkable man, whose wonderful adventures and achievements give to the sober page of history a romantic interest, that, if history were not sometimes stranger than fiction, would seem to belong rather to products of the imagination than to the events of real life. Capt. John Smith had already been distinguished in planting and sustaining the southern Colony of Virginia; and he now gave his unsurpassed energy, and all the influence he possessed, to the foundation of a settlement on the northern coast.

In the employ of some London merchants, he set sail on the 3d of March, 1614, with two ships, and forty-five men and boys, for the coast of New England, or, as it was still called, North Virginia. On the 30th of April, they arrived at the Island of Monhegan, on the coast of Maine. "Our plot," he

* Smith's Description of New England.

says, "was there to take whales, and make trials of a mine of gold and copper." After due trial, this purpose of the expedition was abandoned, and a more profitable occupation was found in trying for fish and furs, which were to be the "last refuge" to secure a saving voyage. While the ships and most of the company were engaged in fishing, Capt. Smith, with a few of his men, in a small boat, sought a more congenial employment in ranging the coast and trading with the natives. The employment was not only congenial, but it was one in which he had had much experience; for he had explored the shores, rivers, and inlets of Chesapeake Bay, a distance of three thousand miles, in an open boat. In this new enterprise, he explored the coast from Penobscot Bay to Cape Cod; within which bounds, according to his own account, he "sounded about twenty-five excellent good harbors." At the latter place he had a skirmish with the Indians; but, within an hour after it occurred, the parties became friends again.

Capt. Smith made a map of the territory he visited, and affixed names to its most prominent parts. The outline of our Cape is not correctly drawn, and the harbor does not appear at all. In his description of the coast, he mentions "Augoam," on his map called Southampton, but now Ipswich. On the east of this place, he says, "is an isle of two or three leagues in length, the one-half plain mairsh grass, fit for pasture, with many fair high groves of mulberry trees and gardens; and there is also oaks, pines, and other woods, to make this place an excellent habitation, being a good and safe harbor." Next he alludes to "Naimkeck," now Salem; and says, "From hence doth stretch into the sea the fair headland Tragabigzanda, fronted with three isles called the Three Turks' Heads. To the north of this doth enter a great bay, where we found some habitations and cornfields." The isle east of Augoam is, of course, Plumb Island; and the "great bay" can be no other than Ipswich Bay.

It is not known that Capt. Smith landed on our Cape. The name he gave it was that of a Turkish lady, who showed him much kindness while a prisoner in her country. After his return to England, Prince Charles substituted for it that of his mother, Queen Ann, consort of James I. The only other name given by Smith to any part of our territory was that of the Three Turks' Heads, to the three islands off the head of the Cape; which were so called in memory of an exploit, by which three Turkish champions were successively slain by him in personal combat. This name seems also to have been soon transferred to another place;* and the three islands have long been known by their present separate appellations. Having received a name which it will probably keep as long as its rock-bound coast shall resist the dashing surges of the Atlantic, Cape Ann does not again appear as a point of interest, or even notice, till about the time of its first occupancy by English residents; though it can scarcely be doubted that it was often seen, and perhaps sometimes visited, by the mariners who in the intervening years resorted to the coast for fishing, trade, or discovery.

Capt. Smith, with one of his ships, carrying his skins and furs and some of his fish, sailed for England on the 18th of July, and arrived there on the 5th of August. Hunt was left on the coast, with the other ship, to prepare his fish for a Spanish market; and, after having got them on board, sailed to Cape Cod, and thence to Spain. At Cape Cod, and another harbor, now Plymouth, this base man committed an act of villany, which consigned his memory to the execration of all mankind. Having, under false pretences, enticed twenty-seven of the natives into his ship, he secured them under the hatches, and carried them off, to sell in Spain for slaves. Seven years afterwards, an aged mother of three of these Indians could not behold any of his countrymen "without breaking forth into great passion, weeping and crying excessively."†

---

* It was borne by another locality as early as 1630. Gov. Winthrop, in the journal of his passage to New England, says, "About four in the afternoon, we made land on our starboard bow, called the Three Turks' Heads; being a ridge of three hills upon the main, whereof the southmost is the greatest. It lies near Aquamenticus." — *Savage's Winthrop*, vol. i. p. 24.

† Young's Chronicles of the Pilgrims, p. 215.

While Capt. Smith was making trial for a mine of gold on the coast of Maine, another expedition, having the same object in view, was fitting out in England. Epenow, formerly mentioned, had fallen into the hands of Sir Ferdinando Gorges. He had art enough to invent a story of a mine of gold in his native place. A voyage was therefore undertaken by Gorges, who despatched a ship in June, 1614, under the command of Capt. Hobson, with Epenow on board, to guide to the desired spot. Epenow's story was, of course, a trick, to which he resorted for getting home; and soon after the arrival of the ship at Martha's Vineyard, where he was to make good his undertaking, notwithstanding every precaution had been taken to prevent his escape, he contrived to slip overboard, and, under cover of a shower of arrows from twenty canoes, to rejoin his countrymen, in spite of all the English could do with their muskets to prevent it. Thereupon Hobson returned to England, though directed how, upon the failure of this scheme, to have spent the summer to good purpose. He must have been on the coast soon after Hunt left it; and the unfavorable termination of his voyage is attributed to the treacherous dealing of the latter with the natives.*

Besides Capt. Smith and his men, other European mariners were in the vicinity of Cape Ann in 1614. He himself informs us, that at a place forty leagues westward from his station, at Monhegan, while he was trying the "conclusions" of whaling and mining, two French ships made a great voyage by trade. This place, it seems from his description of the coast, was in the great bay, north of the "fair headland Tragabigzanda." During the few years following this date, it is certain that vessels from France visited the parts about Cape Cod; where, in 1616 or 1617, one was cast away, the crew of which fell into the hands of the natives, who kept three or four of them, whom they used "worse than slaves," and killed the rest. Hunt's villany left no claim for kindness to shipwrecked mariners here.

To that portion of North Virginia explored by Capt. Smith

* Massachusetts Historical Collections, vol. xxvi. p. 132.

he gave the name of "New England;" and, though he did not plant a colony here, his earnest and well-directed efforts to do so, and the employment of his pen and his influence to encourage colonization in this part of the country, merit, and will always receive, the grateful regard of the people who inhabit it.

The cargoes carried home in Capt. Smith's ships yielded a handsome sum; and preparations were immediately made, by persons of London interested in the South-Virginia Company, to engage in an expedition for fishing and trade to the coast of New England. The command of it was offered to Capt. Smith; but he had already engaged himself to Gorges and others, of the Plymouth Company: and Michael Cooper, msster of the ship in which he had just returned, was appointed to the charge. Besides, the London Company did not design to make any settlement, and Smith had resolved to go only with a company for plantation; "for," said he confidently, "I know my grounds." But a succession of singularly untoward events prevented his coming to settle a colony, and his first voyage to New England was also his last. In pursuance of the engagement of Gorges and his friends with him, two ships — one of two hundred and one of fifty tons — were fitted out. With these ships, — on board of which were fifteen men besides himself, who were to stay in the country, — Smith sailed again for New England, in March, 1615. He had just got clear of the coast when his ship lost her masts and sprung a leak, so that he was obliged to put back to Plymouth. Embarking again in a small vessel of sixty tons, and proceeding on his voyage, he was captured by a fleet of French men-of-war; and though his vessel got clear, and returned to England, Smith himself was detained as a prisoner for some time, but finally escaped in the night in an open boat, and, after twelve hours' exposure in a storm, succeeded in reaching land on the coast of France. In the next year (1616), he published his description of New England, — a work especially designed to awaken an interest in settling the country; and, by zealous and unwearied personal efforts in the cause he had so much at heart, he succeeded in obtaining command of another expedition, which was got ready in the spring of 1617, in three ships, with a number of men to remain in the country. But this design was also frustrated. The ships were wind-bound three months; at the end of which the season was too far advanced, and the voyage was abandoned. Discouraged by repeated failures, his friends could not be induced to make another effort; and Capt. Smith was obliged to content himself at home with the empty title of Admiral of New England, which, in consideration of his services, losses, and disappointments, the Plymouth Company formally conferred upon him for life.*

The four ships fitted out from London under Cooper sailed in January, 1615; and arrived on the New-England coast in March. They were so successful in fishing and trade, that eight ships were sent the next year from the ports of London and Plymouth; six of which arrived safely back the same season, with cargoes of fish, oil, and furs. Two of the ships, sailing late, came by the way of the West Indies, and did not reach the fishing-ground till May, 1617.

Besides the ships before mentioned as visiting the New-England shores in 1615, a voyage of Sir Richard Hawkins for the Plymouth Company is mentioned by Gorges. He left England in October, with how many ships it is not stated; and, arriving on the coast, found war raging among the natives. He sent a ship, laden with fish, to market; and then passed along the coast to Virginia, and thence, with "such commodities as he had got together," to Spain. Whether he wintered on the coast or not, we do not know; nor does it appear at what season his fish were caught.

A zeal for settling a plantation in New England was still kept alive in the Plymouth Company; and Sir F. Gorges, too, was still intent upon prosecuting the work. They seem to have had

* Capt. John Smith died in London, in 1631, aged about fifty-two. His association of two of the most remarkable events of his wonderful life with the territory of Cape Ann invests them with a peculiar interest for us. His grateful recollection, at our Cape, of the kindness of the far-distant Turkish maiden, Charatza Tragabigzanda, is an incident especially interesting. But the story is too long, even for a note. It is well told in the excellent "Life and Adventures" of Capt. Smith, by G. S. Hillard, in Sparks's American Biography.

this favorite object in view in sending Capt. Edward Rocraft on to the coast in one of the fishing-ships in 1618, and in making arrangements for Capt. Thomas Dermer to join him there the same year from Newfoundland. Rocraft came in a ship of two hundred tons, which took a cargo of fish, and returned to England, carrying the crew of a French vessel that he seized in one of the creeks upon his arrival. With this vessel and a company of men, he intended to winter on the coast; but, discovering that some of his company were conspiring to murder him, he put the culprits ashore at Sagadahoc, with provisions for their use, and then sailed to Virginia, where he was killed in a quarrel the next year. Dermer, instead of going from Newfoundland to join Rocraft, returned to England, and was sent from there, in the spring of 1619, by Gorges, with a company, to meet him on the coast. Upon his arrival at Monhegan, he found Rocraft's mutineers, who had spent the winter there; having, without doubt, come to the island from the main in a pinnace, which their captain probably left with them when he put them ashore, and which was now taken possession of by Dermer for his own use. These men appear to have been the second company of Englishmen that spent a winter on the coast of New England.

In his pinnace (an open boat of five tons), Dermer coasted along the shore to Cape Cod, and redeemed at different places two of the Frenchmen who were cast away at that place a few years before. Returning to Monhegan, he found the ship ready to depart; but, instead of going back in her, he embarked in his pinnace for Virginia, "searching every harbor and compassing every headland" as he went along. He spent the winter in Virginia, and came again to New England in 1620. In the region about Cape Cod he met Epenow, who, fearful of recapture, instigated an assault upon Dermer and his company, by which the latter lost three of his men. Dermer received fourteen wounds himself, and barely escaped with one man. He then went back to Virginia for the cure of his wounds, and died there not long after his arrival.

It nowhere appears what particular work Rocraft and Dermer

were commissioned to do; but it undoubtedly had reference to the selection of a place for a planting and fishing settlement, and such general arrangements and information as would promote the ends at which their employers aimed. It was already certain that the best cod-fishing ground yet discovered in the world was on the coast of New England. About Monhegan, "within a square of two or three leagues," where Capt. Smith found the "strangest fish-pond" he ever saw, a single ship, in 1619, got a fare that yielded twenty-one hundred pounds in money; and, the next year, several ships did even better than that. The shores of the country, it is true, were rocky and barren: but inland were noble rivers, forests, and fertile fields; and only industry and enterprise seemed necessary to convert the most favorable spots into flourishing settlements. The common worldly views which influence mankind, would, in time, do this; but who should begin the work? While this great question was occupying the minds of Gorges and others, a few feeble men and women of a despised religious sect, upon the divine idea of conscience, laid the foundation of all the glory and prosperity that New England can justly boast of, and established at Plymouth the first permanent colony. The most important and interesting voyage ever made to these shores, or, we may say, ever undertaken by men, terminated when the "Mayflower" anchored in Cape-Cod Harbor, in November, 1620. About four months before, not far from this place, Dermer had reaped the bitter fruits of the crimes of his countrymen, and had fled, fearfully wounded, for his life. The six or seven fishing-ships that had been on the coast in the summer had long since departed; and it is not known, that, besides the Pilgrim band, a single European was anywhere in the country between Hudson River and the Penobscot.

About the time of the landing of the Pilgrims, a fresh impulse was given to New-England colonization by the grant of a new charter from the king to Gorges and others, "noblemen, knights, and gentlemen," conferring upon them that portion of North America between the fortieth and forty-eighth degrees of latitude, and extending in length from the Atlantic to the

Pacific. The grant gave all that cupidity could crave. This famous corporation is known in history by the name of "The Council established at Plymouth, in the County of Devon, for the planting, ruling, ordering, and governing of New England in America." Their charter, says the annalist Holmes, "was the only civil basis of all the subsequent patents and plantations which divided this country." Under its authority, some portions of the territory were overlaid with patents; and vexatious disputes and lawsuits were the consequences.

One of these patents was that by which, in March, 1621, Capt. John Mason, who had been a merchant in London, sea-officer, and Governor of Newfoundland, obtained from the Plymouth Council a grant of all the land from the river Naumkeag, round Cape Ann, to the river Merrimack, and up each of these rivers to the farthest head thereof; thence to cross over from the head of the one to the head of the other; with all the islands lying within three miles of the coast. This tract of country was called Mariana, and it was the first grant by the council of the territory of Cape Ann; but no use was made of it in the way of settlement.

By virtue of a grant from the same council, Thomas Weston, in 1622, attempted to settle a colony at Wessagusset, now Weymouth; but his agents were ill chosen, and the enterprise soon came to an end. Another attempt to plant a colony on the same spot was made in September, 1623, by Robert Gorges, who remained in the country but a few months. A few of his people were left behind, and were probably the nucleus of the subsequent permanent settlement at that place.

Such were the attempts at colonization on the New-England shores, prior to the first occupation by Englishmen of the territory of Cape Ann. The continued success and increased number of the fishing voyages to the coast* led those engaged in them to seek convenient places for their stages all along the

---

* In 1621 came "ten or twelve ships to fish, which were all well fraughted. Those that came first at Bilbow made seventeen pounds a single share, besides beaver, otter, and martens' skins." In 1622, "from the west of England, thirty-five ships only to fish." — *Smith's New-England's Trials.*

shore, from Monhegan to Piscataqua River; and finally to the establishment, in that region of the country, of plantations for fishing, agriculture, and trade. The late arrival of one of the fishing-ships at the usual resort, in 1623, led to the founding of a similar plantation in the harbor of Cape Ann, and to the settlement of the Massachusetts Colony.

CHAPTER III.

ATTEMPT AT SETTLEMENT.

Dorchester Company in England attempt to plant a Colony at Cape Ann. — Roger Conant Governor of the Plantation. — Failure of the Attempt, and Removal of the Colonists to Naumkeag. — Notice of these First Occupants of Cape Ann.

Twenty-one years had now elapsed since Gosnold passed our Cape, and sailed by the entrance of Massachusetts Bay to Cape Cod and the Vineyard Sound. During this time, numerous fishing voyages had been made to Monhegan and the neighboring coast. All the principal bays and harbors, extending thence many miles westerly, had been explored; and a Colony had been founded by a few noble men, the place of whose landing was destined to surpass in historical interest every other spot on the continent. By all these means, such information had been obtained in England of the state of the country, and of the abundance of fish in its waters, as to induce a belief, in the minds of many of the merchants interested in the fishing voyages to New England, that these voyages might be carried on with more advantage if they could be connected with a plantation where agriculture and other business on the land could be pursued.

The first to begin this work were some "merchants and other gentlemen about Dorchester," who, after raising the necessary capital, despatched a small ship of fifty tons, in 1623, to begin, in the prosecution of her fishing voyage, the foundation of a colony. In this enterprise, a new friend and promoter of New-England colonization appears, — the Rev. John White, of Dorchester, — who with Mr. Humphrey, the treasurer of the adventurers, are the only persons interested in its success whose names are given. Mr. White is not only mentioned as its "instigator," but is also supposed to have had a pecuniary interest in the undertaking. We are so fortunate as to possess from his own pen, as is with good reason believed, an account* of the origin and operations of this company, the foundation of whose Colony on the shores of Cape Ann is the first prominent event of our history.

It does not appear that the Dorchester adventurers had, at the commencement of their enterprise, any particular spot in

---

* This account is contained in a small pamphlet entitled "The Planter's Plea; or, The Grounds of Plantations examined, and usual Objections answered. Together with a Manifestation of the Causes moving such as have lately undertaken a Plantation in New England. London: 1630." In the few lines contained in the following extract, Mr. White gives the whole story of the origin of the Colony established at Cape Ann:—

"About the year 1623, some western merchants, who had continued a trade of fishing for cod and bartering for furs in those parts for divers years before, conceiving that a colony planted on the coast might further them in their employments, bethought themselves how they might bring that project to effect; and communicated their purpose to others, alleging the conveniency of compassing their project with a small charge, by the opportunity of their fishing-trade, in which they accustomed to double-man their ships, that, by the help of many hands, they might despatch their voyage and lade their ship with fish while the fishing season lasted; which could not be done with a bare sailing company. Now, it was conceived, that, the fishing being ended, the spare men that were above their necessary sailors might be left behind with provisions for a year; and, when the ship returned the next year, they might assist them in fishing, as they had done the former year; and, in the mean time, might employ themselves in building, and planting corn, which, with the provisions of fish, fowl, and venison, that the land yielded, would afford them the chief of their food. This proposition of theirs took so well, that it drew on divers persons to join with them in this work; the rather because it was conceived that not only their own fishermen, but the rest of our nation that went thither on the same errand, might be much advantaged, not only by fresh victual which that Colony might spare them in time, but withal, and more, by the benefit of their minister's labors, which they might enjoy during the fishing season; whereas otherwise, being usually upon those voyages nine or ten months in the year, they were left all the while without any means of instruction at all. Compassion towards the fishermen, and partly some expectation of gain, prevailed so far, that, for the planting of a Colony in New England, there was raised a stock of more than three thousand pounds, intended to be paid in in five years, but afterwards disbursed in a shorter time."

As the basis of a Colony, this use of the spare men, who were necessary while the fishing lasted, but useless in navigating the ship, must have been a prominent consideration among the inducements to plant in New England. Indeed, the great charge of double-manning and double-victualling the ships for the fishing voyages to Newfoundland is mentioned among these inducements as early as 1602. — *Tracts appended to Brereton*, in Massachusetts Historical Collections, vol. xxviii. p. 98.

view for the seat of their colony. Their ship came to the usual fishing-ground: but, arriving late in the season for fishing, did not complete her loading there; and "the master thought good to pass into Mattachusetts Bay, to try whether that would yield him any." We know not upon what encouragement he came into these waters, except upon that of the general report that the coast everywhere abounded with cod; for this is the first fishing voyage, of which we have any knowledge, to any part of the New-England shores as far to the west as Cape Ann. Here, however, he succeeded better than he expected; and, having completed his cargo, proceeded with the same to Spain.* Fourteen men, with the necessary provisions, were left "in the country at Cape Anne;" and these, undoubtedly, commenced the work of the plantation.

The expense of this voyage, including three hundred pounds paid for the ship, was eight hundred pounds. The amount returned to the company was not above two hundred; a disproportion which, unless considerable gain was anticipated from the men left here, did not augur well for the success of the undertaking.

Curiosity may prompt inquiry concerning these fourteen men, the first English residents of Cape Ann; but history refuses to gratify us, even to the extent of giving their names. The only other persons of the English race then in New England, besides the people of New Plymouth, were a few men at Nantasket; the remnant of Gorges's plantation at Weymouth; the settlers at Piscataqua River and Saco, who began at these places the same year; a company at Monhegan; and perhaps one or two other residents on the coast of Maine.† The imagination may find a pleasure in dwelling for a moment with the little company at Cape Ann; in looking upon its members, as they were attracted abroad by day to find sources of wonder and delight in new

* Probably to Bilbao. The commencement in Massachusetts of the great trade in fish to that port, which continued down to a period so recent, that some of our aged mariners now living were engaged in it.

† Drake's History of Boston, p. 41; Bradford's History of the Plymouth Plantation, p. 154; Belknap's New Hampshire, vol. i. p. 8; Williamson's History of Maine, vol. i. p. 227; Winslow, in Young, p. 328.

aspects of nature, and as they were occupied during the long hours of the winter evening with recollections of home, and stories of exploits and adventures along the shores and in the wilderness of the New World.

Just as the Dorchester Company had taken possession of Cape Ann, others, perhaps with a knowledge of their occupation of the territory, turned their attention to the same spot. Although the settlement at New Plymouth was now three years old, it is not known that any of the people there had crossed the bay to Cape Ann, or that any of the six or eight ships which had come to their harbor during that time had been in our waters. Edward Winslow, of New Plymouth, sailed from that place, on a visit of business to England, in the fall of 1623; and there obtained, of course, information of the proceedings and intentions of the Dorchester adventurers. He must have learned, one would suppose, before his departure, that their ship was fishing in the bay that summer; and it is quite possible that he knew of the beginning, by some of their men, of the plantation at Cape Ann. The people of New Plymouth, struggling with famine, had not yet engaged in fishing as a business, and were unable to do so without aid from the company of adventurers in England with whom they were connected. To make preparation for prosecuting this business seems to have been one of the objects of Winslow's mission; but whether his attention was directed to Cape Ann as the best place for their fishing-stage, in consequence of its occupation by the Dorchester people, and upon report of the success of their ship, does not appear. It is certain that he and Robert Cushman procured from Lord Sheffield, a member of the Council for New England, a patent, conveying to them and their associates "a certain tract of ground in New England," "in a known place there comonly called Cape Anne." *

* See this instrument, in Appendix I. A beautiful *fac-simile* copy of it may be found in Mr. J. W. Thornton's Landing at Cape Ann, in which it was first published. Mr. Thornton's work embraces a portion of the history of the Dorchester Company's operations, in their attempt to establish a Colony here: but its chief aim is to show that the proceedings of that company were based on this patent; that, under its authority,

This patent was a sufficient basis for the largest operations in the way of settlement. Civil government, churches, and schools were all provided for; but it does not seem that Cushman and Winslow, and the Plymouth adventurers in England, meditated or attempted any thing more than a summer occupation of the territory for fishing-purposes. Their first use of the patent was to send hither the ship "Charity," on a fishing voyage, in the spring of 1624, after she had discharged some supplies at Plymouth. At that place, a man who was sent over to erect salt-works, and a ship-carpenter, entered upon their respective employments. The crew of the "Charity" had help from the Plymouth planters in building their stage at Cape Ann; but the season was too far advanced. The master — one Baker — was a "drunken beast;" most of his men were like their master; and a poor voyage was the natural result. "Mr. William Peirce was to oversee the business, and to be master of ye ship home; yet he could do no good amongst them, so as ye loss was great." Some gain, however, was derived from trading with the Indians for skins.

The Dorchester Company, having already taken possession of Cape Ann at the date of the patent to Cushman and Winslow, and designing to found a Colony at this place, made some arrangement with the patentees for sharing in the benefits conferred by that instrument. Of the particulars of that arrangement, we know nothing at all. The only information that has come down to us respecting it is from Capt. John Smith, who, writing in 1624, says, "At Cape Anne, there is a plantation beginning by the Dorchester men, which they hold of those of New Plymouth." It is probable that they "held" as associates, and not by assignment; for the Plymouth people occupied our territory for fishing purposes nearly to the time of its abandonment by the Dorchester Company. In whatever

---

a Colony was founded at Cape Anne, having laws, magistrates, and a minister; that this Colony removed to Salem, where it was joined by Endicott's company, under a new organization; and that, therefore, Massachusetts begins her history at Cape Ann, and not at Salem. — See the *Planter's Plea*, *Hubbard's History of New England*, and *Bradford's History of Plymouth Plantation*.

way the latter "held," their operations do not appear to have been connected at all with those of the former; nor is there any thing to show that both were under the same local government and superintendence. The proceedings of the Plymouth adventurers, however, with regard to their fishing-business here, are of insignificant importance in comparison with the great work which the Dorchester men were striving to accomplish, and did accomplish, — the foundation of a Colony.

The fourteen men who were left on our soil, in 1623, to carry on the work of the plantation just begun, watched anxiously, without doubt, for the arrival of recruits with stores and tidings from their native land; and, as the New-England fishing came on early, they were probably gladdened some day in February or March by that event. The same ship that left them here now returned, under the command of the same master. She was accompanied or joined by a Flemish fly-boat, of one hundred and forty tons, described by Mr. White as a very unfit vessel for their business, but made, by alteration, to suit their purpose. Encouraged by the success of the last year's fishing at "Cape Anne, not far from Mattachusetts Bay," the two ships tried again the same ground, but now "sped very ill;" and the returns to the company, for the summer's industry, barely amounted to the charges for wages and provision of the men who remained in the Colony.* These were now thirty-two in number; two of whom were John Tylly and Thomas Gardener, as overseers of the business of the plantation, — the first of the fishing, and the other of the planting.

The unfavorable result of their fishing-business, so far, afforded the Dorchester merchants little encouragement to pro-

* Christopher Levett, who visited the eastern coast of New England in 1624, says, "Yet was I never at the Mesachusett, which is counted the paradise of New England; nor at Cape Ann. But I fear there hath been too fair a gloss set on Cape Ann. I am told there is a good harbor, which makes a fair invitation; but, when they are in, their entertainment is not answerable: for there is little good ground; and the ships which fished there this year, their boats went twenty miles to take their fish; and yet they were in great fear of making their voyages, as one of the masters confessed unto me who was at my house." — *Massachusetts Historical Collections*, vol. xxviii. p. 160.

ceed with their design; but the experience of another year was needed to convince them of the delusive character of their hopes with respect to the practicability of establishing a Colony on the plan they proposed. With a praiseworthy determination to give the experiment a fair trial, their efforts in the third year (1625) for the good of the Colony were vigorous and judicious. The two ships of the previous year were again despatched for fishing, the large one being commanded by "a very able master;" and another vessel, of about forty tons, was sent, on board of which were "kine and other provisions." The best results, however, for the prosperity of the Colony, — so far, at least, as the proceedings at the plantation could contribute to it, — were to be expected from the appointment of a very superior man, already in the country, to be its superintendent or governor.

For some time, the "merchant adventurers," as they were called, who in England had aided the Pilgrim colonists, had been divided into two parties; one of which, adherents of the Established Church, succeeded in introducing into the Colony a minister of their own sect, and therefore hostile to the religious sentiments of the Pilgrims. This was the Rev. John Lyford, who found in the Colony a few men holding views similar to his own; but no one to join him in disturbing the peace of the place, except John Oldham. The conduct of both of these men was such that they were expelled from the Colony, — Oldham immediately, and Lyford after a respite of a few months. Their next place of residence was Nantasket; where Roger Conant, "out of dislike" of the "principles of rigid separation" of the Pilgrims, and some few others, "found a place of retirement and reception for themselves and families," not long after Oldham's expulsion.

This is the first mention of Mr. Conant in New-England history. In his native land, his character stood so high, that Mr. White, upon the information he obtained respecting him, acting with the rest of the Dorchester Company, selected him "for the management and government of all their affairs at Cape Anne," and caused him to be notified by their treasurer, in the name of the company, "that they had chosen him to be their governor in that place." Lyford and Oldham were also invited to join the plantation, — the former as its minister, and the latter to trade with the Indians. Lyford accepted, but Oldham declined. The date of Conant's removal to Cape Ann is not known. The notice of his appointment to the office before named, came, probably, by one of the company's fishing-ships, in the early part of 1625: and he entered, without doubt, immediately upon its duties; for there is evidence that he was here early in the spring of that year.

For the plantation, all the elements of success seemed now to be assured, — men in sufficient number, provisions and cattle, a minister, and a competent governor. But the prosperity of the Colony was contingent upon the profitable result of the fishing voyages connected with it; and these, hitherto unfortunate, were destined to continue so, and thus to lead to the abandonment of the work undertaken by the Dorchester Company.

It has been seen that three ships had been sent out by the company in 1625. One of these, the Flemish fly-boat, was disabled on the passage, and compelled to put back to England. After the necessary repairs had been made, she was again despatched; but, on account of the lateness of the season, she proceeded no farther than Newfoundland, where she was laden with all the fish she could carry home. No account is given of the two vessels that came to Cape Ann, further than that one of them returned to England with fish; which, with those brought from Newfoundland, the company were obliged to sell at home for about half the sum they could have obtained for them at another market.

Discouraged by their losses, and by the "ill-carriage" of their "land-men," the company decided, at the end of the third year, to abandon the design of planting a fishing colony at Cape Ann. They therefore sold their ships, and took measures for breaking up the settlement; having lost, as nearly as can be made out from the statement of its business operations, almost all the capital with which they commenced. "In planting colonies," says Mr. White, "the first stocks employed that way are consumed, although they serve for a foundation to the work." So in planting the Colony at Cape Ann: the stock was consumed; but a foundation was laid, on which now rests one of the leading States of a great nation.

The ill-carriage of the land-men of the Colony has been mentioned. Mr. White says they were ill commanded; but does not tell us whether by Conant, or his predecessors Tylly and Gardener, or by all of them. The historian Hubbard has preserved an account of an occurrence here, presently to be noticed, in which Mr. Conant bore a very honorable part; and his subsequent career furnishes grounds for the belief that he discharged well the duties of his office during the few months that elapsed from his entering upon them to the decision of the company to abandon their undertaking.

Notwithstanding the poor success of the Pilgrims' fishing voyage to Cape Ann in 1624, they and their friends in England undertook another enterprise of the kind, with a ship and pinnace, in 1625. The "salt-man," who came over to Plymouth the year before, was now sent to Cape Ann to set up a house and salt-pans here; but this business came to an end in consequence of a fire which destroyed the house and some of the pans. Before the arrival of their ship, another one, despatched by the faction of the merchant adventurers in England who were hostile to the Pilgrims, came into the harbor; and her crew seized the stage and other provisions made for fishing by the crew of the "Charity" and the Plymouth people the year before. When called on to surrender it, they refused to do so, without fighting: whereupon they were allowed to keep it; and the Governor of Plymouth sent some men over to help to build another. It thus appears probable that five vessels came into our harbor in 1625, and made it the chief place of their anchorage while on the coast. The dispute about the fishing-stage — briefly mentioned by one early writer, and nearly in his own language given above — appears, in the more particular account of another, to have been an affair which at one time threatened an unhappy result. According to the latter, the usurping captain, whose name was Hewes, barricaded his company with hogsheads on the stage-head; while the rightful owners, under the conduct of Capt. Miles Standish, stood upon the land, and demanded a surrender. A war of words followed; but happily a more serious encounter was prevented by the prudence and moderation of Roger Conant, and the interposition of Capt. William Peirce,* the master, it is supposed, of the ship in which the Pilgrims were interested, and which was then lying in the harbor. The scene of the dispute is not known; and, if it were, the spot should serve, not so much to remind us of the characteristic courage of the famous Puritan soldier which was undoubtedly displayed on this occasion, as of the higher virtues exhibited by the two worthies who saved our soil from becoming the theatre of a disgraceful fight, and the parties themselves, perhaps, from the guilt of bloodshed.

With the close of this year's fishing, all connection of the Plymouth people with Cape Ann seems to have terminated, though their last vessels were highly successful in taking fish, and both of them, "well laden," "went joyfully home togeather," the master of the larger ship towing "ye lesser ship at his sterne all ye way over-bound."

The efforts of the Dorchester Company also, in the work of founding a Colony at Cape Ann, had now ceased. Most of their men, being sent for, returned to England. Roger Conant, and a few of the most honest and industrious, resolved to stay, and take charge of the property at the plantation; and, as the advantages of this spot consisted only in its convenience for fishing, they removed, some time in the next year, to Naumkeag, now Salem, — a place better adapted to the pursuits of agriculture.

Thus terminated the first occupation of our soil by the coun-

---

* This "godly man and most expert mariner" is distinguished among the early navigators between Old England and New. He attempted to come in the "Paragon" in 1622, but was obliged to put back. He came in the "Ann" in 1623; in the "Charity" in 1624; in one of the ships in 1625; in the "Mayflower" in 1629; in the "Lyon" in 1630, 1631, and 1632. He also made voyages to Virginia and the West Indies. He was killed at one of the Bahama Islands in 1641. — See *Bradford's History of Plymouth Plantation*, and *Winthrop's New England*.

trymen of our ancestors; and Gloucester, instead of being the oldest permanent settlement in the Massachusetts Colony, can only claim the distinction of having within its limits the spot on which that Colony was founded. That spot is plainly marked by tradition; and other evidence is not wanting to indicate the place. It is on the north-west side of the outer harbor. It was well chosen for planting, as the soil is good, and the tract is less rocky than any other of equal extent lying along the shore inside of the Cape. With reference to its early use, probably, it received the name of "ffisherman's field," by which it is designated in the early records of the town. The spot used for landing fish is indicated by the name it has always borne, — the Stage. A high ledge near it affords a delightful view of the town, harbor, and bay; and for many years, while access to it was unobstructed, it was a favorite resort of the people of the town for a short summer's walk. Some of these found, perhaps, in addition to the natural beauty inviting their attention, a source of pleasure in the interesting associations connected with the spot.

Among the causes of the failure of the Dorchester Company, in their design to plant a Colony at Cape Ann, Mr. White mentions "the ill-choice of the place for fishing;" a reason which may seem strikingly inconsistent with the fact, that this place is now the largest fishing town on the American continent, if not in the world. The cause of their failure was in the attempt to combine fishing and planting. The season for one is also the season for the other; and he himself shows why, for other reasons, the two pursuits are incompatible: "First, that no sure fishing-place in the land is fit for planting, nor any good place for planting found fit for fishing; at least, near the shore: and, secondly, rarely any fisherman will work at land; neither are husbandmen fit for fishermen, but with long use and experience." The whole number of men on Cape Ann at the present day, who combine the two pursuits of fishing and agriculture, is not probably so large as that employed here by the Dorchester Company in 1625.

By the encouraging advice and promises of Mr. White,* who has been called the "father of the Massachusetts Colony," Roger Conant was induced to declare his intention to remain at Naumkeag, even if the few companions who accompanied him from Cape Ann should forsake him: which, at one time, they were strongly inclined to do; "secretly conceiving in his mind, that in following times (as since is fallen out) it might prove a receptacle for such as, upon the account of religion, would be willing to begin a foreign plantation in this part of the world." Mr. White redeemed his promise to Mr. Conant. "The business came to agitation afresh in London." New adventurers were enlisted in the work, and the resolution was taken to erect "a new Colony upon the old foundation." At length, on the 6th of September, 1628, the worthy Conant and his little band were cheered by the arrival of the ship with Endicott and his company. The next year followed other ships with more settlers; and finally, in 1630, came the great emigration under Winthrop, and the Colony of Massachusetts Bay was firmly and permanently planted. The ship in which Winthrop himself came passenger first cast anchor in the waters of Massachusetts, inside of Baker's Island. While lying there, most of her "people went on shore upon the land of Cape Ann, which lay very near, and gathered store of fine strawberries." The land of Cape Ann then included, probably, all the territory east of Naumkeag to the head of the Cape.

The names of a few of the first English occupants of our soil have come down to us, of whom Tylly and Gardener are first mentioned. Whither the former went from Cape Ann, we have no information. A John Tylley was admitted a freeman in 1635: probably the same person who, in 1636, was taken by Indians on Connecticut River, and barbarously murdered. Thomas Gardener is said to have come from Scotland. He set-

* The services of Rev. John White in behalf of the settlement of Massachusetts entitle him to a memoir, giving all that can be known concerning him, in some of our historical books. He was born in 1575; and, in 1605, became Rector of Trinity Parish, Dorchester. He was persecuted in the time of the civil war for taking side with the popular party, and went to London. After the wars were over, he returned to Dorchester; and died there, July 24, 1648, in his seventy-fourth year. — *Young's Chronicles of Massachusetts*, p. 26.

tled in Salem; became a freeman in 1637, and representative the same year.

The next and most prominent name among these occupants is that of Roger Conant. Nothing is known of the time or manner in which he came to New England. According to his own statement, he was in the country in the early part of 1623. After Lyford and Oldham "were discharged from having any thing more to do at Plymouth," in the course of the next year he went to Nantasket; whence in the following season he removed to Cape Ann to enter upon his office as "governor" of the plantation. We know but one incident of his career here, and that presents him in the beautiful character of a peacemaker. We follow him to Naumkeag, and behold him the pious and resolute pioneer in planting the first permanent settlement in the Colony of Massachusetts Bay. "The superior condition of the persons who came over with the charter," says Hutchinson, "cast a shade upon him, and he lived in obscurity;" but the memory of his virtues and services has been preserved from oblivion, and his name will always have an honorable place in the annals of our Commonwealth. Indeed, the historian of the "Landing at Cape Anne" considers it entitled to the first place in the list of Governors of Massachusetts. Whether this distinction shall be allowed or not, no one will contend that a want of titular rank can ever dim the lustre of any of the names of those persons in history distinguished for preferring the public good before private interest. "This," says Roger Conant truly, declaring himself in a public manner late in the evening of his life, "I praise God, I have done." The place in which he finally settled in Salem was in that part of the town which is now Beverly. He was admitted a freeman in 1631; was a representative in 1634; and died Nov. 16, 1679, aged eighty-six.

John Woodbury, John Balch, and Peter Palfrey, companions of Conant in the removal from Cape Ann to Naumkeag, are mentioned as having been known to Mr. White to be honest and prudent men; and, on that account, were engaged by him to stay in New England, and await the result of an effort to establish a plantation where they then were.

John Woodbury came from Somersetshire in England. After a residence of three years here and in Salem, he went back to England on business, and returned in 1628. He was made a freeman in 1631, and filled various offices of trust in Salem, besides representing it twice in the General Court. He died in 1641, leaving a son Humphrey; the father, without doubt, of Humphrey, who removed from Beverly to Gloucester about 1677.

John Balch came from Bridgewater, England. He was admitted a freeman in 1631; and was a useful citizen of Salem, where he died in 1648.

Peter Palfrey became a freeman in 1631. He was representative from Salem in 1635; and in 1653 removed to Reading, where he died in 1663.

Besides these men, there were old Goodman Norman and his son, William Allen, and Walter Knight; the last of whom stated to an early settler, according to his deposition given in 1681, that they came over to Cape Ann for the Dorchester Company. William Allen was probably an early settler of Manchester, as he was one of a company for "erecting a village" on that spot in 1640. He was living in 1664.

One other name concludes the list. The Rev. John Lyford was an Episcopal clergyman, and was, without doubt, the first leader in the exercises of public Christian worship in our territory. He came to New England, in the ship "Charity," in 1624, but not with the approbation of the friends of the Pilgrims in England. Soon after his arrival, he engaged in a course of conduct which resulted in his expulsion from the Colony. Historical evidence of the highest authority, recently published, leaves no room to doubt that he was a very bad man. A recital of his guilty deeds would be an unfit narrative for these pages. He is supposed to have remained here till the settlement was broken up; soon after which he went to Virginia, where he died. Tradition has marked the place where the first Christian worshippers on our soil were located; but it has left the imagination to select the spot where they set up their altar, and to picture the scene of their devotions, and all the circumstances of their religious worship.

The first landing of the Dorchester Company's planters on our soil was in 1623; probably in the summer. It is supposed that Mr. Conant and his men abandoned the plantation in the summer of 1626. This period of our history occupies, therefore, about three years. The cattle and other property, including a house, owned by the Dorchester adventurers, were carried to Naumkeag, and sold to the Massachusetts Company, at the commencement of their operations at that place which soon after received its present name, — Salem. On the zigzag path trodden by the cattle, tradition says, the highway from Gloucester to Salem was afterwards made. Some remains of the house are said to be contained in an old building, still standing, at the corner of Court and Church Streets, in the last-named town.*

Though abandoned by Conant and his companions, Cape Ann does not cease from this time to present some point of historical interest every year. It had visitors occasionally for the first five years after the breaking-up of the settlement; and within five or six years, there is reason to believe, there were permanent residents on the spot. Among the visitors was a man named Fells, a shipwrecked adventurer, who, with his paramour, fled hither from Plymouth to escape just punishment from the hands of the Puritans. Another one was Thomas Morton, of Merry-Mount notoriety, who seems to have come to our territory after he was driven away from the other side of the bay. Next we have more respectable visitors. On Saturday, June 27, 1629, the ship "Talbot," with Rev. Francis Higginson and other passengers, who were sent over by the Massachusetts Company to Salem, anchored in our harbor; "where," says Mr. Higginson in his journal, "there was an island, whither four of our men with a boat went, and brought back again ripe strawberries and gooseberries and sweet single roses." The ship remained in the harbor till Monday: and it is probable that some of the company landed on the main, and saw the marks of the abandoned

* Richard Brakenbury, who came with Endicott to Massachusetts, testified, in 1681, that he, with others, was sent to Cape Ann "to pull down the said house for Mr. Endicott's use."

settlement; for William Dixy, without doubt one of the passengers, says, in a deposition which he gave several years after this date, that he arrived at Cape Ann in 1629, but saw no English people here, though there were signs of "buildings and plantation-work."

We have now reached the conclusion of that chapter in the history of the town, which includes its discovery, and the temporary residence of a company of English fishermen and planters on its soil. The next will give an account of the permanent settlement within its borders of those among whom were the ancestors of a considerable portion of its present population. But, before entering upon it, we should allude to the absence of all evidence that Cape Ann was ever the seat of any Indian settlement. Its Indian name was Wingaersheek. Skeletons of the aborgines have been found; and the Indian tools, and collections of clam-shells, discovered many years ago around one spot in Squam, indicate the presence of the natives at some time in considerable numbers: but whether their visits were frequent or rare, and whether the early settlers were welcomed to a friendly wigwam or alarmed by the menacing gesture and suspicious carriage of the red man, no record or tradition is left to tell.

CHAPTER IV.

EARLY SETTLERS.

TRADITIONARY ACCOUNT OF FIRST SETTLEMENT. — THACHER'S SHIPWRECK. — MR. THOMSON, OF LONDON, ENCOURAGED TO ESTABLISH A FISHING PLANTATION AT CAPE ANN. — PERMANENT SETTLEMENT AND INCORPORATION OF THE TOWN. — LIST OF SETTLERS TO 1651, TO 1701; WITH NOTICES OF THESE SETTLERS AND THEIR FAMILIES.

IN entering upon this period of our history, the path is found for a few years to be involved in darkness and obscurity. There is no mention by historians, or in any ancient record, of the story that tradition has handed down concerning the first permanent settlers of Cape Ann. It is natural to suppose that they were attracted to this rocky promontory chiefly by its advantageous situation for shore-fishing; for, though but poor returns could be expected for the most laborious industry upon its soil, they might reasonably hope to find the means of a comfortable subsistence in the treasures of the sea by which it is surrounded. The settlement of a large Colony within convenient distance, and the growing intercourse between Old England and New, afforded increased advantages, and a greater inducement than had yet existed, for pursuing that business; and no improbability forbids credence to the statement that a company from Plymouth came across the bay in search of a suitable place for a fishing-station, and found it on the shores of Cape Ann.*

It is said that these men, led by a son of Rev. John Robinson, landed at Agassquam, and were so well satisfied with its har-

* The source whence the tradition mentioned in this paragraph is derived, with some remarks, will be given in a notice of the Robinson Family.

bor, and other conveniences for the fishing-business, that they concluded to set up a fishing-stage, and to make preparations there for the accommodation of their families. No means exist for determining the year in which this took place. We know that a remnant of Mr. Robinson's Leyden congregation were passengers in one of the ships that brought Winthrop's company in 1630; and a letter in print, written in March of that year, alluding to Mrs. Robinson as intending to come over, authorizes the inference that she, with one or more of her children perhaps, was among the passengers. If, therefore, this traditionary account of the first settlement of Cape Ann may be received as a fact in our history, the date of that event may be fixed about 1631. That there were settlers here as early as 1633, who "met, and carried on the worship of God among themselves, read the word of God, prayed to him, and sung psalms," may be asserted upon authority of the highest respectability; for the statement is made in a printed sermon of one of the most esteemed ministers of the town in the last century, who gives, in the margin, reference to an "ancient manuscript" to warrant his assertion.* It appears probable, therefore, that, from the last-named year, we may date the permanent settlement of Cape Ann.

While Cape Ann was yet but little known to the scattered settlers of New England, it became, in a sudden and wholly unlooked-for manner, a point of melancholy interest to all of them, by the occurrence of one of the most distressing shipwrecks that has ever happened on its coast. On the 12th of August, 1635, a pinnace, having on board Rev. John Avery and family, eleven persons in all, including his wife and six children; Mr. Anthony Thacher, his wife, four children, and another person of his family; one other passenger, and four mariners, — sailed from Ipswich for Marblehead, where Mr. Avery had engaged to

* The sermon here alluded to was preached by Rev. Eli Forbes, September, 1792, on the occasion of re-opening the meeting-house of the First Parish after it had been thoroughly repaired. The text was from Exod. xx. 24, last clause. "Ancient manuscript:" these are the only words of the marginal reference. There is too much reason to fear that this precious document is lost beyond the hope of recovery, and that we must ever experience the vain regret that it was not published instead of the sermon.

settle in the ministry. The wind being unfavorable, they had not doubled the Cape at night on the 14th. About ten o'clock that night, in a fresh gale of wind, their sails were split, and the vessel was brought to anchor; but, before daylight next morning, a furious storm came on, and she began to drag her anchor, and drift about at the mercy of the wind and waves. She was finally driven "upon a rock between two high rocks, yet all was one rock." Mr. Avery and his eldest son, and Mr. Thacher and daughter, were by "a mighty wave" washed out upon the rock, whence they called to those in the pinnace to come to them; but the next wave dashed the vessel to pieces, and swept away those who had gained a momentary foothold upon the rock. After he had been washed about by the sea and beaten against the rock for a quarter of an hour, Mr. Thacher at last felt the bottom, and soon found himself standing on his feet, breast-deep in the water, with his face towards the shore, which he soon reached in safety. His first act, after blessing God, was to look for his family and friends; but the merciless ocean had swallowed them all save one, — the one who, of all that ill-fated company, could most deeply sympathize with him in the loss of his children, and most heartily unite with him in thanksgiving for the wonderful deliverance they had experienced, — his wife. Soon after he reached the shore, he saw her "getting herself forth from amongst the timber of the broken bark;" from which, before he could join her, she cleared herself; and, going to her husband, they sought together a resting-place under a bank. Some provisions and clothing came ashore; as also, fortunately, a "snapsack" containing a steel, flint, and some gunpowder in a dry condition. With these they made themselves comfortable, till, on the second day after the shipwreck, they were taken off, and carried to Marblehead. Mr. Thacher arrived in New England but a few weeks before the distressing event which deprived him of all his children. Public liberality and private benevolence contributed to make up to him the loss of his property, and the lapse of years filled in part the places of his lost children. He settled in Yarmouth, and died there in 1668, aged about eighty; leaving a son, by whose descendants the name is perpetuated in various places. On his departure from the sorrowful scene of his shipwreck, he gave his own name to the island upon which he was cast, calling it "Thacher's Woe;" and the rock on which the vessel was wrecked was called "Avery his Fall."*

The lapse of six years brings us to another attempt to establish a fishing plantation here on foreign account. This enterprise was undertaken by Maurice Thomson, a merchant of London, of whom nothing more is known than that he had been, a few years before, engaged in a trade for beaver in Canada. By an act of the General Court, May 22, 1639, "for the encouragement of Mr. Maurice Thomson, merchant, and others who intend to promote the fishing-trade, it was ordered that a fishing plantation should be begun at Cape Ann, and that the said Mr. Thomson should have places assigned for the building of houses and stages and other necessaries for that use; and shall have sufficient lands allowed for their occasions, both for their fishing and for keeping of cattle, and for corn, &c.; and that such other fishermen as will join in the way of fishing, and inhabit there, shall have such lands and other liberties there as shall be needful and fit for their occasions." The court empowered "Mr. Endicott, Mr. Humphrey, Mr. Winthrop, jun., Mr. William Pierce, and Joseph Grafton, or any three of them, to set out the said plantation, and all lands and other accommodations, to such as should be planted there; and none to be settled there but by their allowance." An act was also passed, granting to fishing

---

* A letter from Mr. Thacher to his brother, written in the most pathetic language, giving a particular account of his shipwreck, has been preserved, and reprinted in Young's Chronicles of Massachusetts, with a valuable note by the editor. The rock lying off the head of Cape Ann, now called "Avery's Rock," cannot be the one mentioned in Mr. Thacher's narrative, for reasons that will be apparent enough to any one who will visit Thacher's Island with the narrative in his hand. Avery's Rock is more than two miles from the island, — much too great a distance for a man to be carried by the sea in a quarter of an hour. Besides, we know that the terrific gale which caught the pinnace off our Cape was from the east, — a direction almost contrary to that which points from Avery's Rock to Thacher's Island. But what settles the question is the fact, that the present Avery's Rock never shows itself, even at low water, above the surface of the sea. Mr. William Hale, late keeper of the lights on Thacher's Island, and several other persons living at the Cape, who have carefully read the narrative, give their opinion, that the fatal rock was a ledge on the south side of the island, about a gunshot distant from it, now called Crackwood's Ledge.

establishments certain exemptions to encourage the colonists themselves to give their attention to this branch of industry, and in expectation that Mr. Thomson would come over and settle. But Mr. Thomson did not come; and, indeed, history is almost silent respecting this new plantation. By one notice only does it appear that that person made any use of his grant; though sufficient evidence exists that our soil, about this time, was the abode of a few fishermen. Our town-records, under date of 4th month, 1650, say, "Will Southmead hath given him that psell of land in the harbour upon which Mr. Tomson's frame stood;" "provided, yt if Mr. Tomson or his agent shall demand it, that then, upon compensation for the charges about it, this said grant is to be surrendered up." From one writer of that period (Thomas Lechford), we learn that our territory was occupied in 1639. He resided in Boston in that year, but soon after returned to England, where he published a work, in which he says, "At Cape Ann, where fishing is set forward, and some stages builded, there one master Rashley is chaplain."* Another early writer calls "Cape Ann a place of fishing; being peopled with fishermen till the reverend Mr. Richard Blindman came from a place in Plimouth Patten." The grant to Southmead was undoubtedly several years before the date of its record; as the grantee was an early settler, and, at that time, had been dead upwards of a year. The mention of "Mr. Tomson's frame," in this grant, suggests a possibility, at least, that the erection of it might have been the extent to which that individual prosecuted his design here. Our early records shed no further light upon this part of our history; and ultimate despair must probably be the fruit of every attempt, in any other quarter, to enlarge the scanty information we possess concerning it. No regret will be felt, therefore, in leaving this period to enter upon that which exhibits Cape Ann as the home of families and the scene of the infant existence of a settled town.

At a General Court, October, 1641, commissioners were appointed to view and settle the bounds of Ipswich, Cape Ann,

* Massachusetts Historical Collections.

and Jeffries' Creek (now Manchester); and the Deputy-governor (Mr. Endicott), and Messrs. Downing and Hathorne, deputies from Salem, or any two of them, were appointed to dispose of all lands and other things at Cape Ann. Pursuant to this authority, as the town-records declare, "the first ordering, settling, and disposing of lots, was made by Mr. Endicott and Mr. Downing, commissioners, 2d month, 1642." How many people were then here is not known: but, about this time, the settlement assumed more consequence, from the arrival of Rev. Richard Blynman with several families from Plymouth Colony; and it was, at a court in May in that year, by the simple form of incorporation then used, established as a plantation, and called Gloucester. This name was probably given by desire of some of the principal settlers, who are said to have come from the city of the same name in England.* Gloucester in England is situated in the Vale of Gloucester, on a gentle eminence rising on the east side from the river Severn, about thirty miles from the junction of that river with Bristol Channel. It was founded by the Britons, who named it Caer Gloew; which signifies the "Fortress of Gloew," a prince of the county of which the city was the capital. Under the Saxons, the name became Gleaucestre,—the etymon of the present appellation. Some writers say that the name is derived from the British words *glaw*, "handsome;" and *caer*, "city." Gloucester is distinguished for its manufacture of pins, and its handsome Cathedral, begun as early as 1047.

Mr. Blynman is said to have been accompanied to New England by several Welsh gentlemen of good note; but the date of his arrival is not known. He had probably been but a short time in the country when he came to Cape Ann. At a court held in Plymouth, March 2, 1641, Mr. Blynman, Mr. Hugh Pritchard, Mr. Obadiah Bruen, John Sadler, Hugh Caulkin, and Walter Tybbot, were propounded to be made free at the next court. All these persons were of Mr. Blynman's company in the removal hither, and some of them followed him when he left. No means exist for ascertaining the names of all his com-

* Rev. E. Forbes's sermon, alluded to on p. 47.

panions. The early records of the town make no discrimination between these settlers and those who preceded and those who followed them. After residing in Gloucester a few years, Mr. Blynman and several of the early settlers removed to New London; and it is probable that those who accompanied him to that place were also of the number that came with him to Cape Ann. The emigrants to New London were Christopher Avery, James Avery, William Addes, Obadiah Bruen, Hugh Calkin, John Coit, sen., William Hough, William Kenie, Andrew Lister, William Meades, Ralph Parker, and William Wellman. Mr. Blynman and Ralph Parker seem to have gone on in advance of the rest: for they received their grants of land there a few months before the others; all of whom, except William Addes and Christopher Avery, had removed thither in 1651. These two followed several years after. Before dismissing this collective body of settlers, it may be stated, as an interesting fact, that their lots in New London were laid out in a new street, long known as Cape-Ann Lane, and now called Ann Street.

Our town-records supply most of the information that can be gathered concerning the early settlers; but these furnish no data for ascertaining, in many cases, the year in which they came. The list of persons which follows is believed to comprise all who are known to have been residents of Gloucester, or proprietors of its soil, from the time of its permanent settlement to the close of 1650:—

William Addes.
Christopher Avery.
James Avery.
William Ash.
Thomas Ashley.
Isabel Babson.
James Babson.
Alexander Baker.
Richard Beeford.
George Blake.
Richard Blynman.
Obadiah Bruen.
John Bourne.
Thomas Bray.
William Brown.
Hugh Calkin.
Thomas Chase.
Mr. Clark.
Matthew Coe.
John Collins.
Thomas Cornish.
John Coit, sen.
John Coit, jun.
William Cotton.
Clement Coldam.
Anthony Day.

William Dudbridge.
Osman Dutch.
William Evans.
Robert Elwell.
Sylvester Eveleth.
Henry Felch.
Mr. Fryer.
James Fogg.
John Gallope.
Charles Glover.
Stephen Glover.
William Haskell.
John Holgrave.
William Hough.
Zebulon Hill.
Samuel Haieward.
George Ingersoll.
Thomas Jones.
Thomas Judkin.
William Kenie.
Thomas Kent.
John Kettle.
Nicholas Liston.
Andrew Lister.
John Luther.
Solomon Martin.
William Meades.
Thomas Milward.
George Norton.
Ralph Parker.
John Pearse.
Capt. Perkins.
Thomas Prince.
Hugh Pritchard.
Phenis Rider.
Abraham Robinson.
Edward Rouse.
Mr. Sadler.
Robert Sadler.
William Sargent.
Thomas Skellin.
James Smith.
Thomas Smith.
Morris Somes.
William Southmeade.
William Stevens.
Stephen Streeter.
John Studley.
Walter Tybbot.
Thomas Very.
William Vinson.
Thomas Wakley.
John Wakley.
Henry Walker.
William Wellman.
Philip Yondall.

Of these eighty-two settlers, about one-third remained in town, and found here their final resting-place. It has been seen that thirteen went to New London; six removed to Falmouth, Me., and about twelve to other places; leaving about twenty who left for parts unknown.

The Babsons, Bourne, Coit, Collins, Fryer, Skellin, Norton, Stevens, Glover, Brown, Elwell, Vinson, and Holgrave, came from Salem. Of the whole list of names of the first settlers, it is supposed that not more than ten are perpetuated by families now living in town, though descendants of several others in the female line are numerous.

In order to present, in this connection, a complete list of all the early inhabitants of the town, the following names are added of persons who settled here between the period to which the preceding list is brought, and the end of the century: —

Joseph Allen.
Ralph Andrews.
Edmond Ashby.
Thomas Bailey.
Giles Barge.
William Bartholmew.
Anthony Bennett.
Richard Biles.
John Briars.
Edmund Broadway.
John Brown.
John Butman.
William Card.
Arthur Churchill.
Peter Coffin.
William Cogswell.
William Colman.
John Cook.
John Curney.
Zacheus Curtis.
John Davis.
Nicholas Denning.
Richard Dike.
Samuel Dolliver.
Moses Dudy.
Peter Duncan.
John Durgee.
William Ellery.
John Emerson.
Peter Emons.
John Fitch.
Bartholomew Foster.
James Gardner.
George Giddings.
Richard Gooding.
John Hadley.
Nathaniel Hadlock.
John Hammons.
John Hardin.
Edward Harraden.
George Harvey.
Samuel Hodgkins.
James Hughes.
John Jackson.
Charles James.
Henry Joslin.
John Lane.
Thomas Lovekin.
Thomas Low.
Edmund Marshall.
Philip Merritt.
Thomas Millet.
Francis Norwood.
Joseph Page.
Elias Parkman.
Jeffrey Parsons.
Thomas Penny.
William Perkins.
John Pool.
Rowland Powell.
Thomas Pulcifer.
Thomas Riggs.
John Ring.
John Roberts.
John Rowe.
Abial Sadler.
James Sawyer.
William Sargent, 2d.
James Sayward.
Robert Skamp.
Morris Smith.
John Smith.
Philip Stainwood.
George Stover.
Harlakenden Symonds.
James Travis.
Robert Tucker.
John Tucker.
Bridget Varney.
John Wallis.
Samuel Webber.
Nathaniel Wharf.
William Whittridge.
Richard Window.
Henry Witham.
Humphrey Woodbury.
Samuel York.

The above list contains the names of eighty-seven persons; of whom, as nearly as can be ascertained, about fifty became permanent settlers, and were residents of the town when they died.

Thirty-five of the whole number are supposed to be represented by descendants living in town, and bearing their names. But further general remarks respecting them are deemed unnecessary in this place, as the biographical notices which follow give all the information worthy of preservation here concerning the settlers whose names have been given, and also of those of their descendants who have been prominent in the history of the town.

WILLIAM ADDES. — He was one of the first selectmen. He is not mentioned as a landowner, otherwise than as a seller of a lot on Eastern Point. He was here in 1649, when he was witness in an action against Charles Glover. He appears in New London, Conn., in 1659; when he was allowed to brew beer, and distil for the benefit of the town. Afterwards he was engaged in trading operations for a company in England. Mercantile employments may have occupied his attention in Gloucester; for, in one of the few instances in which he is mentioned, he is spoken of as building a bark. He had a daughter Millicent, who married William Southmeade.

MARTHA AGAR. — Her daughter Hannah died in 1696, in the tenth year of her age.

JOSEPH ALLEN. — The name of Allen occurs among the first occupants of our territory; William Allen having been one of the adventurers who came over to Cape Ann for the Dorchester Company. He was probably the early settler of Manchester of the same name, and perhaps the ancestor of our Allens. Joseph Allen came to Gloucester in 1674. He was a blacksmith, and was encouraged to settle here by an immediate grant of land and a common right. In 1675, he bought of James Davis, sen., a house and land near the Meeting-house. A house, erected by him on this land, was taken down a few years since by the descendant now owning the property, who built a new one on the same spot. He was frequently elected a selectman, and chosen on committees; and, in 1705, was representative. The title, "captain," often given to him, was a military one; probably derived from his command of a military company. He died Oct. 6, 1724, aged seventy-one. He was twice married: first to Rachel Griggs, in 1680, who died April 26, 1684; and next to Rose Howard, in 1684, who survived him but twenty-one days, and died Oct. 27, 1724, aged about sixty. By these two wives he had seventeen children; namely: Joseph, born in 1681; Jeremiah, 1682; Rachel, 1684; Solomon, 1685; Benjamin, 1687; a son, 1688; Thomas, 1689; Anna, 1691; John, 1692; Rose, 1694; William, 1696; Mercy and Patience, 1697; Jeremiah, 1698; Samuel, 1701; Zerubbabel, 1703; and Moses, 1706. Several of these children died young. JOSEPH, the oldest, engaged in trade, and became a citizen of considerable distinction, taking an active part in town-affairs. He represented the town in General Court four years. He died April 6, 1750, leaving an estate appraised at £5,130. 14s. 6d. His wife was Mary Coit, who survived him. Eight of his children also survived him. Of these, William, born in 1717, built the large house east of the site of the old Meeting-house in Town Parish, where he had a large family of children born to him; the last of whom, Elizabeth, widow of Samuel Stevens, deceased in Portland, in 1850, at the advanced age of ninety-eight. He removed to New Gloucester, Me., on the early settlement of that town. Nathaniel, born in 1718, engaged extensively in fishing and commercial operations. He built the old Long Wharf, and the house near the head of it, recently standing, in which he resided. Becoming bankrupt in business, he removed, about the commencement of the Revolutionary War, to Dover, N.H.; where he died soon after his removal. Mr. Allen was representative five years, and was a gentleman of high character and standing. His real estate became the property of a British subject; and, as such, was leased by the selectmen, in 1779, for the term of one year. The house had been previously occupied as barracks for one of the companies stationed here. Mr. Allen was twice married: first to Mary, daughter of Rev. Joshua Gee of Boston; and next to Sarah, daughter of Epes Sargent, Esq. Although twelve children were born to him by these two wives, no descendant remains. One of his sons (Joseph) graduated at Harvard College in 1774; and, after residing several years in New Hampshire, became cashier of the Gloucester Bank in 1796, and continued in that office till 1829. He died, unmarried, Oct. 8, 1831, aged seventy-five. Thomas, son of Captain Joseph Allen, occupied the paternal estate. He was born in 1689; married Elizabeth Coit in 1711; and died, at an advanced age, about the commencement of the Revolutionary War. Three of his sons married, and had families. Thomas married Jemima Haskell in 1732: David and Isaac married daughters of Rev. John White. His son Jeremiah, born 1717, died young, an undergraduate of Harvard College. William, son of Thomas Allen, jun., born in 1735, was a soldier in the French and Indian wars. He also served, with two sons, in the Revolutionary War. William, one of these sons, received a fatal shot in the arm on the retreat from Long Island. Nathaniel, the other son, left the army, and went on board a privateer. He was in the "Civil Usage" when the commander, Capt. John Smith, was killed; and stood alongside the lieutenant when that officer was struck on the head by a cannon-ball, and killed on the spot. He died in Manchester, about 1843, aged eighty-five. John Allen married Eunice Stone of Beverly in 1716; and, besides daughters, had sons, — Ambrose, John, Nehemiah, and Solomon. He resided at the entrance of the southerly way leading to Hodgkins' Ferry. Samuel married Rachel Day in 1726, and had eight children, of whom five were sons; viz., Samuel, Joseph, Robert, Jonathan, and William. Zerubbabel married Lydia Parsons in 1728, and died Feb. 4, 1749. He had sons, — Ebenezer, Jacob, Joseph, Moses, Stephen, and Zerubbabel. The latter died at sea in 1756.

Ralph Andrews. — This individual first appears in Gloucester on the occasion of his marriage to Abigail Very, Nov. 17, 1681. His life was one of poverty and misfortune. His poverty is inferred from the fact that he appears nowhere as a landholder during his whole life, and from the allusions to the help he received from the town. He did not come upon the town for support till after 1699, when the selectmen were fully empowered to send him to the "Lin doctor, James Kibber, to be cured of his lameness, if the said Kibber doth think he can cure him."

He died Feb. 25, 1718, aged seventy-five. His wife died May 8, 1728, aged sixty-seven. Four children are recorded to him, — Thomas, 1686; Francis, 1689; Abigail, 1692; and Hannah, 1702. Besides these, there was probably a Ralph, who received aid from the town in 1740, and died Nov. 3, 1778, aged eighty-three. These sons are believed to have married. Others of the name appear in town about the commencement of the last century; who were, without doubt, from Ipswich, where families of this name settled early. John Andrews and Sarah Curtis (whom he afterwards married) were warned out of town in 1711. William Andrews settled here about the same time, and was father of William, who was wounded in one of the expeditions to Louisburg, Cape Breton, and died on his passage home.

William Ash. — No land is recorded to him; but he sold a house and land to John Jackson in May, 1651. He married Millicent, widow of William Southmeade.

Mr. Ashley. — A lot in the harbor is mentioned, in 1650, as once belonging to him. Thomas Ashley and his goods were attached in July, 1642, for William Addes and others.

Edmund Ashby was of Salem in 1665, and only appears here at the birth of his son James in 1680.

Christopher Avery and his son James were among the first settlers. They had land in several places; but resided, as nearly as can be made out from the records, at the plantation. Christopher Avery was selectman in 1646, 1652, and 1654. At a court in Salem, June 29, 1652, he took the freeman's oath; was chosen and sworn clerk of the band, constable and clerk of the market. These offices indicate the possession of a fair character; but the criminal records of those times present him to us in various unfavorable aspects. He was presented twice at court for living away from his wife; once for speaking scoffingly of Mr. Blynman: and, in 1655, he commenced an action against James Standish and William Vinson for slanderously reporting that he drank liquor so long, "that he took Inke instead of liquor; and took another man's wife upon his knee, and dandled her, ye foolish man, her husband looking on therewhile." The jury found for defendants. Avery sold his house and land in 1658, and went to New London; whither his son James had removed several years before. The latter married Joane Grinslade, Nov. 10, 1643, and had children, — Hannah, born 1644; James, 1646; and Mary, 1648. In 1651, he sold all his possessions in Gloucester to his father, and removed to New London, where he continued many years a useful and enterprising citizen.

ISABEL BABSON, widow and midwife, was of Salem in 1637, but came early to Gloucester, and had several grants of land. She also bought of Mr. Milward two acres that was Ashley's lot; a portion of which, situated at what is now 75 and 77, Front Street, continued in the family about a century and a half. She died April 6, 1661, aged about eighty-four; leaving an estate inventoried at £27. 6s. Her son James came hither with his mother, and settled near Little Good Harbor. He was a cooper by trade; but he cultivated his land, and left at his death a small farm, which went into the possession of Thomas Witham, who married his daughter. He died Dec. 21, 1683. His wife, Elinor Hill, to whom he was married in 1647, died March 14, 1714, aged eighty-three. His children were — James, born 1648; Elinor, 1651; Philip, 1654; Sarah, 1656, died 1676; Thomas, 1658; John, 1660; Richard, 1663; Elizabeth, 1665; Ebenezer, 1668; and Abigail, 1670. PHILIP BABSON removed to Salem; where, in 1689, he married Hannah Baker, who died in 1692, leaving a daughter Anna. THOMAS enlisted in the Indian war of 1675, and was some time on duty in garrison at Hadley. He probably died young, as his name does not appear after this time. JOHN had a grant, in 1695, of two or three acres at Straitsmouth, to "set up fishing upon." By further grants and purchase, he became possessor of twenty-seven acres there, which he held several years, and probably improved in carrying on the fishery. He sold it in 1721. He married, in 1686, Dorcas, daughter of Josiah Elwell. They both died in 1737. He had several children, three of whom — Elias, born in 1687; John, 1691; and Josiah, 1703 — died within a few weeks in 1720. His son James, born in 1689, is supposed to have been the father of Isaac Babson of Wenham, who died young in Bristol, England, leaving several children; one of whom (Isaac) graduated at Harvard College in 1779, and soon after went on board the privateer ship "Buccaneer" as steward. He spent several years in a seafaring life; but finally settled as a trader in Hopkinton, N.H., in 1786. In 1796, he removed to Manchester; where he died suddenly, July 31, 1800. John Babson, son of John, left two children, — James and William. The former became a sea-captain, and died Sept. 3, 1759, aged forty-two; leaving a son James, who was commander of a privateer in the Revolutionary War, and died Oct. 10, 1790, aged forty-nine. William was lost overboard on a voyage to the Grand Bank about 1749, aged thirty. His son William married Ann, daughter of Rev. John Rogers; and died at the McLean Asylum, Dec. 30, 1831, aged eighty-two. He was bred to a seafaring life; and, after several years spent in privateering and mercantile voyages, settled in business at Annisquam. His oldest son William, after a long and successful career in trade and commerce, died June 29, 1848, aged sixty-nine. Two of his sons have been representatives; William in 1850, and John J. in 1859 and 1860. Of this branch of the family is John Babson, who has held important national and state offices in Maine; and is now vice-consul of the United States for Canada. His residence is in Wiscasset, Me. RICHARD BABSON had a wife Mary, who died Feb. 14, 1718, aged fifty-four. He next married Jane Reading, Oct. 14, 1718. He settled at Fresh-water Cove; and, after living there many years, removed to Falmouth, Me., about 1727. He had eleven or twelve children, but only one son that married. John, born in 1687; married Hannah Hodgkins in 1711, and died before 1743. She died about 1779, over ninety. From the sons by this marriage are descended most of the Babsons on Cape Ann. John, born in 1713, died about the close of the last century, leaving a son Samuel; who, having acquired considerable property in mercantile pursuits here, retired to a farm in Lincoln, Mass., where he died Oct. 8, 1805, aged about sixty-four. Solomon, born in 1715, was the father of John, a merchant, extensively and successfully engaged in business many years in

Gloucester and Newburyport. Becoming reduced in circumstances, he removed to Maine; and died suddenly at Mt. Desert, March 22, 1825, aged seventy-nine. His wife was Catharine, daughter of Rev. John Rogers. William, born in 1721, married Mary Williams. His oldest son, William, was lost in the ship "Gloucester." Three of the grandsons of the latter have held public offices of importance: Gorham, a representative three years, and now collector of the customs; David, for several years surveyor of the port; and Fitz J., representative in 1858 and 1860. The two former have their residence in Rockport. EBENEZER BABSON would have no further notice here if he had not found a place in the "Magnalia" of Cotton Mather, where, in a letter from Rev. John Emerson, he figures in the diabolical work by which, in 1692, the town was kept in a state of agitation and alarm for several months. He may have been distinguished in an encounter with a less ethereal enemy, and thus have been the occasion of the local saying, "The knife that Babson killed the bear with." He died before 1696. James Babson is probably the ancestor of all the Babsons in the United States.

THOMAS BAILEY and wife Mary appear in Gloucester, 1700; when Thomas, their son, was born. Other children were — Samuel, born 1702; Mary, 1704. The father died Oct. 15, 1704.

ALEXANDER BAKER was owner of a house and land early, and may have been for a short time a resident. He lived in Boston many years.

GILES BARGE bought two acres of land in Fishermen's Field in 1653, which he sold in 1655. In the time of Sir Edmund Andros, he petitioned for confirmation of two hundred and sixty acres of land in Scarborough, which some years before he had lived on and improved.

WILLIAM BARTHOLMEW was here in 1657, when he was one of a committee to "seek out for a minister." He had planting-ground and marsh; but, after remaining in town a short time, he removed to Boston.

RICHARD BEEFORD was born about 1608. He is named in an action at a Quarterly Court in Salem, 1637; but he was not probably an inhabitant of Gloucester before 1650, although his children (John, Mary, Hannah, and Ruth) are recorded here as born by his wife Mary before that year. Other children of his were — Nathaniel, born in 1650; and Richard, in 1653. He bought a house and land of Solomon Martin in 1651. He was freeman, 1651; selectman, 1659 and 1660; and then disappears.

Anthony Bennett, carpenter, probably came to this town from Beverly; where a person of the same name, a carpenter, was living in 1671. He had grants of land here in 1679; on one of which, on the east side of Mill River, he settled. He died Jan. 12, 1691: his wife Abigail died Oct. 26, 1733, between seventy and eighty years of age. His two sons (Anthony, born in 1679; and John, in 1686) both married, and had families. John died Feb. 1, 1725, aged thirty-eight years. He came into possession of the ancient mill, with the privilege of the stream; but he found an earnest competitor for the business of the town in John Ring, who had a mill on Sawmill-river Dam. The mill continued in the Bennett Family, and was carried on by them many years. Peter, another son, settled in town, and had several children; but had removed in 1718, when he was living in Georgetown, York County, Me. The name is not borne here now by any descendant; but it survives in New Gloucester and other parts of Maine, whither members of the family emigrated from here.

George Blake had several grants of land; on one of which, near the Meeting-house, he resided. He was selectman, 1649; and freeman, 1651. In 1665, he sold house, upland, orchard, and commonage, to John Fitch; and, in 1669, another house and land, to Thomas Judkin; soon after which he removed to Boxford, where he died Feb. 17, 1698. Dorothy Blake, probably his wife, died at the same place, Dec. 12, 1702. The children of George Blake by his wife Dorothy, recorded on our books, are — Rebecca, born in 1641; Deborah, Prudence, 1647; Elizabeth, 1650; Mary, 1652; Thomas, 1658; and Ruth, 1659.

John Bourne lived in Salem before he came to Gloucester. He had liberty from the General Court in 1646 to set up a cookshop in the former place; not to sell beer above a penny a quart.

He bought a house and land at Trynall Cove, in 1649, of William Hough; and sold it in 1652. In 1651, he was clerk of the writs and of the market. After leaving Gloucester, he went to Barbadoes, where he was in 1661. By his wife Mary he had one child (Bethiah), born here in 1651.

THOMAS BRAY, ship-carpenter, born in 1614, had, with other grants of land, six acres, in 1647, at the head of Little River; and, in 1651, one-quarter of an acre in the bottom, on the north side, of Cow-Island Marsh, "for a house to be sett on." He probably settled at this time in that part of the town, where descendants have continued ever since. John Bray, perhaps a relative, was a shipwright at Kittery in 1663, and had a daughter, who became the mother of Sir William Pepperell. Thomas Bray married, May 3, 1646, Mary Wilson, who died March 27, 1707: he died Nov. 30, 1691. His children were — Mary, born in 1647; Thomas, 1653; John, 1654; Nathaniel, 1656; Hannah, 1662; Esther, 1664; and Sarah. THOMAS had a wife Mary, and several children, of whom five were sons, — Thomas, John, Nathaniel, Moses, and Aaron. Thomas married Elinor Dodge of Beverly in 1716; and had, besides daughters, sons, — Thomas, Edward, and Ebenezer. Thomas, though not an educated physician, practised medicine in his native parish many years; and died there Nov. 26, 1801, aged over eighty. John, second son of Thomas Bray, jun., married Susanna Woodbury in 1716, and had six children, of whom three were sons: one of these (Humphrey) married Lydia Woodbury in 1749, and had a son Silas, whose son Silas was representative in 1838 and 1844. Nathaniel, the third son, married Sarah Haskell in 1733, and had eleven children, among whom were sons, — Nathaniel, Daniel, Benjamin, — and others whose names are not known; and died Jan. 18, 1773, aged seventy-nine. Moses Bray had a wife Mary, and sons, — Samuel, Nicholas, and Moses. He died July 19, 1773, aged seventy-seven. Aaron Bray married Elizabeth Davis in 1727, and Ruth Winter in 1744. Of his ten children, four were sons, — Aaron, Mark, Edward, and Thomas. JOHN, son of Thomas, sen., married Margaret Lambert in 1679, who died in 1725, aged seventy:

he died Sept. 25, 1714. Having no children, he gave the reversion of his property to his nephew John. NATHANIEL, the youngest son, married Martha Wadin in 1684. He died May 2, 1728, aged seventy-six; leaving, it appears, an only son Nathaniel, who married Sarah Davis in 1714, and had sons, — Isaac, Andrew, and Nathaniel.

JOHN BRIARS appears here, in 1652, on the occasion of his marriage to Elizabeth, daughter of John Jackson. The following children are recorded to him: Grace, born in 1655; John, 1658; Benjamin, 1660; and Mary, 1661, who died at birth. In 1858, there was given him a "necke of land liinge over against John Jackson's two or three acres, which was called Peter Mud's Neck." He left town soon after 1661.

EDMUND BROADWAY sold land in Fishermen's Field and other places in 1653 and 1654; but it does not appear certain that he resided here.

JOHN BROWN had, in 1704, built a small house and fenced in a piece of town's land near Sadler's Run. He died March 17, 1732, aged seventy. His wife Rebekah died June 24, 1711. Their children born in Gloucester were — Sarah, born in 1696; Rebekah, 1699; Rachel, 1702; Jonathan, 1705; and Joseph, 1709; besides others that died in infancy. John Brown (probably the preceding) married Elizabeth Somes in 1713; by whom his sons — William, 1714; and Daniel, 1717 — were born. He may have brought children to Gloucester with him; as an Elisha married Hannah Gardner, Nov. 21, 1717; and a John married Hannah Elwell, Jan. 23, 1721. Jonathan Brown married Lydia Elwell in 1728, and Joseph Brown married Mary Elwell in 1732. These three maidens of the same name were sisters; probably daughters of Jacob Elwell. Elisha Brown had eleven children; among whom were sons, — John, Elisha, James, Stephen, and Samuel. The latter was born in 1744, and married Dorcas Elwell in 1765. His business was that of a coaster. He was lost overboard on his passage from Boston to Gloucester about 1790; leaving several children, of whom one was Elisha, who died in Surinam about 1802. John Brown, jun., had two children born in Gloucester; and then removed to Falmouth,

Me. William married Elizabeth Phipps in 1735, and Daniel married Sarah Row in 1741. Descendants of Elisha, and probably of other sons of the first settler, John, continue the name in town.

WILLIAM BROWN was among the earliest settlers, and had several parcels of land. His residence was in the harbor. He was selectman, 1644 and 1647; and, in 1654, he had liberty from a Quarterly Court to draw strong waters during the pleasure of the court. He married Mary, widow of Abraham Robinson, in 1646; and died May 3, 1662, leaving a daughter Mary, born in 1649, who married William Haskell. His widow married, for her third husband, Henry Walker. His estate, which was considerable for the time and place (£223. 7s.) was mostly left to his son-in-law, Abraham Robinson.

OBADIAH BRUEN was the youngest son of John Bruen of Bruen Stapleford, county of Chester, England; a noted Puritan of an ancient family, which dates back to the Norman Conquest. He was baptized Dec. 22, 1606. He came to Plymouth with Rev. Richard Blynman, and accompanied him thence to the various fields of his labor, but parted on the settlement of the latter in New Haven. As nearly as can be ascertained, his residence in Gloucester was on the south-west side of the Meeting-house Green. Land in different places is recorded to him, though not in so large grants as to several other settlers. He was made a freeman in 1642; clerk of the writs, and commissioner to end small causes, in 1643; was a selectman several years, and the representative three years. In 1645, he was licensed at a Quarterly Court "to draw wine." He filled the office of town-clerk during the whole period of his stay in Gloucester; and, when he left, carried the records with him, as it appears by a copy of an extract from them, taken by his own hand after his removal to New Jersey. He sold all his possessions here in September, 1650, and went to New London, of which place he was the recorder many years. He was one of the patentees of the Colony of Connecticut named in the charter granted by Charles II. in 1662. In company with about fifty families from Connecticut, he emigrated to Newark,

N. J.; which place he bought of the Indians in 1667, and where it was the purpose of the settlers, as they declared, to establish a church and commonwealth exactly according to God's word; not permitting any one, except a member of a Congregational church, to hold office, either civil or military. Mr. Bruen had a wife Sarah, by whom two children were born in Gloucester, — Hannah in 1643, and John in 1646. The date of his death is unknown; but he was living in Newark in 1681. Descendants of this respectable stock remain in New Jersey. One (Rev. Matthew Bruen, born in Newark) was an eminent minister in New-York City; and died there in 1829, aged thirty-six.

Richard Byles, weaver, son of Jonathan Byles of Beverly, and his wife Elizabeth Patch, and grandson of Richard Brakenbury (who came to Salem with Gov. Endicott in 1628), was born Nov. 3, 1675; and first appears in Gloucester in 1700. In 1718, he bought of William Sargent a house and land that Sargent bought of John Durge. He had a wife Mary, by whom the following children were born: Charles, 1700; Mary, 1702; John, 1704; Martha, 1706; Sarah, 1710; Elizabeth, 1713; Alexander, 1716; and Jonathan, 1719. He had removed back to Beverly in 1727, where it is supposed his wife died in January, 1746, aged seventy; and he himself died Feb. 12, 1771, aged ninety-six. Charles Byles bought his father's property here, and remained in town. His residence was in the Second Parish, about half a mile from the head of Little River. He commanded a company at the siege of Louisburg in 1745; and again, it is said, at the taking of Quebec. He married Hannah Eveleth, Jan. 17, 1727, who died March 9, 1785, aged seventy-five: he died March 9, 1782, aged eighty-one. He had a son Charles, born in 1732, of whom nothing is known; and another (Nathaniel), born Feb. 5, 1741, whose intention of marriage with Sarah Procter of Ipswich, March 13, 1766, is recorded; and who died at Halifax, of small-pox, in December, 1777.

John Butman is supposed to have come from Salem, where Jeremiah Butman, a fisherman, was living in 1673. A Matthew

Butman resided in Beverly, with his sons Matthew and Jeremiah, in 1714. John received a grant of land on the west side of Annisquam River, in 1693, on condition that he should build upon it in three years; but, in 1696, he exchanged it for a lot of two acres and a half at the head of Lobster Cove, where he built his house, and probably spent the remainder of his life. He married Sarah, daughter of Abraham Robinson, June 30, 1690, and had the following children: Jeremiah, born in 1690; a daughter, 1693; Mary, 1697; Hannah, 1700; John, 1703; Jonathan, 1708; and Samuel, 1711. Jeremiah married Abigail Stevens in 1713; and was lost in a violent gale, coming from Cape Sable, in 1716; leaving a son Jeremiah. John had two wives; but no sons are recorded to him, and only one daughter that lived. Jonathan had a wife Judith, and several children; the first of which was born in Newbury in 1734.

Hugh Calkin, husbandman, was one of Mr. Blynman's company. He had land in various places, but fixed his residence on the neck of house-lots. He was admitted freeman in 1642; was a selectman several years; commissioner for ending small causes in 1645; and representative in 1650 and 1651. In this last year he left Gloucester, and became successively a resident of New London and Norwich; in both of which places, as in Gloucester, various trusts were confided to him by his fellow-citizens. The history of these two towns has been written by a female descendant, — Miss F. M. Caulkins. He died in Norwich about 1690. He had one child (Deborah) born here, by his wife Ann, in 1644. His daughter Rebekah died March, 1651. A daughter (Sarah) married William Hough, and another (Mary) married Hugh Roberts.

William Card married Hannah Coit, widow, Jan. 10, 1693; and from that time resided here. His children were — Mary, born in 1693; William, 1696; Hannah, 1699; John, 1701; and Benjamin, 1710. All we know of his profession or business is that he bore the title of "captain." He died July 7, 1736, aged about seventy-four years. His oldest son William married Rebecca Wallis in 1717, by whom he had three children. He was lost in a schooner, near the Isle of Sables, in

April, 1722. William, his oldest son, married Mary Babson. BENJAMIN CARD married Rachel York in 1732; and died at Canso, of a fever, in 1738, leaving three children.

THOMAS CHASE. — His lot is mentioned before 1650; but there is no other notice of him. A person of this name was an early settler in Hampton; and died in 1652, leaving a wife Elizabeth.

ARTHUR CHURCHILL. — It is uncertain when this individual came to Gloucester; but, from the grant made by the town in 1701 to Richard Tarr, — a condition of which was, that the latter should maintain "old father Churchill during his natural life," — it seems probable that he was in some way connected with Tarr's family, which settled here about 1690. He died Jan. 22, 1710.

EDMUND CLARK. — In the record of land-grants, a Mr. Clark is mentioned a few times before 1650, but only by the title of "Mr.;" which, in accordance with the custom of that period, implied some distinction on the part of the possessor. He is probably the same individual who appears with the baptismal name of Edmund in 1650; and perhaps the same Edmund Clark who was of Lynn in 1636, and afterwards of Sandwich. The name also appears in Haverhill in 1654. Our Edmund Clark was town-clerk from 1657 to November, 1665; when his last record, in a failing hand, was made. He died Feb. 26, 1666; leaving a widow Agnes, who married Thomas Penny; a son John, who resided near Walker's Creek, and died in 1681, probably unmarried; a daughter Abigail, born in 1632, who married William Sargent; and a son Joseph, born in 1650, who was a soldier in the Indian war of 1675, and died in 1696, leaving three sons, — Joseph, John, and Edmund; the first and last of whom married, and had large families in the town. John purchased a lot of land, in 1718, in that part of Windham, Conn., which has since been incorporated by the name of Hampton. He removed thither with his wife, Ruth Haskell, whom he married in 1718; and was the fourth settler of the place. He died Nov. 9, 1782, aged ninety: his wife died July, 1776, aged eighty-three. Edmund was admitted an inhabitant of Falmouth, Me., in 1728; but did not remove thither.

MATTHEW COE, a fisherman, lived in Portsmouth in 1640, but came to Gloucester before 1647; in which year, with Morris Somes, John Wakley, and Davis Wheeler, he was brought before a court at Salem for hunting and killing a raccoon on the Lord's day, in time of public service, to the disturbance of the congregation. In 1651, he had a grant of six acres of land "upon the neck that is on this side of the stage-neck." After having resided here several years, he sold his house and land to Thomas Riggs, in 1661, for forty pounds, and bought, with others, of Richard Tucker of Falmouth, Me., two hundred and ten acres of land on the north margin of Back Cove, in that place; where he died before 1675. He married Elizabeth, daughter of Thomas Wakley, in 1647, and had the following children: John, born in 1649; Sarah, 1651; Mary, 1653; Abigail, 1658; and Matthew, 1660, who died the same year. John settled in Rhode Island. Sarah married Joseph Ingersol of Falmouth, and returned with her husband to Gloucester, the native place of both, about 1690; having left Falmouth probably on account of the continual anxiety and alarm to which they were exposed from the hostility of the Indians, and their repeated murderous attacks on that place.

PETER COFFIN was son of Tristram Coffin of Newbury, where the family settled early. He came to Gloucester in 1688, and occupied the large tract of land, of about five hundred acres, between Annisquam and Chebacco Rivers (originally granted to William Stevens), that his father had purchased the same year of Jonathan Willoughby of London. How long he remained here is uncertain. Two daughters (Hannah and Judith) were born, by his wife Afiah, within three years after he came. His grandson Peter, upon whom the property was entailed, took possession of it about 1747, and resided there till his removal to the harbor. Soon after he came to town, he began to take a part in public affairs; and continued upwards of forty years a prominent and useful citizen. In the earliest stages of the Revolution, he embraced the Colonial cause with enthusiastic ardor; and ceased not to devote all his energies to the public good till independence was established. As his farm was at an inconvenient distance from the village for an actor in the stirring events of the time, he took a house in town about the commencement of the war, and resided there till his death. The high estimate placed upon his services by his townsmen is sufficiently attested by his repeated election to offices of trust and responsibility. He served from 1753 to 1777, excepting two years, on the Board of Selectmen. In 1774, he was first chosen representative to the General Court, and filled this office several times between that period and the last year of his service, — 1792; and also served as one of the senators from Essex County. He was the principal acting magistrate in town for many years. His death took place, Feb. 14, 1796, at the age of seventy-two. Mr. Coffin's wife was Mary Currier of Amesbury. Of his ten children, three were sons, — Peter, William, and Tristram. Peter graduated at Harvard College in 1769, and commenced studying law with Judge Sargent at Haverhill; but, conceiving a dislike for the profession, he abandoned his studies, and took up his abode as a shopkeeper in his native town. In this business he failed of success; and, soon becoming bankrupt, he went on to the farm, where he lived as long as it would yield him a support by the sale of the wood upon it, and then came back to town, and died Aug. 4, 1821, aged seventy-two. He married Polly, daughter of Rev. Eli Forbes, Oct. 21, 1773; who died in 1795, aged forty. He had a son Peter, who died unmarried. He sailed from Boston on a foreign voyage in the capacity of supercargo, and was never again heard from. Two other sons (Charles and Eli Forbes) sailed for the north from Baltimore, where Charles was engaged in business, and were lost on the passage. William Coffin, born June 30, 1756, was educated at Dummer Academy, Byfield; and studied medicine in Boston, where he married Mary Langdon. After serving a short time as surgeon of the public armed vessel "Tyrannicide," he settled in the practice of medicine in his native town about 1779. His residence was at the eastern corner of Front and Short Streets. He was an esteemed physician, and enjoyed an extensive practice for nearly half a century. He died June 20, 1827, after a short illness, during which he made a profession of religion, and received the sacrament of the Lord's Supper. His widow died Aug. 20, 1844, aged eighty-five. Dr. Coffin had a large family of children. Three of his sons lived to mature years, — William, who settled in Boston, where he was cashier of the Columbian Bank many years; Edward L., a shipmaster of Gloucester; and Arthur G., the president of an insurance company in Philadelphia. Tristram, the third son of Hon. Peter Coffin, spent his life in Gloucester in various employments, one of which was that of a school-teacher. He died March 9, 1852, at the venerable age of ninety.

JOHN COIT. — Two persons of this name, father and son, were here early; having probably come from Salem, where the name is found in 1638. John Coit, sen., had his residence at the end of the neck of house-lots, now called Wheeler's Point; where, and on Planter's Neck, he had considerable land. He was admitted freeman in 1647, and was a selectman in 1648. About 1651, he went to New London, and died there Aug. 29, 1659; leaving in that place a wife Mary, a son Joseph, two daughters (Mary and Martha), and "other two sons and daughters" who were absent. JOHN COIT, jun., had land near his father's. He had land granted to him in New London; but, not removing thither, the grant was forfeited. He married Mary, daughter of William Stevens, May 21, 1652. He is supposed to have died before Oct. 3, 1667; when a Mary Coit, who could have been no other than his relict, married John Fitch. His children were — John, born in 1653, died April 15, 1675; Mary, 1655; Abigail, 1657; Nathaniel, 1659; and Job, 1661. Nathaniel Coit had his residence near the head of Little River. He was a citizen of considerable influence; which was derived in part, perhaps, from the large estate given to him by Henry Walker, who in 1690, Coit then living with him, made his will, and gave him all his property, except a few small legacies. He was a selectman six years, and representative in 1714, 1718, and 1719. He died, without any previous indisposition, Jan. 10, 1743, aged eighty-four. The name has not since existed in town, though descendants of his daughters are numerous. He was thrice married: first to Elizabeth Davis, Feb. 16, 1687, who died Feb. 11, 1700; next to Abigail Stevens, Feb. 17, 1702, who died Jan. 8, 1710; and last to Widow Hannah Sargent, Nov. 30, 1711. His children were — Mary, born in 1688; John, March 9, 1691; a daughter, 1693; Abigail, 1695, died 1698; Joshua, born 5th, died 9th July, 1697; Martha, 1698; Abigail, 1703; and Stephen, 1704, who died in 1705. John was probably the graduate of Harvard College, of the same name, of the class of 1712. He was living in Marblehead in 1715. In 1716, he calls himself heir of John Fitch; and in 1719, still of that place, he is called merchant and schoolmaster. He may have removed to Boston, and died before 1743; when Nathaniel, Job, Joseph, and other grandchildren of Nathaniel Coit of Gloucester, were living there. Job, son of John Coit, died Sept. 15, 1690; leaving a wife Hannah, and daughter Mary. The latter died in infancy.

Clement Coldom is supposed to have come from Lynn, where the family name is found among the early settlers. He was here "the last of the last month," 1649, when his daughter Judith died. In 1651, he bought a house and land, on the neck of house-lots, of Andrew Lister; but his own place of residence was on the easterly side of Mill River, towards Goose Cove. If he continued to reside here from that time, he led an entirely obscure life; as his name is hardly mentioned for about half a century before his death. He died Dec. 18, 1703, about eighty years old. His daughter Elizabeth married Francis Norwood. A Mary Coldom died Jan. 26, 1704.

John Collins came to Gloucester from Salem, where he had land granted in 1643. Here he had his residence in the harbor. He was a selectman in 1646, and several times afterwards; and died March 25, 1695, leaving an estate of £139. 4s. 8d. He had a wife Joanna, who died May 25, 1695; and children, — John; James, born in 1643; Mary, 1646; and Anna, 1649. The sons were both mariners. John had nine children born here by Mehetabel, his wife. He removed to Salem about 1675, and died before September, 1677. James married twice, and had a son by each wife. He also removed to Salem; from which place he sailed, in 1685, for Barbadoes, and never returned. Mary had three husbands, the last being Capt. James Davis; and died March 9, 1725, aged seventy-nine. Ann married Charles James. Daniel, supposed to have been a son of the second John, had a grant of land above the head of Goose Cove in 1719; which was increased in 1725, when he had a house there. Ezekiel, another son, born in 1664, married Elizabeth, daughter of Thomas Riggs, in 1692. He settled in the easterly part of the town, towards Little Good Harbor; where his descendants remained till about the commencement of the present century. He died December, 1744, aged eighty; having been often employed, through the course of his long life, in various important town-offices. He left four sons, — John, Ebenezer, Daniel, and Amos. The latter settled in Marblehead. Daniel and John were both mariners. Ebenezer was a shoemaker, and had a son Ebenezer, who removed to New Gloucester, Me., and died about 1804. James, another son of Ebenezer, born Nov. 26, 1724, resided on the family estate, on the Sandy-bay Road. He commanded a company in the first year of the Revolutionary War, and is said to have subsequently attained the rank of major. He had previously been in charge of a ship; and, becoming tired of the camp, he again sought employment on the quarter-deck. He took command of a privateer of eighteen guns, and sailed on a cruise; during which he captured a ship called the "Lady Gage," laden partly with wine. Upon his return home, he was offered the command of a new, large privateer-ship called the "Cumberland." He probably sailed in this ship some time in the year 1778, and neither ship nor crew were ever again heard from. A descendant remembers that the wives of forty young men, called "the flower of Portland," were made widows by this sad loss. Capt. Collins was twice married, and had children by each wife. By the last, who was Abigail, daughter of Elder Warner, he left a son James, who was master of the ship "Winthrop and Mary," on a voyage to India, about 1800; of whose fate, after leaving Sumatra on her passage home, no tidings were ever received. He married Elizabeth Homans of Beverly, and left a son, James Albert, who abandoned a seafaring life in 1833, and has since resided in Griggsville, Ill. The youngest daughter of Capt. James Collins, sen., married Mr. Outien, who was lost at sea in 1799; leaving a son, who was also lost at sea, at the age of nineteen, in 1817; and a daughter, who is the wife of Hon. Charles Kimball of Ipswich. A grandson of Ezekiel Collins, probably, was Daniel, a blockmaker by trade, who was an officer in the Revolutionary War, and subsequently colonel of militia. He died in August, 1810, aged seventy-one.

William Colman, planter, first appears in Gloucester about 1654. He married Bridget, widow of John Rowe, Nov. 14, 1662, who died May 2, 1680: he died April 18, 1680. His house, which was at the "Farms," was burnt. A rock on the northerly side of the road to Rockport, near the place of his residence, perpetuates his name.

John Cook. — The first mention of the name of Cook in town is that of Rachel Cook, who married William Vinson in 1661. She was probably a widow when she married Vinson; as the latter, in his will, speaks of the "son of my son-in-law John Cook." This John Cook married Mary Elwell, a widow, Feb. 2, 1680; and had five children, of whom three died in infancy. The other children were — John, born in 1680; and Mary, in 1688. Either father or son had a grant of land on Eastern Point in 1704; but nothing farther is known of the family after the last date. A Samson Cooke died in April, 1673. Elias Cook had a dwelling-house in Sandy Bay in 1738; but it is not known that he belonged to the first family of that name.

Thomas Cornish married Mary, daughter of John Stone, Sept. 4, 1641; by whom he had a son John, born in 1642. No land is recorded as granted to him; but he had a house, and also owned marsh in Annisquam, and a lot on Planter's Neck. He probably went to Exeter, N.H.; where a person of the same name resided in 1652. This name is also on a list of men, under Capt. Beers, who were slain by the Indians at Squahoge, now Northfield, in 1675.

William Cotton is mentioned in Mr. Blynman's grant. He had a lot which was afterwards Thomas Bray's. He may have resided here early for a short period; but Boston was the place of his permanent residence.

JOHN CURNEY, in 1671, had a grant of half an acre of land where his house was standing. He had then but recently come from Falmouth, Me.; bringing with him, perhaps, Abigail Skelling, whom he married Nov. 18, 1670. He died May 3, 1725, aged eighty: she died Feb. 16, 1722, aged seventy. He had a son Elisha, born in 1672; and a daughter Mary, in 1682. A son John died in infancy in 1678. ELISHA married Rebecca Smith, settled at Eastern Point, and had a large family of children. A John Curney, probably another son of John, married Mary Cook in 1713. He had the title of "captain;" derived undoubtedly from maritime employment, in which he was engaged as master of a brigantine belonging to Salem in July, 1712, when he was taken by a French privateer.

ZACCHEUS CURTIS and his wife Jane are mentioned only as the father and mother of a daughter Mary, born in 1659.

JOHN DAVIS bought of Richard Window, in 1656, his house, barn, orchard, and land. This property was situated probably near Walker's Creek, as Window had a house there in 1651. After a residence of several years in town, Davis removed to Ipswich; leaving here his two sons, — James and Jacob. The former had a house and land, which he sold to Joseph Allen in 1674. A few years later, mention is made of his house on the right hand of the way from Long Cove to Mr. Walker's; perhaps the same occupied by his father. Three generations of his family gave to the town some of its most valued and useful citizens; men who, during a whole century, were constantly in office, and, whether filling civil, military, or ecclesiastical stations, always securing the best reward of public service, — public confidence. JAMES DAVIS was appointed by the General Court ensign to the trainband in 1681; and, in 1689, received his commission as captain. No means now exist for ascertaining what active service he performed in these offices: but we find, that, in 1693, he was "very sickly" in consequence of sickness he received in the "country service in Sir Edmund Andros's time;" and that he received in 1699, from the General Court, a grant of

Straitsmouth Island, for the charge and expense he had been at and the time he had spent in the late wars with the French and Indian enemy. He was repeatedly elected to the office of selectman; and, for eight years, served the town as its representative. His death took place May 1, 1715. By his first wife Mehetabel, who died June 9, 1666, he had four children; of whom two — John, born in 1660; and James, 1663 — lived to maturity. By his second wife (Elizabeth Batchelder of Wenham), whom he married Dec. 6, 1666, he had seven children; one of whom (Ebenezer) became a citizen of considerable prominence. This wife died Jan. 1, 1697; and, Aug. 3 of the same year, Capt. Davis married his third and last wife (Mrs. Mary Cook), who died March 9, 1725, aged seventy-nine. John Davis had three acres of upland between Lobster Cove and Hogskin Cove in 1684; and there he probably fixed his residence. He often served in town-offices, and was also lieutenant of the military company. He died March 16, 1729, aged sixty-nine. His wife, who was Ann Haraden, and two sons (Benjamin and Joseph), survived him. The latter son may have been Joseph of Squam, who married Jemima Haskell in 1732, and died about 1753. His son William, born in 1738, whose posterity is numerous, was a prisoner two years and a half at Halifax, in the Revolutionary War; and died in 1814, leaving several sons, among whom was Epes, an occasional preacher of the Baptist denomination, and father of William, a representative in 1841. James, second son of Capt. James Davis, married Bethiah Leach in 1685, who died Aug. 20, 1733, aged seventy; and he next married, Dec. 31, 1733, Sarah Millet. He had ten children, of whom four were sons, that married and settled in town, — James, Elias, Solomon, and Jedediah. He is generally mentioned by his military title of "lieutenant;" but he best commended himself to the favor of his townsmen by his usefulness in civil office. He served several years as a selectman; and, in 1708 and 1709, as representative. He sold his dwelling-house, near Harbor Swamp, in 1703, to Rev. John White; and bought in 1706, of William Somes, a house and land "on the northwardly and easterly side of a highway leading from ye mill." He died March 5, 1743, aged eighty. His son James, born in 1690, was twice married: first, in 1719, to Mary Haraden, who died June 22, 1753; and next to Mrs. Hannah Saunders. He became one of the most useful and honored citizens of his time. He resided at Squam, and was one of the deacons of the church there nearly half a century. He also filled all the civil offices held by his father and grandfather; serving the town as one of its selectmen for a long course of years, and for seven years as its representative. His death took place, Aug. 15, 1776. He had nine children; one of whom (Sarah), in the early blush of womanhood, accepted for her husband Rev. Amos Cheever of Manchester, who was then far advanced in years. Elias, the next son, born in 1694, had a wife Elizabeth, who died in or before 1733; when he married Sarah Foster. He was a merchant of extensive business, which he probably carried on at Squam Harbor. He died about 1734, leaving sons Job and Mark, and an estate, valued in the currency of the time, when corn was worth six shillings a bushel, at upwards of forty-five hundred pounds. Solomon, born in 1696, married Mary Small of Kittery in 1720, and probably Lydia Cannaby in 1747. Besides several daughters, he had a son Solomon, a Noah, and twin sons James and Samuel. Jedediah Davis, born in 1704, had a wife Dorothy; and, in 1734, was married to Martha Haraden. He had a son of his own name; but nothing is known of either father or son after the last-named date. Ebenezer, son of Capt. James Davis, married Mary Wharf in 1705; and died Oct. 30, 1732, aged fifty-one. He engaged in mercantile employments, and was one of the first in town who entered extensively into such pursuits. The inventory of his estate, amounting to three thousand pounds, shows that his labors were not unrewarded. He had a son Abraham; and, besides other daughters, a Susanna, who married Rev. Moses Parsons, and had among her children Theophilus Parsons, the distinguished Chief-Justice of the Supreme Court of Massachusetts. No efforts to ascertain what descendants of John Davis in this respectable line, bearing the name, and now living on the Cape, have been successful. The families of the following trace their origin to the Fourth Parish, where Lieut. James Davis had his home. Thomas, who perished, with the rest of the company of the schooner "Mary," by shipwreck, on Tinker's Island, April 2, 1786, in a severe snow-storm, coming into the bay from Bilbao; leaving sons, one of whom is Solomon, a venerable citizen of more than fourscore years, yet living; Elias, a shipmaster, who died in October, 1821, aged sixty-two; and Daniel, who settled in Sandy Bay, and had sons Timothy R. and John, both of whom represented the town in General Court. JACOB, the other son of the original settler, John Davis, married Elizabeth Bennet, Jan. 20, 1661, and had nine children; of whom two were sons (Jacob and Aaron), who married in town. He had a grant of land at the head of Long Cove in 1662; and, in 1682, he, with others, had a grant of the stream, at the head of Little River, "to set up a sawmill on." He died Sept. 2, 1685. Half of a sloop, and four canoes, valued at £12. 10s., formed part of his estate. His son Jacob carried on the mill, though he resided for a time in Ipswich. He probably built the old house which still stands near the mill-stream, and arrests the attention of every passer by its venerable and antique appearance. He married Mary Haskell, Sept. 14, 1687; and died Feb. 1, 1716, aged fifty-five, leaving sons Moses, William, Aaron, and Joseph. Aaron settled in Attleborough; from which place his son Zebulon came in his minority to Gloucester, and married Mary Bray in 1752. Moses, son of the latter, removed to New Gloucester, Me. Eliphalet, another son, settled in the Harbor Parish. He kept, in company with Frederick Gilman, a shop on Front Street; and was engaged in foreign commerce. He was treasurer of the town at the time of his death; but his chief public services were those which he rendered in the militia, in which he attained the rank of general. He died Sept. 7, 1804, aged forty-eight. Timothy, brother of Zebulon, also returned to the home of his ancestors. He came from Providence, R.I.; to which place he may have removed from Attleborough. He settled in the Second Parish, where he married Sarah Tyler, June 23, 1768. He was drowned in Little River by the upsetting of a boat; leaving an infant son Timothy, who was an active shipmaster over thirty years, and died at his residence in West Parish, June 30, 1830, aged sixty-two. His son Timothy, also a shipmaster, died of a fever at Montevideo, S.A., May 3, 1825, aged twenty-nine. Timothy, only son of the latter, is the late representative in Congress from the sixth district of Massachusetts, — the only one belonging to Gloucester since the adoption of the Constitution. Alexander P., another son of the second Timothy, was a representative to the General Court in 1839. Aaron, son of the first Jacob, had a wife Hannah; and died April 24, 1718, aged thirty-nine. He had a son Jacob, born in 1704 (the same, probably, who died in the Second Parish, April, 1777, upwards of seventy years old); and a son Abel, whose son Amos settled in early life in New Gloucester, Me.; was a patriot of the Revolution; and died in 1829, aged eighty-eight. Persons bearing the very common name of Davis have been so numerous in Gloucester for a hundred and fifty years, that genealogical inquiry concerning them is attended with great perplexity.

ANTHONY DAY was born in 1616; and came to Gloucester about 1645, probably from Ipswich, where several of the name are found at an earlier date. He did not become a permanent resident here till 1657, when he bought a house and land near Poles. His wife's name was Susanna: perhaps Susan Matchet, whose good name he vindicated before a Quarterly Court in Salem, in 1649, against the aspersions of William Vinson. He died April 23, 1707, aged ninety-one: his wife died Dec. 10, 1717, at the age of ninety-four. Their children were — John, born in 1657; Ezekiel, 1662; Nathaniel, 1665; Elizabeth, 1668; Samuel, 1670; and John Joseph, 1672. Besides these, he had sons Thomas and Timothy. JOHN had a house near Poles. He married Abigail Lead, Dec. 12, 1681; who died Feb. 9, 1726, aged sixty-three. The date of his death is not ascertained. He may have lived nearly to 1742; when Joseph Winslow was administrator of the estate of a John Day, who appears to have been his father-in-law. The latter had several children, but probably no son that lived to mature years. EZEKIEL received a grant of land to set a house upon, between Lobster Cove and Hogskin Cove, in 1694; and was one of the first settlers in that section of the town. He married Mary Rowe, Jan. 27,

1690; and died Feb. 18, 1725, leaving several children. One of these (Ezekiel) died about 1737; at which date three other sons (Pelatiah, Samuel, and Nathaniel) were still living. He also had a son Jonathan, who married Sarah Ingersol in 1730, and died before the birth of his second son David. The latter was a soldier in the French wars and in the Revolutionary War; and died May 1, 1816, aged eighty-four. NATHANIEL, son of Anthony, married Ruth Rowe, Feb. 13, 1690. He had sons Benjamin, Nathaniel, and David, and several daughters; and appears to have deceased or moved from town before 1721. SAMUEL DAY married Rachel Rowe, Aug. 9, 1692. These three last brides were sisters, daughters of Hugh Rowe. The one last named gave birth to two children, and died Sept. 6, 1698; after which, nothing is known of the husband. JOSEPH DAY married Elizabeth Gouge, Aug. 15, 1695. He had sons Jeremiah and William, and perhaps a Joseph, and several daughters. THOMAS DAY married Mary Langton, Dec. 30, 1673. She and her daughter Mary were killed by lightning, in the entry of their dwelling-house, July 15, 1706. He died Jan. 29, 1726, aged seventy-five. Two sons are recorded to him,—Thomas, born in 1675; and Joseph, in 1689. The former was lost on a fishing voyage, at the Isle of Sables, August, 1716, aged forty-one. TIMOTHY DAY married Phebe Wildes, July 24, 1679; who died April 8, 1723, aged seventy. The date of his death is not known; but it appears probable that he was living in 1721. He had his residence on the westerly side of Squam River, where some of his sons also settled. His children were—Timothy, Anthony, John, Joseph, Jonathan, Ebenezer, and Susanna, besides others who died in infancy. John is supposed to have died about 1747, and to have left a son John, who settled in Norwich, Conn. Descendants of Anthony Day have continued to the present time about the spot occupied by their ancestor.

NICHOLAS DENNING appears in Gloucester in 1697; in which year, Nov. 25, he married Sarah Paine. A Nicholas Denning married Elizabeth Davis, Dec. 7, 1699, and had children,—Elizabeth, born in 1703; Nicholas, 1706; Em, 1711; Margaret, 1714; and Hannah, 1717. The marriage of William is recorded in 1706; and that of George, in 1708. Nicolas Denning, perhaps the father of these, died June 9, 1725, aged eighty. George was lost on a fishing voyage, at the Isle of Sables, August, 1716, aged thirty. A William Denning was drowned at Cape Sable in 1729. Each had a family. The widow of George Denning was living, in 1738, in the west precinct; where it is supposed the family originally settled.

Richard Dike. — He is mentioned as a grandson of Walter Tybbot; and probably came to Gloucester when an infant. He resided on the westerly side of Annisquam River; where, in 1668, he bought a house and land of Thomas Kent. He married, Aug. 7, 1667, Rebecca, daughter of Samuel Dolliver; who died April 28, 1726, aged eighty-six: he died May 6, 1729, aged eighty-nine. Their children were — Rebecca, born in 1668; Samuel, 1670; Sarah, 1673; Mary, 1675; Joseph, 1678; Job, 1680; Elizabeth, 1683; John, 1686; Hannah, 1688; and James, 1692. Job died in 1705. Nothing is known of the history and end of any other son, except James, who married Sarah Dolliver. She complained to the General Court, in 1734, that her husband, after twenty years' cohabiting with her, had turned her out of doors, and was going to sea without making provision for her. In his old age, he married Miriam Rust. They both died in 1778, nearly ninety years of age. The name was not perpetuated in town beyond the second generation.

Samuel Dolliver came from Marblehead. In 1652, he bought a farm, at Fresh-water Cove, of Thomas Milward. He died July 22, 1683; leaving an estate, of which ten cows formed a part, appraised at £113. His wife was Mary, daughter of Robert Elwell; by whom he had the following children: William, born in 1656; Samuel, 1658; Mary, 1661; Richard, 1665; Sarah, 1667; and John, 1671. William had the title of "captain;" probably derived from maritime employment. He married Ann, daughter of Rev. John Higginson of Salem; an infelicitous marriage, as appears by record of court in 1683, showing that he was then complained of for idleness, and neglect of family; and that, having left the Colony, the effects he left behind were put into the hands of his father-in-law and his wife. She was under accusation of witchcraft in 1692, but escaped the fatal consequences that followed other cases; and was living, in 1705, in a state of *non compos mentis*, and alienation from all her friends. Mr. Higginson was at heavy expense for her and her children. RICHARD married Agnes Bennet in 1697, and lived on the paternal estate at Fresh-water Cove. His will, proved in 1746, mentions three daughters, but no sons. JOHN married Susanna Mariner, Nov. 1, 1700. She died Feb. 28, 1705; and he next married Elizabeth Wood, Feb. 11, 1706. By these two wives he had eight children born here before 1725; soon after which he removed to Falmouth, Me. He had sons Samuel, John, and William; all of whom appear to have married in North Yarmouth.

WILLIAM DUDBRIDGE had land recorded in 1645; but nothing further is known of him than that he was a party in an action against Henry Walker in 1651.

MOSES DUDY was a servant to Robert Elwell. He was impressed into the service of the Colony; and, in 1676, was in the garrison at Hadley. He received for his military services a lot of land at Kettle Cove, which he sold to John Rowe in 1680; after which date, nothing is known of him.

PETER DUNCAN, called a merchant, bought a house and land in the harbor, of John Jackson, in 1662. A portion of this land, probably, was that point, projecting into the harbor, which long bore his name. His mercantile transactions were on a small scale, and were not attended with much success; as he was reported in 1693 very poor, and not able to work. He died May 6, 1716, aged eighty-six. His wife Mary, daughter of Deputy-Gov. Symonds, died July 21, 1692. Their children were — Mary; Elizabeth, born in 1661; Ruth, 1663; Peter, 1665; Priscilla, 1667; Margaret, 1670; and Daniel, 1672. This name was not perpetuated in town; but there are several descendants of Duncan by his daughter Mary, who married William Sargent, 2d.

JOHN DURGEE, weaver, first appears here in 1695. He probably came from Ipswich, where "John Durgy, ye son of John Durgy," was born in 1689. In 1704, he had land at Chebacco side to set a house on; and, a few years later, other lots. His wife was Elizabeth, daughter of Jeffrey Parsons; and his children, born in Gloucester, were — Jeremiah, born in 1695; Elizabeth, 1697; William, 1700; Thomas, 1702; Patience, 1703; Stephen, 1706; Sarah, 1708; Mary, 1709; and Mary, 1711. The wife died Sept. 23, 1711. Two John Durgees (father and son, probably) were intending marriage in 1713; one with Mary Lee of Manchester, and the other with Anna Low. John and William removed to Hampton, Conn.; where their descendants are numerous.

Osman Dutch is mentioned early as a purchaser and grantee of land; but no date is given. His residence was in the easterly part of the harbor; near the head of which, a miry place was long called "Dutch's Slough." His homestead, it is supposed, was that first owned by Sadler, which Dutch bought in 1651. He was a selectman in 1650. He had a wife Grace; by whom his son Hezekiah was born here, March 29, 1647. He also had children, — Robert, Alice, Grace, Mary, and Hester. The latter was born in 1639, and married Samuel Elwell. Alice married a Meacham of Ipswich, and Grace married a Hodgkins of the same town. They were both living in 1704. Mary married Joseph Elwell. "The humble petition of the poor distressed widow, Grace Dutch," to the General Court, July 21, 1685, in relation to her husband's estate, states that he died in December, 1684, aged above one hundred years, and had lived with her more than fifty years. She died Oct. 10, 1694. His estate was appraised at £83. 10s. Robert Dutch had a wife Mary, and sons John, Robert, Samuel, and Benjamin, and a daughter Mary, born here. He bought land of John Coit, jun; which he probably improved in fishing and agricultural employments. In 1656, he sold to Edward Haraden his house and thirty acres of land on Planter's Neck, with the stage, and all appurtenances belonging to it; and twelve acres upon the Meeting-house Neck, with a barn and orchard; the whole comprising all his possessions in Gloucester. He afterwards lived in Ipswich, and was a soldier in the Indian war of 1675. In one of the skirmishes with the savages, he was wounded, beaten, stripped, and left for dead; but he recovered, and was soon joined and relieved by his friends. He died before 1691.

WILLIAM ELLERY. — The date of his first appearance in Gloucester is that of his marriage, Oct. 8, 1663, to Hannah, daughter of William Vinson. He had his house, without doubt, near that of his father-in-law, at Vinson's, or, as it was sometimes called, Ellery's Cove. His widow was living there in 1708. William Ellery was admitted a freeman in 1672; was a selectman a few years; and a representative in May, 1689. Of his business employments, nothing more is known than that he possessed a sloop. He died Dec. 9, 1696. He was twice married. His first wife died Dec. 24, 1675; and he next married Mary Coit, June 13, 1676. His children were — William, born in 1664; Hannah, 1667; Benjamin, 1669; Susanna, 1673; Mary, 1677; Abigail, 1679; John, 1681; Nathaniel, 1683; Jemima, 1686; Elinor, 1688; William, 1694; and Dependance, 1696. Of his estate, no inventory is preserved. The settlement of it shows a charge for "Rum, wine, sider, and shug' and spis, for funnerall, £2. 5s;" and for eight pairs of gloves, 16s. BENJAMIN ELLERY settled in Rhode Island; first at Bristol; whence he removed to Newport, where, it is said, he served as deputy in the Colonial Assembly, judge of the County Court, and assistant of the Colony. He had a letter of marque from George of Denmark, consort of Queen Anne, in 1702; but nothing is known of his service at sea. A fine, large, old portrait, representing him in full dress, is in possession of a descendant in Rhode Island. He married, July 30, 1696, Abigail, daughter of John Wilkins, a native of Wiltshire, England, who emigrated to Boston, where this daughter was born in 1676. She died in Newport, Dec. 15, 1742: her husband died at the same place, July 26, 1746. By his will he disposed of a large estate; giving, with other property, all his "lands and salt-marsh lying in Gloucester, in the county of Essex, in the province of Massachusetts Bay," to his son William. This was his oldest son, and the third of his nine children. He was born in Bristol, Oct. 31, 1701; and graduated at Harvard College in 1722. He became a wealthy merchant of Newport, and a judge, assistant, and deputy-governor of the Colony of Rhode Island. He married, Jan. 3, 1722, Elizabeth Almy; and died in Newport, March 15, 1764, leaving three sons and one daughter. The second of these sons (William), born in Newport, Dec. 22, 1727, graduated at Harvard College in 1747; and married Ann Remington of Cambridge, Oct. 11, 1750. He settled in Newport, and engaged probably in mercantile business. In 1759, he was appointed naval officer of the Colony of Rhode Island; and, in 1770, commenced the practice of law, in which he continued till his election to the Continental Congress in 1776. Of this body he was an active and useful member, and his name is familiar to all as one of the signers of the Declaration of Independence. On the organization of the present government of the United States, he was appointed collector of the customs for the district of Newport; and retained that office till his death, Feb. 15, 1820. His son by a second marriage (George Wanton Ellery) has been for several years deputy-collector of Newport. Lucy, one of his daughters by his first wife, married William Channing, and became the mother of the distinguished theologian and divine, William Ellery Channing, D.D. In this line of descent, it will be seen that William Ellery, the signer of the Declaration, was a great-grandson of our original settler, William Ellery; and that Dr. Channing was a descendant of the fifth generation from the same settler. John, oldest son of William Ellery of Gloucester by his second wife, also went to Rhode Island; but nothing more is known of him than that he was living in Newport in March, 1708, and then styled himself "mariner." Nathaniel, the next son, is called in a deed "shipwright;" but he is supposed to have been engaged mostly in the pursuits of trade and commerce. In 1711, in company with others, he had a grant of "flatty land," on the westwardly side of Philemon Warner's wharf, to build a wharf on for himself. Nearly opposite this spot, at the foot of Hancock Street, he is said to have built the original part of a house which stood there till about 1840. He had the title of "captain;" which was probably derived from military service, as he had previously borne that of "lieutenant." He was twice married: first, Jan. 1, 1711, to Abigail

Norwood, who survived the union just three months; and next, Feb. 16, 1721, to Ann Sargent, who died Oct. 8, 1782, aged ninety. A fine portrait of this lady, in her advanced years, by Copley, is in possession of a descendant. Mr. Ellery deceased May 30, 1761. His daughter Mary married Rev. John Rogers. His sons were Nathaniel, William, Daniel, and Epes. The first, born in 1726, became a merchant; and was extensively engaged in trade when the Revolutionary War commenced, which brought ruin upon the commerce of the town. The date of his death is not known. He left several sons and daughters; of whom John Stevens, the oldest, married in Gloucester, and had a son of the same name, who acquired a large fortune in commercial pursuits. He left this town when a young man, and spent some time in France; but the latter years of his life were passed in Boston and its vicinity. He died in New York, Nov. 18, 1845, leaving a daughter, the fruit of a marriage he contracted when far advanced in years. The second son of the last-named Nathaniel bore his father's name. He was born in 1753, and graduated at Harvard College in 1772. He was intended by his father for the mercantile profession; but the war put an end to all business in that line, and this young man embarked in privateering. While engaged in this employment, he was taken by the enemy; and did not again reach his home till he had passed through much hardship and suffering. Being a good penman and accountant, he next obtained employment in writing; and by that and other labor gained his livelihood. He died March 1, 1833, aged eighty; leaving an only son William, who resides in Chelsea. Epes, brother of the last Nathaniel, was a shipmaster; and, for one year (1837), a representative. He died Feb. 20, 1846, aged seventy-six. William, son of the first Nathaniel, born in 1730, is supposed to have been in early life a sea-captain; but he afterwards became a merchant. He built and occupied a spacious house, entertained company, and lived several years in comfortable circumstances; but his last days were spent in poverty: and, as if still further to mark the instability of fortune, his aged widow closed her life at the alms-house, Sept. 13, 1805. WILLIAM ELLERY, son of the first William, had, by two wives, a numerous family. He bought a house in the Town Parish, built and formerly occupied by Rev. John White, and still standing to attest the distant date of its erection. He probably went to sea some years, as he did not settle in this abode till middle life, and then bore the title of "captain." He kept a tavern, and engaged in other business. He died Sept. 20, 1771, at the age of seventy-seven. His daughter Lucy married Rev. Samuel Foxcroft, first minister of New Gloucester, Me. His son Capt. Joseph Ellery, a young man of twenty-nine years, of excellent character, was drowned by falling overboard from the bowsprit of a schooner in which he had taken passage from Boston for home, Oct. 11, 1769. Benjamin, another son, occupied the paternal residence; and died Feb. 15, 1825, in his eighty-first year. DEPENDANCE ELLERY married Sarah Warner, Jan. 4, 1722, and had eleven children, concerning whom little is known. He died before 1757. The posterity of Capt. Epes Ellery, and of Benjamin, the last named, comprise all the descendants of the ancient settler, bearing the name of Ellery, now living in town.*

ROBERT ELWELL. — This name occurs in our Colony Records, in 1635, in connection, as a witness, with the outrageous conduct of one Mr. Thomas Wannerton at the eastward. He was admitted a freeman in 1640, and was a member of the Salem Church in 1643. He bought land here in April, 1642; and by further purchases, and grants from the town, became the possessor of several lots; among which was a neck of about thirty acres, lying on the south-east side of the harbor, called the "Stage

---

* Daniel Ellery, son of Nathaniel, born in 1732, intended marriage with Mary Matchett, Dec. 20, 1754; and had a daughter Mary, baptized Jan. 11, 1756. This infant, I suppose, was the subject of the following notice in a Boston newspaper of Feb. 2, 1756: "Gloucester, Jan. 6, 1756. — This day, a child was born that has ten grandfathers and grandmothers, all living; and this child makes the fifth generation; and the firstborn of every one of the generations was a daughter; and every one of the children's name was Mary; and they are all of them now living." These Marys must have been, first, Mary the infant, whose mother was Mary (Matchett) Ellery, born in 1734, the second; whose mother was Mary (Ingersol) Matchett, born in 1718, the third; whose mother was Mary (Stevens) Ingersol, born in 1694, the fourth; whose mother was Mary (Ellery) Stevens, born in 1677, the fifth. The mother of the last was also a Mary, the *second*-born of John Coit and Mary Stevens: she was born in 1655.

Neck." He first resided in the harbor; but it is supposed he finally settled at Eastern Point, where most of his land was situated. He was a selectman in 1649, and several times afterwards; and a commissioner for ending small causes, in 1651. The title "goodman," often affixed to his name, may be defined, it is likely, in its application to him, in its best sense. He died May 18, 1683, leaving an estate of £200: his wife Jane died March 31, 1675. Another wife (Alice Leach), to whom he was married May 29, 1676, died April 10, 1691. He had two daughters, who died young; and the following sons, — Samuel, John, Isaac, Josiah, Joseph, and Thomas, — all of whom married and had families, from which the descendants of this ancient settler have multiplied to a numerous posterity. SAMUEL married Hester, daughter of Osman Dutch, June 7, 1658; and died Nov. 24, 1696: she died Sept. 6, 1721, aged eighty-two. In consequence of sickness and poverty, she, like her mother, was a "poor distressed widow" many years. They had four sons — Samuel, Jacob, Robert, and Ebenezer — and four daughters. Jacob married Abigail Vinson, July 5, 1686, and had ten children, of which four were sons; two of whom (Vinson and William) are supposed to have married. The father was killed by the French and Indians at Cape Sable, May 2, 1710, aged forty-eight. Robert married Sarah Gardiner, Oct. 12, 1687; by whom he had five sons and five daughters. He removed to Kittery, Me.; where he was living in 1730. His oldest son Robert died at Ipswich, "under the doctor's hands," Feb. 2, 1715. Two of his sons (Joseph and John) settled in Biddeford, Me.; and one (Samuel) settled in Gloucester, and married, in 1718, Rebecca Brown, by whom he had several children. One of these (Capt. Robert Elwell) died in March, 1805, aged eighty-four. Ebenezer Elwell married Jane Elwell, Jan. 2, 1695, and had seven children. He was some time held in captivity by the French, and died before 1723. JOHN, son of Robert Elwell, sen., had a wife Jane, with whom he appears in town in 1678; having probably lived previously in Salem. He resided at Eastern Point, where he had a house. He died in captivity in 1710. Four daughters were born to him here; but he also had a son

John, who married Mary, daughter of Abraham Robinson, and who, being "ancient, diseased, and blind," was helped by the town in 1732, and died before 1738. ISAAC was a shoemaker, and lived at the Harbor. He married, first, Mehetabel, daughter of Thomas Millet, who died in September, 1699; and he next married, Dec. 2, 1702, Widow Mary Rowe, who died March 3, 1723, aged sixty-five: he died Dec. 14, 1715. Of the nine children recorded to him, five were sons; only two of whom (Eleazer and Joshua) appear to have married in town. The latter had a son Isaac, who married Susanna Stanwood in 1738, and had eleven children; one of whom was Isaac, who became a sea-captain,* afterwards a merchant, and was for several years the postmaster of the town. He died Jan. 22, 1832, aged eighty-nine. Isaac Elwell, sen., also had a son Jonathan, born in 1670; and his son Eleazer had a Jonathan, born in 1698. Neither of these Jonathans is known to have settled in town: perhaps it was the latter, who, with his wife Lydia, lived in Beverly in 1727, and soon afterwards in Gloucester. He died about 1752. Another Jonathan, with a wife Abigail, appears here in 1727. Connected nearly with one of the preceding, probably, was Jonathan, who married Abigail Stevens, and lived many years on Eastern Point; where he died March 10, 1808, aged ninety-four. He had a son Jonathan, who settled in Maine. JOSIAH ELWELL married Mary Collins, June 15, 1666; and is supposed to have had his residence near the shore of the Harbor Cove. He went to sea, and died abroad about 1679; leaving probably one daughter, and four sons, — Elias, Nehemiah, William, and Josiah. JOSEPH ELWELL married Mary, daughter of Osman Dutch, June 22, 1669; and had sons, — Hezekiah, Joseph, Samuel, and Benjamin. THOMAS married Sarah Basset, Nov. 23, 1675; by

* In the winter of 1779, Capt. Elwell, in command of a schooner coming from the West Indies, was blown off the coast, and had his vessel so disabled that she was driven about upon the ocean for more than six months; during which the crew had no meat or bread. They subsisted on parched cocoa, and West-India rum "burned down;" though they sometimes caught a fish, which they ate raw. They were finally taken off by a passing vessel; and, upon arrival on the coast near New York, were furnished with a boat, in which they came home. Though they endured great suffering, only one man died. Besides this man and the captain, there were on board John Woodward, Jacob Lurvey, Nathaniel Allen, and a Witham.

whom he had three sons — Thomas, William, and Elisha — and two daughters. Both of these last two brothers are supposed to have removed from town before 1688; as their names do not appear among the grantees of lots of land which were that year given to all the tax-paying inhabitants. William Elwell, probably a grandson of the first Isaac, was the father of Paine, who was born in 1744, and went in early life to North Yarmouth, Me.; where he purchased wild land to a considerable extent, and, by his enterprise in business, accumulated considerable property. He returned to Gloucester about 1802, and for several years carried on the fishing business and foreign trade with success. Having secured a competent fortune, he purchased a farm in Bradford, and retired thither, but failed to obtain permanent enjoyment and repose. Injudicious purchases of real estate to a large extent, added to other causes of embarrassment, compelled him to relinquish his property, and return to his native place; where he died March 29, 1820, aged seventy-six. His son Paine was connected with his father in business a few years; but finally established himself in Waldoborough, Me., where he died. Another son (Robert) commenced a mercantile life as a partner with his father; and, after dissolving the connection with him, pursued it alone a few years, till bankruptcy finally closed his commercial career. He went from Gloucester to New York, where he died about 1824. He was colonel of the regiment of militia here, and representative three years.

PETER EMONS and wife Martha first appear in town in 1700, when their daughter Mercy was born. They also had a son Joseph, born in 1708. A Cooly Emons had forty rods of ground, lying near the head of the harbor, in 1707; and, the next year, a grant of timber for a house. A Richard Emons was lost on a fishing voyage, coming from Cape Sables, in 1716. A Daniel Emons married Abigail Davis in 1719, by whom he had ten children. Only two of his sons (Daniel and Peter) lived to maturity. Both married in town. One of them may have been the father of Daniel (remarkable for his small stature), who died, in old age, about thirty years ago; and was probably the last Emons in town of this family.

WILLIAM EVANS had land granted to him in 1647, and was a selectman in 1648. Mention is made of his house, between Bourne and Tybbot; and of his land, running towards the Meeting-house. In 1653, he purchased land near the "New Meadows, called Topsfield," to the amount of £200, and removed thither.

SYLVESTER EVELETH — or EVELEIGH, as he himself wrote it, and which agrees with the present English orthography — may have come from the county of Devonshire, England, where the name existed about the time of the settlement of New England. The name is said to have been anciently spelled Yeverleigh, and to have belonged to an estate, which, at an early period, was in the family of Clifford before it was adopted as a family cognomen. This settler had recorded to him in Gloucester, under date of December, 1648, "twelve acres of swamp and upland on the north side of the Millpond." Immediately following this record, mention is made of "his house, on the Meeting-house Hill; having Capt. Perkins's lot on one side, and the highway on the other." He was a selectman in 1648, a freeman in 1652, and a representative in 1673. He did not live on good terms with the church in his early residence here; and, for defaming it, was ordered to make a public acknowledgment, or pay a fine. In 1666, he was licensed to keep an ordinary, or public-house of entertainment; and, at the same time, was excused from common training by paying two bushels of Indian corn yearly. He was then probably living on the west side of Annisquam River, where he had become possessor of large tracts of land; on one of which (in possession of a descendant) still stands an old house built by his son or grandson a century and a half ago, and which is a good specimen of the best dwellings of the time of its erection. Proof of its early construction is to be found in the projecting upper story, the large oak timbers composing its frame, its rude workmanship, and the venerable appearance it presents throughout. His wife Susanna died Sept. 14, 1659; and he married Bridget Parkman, Sept. 6, 1662. He died Jan. 4, 1689. His daughter Mary married Thomas Millet. He had two sons, — Joseph and Isaac. The former married Mary, daughter of Edward Bragg of Ipswich, in 1667. He removed to Chebacco Parish, Ipswich, now Essex, about 1674; and died Dec. 1, 1745, at the extraordinary age of one hundred and five years. He was a man of rigid puritanical piety. A venerable descendant, not long since deceased, remembered to have often heard his mother, who was born in 1730, describe the life, person, and character of Joseph Eveleth, who was her great-grandfather, and with whom she was fifteen years contemporary. Among her interesting recollections of her aged ancestor was that of a visit made to him, just before his death, by the celebrated Rev. George Whitefield. Her mind always retained a vivid impression of the solemnity of the scene that was presented, when Mr. Whitefield knelt upon the floor, and received, from the lips that could relate a Christian experience of a hundred years, a truly patriarchal blessing. He was one of the jurors who signed a humble and solemn declaration of regret for the part they had borne in the trials for witchcraft at Salem in 1692. Isaac, the other son of Sylvester Eveleth, married Abigail Coit, Nov. 13, 1677; and died Nov. 2, 1685. From a portion of the effects composing his small estate (a third of a sloop, and seafaring books and instruments), it is supposed he led a maritime life. He left sons Isaac and Job. The latter was a ship-carpenter; and, in 1717, had his residence at the Harbor. He had a son Isaac, who married, and settled somewhere within the limits of the First Parish, but does not appear after 1754. Joseph Eveleth had several children born in Gloucester and Ipswich. The oldest (John), born Feb. 18, 1670, graduated at Harvard College in 1689; and, in the same year, entered upon the office of preacher at Manchester, where he remained till 1695; after which he appears for a short time at Enfield; and next in Stow, where he was installed in 1699. He remained in Stow till 1719; when he removed to Maine, and, for a few years, divided his services between Arundel (now Kennebunkport) and Biddeford, till one of the towns determined to have a "whole minister." After three years more, he, in 1726, left the ministry. The people of Arundel were unwilling to part with him; as he was not only their minister and schoolmaster, but a good blacksmith and farmer, and the best fisherman in town. His wife was Mary Bowman of Cambridge, by whom he had several children, some of whose descendants are living in Stow and in Maine.* Isaac, son of Joseph, removed into town soon after the death of his grandfather, and took up his abode on the family estate, near Little River. He died March 23, 1755, in his seventy-ninth year. By his wife Sarah he had ten children. He left an only son (Isaac), who survived his father about four years. This son married Elizabeth Parsons in 1729; who died Feb. 12, 1799, aged about ninety. A numerous offspring was the fruit of this marriage. Nathaniel settled in New Gloucester, Me. Joseph served in the Revolutionary War; and died June 30, 1806, aged sixty-five. Isaac became a major in the militia; and died June 12, 1805, aged fifty-one. Edward, son of Joseph of Ipswich, was a shopkeeper in that town. He served in the expedition to Cape Breton in 1745, and remained there on duty some time after the reduction of the fortress. He died Nov. 5, 1759. This name has long been extinct in Gloucester; but it is borne by families in the neighboring town of Essex, and is also found in many other places. All who bear it are undoubtedly descended from the ancient settler in Gloucester, Sylvester Eveleth.

HENRY FELCH was here in 1642, and was the owner of "six acres of hoed ground," of which there is no grant in the records. From this fact, it may be inferred that he was a settler before the incorporation of the town. He also had a house and land, which he sold to James Avery. He may have removed to Reading, where a person of the same name resided in 1647; and next, perhaps, to Boston, where the name is found in 1657. He had a daughter, who married Samuel Haieward.

JOHN FITCH bought a house and land of George Blake in

---

* "The following is the inscription upon the tombstone of the minister of the Episcopal Church in Kittery, near Eliot; which church, it is supposed, became extinct at the time of his death. The grave is in a field belonging to Mr. Fernald.

"Here Lyes Buried the Body of the Rev^d Mr. John Eveleth, who departed this Life, Augt 1st, Anno: Dom: 1734, aged 65 years." — *N. E. Hist. and Genealogical Register*, vol. iv. p. 38.

1667; and, in the same year, married Mary Coit, widow. He was in England in 1672, but returned to America, and was in the service of the Colony as a soldier; for which he received a lot of land at Kettle Cove. He died May 9, 1715, aged about seventy-nine: his wife died Nov. 7, 1692.

James Fogg is mentioned as an owner of land in 1651; but he was probably a resident of Gloucester, February, 1649, when he was presented at a court in Salem for disturbing the church here in time of their meeting. In 1651, he was again a defendant in court in an action of battery; and this is the last date of his appearance in Gloucester.

Bartholomew Foster bought a house and land situated near the westerly end of Front Street, of Bridget Varney, in 1669. He married Hannah, daughter of Thomas Very, Nov. 9, 1668; and died Dec. 5, 1689. His widow married Thomas Sawyer. He is one of the few early residents who are mentioned as possessors of property employed in maritime pursuits. Among the effects composing his estate at his death was a sloop, valued at £30. His children were — Bartholomew, born in 1670; John, 1673; Thomas, 1676; Samuel, 1678; Edward, 1681; Andrew, 1682; Ephraim, 1683; Edward, 1685; Francis, 1688; and Benjamin, 1689. Of these ten sons, eight are mentioned in their father's will. Bartholomew was living in Hartford in 1694. Samuel and Benjamin married and had large families in Gloucester; but it does not appear that the name is now borne here by any of their descendants.

Mr. Fryer was probably Thomes Fryer, who was of Salem in 1639. He was one of the persons appointed to order prudential affairs in 1642, but does not appear after that date. He may have been the husband of Elizabeth Fryer, whose lots of land on the neck of house-lots are named in Hugh Calkin's grant. In 1668, the town agreed with Thomas Judkin to take care of her, during the remainder of her life, for ten bushels of Indian corn yearly, and the use of her house, land, and cow. She died Sept. 9, 1685.

John Gallope is mentioned only as the seller of upland in the Harbor, and of marsh at Little Good Harbor, before 1650.

A John Gallop was an early inhabitant of Boston. He was a fisherman and pilot; and was some time wind-bound in Cape-Ann Harbor, in 1632, in a voyage to Piscataqua for the Colony Government, to gain information of some Englishmen at the eastward who had turned pirates.

JAMES GARDNER came to Gloucester about 1661, when William Vinson gave him land. In 1668, he exchanged real estate with Hugh Rowe, and perhaps settled in the remotest easterly section of the town which was at that time inhabited. He married Elizabeth, daughter of William Vinson, June 16, 1661; and had the following children: George, born in 1664; Elizabeth, 1666; Sarah, 1669; Joseph, 1672; Rebecca, 1675; John, 1678; and James, 1681. He died Dec. 8, 1684: his wife died March 4, 1684. The three sons last named married in town. Joseph had his home on Eastern Point, and was living in 1749.

GEORGE GIDDINGS is said by descendants to have come from Ipswich about 1690. May 19 of that year, he married Mary, daughter of Robert Skamp; who died April 9, 1706. He had a second wife (Elizabeth), who died May 10, 1727, aged fifty-six. His children were — Lydia, born in 1692; Mary, 1695; John, 1698; Robert, 1700; Zebulon, 1703; Mercy and Deliverance, 1708; Sarah, 1710; George, 1714; and Joseph, 1717. Joshua and Thomas Giddings were here soon after 1700, and had families. The former was lost at sea, October, 1716, aged thirty-eight. Land was granted to a Lawrence Giddings in 1717. Three of the sons of George Giddings (Robert, George, and Joseph) married here, and had children; but the families of the last two did not probably remain in town. Zebulon seems to have gone to New Hampshire. Andrew Giddings, son of Robert, was a shipmaster; and was lost at sea during the Revolutionary War, leaving, with other children, a son (Andrew Robinson), who at his father's death left Dummer Academy, of which he had been several years a member, and embarked on a seafaring life; which he abandoned after a few years' trial, and removed to Danville, Me., where he lived to an advanced age. His son, Rev. George P. Giddings, is an Episcopal clergyman in Illinois.

CHARLES GLOVER was a ship-carpenter; and was made freeman in 1641, then living in Salem, where he was admitted to the church in 1640. He was a selectman here in 1644. Under the year 1645, land on Planter's Neck is recorded to him; but he also had land in the settled portion of the town. He had a wife Elizabeth, who died March 6, 1647; and another wife who, in 1649, at a court in Salem, was found guilty of adultery. She did not long survive her disgrace; for he married again, Feb. 12, 1650, Widow Esther Sanders, and soon after disappears. By his wife Elizabeth he had a son Samuel, born June 20, 1644.

STEPHEN GLOVER was born in 1625, and first appears in Gloucester in 1649. August, 1651, he had a grant of an eighth of an acre of ground before the door of his house, in the Harbor; where he probably resided till his death. He was a selectman in 1659, 1667, and perhaps in the intervening years, for which the list is wanting; and from 1669 to his death, which took place Dec. 10, 1686. He married, Oct. 7, 1663, Ruth, daughter of William Stevens; who died Aug. 16, 1664, having given birth to a son on the 2d, who died on the 5th of the same month.

RICHARD GOODING (or GOODWIN) is called son of Richard Window. In 1662, he had a grant of six acres of land between Stony Cove and Long Cove. He married Hannah, daughter of Thomas Jones of Manchester, Nov. 20, 1666; and had the following children: Hannah, born in 1667; Richard, 1670; Thomas, 1672; Mary, 1674; Joseph, 1677; Elinor, 1680; Daniel, 1685; and Sarah, 1687. He died March 5, 1709: his wife died Feb. 4, 1725, aged eighty; having received assistance from the town for several years. DANIEL died in April, 1717. The family was not perpetuated here beyond the second generation.

JOHN HADLEY had half an acre of upland ground to set a house upon, on the left hand of the way to Little Good Harbor, in 1683. Nothing further is known of him than that he died Oct. 22, 1711. His nephew (John Hadley, jun.) had land near his uncle's in 1709. He married Hannah Low, Nov. 8, 1707; and had several children. He was probably living in 1765. It appears by the records that three of his sons were married in town: Daniel, to Susanna Milberry in 1736; John, to Sarah Witham in 1737; and Benjamin, at the age of eighteen, to Sarah Elwell in 1744. Daniel Hadley died June 10, 1737, on his passage from Canso. Several children are recorded to John Hadley, and one to Benjamin.

NATHANIEL HADLOCK had land near Ipswich line, where he probably lived. He married Remember Jones, May 1, 1673; who died March 2, 1718, aged sixty-four. His children recorded are — Nathaniel, born in 1677; Deborah, 1679; John, 1682; James, 1684; Samuel, 1687; Mary, 1696; and Benjamin, 1700. Besides these, he had Joseph and William. The latter married Penelope Firbee in 1717; had a daughter, and a son Nathaniel; and was drowned near the Ferry, Sept. 14, 1730. BENJAMIN had a wife Dorcas, by whom he had eight children; of which were sons Benjamin and John.

SAMUEL HAIEWARD is not mentioned as an owner of land, nor in any other connection than that of husband and father. His marriage with a daughter of Henry Felch, March 2, 1641, is the earliest in the records. His children were — Samuel, born in 1642; and John, 1643.

JOHN HAMMONS, in June, 1663, had land lying between Thomas Riggs's and the run going to Goose Cove. He married Mary, daughter of Morris Somes, Oct. 17, 1660; and had the following children,: Elizabeth, born in 1661; John, 1664; Mary, 1666; Timothy, 1668; and William, 1674. He died before 1686; and a Mary Hammons (probably his wife) died May 6, 1689. JOHN HAMMONS, the only son of the foregoing of whom any thing is known, had land in 1701, on Eastern Point, to erect a house on. He was twice married: first to Ruth Stanwood, July 7, 1686, who died April 17, 1689; and next to Agnes Penny, Jan. 20, 1691. He died at Casco Bay, January, 1718, aged fifty-four; leaving five daughters, and a son John, who died Feb. 3, 1725, aged twenty-five.

JOHN HARDIN, said to be of Weymouth, bought four acres of upland of William Sargent in 1652; in which year, April 22, he married Widow Tybbot. He was a selectman in 1664. In 1665, he recorded land to John Davis; and his name does not again appear in town.

EDWARD HARADEN came from Ipswich. In 1657, he bought of Robert Dutch a house, barn, and all his land, in Gloucester. Part of this property was on Planter's Neck, where Dutch had a fishing-stage. Haraden added to his possessions at this place by subsequent purchases, and appears to have been the first permanent settler in that section of the town. The place of his residence and business was undoubtedly Squam Point. He died May 17, 1683, leaving an estate of £285: his wife Sarah died March 4, 1691. His children, born in Gloucester, were Andrew, born in 1658; Ann, 1661; John, 1663; Thomas, 1665; Joseph, 1668; Sarah, 1670; and Benjamin, 1671. EDWARD, son of the preceding, born probably before his father removed to Gloucester, had land at Plum Cove in 1707; near which he was employed by the town, in 1704, to build a watch-house. He was one of the grantees of soldiers' lots at Kettle Cove in 1679; and his name often appears in later years with the military title of "sergeant." He married Sarah Haskell, Feb. 5, 1684; and Hannah York in 1693. The births of eighteen children, by these two marriages, are recorded. JOHN HARADEN, son of Edward, first named, engaged in maritime employments; and, in 1709, was in the service of the Colony as master of one of the sloops fitted out to attempt to take a vessel, supposed to be a French privateer, forced by a storm to anchor off Nahant. In 1711, he was pilot of the ship "Montague," in the disastrous expedition against Canada; and, for his expense and wages, received an allowance from the General Court in 1714. He died Nov. 11, 1724; having survived his wife Sarah Giddings, by whom he had several children, about two years. His son Andrew died Dec. 12, 1724. JOSEPH HARADEN was twice married; but no children are recorded to him. He died May 19, 1716. BENJAMIN HARADEN married Deborah Norwood, Jan. 15, 1696; and died Feb. 3, 1725. Among his children were sons Caleb, Joseph, and Ebenezer, besides others who died in early life. Jonathan Haraden, without doubt a descendant of Edward, was born in

Gloucester in 1744; removed early in life to Salem, and went to sea. In the Revolutionary War, he was lieutenant of the "Tyrannicide," and afterwards commander of a privateer. He was engaged with the enemy in several actions, and evinced great bravery on all occasions. He died in November, 1803.

GEORGE HARVEY had a son Benjamin born here in 1697. He came from Salem; where, by his wife Sarah, his three children (Sarah, Nehemiah, and Rose) were born. In 1707, he and his son George had a grant of land on the way leading from the Meeting-house to the back side of the Cape. His residence was probably near the Meeting-house, in the vicinity of that of Anna Judkin, the mother of his wife. He died Dec. 23, 1723, aged seventy. His son GEORGE married Sarah Butman in 1713, who died Nov. 29, 1718, aged twenty-five; and Patience York in 1720. He died Nov. 24, 1724, aged thirty-seven; leaving a son Nehemiah, who married Abigail Hodgkins in 1741, and had sons Nehemiah and Benjamin.

WILLIAM HASKELL was born about 1620, and was connected with the family of Roger Haskell of Salem. He first appears in Gloucester in 1643; and, in 1645, mention is made of his land at Planter's Neck. He probably resided here a few years following the last date; but the hiatus in the recorded births of his children affords ground for conjecture that he was not a permanent resident from that time. If he left town for a season, he had returned in 1656, and settled on the westerly side of Annisquam river, where he had several pieces of land; among which was a lot of ten acres, with a house and barn, bought of Richard Window, situated on the west side of Walker's Creek. His sons took up land on each side of this creek, which is still occupied by descendants. The public offices to which he was elected afford sufficient proof that he was a prominent and useful citizen. He was a selectman several years, and representative six times in the course of twenty years. In 1681, he was appointed, by the General Court, lieutenant to the trainband, of which he was afterwards captain. He was also one of the first two, of whom we have any knowledge, that were deacons of the First Church. He married Mary, daughter of Walter Tybbot,

Nov. 16, 1643. She died Aug. 16, 1693; and he four days after (on the 20th), leaving an estate of £548. 12s. His children, whose births are recorded, were — William, born in 1644; Joseph, 1646; Mark, 1658; Sarah, 1660; and Elenor, 1663. Besides these, he had sons Benjamin and John, and daughters Ruth and Mary. Ruth married a Grover, and Mary married a Dodge. Elenor married Jacob Grigs. Sarah married Edward Haraden. WILLIAM married Mary Walker, July 3, 1667; who died Nov. 12, 1715, aged sixty-six. She was the daughter of William Brown; but took the name of her step-father, Henry Walker. He died June 5, 1708, aged sixty-four. Twelve children are recorded to him; of whom four were sons that survived their father, — William, Joseph, Henry, and Jacob. William, born 1670, settled on or near the ancestral property; which being favorably situated for maritime pursuits, he engaged in both fishing and agricultural employments. He was usually called Ensign Haskell, from an office he held in the military company. He also held the office of deacon in the Second Church a few years before his death. He married Abigail Davis in 1692; and died Jan. 17, 1731, leaving an estate of £2,565, of which vessels, warehouse, salt, and a negro man, formed a part. He also left sons William, Mark, and James; the latter of whom, with his wife, received dismission from the Second Church to the church in Attleborough in 1756. Joseph, the next son of William Haskell, jun., born in 1673, married Rachel Elwell in 1696, and died April 11, 1718. He had several children; among whom were Joseph, who removed to Harvard in 1735, and lived to be upwards of ninety; and Abraham, who removed to Stratham in 1732. Henry, the next son, born in 1678, had a wife Ruth, and removed with his family to Harvard in 1735. Jacob, the youngest of these four brothers, born in 1691, married Abigail Marcy in 1716. He became a deacon in the Second Church, and died Aug. 6, 1756: his wife died April 10, 1778, aged eighty-three. Six sons survived him, — Jacob, Abner, Alexander, Israel and Amos (twins), and Zebulon; all of whom, except Abner, married in town. Alexander and his wife were dismissed to Attleborough Church in 1756. Zebulon was born in 1734; and died at the age of eighty-four, leaving a son of the same name, still living, a venerable citizen, in his ninetieth year. JOSEPH HASKELL, son of the first William, married Mary Graves of Andover, Dec. 2, 1674; and died Nov. 12, 1727, aged eighty-one: she died April 8, 1733, aged eighty. He was a deacon of the First Church; and, upon the formation of the Second, was chosen to the same office in that. Of his ten children, three were sons, who married in town, — Joseph, Daniel, and Ebenezer. Joseph, born in 1681, married Sarah Davis in 1705; and died Dec. 13, 1768. His son David died in 1791, at an advanced age; leaving a son Aaron, who died in 1834, aged eighty-three; the father of Thomas, representative in 1836. Isaac, another son, born in 1716, died April 27, 1804; leaving a son Adoniram, who died Aug. 5, 1845, aged eighty-four. Daniel, son of Joseph, sen., born in 1688, married Sarah Haskell in 1716, and died Dec. 4, 1768: she died July 10, 1773, aged eighty. His son Caleb settled in Newbury; and another son, Moses, in New Gloucester, Me. Ebenezer, youngest son of the first Joseph, born in 1690, had a wife Elizabeth, and several children; one of whom (Elijah) is said to have settled in Salem. BENJAMIN, son of the original settler, was born about 1648. He married, Nov. 21, 1677, Mary, daughter of Thomas Riggs. She died Jan. 29, 1698. The date of his death is not known; but his age, at his decease, was ninety-two. His will was proved May 25, 1741. He was often a selectman, representative in 1706 and 1707, and deacon of both the First and Second Churches many years. The sons who survived him were Benjamin, Josiah, Thomas, and William. Benjamin had a wife Elizabeth, who died in 1724, aged thirty-five; and a second wife, Elizabeth Bennet, who died Dec. 23, 1774, probably eighty-four years old: he died Feb. 9, 1764, aged eighty, leaving no male issue bearing the name. Josiah, born in 1687, married Mary Collins, Dec. 7, 1715. He is supposed to have settled in the Harbor Parish about 1738. He had sons, — John, Joshua, Josiah, and Adoniram; the last two of whom are said to have been lost at sea together in 1764. John married Mary Bray in 1743; and had a son Josiah, who, before completing his eighteenth year, married Abigail Fellows of Ipswich, who was twenty-eight. He resided at the Harbor; and died Feb. 16, 1821, aged about sixty-seven, leaving a son Josiah, who settled at Sandy Bay, and was the father of Benjamin, who graduated at Amherst College, is now a practising physician in his native place, and author of "Essays on the Physiology of the Nervous System;" and of James, who has been a senator from Essex County. Thomas, the next son of Benjamin Haskell, removed in 1725 to Falmouth, Me., where he was long a respectable and worthy inhabitant. He died there, in 1785, at the age of ninety-five, leaving a numerous posterity. William, the next and youngest son, lived in his native parish; where he died July 21, 1778, aged eighty-four. JOHN, son of the first William, married Mary Baker, Nov. 20, 1685; and died Feb. 2, 1718, aged sixty-nine: she died Nov. 24, 1723, aged fifty-eight. He had several children; of whom Mary, Edith, Ruth, and John were living at the time of his death. Mary and Edith died unmarried, the latter at the age of eighty. Ruth married John Clark, and removed to Windham, Conn.; where she died, at the age of eighty-three. John died Sept. 30, 1774, aged seventy-nine, childless, if not a bachelor: the name was, therefore, not perpetuated in this branch of the family. MARK, youngest son of the first William, married Elizabeth Giddings, Dec. 16, 1685; and died Sept. 8, 1691. His widow married John Dennison of Ipswich. Two sons (Mark and William) survived their father. Mark married Martha Tuthill in 1710; and died in 1776, aged eighty-nine. Of his nine children, two were sons, — Mark and George. William married Jemima Hubbard of Salisbury; and died Dec. 10, 1766, aged seventy-seven: she died in 1762, at the same age. He was a selectman, a deacon of the Second Church many years, and representative in 1736. He was an eminently pious man, and his last broken accents were heard to express his lamentations and supplications for the church of Christ. He had eight children; two of whom died in infancy, one on her twenty-third birthday, and five attained very advanced age. One of them was a daughter Comfort, who married a Sawyer; and died in 1809, aged ninety-two. Job, the oldest son, settled in Hampton; but is said to have died in New Gloucester, Me., in 1806, aged ninety. Nathaniel married Hannah, daughter of Rev. John White; and died July 31, 1808, in his ninetieth year. He was deacon of the Second Church about fifty years; and, from papers found among his effects, it is evident that he was a thoughtful, prayerful Christian, and that his mind was much exercised with the subtle, doctrinal points in theology, which were deemed of so much importance a century ago. Nathaniel, the oldest of his ten children, settled in town; and died Jan. 7, 1827, aged eighty-four, leaving a son Nathaniel, who deceased at Portland, Me., about ninety years old. Hubbard, the next of these four brothers, died April 9, 1811, aged ninety. He was a sailmaker by trade, and was also engaged in commerce. In accordance with his pious parentage and education, he was a religious man, and creditably sustained for thirty-nine years the office of deacon of the First Church. His wife was Anna Millet, who survived her husband six months, after a conjugal union of more than seventy years; and died at the age of ninety-three. Of the ten children of Hubbard Haskell, three were sons that lived to maturity, — Hubbard, Nathan, and William. The first settled in Newburyport; and died in September, 1831, aged eighty-seven. Nathan went in early life to New Gloucester, Me.; and died there in 1838, aged eighty-seven. William lived in Gloucester; and died Oct. 16, 1843, aged eighty-three. His son John W. was representative in 1853. William, the youngest brother of Deacon Hubbard Haskell, settled in his native parish; and died April 27, 1806, aged eighty. He had three sons at least; one of whom was Elias, father of Eli, whose son William H. was representative in 1851. The posterity of William Haskell is believed to be much more numerous than that of any other early settler. A large number of his descendants remain in town, but a still greater number are scattered abroad over the country. From six generations of this prolific stock, emigrants have gone forth, who, whether they braved the dangers and hardships of pioneer life in the forests of Maine, or sought a kinder soil than their own in more settled and cultivated regions, or engaged in handicraft and trade in the marts of business, have generally sustained the character for usefulness and respectability which the family has always borne in its ancient seat.*

ZEBULON HILL was born about 1621. He was from Bristol, England; and, by trade, was a cooper. Land in several places is recorded to him before 1650. One of the lots was "the bank that lyes in the harbour." This was on the present Front Street, and was laid out to his heirs in 1709. He sold his house, homelot, and other lands, to "Goodman Elwell," in 1657, and removed to Salem, where he died about 1699. He married Elizabeth, daughter of Agnes Clark, Nov. 16, 1651. His will mentions several children, and a brother John of Beverly.

SAMUEL HODGKINS first appears in Gloucester with his wife Hannah in 1684. A William Hodgkins was an early inhabitant of Ipswich, and had a son Samuel born there in 1658. Our Samuel Hodgkins was appointed, in 1694, to keep the ferry at Trynall Cove, where he had already built a house. He was a shoemaker; and a descendant of the same trade was living, near the close of the last century, where his ancestor settled, and was the last ferryman at the place. Samuel Hodgkins's wife died July 28, 1724, aged sixty years; and he next married Mary Stockbridge, May 3, 1725. The date of his death is not known. Fifteen children are recorded to him: namely, Samuel, born in 1684; Hannah, 1686; John, 1688; Philip, 1690; William, 1691; a daughter, 1694; Jedediah, 1696; Patience, 1697; Abigail, 1699; Mercy, 1700; David, 1702; Martha, 1704; Anna, 1705; Jonathan, 1706; and Experience, 1708. Of the seven sons, but little information can be given. SAMUEL married Hannah Pilkington, Sept. 28, 1708; and appears to have been living in 1758. He had nine children, of whom only

* A William Haskell was killed, in 1759, in the king's service; and an Isaac was killed, in 1778, on board of a privateer.

Roger Haskell of Salem was, without doubt, brother of our William; as he mentions in his will (1667) brothers William and Mark. William of Gloucester was guardian to Roger's son Samuel in 1679. It would be difficult to find among the early settlers of New England a single family whose genealogy would interest more persons than that of the Haskell Family.

the two youngest were sons, — Samuel, born in 1729; and James, born in 1732, who died the same year. It was this last Samuel who was the last ferryman at Trynall Cove. He married Abigail Sayward in 1753, and had sons Samuel and James. The former married Jemima Allen in 1776. Several descendants in this line live in the Fourth Parish, not far from the home of their ancestor. Of JOHN, nothing further is known; unless he was the same who married Mary Knowles about 1752, though he was then sixty-four. The children of this marriage were John, Mary, and Timothy: the latter, who was a soldier of the Revolution, died in October, 1830, aged seventy-three. PHILIP and JEDEDIAH HODGKINS probably went to Falmouth, Me. The latter married Sarah Millet in 1722, and had daughters Sarah and Judith born here. DAVID married Abigail Haskell in 1735, and had sons, — David, born in 1737; and William, in 1740. JONATHAN married Mary Stockbridge in 1733, and Widow Sarah Stockbridge in 1749. By these two wives he had ten children; of whom three were sons, — Jonathan, Benjamin, and John. A Christopher Hodgkins had a son Hezekiah born here in 1699.

JOHN HOLGRAVE was an early resident in Salem, where he filled important offices, besides representing the town in the first General Court at Boston, and again in 1634 and the following year. He kept an inn at Salem, but is not mentioned there after 1639. He had land here in 1647; and, in 1649, a house in the Harbor, near the pond. He is not mentioned here after 1653, when both he and his wife had so conducted themselves as to leave no occasion to regret their departure.

WILLIAM HOUGH was a house-carpenter, and lived at Trynall Cove, where, and on Biskie Island, opposite, he had land. He was a selectman in 1649 and 1650. His departure is spoken of in the latter year, when he joined the emigration to New London. He married Sarah, daughter of Hugh Calkin, Oct. 28, 1645; and had three children born in Gloucester, — Hannah, born in 1646; Abiah, 1648; and Sarah, 1651.

JAMES HUGHES's name occurs only in connection with the births of his children. He had a wife Elizabeth, by whom a daughter Elizabeth was born in 1670; and a son Jonathan in 1672, who died in 1689. A Rachel Hughes died in 1689.

George Ingersol was born in 1618, and was son of Richard Ingersol, a Bedfordshire man, who was one of the early emigrants to Massachusetts. His first appearance in Gloucester is in 1646; when, by his wife Elizabeth, his son Joseph was born. Other children of his, born here, were — Elizabeth, born in 1648, died in infancy; Elizabeth, born in 1651; and Mary, 1657. He was a selectman in 1652; and, in the same year, was licensed to keep an ordinary. He had a house in the Harbor, and owned land in several places; which he sold, and afterwards removed to Falmouth, Me. He was lieutenant, at that place, of the military force for protection against the Indians; and, in the attack of the savages in 1675, had a son killed, and his house burned. His letter, describing other destruction of life and property (that of the Wakleys, probably, who had also emigrated from Gloucester), is in our State archives. He returned to Salem, and was living there in 1694. Besides the children already mentioned, he had sons, — George, Samuel, and John. George was a shipwright. He resided in Falmouth and Boston, and died in the latter place before 1730. Samuel was also a shipwright. He came to Gloucester soon after 1700, and settled on Eastern Point, where he built several small vessels. He was one of the five Gloucester men composing part of the company to whom, in 1733, the township of Amherst, N.H., then called Narraganset, No. 3, was granted for services rendered by themselves or their ancestors in the Narraganset War in 1675. He conveyed this right to his son Joel in 1734; saying in the deed, that he was a soldier in the Narraganset War, called "Philip's War." His wife Judith died May 11, 1721, between fifty and sixty years old. By her he had two sons, born in Gloucester, — Nehemiah, in 1705; and Joel, 1709. He had a son Samuel, who married here in 1708, and had several children. John is not known to have ever resided in Gloucester. He was living in Kittery, Me., in 1713. Joseph, the only son of George Ingersol known to have been born in Gloucester, went to Falmouth with his father, and became a joiner. He married there Sarah, daughter of Matthew

Coe. He probably returned to Gloucester soon after the second destruction of Falmouth by the Indians; as he had a daughter Hannah born here in 1693. He died in 1718, aged seventy-two: his wife died May 29, 1714. His son Benjamin had several children born here; but he removed to Falmouth on the re-settlement of the place, took possession of his father's grant, and was a useful inhabitant. He removed to North Yarmouth previous to 1735. Besides those already named of this family, there were other Ingersols here in the early part of the last century, who were probably descendants of our early settler, George. Joseph married here in 1707; Josiah, in 1712; Jonathan, in 1717; and David, in 1718; and all of them had children. Jonathan was keeping a tavern at the Harbor, where he died about 1745. David was drowned on a fishing voyage to the Banks in 1730.

John Jackson was a fisherman. He bought a house and land in the Harbor, of William Ash, in 1651; which he sold, in 1662, to Peter Duncan. He lived in Gloucester seven years. He had a wife Eleanor, who was born in 1602. His son John married Susanna, daughter of Thomas Jones, July 12, 1659: she died April 10, 1662; having had a son John, born in 1660.

Charles James was here in 1673, when he married Ann Collins. From the infrequent mention of his name, and its non-appearance on the list of grantees of the Cape lots in 1688, it is supposed that he was not a permanent settler from the date of his marriage. In 1699, he had six acres of land near Kettle Cove, which he exchanged with Morris Smith for a lot at the Cape. He died Sept. 11, 1720, about sixty-nine years old. The births of two children born to him in Gloucester are on our records, — Charles, born in 1674; and Francis, in 1677. The latter married Elizabeth Hallee, or Hallet, in 1703, and had several children; but none by whom the name was perpetuated in town. A Thomas James (not known to be connected with this family) had, by his wife Susanna, a son Thomas, born here in 1752.

Thomas Jones was born in 1598. He was in Gloucester as early as 1642, and owned a house and land near the burying-place. He was admitted freeman in 1653; and died in 1671, leaving an estate of £147. 15s. His wife was Mary, daughter of Richard and Ursula North: she died in 1681. The children recorded to them are—Thomas, born in 1640, died in 1672, probably unmarried; North and Ruth (twins), 1644 (the latter married Thomas Howard of Salem); Samuel, 1647; Ephraim, 1649 (was apprenticed for twelve years to a Manuel *alias* Nathaniel Ffryar); Benjamin, 1651; and Remember, 1653, who married Nathaniel Hadlock. Besides these children, there were Susanna, who married John Jackson; a daughter who married a Winslow of Salisbury, and another who married a Kent. BENJAMIN JONES married Elizabeth Wills, Jan. 22, 1678; and had four children born here. None of the name of this family appear here after 1686. Benjamin may have removed to Hull, where a person of the same name lived in 1693.

HENRY JOSLYN.—The orthography of this name is variously given: that of the Gloucester Records is here followed. Henry Joslyn, son of Sir Thomas Joslyn of Kent, came to New England about 1634, as an agent for Capt. Mason; but he soon left his service, and, in 1638, had settled at Black Point, now Scarborough, in Maine. He bore a distinguished part in all the political transactions of that Province till October, 1676; when the Indians attacked Black Point, and compelled the people to flee. The fate of Joslyn is not known; but there can scarcely be a doubt that his son Henry was the person of the same name who settled in this town. He and John Wallis, driven the year before in like manner from Falmouth, were probably the first reflux of the tide of emigration which, about twenty years before, began to set towards Maine from our town. His name first appears here on the occasion of his marriage, June 4, 1678, to Bridget Day. The next year, he had a grant of land between the lot of Timothy Somes and Thomas Riggs's house. In 1693, he appears to have sold this land, and a dwelling-house standing on it, to Nathaniel Wharf. By his wife Bridget he had a son Henry, born June 28, 1679; and a daughter in 1682, who died in infancy. His wife died Sept. 7, 1684; and he next married, Nov. 9, 1685, Mary Lambert. His children by her were—

Ebenezer, born 30th July, died 20th November, 1686; Margaret, 1687; Mary, 1689; Constantine, 1691; Benjamin, 1695,—lost at sea in 1716; and Mercy, 1703. Henry Joslyn, sen., was admitted to the church in 1704. All who were householders that year, and were living in town in 1721, had, at the last date, a grant of land; and, as none of this family appear among the grantees, it is reasonable to infer that the elder Joslyn had either died or removed before that year. HENRY, supposed to be the son, married Sarah Litheam,* Dec. 6, 1703; and had a son Richard, born March 26, 1704; after which, nothing more is known of them. CONSTANTINE married Agnes Tenny, Dec. 9, 1713; and had six sons and one daughter. He was living in 1747. Three of his sons — Constantine, Henry, and William — were married; but we know nothing more of their history, except that the first had several children, one of whom (Ebenezer), born in 1738, addressed a letter to his mother from the camp at Long Island, July 5, 1776. One member of this family received at death a special mark of distinction from the town; which paid, February, 1745, eight shillings and tenpence for four pounds of sugar and two ounces of allspice, and twenty-six shillings for four pairs of gloves "for Mother Josselyn's funnerall."†

THOMAS JUDKIN is mentioned as a landowner several times before 1650. In 1665, he bought of George Blake a house and land near the Meeting-house. He married, in 1665, Anna, widow of Nehemiah Howard of Salem. By the previous husband she had had three daughters, — Hannah, who married John Sargent; Rose, who married Joseph Allen; and Sarah, who married George Harvey. He died Feb. 23, 1695, leaving an estate of £271: she died Jan. 27, 1706, aged about sixty-eight. It is probable that Judkin kept a tavern, and that the business was carried on by his wife after his decease; for, in November, 1695, a committee of Ipswich gentlemen met at her house to settle a difference between the town and Francis Nor-

* Perhaps Littlehale. Jan. 7, 1704. — Henry Josslin of Gloucester, and Sarah his wife, convey to Isaac Littlehale of Ipswich "land that was formarly my Grandfather Richard Littlehale's of Haverhill."

† See New-England Hist. and Gen. Register, vol. ii. pp. 204–306.

wood in relation to Thatch Banks, and expended there eighteen shillings. The selectmen also often met at "Landlady Judkin's;" and, in 1704 and 1705, contracted a debt of upwards of a pound in each year, which was paid by the town. The descendants of the landlady by her three daughters are numerous.

WILLIAM KENIE had a house and land, which he sold to Thomas Prince in 1652; having previously removed to New London. His daughter Susanna married Ralph Parker.

THOMAS KENT may have been connected with Richard Kent of Ipswich, who received a grant of land near Chebacco River in 1635. Thomas Kent had a house and land near the burying-ground, recorded under the year 1649; but earlier in his possession, probably: and he bought several lots of William Meades, which, in 1655, he recorded to his brother, Samuel Kent. A Thomas Kent, sen., died May 1, 1658, and Widow Kent, Oct. 6, 1671; leaving Thomas and Samuel above mentioned, who, it is likely, were their sons. These brothers bought of Thomas Prince, in 1657, eighteen acres of land on the west side of Little River, where a house and land were situated that Thomas sold to Richard Dike in 1667. THOMAS married Joan, daughter of Thomas Penny, March 28, 1658; and died Aug, 2, 1696. The children recorded to him are — Josiah, born in 1660; Sarah, 1662; Mercy and Joan, 1664; James, 1666; and John, 1676. SAMUEL married Frances Woodall, Jan. 17, 1654; and had the following children: Sarah, born in 1657; Mary, 1658; Samuel, 1661; and John, 1664. John removed, about 1680, to Suffield, Conn.; where was born, in 1704, Elisha, son of John Kent, grandfather of the distinguished chancellor of New York, James Kent. Josiah Kent married Mary Lufkin in 1689; and died in 1725, aged sixty-five. One of the Johns, probably the brother of Josiah, also married. Both of these had families, and the name continued in the Second Parish down at least to the death of John. He received help from the town for several years, on account of his inability, through weakness of mind, to earn his own living; and died about April 19, 1743, when Col. Epes Sargent was paid by the selectmen "£2 for four pairs of gloves, to be given at ye burial of John Kent."

JOHN KETTLE was born about 1621. He had a house in the Harbor before 1650, and resided here several years. In 1664, he sold a house and land situated near the Meeting-house. By his wife Elizabeth he had the following children born here: John, in 1654; William, 1656, died 1677; Elizabeth, 1657; Mary, 1659; Samuel, 1662; and James, 1665. None of this family appear in town at the granting of six-acre lots in 1688. A John Kettle, a minor, living at Mackerel Cove, was brought before a court at Salem in 1641 for breach of the sabbath and for stealing.

JOHN LANE was born about 1653; and, with his wife and children, came to Gloucester, about the close of the seventeenth century, from Falmouth, Me.; driven thence, probably, on the second destruction of that place by the Indians. He was son of James Lane, and went, in 1658, with his father, from Malden to Casco Bay; where they lived till driven away by the Indians in the first Indian War. His father was killed in a fight with the Indians; and, besides John, left sons Henry, Samuel, and Job. John Lane received from the town a grant of a common right in 1702; and, in 1704, ten acres of land at Flatstone Cove, where he had already settled, and to which his own name was subsequently given. He married a daughter of John Wallis, an early inhabitant of Falmouth. Her baptismal name was Dorcas, if she was the wife that accompanied him to Gloucester. The children recorded as born to them here are — Hepzibah, born in 1694; Mary, 1696; Joseph, 1698; Benjamin, 1700; Deborah, 1703, died in 1729; and Job, 1705. Besides these, there were James, John, Dorcas, Josiah, Sarah, and David. Five of the sons were living when their father died. He was living in 1734, at the age of eighty-one; but the date of his death is not known. JAMES married Ruth Riggs in 1710, who died the next year, aged twenty-one; and Judith Woodbury in 1715. He became a deacon of the Third Church; and died about 1751, leaving sons William, James, and Josiah, and daughters Mary and Ruth. JOHN LANE, jun., married Mary Riggs in 1713; and was killed by Indians at Penobscot, June 22, 1724, at the age of thirty-six. He left an estate of nearly £500; consisting, in part, of half of a coasting and half of a fishing vessel. He had six daughters and two sons. One of the latter (David) appears to have married in town. JOSIAH married Rachel York in 1713; after which nothing is known of him. JOSEPH married Deborah Haraden in 1721, and had sons Joseph, Caleb, and Solomon; besides daughters, one of whom (Deborah) was first married to John Langsford, and next to William Lane. One of these husbands met his death at Owl's Head. He was returning from a fishing voyage, and put in there for a harbor. While walking on the shore with a companion, he was shot at by some Indians who were lying in ambush, and killed on the spot. BENJAMIN LANE married Elizabeth Griffin in 1725; by whom, besides two daughters, he had sons Thomas, Benjamin, Jonathan, John, and Hezekiah. JOB married Mary Ashby in 1734, and had sons Job, Ebenezer, and Andrew. Descendants of John Lane and of Samuel, who came subsequently, are numerous in town; and many are scattered abroad in various parts of the country. Of those of the later generations, some have been prominent citizens. Samuel was a representative from 1829 to 1832 inclusive, and subsequently a senator from Essex County; George, a representative in 1833; and Gideon, a representative in 1833 and 1834. A John Lane was killed, May 29, 1778, in an engagement with a British ship of twenty guns; and is mentioned as the first victim of the war from Squam.

ANDREW LISTER was here as early as 1642, and had a house on the neck of house-lots, and a lot on Planter's Neck. In 1648, he was licensed to keep a house of entertainment, and to sell wine and strong water here. He sold all his property in Gloucester to Clement Coldom, and left town with the company that went to New London about 1651. His wife's name was Barberie; and his children, born here, were — Daniel, in 1642; Andrew, 1644; Mary, 1647; and Anne, 1651.

NICHOLAS LISTON was probably an early but brief sojourner. Under the date of 1645, there is a mention of marsh in Annisquam first given to him; and there is a record, without date, of two acres of upland in the Harbor, purchased of him.

THOMAS LUFKIN, OR LOVEKIN, as the name, in conformity with its manifest derivation, was anciently spelled, came to Gloucester about 1674. In 1680, he had a grant of land above Deacon Haskell's sawmill; and, in later years, lots in other places. His wife's name was Mary. She died in December, 1730, aged eighty-six: he died Nov. 3, 1708. His children, natives of Gloucester, were — Joseph, born in 1674; Ebenezer, 1676; Abraham and Isaac, 1678; Abigail, 1682; Henry, 1684; and James and Elizabeth, 1686. Besides these, there was probably a Thomas, born before the removal to Gloucester, who had a grant of land in 1690. He married Mary Myles in 1690, who died the same year; and Sarah Downing in 1692. His name does not again occur; unless he is the same person who in 1720, then belonging to Ipswich, married Rachel Riggs of this town. Joseph, Ebenezer, and Henry Lufkin all married here, and had children. Benjamin Lufkin was here in 1713, and Jacob in 1720; and both had families. A Jacob was wounded in an engagement with the enemy in the eastern parts of the Province in 1699.

Thomas Low. — This settler was, without doubt, a descendant of the Ipswich Family of the same name; which, according to an account of some of its members, had for their English ancestor Capt. John Lowe, master of the ship "Ambrose" in the great emigration to Massachusetts in 1630. Whether this statement rests upon good authority or not, it is certain that a Thomas Low was of Ipswich as early as 1643. He died Sept. 8, 1677, leaving a son Thomas; also a grandson Thomas, not then twenty-one years old. The son, it is supposed, was Deacon Thomas Low of Chebacco Parish, now Essex, who died April 12, 1712, aged eighty; and the grandson, Thomas, who settled in Gloucester about 1692. The latter had married, before the last-named year, Sarah, daughter of Harlakenden Symonds, who was born here in 1668, probably in the house which her father owned near the Meeting-house, and to which, after an absence of some years from town perhaps, Mrs. Symonds returned again with her daughter and son-in-law. He survived the removal but six years, and died Feb. 8, 1698, leaving sons Symonds, Thomas, and John, and a daughter Elizabeth. The inventory of his personal estate amounted to £80; of which amount, his house is set down at £45. His real estate was valued in 1740 at £838. SYMONDS was twice married, and had three sons and six daughters. One of the sons died in infancy: neither of the other two appears to have settled in town. JOHN, third son of Thomas Low, married Mary Allen, Jan. 20, 1726. His second son (John), born May 17, 1728, became one of the most prominent citizens of his time. He had his home on or near the ancestral property, and owned there a valuable farm; but the business to which his own attention was chiefly given was that of trade and fishing. The latter he carried on from Squam River; which, for several years before the Revolutionary War, was the scene of an active business in this line. In these pursuits he acquired property; and, being a man qualified by education, character, and talents, for public employments, the town found in him, at the period of its need, a ready and faithful servant. In 1775, he had advanced to the rank of lieutenant-colonel in the militia; and afterwards became a colonel, — a title which he retained to the end of his life. He was a representative to the General Court held in Watertown, May 27, 1776; a delegate to the Convention for forming the State Constitution, and to that for ratifying the Constitution of the United States. He also served several times as representative in the General Court of the Commonwealth. Besides serving the town in these elevated stations, he often filled the office of selectman, and held for many years the place of deacon of the Fourth Church. It was while on the road, returning to his home from a meeting of the selectmen, that the career of this good man was suddenly ended by death, Nov. 3, 1796. A sermon was preached at his funeral by the Rev. Eli Forbes, from Isa. lvii. 1, 2; in which the virtues of the departed were portrayed by the venerable pastor with touching simplicity and truthfulness. Col. Low married, April 30, 1752, Sarah, daughter of Rev. Joshua Gee of Boston; who died about twenty years before her husband, during which he remained a widower. He had ten children. His oldest son (John), born Sept. 1, 1754, graduated at Harvard College in 1773; became a merchant in his native town; and died Feb. 10, 1801. David, the second son, spent the first part of his life in maritime employments; and the latter in the pursuits of husbandry, and died March 28, 1840, aged eighty-one. Among his children were — David, a merchant of Boston, who died at Havre, in France, Jan. 2, 1829; and John Gorham, also a merchant of Boston, who perished in the destruction of the steamer "Lexington" by fire, on Long-Island Sound, Jan. 13, 1840. Joshua Gee, another son of Col. Low, was the father of Frederic G. Low, who has filled the office of collector of the customs for this port. William, son of the first John Low, married Dorcas Ellery in 1751, and had eleven children; the oldest of which (William) is said to have been an officer on board a letter-of-marque from Newburyport in the Revolution, and to have been taken by a British ship and carried to New York, where he experienced all the horrors of sickness on board of a prison-ship, in which he was confined a year. After his escape or discharge, he walked home to Gloucester barefooted and bareheaded, begging his food by the way.

John Luther is only mentioned as a seller of land in the Harbor to John Collins, recorded in 1649.

Solomon Martin may have been the person of the same name who came to New England in the ship "James" in 1635, being then sixteen years old. He was a ship-carpenter, and owned a house and several house-lots of land, which he sold to Richard Beeford in May, 1652, when he was a resident of Andover. The Gloucester Records show that he was twice married: first to Mary, daughter of Henry Pindar, in 1643, who died in 1648; and next, in the same year, to Widow Alice Varnum of Ipswich. His children were — Samuel, born in 1645; and Mary, 1648.

Edmund Marshall only appears as a seller of house and land near Poles, which he bought of John Bourne, to Anthony Day, in 1657. Before this date, the same name occurs in Salem, and subsequently in Ipswich and Newbury.

Philip Merritt only appears here at the birth, by his wife Mary, of a son Jacob, Oct. 21, 1700.

WILLIAM MEADES had a lot near the burying-ground. He had been here several years, probably, when he sold land in three places, in 1647, to Thomas Kent. In 1648, the date of his last appearance in Gloucester, he took the freeman's oath; was a selectman and constable. March, 1651, he was a grantee of land in New London.

THOMAS MILLET came to New England in 1635, in the ship "Elizabeth" of London, with his wife Mary and son Thomas, and settled in Dorchester, where he resided several years. The records of that town show that he had the following children born there: John born in 1635; Jonathan, 1638, died the same year; Mary, 1639; and Mehetabel, 1641. Another (a son Nathaniel) was born in 1647. In 1655, Millet bought of William Perkins, who had been a teaching elder in the church here a few years, all the property the latter owned in the town. He came here with the rare title of "Mr.," — a distinction to which he was entitled by the place he filled in the church; for he was the successor of Mr. Perkins in his religious office, as well as in the possession of his lands. His name does not appear among the ministers of his time; but it is certain that he labored here in spiritual things, though perhaps his office in the church was an anomalous one. Its pecuniary rewards were not always voluntarily bestowed, as the Court Records testify; and, indeed, these alone furnish information that he was engaged here in the work of the ministry at all. It is supposed that he removed from town several years before his death, and became a citizen of Brookfield; at which place, he and his wife gave their consent, June 3, 1675, to the sale of a house and land on Town Neck to Francis Norwood. He died within a year from that time; and his wife was deceased, Sept. 27, 1682. His oldest son THOMAS, born in 1633, had land of his father, lying near the old Meeting-house Plain in 1655. He held the office of ensign in the military company, and served a few years as a selectman; but, otherwise, his name does not prominently occur. He came into possession of the land at Kettle Cove originally granted to Mr. Blynman. This was situated near the Manchester bounds, which Millet passed, and became, in the last years of his life, a resident of that town. He died there June 18, 1707; but was brought to Gloucester for burial. He was twice married: first to Mary, daughter of Sylvester Eveleth, May 21, 1655, who died July 2, 1687; and next to Abigail, widow of Isaac Eveleth, who survived him, and died March 19, 1726, aged sixty-eight. It is not known that he had other children than Thomas and John, both by his last wife. JOHN MILLET, son of the first Thomas, married Sarah Leach, July 3, 1663; and died Nov. 3, 1678. He has the births of seven children recorded in the Gloucester Records. Two of their children were sons, — John and Thomas. The latter, born in 1671, married Martha Ingersol in 1695, and had several children. The father and his son John, with their families, removed to Falmouth, Me., about 1724; where the former died Jan. 21, 1730. He left in Gloucester a son Morris, who married Jemima Hodgkins in 1728, and had sons Joseph, James, Thomas, and Samuel. NATHANIEL MILLET received grants of land on the westerly side of Annisquam River; and, it is probable, had his residence there. He finally settled at Kettle Cove; where, in 1700, he and his sons had land granted to them, which was not to be alienated from the family so long as any of them survived. He married Ann Lister, May 3, 1670, who died March 9, 1718, aged sixty-six: he died Nov. 7, 1719, aged seventy-two. Of his eleven children, it appears that three were sons who married in town, — Thomas, born in 1675; Andrew, in 1681; and Nathan, in 1685. These sons all settled near their father, at Kettle Cove; and each had a family that included sons. Thomas was drowned at Casco Bay, March 1, 1722, "by a land flood overflowing ye cottage, and carrying of it away."* Nathan was drowned near Manchester Neck, Jan. 6, 1724. Andrew died March 25, 1718. Descendants of Thomas Millet, bearing the family name, have lived in town down to the present time; but they have never been numerous, and the race is now almost extinct in Gloucester.

* Rev. T. Smith of Falmouth, Me., says, in his journal, that Millet and one Ingersol "were drowned at Presumpscot by the damming of the ice; raising an head of water in the night while they were asleep."

Thomas Milward, a fisherman, was one of the selectmen in 1642. No grants of land are recorded to him; though he sold, as early as May, 1642, two acres in the Harbor to Robert Elwell. He removed to Newbury, where he resided in 1652, when he sold his farm at Fresh-water Cove to Samuel Dolliver of Marblehead. He died in Boston, Sept. 1, 1653.

George Norton had been in Salem several years when he became one of the company, which, in 1640, had leave from the General Court to erect a village at Jeffries Creek, now Manchester. His name does not appear in the Gloucester Records as a grantee or purchaser of land; but he was here as early as 1642, and probably received then from the commissioners the grant of the farm at Little Good Harbor, which he sold to William Vinson. He was prominent among the first settlers; being one of the first board of officers chosen by the town for ordering its affairs, and the representative in 1642, — the first one; and in 1643 and 1644, — the latter date being the last mention of his name in Gloucester. He died about 1659. He had a daughter Mary born here by his wife Mary, Feb. 28, 1643. A Mary Norton, widow, contemplated marriage with Philip Fowler of Ipswich in 1659.

Francis Norwood, according to a tradition in the family, fled from England with his father, at the restoration of Charles II., on account of the trouble in which the father feared they might be involved for the part he had taken in the civil wars of that period. The son came to New England, and is said to have kept a tavern in Lynn. He came to Gloucester about 1663, and settled at Goose Cove; at which place, by grants from the town and by purchase, he became possessed of considerable land. He married Elizabeth, daughter of Clement Coldom, Oct. 15, 1663; and died March 4, 1709. His children were — Thomas, born in 1664; Francis, 1666; Elizabeth, 1669; Mary, 1672; Stephen, 1674; Deborah, 1677; Hannah, 1679; Joshua, 1683; Caleb, 1685; and Abigail, 1689. Thomas, the oldest son, only re-appears, after his birth, to be noticed in his father's will in 1709; and is not again mentioned. Francis married Mary Stevens, Jan. 24, 1693. She died Nov. 19, 1724, aged fifty-two: the date of his death is not known. His sons William and Jonathan survived him, and had families; the latter a very large one. These brothers lived at Goose Cove, and there carried on the fishing business. William died in February, 1781, aged seventy-three; and Jonathan died Feb. 21, 1791, aged seventy-nine. The funeral procession which accompanied his body to the grave was stopped by one of his creditors for the execution of a legal process, which the law then permitted for the recovery of a debt. A son-in-law stepped forward, and satisfied the demand; when the train, almost petrified with horror at the rude and unwonted interruption, resumed its solemn march. Gustavus, one of the youngest of his sons, died in 1841, in his ninetieth year. Abraham, a grandson, settled in Maine, and was the father of Abraham, a Universalist preacher. Stephen Norwood married Elizabeth Ingallbe, February, 1702, and died Jan. 7, 1703. Joshua married Elizabeth, daughter of Ensign William Andrews of Chebacco, Sept. 25, 1704. He was among the early possessors of land at the Cape, and probably resided there most of his life. He had four sons and eleven daughters. One of the sons (Caleb) was born in Attleborough, where his father lived a few years. His son Caleb was a representative in 1806 and 1807, and died about 1828. Another son (William), still living, is a venerable citizen of Rockport. His son George was a representative from Gloucester in 1857. Joshua Norwood became poor in his old age, and lived with his children. He died in 1762, in his eightieth year: his wife is said to have died Nov. 1, 1774, aged about ninety. A still greater age was attained by her daughter Mary, who married Nathaniel Gamage of Cambridge in 1731, and is reported to have died in Bristol, Me., at the age of one hundred and five years. To this branch of the family belongs Francis Norwood, who was born in 1795; graduated at Dartmouth College in 1818; studied theology at Andover; and is now settled in the ministry at Phipsburg, Me. Caleb, youngest son of the first Francis, married Alice Donnel of York. He had a grant of land near Halibut Point in 1710, and had several children born in Gloucester; but finally removed to Boston, and was an innholder there Nov. 29, 1735, when he made his will, which mentions a son Gustavus and five daughters. The former settled in York, Me. The widow became the third wife of Rev. John White.

RALPH PARKER had recorded, under the year 1647, land in the Harbor, on the westerly side of his house, which was near Governor's Hill. He sold his possessions in Gloucester to Phineas Rider in 1651; about which time he removed to New London. He is not mentioned here as having a family; but the New-London Records state that he had a wife who was a daughter of William Kenie.

ELIAS PARKMAN was of Boston in 1651. He is mentioned, in our records without date, as purchaser of a house and land, in Fisherman's field, of Christopher Avery. In 1655, he had a grant of "wood and timber from the run of water as runneth out at the beach by the salt-work; in consideration of which he is to let the town have salt, for their own proper use, 6d. per bushel cheaper than he sell out of town, for such pay as the town can pay him at pris currant." If he resided in town at all, it was probably only for a brief period.

JOSEPH PAGE had, in March, 1699, a grant of half an acre of land near Clay Cove to set a house upon, on condition that he should take care of his mother. He married Elizabeth Row in 1705; and died March 18, 1725, aged about forty-eight. A George Page had, in 1709, a grant of land near the head of the Harbor. The birth of his daughter Mary in Antigua, in 1705, by his wife Joanna, and the decease of Joanna Page in 1707, are recorded in the town-records.

JEFFREY PARSONS, born in 1631, left England when quite young, and went with an uncle to Barbadoes, where he lived several years, and came thence to New England. He left in his native country a brother James, who died there about 1708, leaving several children; one of whom, Elizabeth Morgan, was living in 1714 at Ashprington, near Dartmouth, as appears by her letter to her cousin James in New England, dated 1714; copies of which are preserved in the family. In April, 1655, he bought of Giles Barge an acre and a half of land in Fisherman's Field. He also bought, about the same time, a house and land at the same place, which had once belonged to George Ingersol, and still earlier to George Norton. There he fixed his residence; and descendants still live around the spot first occupied by their ancestor. Tradition has preserved the romantic incident that determined his choice of a partner for life. While walking on a hot summer's day, he was overcome with fatigue and thirst, and stopped at Vinson's Spring for rest and refreshment. The house of Vinson was near by, and a benevolent impulse prompted his beautiful daughter Sarah to approach the weary stranger with the tender of a drinking-cup. The charms and kind attentions of the fair one made a deep impression on the heart of Jeffrey; and, as she reciprocated the sentiments she had inspired, she ere long became his wife. They were married Nov. 11, 1657. He was selectman several years; and died Aug. 16, 1689, leaving an estate of £317. She died Jan. 12, 1708. Among their descendants, besides the distinguished Chief-Justice of Massachusetts, are several eminent merchants. The children of Jeffrey Parsons were — James, born in 1658; Jeffrey, 1661; Sarah, 1663; Elizabeth, 1665; John, 1666; Jeremiah, 1672; Nathaniel, 1675; Abigail, 1678; Ebenezer, 1680, died 1680; and Ebenezer, 1681. James was one of the most useful citizens of his time. He was a selectman, elder of the church, town-clerk eleven years, and representative five years. His residence was at the corner of the old road leading from the Manchester Road to Ipswich; and the old house still standing there bore till recently indubitable marks of age, which render it probable that he was the builder. He married, Dec. 18, 1688, Hannah Younglove of Ipswich, who died March 11, 1733, aged seventy-eight: he died Oct. 1, 1733, aged seventy-five. His sons were James, Eliezer, and Joseph. James, born in 1690, died Nov. 15, 1761; having lost two sons in the military service of the Colony: namely, James, who was a soldier in the expedition to Cape Breton, — returned home ill, and died Aug. 20, 1745, aged about twenty years; and Eliphalet, who enlisted in the army sent against the French at Crown Point in 1756, and died at Albany, Aug. 9 in that year, aged twenty-four. Eliezer married Mary Day in 1720, and had five sons and three daughters.

Joseph, the other son of Elder James Parsons, a student of Harvard College, died at Cambridge, Oct. 30, 1722, aged about twenty-nine. JEFFREY received, in 1685, a grant of land situated on the road to Starknaught Harbor; where he erected a house, and settled. He married Abigail Younglove of Ipswich, May 5, 1686; who died in June, 1734. The date of his death is unknown. His will, made in 1734, was proved in 1750. Most of the Parsonses on the Cape are descended from this son. In his will, three sons are mentioned, — Jonathan, Samuel, and Jeremiah. Jonathan married Lydia Stanwood in 1711, and had the following sons: Jonathan, who had several children; John, who died about 1796, aged eighty, leaving a wife Anna (Clark), who died at the age of ninety; James and Joseph (twins), the former of whom settled at Sandy Bay, and has, among his descendants, Gorham, for several years postmaster of Gloucester, whose son James C. graduated at Amherst College in 1855; and William, representative in 1841 and 1842, now a merchant in Boston. Joseph, the other twin, was lost on the Grand Bank about 1785, aged sixty-three. David, the next and youngest of these brothers, had his home at the "Farms;" and died in 1808, aged eighty. Samuel, second son of Jeffrey Parsons, jun., married Ruth Lee of Manchester in 1713. The records show that he had eleven children, and that two of his sons (Samuel and Nehemiah) married in town, and perpetuated the name. Samuel and his brother David were among the first settlers of New Gloucester, Me. Jeremiah, the other son of Jeffrey Parsons, jun., married Susanna Cogswell of Ipswich in 1721; and had sons Jeremiah, Jeffrey, and Zaccheus. The first of these sons appears to have married in town, and to have had sons Jeremiah and Zaccheus. Jeffrey, son of John and Anna above mentioned, born in 1746, a soldier in the battle of Bunker Hill, was drowned near Salt-Island Ledge in 1792. JOHN PARSONS, third son of Jeffrey, sen., settled at Fisherman's Field. He married Isabella Haynes, Jan. 19, 1693, who died Nov. 20, 1700; and he next married Sarah Norton, July 29, 1701. She died July 25, 1726, aged fifty-six. He died Dec. 1, 1714; having had, by his two wives, nine children. John, his oldest son, married Elizabeth

Haskell in 1716, by whom he had twelve children; of whom five were sons, that married and had families. He was a ruling elder of the First Church, and was living in 1762. Josiah, the next son, married Eunice Sargent in 1719; had ten children born here; and afterwards removed to New Hampshire. Thomas, the third son, married Rachel Baker in 1729; and died March 13, 1732. Daniel, the next, married Susanna Warner in 1732; and died in Antigua, probably about 1738, leaving no son. Solomon, the youngest, married Abigail Knowlton, who died Feb. 15, 1741, aged thirty-four; and next, July 26, 1741, Sarah Dodge of Wenham, who died Jan. 29, 1779, aged sixty-four. He died March 24, 1779, aged seventy-four; leaving an only son Solomon, as appears by record, who died Oct. 5, 1807, aged sixty-eight. Jacob, son of the latter, emigrated with sons to Illinois. These two Solomons lived near the spot on which their ancestor first settled at Fisherman's Field. JEREMIAH, son of the first Jeffrey, was impressed on board of a man-of-war when young; and, having escaped from her, is said to have settled in Virginia. NATHANIEL, the next son, married Abigail Haskell, Dec. 27, 1697; and died of small-pox, May 21, 1722. He engaged in mercantile business; and, at the time of his death, was the owner of several vessels and a shop and wharf. His oldest son (Nathaniel) died of small-pox in 1721. The next (William) became a merchant, and acquired a handsome fortune. He was a man of excellent character; for which his townsmen showed their regard by electing him to the highest offices. He was deacon of the First Church, and representative six years. He died July 10, 1755, aged fifty-five. He was twice married: first, to Mary Haraden, who died in 1751; and next to Mrs. Abigail Beck of Newbury. The youngest of his numerous family of children was Obadiah, minister of the Fourth Parish in Gloucester. Stephen, brother of Deacon William Parsons, married Abigail Robinson in 1732; and was lost in a hurricane in the West Indies, leaving sons Enoch and Daniel. Of this branch of the family is Mrs. Sarah A. Parsons Nowell, author of a volume of poems and a volume of tales. EBENEZER, youngest son of Jeffrey Parsons, married Lydia Haskell; who died in 1734, aged fifty-three. His intention of marriage with Mrs. Alice Norwood was published April 11, 1741; and with Mrs. Jemima Todd of Rowley, Dec. 4, 1742. She became his wife, and died April 25, 1752, aged sixty-five. He next married Mrs. Elizabeth Andrews of Ipswich, Oct. 31, 1754. His death took place Dec. 19, 1763, at the age of eighty-two. His business was that of a trader. He was often a selectman, several years a deacon, and finally ruling elder of the First Church. Each generation of his descendants has furnished distinguished men. His oldest son Ebenezer was lost overboard between Cape Ann and Cape Sable, October, 1732, aged twenty-six years. Jacob, the second son, married Sarah Redding in 1732. Nothing is known of him after the birth of a second son Jacob in 1734. Isaac, the next son that lived to maturity, married Hannah Burnham of Ipswich in 1734; became a deacon of the First Church; and died July 5, 1767, leaving sons,—Isaac, born in 1740, a pioneer in the settlement of New Gloucester, Me.; Nehemiah, born in 1746; and Thomas, 1756, a representative four years, both of whom engaged in commerce in Gloucester, whence they removed to Boston; and Aaron, born in 1759, who also became a merchant in his native town, and died in 1809. Moses, the youngest son of Ebenezer Parsons, born in 1716, graduated at Harvard College, 1736; and taught a school here several years, preparing himself for the work of the ministry, to which he was ordained in Byfield, June 20, 1744. He had preached here occasionally; and, in 1742, was chosen to assist Rev. John White of the First Parish; a measure designed to heal the dissensions that had long existed in the parish: which did not, however, suit the malecontents; and Mr. Parsons accepted a call to Byfield, where he remained till his death, which took place Dec. 14, 1783. He was distinguished as a preacher, particularly excelling in the gift of prayer; and was eminent for all the graces that adorn the character of the true Christian. His wife was Susanna, daughter of Ebenezer Davis; to whom he was married Jan. 11, 1742. She died in Boston, Dec. 18, 1794, aged seventy-five. He had several sons,—Moses, born in Gloucester in 1744, graduated at Harvard College 1765, and died in 1801;

Eben, born in 1746, married Mary Gorham of this town, daughter of Col. John Gorham of Barnstable, in 1767, — was extensively engaged in commercial pursuits in Boston and Gloucester, and died in Byfield in 1819, leaving an only son Gorham, who was born in Gloucester in 1768, became a wealthy merchant in Boston, and died at his farm in Byfield in 1843; Theophilus, the eminent Chief-Justice of Massachusetts, distinguished also for his learning and wit, and for the great influence he exercised in the party divisions of his day, died at his residence in Boston, Oct. 30, 1813, aged sixty-three, leaving several children, one of whom is Theophilus, formerly a distinguished citizen of Boston, now professor in the Law School at Cambridge. Theodore, the next son of Rev. Moses Parsons, born in 1751, graduated at Harvard College in 1773. He sailed from Gloucester in March, 1779, on board the privateer brig "Bennington." A letter was received from him, dated in May following; after which he was never again heard from till accounts were received from London that the brig was sunk in the English Channel in an engagement with a British vessel of superior force. William, the youngest child, born in 1755, eminent for a long and successful commercial career in Boston, and for the exalted character he bore to its close, died March 19, 1837, aged eighty-two. Few of our early settlers are represented by more numerous families than those who perpetuate the name of this respectable stock.

John Pearce, styled "a husbandman," was an early settler, and had land on the narrow projection, between Mill River and Annisquam River, which was formerly called "Pearce's Point." He was made a freeman in 1651; but the church-membership, then a necessary qualification for that privilege, is somewhat dishonored by the contumacious spirit, which, according to the records of the Quarterly Court, he often manifested. Within a period of four years, he was dealt with successively for reproaching the minister and ministry; for absenting himself from public worship; for speaking evil words of a magistrate; and finally, as a juryman, for dissenting from the rest of the jury. He had a wife Elizabeth, to whom he was married Nov. 4, 1643. She died July 3, 1673; and he next married, Sept. 12, 1673, Jane Stanwood, who died Aug. 18, 1706: he died Dec. 15, 1695. His children were — Mary, born in 1650, married James Travis; and John, born in 1653, to whom he gave land to set a house upon in 1680. JOHN PEARCE, jun., had a wife Mary, and children, — Rachel, John, Stephen, and Silas. He sold to Francis Norwood his house and land on the south-east side of Goose Cove in 1682; and there is no mention of his name after that date.

THOMAS PENNY bought, in 1652, a house and three acres of land of Thomas Bray, and a house and home-lot of Thomas Jones. The first he sold back to Bray. In 1658, he bought land at Little River; and, in 1679, had a grant next to William Haskell's land. These notices indicate that his residence was in the westerly part of the town. His wife Ann died April 26, 1667; and he next married Agnes Clark, June 15, 1668, who died Feb. 23, 1682. He was again married, May 17, 1682, to Joan Braybrook. He died about 1692; leaving a daughter Joan, who married Thomas Kent, and is the only child named in his will. Persons of this name lived in town early in the next century, between whom and the preceding it would be natural to suppose that a connection by blood existed. Thomas Penny married Miriam Elwell in 1721, and had five children: one of whom was a Thomas, who married here, and had a son Thomas, born in 1750; the same, perhaps, who died in New Gloucester, Feb. 28, 1813, aged sixty-two. An old Mrs. Penny died April 1, 1758; and a Thomas Penny, in February, 1774.

JOHN POOL, according to family tradition, was born, about 1670, in Taunton, England. Persons of the name of Pool were among the first settlers of our State. A John was of Cambridge in 1632. Elizabeth, "the virgin mother" of Taunton, was there as early as 1639. Our John Pool was a carpenter, and resided several years in Beverly; whence he removed to Gloucester in 1700. While living in Beverly, he worked at his trade with Richard Woodbury; who died May 20, 1690, on his return from the expedition to Canada, and was buried in Boston, leaving a widow, who became Pool's wife. Her maiden name was Sarah Haskell. He bought of John Emerson, jun., in April,

1700, a certain "farme, messuage, &c., at a place commonly called ye Cape," for £160. Pool found one family only at Sandy Bay on his removal to that place, — that of Richard Tarr, who had settled there a short time before. Unquestionable evidence exists to show that he was a man of great industry and enterprise. He is said to have furnished the builders of Long Wharf in Boston, in 1710, with a large quantity of timber, which was carried thither in a sloop built by himself. He became possessed of a large landed property, sufficient to accommodate each of his sons with a farm. He was careful to provide a good education for his children, by sending the oldest son to Beverly to attend school, in order to be qualified to become the instructor of the rest. He died May 19, 1727;* leaving an estate of £2,832. His first wife died Nov. 13, 1716, aged about fifty-five years. His second wife was Deborah Dodge of Ipswich; who died Feb. 1, 1718, aged about thirty-three years. His next wife was Elizabeth Holmes of Salem, who survived her marriage less than two years; and died July 13, 1721, aged between thirty and forty. His fourth and last wife was Abigail Ballard of Lynn. Notice of his intention of marriage with her was published May 19, 1721; which was probably soon followed by the nuptial ceremony, making the bride the fourth wife the bridegroom had had within less than five years. His children were — Jonathan, born in 1694; Miriam, 1695; Robert, 1697; Ebenezer, 1699; and Joshua, 1700 (these were all borne by the first wife, in Beverly). Caleb, 1701, and John, 1703, were born in Gloucester. By his last wife he had Return, born in 1722; and Abigail, in 1725. The latter married John Dane. The uncommon baptismal name given to the former is said to have been bestowed by his father in commemoration of the joy with which he heard the relenting voice of Abigail Ballard bid him to *return*, after she had once rejected

---

* He was buried on his own land, on a spot now in the yard of Deacon Thomas Giles; where his gravestone is still to be seen, bearing the following inscription: —

HERE LYES Y^E^ BODY
OF Mr JOHN POOL,
AGED ABOUT 57
YEARS. DEC^D^ MAY
Y^e^ 19, 1727.

the offer of his hand. JONATHAN married Hannah Burnham of Ipswich, Jan. 4, 1722; and died in 1776. He had several children; of whom four died, in 1738, of a throat distemper, which was at that time prevalent in Sandy Bay with distressing fatality. ROBERT married Anna Sargent, Jan. 1, 1724. Of his six children born here, three died within a month in 1736. He removed to Boston about 1745; thence, in his old age, back to Gloucester; and finally to Maine, where he died. EBENEZER married Elizabeth Norwood, Jan. 30, 1724; and died of small-pox in 1779. He had ten children; one of whom was father of Francis, who was killed in the battle of Bunker Hill.* JOSHUA married Deliverance Giddings, Dec. 28, 1725. He lost his life in Sheepscot River, Me., by falling overboard from a boat in which he and Samuel Tarr were engaged in weighing an anchor, June 27, 1739, in consequence of the parting of the buoy-rope. They were heard to call out for help; but, before any one could reach them, they were both drowned. The body of Pool was recovered, and buried in Wiscasset. Several of his children died young. Joshua, the oldest son, was lost in the ship "Tempest;" and Mark, who was born after his father's death, served in his early youth in the French War, and fought on Bunker Hill as lieutenant of Capt. Rowe's company. In 1778, he joined the army under Sullivan, with a volunteer company raised by himself; and was engaged in the action which occurred near Newport, Aug. 29. After the peace, he held the rank of major in the militia. He died Feb. 11, 1815, aged seventy-six; having been always held in high esteem for the undaunted bravery of his military career. CALEB POOL married Martha Boreman of Ipswich, March 28, 1727. She died in 1760. Four of their children died, in 1738, of the throat distemper then prevailing. He is said to have married again twice. His last wife died, in 1779, of small-pox; of which disease he also died about the same time. He left a son Caleb, whose religious experience places him among those who have been "blasted with excess of

* A grandson of another is Mr. Ebenezer Pool of Rockport, who has a large collection of historical and genealogical facts relating to Sandy Bay and its early settlers. I am indebted to him for several items of information contained in this work.

light." His own account is still extant in print, to show the "signs, wonders, and visions" by which God spoke to him for many years.* JOHN POOL married Jemima Elwell, Oct. 29, 1729. They lost four children, in the fatal year of 1738, by the throat distemper. Four more were subsequently born to them; of whom one was Isaac, who married a daughter of Rev. E. Cleaveland. RETURN POOL went with his brother Robert to Boston, where he is supposed to have died without issue.

ROWLAND POWELL recorded land, in 1659, to John Collins, which had the same day been recorded to him by Collins. His name occurs so seldom, that the births of his children may be supposed to indicate the length of time he resided in Gloucester. He had a wife Isabella; and a son Rowland and a daughter, twins, born in 1657; a daughter Mary, born in 1660; and a son Stephen, 1662.

HUGH PRITCHARD undoubtedly came to Gloucester with Mr. Blynman, with whom he is found in company in Plymouth Colony in 1641. He had thirteen acres of land on the neck of house-lots, which he sold to Thomas Wakley. He was selectman in 1645, and soon afterwards removed from town. He was representative from Roxbury in 1649.

THOMAS PRINCE is called brother-in-law of Thomas Skillings. He came to Gloucester before 1650, and settled at the Harbor, on what is now Front Street; where the family continued to reside more than a hundred years. He also had land in Fisherman's Field. He had a wife Margaret, who died Feb. 24, 1706. He died Jan. 17, 1690, aged seventy-one; leaving an estate of £153. His children were — Thomas, born in 1650; John, 1653; Mary, 1658; and Isaac, 1663. THOMAS PRINCE, jun., married Elizabeth Haraden, Sept. 27, 1676; and died Jan. 11, 1705, leaving sons John and Isaac, and probably daughters. John became a sea-captain; and died April 19, 1767, aged ninety. He had eight children, of whom two were sons. One of these died in youth; and of the other (Isaac), born in 1718, nothing is known.

* This account is in a pamphlet of thirty-one pages, entitled "News from Heaven by Visions communicated miraculously to and explained by Caleb Pool of Gloucester." It was printed in Salem, 1805.

John and Isaac, sons of Thomas Prince, sen., do not appear to have married in town. Isaac received a soldier's lot at Kettle Cove in 1679, instead of John; and was here ten years later, but afterwards disappears. Isaac, son of Thomas Prince, jun., born in 1683, is supposed to be the same who married Honor Wonson, widow, in 1730. The only male issue of this marriage recorded is a John, born in 1734. He is perhaps the early settler of New Gloucester, Me., of that name. No descendants of Thomas Prince, bearing the name, have resided in town for many years.

John Pulcifer, or Pulsever, settled about 1680, according to tradition, near a spot still occupied by one of his descendants, on the old road leading to Coffin's Beach. In 1688, he had a piece of land "given to the house where he then lived." He married Joanna Kent, Dec. 31, 1684, and had children, — John, born in 1685, and died in 1707; Joanna, 1688; Mary, 1691; a son, 1693; Ebenezer, 1695; Mary, 1697; David, 1701; and Jonathan, 1704. Ebenezer married Huldah Silley, Feb. 11, 1720; and had many children. David had a wife Mary and children. Jonathan married Susanna Hadley, Dec. 11, 1729; and had children, — Susanna, Jonathan, and Samuel. The son born in 1693 was named Thomas, who lived on the old homestead. He married Sarah Grover, Jan. 6, 1726, who died in 1728; and he next married Hannah Woodward, Oct. 29, 1730. She died in September, 1778, at an advanced age; and he on the succeeding day, aged eighty-five. They were buried at the same time. One of his sons (Nathaniel) was a soldier in the French wars, and narrowly escaped massacre at the surrender of Fort William Henry. He died at a very advanced age; leaving a son Nathaniel, — an aged citizen, now living on the ancestral estate.

Phineas Rider was here as early as 1649, perhaps before; and had his residence in the Harbor, near Governor's Hill. He left Gloucester in 1658, and went to Falmouth, Me.; where he was town-commissioner in 1670 and 1671. He lived there in 1675, before the destruction of the town by the Indians; but his name is not afterwards met with.

THOMAS RIGGS first appears in town as a grantee of land at Goose Cove in 1658. In 1661, he bought houses and lands of Matthew Coe and Thomas and John Wakley, also situated near Goose Cove. A part of an old house in that section of the town is still shown as the original tenement erected by him. He is said to have been educated in England for the profession of a scrivener; and his ability in that line made him a welcome acquisition to a community, of whose men one-half were unable to write; while his repeated election to the most important offices sufficiently attests the estimation in which he was held by the citizens. He was town-clerk from 1665 to 1716 (fifty-one years), selectman upwards of twenty years, and representative in 1700. Besides filling these offices, he often served on committees, and sometimes officiated as schoolmaster. He married, first, Mary, daughter of Thomas Millet, June 7, 1658. She died Jan. 23, 1695; and he married, next, Elizabeth Frese, Oct. 30, 1695, who died June 16, 1722, aged eighty: he died Feb. 26, 1722, aged ninety. His children were — Mary, born in 1659; Thomas, 1660; Sarah, 1662; Anna, 1664; Thomas, 1666; John, 1670; Elizabeth, 1672; Abigail, 1678; and Andrew, 1682. THOMAS settled near his father. He married Anne Wheeler of Salisbury, Nov. 22, 1687; who died Sept. 28, 1723, aged fifty-six. He had a second wife (Elizabeth); who died May 19, 1729, aged fifty-nine. He died in August, 1756, in his ninetieth year. Of his eleven children, four were sons, who married and had families in town, — Thomas, Moses, Aaron, and Joshua. JOHN settled on the westerly side of Annisquam River, and resided there during his life. He married Ruth Wheeler, Jan. 1, 1690; and died Jan. 12, 1748, aged seventy-eight. He also had eleven children, of whom four were sons. One of these died in infancy: the others — John, Jeremiah, and Jonathan — married in Gloucester. Jeremiah was a tanner, and removed, about 1725, to Falmouth, Me.; where he carried on his trade, and died. He had several children, one of whom (Wheeler) was killed in the expedition to Penobscot in 1779. ANDREW RIGGS married Mary Richardson, Jan. 24, 1704. He must have attained a very advanced age; for it appears that he was living in 1771.

Besides six daughters, he had three sons, — William, Joseph, and George, — who settled in their native town. Two descendants of Thomas Riggs — David and Thomas — were soldiers in the French wars of the middle of the last century; and some still live on and around the spot occupied by their ancestor.

JOHN RING is first mentioned in 1697; when, as the agent, it is said, of Thomas Witham, he bought the Babson Farm at Little Good Harbor. A family of Rings were early inhabitants of Ipswich. John, of that town, married Mary, daughter of Thomas Bray of Gloucester, Nov. 18, 1664. She died here April 11, 1725, aged seventy-seven; the wife or mother, probably, of our settler John. William, Daniel, and David, who were all in town about 1700, might also have been her children. John bought, in 1709, the tide-mills on Sawmill River, and, without doubt, fixed his residence in that locality; though, in 1719, he also had a house in the West Precinct, near Ensign Haskell's. He served as a selectman several years; and, in 1705, kept the town-school. The date of his death is not known. William Ring married Mary Sawyer, Dec. 5, 1699; who died Dec. 18, 1717, aged forty-five. They had a son John, born in 1703; and a William, in 1713. It appears that he was the same who married Mary Bray in 1720, and had six sons and a daughter. He died about 1737; and, in 1744, his real estate — consisting of a cornmill, sawmill, and house — was divided among his heirs. One of his sons (Moses) came into possession of the mills; and, in 1757, petitioned for a license to keep a house of entertainment near them. He came home from Canada; and died Nov. 19, 1759. Another son (Job) enlisted as a soldier in the Provincial army sent against the French in 1758; and died at Lake George, Oct. 1 of that year. Daniel Ring had a house and land that he bought of Jacob Davis. His earliest grant of land was in 1704. A Daniel Ring married Ann Denning in 1733, and had children; one of whom, named Daniel, or the father, was lost at sea on a fishing voyage in 1755. David Ring had land near his father Haskell's house in 1706. This Haskell was Benjamin, whose daughter Elinor he had married. She died in 1713; and he next married Susanna Day, who died in 1720. He had, for a third wife, Martha Winslow; to whom he was married in 1722. He had several children: but the only son having any known progeny was David, who married Abigail Parsons in 1756, and had David, who was lost at sea on a fishing voyage; William, who became mate of a vessel, and perished by shipwreck on Tinker's Island in 1786; and Job, who lost his life in effecting his escape from the Jersey prison-ship in New York in the Revolutionary War. Bartholomew, son of the latter, formerly a sea-captain, has been a representative in the General Court. It is only by his family that the name is continued in Gloucester. A Mary Ring died Feb. 17, 1758, more than eighty years old.

JOHN ROBERTS, called a planter, may have belonged to the family of Robert Roberts, an early settler of Ipswich, who had a son John, born in 1646. Land is not recorded to him till several years after his first appearance in town; which was on occasion of his marriage to Hannah, daughter of Thomas Bray, Feb. 4, 1677; the bride then not having quite completed her fifteenth year. In 1695, he had a grant of six acres by the land of Nathaniel Hadlock; and, in 1705, six acres near Hadlock's house, "by the side of the lot that said Roberts formerly had for going out a soldier." Hadlock's land bordered on Ipswich line; and this land, mentioned as granted to Roberts for military service, may have been given by the neighboring town. He died Jan. 10, 1714: his wife died March 23, 1717, aged fifty-five. Their children were — Nathaniel, born in 1679; John, 1680; Samuel, 1685; Thomas, 1687; Ebenezer, 1690; Mary, 1696, died in 1717; and Job, 1701, died in 1725. NATHANIEL had a wife Mary; and a son Jonathan, born in 1708. JOHN married Patience, daughter of Benjamin Haskell, March 17, 1703. He spent his whole life near the place of his birth, in the West Parish, esteemed by his neighbors and friends as a just and upright man. He was a selectman several years. He died May 3, 1767, aged eighty-seven: his wife also lived to advanced age. They had three sons, who settled in their native parish, and lived to old age. Benjamin, the oldest, married Ruth Martin in 1728; had several children; and died April 4, 1777, aged seventy-three. John, another son, married Mary Lane in 1735. He was deacon of the Second Church many years; and died about 1794, aged eighty. He had several children; one of whom was Levi, who died in June, 1818, aged seventy-two. Charles L., son of the latter, was a trader on Front Street many years; and died of consumption, Nov. 3, 1831, aged forty-eight, leaving several children, all of whom have settled away from their native town. Ephraim, youngest son of the second John, died July 25, 1806, aged eighty-five. EBENEZER, son of the first John, had a wife Sarah, and three children born, before 1721. In 1727, he was admitted a resident of Falmouth, Me.

ABRAHAM ROBINSON. — A traditionary account of the most respectable character affirms that this individual was a son of Rev. John Robinson, whose name and praise are familiar to New-England ears as the faithful pastor of that band of Pilgrims, who, after bitter persecutions in their native land, and a sojourn of several years at Amsterdam and Leyden in Holland, found a final resting-place at Plymouth in New England; whither a part of the church emigrated in 1620, and most of the remainder in subsequent years. Various obstacles frustrated Mr. Robinson's design of coming over, and he remained at Leyden till his death; which took place March 1, 1625, at the age of forty-nine. His widow and children are said to have come to New England. Mrs. Robinson probably arrived in the summer of 1630, in the ship "Lyon;" which vessel is known to have brought a remnant of the Pilgrims that year: and James Shirley, one of the Plymouth adventurers in England, writing to Gov. Bradford at Plymouth, New England, March, 1630, says, in reference to some of the Leyden people about to embark, "Their indiscreet carriage hath so abated my affection towards them, as, were Mrs. Robinson well over, I would not disburse one penny for the rest." Isaac, a son of the Pilgrim pastor, came to New England in 1631, and settled in Plymouth Colony, where he was living in 1634. He finally settled in Barnstable, and lived to a very advanced age. The tradition before alluded to asserts that Abraham, another son, settled at Cape Ann, and had several children born here; one of which (Abraham) was the first child born of English parents on this side of the Bay, and died at the extraordinary age of one hundred and two years. In our early grants and sales of land, incidental allusion is twice made to lots belonging to Abraham Robinson; and, in 1708, his son Abraham received a common right for the house his father built, and in which he died Feb. 23, 1645. The inventory of his estate amounted to £18. 11s. He left a widow Mary, who married William Brown, July 15, 1646; and, again becoming a widow in 1662, married Henry Walker in the same year, and died April 17, 1690. His son ABRAHAM, on coming to maturity, received several lots of land bequeathed to him by his step-father Brown; and, in 1668, grants at Eastern Point, where he fixed his residence, and lived in obscurity to a great age. Neither the date of his birth nor death has been yet ascertained; and the statement that he died at the age of one hundred and two years is not confirmed by any contemporaneous record. The probate-books, however, furnish evidence that he was living in 1730, — eighty-five years after his father's death. From the mention made of him in his step-father's will, the date of his land-grants, and the time of his marriage, it may be reasonably inferred that he was in early childhood at the period of that event; and that, if he lived to be a centenarian, his death must have occurred about 1740. Family tradition has preserved the memory of an ancient silver vessel once in his possession, which is said to have been used by his celebrated ancestor on baptismal occasions, and which is now owned by a descendant in Philadelphia.* A few articles of ancient Delft ware † are also preserved by one of his posterity in Lowell, as precious memorials of his Pilgrim descent. This second Abraham Robinson married Mary, daughter of Edward Haraden, July 7, 1668: she died Sept. 28, 1725,

* George W. Sargent, son of Gov. Winthrop Sargent, deceased; whose mother was grand-daughter of Capt. Andrew Robinson.

† Delft ware is a kind of pottery covered with an enamel, or white glazing, which gives it the appearance of porcelain. It has its name from Delft in Holland, where it is made in large quantities. Delft Haven, where the Pilgrims embarked, is only a few miles from Leyden; and it is quite likely that articles of this ware composed a part of their scanty furniture. I do not know whether it was in common use in England at that period or not: I have not found it in possession of any other Gloucester family than this. It is mentioned as part of the effects of two of the grand-daughters of the second Abraham Robinson.

aged seventy-six. They had the following children: namely, Mary, born in 1669, married John Elwell; Sarah, 1671, married John Butman; Elizabeth, 1673, married Timothy Somes; Abigail, 1675, married Joseph York; Abraham, 1677; Andrew, 1679; Stephen, 1681; Ann, 1684, married Samuel Davis; Dorcas, 1685, married Jonathan Stanwood; Deborah, 1688, married John Stanwood; Hannah, 1691, died in 1717, unmarried; and Jane, 1693, married John Williams. Abraham, the oldest son, was one of the earliest settlers on the north side of the Cape. He had, in 1706, a grant of four acres of land on the south-west side of the brook running into Plum Cove; and, in 1710, he and his brother-in-law, Joseph York, had a grant of land "to try whale's oyle on." To what extent he carried on the whale-fishery is not known; but the inventory of his estate shows that he possessed some of the implements of the business. He married, Feb. 10, 1703, Sarah York, who died Aug. 9, 1718; and he next married Anna Harvey, Feb. 14, 1721. He died Dec. 28, 1724, aged forty-seven, leaving five sons and four daughters. Jonathan, his grandson, removed, upwards of fifty years ago, to Lisbon, Me., and lived to be about eighty years old. He left behind a son Jonathan; who died Nov. 28, 1843, aged eighty-five. Other descendants remain at Squam, one of whom (Daniel) was a representative in 1840. Andrew, the second son of Abraham Robinson, sen., was one of the most remarkable men that Gloucester has ever produced. Of his youth nothing more is known, than that, at the age of eleven years, he was living with his paternal grandmother, and her husband, Henry Walker, who left him, by will, a legacy of twenty pounds. In the vicinity of this early home, which was surrounded for many miles by a dense forest, he probably acquired the passion for hunting; which in manhood often led him several days at a time upon distant excursions, from which he always returned with abundant proof of his courage and skill. On arriving at the age of twenty-one, he received a grant of land near his father's, on Eastern Point; on which he built "the great house," which was his home during the remainder of his life. Near by was his wharf, and the yard in which he sometimes built vessels, and from which he launched, in 1713, the strangely rigged craft, that, on gliding from the stocks, received from him the appellation of "schooner," and thus secured him a more than local renown. There he also engaged in the fishery; going often on to the Banks himself, and giving his men such an example of persevering industry that he rarely failed to make a successful voyage. In this employment he often came in contact with the Indians about Cape Sable; who, as is well known, harassed and annoyed, for a long series of years, the fishermen who frequented their coasts, — sometimes capturing and murdering them. The first account of him in connection with these savages occurs in 1708, when he ransomed the sloop "Peacock," a vessel belonging to him which they had taken. He was not the man to suffer a second time in the like manner; and accordingly, the next year, having armed and equipped his vessel, and received a commission from the governor, he sailed on a fishing voyage, intent also upon making reprisals, and taking revenge for the injury of the preceding year. Sailing into a place called Margaret's Bay, under French colors, he decoyed two Indians, who were in a canoe, within reach of his guns, and shot them, preserving their scalps; which, on his return home, were presented at the proper place in Boston for the bounty allowed by the government.* This, however, was not obtained; but the government granted him, by a special act, a reward of twenty pounds, and commended the deed as "a good service." In October of that year, — which was one of considerable excitement in Massachusetts, on account of the extensive preparations for a contemplated expedition against the French possessions in America, — Capt. Robinson was ordered by the governor to proceed in his vessel, in company with another from this town, to attempt to take a vessel, supposed to be a French privateer, which had been driven in by a violent storm, and forced to anchor off Nahant. He embarked in this enterprise, but returned without accomplishing its object. For this service also he received, besides the proper pecuniary satisfaction, the favorable notice of the

* This bounty was a reward of forty pounds, offered by the General Court, in 1708, for every Indian scalp, to encourage small parties to hunt the savages.

General Court for his laudable zeal in the public employment. In February following, Capt. Robinson proposed to the government to man his sloop with fifty men, and cruise against the enemy; but, before any arrangement was completed, he received an order from the governor to man and equip his vessel immediately, and sail in pursuit of a French privateer which had been seen off Cape Cod. The enterprise was not an inviting one to men who had neither the iron constitution of the leader, nor the daring spirit, and contempt of danger and hardship, for which he was distinguished. The captains of the military companies were called on for assistance, and the drums were beaten for volunteers: still enlistment went on too slowly for the impatience of the commander, and impressment was threatened. But our people were inveterately averse to the enterprise, and even fled from their homes under fear of compulsion to engage in it; so that it was probably abandoned. Exculpatory letters were addressed to the governor by Capt. Robinson, the militia-captains, the magistrate, and the minister. The latter, with a true pastoral regard for the comfort of his flock, said in their behalf, that "it made them quake to think of turning out of their warm beds and from good fires, and be thrust into a naked vessel, where they must lie on the cold, hard ballast, instead of beds, and without fire, excepting some few who might crowd into the cabin." It is not known that Capt Robinson was again employed in the public service till 1722, when he fitted out at Canso in quest of some Indians who had recently taken several fishing vessels. This cruise was so far successful, that he came up with a canoe containing seven of the enemy, six of whom he killed. The next year (1723), the Indians, instigated by the French, united in a general war. In the latter part of July they surprised Canso, and took sixteen or seventeen Massachusetts fishing vessels. Two sloops were manned, and sent in pursuit of the enemy. One of these was commanded by Capt. Robinson, who retook two of the vessels, and killed several of the men.* In consideration of his

* Hutchinson (History of Massachusetts, vol. ii. p. 295) erroneously gives our Indian slayer the baptismal name of John.

services in the war with the French and Indians, and the expenses he had incurred, which had not been re-imbursed, the General Court, in 1730, granted him three hundred acres of the unappropriated land of the Province.* The last service in which Capt. Robinson was engaged for the government was the erection of a fort and truck-house at St. George's River, Me. This was an important work; and Capt. Robinson's knowledge of the Indian character, together with the uncommon bravery and tact he had often exhibited in his dealings with the savages, might well have designated him as a suitable person to superintend it. Gov. Shirley testified to his faithful performance of this duty while he was engaged in it; for, before its completion, he was taken sick with a lung-fever, which, after a short illness, caused his death. He was attended in his last sickness by one of his daughters, who deposited his remains in one corner of the fort.†

Capt. Robinson was possessed of great bodily strength, a courage that never quailed, and resources of mind, by which he was often extricated from impending destruction. The accounts of his marvellous exploits with the Indians, his surprising feats of bravery and daring, and his hair-breadth escapes, were, for many years after his death, the oft-recurring theme of fireside story. The account of one of his exploits may, perhaps, be properly preserved in this place from the oblivion to which time is fast consigning the details of his personal history.

Being, on one occasion, in a harbor at the eastward, with his sloop and two men, he was surprised by the Indians, and captured. The savages soon despatched his men, and reserved the captain himself for such a death as they could celebrate and accompany with the highest exultation and rejoicing; but, as was customary with the savages when they could get rum, when night came on, they were all drunk but one, who, not being so badly off as the rest, was appointed guard. Robinson feigned

* This grant was probably laid out at Mine Hill, Worcester County. — *Whitney: History of the County of Worcester.*

† The site of the old fort is still shown near the mansion of the late Gen. Knox, in Thomaston, Me.

sleep; and as soon as he had reason to believe that all the Indians, except the guard, were buried in slumber, he attacked the latter, and killed him. He then made his way for his vessel, which was some miles distant; and, as soon as he reached her, prepared to sail. Daylight coming on, he got under way, and put out to sea; but he had not proceeded far when he descried the Indians, who, having recovered from their stupor and missed their captive, had now reached the shore in pursuit of him. They immediately started off in their canoes to recapture him; and, as the wind was light, they rapidly approached the sloop, and soon Robinson could hear their exulting shouts. These, however, were shortly exchanged for yells of desperation and madness; for the fertile mind of Robinson had prepared for them a reception which they little expected. He had on board his vessel a large quantity of scupper nails, well known for their peculiar shape; being short, and having a sharp point, and a large, flat head, with a sharp edge. These were at once brought forth, and scattered thickly upon such parts of the deck as the Indians would alight upon when they came over the side. The savages came boldly on, notwithstanding the brisk firing of the captain, which brought down a red man at every shot; and, having got alongside the sloop, sprang, with tomahawk in hand, like infuriated demons upon the deck; upon which, as the sharp nails suddenly pierced their naked feet, they fell headlong, and were quickly despatched by Capt. Robinson, who threw them overboard in such rapid succession, that those of the savages who had not yet boarded, convinced that their great foe not only bore a charmed life himself, but brought death to every Indian enemy that came within his reach, quickly paddled away in consternation and amazement. The captain now made the best of his way home, where he soon arrived, to astonish his friends and townsmen by the relation of an adventure distinguished for boldness, bravery, and cunning.

Capt. Robinson was representative in 1738 and 1739. He died in 1742, leaving an estate of £2,372. His wife was Rebecca Ingersol; to whom he was married Dec. 7, 1704. She died Nov. 11, 1743, aged fifty-seven. They had one son and nine daughters. The son and one daughter died in infancy. Rebecca,* born in 1705, married Robert Giddings, and died

---

* Her daughter Rebecca married Alexander Smith, and had a daughter Rebecca, who married Samuel Webber, late President of Harvard College. From a statement in the handwriting of this lady, I have derived the tradition mentioned in the text. The early history of Gloucester is so little connected with matters of general historical interest, that this tradition, relating to a subject to which no student of New-England history can be indifferent, seemed to demand investigation. I have explored every quarter from which information might be reasonably expected, and have embodied the scanty result in the above article. Better success may reward some future explorer. The paper of Mrs. Webber was found by me in possession of Samuel L. Dana, LL.D., of Lowell; having come into his hands among the effects of his brother, the late James F. Dana, Professor in Dartmouth College. These brothers are descended from Mary, the oldest daughter of Abraham Robinson, who married John Elwell. From her the Delft ware alluded to has been handed down to Dr. Dana of Lowell. The paper was written, about the year 1824, at the request of Professor Dana, who was the husband of Mrs. Webber's daughter Matilda. Mrs. Webber was then sixty-two years old, and was in the full possession of a very excellent memory. She was contemporary many years with several of Andrew Robinson's daughters, her great-aunts, who, of course, had lived in neighborly and familiar intercourse with their grandfather, the centenarian; and are said, by their descendants, to have been women of uncommon intelligence and superior education. Her mother was born in 1730; and could, therefore, probably remember her venerable ancestor. She resided in Mrs. Webber's family at Cambridge during the last years of her life, and died at her house in 1810. Mrs. Webber's children remember that the Pilgrim ancestry of the family was often the subject of conversation in the domestic circle, and that one visitor — Chief-Justice Parsons — was particularly interested in it. The late Gorham Parsons, nephew of the latter, in a letter which I have seen, gives the substance of Mrs. Webber's statement, and connects his own branch of the Parsons Family with the Robinsons. But he is mistaken: there was no mingling of the blood of the two families in his line. The grandmother of Rev. Moses Parsons, on the mother's side, was daughter of the first Abraham Robinson's wife by her second marriage. Mrs. Webber's account contains anachronisms; which, considering that even a good memory often errs in dates, do not affect its value, if otherwise entitled to confidence. It also mentions four sons and one or more daughters of the first Abraham Robinson, concerning whom we have no further information. Here follows her account: —

"When the Pilgrims left Holland to seek an asylum in America, where they hoped to enjoy liberty of conscience, they left behind them their venerable pastor, — the Rev. John Robinson; who promised to join them the next year, but was prevented by death from fulfilling his promise. About two years after the first landing of the Pilgrims, they were followed by Mr. Robinson's widow and two sons. They continued in the Colony of Plymouth till the year 1626. Early in the spring of that year, one of the sons with several others left Plymouth to explore the Bay, in order to find a suitable place for a fishing station. They landed at Agassquam, since called Cape Ann; where, finding a commodious harbor and plenty of materials for building, they concluded to set up a fishing stage there, and make preparations for removing their families from the other side of the Bay, and establish a permanent settlement at that place. Very soon after they had got settled there with their families, Mr. Robinson had a son born, whom he called Abraham. He had four other sons, — Zebulon, Samuel, Jonathan, and Stephen, — and one or more daughters. Abraham married young, and

about 1784. One of her daughters married an Averill, and died in Boston about 1825, aged ninety-six. Mary (1709) married Benjamin Perkins, who was lost at sea. She kept a tavern several years, and died in 1759; having previously become blind. Judith (1711) married Thomas Sanders, and died in 1770. Abigail (1715) had three husbands, — a Parsons, a Ring, and a Sargent, — and died in 1781. Dorcas (1717) married Samuel Hidden. Hannah (1720) married James Pearson. Ann (1723) married Nathaniel Kinsman, and died suddenly about 1790. Sarah married Richard Palfrey, and died at an advanced age. Stephen Robinson married Sarah Smith, Nov. 25, 1703, who died Oct. 15, 1720; and he next married Elizabeth Ingersol, May 10, 1721. He settled somewhere near the Meeting-house, and only emerges from obscurity as its sexton for several years. He is supposed to have died before May, 1742; when Jeremiah, his son, was paid by the town for taking care of his mother ten months. His sons that lived to maturity and married were Stephen, Smith, and Jeremiah. The former, born in 1709, married Mary Clark in 1730, and had a daughter Sarah; and probably the Stephen, son of Stephen,

---

had twelve children, — three sons (John, Stephen, and Andrew) and nine daughters, two of whom died young: the other seven were married, and left families, — Elwell, Davis, Butman, Williams, Somes. Mr. Abraham Robinson lived to the age of a hundred and two years, much beloved and respected by his friends and acquaintance for his piety and strict integrity. It was engraved on his tombstone, that he was the first child born of English parents on that side of Massachusetts Bay."

The material part of this statement was believed by Professor Dana to be well founded; and to me it has always appeared to bear the impress of truth. Recent research has added considerably to our knowledge of the Robinson Family. As this work is about to go to press, we learn, from the remarks made by Mr. George Sumner at Plymouth, Aug. 2, 1859, that in the registry of the census of Leyden, taken in 1622, and still preserved there, he "found inscribed the inmates of the house of Robinson, — himself, his wife, six children, and one maid-servant. Thus stands the record: —

"Jan Robberson, preacher.

"Brigetta (Briget) Robberson, his wife.

"John, Bridget, Isaac, Mercy, Favor, Jacob Robberson, his children.

"Maria Hardy, his maid-servant."

From this it appears that Mr. Robinson had sons to whom he gave the patriarchal names, Isaac and Jacob; and that, unless he also had an Abraham who was not an *inmate of his house* in 1622, some other parentage must be sought for our early settler of that name. — See Historical Magazine, vol. iii. p. 332.

who was baptized in 1736. This last Stephen is supposed to be the same who, with his wife, was helped by the town in 1765, and, in 1775, was buried at its expense; leaving no known issue, unless Stephen, who died Oct. 20, 1829, aged sixty-nine, was his son. Smith Robinson, born in 1712, appears to have settled in Salem, and to have died before 1742; when Mary Robinson presented an inventory of his estate, which was of very small amount. Jeremiah, born in 1719, married Elizabeth Lufkin in 1741. He resided on the old back road to Sandy Bay. He was the grave-digger at the old burying-ground about sixty years; and is remembered by some of our elderly people, tottering, under the weight of his tools and the infirmities of age, to his melancholy employment. He died about 1800. It is not known that he had more than one son (Jeremiah), who married in town, and had an only son of the same name. The latter died, unmarried, just after he had returned home sick from a voyage.

John Rowe settled in that part of the town which has long been known as the Farms. He bought land there, in 1651, of Thomas Drake; into whose possession it passed from Nicholas Norton of Weymouth, who bought it of William Vinson; to whom it was sold by George Norton, the original grantee. He was the first settler on this remote and lonely spot. A dense forest surrounded him, separating him on one side from the ocean, which was not far distant; and on the other from his townsmen, most of whom were more than two miles off. He did not, however, find repose in this retired place: for he appears in 1656, intimating a "mind to set his house on fire, and run away by ye light;" and expressing a desire "to live no longer among such a company of hell-hounds." He continued there, nevertheless, till death relieved him from all earthly trouble, March 9, 1662. He left a widow Bridget, who married William Colman; and two sons, — John and Hugh. John had a portion of his father's property, which he occupied till his death; which took place, Sept. 25, 1700. He was twice married: first to Mary Dickersonn, Sept. 27, 1663; who died April 25, 1684. By her he had children, — John, born in 1665, died in 1690; James, 1666; Thomas, 1668; Mary, 1670; Elizabeth, 1673; Stephen, 1675; Samuel, 1678; Ebenezer, 1680, died in 1692; Andrew, 1683, died 1700. He next married Sarah Redington, Sept. 1, 1684; who died Feb. 15, 1701. Of his four children by her, all but the last (Rebekah) died in childhood. Only two of his sons are known to have married: Stephen married, first, Martha Low in 1699, who died Dec. 4, 1718, aged thirty-nine; and, next, Elizabeth Curney in 1721, who is said to have lived to be nearly a hundred years old. He died April 28, 1731, aged fifty-six. He had sons Stephen; John; Thomas; Joseph; Benjamin; David, who was an ensign in the expedition against Crown Point in 1755; and Jonathan. The second son (John), born in 1714, settled at Sandy Bay; where he married Mary Baker in 1736. He was lieutenant of a company raised in town, in 1755, for service in the campaign against the French that year. His son John, born in 1737, married Sarah Pool. He was sergeant in the company with his father in 1755; and, at the commencement of the Revolutionary War, took command of one of the Gloucester companies that fought at Bunker Hill. Being at home on furlough in the summer of 1776, he engaged in an attack upon a British vessel off the Cape, and was taken, and carried, a prisoner, to New York. He became a major in the militia, and died on his farm at Pigeon Hill about 1800. His son John, although a youth of only sixteen years, enlisted in his father's company, and fought on Bunker Hill. He served in the army throughout the war, and was engaged in many important battles. He commanded a company in Shay's Rebellion, and was appointed to head a column which attacked the rebels, and drove them from a strong fort, where they threatened defiance. At the commencement of the last war with Great Britain, he had the offer of a high command in Hull's army, but declined the service; foreseeing and predicting, it is said, its disastrous fate. He was an accomplished officer, and showed rare skill and courage in military tactics. At the time of his death (October, 1820), he was residing in Maine. Jabez, another son of the Sandy-Bay settler, served in the expedition against Canada in 1759. He had a son Jabez; whose son, David Sawyer Rowe, graduated at Bowdoin College, and was several years Principal of the State Normal School at Westfield. Isaac, brother of the elder Jabez, served in the Revolutionary War; and died in January, 1852, aged ninety. Thomas Rowe, born in 1717, occupied the paternal acres; and died about 1790, leaving a son William, who died Sept. 24, 1856, aged ninety-three; having, just before his death, removed from his old home on the estate* which had been in the family more than two hundred years. Samuel Rowe, born in 1678, married Dorcas Ingersol in 1709; and died in 1742, leaving sons James and Jonathan, and a daughter Judith. James married Abigail Rowe in 1736; and besides a son James, who died March 26, 1819, aged eighty-one, had sons Samuel, Benjamin, David, and Nathaniel. Jonathan married Abigail Parsons in 1742, and removed to New Gloucester, Me., in 1763. One of his sons (Zebulon) died there in 1848, aged ninety-four. HUGH, son of the first settler (John), married Rachel Langton, June 10, 1667. She may have been a daughter of William Vinson, who, in a deed, calls Rowe his son-in-law. He enlisted in the Indian War of 1675, and received a grant of land at Kettle Cove for his services. His wife died March 7, 1674, leaving three daughters, who married three sons of Anthony Day. He next married Mary, daughter of Thomas Prince, Sept. 10, 1674; and had, by her, sons Abraham, Isaac, Jacob, Joseph, and Benjamin, and three daughters. Abraham married Bethiah Elwell; and died July 8, 1706, leaving no children. Isaac is supposed to have died unmarried, Feb. 23, 1723. Jacob married Mary Curney in 1713. In 1723, he was engaged in the military service of the Colony; and died, in 1730, of small-pox; leaving, probably, a son Jacob. Joseph married Abigail Smith in 1712, and had five children. He served in the expedition againt Port Royal in 1707, and received several

* It may, perhaps, be deserving of mention in this chapter of family history, that on this spot, his present home, the writer is now penning these lines; and that on an adjoining estate, now separated from this by a road, his ancestor, James Babson, fixed his permanent abode two centuries ago.

dangerous wounds; in consequence of which, the General Court, in 1735, granted him one hundred and fifty acres of land.

EDWARD ROWSE. — Nothing more is known of this person than that he bought land, on the neck of house-lots, of Morris Somes; and sold, in 1651, house and land to Robert Tucker.

JOHN SADLER. — More information concerning him would be desirable. Although he was one of Mr. Blynman's company, one of the first selectmen, and a proprietor of lots in several places, he is not mentioned in the records as a grantee of land. In the frequent incidental allusions to him, he is variously distinguished by the title of Mr., Captain, and Major, but never designated by his baptismal name. He was made a freeman in 1642. Whither he went from Gloucester, is not known. The only further account we have of him is contained in the entry on our records of a commoner's claim, made in 1704 by the heirs of Osman Dutch, "by virtue of a house and land which was given to Robert Sadler by his father Captain Sadler, when he sent for his wife into England," and which Dutch purchased of Hugh Calkin, Sadler's attorney, in 1651.

ABIAL SADLER had, in 1689, three acres of land above the head of Stony Cove. Before that date, he had been a soldier in the Colony service, from Essex County. He had a child born here by Rebekah, his wife, March 13, 1693. She was probably a daughter of Richard Dike; and, after the death of Sadler (Sept. 15, 1697), is supposed to have married Josiah Tainer. Another supposition might identify the child above mentioned, or a previous one, with John Sadler, who, in 1713, married Sarah Scott of Rowley; and in 1720, then living in Rowley, sold a house and land situated in the Second Parish, in the deed of which he calls Josiah Tainer his father-in-law.

JAMES SAWYER was a weaver, and may have been a son of William Sawyer, who came to New England about 1640. A William Sawyer, sen., was living in Newbury, in 1697, in advanced age. James Sawyer's wife was Sarah, daughter of Thomos Bray. He first appears in Gloucester on the birth of his son Nathaniel in 1677. His other children were — Abraham, born in 1680; Sarah, 1683; Isaac, 1684; Jacob, 1687; James,

1691; and Thomas, John, and Mary, who were born, probably, before he came to this town. He was a grantee of a six-acre lot on the west side of Annisquam River in 1688; and in 1690 he bought land in that section of the town, and had his residence there. He died May 31, 1703. His wife survived him many years; and was living in 1726, with her son Abraham, on the family homestead, probably, on the way leading to Coffin's Farm. This son is not known to have been married. His estate was divided in 1752. THOMAS married twice: first to Hannah Millet, in 1690; and next to Hannah Foster, in 1691. This last wife had had ten children by a previous husband, eight of which she brought to these nuptials. The new union was blessed by an addition of two, — James, born in 1692; and Francis, who died in infancy. Thomas Sawyer bought the house which had been the home of his last wife, and there settled. It was situated at the Harbor, near the Beach. He died Jan. 12, 1711. JOHN married Rebekah Stanford in 1701, and had several children born here before 1719; when he removed to Falmouth, Me. NATHANIEL married Hannah Parker, Nov. 4, 1706, and died about 1741. Nine children are recorded as the offspring of this marriage. ISAAC had a wife Martha (to whom he was married in 1706) and several children. He removed in 1725 to Falmouth; where he died in 1772, aged eighty-eight. JACOB married Sarah Wallis in 1716, and had five children born in Gloucester before 1726; soon after which, he joined the emigration to Falmouth. JAMES, the youngest of these brothers, and James, son of Thomas, were both married in 1714: the latter, it is supposed, to Elinor Ellery; and the former to Hannah Babson, Dec. 23 of that year. He settled at Fresh-water Cove, on a place still owned in the family. When he became old, he moved into a house he owned in the woods, and died there some time in the Revolutionary War, at a very advanced age; leaving a son Abraham, who was married at Mrs. Wheeler's, in presence of "a great company," April 13, 1758, to Mary Sayward. He died about 1815, aged seventy-eight; and his wife died at the age of eighty. He was a sailmaker by trade; and therefore had his residence at the Harbor, where he built, in 1760, a house on Front Street, which came into possession of his son Abraham, and was owned and occupied by him till his death, May 3, 1856, at the venerable age of ninety-five. Descendants of James Sawyer are not numerous here; but many are living in Portland and its vicinity.

William Sargent had grants of land in 1649; and he became the possessor of the houses and lands of Streeter and Baker. One of these houses was near the burying-ground,— probably on its western side; and there he seems to have fixed his residence. He was a selectman several years, and representative in 1671 and in 1691. He married Abigail, daughter of Edmund Clark, "at a general traine at Ipswich," Sept. 10, 1651; and died Feb. 19, 1717, aged ninety-three, having survived all his compeers in the early settlement of the town. His wife died March 8, 1711, aged seventy-nine. Their children were — John, born in 1653; Andrew, 1655; William, 1658; Samuel, 1660; Nathaniel, 1663; Abigail, 1665; Nathaniel, 1671; Joseph, 1675; and Mary, 1678. John married Hannah, daughter of Nehemiah Howard of Salem, Dec. 24, 1679, and settled on the westerly side of Squam River. He was a selectman several years. In 1710, he engaged in the expedition against Port Royal; where he was drowned by the shipwreck of the transport under Capt. Foye, of which he was pilot. His widow married Nathaniel Coit. He left five sons and seven daughters. John, the oldest son, born in 1683, married Bethiah Davis in 1714, and Widow Mary Ring in 1738. He died about 1754, leaving a son Thomas, and daughters Bethiah and Abigail. Thomas, the next son, born in 1685, married Elizabeth Haskell in 1710, and had several children. He died about 1745. Andrew, the third son, born in 1691, perished by shipwreck in 1716. Joseph, the fifth son, born in 1702, married Martha Day in 1727; had two children (David and Joseph), and died about 1733. Andrew, second son of William Sargent, sen., is not known to have married; nor is any thing known of him after 1679, when he was a grantee of a six-acre lot on the west side of Annisquam River. William Sargent, jun., married Naomi Stanwood, Oct. 26, 1681. She died March 13, 1702; and he next married

Hannah Short, Sept. 14, 1703. In 1679, he had a grant of "half an acre of land to set a house upon, on the left hand of the way that people goe to the head of the Harbor, at the head of William Vinson's lot;" but in 1694 he was living near his father, "on the south-west side of ye river leading up to ye Cut." He had eleven children by his two wives. It is not known that he died in town, nor does it appear that any of his three sons married here; and, as he did not participate in a division of land in 1721, it is supposed that he had removed from town before that time. SAMUEL married Mary Norwood, May 24, 1689. She died April 27, 1718; and he next married, June 19, 1725, Mrs. Ruth Newman. His father gave him, in 1694, the western end of his dwelling-house; but the place of his permanent residence was at Hogskin Cove. He had a grant of land on the easterly side of the cove, in 1695, "to set up fishing upon;" and was one of the first settlers in that section of the town. He frequently served as a selectman, and, in 1729, as representative. The date of his death is not known; but it is certain that he was living as late as 1746. Of his ten children, six were sons, of whom four appear to have married in town. The oldest (Samuel), born in 1690, married Mary Emerson in 1713; and died about 1762, leaving a son Samuel, and a grandson Samuel not then twenty-one years old. The latter may have been the same Samuel who died in April, 1833, aged eighty-four. William, second son of Samuel Sargent, sen., born in 1692, married Susanna Haraden in 1726, and had several children. Francis, the next son, born in 1694, married Mary York in 1722, and had the birth of nine children recorded on the town-books. Solomon, the youngest of these sons, born in 1708, married Sarah Somes in 1735, and had three sons and a daughter born before 1742. NATHANIEL SARGENT married Sarah Harvey, Jan. 24, 1695, who died Feb. 5, 1706; and he next married Mary Stevens, March 26, 1710. He was a selectman several years; and, in 1727, appears to have kept a tavern.*

* Perhaps this tavern was at Done Fudging, where his father had lived, and where tradition reports that a house of entertainment was kept for several years, in the early part of the last century, for the accommodation of mariners passing through the Cut.

He died Dec. 12, 1732. Of his twelve children, five were sons; and, of these, three are supposed to have married in town. Nathaniel, born in 1702, married Judith Parsons in 1725, and had sons Nathaniel and David and four daughters. It was this Nathaniel, probably, who kept the tavern at the corner of Middle and Pleasant Streets, about ninety years ago. Daniel, born in 1714, married Lydia Stanwood in 1744, and had a son William and a daughter. This son was born in 1750. Just before the commencement of the Revolutionary War, he was impressed on board of a British man-of-war; but, arriving at New York in 1776, he managed to escape, and join the American Army on Long Island. He was killed on the retreat from the island. His only child, a son William, is the venerable citizen of the same name still living, — the oldest representative, probably, of this ancient family. Peter, born 1721, married Rebekah Ingersol in 1743, and had several children; one of whom (Jonathan), born in 1746, died Feb. 4, 1830. JOSEPH, youngest son of William Sargent, sen., born in 1675, married Martha Baker of Topsfield in 1712; who gave birth to a son (Joseph), May 16, 1713, and died on the 27th of the same month. He next married Hannah Haraden, Sept. 16, 1717; and died about 1750, without any known issue by the second marriage.

WILLIAM SARGENT, 2d, was son of William Sargent and Mary Epes, and was born in Bristol, England. His father went from Exeter, England, to Barbadoes, when young, and was educated there. He returned to his native country, and there married Mary Epes, who stole from her home in the habit of a milk-maid to become his wife. Such is the family tradition. The son who came to Gloucester first appears here in 1678, when he had a grant of two acres of land at Eastern Point, where he built a house. He was a mariner, and

---

At that time, an active business was carried on in the exportation of wood and timber from the westerly part of the town through this channel. The opposite currents met at Done Fudging; and there the vessels were sometimes anchored to wait a change of tide. The attractions of a tavern added other inducements to stop. The singular name given to this place is said to have been derived from the fact, that persons, poling or "fudging" a boat or raft on the river against the current, here took a fair tide, and were therefore "done fudging."

owned a sloop, which he probably employed in coasting. The date of his death is not known: but it is certain that he died before June, 1707; perhaps at sea, as, in the settlement of his estate, no charges are made for sickness or funeral expenses. The inventory of his property amounted to £278. He married, June 21, 1678, Mary, daughter of Peter Duncan; who died Feb. 28, 1725, aged sixty-six. Their children were — Fitz William, born in 1679, died in 1700; Peter, born in 1680, was living in Boston in 1711, and died Feb. 11, 1725; Mary, 1681; Andrew, 1683; Daniel, 1686, became a blacksmith, and was killed by lightning, July 21, 1713; Jordan, 1688, died in 1689; Epes, 1690; Ann, 1692; Samuel, 1694, died 1699; Fitz John, 1696, died 1698; Machani, born and died in 1699; Jabez, born and died in 1700; Fitz William, 1701, living in 1738; and Winthrop, 1704. It is only by one of these sons (Epes) that the name has been perpetuated. He was a prominent citizen; and several of his descendants have been distinguished men. He was twice married: first to Esther Maccarty, April 1, 1720; and next to Mrs. Catharine Brown of Salem, Aug. 10, 1744. Soon after this last marriage, he removed to Salem; where he died Dec. 6, 1762, aged seventy-two. His children by his first wife were — Epes, born in 1721; Esther, 1722; Ignatius, 1724; James, 1726, died in 1727; Winthrop, 1728; Sarah, 1729; Daniel, 1731; William, 1734; and Benjamin, 1736. By his second wife, he had Paul Dudley and John. His remains were brought to Gloucester, and placed in the family tomb. He acquired considerable property here as a merchant; was the principal acting magistrate in town for several years, and its representative in 1740. In Salem, he took an active part in public affairs; was colonel in the militia; and long a Justice of the General Sessions Court. An obituary notice, in a newspaper of the day, gives him a high character as a merchant, magistrate, and Christian. His son Epes married Catharine, daughter of Hon. John Osborn of Boston, in 1745. She died Feb. 7, 1788. An obituary notice, contained in a Salem paper of the 19th of that month, describes her as a lady of eminent virtue. Mr. Sargent died of small-pox in 1779; in which year, by vote of the town, a general inoculation of the citizens took place. He had a presentiment that the disease would prove fatal to him, and therefore desired an exception in his favor; but the authorities were inexorable, and he submitted to the fate he apprehended. Early in life, he engaged in mercantile pursuits, in which he acquired a large property. A few years prior to the Revolutionary War, he owned ten vessels, which were employed in the fishery and foreign commerce; and he was carrying on at that time a very extensive trade: but the total suspension of his business which the war occasioned, together with the embarrassing situation into which he was thrown by joining the unpopular side in the contest with the mother-country, caused heavy pecuniary losses, by which his property became greatly reduced. In common with all who held his political principles, he was made the mark of obloquy and reproach. He was, on one occasion, cited before the assembled voters of the town, and required to give satisfaction that he was a harmless citizen: but he would not obey the summons; and the excited meeting proceeded to forbid all persons to have any commerce with him or his abettors; intending to compel him, through fear of starvation, to quit the town. This measure had the desired effect. He went to Boston, where even greater indignities were heaped upon him. His son Epes had embraced the patriotic cause; but he could not divert from his father the torrent of hatred and contempt which overwhelmed all who were of his political faith. The latter, therefore, determined to seek refuge in another part of America, and made every preparation to embark for Halifax; but, on assembling his family for leave-taking on the evening before his intended departure, his spirits were so much oppressed with the pangs of separation, that he resolved to return to his home, and endure, as he best could, the fortune that might await him. In addition to the bitter political proscription of which he had been the object, he was made to feel, in the keenest manner, the effects of religious bigotry and intolerance, on account of the hearty welcome he had extended to the Rev. John Murray, and the avowal of his belief in the doctrines of that preacher. His whole life had exhibited the proper fruits of the Christian spirit, and he had sat for many years at the table of the Lord in affectionate communion and entire unity of religious sentiment with his brethren of the Christian faith : but these now coldly turned from him ; and so, with fortune wasted and friendships broken up, he "endured as seeing Him who is invisible," and, rich in faith and the memories of a just and pure life, passed away to the tomb. Mr. Sargent left two sons, — Epes and John Osborn. The former graduated at Harvard College in 1766, and made several voyages to sea for his father before settling in business. On the organization of the present National Government, he received the appointment of collector of the customs for this port, which he held till 1795 ; when he removed to Hampstead, N.H., where he lived a short time, and thence went to Boston. In the latter place, he was president of an insurance company several years. He died in April, 1822, aged seventy-four. His wife (Dorcas Babson), to whom he was married in 1772, died in 1836, aged eighty-seven. They had several children, one of whom (Charles Lenox) published a book entitled "Alexander Smith." Smith was a Gloucester man, as represented in the story ; but his career, as related by Mr. Sargent, is believed to be wholly fictitious. John Osborn Sargent married, and left an only son (Epes), who was a sea-captain in early life, but afterwards became a merchant, and settled in Roxbury, where he died. Three of his sons are men of distinction, — John Osborn, who graduated at Harvard College in 1829, studied law, and, after several years' practice in Boston and New York, settled in Washington, D.C., where he now resides ; Epes, extensively known as a poet and dramatist, and the author of a popular series of school-books ; and George B., who emigrated to the Western country in his youth, and settled at Davenport, Io., of which city he has been the mayor. Winthrop Sargent commenced business as a seafaring man, and was early in command of a vessel ; but he soon established himself as a merchant, and continued in commercial pursuits till his death. In the contest with the mother-country, he warmly espoused the patriotic side. He served on the Committee of Safety in 1775 ; was a government agent here during the war; and, in 1788, was one of the delegates to the State Convention for ratifying the new Federal Constitution. He was one of the first adherents of Rev. John Murray; and remained, as long as he lived, one of his firmest friends and supporters. His general character was that of an intelligent and benevolent man, whose qualities of head and heart secured him universal esteem. He died Dec. 3, 1793. His wife was Judith, daughter of Thomas Sanders. She died July 27, 1793. Winthrop, their son, born in 1753, graduated at Harvard College in 1773. He was twice married: first, in Ohio, to a daughter of Gen. Tupper; and next to Mary, widow of David Williams, a planter in Mississippi. She died in Philadelphia, Jan. 9, 1844: he died of gout in the stomach, at New Orleans, on board of a steamboat in the river, June 3, 1820. He is one of the few natives of Gloucester that have attained a high station in public life. Little is known of his early history. At the commencement of the Revolutionary War, he was absent on a voyage to the West Indies, in a vessel belonging to his father; and, immediately on his arrival home, joined the army, taking the command of a company of artillery in Crane's regiment. He was at the battles of Trenton and Brandywine; was some time an aid-de-camp to General How of North Carolina; and finally a major in the army. He remained in service till the close of the war. In the disastrous defeat of St. Clair at the battle of the Miamis, Nov. 3, 1791, he was adjutant-general, and was wounded in the engagement; in which he also lost all his private papers. The carnage of that dreadful day was commenced by the unexpected onslaught of the Indians early in the morning. When first heard by Gen. Sargent, he was lying in his litter, in torment from the gout. He sprang up, and mounted his horse as soon as possible; having first filled his military boots with water, into which he thrust his gouty feet. He was accustomed to describe the attack, rendered more horrible by the hellish yells of the savages, as an appalling spectacle, and to reflect with admiration upon the good conduct of the troops. Mr. Sargent's name frequently occurs in the records of the Ohio Land Company. He was Secretary of the North-west Territory, and, for a time, acting Governor. While there, his residence was at Marietta; to which place, it is said, he gave that name. He finally selected a spot near Natchez, where he built a large brick mansion, and called it, after the place of his nativity, Gloster Place. In 1796, a territorial government was established for the Mississippi country; and soon afterwards Mr. Sargent was appointed its Governor. Difficulties soon beset him in this office. The people had probably been little used to the restraints of authority, and a few of the leading men commenced an early opposition to the Governor's administration. In course of time, they proceeded to violent measures, and made representations to Congress, setting forth their causes of complaint. The Governor's course was vindicated in a long letter from Col. Clark, a military and judicial officer of high standing, to the Chairman of the Mississippi Committee in Congress, and in letters addressed by himself to the Secretary of State. In one of these, the Governor complains that he had not received fair treatment from the Congress Committee; and concludes in the words of a Latin poet: —

"Durum, sed levius fit patientia,
Quicquid corrigere est nefas."

Early in 1801, he took leave of absence for the purpose of giving personal attention to his affairs at the seat of the National Government. Previous to his departure, he received addresses from the judges, military officers, and principal inhabitants, expressing their full approbation of his official conduct, and the high esteem in which they held his private character. On his arrival at Washington, he found that an effectual stop had been put to further proceedings with the government. Mr. Jefferson's administration had come into power, and Mr. Sargent's name was on the list of the proscribed. The people had not then become so familiar with the removal of public functionaries as to disconnect it with demerit on the part of the officer displaced; and, by particular desire of his friends, Mr. Sargent immediately published a pamphlet, containing papers in relation to his official conduct, on which he relied for his vindication before the country. He returned to Mississippi, where he resided as a private citizen during the remainder of his life, occasionally visiting the distant place of his birth. He left two sons, both by his second marriage, — William Fitz Winthrop, who graduated at Harvard College in 1817, and died in Philadelphia in 1822; and George Washington, who graduated at the same college in 1820, and now resides in Philadelphia. Winthrop, son of the latter, graduated at Harvard in 1847, and is already widely known as an historical writer. Fitz William, another son of Winthrop and Judith Sargent, born in 1768, engaged in commercial pursuits in his native town, and was an enterprising and successful merchant. After suffering severely for many years from gout, he died of that disease, Oct. 6, 1822; leaving an only son Winthrop, who was the representative in 1823. He continued his father's business till 1829, when he removed to Philadelphia; where he has since resided, with the exception of a few years spent in Byfield Parish, Newbury, of which town his son Gorham P. was the representative in 1859. Daniel, son of Col. Epes Sargent, married Mary Turner of Salem. He was engaged in the fishing business and in foreign trade in Gloucester till the commencement of the Revolutionary struggle, when he removed to Newburyport. He went thence to Boston, where he lived many years a highly respected merchant; and died Feb. 18, 1806. Four of his six sons became prominent men. Daniel, the oldest, was a merchant, and lived in Boston. He was held in high estimation; one evidence of which was his election to the office of Treasurer of the Commonwealth. Towards the close of his life, he manifested his interest in his native town by placing a handsome wall and iron gate at the entrance of the ancient burial-place which contains the family tomb. He died in Boston, April 2, 1842, aged seventy-nine. Ignatius carried on mercantile business in Gloucester till about 1800, when he removed to Boston. His name is still mentioned with grateful remembrance as a friend ever ready with kind offices for our citizens in both places of his residence. While he lived in Gloucester, he took an active interest in military affairs, and attained the rank of major. He died in Boston,

Jan. 20, 1821; leaving a son of the same name now residing there. Henry, another son of Daniel Sargent, was a painter of considerable celebrity. One of his largest works, — an historical painting of the Landing of the Pilgrims, presented by himself to the Pilgrim Society of Plymouth, whose hall it adorns — has been much admired. Lucius Manlius, the youngest of these four brothers, is a writer of established reputation and popularity. He has an office in Boston, but resides in Roxbury. Col. Epes Sargent left two sons by his second wife, — Paul Dudley (born in 1745) and John. The former was brought up in Gloucester, and married here Lucy, daughter of Hon. Thomas Sanders, in 1772. He was an early asserter of the rights of the Colonies, and one of the first to take up arms in their defence. He attained the rank of colonel in the Revolutionary War, and was an active and valuable officer. After the war was closed, he engaged in commercial pursuits, but was unsuccessful; and finally retired to a farm in Sullivan, Me. He represented that town in the General Court, and held a number of offices under the State and National Governments. He died about 1823, leaving a widow and a large number of descendants. His brother John espoused the unpopular side in the Revolutionary contest, and sought a home where he could find congenial political sentiments. He removed to Barrington, N.S. None of the descendants of William Sargent, 2d, bearing the family name, remain in town; but his progeny by his daughter Ann, who married Nathaniel Ellery, is numerous.

James Sayward came to Gloucester about 1696, perhaps from York, Me.; where, in 1661, was a "Samuel Sayward, son of Edmond Sawyer," as it is written in a deed, "sometimes inhabitant of Ipswich." He had a grant (March, 1690) of half an acre of land at Cripple Cove, where he built a house. This property has continued in the family down to the present time. He was an elder of the First Church, a selectman, and for seven years a representative. These official distinctions give evidence that he was a useful citizen. He had a wife Deborah, the mother of all his children, who died July 13, 1734, aged sixty-seven; and a second wife, Widow Mary Davis, to whom he was married

Jan. 30, 1735. He died Feb. 13, 1736, aged sixty-seven. His children were — Deborah, born in 1694; James, 1697; James, 1699; Samuel, 1701; Henry, 1704; Mary, 1706; Joseph, 1708; Hannah, 1713; and Elizabeth, born before he came to Gloucester. SAMUEL married Lucy Norwood in 1729, and had two children, — Samuel and Judith; the former of whom married Susanna Lord of Ipswich in 1761. HENRY married Abigail Sargent in 1730; by whom he had two daughters, and a son Stover. JOSEPH married Sarah Giddings in 1730, and had several children. His oldest son Joseph, a sea-captain in early life, was the keeper of Thatcher's-Island Lights nineteen years; and died in April, 1814, aged eighty-two; leaving, besides other children, a son William, the well-known pilot of our harbor and coast. James, son of the first Joseph, died young at sea. George, another son, married and had several children in Gloucester; but finally settled in Camden, Me.

ROBERT SKAMP had a grant of three acres of land, in 1674, by the pasture of John Collins; whose daughter Jane he married Dec. 25, 1661. She died in 1662; having given birth to a daughter Mary, who had a son named Unconstant Langworth, born in 1682. Robert Skamp died April 23, 1691.

THOMAS SKELLIN was one of the first settlers, and had land near the burying-ground. He was in Falmouth, Me., in 1651; and probably removed thither before 1658, when he purchased land there. "Suspicious carriages" with Thomas Patten sullied the name of his wife Deborah, for whose good behavior her husband was bound at a court in 1653. He died at Falmouth in 1667, leaving legacies to sons Thomas (born in 1643) and John. The birth of his daughter Deborah in 1640 or 1648 is on our books. His eldest son THOMAS married Mary Lewis of Falmouth, by whom he had two sons, — John and Benjamin; and died in Salem, Dec. 30, 1676. She was living in Salem in 1732, seventy-eight years old.

JAMES SMITH. — Land was given him by the commissioners, in 1642, as appears in the recorded sale of the same to James Avery in 1651. Nothing further is known of his connection with Gloucester.

THOMAS SMITH was an early settler and proprietor, and one of the commissioners for ending small causes, in 1645. He had a son Thomas, born in 1643. These first Smiths remained in town but a short time. The name re-appears in subsequent years; but it is not known that the persons who bore it were connected with the early Smiths or with each other. A Thomas Smith, late of Ipswich, died in town, April 24, 1706.

MORRIS SMITH had a grant of two acres of land above the old Cornmill in 1685; but he is first found in town on the occasion of his marriage, Nov. 4, 1681, to Sarah Millet, who was probably the widow of John Millet, and who died Jan. 20, 1725, aged eighty: he died May 13, 1726, aged seventy. They had two children,—Sarah, born in 1683; and Morris, 1686. The latter died in infancy. Morris Smith was the sexton of the town for several years; and was succeeded in that office by Stephen Robinson, who married his daughter Sarah.

A Richard Smith has recorded in our books the birth, by his wife Mary, of Thomas, born in Falmouth in 1684; and of Richard, born in Marblehead in 1689.

JOHN SMITH.—Three persons of this name appear in town between 1692 and 1702. Taking them in the order of time, the first John had a house, in which he dwelt, on Eastern Point, near Peter Mud's Neck, before 1701. He had a wife Rebekah, and children,—Daniel, born in 1692, his oldest son; Mary, 1696, died in 1697; Joseph, 1699, died in 1701; and Jonathan, 1702. DANIEL married Lydia Sargent in 1717, and had four sons and four daughters. One of the former (John), born in 1723, is supposed to be the same who married Abigail Fleming in 1746, and died Jan. 9, 1789. He had seven sons and three daughters. Two of his sons were John and Sargent, who were commanders of privateer letters-of-marque in the Revolutionary War, and were both distinguished for their bravery in engagements with English vessels of superior force. JONATHAN SMITH married Mary Carlisle in 1723, and had three daughters and a son Jonathan. The second John Smith may have been connected with the first, but does not appear to have been his son. He had a wife Susanna (who died a widow, March 2, 1725, aged forty-six) and several children; among whom was a Joseph, born in 1709: the same, probably, who married Abigail Gardner in 1730, and had sons Joseph, John, James, and Benjamin, and two daughters. The third John Smith has no further known connection with us than his marriage to Elizabeth Elwell in 1702.

MORRIS SOMES, born in 1614, was one of the earliest settlers, and a proprietor of land on the east side of Mill River, where it is supposed he had his residence. By his wife Margerie, who died Jan. 22, 1646, he had Mary, born in 1642; Sarah, 1643; and Timothy. His next wife, to whom he was married June 26, 1648, was Elizabeth, daughter of John Kendall of Cambridge. She died Jan. 4, 1697: he died Jan. 16, 1689, leaving an estate of £198. The children of his second marriage were — John, born in 1648; Lydia, 1649; Nathaniel, 1651; Patience, 1652; Joseph, 1654; Abigail, 1655; and Hannah, 1658. TIMOTHY was the only son of Morris Somes, who married and settled in Gloucester; and all who have ever borne the name in town have descended from him. He married Jane Stanwood, April 2, 1673; by whom he had ten children, whose births are recorded; and probably a Morris, who was lost at sea in 1716, aged twenty-four. The last of these children were — Mercy, born Oct. 29, and Patience, Oct. 30, 1696; on which day the mother died. He next married Hannah Despar, March 11, 1697, and had six more children; the last of which was born after his death, which took place Feb. 1, 1706. Timothy Somes's home was also near Mill River. Of his seventeen children, eight were sons; and it appears to be by one of these alone that the name has been perpetuated in town to the present time. The oldest (Timothy), born in 1673, married Elizabeth Robinson, Dec. 31, 1695; and had sons Stephen, Timothy, Joseph, Nehemiah, Abraham, and Isaac. The date of his death is not known; but there is reason to suppose that he was not alive in 1721. Stephen Somes married Rachel Brown in 1719, and had several children. Two of his sons (William and Samuel) were progenitors of families now living in town. John, son of the former, was representative in 1808 and 1809;

and died Sept. 3, 1820, aged fifty-three. Another John, son of Samuel, also aged fifty-three, was found drowned, on the last-named day, on the back side of the Fort. Timothy, brother of Stephen, married Abigail Springer in 1721, and had sons Timothy and Jonathan. Joseph, the next of these brothers, married Sarah Harvey in 1731, but has no offspring recorded in town. Nehemiah Somes was twice married, if, as is supposed, he married Lucy Rogers of Truro, with whom he was intending marriage, September, 1734. His son Nehemiah, born here in 1737, was probably the Boston merchant, of the same name, who was the agent and part owner of the privateer "Active," one of Manly's fleet, in 1779. Abraham and Isaac Somes were twins, born in 1707. Abraham married Martha Emerson in 1730. They had a large family of children, and both died in advanced age. Abraham, the oldest son, settled on Mount-Desert Island, Me.; lived to be over eighty years old; and left at his death a numerous posterity at that place. Benjamin, the next son, was a soldier in the Revolutionary War, a mariner, and finally the keeper of a noted tavern on Front Street. He died about the 1st of February, 1805, aged seventy-three. His daughter Abigail married Frederic Gilman. Isaac, the next brother of this family, was commander of the privateer letter-of-marque ship "Tempest," in which he was lost, in the Revolutionary War. John, another brother, was also a mariner, and engaged in privateering during the war, and in commercial pursuits afterwards. He was many years President of the Gloucester Bank; and, in 1806 and 1807, a representative. In political action, he was a warm supporter of Mr. Jefferson. He died in August, 1816, aged seventy-one; leaving a wife, who died April 13, 1846, aged ninety-one. Her maiden name was Anna Dolliver. She had a husband (Capt. John Colson) previous to her marriage to Capt. Somes, of whom she was the second wife. There was no offspring by either of the marriages. Daniel, the youngest son of Abraham Somes, removed to Maine or one of the British Provinces, and had a son Daniel, who went to the East Indies, and settled in Manilla. Isaac, twin-brother of Abraham, married Eunice Godfrey in 1730, and Widow Lydia

Reading in 1744. He was lost at sea in 1755, leaving a son Samuel, who was a soldier in the early part of the Revolutionary War; afterwards a sea-captain and merchant; and died Mar. 27, 1796, aged forty-one. The latter left a son Samuel, who became an intelligent ship-master, and died in New Orleans in August, 1839; and a son Isaac, the present President of the Gloucester Bank, who is probably the sole male representative of this branch of the family. Joseph, son of Timothy, sen., born in 1679, died, probably unmarried, about or before 1719, when his brother Nathaniel administered upon his estate. William, the next son, born in 1681, is supposed to be the person of the same name who was of Amesbury, and was deceased before 1707. Ichabod, another son, born in 1687, is only mentioned as the father, by his wife Abigail, of a son William, Aug. 16, 1713; and in the warning, June 4, 1723, to Abigail, wife or widow of Ichabod Somes, to leave the town, and return to her last abode. Nathaniel, born in 1695, married Susanna Whittredge in 1722, and had two children born before 1726. Timothy Somes had sons Ebenezer and Abiel by his second marriage, who are not known to have married in town. The former, born in 1700, was living in 1721. John, son of Morris Somes, born in 1648, became a cooper, and settled in Boston. Joining the Quakers, he shared in the persecutions of that sect; and was twice apprehended in 1677, at their usual place of worship, and whipped. He had previously been represented to the Colonial authorities as one who derided the government, and aspersed juries by accusing them of false judgments. He died Nov. 16, 1700; and a gravestone in Copp's-Hill Burying-ground still marks the place of his interment. Nathaniel, third son of Morris Somes, born in 1651, died July 12, 1690. It does not appear that he was ever married. Joseph, the youngest son of Morris, born in 1654, was killed in the fight with the Indians at Narraganset Fort, December, 1675.

William Southmeade was one of the early settlers, and had a grant of the lot on which Mr. Thompson's frame stood. He married Millicent, daughter of William Addes, Nov. 28, 1642; by whom he had sons, — William, born in 1643; John,

1645, who died the same year; and John, 1646. The oldest of these sons settled in Middletown, Conn.; and died in 1702, leaving eight sons. The death of our settler is not recorded; but it occurred before 1649, when an inventory of his goods and chattels was made by Christopher Avery and William Addes. The augers, tools, and other instruments, mentioned in the inventory, authorize the conjecture that he was a ship-carpenter. His widow married William Ash, and probably left town with him about 1651.

PHILIP STAINWOOD.—The original orthography of this name, which indicates its probable derivation, was not continued beyond the second or third generation. This settler first appears in Gloucester in 1653. In 1654, he bought a house and land of Robert Tucker; and, in the same year, had a grant from the town of six acres on the east side of Lobster Cove. He was a selectman in 1667; and died Aug. 7, 1672, leaving an estate of £87. 10s. His widow Jane became the second wife of John Pearce, Sept. 12, 1673; and died Aug. 18, 1706. The children of Philip Stainwood were — Philip; John, born in 1653; Jane, 1655; Samuel, 1658; Jonathan, 1661; Naomi, 1664; Ruth, 1667; and Hannah, 1670. Three of these sons (Philip, John, and Samuel) received grants of soldiers' lots at Kettle Cove, in 1679, for military service in the wars of that period. PHILIP married Mary Blackwell, Nov. 22, 1677. She died Jan. 3, 1679; and he next married Esther Bray, Oct. 30, 1683. He died Sept. 24, 1728. Two of his sons married and had families in town. Philip, born in 1690, married Sarah Haraden, Dec. 18, 1718; and had three sons (John, Job, and Zebulon) and three daughters. Job lost his left arm in the expedition against Louisburg in 1745, and for this loss was made a pensioner for life by the General Court of Massachusetts. He married Hannah Byles in 1749; who died March 1, 1753, aged twenty-four, leaving one son (Zebulon), who engaged in agricultural and commercial pursuits. He had his residence in the Second Parish; where he died in August, 1838, aged eighty-seven, leaving several descendants. His son Theodore, an intelligent shipmaster, married Sarah, daughter of Rev. John

Rogers; and died on his passage from Russia in 1814. His only child settled in town is the wife of Hon. John W. Lowe: another daughter is the wife of Rev. Andrew Bigelow, D.D., of Boston. David, the other son of Philip Stanwood, jun., married Susanna Davis in 1720, and had several children. One of his sons (Solomon) was the father of a venerable citizen still living, — Richard G., whose son, of the same name, was representative in 1839. JOHN, son of the original settler, married Lydia Butler, Dec. 9, 1680; and died Jan. 25, 1706. Of his nine children, three were sons (John, Jonathan, and James), who married in town, and had families. The two latter were probably the persons of the same names who were admitted residents of Falmouth, Me., in 1728. SAMUEL had a wife Hannah, to whom he was married Nov. 16, 1686; and had five children born in town before 1695: soon after that date, he removed to Amesbury. He had a son Ebenezer; the same, perhaps, who has two children recorded in our books as born at Brunswick, besides others born here. JONATHAN, son of Philip Stanwood, sen., married Mary Nichols, Dec. 17, 1688. According to the records, he had ten children; of whom three were sons (Ebenezer, David, and Nehemiah), who married and settled in Gloucester. David was a soldier in the expedition to Cape Breton in 1745, and received a wound which induced him to apply to the Colonial Government for relief. In the early generations of this family, there was promise of a numerous posterity; but the name is now borne here by only a few families. Many of the stock emigrated, probably, during the first century of our history. Perhaps all who bear the name in this country are descended from our settler.

WILLIAM STEVENS, a ship-carpenter, was one of the first settlers; and is entitled to honorable mention for his mechanical skill, his inflexible honesty, and his services in various public offices. He came to New England before 1632, and probably had his residence in Boston or its vicinity. From his ability as a mechanic, it may be inferred that he was the Mr. Stevens, who, in March, 1634, was to receive, by order of the General Court, £10 for seeing to the erection of a movable fort to be built in Boston. He was in Salem in 1636; where, in 1639, his children, Isaac and Mary, were baptized, and, in 1641, his daughter Ruth. He was admitted a freeman in 1640; and, in 1642, appears in Gloucester as one of the commissioners appointed by the General Court for ordering town-affairs. His standing among the early settlers, and the importance of his aid in promoting the prosperity of the town, are sufficiently indicated by the extraordinary grant he received of five hundred acres of land lying between Chebacco and Annisquam Rivers. He also had a grant of six acres on the Meeting-house Neck; but his residence was at the Cut, near the Beach, where he had eight acres of land. He was a selectman several years, commissioner for ending small causes, town-clerk, and four years representative. Proof of his mechanical skill and honesty is preserved in the following extract from a letter * written by Emanuel Downing, one of the Massachusetts Company, to an officer of the English Government: —

"Being last night at the Exchandge, I enquired what ship-carpenters Mr. Winthrop, the Governor, had with him in New England: when I was informed by Mr. Aldersey, the lord-keeper's brother-in-law, and Mr. Cradock, that the Governor hath with him one William Stephens, a shipwright; soe able a man, as they believe there is hardly such an other to be found in this kingdom. There be 2 or 3 others; but, for want of their names, I could not be satisfied of them. This Stephens hath built here many ships of great burthen: he made the 'Royal Merchant,' a ship of 600 tonns. This man, as they enformed me, had more reguard to his substantiall performance than the wages he was to receive, and soe grew to poverty: whereupon he was preparing to goe for Spayne, where he knew he should have wages answerable to his paynes, had not some friends perswaded him to N. England, where he now lives with great content. Had the state of Spayne obteyned him, he should have be'n as a pretious Jewell to them."

He also had a New-England fame; being, undoubtedly, the "very sufficient builder" mentioned by Johnson, one of our

* This letter forms a part of the interesting "Gleanings for New-England History, collected in England, in 1842, by Hon. James Savage, and published in vol. xxviii Mass. Hist. Coll.

early historians.* Nothing is known concerning the particular vessels he built here, except in two instances, to be hereafter mentioned. This worthy citizen was no less distinguished for his action in relation to political affairs. He was a member of the General Court in 1665, when the Colonial Government made a noble resistance to the proceedings of the commissioners sent over by the king to interfere in the legislation of the Colony, in a manner which was justly esteemed to be an infringement of Colonial rights and privileges. It was a grave offence, in those days, to speak evil of rulers; and discretion would have counselled silence: but the honest indignation of our townsman, spurning all restraint, found utterance in no softened terms of dislike. Four of his neighbors testified at a Quarterly Court in Salem, in 1667, to his declaring "that he would bear no office within this jurisdiction, nor anywhere else, where Charles Stewart had any thing to do; and that he cared no more for Charles Stewart than any other man, as king; and that he abhorred the name of Charles Stewart as king." For this bold and rash expression of his hatred of the king, the offender was sentenced to a month's imprisonment; to pay a fine of £20 and costs; and to be deprived of his privileges as a freeman. Soon after this, his wife, in a petition to the General Court for relief, represents him to be deranged, and herself as aged and having a family. There is no record of his death, or of the settlement of his estate; for he again "grew to poverty," having mortgaged part of his property, in 1667, to Francis Willoughby of Charlestown, from whom it never returned to him. The property conveyed to Willoughby was the five hundred acres near Chebacco, on which were a dwelling-house, barn, and out-houses; and his estate at the Cut, with "said gutt, or passage, for boats running through as they pass between Cape-Ann Harbor and Annisquam." Another portion of his property, consisting of a new house and land, was put into the hands of his sons James and Isaac, in trust for their mother Philippa, who died Aug. 31, 1681. No other mention occurs of Isaac. Mary

* Wonder-working Providence; Mass. Hist. Coll., vol. xvii. p. 82.

married John Coit: Ruth married Stephen Glover. JAMES, the only other son of William Stevens of whom we have any knowledge, received a grant of land on Town Neck, near Trynall Cove, in 1658. He married Susanna, daughter of Sylvester Eveleth, Dec. 31, 1656; and died March 25, 1697, leaving an estate of £239. 19s. The ship-carpenter's tools and oak plank mentioned in his inventory render it probable that he followed the trade in which his father was so distinguished. His repeated election to the highest offices in town shows that he possessed the public confidence in a high degree. He was a deacon in the church; a military officer; selectman in 1667, and from 1674 to 1691 inclusive; and representative ten years. He had eleven children; of whom William, Samuel, Ebenezer, David, Jonathan, Mary (the wife of Francis Norwood), and Hannah, were living at the time of their father's death. William married Abigail Sargent, June 15, 1682. He was lieutenant of the military company here, selectman two years, and representative in 1692. He died Sept. 24, 1701, aged forty-two; leaving an estate, which consisted, in part, of an interest in three sloops, a negro woman and a boy, and the privilege called the Cut, the latter valued at £30. James, supposed to be his son, married Deborah Sayward in 1717; and disappeared in 1721, on the birth of his third child. Samuel, son of Lieut. William Stevens, born in 1691, married Anna Allen in 1713. He inherited the Cut, which occasioned him considerable trouble and vexation. He resided on the family property there, and was called Cut Stevens, to distinguish him from an uncle of his own name. He is said to have lived to old age; but the date of his death is not known. His daughter Abigail married Jonathan Elwell. Of his two sons William and Samuel, the former only appears to have married in town. He married Anna Davis in 1740, and died about 1743, leaving a son William. Samuel, son of Deacon James Stevens, born in 1665, married Mary Ellery in 1693. He was a merchant, and took an active part in public affairs; filling the most important offices, among which was that of representative, which he held six years. His residence was on Front Street, between Hancock and Centre. He died Nov. 16, 1756, aged ninety-one. His wife survived him, and, though past fourscore, accepted a matrimonial offer from Elder Grover in 1758; but their marriage was soon dissolved by the death of the aged bride. Mr. Stevens had a son Samuel, who married Abigail York in 1718, and had sons York and Joseph. He was lost at sea, near Sable Island, April, 1722, aged twenty-six. James, another son, born in 1699, was probably the same who kept a tavern near the Meeting-house several years. Two other sons were prominent actors in the affairs of the town. John, born in 1707, married Rachel Allen in 1729; and, in 1754, Mrs. Elizabeth, widow of Col. John Gorham of Barnstable, an officer who rendered valuable aid in the siege of Cape Breton in 1745, and died in London, of small-pox, about 1750, while prosecuting his claims for expenses in that expedition. Mr. Stevens sustained a high character as a merchant. In military affairs he took a strong interest, and attained to the rank of colonel. He died April 13, 1779, aged seventy-two: his wife died Dec. 25, 1786, aged seventy-three. William, another son of Samuel Stevens, born in 1713, married Elizabeth Allen in 1733. He engaged in maritime pursuits and in the cultivation of the soil: but neither yielded him profit; for, though he died possessed of a considerable estate, his debts were more than sufficient to absorb the whole of it. He was representative in 1753 and 1754, and from 1756 to 1760 inclusive. He died May 10, 1767, aged fifty-four; leaving, with other children, John and Samuel. The former married Judith Sargent. He was a merchant and trader, in which occupations he met with no success; and finally became a bankrupt. To avoid being arrested for debt, he fled, in a vessel belonging to his father-in-law, to St. Eustatia, where he died. His widow married Rev. John Murray. Samuel married Elizabeth Allen in 1748, and for many years kept a shop on Fore Street. He died Dec. 9, 1795, aged forty-eight; leaving a wife and children, who removed to Portland, Me., where Mrs. Stevens lived to be nearly a hundred years old. Ebenezer, son of Deacon James Stevens, born in 1670, is supposed to have married Widow Mary Day in 1723. No offspring is recorded; but the books show the marriage of an Ebenezer, jun., in 1751.

The elder Ebenezer was supported by the town several years, and died about 1757. David, born in 1677, and Jonathan, 1679, other sons of Deacon James Stevens, married in town, and were both dead in 1709. Jonathan left a son of the same name. No descendants of our eminent shipwright, bearing the family name, are known to be now residents of the town.*

STEPHEN STREETER may have preceded the settlers of 1642, as Mr. Blynman's grant includes a lot "primarily given" to him. He had a house here, but did not remain in town long after its permanent settlement; for, in 1644, he was residing in Charlestown.

JOHN STUDLEY appears as an owner of land in 1649; and also, in the same year, as a witness in an action against Charles Glover and his wife for fighting.

HARLAKENDEN SYMONDS was son of Deputy-Governor Symonds. He bought of John Kettle in 1664, for £100, a house and land, and "the timber of the old Meeting-house." From the description of this land, it must have been the lot directly opposite the south part of the Meeting-house Green, on the easterly side of the road. He had by his wife Elizabeth a daughter Sarah, born here in 1668. In August, 1672, he was at Weathersfield, England, waiting for a power of attorney. His subsequent career and end are not known. He may have returned to Ipswich, the place of his father's residence; whence his widow, with her daughter, who married Thomas Low, came back to

---

* A William Stevens married Anna Lufkin in 1725, and has nine children recorded in our books. He lived in the Second Parish; where he died June 17, 1773, aged seventy-eight: his wife died April 3, 1780, aged eighty. I can trace no connection between him and our early family of that name, though there might have been one. His son, or grandson, Nathaniel, went to New Gloucester, where he had a son born, who was adopted by George Clark. Clark was an Irishman, and, it is said, fought on the English side at the Battle of Bunker Hill, and was taken prisoner, and confined in Ipswich Jail. Upon regaining his freedom, he went to live on Hog Island, Chebacco; and finally settled in the West Parish of this town. His adopted son Stevens took his name, and transmitted it to our present citizens, George Clark and Col. John Clark.

There was a William Stevens, too, among the early settlers of New Gloucester. He was born in 1718; and died Dec. 30, 1789, leaving a wife, who was a Woodbury of this town. It would be natural to expect to trace him to the parent town; but it does not appear that he emigrated hence.

Gloucester about 1692. Mrs. Symonds died here Jan. 31, 1728, aged ninety.

George Stover had, in 1698, a grant of half an acre of ground to set a house upon on the south side of Cripple Cove. He married Abigail Elwell, Jan. 25, 1692; by whom he had the following children: Josiah, born in 1694; Jonathan, 1696, died in infancy; Isaac, 1697; Hannah, 1702; Abigail, 1703; Mehetabel, 1706, died the same year; Abraham, 1707, died in 1707; John, 1709; and David, 1712. This family is supposed to have removed from town, as none of its members appear here at the division of lands in 1721.

Richard Tarr. — Tradition has preserved an account of this settler; which states that he was born in the west of England about 1660, and settled in Marblehead soon after 1680, where he married his wife Elizabeth. A person of this name, of Saco, was a petitioner to Sir Edmund Andros for confirmation in the possession of land he bought there, three years before the time of his petition, of John Seilye, fisherman. The date of our settler's first appearance in town is not known. All of his children born after 1690 are recorded in our books; but his will shows that he had two who were born before that year. In April, 1697, he had a grant of a piece of land, for three or four years, where his house stood; and, in 1701, another grant, of ten acres, with the condition annexed, that he should support "old Father Churchill" for life. This land was situated in Sandy Bay, near Davison's Run. He died about 1732; leaving an estate of £399, and the following children: William; John; Elizabeth, born in 1691; Honour, 1693; Richard, 1695; Joseph, 1698; Benjamin, 1700; Caleb, 1703; Samuel, 1706; and Sarah, 1716. William married Elizabeth Felt in 1708, and had several children; but none of the name now in town trace back to him. John was intending marriage with Elizabeth Heans of Marblehead in 1714; and, by his wife Elizabeth, a daughter of the same name was born in 1719. Richard married Grace Hodgkins, Feb. 20, 1722; and had by her Hazelelponi,* born in 1722;

* I think few of my readers will remember ever before to have met with this name, unless they are familiar with a portion of the Bible not much read. — See 1 Chron. iv. 3.

and William, 1724. Joseph married Sarah Sargent, July 28, 1719; and had a daughter Abigail, and three sons — Joseph, Benjamin, and Nathaniel — born before 1726. He removed to Parker's Island, Georgetown, Me.; where descendants are still living. Benjamin married Rebecca Card, Feb. 4, 1724. His posterity includes the larger part of all who now bear the name on the Cape. One of his sons (Benjamin) died about 1814, aged eighty-eight, having had several children. Daniel Barber, one of them, was a soldier in the Revolutionary War; and died April 16, 1840, aged eighty-six. Jabez, another, was also a soldier in the same war; and died Nov. 25, 1844, aged eighty-five, — the last of the Gloucester soldiers who fought on Bunker Hill. Moses, the next son, was lost at sea in the privateer ship "Tempest." Caleb Tarr had a wife Martha and twelve children. He died about 1752; leaving a son Caleb, who settled at the Harbor. Samuel, the seventh and youngest son of Richard Tarr, married Elizabeth Williams, Oct. 12, 1726, by whom he had four sons before 1739; when he was drowned in Sheepscot River, Me. Three other Tarrs besides the one mentioned above were lost in the "Tempest," — James and William, sons of James; and Henry, son of Henry. Another Richard Tarr appears in town in 1722. He married Sarah Beal at Beverly in 1719; and had a son Richard, born here in 1722. He is supposed to be the same Richard who was killed by Indians at Fox Islands in 1724.*

James Travis, or Travers, perhaps son of Henry of Newbury, born in 1645, bought, in 1667, land and the frame of a dwelling-house, situated near Poles, of Samuel Peacock of Boston. April 18 of the same year, he married Mary, daughter of John Pearce, of whom his daughter Elizabeth was born, Feb. 8, 1668; in which year he sold his house and land to Thomas Millet, sen., and appears no longer in town.

Robert Tucker may have removed hither from Weymouth,

* The town of Rockport has erected a granite monument, with an appropriate inscription, to the memory of Richard Tarr, its first settler, on the spot which tradition has marked as that of his burial. This spot was his own land; and, having been enlarged and enclosed, became finally the Parish Burying-ground.

where a person of this name lived in 1639. He first appears in Gloucester in 1651, when he bought a house and land of Edward Rowse. He was selectman in 1652, and town-clerk from 1652 to 1656. He had a wife Elizabeth, by whom he had Expedance in 1652, and Ephraim in 1653; the former of whom died in infancy. A son Ebenezer died in 1653. His residence here appears to have terminated with the expiration of his clerkship, and to have been transferred back to Weymouth.

JOHN TUCKER is not known to have been of the same family as the preceding; nor has any information concerning him come to light, further than that furnished by our records in giving his marriage and the births of his children. He does not appear among the grantees of six-acre lots in 1688; nor does he or any of his family appear in the division of land, in 1721, to persons who had been householders seventeen years. From the latter circumstance, it may be inferred that he and his wife had both deceased or removed before that year. His wife was Sarah Riggs, to whom he was married May 9, 1681; and his children were — Mary, born in 1682; Sarah, 1685; John, 1686; William, 1690; Thomas, 1692; Richard, 1695; Abigail, 1697; Joseph, 1701; and Grace, 1706. JOHN married Mary Lane in 1714, and has the births of twelve children recorded. WILLIAM married Dorcas Lane in 1713; and had issue two sons and three daughters, as appears by the records. John, one of these sons, born in 1725, married Mary Davis in 1746; and had sons John and Nathaniel, who served in the Revolutionary Army, and lived to old age. John attained the rank of lieutenant in the army, and afterwards that of colonel in the militia. He was an active Federalist; and, during the rule of his party in town-affairs, was seven times elected representative. He died in January, 1831, aged eighty-two. THOMAS TUCKER was drowned in Carolina, April 20, 1717. RICHARD married Abigail Harvey, Jan. 16, 1718; and died before 1734. He had several children; one of whom (JOSEPH), born in 1728, was probably the same who died Jan. 16, 1816, aged eighty-nine. A Richard Tucker and wife Bethiah appear in town at the birth of their son Richard in 1704; and a Lewis Tucker has recorded here the births of five children by Joan, his wife, at Kittery side, on Piscataqua River, at the commencement of the last century.

WALTER TYBBOT was born in 1584, and came to Gloucester with Mr. Blynman. He was admitted a freeman in 1642; and was a selectman that year, and in several of the subsequent years. In 1647, he was licensed to draw wine, and exempted from common training. The records do not indicate the place of his residence, though they furnish evidence that he was one of the largest proprietors of land. He gave his attention to agriculture; and the inventory of his estate shows that he did not cultivate our unpromising soil in vain. He died Aug. 14, 1651, aged sixty-seven, leaving a widow (who married John Harding, April 22, 1652), and a daughter Mary, by whose marriage with William Haskell his descendants are numerous. No other child of Tybbot is mentioned; but Agnes, wife of Edmund Clark, may have been his daughter, as her husband is called son-in-law of Tybbot. She had had a previous husband (Dike), by whom she had a daughter Elizabeth, and perhaps the Richard who is noticed in this work; as he is mentioned as a grandson of Tybbot, and of Harding, who married Tybbot's widow.

BRIDGET VARNEY was of Ipswich in 1663. In 1669, then a widow, she sold house and land, with the harbor and neck of land on the south-east, to Bartholomew Foster. This property was situated near the present Mill Street. She died Oct. 25, 1672. Her will mentions sons Humphrey and Thomas, son Jeffrey Parsons, daughter Rachel Vincion, and son-in-law William Vincion.

THOMAS VERREY, or VERY, was born about 1626. He was a fisherman, and was here before 1650. He had several lots of land, the location of which indicates that his residence was at the Harbor. He married Hannah, daughter of Thomas Giles of Salem, July 6, 1650, who died Aug. 25, 1683: he died March 28, 1694. His children were — Ephraim, born in 1652; Hannah, 1653; Bridget, 1654; Thomas, 1656; Samuel, 1659; Abigail, 1661; Edward, 1663; Elizabeth, 1665; and Francis, 1668. This last son was living in the city of Waterford, in Ireland, in 1716. The name was not perpetuated in Gloucester beyond the second generation; but it is still found in other places in Essex County.

WILLIAM VINSON was of Salem as early as 1635, but removed to this place on the first settlement of the town. He is called, in the records, "potmaker." By grant and purchase, he became an owner of several lots of land; on one of which, probably, was the spring that perpetuates his name. He was also the original grantee of Five-pound Island. He was admitted a freeman in 1643; and in 1646, and several times subsequently, was one of the selectmen. He had a wife Sarah, who died Feb. 4, 1660. He next married, June 10, 1661, Rachel Cooke, a widow, who died Feb. 15, 1707: he died Sept. 17, 1690, aged about eighty. His children were — Elizabeth, born in 1644; Richard; John, 1648; William, 1651; Richard, 1658; Thomas, 1662; Abigail, 1668; and Sarah and Hannah, born before he came to Gloucester. The four daughters married here, and had children. Of the sons, the first Richard died in childhood; the second, and Thomas and William, died in December, 1675; John was dead in 1683. The name was not continued here beyond the second generation; but the descendants of his daughters are numerous.

THOMAS WAKLEY, called a yeoman, lived in Hingham in 1635. He bought thirteen acres of land, on the neck of house-lots, of Mr. Pritchard; besides which, he owned several other parcels. He was a freeman in 1636, and one of the selectmen in 1646. He and his son John had houses and land on the south side of Goose Cove; which, in 1661, they sold to Thomas Riggs, and, with another son (Isaac) and a son-in-law (Matthew Coe), went to Falmouth, Me., where they purchased a large tract of land, on which they settled, and remained till the destruction of the place by the Indians in 1675, when Thomas Wakley and his wife Elizabeth, and John and his wife and two children, were barbarously slaughtered by the savages. Elizabeth, daughter of John, was carried off; but, after some months' captivity, was taken by Squando, the Saco sachem, to Major Waldron at Dover, where she subsequently married Richard Scamman, a Quaker. ISAAC WAKLEY was killed by the Indians, at Falmouth, in 1676. JOHN WAKLEY married Elizabeth, daughter of Johanna Somars, June 10, 1657; and had, by her, Hannah, born in 1657; Thomas, born 3d, died 7th September, 1659; and Elizabeth, 1661. Old Thomas Wakley was often heard to bewail with tears his removal from places where he had enjoyed gospel privileges "to a plantation where there was no church at all, nor the ordinance and institutions of the Lord Jesus Christ."

HENRY WALKER is mentioned as an owner of land before 1650. He married, Sept. 26, 1662, Widow Mary Brown, who first appeared here as the wife of Abraham Robinson. He had his residence on the west side of Annisquam River, where a creek still perpetuates the name. He was selectman in 1667 and several subsequent years. He died Aug. 29, 1693: his wife died April 17, 1690. His estate, the largest that had then been accumulated in town, was appraised £922. 10s., consisting chiefly of land. Having no children, he left legacies to the descendants of his wife by her two previous husbands; and gave the remainder of his property to Nathaniel Coit, who resided with him.

JOHN WALLIS.—He and Nathaniel Wallis, who was born in the county of Cornwall, England, 1632, were early inhabitants of Casco; whence John was driven away at the time of the destruction of the settlements there by the Indians in 1675. He is only mentioned here as the father, by his wife Mary, of a daughter Elizabeth, Sept. 12, 1678; and as having deceased Sept. 23, 1690. The silence of our records concerning him, between these two dates, is explained by the fact, that he returned to Falmouth, and remained there till the second attack on that place by the Indians compelled him again to flee. He had sons Josiah, Benjamin, Joseph, and James. JOSIAH was born about 1662. He first appears here in 1696 with his wife Mary; by whom his son John was born in the same year, and his daughter Susanna in 1699. About 1702, he went back to Falmouth, and built a house at Spring Point, on the Purpooduc side of the river, where his three brothers then lived. Here, however, he enjoyed but a brief season of repose. The French and Indians, in August, 1703, attacked all the settlements from Wells to Casco; and, in the destruction of the latter, the Wallis families were severe sufferers. The wives of Josiah and Benjamin Wallis were killed, and Joseph Wallis's wife was carried into captivity. Josiah Wallis himself made his escape to Black Point; carrying his son John, who was then about seven years old, part of the way on his back. He again took up his abode in Gloucester, where he is found with a wife Sarah, to whom he was married Dec. 19, 1706. By her he had a son Josiah, born in 1708; and Samuel, 1711. Besides these and the children by his previous wife, he had a daughter Sarah, who married Jacob Sawyer, and removed to Falmouth; and a daughter Mary, who married Paul Dolliver. He died Feb. 7, 1741. JAMES WALLIS had, in 1704, half an acre of land near the Harbor Swamp. How long before that he had removed hither, is not known. The birth of his daughter Rebekah, in 1699, is recorded in our records: after her he had Martha, Joseph, Benjamin, and Jonathan; and, before her, Elizabeth and James. The father, with his sons James and Joseph, was taken by the Indians, in Fox Harbor, in June, 1724. The two sons were killed; but the father escaped, and returned home. In his will, made in 1731 and proved in 1743, he mentions his son Benjamin in captivity, and a son Jonathan. John Wallis, who married Patience Hodgkins in 1719, and had several children born here before 1738, was probably the son of Josiah, and is supposed to be the John Wallis who was an inhabitant of Cape Elizabeth in 1768. The name has continued here down to the present time, though the individuals bearing it have never been numerous.

SAMUEL WEBBER is first presented to our notice as an inhabitant of Falmouth, Me., in 1681. In 1692, he was a witness at the trial of Rev. George Burroughs at Salem for witchcraft, and testified to his great strength. He appears in Gloucester in 1695; when, by his wife Deborah, a daughter of the same name was born. Besides her, Waitstill and Patience, twins, were born here in 1698. He had a house and fifteen acres of land at Goose Cove, which he sold in 1696 to Thomas Riggs. He probably left town before 1700, and went to York, where he died in 1716.

His wife Deborah and nine children survived him. A Michael Webber and wife Deborah had a daughter Mary born here May 16, 1701. He is probably the person of the same name who was a fellow-sufferer of the Wallises in the destruction of the settlement at Purpooduc by the Indians in 1703. The savages killed Webber's wife, who was pregnant, and mangled her body with shocking barbarity. The same, or another Michael, was here in 1716, and became a permanent settler. He had a wife Sarah, by whom ten children were born to him in the subsequent twenty years. One of his sons (Michael), born in 1716, married Hannah Sawyer in 1739, and was lost at sea in August, 1760; leaving two sons (John and Michael), who settled in New Gloucester, Me.; whence Gen. John Webber, son of the latter, came to Gloucester, and was a prominent citizen till his death, Dec. 16, 1858, at the age of seventy-two. His son John S. was a representative in 1855 and 1857. Another son of Michael Webber, sen. (Benjamin), born in 1726, married Hannah Babson in 1750. He fell dead suddenly, in advanced age, at the door of his dwelling-house, to which he was returning with a burden of fuel from the adjacent woods. He was the father of Benjamin, who was a soldier in the battle of Bunker Hill, a sea-captain and merchant, and died Jan. 9, 1841, aged eighty-five; and of Joseph, who was killed by the accidental discharge of a musket, on board the privateer "Black Prince" of Salem, about 1779. Ignatius, youngest son of Michael Webber, born in 1733, married Elizabeth Stewart in 1757, and had several daughters, and a son Ignatius, who became a shipmaster, and, with a good reputation in his profession, acquired also a competent estate, a part of which was unprofitably invested in the erection of an expensive windmill on the spot now occupied by the Pavilion Hotel. He died Feb. 1, 1829, aged seventy-two. A James Webber was here in 1704; when, by his wife Patience, he had a son Nathan born. The ancestor of all these Webbers may have been Michael, who died here Jan. 12, 1729, aged nearly ninety. The date of his first appearance in town is not known. A Michael was a householder here in 1704; and, in 1725, received a grant of land near his house, at Fresh-water Cove; where the family name has continued to the present time.

William Wellman was son-in-law of Major Sadler, and probably came to Gloucester with him. He does not appear as a grantee of land, though he had several lots; one of which was in the Harbor, and one in Fisherman's field. He was one of the company that went to New London, where he received a grant of land in 1651.

Nathaniel Wharf was son of Nathaniel Wharf of Falmouth, Me., by his wife Rebecca, daughter of Arthur Macworth. The father died in 1673; leaving Nathaniel, then eleven years old, who came to Gloucester, and married, Jan. 30, 1684, Ann, daughter of Thomas Riggs, by whom he had the following children: Nathaniel, born in 1685; Rebecca, 1686; Mary, 1687; Charity, 1688, died in infancy; Thomas, 1689; Mercy and Experience, 1690; Hannah, 1691; Arthur, 1694; John, 1696; Patience, 1697, died in infancy; Abraham, 1699, died in 1706; and Lydia, 1701. The mother died Dec. 17, 1701, a few weeks after the birth of this last child. Nathaniel Wharf was living in 1734. His oldest son (Nathaniel) married Hannah Stevens, Feb. 7, 1715, and had sons Thomas and Isaac. Thomas married Dorcas Lane in 1738, and had sons Job, John, Nathaniel, Thomas, David, and Eliphalet, and two daughters. He was supposed to have been lost at sea in the fall of 1753. His son Thomas settled in New Gloucester, and died there Jan. 22, 1835, aged eighty-seven. Isaac married Catherine Connelly of Newbury in 1744, and had sons John, Isaac, and Humphrey, and two daughters. Arthur Wharf is supposed to have married Martha Lee in 1737. Sons Abraham, John, and Samuel were the offspring of this marriage. John, youngest son of Nathaniel Wharf, married Hannah Cleigh in 1719, and had sons James and Arthur and three daughters. By these descendants of Nathaniel Wharf, the name has been perpetuated in town; but the persons bearing it are not numerous.

William Whittridge had a grant of a common right in 1692; but first appears here at his marriage, March 4, 1684, to

Hannah Roberts. The fruits of this union were — Hannah, born in 1685; Samuel, 1692; and Susanna, 1697. He died Aug. 8, 1726, aged seventy. SAMUEL married Hannah Whiston of Barnstable in 1720, by whom he had four daughters and a son William; and was drowned at Sable Island, May 10, 1732, aged forty. His son William married Mary Saville in 1755, and had sons William and Oliver Saville and a daughter Mary.

RICHARD WINDOW, a carpenter, had, as early as 1651, a house and ten acres of land near Walker's Creek; which, at a date not known, he sold to William Haskell. He was a selectman in 1654. In 1655, he bought of John Coit a house and land on the east side of the river, where he probably lived during the remainder of his life. He had previously bought a house, near Trynall Cove, of William Sargent. In 1648, the Quarterly-Court Record says that he was presented for living away from his wife: but it was proved that he had sent for her, and had heard that she was dead; and he was therefore discharged. His Gloucester wife was named Elinor, by whom he had a daughter, born in 1654; and by the loss of whom, May 16, 1658, he again became a widower. He next married Bridget, widow of Henry Travis of Newbury, March 30, 1659. In 1662, land was granted to him for his son Richard Goodwin; and the date of his will (May 2, 1665) completes our knowledge concerning him. In that he mentions a daughter Ann, his "true and laful aire;" Anthony Bennet, his son-in-law; and Elizabeth his daughter-in-law.

HENRY WITHAM may have been a son of Thomas Witham, who died in 1653. Our information concerning him is of the slightest kind. The spot on which he resided is not known; though it is indicated, perhaps, by his possession of eighteen acres of land lying near Lobster Cove. He married, first, Sarah, daughter of Morris Somes, June 15, 1665, who died May 11, 1689; and, second, Lydia Griffin, Oct. 23, 1691, who died Nov. 1, 1702: he died April 17, 1702. His children were — Thomas, born in 1666; Henry, 1668; John, 1670, died same year; Samuel, 1672; and Joseph, 1676. Only two of these sons (Thomas and Samuel) appear to have married and settled in town. THOMAS married Abigail Babson, July 8, 1691; from whose mother he received a gift of land situated near her own residence, at the Farms, where he built a house, which he made his home for life, and which has been owned and occupied by his descendants down to the present time. He filled the office of selectman several times, and appears to have been a worthy citizen. He died Aug. 1, 1736, aged seventy: his wife died Feb. 25, 1745, aged seventy-three. They had seven sons and four daughters. One of the sons died in youth: the rest were married, and had families in town. The six brothers had sixty-four children; and the youngest son of the youngest brother is now living, at the age of eighty-two, — a hundred and fifty-two years after his father's birth. One of the sons (Daniel), born in 1700, graduated at Harvard College in 1718. Soon afterwards, he taught a school in Dorchester; and, in 1729 and 1730, was engaged in the same employment here. He next entered upon the practice of medicine, and continued in it during life. Tradition and history are both silent concerning his professional career and reputation; but the written testimony of his ability, and usefulness as a citizen, is ample and conclusive. He began in early manhood to take an active part in town-affairs, and gained a popularity which he preserved to the end of his life. He was town-clerk forty-two years, and selectman thirty-seven years; and, besides these permanent offices, was frequently called upon to serve in others of temporary, but no less important character. Being qualified by education, experience in public affairs, and interest in the general welfare, his services were often in requisition in the preparation of resolves and addresses for the expression of the sentiments of the people at the anxious and excited period which immediately preceded the Revolutionary War; and he fully shared the patriotic indignation which filled the breasts of his townsmen, when assembled to consider the oppression and wrongs which the mother-country made them so sensibly to feel. Dr. Witham married Lydia Sanders, Jan. 7, 1735; and had by her twelve children, several of which died in infancy and childhood. His son Thomas died at Bayonne, whither he was carried as a prisoner, July, 1757, aged nineteen. Daniel, the youngest son, and the only one that survived his father, was a tailor, and had a shop on Middle Street, on the lot next west of the present Orthodox Meeting-house. The date of Dr. Witham's death is not known; but it was about 1776. Ebenezer, brother of Daniel, born in 1702, had sons Asa, Jeremiah, and Ebenezer, who are said to have removed to New Gloucester; whence Asa returned to his native town, and embarked on a privateering cruise, on which he was taken and carried to England, where he died in prison. Zebulon, the youngest son of Thomas Witham, born in 1708, was twice married, and, by his two wives, had eighteen children. His youngest son, born in 1778, is still living. He was some time a ship-master; and our Massachusetts State archives contain his deposition concerning his capture, robbery, and release by a Spanish privateer, on the coast of Cape Charles, November, 1740. He died June 22, 1794, aged eighty-six. SAMUEL WITHAM married Rebekah Gardner, Dec. 5, 1705, and had sons Samuel and John and a daughter Rebekah, and died before 1723. His residence was on Eastern Point.

HUMPHREY WOODBURY is supposed to have been a grandson of John, who came from Somersetshire, England, for the Dorchester adventurers, and was one of the first English occupants of our territory. The latter had a son Humphrey; who was undoubtedly the same person to whom, by his wife Elizabeth, our Humphrey was born, in Salem, in 1646. He became a citizen of Beverly by the separation of that town from Salem, and there married Ann Winder,* Jan. 8, 1671. The first mention we have of him in Gloucester is in 1677, when he purchased land on Biskie Island of Joseph Clark. He came into possession of other lots on that island, and built a house there; which was his residence, probably, at the time of his death. He died April 9, 1727, aged eighty: his wife died Feb. 28, 1728, aged seventy-five. His children baptized in Beverly were — Bethia, 1672; Abigail, 1674; Humphrey, 1677, died in 1695; Anna,

* Perhaps Ann Window, daughter of our Richard. She might have had Beverly connections in the Bennett Family of that town.

1680; Nehemiah, 1686; Abel, 1688; Nathan, 1691; and Israel, 1693. The births of Elizabeth, 1682; of Nathaniel, 1684; of Susanna, 1695; and of Humphrey, 1698, — are recorded in Gloucester. NATHAN married Hannah Giddings in 1712, and had three children. HUMPHREY married Abigail Bray in 1726, and, after living several years on the island where his father settled, removed to New Gloucester with the first permanent settlers of that town. He left here a son Abel, who became a sea-captain, and was taken in the Revolutionary War, and carried a prisoner to New York; where he died, on board a prison-ship, in 1778. Abel's daughter Jerusha, widow of Israel Rust, died April 9, 1854, aged ninety-seven.

SAMUEL YORK. — A Richard York was of Dover in 1661; and, in that year, sold land there which he had bought of William Hilton. He appears to have removed to Oyster River, now Durham, N.H.; where he owned land, which his son John sold in 1676. The latter had a wife Ruth, and may have been the same John who, in 1684, was living in North Yarmouth, Me.; where a Samuel also had land about the same time. No other Samuel appearing, further conjecture might identify him with our settler, and make him the father of Samuel and Benjamin, who were living in Falmouth, Me., on the second destruction of that place; as our Samuel had sons bearing these names. In 1700, he bought of Timothy Somes eighteen acres of land, with a house and barn. This land had the sea on the northern end, and Lobster Cove at the southern. His first appearance in Gloucester is at the birth of his son John, by his wife Hannah, in 1695. This son and another (Thomas) died in 1699: the father died March 18, 1718, aged seventy-three. A Mrs. York died Nov. 28, 1724, aged seventy. Samuel York mentions in his will sons Samuel (who had a son Samuel, a minor), Benjamin, and Richard, and three daughters who were married. The first of these sons is not known to have ever resided here. A Samuel York, with his wife Mary, was living in Ipswich in 1713; and, "being arrived at old age," made his will in 1767. He was the same, probably, who is mentioned as executor of the will of our Richard in 1729; and may have been his brother. BENJAMIN married Mary Giddings in 1704, and had six children born in town before 1728. His name is among the number of admitted residents of Falmouth, Me., in 1727 and 1728; whither he probably removed. RICHARD married Patience Hatch in 1711; and died May 2, 1718, aged twenty-nine, leaving a widow, sons Thomas and Richard, and daughters Patience and Mary. He owned two sloops and a schooner, and is supposed to have carried on the fishing business at Squam. Besides the above Yorks, Joseph settled here in 1700; when he married Abigail, daughter of Abraham Robinson. He bought, in 1701, eighteen acres of land near Lobster Cove, where he carried on the fishing business. He died Oct. 13, 1728, leaving an estate of over £1,400 after his debts were paid. He had several daughters and a son Joseph; but the name does not appear to have been perpetuated on the Cape by any one but Thomas, son of Richard.

PHILIP YOUDALL. — Not much is known concerning him. Mention is made in the town-records of land once belonging to him; and the Quarterly-Court records, under date of 1648, have preserved his name in connection with a criminal offence.

Although the date of the first settlement of Gloucester cannot be ascertained, it appears probable that Felch, Streeter, Thomas Smith, Baker, and Cotton, were here before the incorporation of the town, and were located at Done Fudging; and that Ashley, Milward, Liston, Luther, and perhaps two or three others, were also here before that date, and had lots at the Harbor. These persons may have been here in the employment of Mr. Thomson; or they, or some of them, may have been companions of Robinson in the removal from the other side of the Bay, if such removal actually took place. Of the whole number who were here before 1651, it appears that about thirty had their habitations at the Harbor, and that nineteen of these lived on the north border of the Harbor Cove; five had lots at Vinson's Cove; three resided on Duncan's Point, between the two coves; and two lived on the south-east side of Governor's Hill. About forty of the first settlers had houses on the "neck of house-lots;" by which term they usually designated that portion of the territory stretching north from Governor's Hill, and lying between Annisquam River and Mill River. Of the rest of these settlers, there is nothing to indicate the place of residence. The first settlers, or those before 1651, were not all here at one time. The records show frequent changes in the ownership of lots; and other circumstances give evidence that many of the persons who lived in town before that date were only brief sojourners. Of all the first-comers, not more than thirty became permanent citizens of the town. Before 1651, it is not certain that there was a single family residing in any other part of the town than the two sections above named, excepting one or two on the easterly side of Mill River; but, soon after that year, settlers are found near Little Good Harbor, at Walker's Creek, at Little River, at Fresh-water Cove, and at Annisquam. A few years later, inhabitants gathered around the coves on the north side of the Cape; and finally, about the end of the century, the head of the Cape itself received a few permanent occupants; Kettle Cove had become the abode of one family or more; and no considerable district of the town now remained unoccupied to attract the attention of new-comers.

The spots selected by most of the early settlers for their homes were chosen with reference to the fitness of the soil for agricultural purposes; and such is the rugged and broken character of the territory, that even the small number of people that then composed its population covered almost every acre of land that could be easily cultivated. Nearly all of the first settlers had land in several different places. Besides their home-lots, those who resided in the Harbor had grants at Fisherman's Field; and those living on the neck of house-lots had them on "Planter's Neck, between Lobster Cove and the sea." Possessing thus different lots in widely separated places, without, in many instances, any mention of a house, the exact spot on which every settler located himself cannot be ascertained. Many of them had grants which were not recorded; and, of those which are recorded, a few are stated to have been made by the commissioners of the General Court: some are entered simply as given, some as purchases, and some as possessions. Planter's

Neck, where lots were early laid out and numbered, was at Annisquam,—the spot which tradition has always reported to have been the first to receive permanent occupants. Abraham Robinson and his companions may have set up their fishery there, as early mention is made of a "stage" at that place; but no evidence exists now to show that any of the earliest families resided there. Robinson owned land, and a house, the location of which no one can tell; but in it, says the record, "he lived and died,"—the first of the early settlers that passed away to the great congregation of the dead.*

* The sources from which I have derived the information given in this chapter are too numerous to be mentioned here in detail. The town-records, of course, have furnished a considerable portion; and, of these, it is proper that this work should give some account. The first book is a folio of medium size, with a thin parchment cover, and is much dilapidated and worn. Its continued preservation is secured by the use of a copy made in 1850, having a full index, and the certificate of J. P. Trask, Esq., the town-clerk that year, to its correctness. The first part of the venerable original is itself a copy from a previous book, as appears by the first entry, in these words: "Gloucester Records of all the Land, drawn out of the first Book of Records, from the first ordering, settling, and disposing of it, until the 15th of August, 1650; and by whom disposed." The first recorder was Obadiah Bruen, who removed to New London in 1650, and carried with him the original record. Tradition says that he took it because the town would not pay for the book; but this seems improbable, considering that he left in another volume, in his own handwriting, what we must conceive to have been the most important part of that which he carried away. In our book, next to the first entry above extracted, follows a notice of "the first ordering, settling, and disposing of lots by Mr. Endicott and Mr. Downing, commissioners in 1642;" then a list of the persons appointed by the commissioners to order the prudential affairs of the town that year, and of those chosen by the town for the same business in the eight years immediately following; next come "Orders made and published for the good of the town since the first settling of it," in Mr. Bruen's chirography, till 1650; and then follows "Land given and disposed of, and to whom." The rest of the volume is almost entirely occupied with records of grants, and transfers of land, till we come to a few pages at the end, which contain lists of the selectmen and a few other town-officers for a number of years, and some proceedings in town-meetings. A regular and orderly record of transactions in town-meetings is commenced in the second volume of the records, in 1693; and is continued, with a slight hiatus, down to the present time. The second and third volumes have been rebound within a few years, and furnished with full indexes. Two volumes of commoners' records contain the proceedings of that body after they ceased to be mixed with those of the town, and all the divisions and grants and sales of land not recorded in the book first mentioned. These three books give the original individual ownership of nearly every acre of our territory. The commoners' books have been recently furnished with indexes, and rebound; and are now in excellent condition. The selectmen's proceedings are recorded in several books, commencing as far back as 1698. The earlier volumes contain a variety of interesting transactions. They need a new binding, and are well worth the additional expense of an index. Three small, narrow books, two of which are quite thin, contain

the births, deaths, and marriages to about 1785. To that date, these records show but few omissions: but, after that time, very few deaths are recorded for more than a hundred years; and it is evident that many births also are not entered. The fourth volume continues the marriages and births to about 1776. Two of these volumes are not fit for use; and, fortunately for their preservation, there is little occasion now to refer to them, as their contents have been transferred, in an abbreviated form, to a new volume, in which they are alphabetically arranged. Such are the early town-records. The church and parish records have also furnished information for the last chapter. The records of the First Church commence with the ministry of Rev. John White. Those of the other churches and of the parishes begin with the organization of the parishes respectively. The records of the several churches are valuable for their lists of baptisms; and these should secure their careful preservation. In the preparation of this work, I have minutely examined twenty volumes of these local records; and I trust that no more serious fault will be found with the use I have made of them, than that I may have failed to reduce their various spelling of proper names to a uniform orthography. The town-records were kept at the house or place of business of the town clerk till 1844, when a Town House was erected, in which a safe place of deposit was provided for them.

CHAPTER V.

First Selectmen. — Ship Built in the Town. — First Church. — Rev. Richard Blynman: his Ministry, Removal, Death, and Character. — First Meeting-House. — First Tax. — William Perkins, Minister of the Town: his Removal and Death. — Mill. — Rev. John Emerson Settled: his Ministry, Death, and Family. — New Meeting-House.

Under the authority with which they were invested by the General Court before the town was incorporated, the commissioners appointed eight men to manage the affairs of the plantation for 1642. These were William Stevens, Mr. Sadler, Obadiah Bruen, George Norton, Mr. Addes, Mr. Milward, Mr. Fryer, and Walter Tybbot. They were to order all the concerns of the settlement; and probably did so till they were superseded in the next year by selectmen* chosen by the town. The regulations made by these men, and many of the orders passed by the town, in the course of the ten following years, relate to trees and timber. One of them mentions, "11th, 9 mo. 1642," a highway † to be laid out through the lots of Messrs. Fryer, Tybbot, and Calkin.

Another, passed a few years later, indicates the employment of a portion of the settlers. It declares that "all ship-carpenters that build vessels of greater or lesser burthen shall pay unto the Town, before the Launching of any vessel, one shilling a Ton unto such as the Townsmen shall appoint; or pay, as a delinquent of Town order, ten pence a tree. Neither shall they be permitted to improve or transport boards, planks, clapboards, boults, hoop staves, fire wood, or any Timber more than other

* See Appendix, II. † See Appendix, III.

men, but only in building vessels in the Town." A ship was built in the town as early as 1643, by Mr. Stevens and other ship-carpenters, for one Mr. Griffin. Unhappily for the credit of some of the workmen, a letter has been preserved, which shows that they were guilty of such misdemeanors as required the interference of the Colony Government, and called forth an order to proceed against them with force.* An historian† of this period takes notice of the "good timber for shipping" to be found here, and of several vessels that had been built in the town. He also mentions "a very sufficient builder;" in allusion, without doubt, to our eminent shipwright, William Stevens: but neither from him nor any other source is any further information to be derived concerning the employment of our early settlers in this interesting occupation.

A committee, appointed by the General Court to settle the westerly boundary of the town, made their report on the 3d of the third month, 1642; in which they say, "That all the land lyinge between Ipswich and Cape-Ann Meeting-house shall be divided, six miles to Ipswich, and four to Cape Ann, where there are ten miles, and soe by proportion where lesse; that is, by ffyftes; three parts to Ipswich for two to Cape Ann; and, where there is more than ten myles, the remainder to lie to Jefferie's Creek, and this to be measured by the next General Court."

The settlers of Cape Ann, with a minister among their number, were, of course, soon organized into a church government. But, before proceeding to this part of our history, it is necessary to allude to the Christian worship of which our territory was the scene for a few years immediately preceding the arrival of Mr. Blynman in 1642.

Religious motives and feelings have ever been among the chief springs of human action. Under their influence, a band of Christian Pilgrims established the first permanent settlement in New England, at Plymouth; and, though religion was of less weight among the moving causes that led to the foundation of

* See Endicott's letter to Gov. Winthrop, in Hazard's Coll.

† Johnson; Wonder-working Providence. — Mass. Hist. Coll., vol. xvii. p. 32.

the Massachusetts Colony, it entered largely into the hopes and views of the settlers. It has been seen that provision was made for the religious wants of the first occupants of our soil; and, of those who came next, it has been stated, that "the first settlers of Cape Ann were early solicitous to set up and maintain the public worship of God among them. Though they were few in numbers, and strangers in the land, yet, like Abraham, as soon as they pitched their tent, they set up an altar; i.e., they agreed on a place where they might meet for the public worship of God on the sabbath."* So they continued, probably, to carry on their exercises of prayer and praise, till they had the services of "master Rashley," who was found here as chaplain, by an English visitor to the country, about 1640. By whose invitation he came, whether by that of Mr. Thomson (if he, indeed, established a company here) or by that of settlers on the spot, can never probably be known. He was some time member of the church in Boston; and, in 1652, was officiating as minister at Bishop-Stoke, England.

The first gathering of believers here into organization as a church was the work of Rev. Richard Blynman. This took place in 1642; and the church then gathered, and of which he was the first pastor, was the nineteenth, in the order of formation, in the Colony of Massachusetts. Neither record nor tradition has handed down any account of its members or its early proceedings; nor, in fact, of its history for sixty years.

Mr. Blynman was a native of Great Britain, and was minister of Chepstow in Monmouthshire. He came to New England, with several Welsh gentlemen of good note, by invitation of Edward Winslow of Plymouth; and settled near him, at Green's Harbor (now Marshfield), in that Colony. Dissensions soon arose, of which no particular information is preserved; and Mr. Blynman crossed the Bay, and fixed his residence here. Concerning these dissensions, an early work† on affairs in New England, in a note of "occurrences touching Episcopacie," says,

* Rev. E. Forbes's Sermon, preached in September, 1792.

† Lechfords Plaine Dealing.

"Master Wilson* did lately ride to Green's Harbor, in Plymouth Patent, to appease a broyle between one master Thomas, (as I take it his name is) and master Blindman, where master Blindman went by the worst;" and concludes with an intimation that the latter was forced to leave.

Mr. Blynman received several grants of land here; among which was one of eighty acres at Kettle Cove, long called the Blynman Farm. His dwelling is supposed to have been near the Meeting-house, where it is known that he had a lot. He continued his labors here till 1649. The exact date of his departure is not known; but an entry in the Massachusetts-Colony Records makes it appear that he was here in September, 1649, when Anthony Day petitioned the court against him for tearing a writ he had taken out against William Vinson. Mr. Blynman was called before the court for this offence, and acknowledged the fact; and as he did not do it out of any contempt of authority, but only to stop the proceeding that the matter might be privately healed, he was let off with an admonition "to beware of the like rash carridge for time to come." He was living in New London, November, 1650; having gone on in advance of the rest of the company which, about that time, emigrated from Gloucester to that place. He remained there, preaching to the Indians as well as to his own people, till 1658, when he removed to New Haven; and, after a short stay in that place, returned to England. On his way, he stopped at Newfoundland; where he declined an invitation to settle, notwithstanding his ministry was "acceptable to all the people, except some Quakers, and much desired and flocked unto." Having reached his native land, he took up his abode at Bristol; and, in 1670, was living with his wife in the castle in that city. He died at an advanced age. A short time before his death, he published an essay tending to settle the controversy about infant-baptism. His wife's name was Mary; and their children, born in Gloucester, were — Jeremiah, born in 1642; Ezekiel, 1643; and Azarikam, 1646.

Unhappy dissensions drove Mr. Blynman from the scene of

* Rev. John Wilson of Boston Church, probably.

his first ministry in New England; and the ill-treatment he received from some of his people here may have hastened, if it did not induce, his departure from the town. His church was defamed; his public meetings were disturbed; and he himself was scoffingly spoken of for what he had formerly delivered in the way of the ministry.* But he appears to have worked undisturbed in the other fields of his labor, and to have lived in peaceful and harmonious relations with all. He was greeted with the loving salutations of eminent men; and a contemporary writer† describes him as a man "of a sweet, humble, heavenly carriage," who labored much against the errors of the times. The same writer also makes him the subject of the following lines: —

"Thou hast thy prime and middle age here spent:
The best is not too good for him that gave it.
When thou didst first this wilderness frequent,
For Sion's sake it was, that Christ might save it.
Blindman be blith in him, who thee hath taken
To feed his flock, a few poor scattered sheep.
Why should they be of thee at all forsaken?
Thy honor's high, that any thou mayst keep.
Wait patiently thy Master's coming: thou
Hast hitherto his people's portions dealt.
It matters not for high preferment: now
Thy crown's to come, with joyes immortal felt."

There is nothing in the town-records about the erection of the first Meeting-house;‡ but these records show that the first settlers had a place of public worship, and they corroborate the tradition which points out the spot on which it was located. An order passed for assigning a piece of land for a burial-ground, Feb. 8, 1644, says, "that, at the end of these lots (viz., Mr. Blynman's, Thomas Jones's, Thomas Kent's, and Tho. Skillings's, betwixt and the old meeting-house place) shall be half an acre laid out for a common burial-place." This language

* One of these disturbers of the peace of the church, John Stone of Gloucester, was fined fifty shillings at a court, Aug. 27, 1644. Besides the marriage of a daughter in town, he is not otherwise connected with our history.

† Johnson, in his Wonder-Working Providence, Mass. Hist. Coll., vol. xvii. p. 32.

‡ Rev. E. Forbes, in his sermon at the dedication of the Town Grammar-school House, 1795, says, "So long ago as in 1638, the first settlers of this town consecrated a house for public worship."

will perhaps justify an inference, that, even at this early period, the second Meeting-house had been built, and that the one mentioned in the order was erected by earlier inhabitants than Mr. Blynman and his company. In a grant of land to Sylvester Eveleth, recorded next after a grant bearing date December, 1648, allusion is made to his house on Meeting-house Hill: and in April, 1653, it is recorded that Christopher Avery and John Collins measured the Meeting-house plain, and found it "39 rods from the creek and William Evans's fence; and from the north-west corner of Goodman Wakley's fence to Mr. Perkins's fence, 20 and a half rods; and from Mr. Perkins's garden fence over straight east to Goodman Wakley's fence, 17 1–2 rods." From these allusions, and other notices of the Meeting-house Plain of subsequent date, it appears probable that a house of worship was erected, soon after the incorporation of the town, on or near the spot occupied by three successive buildings for this purpose, about half a mile north of the place indicated as the site of the first one.

At a General Court held the 8th September, 1642, it was ordered "that Glocester is to have ten muskets of the country's lent them;" and in 1644, at the request of the town, the court ordered that George Norton, as their eldest sergeant, should exercise their military company.

The rank of the town the first year of its incorporation, in pecuniary importance, is shown in the proportion of a Colony rate levied upon it of a tax of £800. The proportion for Gloucester was £6. 10s.; that of Ipswich being £82; Salem, £75; and Lynn, £45.

The first deputy or representative* to the General Court was George Norton, who served in 1642, 1643, and 1644. The first board of selectmen, or, as the records call them, officers for "ordering town affairs," chosen by the town, consisted of William Stevens, Walter Tybbot, George Norton, Hugh Calkins, and Obadiah Bruen. Three of these — Stevens, Norton, and Bruen — also acted under authority of the General Court as

* See Appendix, IV.

commissioners to end small causes. Other persons who received appointment to public offices soon after this time were Thomas Smith, William Stevens, and Walter Tybbot, commissioners to end small controversies; Christopher Avery, measurer, to lay out lots granted by the town; also constable, and clerk of the market and of the band. Walter Tybbot was allowed to draw wines, paying twenty shillings per annum rent or fine.

The removal of Mr. Blynman to New London not only deprived the church here of its pastor, but weakened its ability to procure another to supply his place; for, as has been before stated, his departure was followed by that of a considerable portion of the settlers, who accompanied him thither. It does not appear that any measures were immediately taken by the town to settle a minister; but religious worship was not neglected. The pious edification and instruction of the people became the subject of attention soon after Mr. Blynman left, as appears by an order of the selectmen passed on the 30th December, 1649, providing "that 10 acres of upland shall be reserved, and laide out, for a teaching Elder, near to the place of the old meeting-house, upon the plaine lying neere to the Swampe betweene the harbor and the plantation; and soe to be reserved unto the use of teachinge Elders unto all posteritie. Alsoe half an acre of Upland reserved for the Towne to build an house upon for the use of teachinge Elders under the meeting-house where now it stands. Likewise 10 acres of fresh marsh in the marsh yt lyeth above the head of Little River."

Other encouragement was probably held out, which induced the removal hither, from Weymouth, of William Perkins, to become the spiritual guide of the little band of worshippers then living here. He settled in Gloucester in 1650. In September of that year, ten acres of land at the head of Mr. Blynman's lot, called the Plains, were granted to him. This was undoubtedly the same lot mentioned in the order above given. He also had the marsh reserved for teaching elders, and bought of Obadiah Bruen "all that was his right in Gloucester." A Captain Perkins owned land here in 1647; and, though the change from the military to the clerical profession is an unusual one, there is sufficient reason to believe that he was the same person who afterwards became the minister of the town.

Mr. Perkins was son of William Perkins, merchant-tailor of London, by Katharine his wife; and was born Aug. 25, 1607. It is supposed that he was in New England as early as 1633, and that he was one of the company that went with Mr. Winthrop that year and commenced the settlement of Ipswich. He was made a freeman in 1634. He married Elizabeth Wootten, Aug. 30, 1636, at Roxbury. He removed from Roxbury to Weymouth; and, in 1644, was representative from that town, and leader of its military band. He remained in Gloucester till 1655; when he sold his houses and land here to Thomas Millet, sen., and removed to Topsfield, where he died May 21, 1682. He had several children. Mary, the only one whose birth is recorded here, was born in 1651, and married Oliver Purchas, September, 1672. The town-records were left by Mr. Bruen in the hands of Mr. Perkins; who delivered them by vote of the town, Aug. 24, 1651, to William Stevens.

Tradition says that Mr. Perkins preached in Topsfield five or six years immediately following his removal into the town. No means exist for ascertaining his rank in the church, nor the exact office that he filled in it. It is not known that he was ever set apart for the work of the ministry by ordination, or that he was recognized by the ministers of his time as a fellow-laborer of equal standing and authority in the vineyard of the Lord. Our records are silent, and tradition has not one word to say, in reference to his office or his labors here; and it is only by the Quarterly-Court Records that he appears at all to have been a laborer in spiritual things. These present him as a defendant in actions brought by a factious member of his congregation; but they contain nothing more serious against him than the reason alleged by a silly woman, in justification of her absence from meeting, that the teacher was "fitter to be a lady's chamberman than to be in the pulpit."

Although, as has been stated on a preceding page, vessels had, at this period, been built in the town, and many of the orders passed by the settlers and the selectmen were for the regulation of their proceedings with respect to timber, boards, and plank, there is no mention of a sawmill before 1653. As early as 1644, the Colony Government granted the town twenty pounds out of a fund left to it for benevolent purposes by Richard Andrews, a godly man of London. This sum was to be expended towards erecting a mill here; but it is not known that it was applied to that use. In February, 1653, a vote was passed by the town, authorizing the erection of a sawmill without naming the stream on which it was to be located, or mentioning the grantees of the privilege. The latter were to enjoy their grant twenty-one years, with the condition that they should sell to inhabitants of the town "1s. per hundred Better cheap than they sell to strangers," and receive such pay as was "Raised in the towne."

The population of the town at this time was small, and, in regard to number, stationary. No accession of inhabitants had supplied the places of the large portion of the first settlers who had removed. Those, therefore, who still remained, wanting numerical strength, and needing all the scanty products of an ungenial soil and an uncertain fishery for their own support, contented themselves, for a few years after Mr. Perkins's departure, with such religious edification as the most gifted of their lay-brethren could afford. Here, again, the court-records are our chief source of information; and these, unhappily, present as litigants the two most gifted in endowments for teaching and exhortation. They show, under date of March, 1658, Thomas Millet, plaintiff, in an action of the case against William Stevens "for withholding a wrighting of the subscription of the inhabitants of Gloster for payment of their several sums to Mr. Millet for his labours among them, and his own proportion included, which is 50 shillings." The jury gave their verdict in favor of the plaintiff; but no permanent estrangement between the two brethren was produced, as may be inferred from their appointment by the court, in June, 1659, to exercise their gifts jointly for the edification of the inhabitants, who were ordered to meet in one place together to attend the public worship of God on the Lord's Day, and so to continue till Mr. Emerson should be here or come to settle.

Nearly two years before the date last given, the town had voted unanimously "to seek out in convenient time for a meete person to come and preach the word of God," and had also voted to raise fifty pounds a year for the maintenance of a minister or elder. From the allusion to Mr. Emerson in the court order, it is reasonable to conclude that the committee, composed of Mr. Stevens and Mr. Bartholomew, who were appointed to seek a minister, had already given him an invitation to settle here. A committee was chosen, in 1659, to treat with him; but it does not appear from any action of the town that he commenced his labors here before 1661. In July of that year, his salary was fixed at sixty pounds per annum as long as he should continue in the ministry; and he was to receive it in Indian corn, pease, barley, fish, mackerel, beef, or pork. From this time, therefore, Rev. John Emerson may be considered the settled pastor of the church.

Mr. Emerson was son of Thomas Emerson of Ipswich. He graduated at Harvard College in 1656; and was ordained as pastor of our church, Oct. 6, 1663. Rev. Mr. Higginson of Salem, with Messrs. Lothrop and Allen of his church, attended the ordination.

In 1672, the town voted that Mr. Emerson should have one-eighth of his salary in money; and afterwards, for several successive years, by a similar vote, he received one-fourth of it in money. In 1679, an addition of eight pounds was made to his salary, to provide him firewood; for which he was to preach a lecture every three weeks, from March to September. He had similar grants in after years, with like conditions annexed. It is not improbable that disputes sometimes arose in regard to the articles in which he received the largest part of his salary: so much, at least, may be inferred from a vote of the town, passed in 1684, appointing John Fitch, Thomas Judkin, and Joseph Allen, "to judge of any pay brought to Mr. Emerson for his salary, whether it be merchantable, and fit to pass from man to man." In 1673, the town voted that he should have eighty pounds to provide himself a house to dwell in. The place of his residence was on the south side of the highway leading from the Meeting-house Green to Fox Hill. He had thirty acres of land about his homestead, and thirty acres near the burying-place, besides other smaller lots. He was not indifferent to the secular concerns of life; for he became the sole or chief owner of the three principal mills in town: and, though not favorably located for the accumulation of property, he died possessed of a considerable estate. In addition to his property in Gloucester, he owned farms in Ipswich, which probably came to him by inheritance from his father. From the various sources of his worldly prosperity, he derived the pecuniary ability to settle one hundred pounds on his daughter Mary on the day of her marriage.

Mr. Emerson died Dec. 2, 1700, aged seventy-five. No information has come down to us concerning the rank he held among the ministers of his time; but, in the absence of all evidence to the contrary, it may be taken for granted that his character was such as to secure him a large place in the affections of the little flock, whom, to use the language of one of his successors, "he served more than forty years in the gospel of God's dear Son." But one article from his pen is known to be extant, — the account furnished by him, in a letter to Rev. Cotton Mather, of the strange and wonderful occurrences here in 1692. If we call to mind the witchcraft delusion of that year, by which a neighboring town was made the theatre of the most awful tragedy ever enacted in New England, we shall indulge in no astonishment that Mr. Emerson ascribed the cause of the excitement here to diabolical agency.

Mr. Emerson's wife was Ruth, daughter of Deputy-Gov. Symonds. She died Feb. 23, 1702. His children were — Ruth, born in 1660, married, first, John Newman, Esq., Dec. 1, 1683, and next, probably, Samuel Sargent; Martha, 1662, married William Cogswell* of Ipswich; Mary, 1664, married Samuel Phillips of Salem, May 26, 1687, and died Oct. 4, 1703; Elizabeth, 1667, died in 1683; John, 1670; Dorothy, 1675, married a Henchman; and Samuel, 1678, who died in 1687.

* William Cogswell is placed in the list of early settlers; but there appears to be no other reason for putting him there than that he had a son Edward born here Aug. 18, 1686.

JOHN, son of our minister, was a graduate of the first class of Harvard College that contained a native of Gloucester. He and John Eveleth, another native of the town, were both graduates of the class of 1689. He appears to have spent the first few years, after graduating, at home with his father; probably in preparation for the ministry. He preached a short time in Manchester; and, in 1701, was residing in Salem, from which place he removed to Ipswich, and in 1703, in a deed, called himself "gentleman" of that town. In May of the last-named year, he received an invitation to settle in the ministry at Newcastle, N.H., and was soon after ordained in that town; where he remained till 1712, when his pastoral connection with the church there was dissolved. He went from Newcastle to Portsmouth, where he was installed in 1715; and continued there till his death, June 21, 1732. Mr. Emerson made a voyage to England in 1708, spent some time in the city of London, and was handsomely noticed by Queen Ann. He married Mary, daughter of Edmund Batter of Salem, by whom he had six daughters who survived him, and several other children who died young.*

These may Certify whom it doth
Concerne that Neighbour Riggs
hath payd all his Rates to the Ministry
for former yeares & also for the
yeare Eighty Nine. John Emerson
Jan: 8: 1689.

---

* Who was the Mr. John Emerson, "a worthy preacher at Berwick," that narrowly escaped the sad fate of Major Waldron and twenty others, who were slain by the Indians at the destruction of the garrison at Dover, on the night of the 27th June, 1689, by declining an urgent invitation to lodge there that night? Belknap's History of New Hampshire, vol. i. p. 268, says he was the future minister of Newcastle and Portsmouth; but *he* was then only just nineteen, and had not graduated. Our State archives contain a document in these words: "1689, — This may certify, that, being sent eastward by the Governor and Council, when I came to Newichewannock (Berwick), Mr. John Emerson being about leaving that place, being helpful to us in his advice and council, and finding himself both house and furniture, served 11 weeks, — from 7th Sept., 1689, to Nov. 28, 1689." The same archives show that "Mr. Emerson, with Mr. Wise, Mr. Hale, and Mr. Rawson," were desired by vote of the Governor and Council, July, 1690, to accompany the general and forces in the expedition against Canada, — to carry on the worship of God in that expedition.

About the time of Mr. Emerson's settlement, a new meeting-house was erected, and was probably the third one built in the town. In 1660, the inhabitants agreed to gather by rate the sum of sixty pounds to build it, besides the boards that should be used upon it; and chose Robert Elwell and Clement Coldam to set forward the work. It was completed before 1664; as, in May of that year, the timber of the old one was in possession of John Kettle, who sold it, with a house and land in the vicinity of the Meeting-house, to Harlakenden Symonds. The building erected stood less than forty years. In 1686, the town voted to build two galleries in it, — one in the eastern, and one in the western end. Of its form, size, or the exact spot it occupied, no knowledge can now be obtained. It is known that it was located on the Meeting-house Plain; and the following item of expenditures upon it, in the year 1698, shows that it was furnished with a bell: —

" Building a galerie and ground celling some of ye house, and under pinning ye house	7.	7.	0.
Ringing the bell and sweeping the house	1.	4.	0.
A man halfe a day to bargain with a carpenter, and drink at ye same time		3.	0.
A paire of hinges for ye door cost money		1.	10."

No further occasion for allusion to the religious concerns of the town will present itself during the remainder of this century. Mr. Emerson's peaceful ministry expired with the closing month of this period. His congregation, small and weak at the time of his settlement, had about trebled in number; and was left by him in a state of increasing growth and prosperity, which enabled it, in the course of a few years, to send forth companies of worshippers to set up their own places of public religious devotion in remote sections of the town.

CHAPTER VI.

SHIP-BUILDING. — MILL. — CORD-WOOD. — MASON'S CLAIM. — INDIAN WAR OF 1675. — SAWMILL. — FIRST GENERAL GRANT OR DIVISION OF THE SOIL. — LIST OF GRANTEES. — ANDROS'S GOVERNMENT. — WITCHCRAFT. — TAX-LIST, 1693. — FERRY. — NEW MEETING-HOUSE. — BURYING-GROUND. — SCHOOL. — INDIAN CLAIM. — HOUSES AND FURNITURE OF FIRST SETTLERS. — SOME OF THEIR CUSTOMS.

THE early history of a New-England town of obscure situation, and insignificant importance in regard to business and population, must include, in order that its series of chronological events may not present too wide intervals, notices of many occurrences that derive their chief interest from the distant point of view from which they are contemplated, and from the fact that these occurrences took place on the scene of our own daily acts, and occupied the thoughts and conversation of the remote generations that preceded us here.

After a lapse of nearly twenty years, the noted shipwright of Gloucester, William Stevens, re-appears as the builder of a ship in the town. He may have built several during this period; but not till 1661 can any particular instance be given. In June of that year, he agreed with "John Brown, for himself and Nicolas and John Balbach of Jarssy, to build 1 new ship of 68 foot long by ye keele, and 23 foot broad from outside to outside, and 9 1-2 foot in ye hold under ye beam; with two decks, forecastle, quarter deck; ye deck from ye mainmast to ye forecastle to be 5 foot high, with a fall at ye forecastle 15 inches, and a raise at ye mainmast to ye quarter deck of 6 inches. The great cabbin to be 6 foot high. The sd Stevens to be paid the sum of £3. 5s. for every tunn of said ship's burthen." For part of his pay, he was to receive "£150 in good muscovadoes Shugar, at 2d. by the pound at Barbados." To how great an extent the business of ship-building may have been carried on for thirty or forty years subsequent to this time, cannot now be ascertained; but, in the early part of the next century, the town became the scene of great activity in this employment, and of the appearance of a remarkable man, who, by his connection with its marine interests, conferred upon it a wider and more enduring fame than had been gained for it by the builder of the great "Royal Merchant" of London.

Means of procuring daily food, and conveniences for preparing it, are matters of chief interest and concern at all times: and a mill for grinding their corn was therefore erected by the first settlers of the town; but no mention is made of the date of its erection. In 1664, the inhabitants granted the mill then standing and in use, with all the rights, privileges, ponds, and streams belonging to it, and all the fresh meadow above the mill, to their pastor, Mr. Emerson, on condition that he should maintain and keep that, or some other mill, in such "frame and order" that it could grind for the use of the town. They also signed a document, the intention of which, as far as can be judged from its loose phraseology, was to secure to him the patronage of the whole town. Some difficulty occurring in relation to this grant in 1695, three of the signers testified that it contained the names of all who were inhabitants or proprietors of the town, with one or two exceptions, at the time it was made. It possesses an interest, therefore, distinct from the subject to which it relates, as a source of information concerning the accession of settlers from 1650 to the period of its date. The names of these, affixed to the grant, were Samuel Abearsoke,* William Coleman, Samuel Deliber, Peter Duncan, John Davis, sen., James Davis, Jacob Davis, William Ellery, Richard Gooding, James Gardner, Edward Haraden, John Hammons, Thomas Millet, jun., Francis Norwood, Rowland Powell, sen., Jeffrey Parsons, Thomas Pinny, John Row, Thomas Riggs, Philip Stainwood, Richard Window, and one too illegibly written to be ascertained. From certain votes of the town, passed some years later, an inference may be

* This name is plainly written, but does not again appear in our records.

drawn that Mr. Emerson did not for a long period make any use of this grant; as, Feb. 18, 1677, the town voted that a cornmill should be set up and erected on the Sawmill Dam: and, "things not being made clear concerning the old saw-mill," a town-meeting was called on the 11th of March following; when, "upon much discourse about the mill, Mr. John Emerson, having undertaken to erect a corn mill, did promise in said meeting to set it upon the saw-mill dam, and to supply the town." At the same meeting, Mr. Emerson, John Fitch, and Thomas Riggs, were named as the proprietors of the old Sawmill, which they were to repair, and to have the privilege of cutting timber enough to make twenty thousand feet of boards yearly, for seven years. They were also to saw "at the halves," and to sell boards on a credit of three months to those who needed credit. No other mention of a cornmill is found till May 13, 1690; when William Haskell and Mark Haskell had liberty to erect one upon Walker's Creek.*

---

* The first mill in the town was undoubtedly erected, at a very early date, on the spot where part of an old dam is still to be seen, at the westerly end of the stream running from Cape Pond. Further information concerning the mills of the town may be desired by some; and I add it here.

1644. — The General Court granted to Gloucester £20 out of a gift of Richard Andrews, a godly man of London, towards erecting a mill.

Mention made of a mill in the grants to Hugh Calkin and Sylvester Eveleth.

1652. — "There was given by the town-meeting liberty to build a saw mill where they think fit," &c.

1661. — Town gives William Vinson leave to stop the water at the "fresh medoes," above his mill, and to make use of it for his mill.

1664, May. — William Vinson sells to Mr. Emerson, for £55, his gristmill and three and a half acres of land; the same being near Mr. Emerson's house.

1677, Feb. 18. — Town votes "that there should be a Corn Mill set up and erected on the saw-mill dam," and "that the town give the stream to belong to the Corn Mill." The "saw-mill dam" here mentioned is the place now occupied by the tide-mills of Messrs. Brackett and Brown.

1682. — Jacob Davis and others have liberty of the stream at the head of Little River to set up a sawmill. Jeffrey Parsons, sen., Samuel Sargent, and Job Coit, have liberty of a stream, or brook, between Fresh-water Cove and Kettle Cove, to set up a sawmill.

1689. — A committee chosen "to see that the Corn Mill be fitted to supply the town with grinding of their corn into meal, or els to see that another corn-mill may be set up."

1690. — "William Haskell, Jr., & Mark Haskell, made request to have liberty to set down a corn-mill upon a creek called Walker's Creek." Mr. John Emerson, William Vinson, Peter Duncan, and William Sargent, sen., "did protest against the voit."

The early inhabitants of the town were undoubtedly indebted to the forests, which covered their whole territory, for a considerable part of their living. The various acts of the town in reference to wood and timber authorize a belief that a traffic in these was early commenced. A few of the votes in relation to this matter, passed in town-meeting about this period, possess some interest.

Jan. 20, 1667, it was agreed "by the whole town" that cord-wood should be cut "from the eastern side of Brace's Cove to Little Good Harbor, forty poles from the sea side up into the woods; and from Little Good Harbor, round the head of the Cape, to Plum Cove." — "No cord-wood shall be cut to sell out

---

1693. — Joseph Allen and others had a grant of the stream formerly granted to Jeffrey Parsons and others, "that they forfitted."

1698. — John Row is about to repair his sawmill.

In division of Rev. J. Emerson's estate, John Newman has the fulling-mill, "standing on a creek, or small river, on the northwardly side of a lane or highway leading from the Meeting House up into the woods:" and William Cogswell has "a quarter part of the grist-mill and saw-mill standing on the saw-mill river, so called; and a quarter of the house and three acres of land belonging to said mill."

1701. — Thomas Witham and John Pool have liberty to set up a grist or corn mill on Davison's Run, at Sandy Bay.

1702. — John Haraden has the privilege of the stream that runs into Hogskin Cove.

1704. — William Cogswell represents gristmill on Sawmill River out of repair; and proposes to put it in order, and supply the town.

1709. — Children of William Cogswell sell mills, &c., in Gloucester, to John Ring.

1720. — Town grants to John Bennet "the privilege of the brook called the fulling mill brook, whereon to set a corn-mill on the lower end of the brook, near where the tide ebbs and flows, so long as he keeps a corn-mill on said stream, and no longer."

1721. — Ruth Newman and her children sell Fulling-mill Stream to John Bennet, with mill Bennet had built.

1724. — John Ring, in a lawsuit against John Bennet, claims certain privileges, and the stream on which Bennet's mill stood, under various grants to Mr. Emerson. Judgment in favor of Bennet is carried by Ring to a higher court. The town favors Bennet's cause.

1755. — "Francis Norwood entered miller of that gristmill whereof his father Jonathan Norwood is owner."

1776. — Town chooses a committee to see that Ring's Mills are put in good repair.

1777. — Isaac Bennet, miller for Ring's Mills, engages to repair the same.

1832. — Town chooses a committee to appraise and dispose of privileges at Goose-cove Dam.

1833. — Town sells to Zachariah Stevens, by quitclaim deed, Bennet's-Mill Stream, for $350. Mr. Stevens was then the owner of "Ring's Mills."

A valuation of Massachusetts in 1771 has, for Gloucester, "15 1-2 grist-mills, fulling mills, and saw-mills."

of town upon the south side of the path that goes to Salem, till they come to the Great Swamp." The forfeit for violation of this order was ten shillings for every cord of wood cut in disobedience of it. At the same time, the town also vote that "there shall be none cut on the north-east side of the path that we used to go in before the new way was marked out from Goodman Parson's house, round the head of Little River, to Goodman Haskell's."

Dec. 29, 1669.—"It was agreed that there should be no cord-wood sold out of town under three shillings and sixpence per cord." At the same time, liberty is given to cut cord-wood at a place near Goose Cove, with the restriction that no family should cut above twenty cords. Many other votes concerning the cutting of wood were passed in following years; and they all indicate a watchful care of the forest. For several successive years, every family was permitted to cut twenty cords on the town's Common for its own use; but measures were taken to see that all who exceeded this quantity were called upon for the penalty for so doing.

An early emigrant to Massachusetts mentions a report, that "lions have been seen at Cape Ann;" but foxes appear to have been the first wild animals concerning which the early settlers were called to take public action. "25th 11mo. 1668.—The order, that there should be two pence given by the town to every inhabitant for every fox that they did kill, was voted down."*

The inhabitants of Gloucester were deeply interested in a law which was early passed in the Colony, giving to riparian proprietors of the soil certain privileges to low-water mark: but these privileges were not so clearly defined as to satisfy the people; at least, so much may be inferred from an answer of the General Court to a petition of our people in relation to thatch-banks in 1669, wherein the court declares, "that where towns do not grant their lands to the rivers, but otherwise bound men's

* The early records mention a wolf-pen. In 1707, Ezekiel Woodward killed three wolves. In 1713, John Lane, sen., was paid £1. 10s. for killing "a grown wolve." In 1754, the town allowed £4 for killing a grown wolf, and £2 for killing a young one within three and a half miles of the north line of the town.

lands that lie by the river-side, that they have not liberty to claim further right by the said law."

In 1671, the town again appears as a petitioner to the General Court. In their petition, they refer to the original boundary of the town granted by the court, which, they state, "they have quietly possessed and enjoyed, till now of late years, to our great damage and wrong, we are disturbed and disquieted." They conclude by praying the court to maintain and confirm the rights formerly granted to them, "against their disturbers and opposers." These disturbers were probably the heirs of Capt. John Mason, who, by virtue of the grant of a large tract of country, including Cape Ann, made to their ancestor, were now endeavoring to enforce their claim to the territory. This claim was allowed by an inhabitant of Salem, and satisfied by the payment of a small annual rent; but, after the opinion of eminent legal authority in England against its validity had been pronounced, it was treated generally as groundless and extravagant, and entitled to no regard. The people of Gloucester, Ipswich, and Beverly, strenuously resisted it in 1681; and, soon after, appear to have been relieved from all annoyance respecting it.

Among "memorable accidents" at this period, an historian* of New England mentions, that, in 1671, "a whirlwind at Cape Ann passed through the neck of land that makes one side of the harbor, towards the main sea. Its space or breadth was about forty feet from the sea to the harbor; but it went with such violence, that it bore away whatever it met in the way. Both small and great trees, and the boughs of trees that on each side hung over that glade, were broken off, and carried away therewith. A great rock, that stood up in the harbour as it passed along, was scarce able to withstand the fury of it, without being turned over."

A few years following this event are marked with no occurrences in the history of the town deserving permanent record; but a period was now approaching which was to include the most

---

* Hubbard, 628.

exciting and important transactions that had agitated and alarmed the public mind since the settlement of the country. The chapter which relates these memorable events is filled with deeds of savage warfare and barbarity, and impresses our mind with painful reflections upon the sad fate of those who fell in ambuscade or open fight before the Indian foe; and the more melancholy doom of the helpless women and children, who, overcome with dread and terror, became the unresisting victims of the tomahawk and scalping-knife.

The Indian War of 1675 afflicted few of the small settlements of New England less than it did Gloucester. The isolated situation of the town, bounded on the west by a tract of country too thickly peopled to be crossed by the enemy, and, on every other side, protected by the sea, must have saved it from great apprehensions of assault, though not, perhaps, from some degree of alarm. In all this troubled period, there is no record that any hostile Indian set his foot on our soil; nor is it known that more than one person belonging to the town fell in fight during the war. Hostilities first commenced in Plymouth Colony, in June; but the theatre of the war was soon changed to the western part of Massachusetts, whither the great chief and leader of the savages (King Philip) had fled. In this section many depredations were committed by the enemy, and severe losses by fight and surprise were sustained by the English. In the fall, a large force was called out for the more vigorous prosecution of the war; and, as it was raised by levy upon all the towns, Gloucester was required to contribute its proportion of soldiers from the military company of the place. The persons thus draughted were Andrew Sargent, Joseph Clark, Joseph Somes, Joseph Allen, Jacob Davis, Vincent Davis, Thomas Kent, and Hugh Rowe; "all wch," as added by the officer who made return of the names of the men draughted, "due want warm cloathing, and must have new coates."

It is not known how many of the above-named persons served in the war; but it is quite probable that some of them provided substitutes. We are able to add to this list several names of Gloucester soldiers, though no information can be given of the time or place of their service. The town-records furnish these additional names, and show, that, Dec. 16, 1679, the persons who bore them had lots of land granted at Kettle Cove for their "service in the Indian war." Among these grantees appear only Joseph Clark and Hugh Rowe of the foregoing list; though Timothy Somes drew a lot for Joseph Somes, who fell in the war. The remaining eleven of the fourteen, which was the whole number of the grantees at this date, were John Bray, Nathaniel Bray, John Day, Moses Dudy, John Fitch, John Haskell, Edward Haraden, Isaac Prince, Samuel Stanwood, John Stanwood, and Philip Stanwood. In 1696, John Babson had a lot that fell to his brother, Thomas Babson; and the records show that Benjamin Jones was also entitled to a lot. In 1676, Dudy and Babson were both on duty in the garrison at Hadley; and a request was sent to the General Court for their discharge. It seems, then, that sixteen men from Gloucester enlisted in this memorable war; a number equal, it is supposed, to nearly one-fourth of all its male citizens at that time who were capable of bearing arms. This large levy shows the exigency of the occasion, and proves that the struggle on both sides was for the possession of the soil.

A committee of the General Court, appointed to ascertain the preparations made for defence by certain towns, reported that Cape Ann had made two garrisons besides several particular fortifications. This was in March, 1676; about the same time that the Indians were committing some depredations at Andover and other places in its vicinity, and when they seemed too near for the town to be left without sufficient means of defence. Before the end of the summer, the great leader of the Indians, and the master-spirit who was at the head of the general rising of his race in arms, — Philip, — was slain on Mount Hope; leaving a name that will always be associated with every thing ferocious in savage warfare, and with the highest bravery and patriotism of the most renowned chieftains of the civilized races of men.

Up to this period, no general division or grant of any part of the territory of the town had been made; but on the 27th February, 1688, the town voted, that every householder and young man, upwards of twenty-one years of age, that was born in town, and was then living in town, and bearing charges to town and county, should have six acres of land. Among the conditions annexed were one, that the inhabitants should be permitted to cut wood upon these lots for their own use; and another, securing to the people a free passage through them for certain purposes to the water-side. In accordance with this vote, eighty-two lots, all numbered, — beginning at Flat-stone Cove, and terminating at Back Beach, Sandy Bay, — were laid out to persons living on the easterly side of the Cut. The inhabitants on the westerly side of the Cut had their lots where they chose to select them in their part of the town. The Cape lots were drawn by the following persons; namely: —

Joseph Allen.
Richard Babson.
John Babson.
Ebenezer Babson.
Anthony Bennett.
Nathaniel Bray.
John Bray.
Joseph Clark.
Joanna Collins.
Ezekiel Collins.
John Cook.
Job Coit.
Anthony Day.
Ezekiel Day.
John Day.
Thomas Day.
Nathaniel Day.
James Davis, jun.
William Dolliver.
Peter Duncan.
Isaac Elwell, sen.
Isaac Elwell, jun.
Jacob Elwell.
Robert Elwell.
Samuel Elwell.
William Ellery.
Rev. John Emerson.
John Emerson, jun.
Isaac Eveleth's heirs.
Sylvester Eveleth.
John Fitch.
Bartholomew Foster.
Joseph Gardner.
Stephen Glover.
John Hadley.
Edward Haraden.
John Haraden.
Sarah Haraden.
John Hammon.
Samuel Hodgkins.
Henry Joslyn.
Thomas Judkin.
Thomas Millet, sen.
Same, another lot.
John Millet.
Francis Norwood.
Francis Norwood, jun.
Jeffrey Parsons.
John Pearce.
Isaac Prince.
Thomas Prince, sen.
Thomas Prince, jun.
Thomas Riggs, sen.
Thomas Riggs, jun.
Abraham Robinson.
Hugh Row.
James Row.
John Row, sen.
John Row, jun.
William Sargent, sen.
William Sargent, jun.
William Sargent, 2d.
John Sargent.
Samuel Sargent.
Nathaniel Somes.
Timothy Somes.

Morris Smith.
Robert Skamp.
James Stevens.
James Stevens, jun.
William Stevens.
Samuel Stevens.
Philip Stanwood.
Samuel Stanwood.
John Stanwood.
Jonathan Stanwood.
Thomas Very.
William Vinson.
Thomas Witham.
Henry Witham.

Here are but eighty names. John Elwell claimed and received a lot in another place, in 1707, on the ground of his absence when the Cape lots were given.

On the westerly side of the Cut, thirty-one lots were laid out, according to the following alphabetical arrangement of the grantees' names; namely: —

Thomas Bray, sen.
Thomas Bray, jun.
John Clark.
Peter Coffin.
Nathaniel Coit.
Richard Dolliver.
Jacob Davis.
James Davis.
Richard Dike.
Timothy Day.
William Haskell, sen.
William Haskell, jun.
Benjamin Haskell.
Joseph Haskell.
Mark Haskell.
Nathaniel Hadlock.
Josiah Kent.
Thomas Lufkin.
Thomas Lufkin, jun.
Nathaniel Millet.
John Pulcifer.
Thomas Penny, deceased.
Jeffrey Parsons, sen.
James Parsons.
John Parsons.
Andrew Sargent.
John Sargent.
James Sawyer.
Henry Walker.
Rev. John Wise of Chebacco, for house bought of Thomas Penny.
Humphrey Woodbury.

Of the foregoing list of persons, Dolliver and the Parsonses were probably the only ones living on the Manchester Road; the rest being on the Chebacco side of the town, on or near the highway leading to Ipswich.

These lists exhibit one extraordinary fact in the history of the town, — the small increase of its population by immigration for a period of twenty-four years. At the time these grants were made, it does not appear that there were then living in the town more than fifteen males of adult age who had emigrated hither since 1664; nor does it seem that the number of transient settlers in the same time had been considerable: a fact which shows the unattractiveness of the spot in those early times for all but such as had occasion to "go down to the sea in ships, and do business in great waters." These, however, began to multiply in a few years, as the town became engaged in different branches of maritime pursuits.

While the people were thus adding to their individual property, the value of their estates was impaired by the unjust and tyrannical measures of the Governor of New England, — Sir Edmund Andros; the creature of the hated monarch, whose advances towards despotism were happily checked by the revolution which placed the Prince of Orange on the English throne. The Colony Charter, under which the people of Massachusetts had enjoyed liberty and prosperity from its settlement, had, after ineffectual struggles on their part to retain it, fallen into the king's hands. The death of the king, the next year, left the colonists at the mercy of his successor, James II.; who found in Andros a fit instrument for the exercise of his hostile designs against them. The rule of this governor, so arbitrary and oppressive, and exercised upon a people accustomed to great political privileges, aroused, as might have been expected, deep indignation and open resistance. Some "feeble but magnanimous efforts of expiring freedom" were exhibited in the refusal of several towns to assess the taxes which the Governor and his Council levied upon them. One of these towns was Gloucester, seven of whose citizens — namely, William Haskell, sen., James Stevens, Thomas Riggs, sen., Thomas Millet, Jeffrey Parsons, Timothy Somes, and William Sargent, sen. — were fined at the Superior Court in Salem for the non-compliance of the town with a warrant for the assessment of one of those odious taxes in the year 1688. The first five of these citizens were the selectmen of the town in that year, and Somes was its constable. In their "complaint" of the abuses and wrongs to which they were subjected, they mention the visit to the town of the justices to bind them over for their appearance at court, and their payment, in addition to the expense of the bonds, of "the Shott for said justices by their order at the Taverne;"

stating that the "Totall for the first bout was three pounds fifteen shillings money." At court, all but Somes were fined forty shillings each; to which three pounds one shilling each were added for fees. Somes was let off with the payment of fees only, on the evidence of the rest, that he, as constable, had but fulfilled his duty in the matter. The whole amount of expenses in the case was forty-two pounds seven shillings.

From the events just related, it may naturally be inferred that the daring rise of the people in Boston against the governor, and their imprisonment of him and his most obnoxious associates, met the cordial approbation and received the warm support of the inhabitants of Gloucester; and that, when the question came up in town-meeting soon afterwards, in regard to re-assuming the old government under the charter, and defending it with their persons and estates, there "was a full and clear vote in the affirmative," as a record of the meeting states.

The arrival of Sir William Phips, Governor, with the new Charter, in May, 1692, terminated the political anxieties of the people of Massachusetts, though their former privileges were not fully restored. The people, however, only emerged from a condition of suspense and fear, with regard to their political affairs, to be cast into one of unutterable sorrow and dismay on account of the awful descent of evil spirits from the invisible world. The memorable and extraordinary delusion of witchcraft, which distinguishes this year from all others in the history of the State, began its work early in 1692, and continued till the beginning of the next year. The scene of its terrible results is well known. Among those first imprisoned, charged with this fancied crime, was Abigail Somes, who is supposed to have been the daughter of Timothy Somes of this town. She was confined in Boston Jail from May 23, 1692, to Jan. 3, 1693, but escaped trial and death. Ann, wife of Capt. William Dolliver of Gloucester, was also accused of witchcraft, but did not become a victim. About the time that reason was beginning to re-assume its sway over the minds of the people, some "accusers were sent for to Gloucester, and occasioned four women to be sent to prison." Again they were sent for, by Lieut. Stephens, who was told that a sister of his was bewitched; and, though they started for the town, it is not known that they continued their journey till they reached it.

Although our people were drawn into no very intimate connection with the Salem tragedy, they were not saved from great excitement and alarm, which were attributed to the same cause. About midsummer, 1692, Ebenezer Babson and others of his family, almost every night, heard a noise as if persons were going and running about his house. One night, on his return home at a late hour, he saw two men come out of the house, and go into the corn. He also heard them say, "The man of the house is come now, else we might have taken the house." The whole family went immediately to the garrison, which was near; whither the two men followed. They were heard and seen about the garrison several nights. One day, Babson saw two men, who looked like Frenchmen: and, at another time, six men were seen near the garrison; whereupon several went in pursuit. Babson overtook two, and tried to shoot at them; but his gun missed fire. Soon after, he saw three men together, one of whom had on a white waistcoat. He fired, and they all fell: but, as soon as he came close to them, they all rose up, and ran away; one of them discharging a gun as he went. One of these strange beings was at last surrounded by his pursuers, and all means of escape were cut off. He approached Babson, who shot at him as he was getting over the fence, and saw him fall from it to the ground; but, when Babson came to the spot where he fell, the man could not be found. Afterwards several were seen lurking about the garrison, and great discoursing in an unknown tongue was heard in a swamp near. After this, men were seen, who were supposed to be French and Indians. Babson was fired upon on his way to the harbor to carry news; and finally, after enduring these disturbers of the peace of the town for a fortnight, the people sent abroad for help. July 18, sixty men arrived from Ipswich to assist in the protection of the town, and the deliverance of it from these mysterious invaders: but it does not appear that any of the latter were taken; which can scarcely be a matter of surprise, considering that they were too ethereal to leave a foot-print upon the soft and miry places over which they were pursued.*

All these occurrences, and many others, were reported with great particularity by the minister of the town to Rev. Cotton Mather, and were published in his "Magnalia." Looking back upon them at this distance of time, they can excite in us no wonder or sorrow; nor, considering the mists that then clouded the reason of the wisest and best, should we dismiss them with the ridicule that would now attach to all such delusions.

The first assessment of a tax in Gloucester, showing the names of the individuals upon whom it was assessed, is one laid in 1693, which appears to have been the town's quarterly instalment of its proportion of a tax for £30,000 levied by the Colony Government. It exhibits the relative standing of our people at that time in regard to property; and is, therefore, here given as copied from the State Records. The names seem to be arranged according to the section of the town in which the individuals who bore them resided.

	£	s.	d.
Wm. Haskell	1	10	0
Joseph Haskell	1	4	0
Benj. Haskell	1	1	0
2d Wm. Haskell	1	12	3
Henry Walker	1	1	8
Nath[l] Coit	0	13	2
Peter Coffin	2	18	6
Rich[d] Tarr	0	12	8
James Sawyer	1	4	0
Timothy Day	0	14	10
James Davis	0	16	0
Nath[l] Millet	1	6	9
John Roberts	0	17	8
Thomas Bray	0	16	10
Richard Dike	0	10	6
Jacob Davis	1	3	8
John Sargent	1	5	7
James Parsons	1	0	0
John Parsons	1	2	5
Rich[d] Dolliver	0	17	4
Wm. Stevens	1	0	4
Thomas Prince	0	14	6
John Babson	0	11	7
James Davis	0	12	10
James Sayward	0	14	0
Wm. Sargent, 2[d]	0	18	0
John Tinny	0	15	0
Wm. Ellery	1	2	3
Jacob Elwell	0	16	3
Hugh Rowe	0	17	6
John Hadly	0	6	0
John Rowe	1	2	1
Jeffrey Parsons	0	18	4
Wm. Haskell, Jr	0	11	0
Ebenezer Babson	0	14	4
Samuel Elwell	0	18	9
John Elwell	0	12	2
Robert Elwell	0	11	0

* "For the truth of these strange occurrences, we have the testimony of this Babson, Day, Hammond, Ellery, Dolliver, who, with others, fired at them, but to no purpose." — *Niles's History of Indian and French Wars*; Mass. Hist. Coll., vol. xxvi. p. 282.

	£	s.	d.
Nath[l] Wharf	0	12	10
John Hammons	0	13	3
John Curney	0	11	1
Widow Coit	0	8	0
Francis Norwood	1	2	6
Henry Witham	0	13	6
Edward Haraden	1	9	7
John Davis	0	14	0
Widow Haraden	0	18	0
John Haraden	0	11	0
Joseph Haraden	0	12	6
Samuel York	0	13	6
Thomas Sawyer	0	17	0
Isaac Elwell	0	11	3
Wm. Sargent, Sen.	0	16	0
Wm. Sargent, Jr.	0	14	4
Thomas Low	0	15	3
Morris Smith	0	16	9
Jonathan Oris *	0	11	6
Wm. Whitredge	0	10	6
Ezekiel Day	0	11	3
Joseph Allen	0	17	0
Sam[l] Hodgkins	0	12	0
Joseph Clark	0	12	0
John Bray	0	14	8
Nath[l] Bray	0	13	0
Widow Mary Bray	0	1	8
Thomas Day	1	6	0
Jonathan Stainwood	0	12	0
Philip Stanwood	0	13	9
Nath[l] Day	0	10	6
Deacon Jas. Stevens	0	8	0
Sam[l] Stevens	0	12	10
Thomas Millett	1	4	9
Anthony Day	0	18	0
John Day	0	14	2
Sam[l] Stanwood	0	10	10
John Stanwood	0	14	0
Thomas Judkin	0	8	9
John Fitch	1	12	3
Thomas Witham	0	15	7
Henry Witham	0	10	10
Widow Abigail Benet	0	1	2
Timothy Somes	1	9	9
Henry Joslyn	0	10	9
Thomas Riggs, Sen.	0	11	8
Thomas Riggs, Jr.	0	11	7

The whole amount of the assessment was £68. 11s.; of which the tax on heads or polls was £39, the number of heads taxed being seventy-eight. Several were exempted from paying the poll-tax, upon the representation of the selectmen that they were diseased or disabled. The list of these furnishes information concerning the bodily condition of many of the old settlers. It says, —

"Capt. Haskell hath been sick almost this half-year, and still remains.

Mr. Henry Walker, very aged; not able to do nothing.

Capt. Davis is very sickly by reason of sickness he rec[d], in S[r] Edmond's time, in the country service.

Richard Dike being distempered in ye head.

John Hadley, a cripple, going by two crutches.

Francis Norwood hath been ill a great while.

Anthony Day, very aged.

* The names of Tinny and Oris are unfamiliar. They do not again occur; except that Oris is mentioned, in 1691, as an appraiser of Alice Elwell's estate.

Deacon Stevens is lame in his foot and one shoulder.
Samuel Stevens, a cripple in one hand.
William Sargent, Sen[r], is aged.
Thomas Judkin is not able to do nothing.
Thomas Riggs, Sen[r], is decrepit in his lims.
John Row hath been very sick a considerable while.
John Pearce very old, almost bed-rid; and relieved by the town.
Thomas Kent relieved by the town, being aged.
Richard Gooding, very poor.
Thomas Lovekin, aged and very poor.
Mr. Peter Duncan is not able to work, and very poor."

By the record of the foregoing list of taxes, it appears that John Sargent, James Sayward, William Sargent, 2d, John Tinny, and William Ellery, each had a sloop. Three others together owned one, and a boat and a shallop were also owned in partnership. If these were all the vessels owned in town then (and there is no evidence to the contrary), some surprise will naturally be excited by the neglect of maritime pursuits which this small amount of tonnage indicates. But this subject will be again considered in a subsequent chapter; and may, therefore, be dismissed without further remark here.

It has been already seen in this chapter, that, in 1688, about one-fourth of the population of the town were residing in that section now called West Parish. The distance round the head of Annisquam River, with the bad state of the roads at that period, without doubt caused most of the travel between that part of the town and the "Plantation" to be performed by crossing the river. In summer, probably, all these distant settlers made use of the short and pleasant route by water to reach their place of worship on the sabbath. The amount of travel by this mode of communication between these two chief sections of the town, had, in 1694, become of sufficient importance to lead to the establishment of a public route by ferry from Trynall Cove to Biskie Island, and thence over the marsh by a causeway to the mainland near the head of Stony Cove. In July of that year, Samuel Hodgkins was chosen to keep this ferry for seven years, on condition that he should keep a good canoe to carry over single persons; and a good boat that would carry two horses at a time in bad weather, and three in good. The ferriage was a penny for each person, and twopence for a horse. This way was continued in use about a hundred years; during all which time, perhaps, the office of ferryman was held in one family, as the last person who carried a passenger over this ancient and now forgotten route was a descendant of the same name of the Hodgkins who commenced it.

The erection of a new Meeting-house seems to have been the last matter of much importance that engaged the attention of our people in the century whose end we are now approaching. One place of public worship still served for the whole town; and the building of a new one was, of course, an affair of public interest, much debated and "discoursed" about in town-meeting. At a meeting on the 23d of December, 1697, there "was discourse concerning a new meeting-house of fourty foot square, and sixteen foot stud between joynts;" and Benjamin Haskell, John Parsons, and Samuel Sargent, were chosen a committee to manage the building. The work appears to have been delayed some time; as in January, 1699, the committee had power to order the dimensions of the building, and the selectmen were authorized to assess the first tax towards its cost. A short time afterwards, "the inhabitants did pass an act, that the meeting-house which is to be now erected should be plaistered with lime and hair." But the work still went on slowly; for not till May, 1700, was it ready to be raised. The town then voted "to provide vitls and drink for as many men as the selectmen should think convenient for the raising." In September, it was voted in town-meeting, that room should be left for pews; that the "draught of seats to be built should be after the form of three front seats, as was showed in the meeting-house at the meeting; and that the women should be seated in the east gallery." The last act of the town at this time concerning it, was the appointment of a committee, in December, 1700, consisting of the two deacons and three other prominent citizens, to seat the people in it.

The house of worship now erected stood on the Meeting-house Green, a short distance, probably, from the old one. It was the third building, devoted to the same purpose, which had been set upon this spot; and was, without doubt, an imposing structure, considering the number and circumstances of the worshippers. The amount raised to pay for it in three assessments was £253. It was furnished with a bell, as may be inferred from the fact that a sexton was paid for ringing one.

The other rates assessed upon the people of the town, besides the tax for the meeting-house, during the last three years of this century, were as follows; namely: —

	County.	Town.	Minister's.	Province.
1698 . . .	£25. 9s. 2d.	£19. 11s. 4d.	£74. 11s. 7d.	£48. 19s. 7d.
1699 . . .	£28. 19s. 6d.		£74. 6s. 6d.	
1700 . . .	£5. 12s. 2d.		£72. 12s. 3d.	£86. 15s. 4d.

Notice has been taken in a previous chapter of an order passed by the first settlers, setting apart a lot of land for a burial-ground. This place of interment was, it is supposed, the sole depository of the dead for the whole town till 1698; when the inhabitants on the westerly side of Annisquam River had a grant of land for the same purpose. The first burial-place was situated in a central part of the "Plantation," near the spot where the first meeting-house was erected, and adjoining the lots of several of the settlers. It has been enlarged from time to time; and a further increase of size, or disuse as a place of sepulture, is now necessary to secure its occupants undisturbed quiet in their last repose. As none of the first settlers have gravestones, the place of their burial is not known; and it is not improbable that most of the dust of Death's early harvests here has been scattered to the winds, in the accidental exhumations which have been of frequent occurrence for many years. In this ancient cemetery, at the period in our annals which we have now reached, nearly all the forefathers of the town were sleeping the sleep of death. All but two of those who had given the vigor of early manhood to the pioneer work of the settlement had reached the end of that solemn procession of the generations of men which terminates at the grave.

It is the boast of Massachusetts, that her legislators, at a very early period of her history, displayed a wise appreciation of the advantages of education, and took measures to secure this blessing for all her children, by passing a law to compel all the towns containing as many as fifty householders to support a public school. Gloucester contained the requisite number; but they were so far apart, that no considerable portion of the children could be gathered conveniently in one school. This fact, and the attention given by the people to private instruction, probably caused the neglect of the town to comply with the law to be overlooked. Private or domestic instruction in the elements of learning must have been common among the early settlers; an instance of which is found in the settlement of the estate of Hugh Row, where six shillings is charged as paid to Ezekiel Collins for teaching his children to write. At length, in 1696, education began to be a matter of public concern; and, at a town-meeting in that year, the selectmen were ordered to provide a schoolmaster "in convenient time." But no schoolmaster was obtained till 1698; when, at another town-meeting "about a schoolmaster, whether they would choose one or no, the vote carried it to choose one;" and Thomas Riggs, sen., was chosen to that office, "to have one shilling and six pence a day during the town's pleasure, and the said Riggs's likeing to carry it on."

Unless Cape Ann formed a part of the Naumkeag territory, which was granted to the first settlers at Salem by its sagamore, such right as the Indians might have to our township was not extinguished till 1700; when the town paid to Samuel English, an Indian, seven or eight pounds to satisfy his claim to it. This Indian was probably one of the grandchildren of the above-named sagamore. In the same year, he set up a claim to Beverly; which was cancelled by the payment of a small sum of money.

The Indian claim for justice satisfied, the town closed its public acts for the seventeenth century by a "full vote and consent of all" to keep the second Wednesday in the next as a day of humiliation and prayer.

The imagination dwells with an ever-increasing interest upon that portion of our history which the present chapter concludes. It loves to meet the early settlers as they land upon our shore, and follow them through all the scenes of the new and interesting life upon which they entered here; for though the great concerns of human existence are the same at all times, and the passions and pursuits of men have always nearly the same objects, there was yet so much of novelty, adventure, and danger, of hardship and suffering, to distinguish the period of settlement in New-England history from other epochs, that all the details of personal experience, domestic life, and manners and customs, relating to the first-comers, will ever afford an interesting subject of contemplation to their descendants. But few of those details with respect to our settlers are known; and the imagination may find abundant occasion for the exercise of its powers in filling up a picture from such imperfect outline as we can draw.

The first care of our ancestors was to procure a shelter from the weather. We have reason to suppose that this was generally, at first, of the rudest kind; being a log-house of the simplest construction, containing a single room; a chimney, built of stones and clay; a door, always facing the south; and probably one small window. The value of William Southmead's house, as given in the inventory of his goods, Feb. 16, 1648, was £8; and that sum was just the value of his "bedstead, feather-bed, & appurtenances." Framed buildings were, of course, erected early. In 1668, James Gardner bought of John Rowe the frame of a house; "he to be at the charge of making up the back and oven, to daub the house sufficiently upon both sides and ends, and to furnish thatch to cover it." The daubing was of clay, which soon went out of use for that purpose, but did not yield entirely to lime, in the building of chimneys, for more than a hundred years. The furniture of these humble abodes was enough for comfort, perhaps; but it certainly contributed little to luxurious living. Besides the items mentioned above of William Southmead's furniture, his inventory contains the following articles, with their value: "1 flock-bed and pillow, £1. 10s.; 1 doz. napkins, table cloth, & 2 towels, £3; pewter & tinne vessels, £1. 10s.; 1 pr. of pillebeers, 10s.; 2 brass kettles, 1 brass pot, two skillets, £3; chests, £2." The dwelling-house, barn, and cow-house of Walter Tybbot, a prominent settler, together with fifty acres of land, were valued at only sixty pounds, and his furniture at twenty-seven; while his live stock is set down at sixty-three, the value of a yoke of oxen being sixteen pounds. Such were the houses and furniture of the early settlers. With regard to the tenements, time must have brought improvement; but there is no reason to suppose that a single house was erected, before 1700, at all comparable with the few specimens still standing of a date a little later than that year.

The distribution of the substantial comforts of life was probably quite as nearly equal among the first settlers as it has ever been since. None were so poor, so far as we know, as to wish in vain for food; and none were rich enough to have much left for luxury after their daily necessities were supplied. We have seen in what staple articles of food the minister was paid; and these articles, the product of their own industry on the sea and land, furnished, without doubt, the chief means of their subsistence. Some articles of foreign production, in daily use among us, were unknown to them; and some, now considered necessaries of life in the humblest abode, had not then descended from the rank of luxuries.

Those important events of life, birth, marriage, and death, excited, of course, in our small community of early settlers, the interest and sympathy of all. There was little form or ceremony attending the entrance of a human being into life, not common to our own time. They had, at least, one professional midwife; and, as no physician settled in the town till it had been incorporated eighty years, it may be supposed that the obstetric branch of the medical practice was chiefly attended to by individuals of the female sex.

Their marriages were not solemnized by clergymen for about half a century after the settlement of the place. One of the early settlers was married at Ipswich, "at a general traine;" and as the records show that the ceremony was always performed by a magistrate, in some instances by the chief, or him who had been chief, it is probable that most of those who intended wedlock went to the neighboring town of Ipswich or Salem, or to

Boston, to be united, as there was no magistrate in Gloucester till about 1700. Our Puritan ancestors guarded with great care the intercourse between young unmarried persons. To this end, the Colonial Legislature passed severe laws, which, though not attended with the awful penalty of death affixed to laws enacted for the same purpose in the mother-country during the control of government there by the Puritan party, were yet so severe as to be deemed by the looser morality, or stricter sense of justice, of the present day, harsh and oppressive in the extreme. The Court Records show that a few of our people were sentenced for a transgression of these laws. One married pair, to whom a child was born so soon after marriage as to prove their guilt, were sentenced to be whipped, or pay a fine, with costs of court.

In only one respect does a death-bed scene in Gloucester now differ from the same solemn sight in the days of our ancestors. They seem to have deemed the minister an indispensable attendant at the closing hour; not so much, probably, for the consolation of the living, as for the service he might yet be to the departing soul. At their funerals, also, there was a prevalent custom, which has fallen now entirely into disuse. On these occasions, liquors were furnished in abundance; and sometimes gloves were distributed to the bearers and others. The expenses for drink at the funeral of Hugh Row were one pound sixteen shillings and nine pence; and for "rum, win, sider, and shug' and spis," and eight pairs of gloves, for the funeral of William Ellery in 1696, upwards of three pounds were paid; the sums in each case amounting to no inconsiderable portion of the estate of the deceased.

In the early times of which we write, the news of the day could hardly have had a general circulation in town oftener than once a week; for it is not probable that many of the people met each other, except on the sabbath, when they gathered around the meeting-house before the hour of worship. To their holy temple they went up with the true spirit of devotion; and it is no impeachment of their religious character to suppose that their steps were sometimes hastened thither by such an interest in human affairs as would lead them to inquire concerning the exciting events constantly taking place in both the Old World and the New.

With regard to the minor matters in the customs and manners of the early New-England settlers, the curious reader may find, in written accounts and abundant traditions of the olden times, all the information he will need; and will therefore be willing to pass on, and proceed with the events of our particular history.

CHAPTER VII.

FIRST CHURCH. — REV. JOHN WHITE: HIS SETTLEMENT, MINISTRY, AND DEATH; HIS FAMILY. — SCHOOL. — COMMONERS. — DIVISION OF LAND. — TOWN-WATCH. — NEW SETTLERS.

THE religious exercises on the day of humiliation appointed by the town, at the commencement of the eighteenth century, were probably carried on by the most gifted of the lay-brethren of the church; for they were then without a minister. But our ancestors valued the privileges and enjoyments of public worship and a settled ministry too highly to be contented for any considerable time without them. They began, therefore, shortly after the decease of Mr. Emerson, to take measures to supply his place. In February, 1701, the town concurred with the church in a vote to call Mr. Jabez Fitch, who was then residing in Cambridge as a tutor in Harvard College. Several months were spent in treating with him, and liberal terms were offered. His final answer, submitted to the town on the 11th September, was so unsatisfactory, that a committee was appointed to go to Cambridge, and have an interview with him in reference to it, and to the "reason of his leaving the town as he had." But no further proceedings are recorded concerning this effort to obtain a pastor.*

After the lapse of a few weeks, another attempt was made; when the choice of the church fell upon Mr. Joseph Coit, and the town concurred: but, in town-meeting, the vote concerning the sending of messengers to him about his settlement was "tied in an equal balance," as the record states; and the meeting was dissolved, without taking any decisive action. A short time

* Mr. Fitch was ordained, in 1703, as colleague with Rev. John Rogers of Ipswich; where he remained upwards of twenty years. In 1725, he settled in Portsmouth, where he had supplied a pulpit some time. He died in 1746, in his seventy-fifth year.

afterwards, Deacon Joseph Haskell and Nathaniel Coit were chosen messengers to go to Mr. Coit, and inform him of his call; and the neighboring ministers were consulted: but, after several months' delay, this attempt ended, like the preceding, in failure.*

Not discouraged by the ill-success that had attended their efforts to find a minister for their vacant pulpit, the church proceeded, in a few weeks, in a renewed attempt to obtain one. They met on the 11th September, 1702, and, out of four who were proposed as candidates, unananimously made choice of Mr. John White; who accepted the call, and immediately entered upon the duties of his ministry. By the terms of his settlement, Mr. White was to have £65 for the first year, £70 per annum for the next two years, and £80 per annum during the remainder of his ministry. He was also to have £100 for settlement, to be paid in yearly sums of £50 each; and to have as an "overplush" what strangers might give by way of contribution. It was further stipulated that he should preach a lecture once a month, from April to October annually.

Mr. White was a son of Joseph White of Watertown, and was born in 1678. He graduated at Harvard College in 1698; and, at the time of his call here, was chaplain of Saco Fort. His ordination took place April 21, 1703. The ministers who assisted in the exercises were Rev. Mr. Gerrish of Wenham and Rev. Mr. Wise of Chebacco. About the same time, the church adopted for the rule of its order and government the Platform of Discipline agreed upon by the synod at Cambridge in 1649, and entered into the following covenant: —

"We do give up ourselves to that God whose name alone is Jehovah, — Father, Son, and Spirit, — as the only true and living God; and unto our Lord Jesus Christ, as our only Redeemer and Saviour; as the only Prophet, Priest, and King over our souls, and only Mediator of the covenant of grace; engaging our

* Mr. Coit was grandson of our early settler, John Coit, who removed to New London. He was born in that place in 1673, and graduated at Harvard College in 1697. Before he became a candidate for the vacant pastorate here, he preached in Plainfield, Conn.; and was settled there early in 1705. He was dismissed in 1748; and died in Plainfield, July 1, 1750, aged seventy-seven.

hearts unto this God in Christ, by the help of his Spirit of grace, to cleave unto him as our God and chief good; and unto Jesus Christ, as our Mediator by faith, in a way of gospel obedience, as becometh his covenant people for ever.

"We do also give up our offspring unto God in Jesus Christ; avouching the Lord to be our God and the God of our children, and ourselves, with our children, to be his people; humbly adoring the grace of God in Christ Jesus, that we and our children may be looked upon as the Lord's. We do also give up ourselves one to another in the Lord, according to the will of God, to walk together as a church of Christ in all the ways of his worship and service, according to the rules of the word of God; promising in brotherly love faithfully to watch over one another's souls, and to submit ourselves to the discipline and government of Christ in his church; and duly to attend the seals and censures, and whatever ordinances Christ hath commanded to be observed by his people, according to the order of the gospel, so far as the Lord hath or shall reveal himself unto us."

The church consisted at this time of twenty-one males and forty-nine females, besides several who had removed from the town, but had not been dismissed to other churches. Two deacons of the church had deceased a few years before; and their places were probably supplied by Joseph Haskell and James Parsons, who were now set apart by Mr. White for their duties by solemn ordination. A long and peaceful ministry of more than half a century followed the connection now formed between pastor and people, and few incidents of interest are to be noted in its quiet progress. In 1716, Mr. White's salary was raised to £90; and, in 1718, £100 were voted to him, to be paid in bills of credit. Until 1716, the town had, from its settlement, constituted one religious body; but, in that year, the inhabitants of the westerly precinct were set off as a distinct parish, in order to the settlement of a minister among themselves. The parish-affairs continued, however, to be regulated in town-meetings for several years; and, till 1729, Mr. White's salary was assessed by the selectmen. At the annual March meeting in 1724, Mr. White presented a complaint, that his salary was, in general, insufficient for his support; and it was thereupon voted, that he should have, that year, £160 in good bills of credit, and the same sum from year to year during the town's pleasure. The town appears, by this act, to have anticipated a duty enjoined upon all the religious societies in the Province, by a resolve of the General Court, passed in the following year, that they ought to make such additions to the salaries of their ministers as would honorably support them, and to have respect to the time and terms of contract, and also to the greatly increasing difference in the value of the bills of credit from what it had been.

In 1728, another church went forth from the parent stem. The people on the northerly side of the Cape had so increased, that they were set off in that year as a distinct parish; and the concerns of the First Parish ceased now to be managed in town-meetings. Nothing further of particular interest in the parish or church history occurs for a number of years. A nominal increase of salary, rendered necessary by the depreciation of the currency, was voted to Mr. White in 1735. In 1738, a new meeting-house was erected by members of the parish in the Harbor, a mile distant from the old one; and Mr. White immediately commenced preaching in it. The people in the northerly part of the parish regarded this an abridgment of their sanctuary privileges; and were only reconciled to the measure by being set off, in 1742, as a separate precinct, taking numerical rank as the Fourth Parish. Soon after the formation of the Fourth Church, Mr. White said, in a letter to a brother in the ministry, using an appropriate figure of speech, that he had not ordinarily fished for souls with a net, but with an angling rod. His success commends his method. At the time of his settlement, his church consisted of seventy members. In the course of his ministry, two new churches had been formed by members of his flock; now upwards of eighty were dismissed to constitute the Fourth; and there remained in the parent church two hundred and sixty members.

A season of unusual religious awakening occurred throughout

New England about 1742, and Mr. White's church was plentifully refreshed with the dews of divine grace. The first visible indication of the special presence of the Lord occurred soon after a day of solemn fasting and prayer, which had been set apart to ask the gift of the Holy Ghost. This was soon followed by an effusion of the Spirit, for which the joyful pastor could find no parallel but that which came to the primitive church, — "a sound from heaven as of a rushing mighty wind." The disciples were now also "with one accord in one place," and the spirit of prayer was poured down upon young and old. Even children of tender years were made instruments in this wonderful work of God, and led the congregation in effectual appeals to the throne of divine grace.

The continued depreciation of the bills of credit induced complaints from Mr. White: and the parish, in 1747, voted him £560, old tenor; and ordered a new valuation of the estates of the parish, in order to make the rate in a more equitable manner than had been the practice before.

Mr. White's health did not begin to fail till he had nearly completed a ministry of half a century. In January, 1750, the church made choice of Samuel Moody as colleague to their pastor; and the parish concurred, though not without a strong dissent on the part of several of the members, who stated their objections in a formal protest; giving as reasons for their course, that Mr. White was still able to perform the necessary parts of the minister's office, — administering the sacrament and marrying; that increased expense should not be incurred, because a change in the currency, about to take place, would render money very scarce, and the parish was already in debt about £500; and that the church had not treated the parish properly in excluding three other ministers, who had preached before Mr. Moody, from being candidates. No further action was taken at this time; but, a few months afterwards, both bodies, united in an invitation to Rev. Samuel Chandler to assume the active duties of the ministry as colleague with Mr. White.

The venerable pastor, though now beyond the allotted period of human life, continued several years longer with the people whom he had faithfully and acceptably served; and at last dropped gently away, while sitting in his arm-chair, Jan. 17, 1760, in the eighty-third year of his age and the fifty-eighth of his ministry.

No description of the personal appearance of Mr. White has come down to us, and we have no particulars concerning the manner in which he discharged his duties in the various relations of life. He was ranked by a fellow-laborer in the ministry as one of the learned, pious, humble, prudent, faithful, and useful men of his day; and the few productions of his pen that have come down to the present time, confirm, as far as they go, the judgment that assigns him such a place.

Mr. White's printed productions were, 1st, "A sermon preached after the funeral of Rev. John Wise of Chebacco," from these words of the apostle: "For we have this treasure in earthen vessels." 2. "New-England Lamentations," a pamphlet of thirty-four pages, in which he states the causes of lamentation to be, "the decay of the power of godliness; the danger of Arminian principles; and the declining state of church order, government, and discipline." The means leading to the decay of godliness are summed up under these heads: 1. "An ill-treatment of the spirit of grace and holiness. 2. An ungrateful neglect and contempt of the Holy Scriptures, especially of the precious promises thereof. 3. The neglect or profane observance of gospel ordinances. 4. Inobservance of God's footsteps in the course of his common providence. 5. Restraining prayer before God." This work was published in 1734. His last printed publication was a letter, describing the revival in his parish in 1742, and its effects, prefixed to a sermon preached during its progress by Rev. B. Bradstreet of the Third Church, and published in a periodical called the "Christian History."

Mr. White was concerned in the celebrated Land Bank, to which he mortgaged his real estate for £75; and, in common with other sufferers by that unfortunate financial enterprise, was called upon to pay several assessments for the redemption of its bills. In a note to a letter to the Governor and Council in 1741, he offers his difficult and perplexed circumstances as an excuse for being concerned in it. Considering his large family, and the fact that he educated two sons at college, it may well be supposed that he was sometimes in a straitened condition: but nothing more is known of his pecuniary affairs than that he left an estate of £441; of which his library, consisting of about seventy volumes, was valued at £21. 5s. 8d.

Mr. White was thrice married: first, June 9, 1703, to Lucy, daughter of Rev. John Wise of Ipswich, who died March 5, 1727, aged forty-six years; next to Widow Abigail Blake, daughter of Rev. Increase Mather of Boston, who died Dec. 10, 1748, aged seventy; and last, June 1, 1749, to Mrs. Alice Norwood of Gloucester, who was buried Jan. 27, 1763. His children were all by his first wife. John, born in 1704, was probably the same who was admitted inhabitant of Falmouth, Me., in 1728; and had a wife Jerusha, and a daughter Lucy, who was born in 1732. He died before his father, leaving four daughters. Lucy, oldest daughter of Rev. John White, born in 1706, married Rev. Joseph Moody of York, Nov. 11, 1724. He had previously been bewildered by the attractions of Miss Hirst, who became the wife of Sir William Pepperell. Mrs. Moody also died before her father, leaving four children,— Samuel, the famous Master Moody of Dummer Academy; Joseph; Thomas; and Hannah, who married Dr. Samuel Plummer of this town. Joseph, the next child, born in 1708, died in infancy. William, born in 1709, probably settled in Falmouth, Me. (where one of this name appears, in company with John, in 1728), and married Christian Simonton in 1736. Mr. White's will mentions "the heirs of my son William;" and the settlement of his estate shows that these heirs were seven children, then living in Falmouth. Thomas White, born in 1712, was living in 1738, when his father drew a lot for him in the division of lots at New Gloucester, Me.; but probably died young. Joseph, born in 1716, died in 1718. Benjamin, born in 1718, graduated at Harvard College in 1738. He taught a school here in 1740; but nothing further is known of him. Abigail, born in 1720, married Isaac Allen in 1751, and died before 1759. Hannah, born in 1721, married Nathaniel

Haskell in 1740; and died Oct. 26, 1814, aged ninety-three. Mary, born in 1723, married David Allen in 1745, and died before 1766. Samuel, the eleventh and youngest child of Mr. White, born in 1725, graduated at Harvard College in 1741, at the early age of sixteen. He became a schoolmaster, and was probably employed in that vocation in his native town in 1743 and 1749. He died before his father. A person of the same name, a physician, removed from York to Saco about 1750; and died, soon after 1756, of consumption.* Our Samuel might have been attracted to that region to visit his sister Lucy, who resided in York.†

Mr. White received, soon after his settlement here, a grant of land, just below the plain on which his meeting-house stood; and undoubtedly built on that spot the house still standing there, which is accurately represented in the engraving below. He

removed from it, several years before his death, into the house which he built and occupied during the remainder of his life, on

---

* Folsom, History of Saco and Biddeford. In Rev. S. Chandler's diary, under date of April 26, 1758, I find the following entry, which probably refers to this son: "I attended the Society for prayer; partie case, Mr. White's son, in a consumption, & fear whether prepared for death."

† The meagre information I have given of Mr. White's sons is the entire result of extensive inquiry. I am able to add the recollections of one of his grandsons (Mr.

the lane leading to the old burying-ground. His former dwelling was bought by James Stevens, who kept a tavern there till 1740; when he sold it to Capt. William Ellery, who continued it as a house of entertainment several years. It yet remains in possession of his descendants; and probably presents the same external appearance as it did when first erected, with the exception of the wooden balls which once ornamented the projecting part of the upper story. The parish voted twenty pounds to defray the expenses of Mr. White's funeral. A brick monument, covered with a slab of freestone, marks the spot of his interment in the old burial-place. A slate tablet, inserted in the slab, has the following inscription: —

HERE LIES THE REMAINS OF THAT
ZEALOUS, FAITHFUL, AND EXCELLENT DIVINE,
THE REV · Mr JOHN WHITE, WHO DIED
JANy 16, 1760, IN THE 83rd YEAR OF
HIS AGE, AND 58th OF HIS MINISTRY.
ΤΟ ΖΗΝ ΧΡΙΣΤΟΣ, ΤΟ ΘΑΝΕΙΝ ΚΕΡΔΟΣ.

The town, having discontinued the school it had provided in 1699, was, in 1701, presented at a Quarterly-Session Court in Salem for neglect in this matter. Early in the next year, the selectmen were instructed to apply to the General Court, and to procure, if they could, one or two members of the Council to visit the town, and see how it was "circumstanced with respect to a school." It is not likely that any peculiarity in the condition of the town, then existing, could prevail on the court to excuse it from compliance with the law: and accordingly, in January, 1703, an agreement was made with Mr. John Newman to keep a school till the 4th of March next ensuing; to be allowed suitable satisfaction for his pains by the town, besides such pay

Isaac Allen), who died in 1855, at the age of ninety-nine, in the town of Minot, Me. He remembered to have heard his aunt (Mrs. Haskell) speak of two of her brothers who were engaged in an iron-foundery somewhere in Massachusetts. They both embarked in a small vessel employed to carry their ware to market, and nothing was ever afterwards heard of them. Mr. Allen removed to New Gloucester about 1771, and then found, in the vicinity of Portland, a cousin White, whose baptismal name he thought was William. He died in 1777, leaving a child, who was said to be the only descendant of Rev. John White that bore the family name. In a later period of his life, Mr. Allen made inquiries for this relative; but all he could learn concerning him was that he had gone back into the country.

as he should receive from young men whom he might teach "to wright and cypher."

In June, 1704, another agreement was made with Mr. Newman to keep a school till the next March meeting; to have five pounds for his services, besides the income of the scholars who paid by the week. Though Mr. Newman's term of employment was not of long duration, he became a constant resident; and his service as a teacher, and other honorable connection with the town, entitle his name and family to a brief notice in this place.* He first appears in Gloucester on his marriage, Dec. 13, 1683, to Ruth, daughter of Rev. John Emerson; but did not reside here till after the death of the latter; by which event, he came into possession of Mr. Emerson's house, fulling-mill, and a considerable portion of his land. Besides his distinction as the second schoolmaster of the town, he was prominent in offices which were then of higher rank. He was the first magistrate belonging to the town; was a selectman several years, and representative three years. He died Jan. 2, 1720, aged fifty-nine, leaving children, — John, Ruth, and Ann. The latter married Dr. David Plummer. John Newman, jun., seems to be connected with our history in no other manner than by the birth of three children, of whom two died in infancy. He had a wife Mary, who died in Edgartown, Sept. 28, 1755, aged seventy-one. His son John, born here March 14, 1716, graduated at Harvard College in 1740, and became chaplain of the garrison at Louisburg. At that place he contracted an acquaintance with several military men from Martha's Vineyard, which led to a call by the church at Edgartown, inviting him to be their pastor. He was ordained over that church, July 29, 1748; and sustained a ministerial relation to it till 1758, when, at his own request, it was dissolved. He left the ministry, and engaged in trade, and also became a colonel in the militia. He died Dec. 1, 1763; and was buried in the Edgartown burying-ground, by the side of his mother. He left a widow, who married Mr. Metcalf of Dedham.

* He was son of Rev. Antipas Newman of Wenham, whose wife was Elizabeth, daughter of Gov. John Winthrop.

Mr. Newman's successor in the school was John Ring, a townsman, who was chosen to that office at a town-meeting in March, 1705. In 1707, the faulty conduct of the town about the school appears to be again a subject of complaint at court; but further proceedings against it were stopped by the engagement into which it entered, in May of that year, with Mr. Joshua Gardner, to keep the school for three months. He continued in office till February, 1709; and probably then left town for some other field of labor. In the latter part of the same year, an agreement was made with Mr. Joshua Moody to teach one quarter for eight pounds. In addition to the common branches, he was "to teach lattine, if scholars appear." His engagement was renewed at the same rate of compensation, and terminated in March, 1711. In the ensuing fall, another teacher was engaged; and, from this time, the school seems to have been one of the permanent institutions of the town. The salary of this last teacher was eight pounds per quarter, and so much in addition as he should be obliged to pay above four shillings a week for his board.

The first schoolhouse in the town was built in 1708, and was situated on the easterly side of the Meeting-house. Its dimensions, as ordered by the town, were — length, twenty-four feet; width, sixteen feet; height of stud, six feet. The cost of the building was twenty-four pounds fifteen shillings. Up to this time, the Meeting-house had been used for a schoolroom.

At the beginning of the eighteenth century, a considerable portion of the territory of the town was held by individual ownership; but there still remained large tracts that had not been granted. A liberal spirit seems to have prevailed, from the first, in the disposal of the land; but, with the exception of the extraordinary grant to William Stevens, the liberality of the town appears to have been governed by the wants of the settlers. All business in relation to the common soil was transacted in town-meeting for more than fifty years; partly, perhaps, because nearly all the inhabitants qualified to act in town-affairs were commoners; and partly, it may be, because no great value was yet attached to the right of commonage: for, as late as 1697, the sale of one produced but thirty shillings. Previous to 1661, every dwelling-house erected entitled its proprietor to a right in the common land; but after that date, by an act of the General Court, such right could be obtained in that way only by consent of the town. The practice of Gloucester, however, appears to have been more liberal, as may be inferred from the discussion in town-meeting, in the year 1700, of the question, "whether any parcell of land given to any to build a house upon, or set or erect any house, such parcell of land shall carry a common right with it or no;" and from the decision, the next year, that "no land granted by the town from henceforth and forwards shall have any common right, except it be included in the respective grant." This privilege came soon to be more highly valued than it had heretofore been. The accession of new settlers, to a considerable extent, warranted an anticipation of this increased value, and probably led the commoners to adopt measures for ascertaining the rightful claimants of the privilege, to the organization of themselves into a distinct body, and to those extensive transactions in relation to the common lands which seem to have engrossed a large share of the attention of our fathers during the first quarter of the last century.

At a town-meeting, March, 1703, a committee was chosen to receive claims to common rights, and report the same to the next town-meeting. At that meeting, held in January, 1704, the list was presented and read, and ordered to be recorded. The whole number of rights claimed and allowed at this time was one hundred and twelve, which was increased by subsequent grants and claims to about one hundred and thirty in 1710. A few were claimants of more than one right; and one, Thomas Riggs, was the owner of five. The exact number of commoners at any one time cannot be determined. New claimants often appeared; and, in 1720, it was found necessary to make a "more intelligible list." In 1757 (the latest period in which any number of rights is mentioned), they recognized one hundred and forty-five. The market value of one of these rights, in the currency of the time, was, in 1718, ten pounds eight shillings; and, in 1730, two pounds.

Between 1700 and 1707, numerous grants of land were made to individual applicants; and, in the last-named year, each commoner and the minister received by vote a lot of six, eight, or ten acres. The committee appointed to lay out these lots was empowered to dispose of any parcel of land, not exceeding eight acres, to any person or persons then dwelling in town, by selling or letting, with the consent of neighbors; the money to be received for it to go into the town-treasury. It is supposed that down to this time, and for a few years later, all money received for the sale of land was appropriated to the public use; but this disposition of it probably ceased as soon as it was found that a considerable number of citizens were non-commoners. No small portion of their funds must have been used by the commoners to defray the expense of law-suits, in which they were often engaged. In 1732, they had a balance of seventy-three pounds in their treasury; and, in 1757, a dividend of thirty shillings to each right was made; amounting, in all, to upwards of two hundred pounds. They afterwards had, at times, a considerable amount on hand, and dividends were proposed: but the records do not show the amount divided at any time after 1757; though there can scarcely be a doubt, that from that time, for more than fifty years, to the dissolution of the body of commoners, several hundred dollars were apportioned among them.

Before 1708, but one general grant of land in contiguous lots had been made to all the commoners. On the 22d June of that year, they voted to lay out the common thatch-banks in separate lots to each one holding a common right. They also voted to each commoner a lot, at the head of the Cape, "of four, six, or eight acres, according as the land is, between the South side of Long Cove, at Sandy Bay, and the head of Starknought harbor and the great fresh pond; reserving the way that is made use of from Starknought harbor to Sandy Bay, and likewise the ways that go down to several landing places along the shore where people used to load in wood; likewise to all the commoners to have ten or twelve acres of ground each joining to the line between Ipswich and Gloucester and Manchester." The commoners met, for the purpose of drawing their lots, Jan. 25, 1709, at the Meeting-house. Nearly all of them are recorded in their books; according to which, the highest number drawn in each section was one hundred and twenty-two. From this time to the next general division, the commoners were constantly selling their land, confining the privilege of buying chiefly to their own number; though new settlers seem to have had no difficulty in procuring from them, on favorable terms, enough for a house-lot.

In 1719, the commoners voted to make another division of woodland, but delayed choosing a committee to lay it out into lots nearly two years; and two years more were occupied in completing the transaction. The number of lots laid out was two hundred and seventeen, — situated on the Cape, at Chebacco side, and in the section between Gloucester and Manchester. Besides the lot granted to every common right, the eldest son of every commoner, being himself a non-commoner, was to have a quarter of a lot; and, if the commoner had no son, then he was to have a quarter of a lot for himself. All who had been householders in town since 1704, and were not commoners, also had a quarter of a lot each. The widows and heirs, too, of such as were householders then, if they themselves had continued householders, had a quarter of a lot. Under these provisions, two hundred and one lots were taken up: three were given to ministers of the town, ten were sold to different persons, and three were not disposed of. The record of these proceedings assists greatly in the attempt to estimate the population of the town as it was in 1704; for it is manifest, that, in the different classes of the grantees, nearly every male citizen of the town, twenty-one years of age and upwards, must have been included. From this and other sources of information, the number of such citizens in that year is ascertained to have been one hundred and seventy at least;* and the entire

* They are here given: —

Joseph Allen.
Joseph Allen, jun.
Ralph Andrews.
Benjamin Averill.
John Babson.
Richard Babson.
Anthony Bennett.
Richard Byles.
Thomas Bray.
Nathaniel Bray.
John Bray.
John Brown.

population at that time is supposed to have been about seven hundred.

While the last division of woodland was in progress, the commoners were making preparations for an apportionment of the herbage land; and for this purpose appointed a committee, in 1723, to make a survey, and report the location and number of acres of it. The committee reported the number of acres in

John Burrill.
John Butman.
William Card.
Ezekiel Collins.
Nathaniel Coit.
John Curney.
Elisha Curney.
Capt. James Davis.
Lieut. James Davis.
John Davis.
Jacob Davis.
Ebenezer Davis.
Aaron Davis.
Samuel Davis.
Anthony Day.
Nathaniel Day.
Ezekiel Day.
Joseph Day.
Timothy Day.
John Day.
John Day, jun.
Thomas Day.
Joseph Day, jun.
Nicolas Denning.
Richard Dolliver.
John Dolliver.
Peter Duncan.
Moses Durin.
Richard Dike.
John Durgee.
Robert Elwell.
John Elwell.
John Elwell, jun.
Isaac Elwell.
Elias Elwell.
Jacob Elwell.
Ebenezer Elwell.
Eleazer Elwell.
Nathaniel Ellery.
Isaac Eveleth.
Job Eveleth.
Peter Emons.
John Fitch.
Samuel Foster.
James Gardner.
Joseph Gardner.
John Gardner.
George Giddings.
John Gilbert.
James Godfrey.
Richard Goodwin.
Samuel Gott.
Samuel Griffin.
Daniel Gutridge.
John Hadley.
Edward Haraden.
Joseph Haraden.
John Haraden.
Benjamin Haraden.
John Harris.
George Harvey.
William Haskell.
William Haskell, jun.
Joseph Haskell.
Joseph Haskell, jun.
Joseph Haskell, 3d.
John Haskell.
Benjamin Haskell.
Benjamin Haskell, jun.
Henry Haskell.
Benjamin Hoppin.
Nathaniel Hadlock.
John Hammons.
Samuel Hodgkins.
Joseph Ingersol.
Samuel Ingersol.
Charles James.
Francis James.
Henry Joslyn.
Josiah Kent.
John Kent.
Thomas Lufkin.
Ebenezer Lufkin.
John Lane.
Thomas Millet.
Thomas Millet, 2d.
Nathaniel Millet.
William Manning.
John Newman.
Francis Norwood, sen.
Francis Norwood, jun.
Joshua Norwood.
Joseph Page.
William Pain.
Jeffrey Parsons.
James Parsons.
Nathaniel Parsons.
John Parsons.
Ebenezer Parsons.
John Pool.
Thomas Prince.
John Prince.
John Pulcifer.
Thomas Riggs, sen.
Thomas Riggs, jun.
John Riggs.
Andrew Riggs.
William Ring.
John Ring.
David Ring.
John Roberts.
John Roberts, jun.
Abraham Robinson, sen.
Abraham Robinson, jun.
Stephen Robinson.
Andrew Robinson.
Stephen Row.
Abraham Row.
Isaac Row.
Samuel Row.
Thomas Sanders.
Nathaniel Sanders.
William Sargent, sen.
William Sargent, jun.
William Sargent, 2d.
John Sargent.
Nathaniel Sargent.
Samuel Sargent.
Thomas Sawyer.
John Sawyer.
Nathaniel Sawyer.
Abraham Sawyer.
James Sayward.
Morris Smith.
John Smith.
John Smith, jun.
Timothy Somes.
Timothy Somes, jun.
Philip Stainwood.
John Stainwood.
Jonathan Stainwood.
Samuel Stevens.
David Stevens.
Jonathan Stevens.
George Stover.
Richard Tarr.
John Tucker.
James Wallis.
Michael Webber.
Nathaniel Wharf.
William Whittredge.
Rev. John White.
Thomas Witham.
Humphrey Woodbury.
Ezekiel Woodward.
Samuel York.
Joseph York.
Benjamin York.

different sections of the town, amounting in all to thirteen hundred and twenty-five and one-half acres, which were laid out to the commoners in 1725. It was the last division of the soil among its proprietors. Several pieces of land and flats remained to be disposed of: but these were gradually taken up; and finally, in 1808, the commoners record their last sale, which was a lot on which to erect a schoolhouse in the middle district at Sandy Bay. The most important sale they had ever made, considering the amount of money realized, was that of the sand-banks on the westerly side of Annisquam River, to Peter Coffin, in 1799, for four hundred dollars. Mr. Coffin's grandfather came into possession of the large tract of land there, originally granted to William Stevens; which tract was bordered for some extent by a beach of fine sand. As no bounds were affixed to Mr. Stevens's grant, a controversy arose between Mr. Coffin and the commoners with regard to it; the subject of dispute being chiefly the right of the parties to take the sand. This article was then extensively used on the floors of dwelling-houses; and the quality of this sand was such, that it commanded a better price than any other. The matter was settled in 1722 by an agreement which continued in force till the sale already mentioned, — that the income of the property should be equally divided between the parties. In 1725, the price of the sand was fixed at a halfpenny a bushel.

The commoners' organization seemed properly to come to a dissolution, when there was no longer any thing to give it life: but, after nine years of suspended animation, it was revivified, and maintained a feeble existence for about eleven months; at the end of which, on the 3d of June, 1820, at the tavern of Gen. James Appleton, it ceased to exist.

The first notice of the establishment of a watch to guard the safety of the town occurs in 1705. In the early part of that year, a watch-house had been recently built on Elwell's Neck, near Hogskin Cove; and another was situated in the Harbor, probably near the place now occupied by the ruins of the old Fort, as may be inferred from the name of Watch-house Neck given to that locality, and from the employment of Thomas

Sawyer, who resided in the vicinity of it, to repair the building and furnish wood for the watch. Demonstrations of French and Indian hostility in 1704, and the landing of pirates in the town in that year, may have excited an unusual degree of alarm, and led to vigilant measures. The pirates alluded to were some of the crew of John Quelch, who was hung for piracy in 1704, a few days after two of his men had been apprehended here and carried to Salem Jail. The watch was kept up for a number of years; and was not discontinued, probably, till all apprehensions of danger ceased to exist.

From the year 1700 to the year 1705, several persons removed into the town, and became permanent settlers. Many of them were useful citizens; and of a few of them the names are still worthily borne by descendants, to some of whom the following notices may afford acceptable information.

Samuel Griffin first appears in Gloucester on his marriage to Elizabeth York, Dec. 15, 1703. There was a family of this name early settled in Ipswich. Humphrey Griffin, of that town, in 1641, who died about 1660, may have been the ancestor of Samuel above named, and of still another Samuel, who is said to have removed hither from Newbury about 1736. Our first Samuel had, in 1707, two acres of land where he had set up his house, near Benjamin York's land; and four acres on the east side of the way leading from Lobster Cove to Sandy Bay. He had sons Samuel, Adoniram, and Daniel. Samuel Griffin, jun., for many years a member of the church at Annisquam, and a useful citizen, died Jan. 15, 1781; and Deacon Samuel Griffin, of the same church, died about Jan. 1, 1794, aged eighty. The family has long been numerous in Squam. Four Samuels were living there in 1754. Josiah, born there, settled in Sandy Bay; was a representative in 1833 and 1834; and died in 1858, aged about seventy.

Samuel Gott, weaver, came to Gloucester from Wenham, where Charles Gott, who was without doubt his ancestor, was an early settler; having removed thither from Salem, to which place he came as early as 1628. Samuel Gott was residing in this town, Oct. 23, 1702, when he bought of William Cogswell of Chebacco, for sixty pounds, lawful money, eight six-acre lots lying upon Halibut Point, and fixed his abode in that remote section of the town. His wife was Margaret, daughter of William Andrews of Ipswich. She died Oct. 30, 1722, aged forty-six; and he married next, in 1723, Bethany Cogswell of Ipswich, who died April 23, 1755, aged sixty-seven. Mr. Gott died Nov. 3, 1748, about seventy-one years of age. He had a large family of children, of which the names of five are mentioned in his will. Some of his descendants have filled stations of the highest respectability and usefulness. Among them may be mentioned here John, who was a representative two years; and Lemuel, his son, a physician for several years in his native place, but now practising in Berlin, Mass.

JOHN GILBERT. — The early home of the Gilberts, in England, was Devonshire County; where Sir Humphrey Gilbert, the distinguished navigator (who found a grave in the Atlantic Ocean, Sept. 9, 1583), was born. A Humphrey Gilbert was of Ipswich in 1648. From an adjoining town (Wenham), John Gilbert removed to Gloucester in 1704. He sold possessions in that place, December, 1703; and in April, 1704, for thirty-six pounds, bought of Morris Smith twenty acres of land, lying partly in Manchester and partly in Gloucester. In June of the same year, he had liberty from the town to get timber for a house-frame twenty-four feet long and eighteen wide. By his wife Martha he had two sons (William and Jonathan) and three daughters, born in Gloucester. Another son probably, born in Wenham, was John Gilbert, jun., who married Mary Coy in 1734, and had a son Coy, who was drowned in Boston, Nov. 7, 1755, aged twenty. JONATHAN GILBERT married Abigail Rogers of Newbury, and died about 1800, aged eighty-six. He had several children; one of whom (Jonathan) died in May, 1836, aged eighty-six. Three of his posterity (two sons and a grandson) have been representatives, — Samuel, in 1832; Addison, son of the latter, in 1836 and 1837; and Moses, in 1846.

JOHN HARRIS, with his wife Susanna (who was a daughter of William Ellery), first appears in town, Nov. 29, 1702; when their son John was born. Another son (William) was born Jan. 10, 1705; and the death of the mother followed in five days. By the county-records, he is shown, March, 1709 (then of Ipswich, locksmith), as the purchaser of certain parcels of land at Sandy Bay, of Richard Tarr; and in another purchase at the same place, in 1712, he is said to have been of Gloucester: but it is probable that he had removed back to Ipswich at the time of his death, which was before 1716. Thomas Harris and his family were warned out of town in 1711. In 1720, he had a grant of land near his own, at Pigeon Hill; and was then, without doubt, residing in that locality. Thomas Harris, jun., married Sarah Norwood in 1727, and had eleven children.

Thomas Sanders and Nathaniel Sanders made their appearance in town, simultaneously, in 1702. Joseph Sanders, shipwright, is mentioned in 1708. A Widow Mary Sanders, perhaps the mother of all the preceding, died Dec. 21, 1717, aged sixty. Nathaniel had a wife Abigail, and nine children recorded in our records. Thomas Sanders married, Jan. 7, 1703, Abigail Curney; who died Feb. 12, 1767, aged ninety. He had three sons and four daughters; and died July 17, 1742, aged sixty. In March, 1704, he had of the commoners an acre of ground between the head of the Harbor and Cripple Cove; and, in 1706, a piece of flats below where he built vessels. He was a shipwright himself, and carried on the business of ship-building extensively. From the frequent occurrence of his name in connection with grants of ship-timber, it is evident that he was a man of great enterprise. In 1725, he commanded the government sloop "Merry-meeting." His oldest son Thomas, born in 1704, married Judith, daughter of Capt. Andrew Robinson, in 1728; and died Oct. 24, 1774, aged seventy: she died Aug. 30, 1770, aged sixty-six. He was commissioned as lieutenant of the sloop "Merry-meeting" in 1725, and passed a large portion of his life in the service of the Province, as commander of a government vessel. On one of his voyages to the eastward, he was taken by a party of French and Indians. Under the guise of a happy and contented appearance, he allayed all their apprehensions of his escape; and, at Owl's Head, took an opportunity, when they were sound asleep, to abscond with their bag of money, amounting to about two hundred dollars. This he hid under a log, and then made his way to the fort at St. George's. Many years afterwards, returning from Louisburg with Gen. Amherst on board, he related the adventure to that officer; and, becoming becalmed near Owl's Head, requested the general to go on shore with him, and assist in looking for the money. The latter was somewhat doubtful about the story; but complied, and, soon after they had reached the shore, saw Sanders lay his hand upon the prize. In January, 1745, he sent a memorial to the Governor, urging his inability to support himself, and to get good able-bodied men to navigate the Province sloop under the scanty allowance made them, and praying for an addition to the wages of himself and company, and to the allowance for the hire of the sloop "Massachusetts." The Governor, in communicating the memorial to the House of Representatives, says, "I am satisfied with the reasonableness of Capt. Sanders's request, and am extremely loath to lose so faithful and experienced an officer. I must desire you would give him such relief as may make him easy in the service." The wages and pay referred to were — for the sloop, five shillings a ton per month; to the captain, five pounds a month; to the mate, a trifle less; and to the sailors, fifty shillings a month each. Capt. Sanders was engaged in the expedition to Cape Breton the same year; and, during the siege, had command of the transports in Chapeau Rouge Bay. A public notice of his death says, "He was a gentleman well respected among those who had the honor of his acquaintance, and died greatly lamented." He had eleven children, of whom three were sons, who married in town, — Thomas, Joseph, and Bradbury. Thomas became a distinguished citizen. He married, about 1752, Lucy, daughter of Rev. Thomas Smith of Falmouth, Me.; and died Jan. 10, 1774, aged forty-five. His widow became the second wife of Rev. Eli Forbes; and died June 5, 1780, aged forty-eight. She lies buried by the side of her first husband, and her gravestone is inscribed with the name that she received by her first marriage; a circumstance which tells enough of its own history. Mr. Sanders was fitted for college by Rev. Moses Parsons of Byfield, and graduated at Harvard in 1748. It is not known that his education was designed to fit him for any learned profession; and it is believed that his life was chiefly devoted to commercial pursuits. He was representative from 1761 to 1770 inclusive, and afterwards a councillor. He resigned his seat at the Council Board in June, 1773. He built, though not in its present shape, the large mansion next east of the Unitarian Meeting-house, where he resided a number of years. His death took place at a critical political period; and, if his life had been spared, he would have borne, without doubt, in the events which followed, the conspicuous part for which his education, patriotism, and experience in public affairs, so well qualified him. His character was thus highly eulogized in a newspaper of the day: —

"Exalted sentiments of generosity, humanity, piety, probity, and public spirit, animated his soul with many noble resolves, and prompted him to vigorous exertions in public and private life. With an uncorrupt and truly patriotic spirit, he served the town for several years as representative; and, for several years, had a seat at the Council Board: in which political spheres, a laudable ambition of being extensively useful engaged the liberal movements of his soul in assiduous efforts to be a guardian to the civil Constitution, for which he had a tender solicitude. Loyalty, virtue, and public spirit, bloomed in his mind, and merited approbation; till the springs began to fail; until infirmities brought on a relaxation of nature and a languor of spirit, which caused him to resign his public posts, and retire. In the uneven traces of life, he exemplified the grace of patience, and preserved a calm and harmony within himself. Christian fortitude encircled his soul in variegated trials; and he viewed the approach of death with Christian confidence, and is doubtless gone to rest in an unchangeable state of everlasting bliss." This obituary is undoubtedly from the pen of his pastor, — Rev. S. Chandler.

Mr. Sanders had twelve children; but none of his descendants remain in town. His son Thomas, born in 1759, settled in Salem, and died, a wealthy citizen of that place, June 5, 1844, leaving several children, one of whom was the wife of Hon. Leverett Saltonstall. Joseph, the youngest son of Hon. Thomas Sanders, became a seafaring man. He was for some time a naval officer, serving as lieutenant on board the United-States frigate "Constitution." He married, and had his home in Edgartown; where he died July 13, 1804, aged thirty-two. Joseph Sanders, son of the first Thomas, born in 1707, had a wife Elizabeth, and died before 1743, leaving a son Joseph, who was drowned on his passage to George's River, Me., April 6, 1757. The latter left a son Thomas, who was born at Pleasant Point, George's River, June 15, 1753. On the death of his father, he was taken into the family of his kinswoman, Mrs. Gibbs; by whom the expenses of his education were defrayed. He graduated at Harvard College in 1772; and, excepting occasional employment during the war in privateering, is believed to have spent his whole after-life in teaching school. After keeping the town-school several years, he was hired by a number of individuals, who erected the building long known as the Proprietors' Schoolhouse, to take charge of a select school. He had been in their employment but a short time, when, in consequence of severe and unmerited censure of his course as a teacher, a depression of spirits was brought on, and induced such a state of mind as caused him to put an end to his existence, April 23, 1795. He was lamented as a capable and faithful teacher and an excellent man. John, third son of the original settler Thomas, born in 1713, died Jan. 17, 1742, leaving an only son John, who died Oct. 24, 1807, aged seventy-two. Descendants in this line, bearing the name, still remain in town. One (Henry) was representative in 1840 and 1843.

Ezekiel Woodward has the birth of a child recorded here in 1702; but he did not become a landholder till 1707, when he bought a messuage and one hundred acres of land, at Little River, of Jacob Davis. Though there were several persons of the name of Woodward, early residents in Massachusetts, it is reasonable to suppose that this Ezekiel was the son of Ezekiel who bought a house and lot in Ipswich in 1661, and who had a son of the same name born there in 1666. Ezekiel of Gloucester had several children by his wife Hannah, who died Feb. 2, 1719, aged forty-eight. He next married Mary Davis, April 15, 1719; who died, Nov. 1, 1721, of small-pox, aged fifty-three. It appears that he was thrice married after the death of the last-named wife: to Rachel Haskell, June 22, 1722; to Anna Low of Ipswich, April 13, 1732; and to Widow Rebekah Bennet, Nov. 24, 1740. He died Jan. 16, 1743. His sons Ezekiel and Beamsley married in town; the former to Elizabeth Davis, Nov. 30, 1720. He settled at the Harbor about 1738, and carried on the fishing business. He was a deacon of the First Church several years, and otherwise a prominent citizen. He was living in 1761. He had nine children; of whom Ezekiel, the oldest son, married Abigail Sanders, and had several children. She became a widow before 1770, when she married Rev. John Rogers. Moses and Davis, two other sons of Deacon Woodward, married, and removed from town, — the former to Portsmouth, N.H.; and the latter to New Gloucester, Me. It is only by a grandson of the last-named Ezekiel — Hon. John Woodward Lowe — that the name has been borne in town for many years. Besides the preceding, the following-named persons moved into town at this time: —

Moses Durin, by his wife Sarah, had a son Jonathan born here in 1702, who died March 10, 1725. He also had a daughter Sarah, and a son Nathaniel, who married Hannah Elwell, Feb. 7, 1717, and had four children. None of the family appear here after 1725. Moses Durin had, in 1707, a grant of land on "the west side of his now dwelling-house;" and, in 1719, his son Nathaniel had half an acre, on which he had built his house.

William Manning had a son William, born Feb. 16, 1702, by his wife Sarah, who died March 3 following. This son was probably the William Manning who married Mary Boyles in 1723, and had several children born in town.

Benjamin Averill came in 1703; and, by his wife Mary, had ten children born here. Three of his sons appear to have married in town. He had a grant of land, in 1707, on Eastern Point, adjoining Samuel Ingersol's.

James Godfrey has the births of three daughters recorded on our books, the first of which was in 1703. He had a house in the Second Parish, and probably lived there. James, who married Hannah Haskell in 1723, is supposed to have been his son.

Benjamin Hoping, or Hoppin, has the birth of a son Benjamin recorded here in 1703, a daughter Hannah in 1705, and a son John in 1707. In the latter year, he had four acres of land on the west side of Gallop's Folly Brook, where he then lived.

Daniel Gutridge, or Goodridge, had a wife Mary, and a son Daniel, born in 1704. He also had two daughters. John Goodridge appears here in 1710, and has several children recorded. Two of his sons are supposed to have married in town.

John Burrill and wife Hannah appear here in 1704, when John, their son, was born. The birth of two daughters afterwards completes our knowledge concerning him.

It is worthy of remark, that two of these settlers sought their homes in opposite extremities of the town: John Gilbert, on the Manchester line, where the Millets were probably his only near neighbors; and Samuel Gott, at Halibut Point, where he was the first known settler. His nearest neighbors on one side were at Lane's Cove, and, on the other, at Sandy Bay; both inconveniently distant for social intercourse, or friendly offices in case of sudden need. At the latter place, Richard Tarr and John Pool, the pioneer settlers, still had the territory all to themselves; with the exception, perhaps, of John Babson's occasional use of his grant at Straitsmouth for fishing. The first, and for many years the only, neighbors of Samuel Gott, on the Sandy-Bay side, were — William Andrews, who owned land near his in 1707, and who was a brother of his wife; Joshua Norwood, who was also connected with him by marriage, and had a large tract of land in that part of the town, on which he settled, probably, soon after Mr. Gott fixed his residence there; and Jethro Wheeler, who, in 1712, bought of Joshua Norwood, for one hundred and fifty pounds, about one hundred acres of land near Pigeon Cove.

Wheeler had lived in Newbury before 1695, and subsequently in Rowley, where he sold land in 1704. Nothing further is known concerning him. Jethro Wheeler, jun., appears in 1723: the same, it is supposed, who married Sarah Haraden in 1717, and had four children recorded in the registry of births; namely, Jethro, Sarah, Moses, and Haraden. About the time of Wheeler's settlement, or not long after it, Thomas Harris was permanently located at Pigeon Hill; and in May, 1716, Edward Bragg had come from Ipswich, and was living in a house somewhere on the back side of the Cape. Passing along by Pool's and Tarr's to the south-east end of the Cape, Mr. Gott could find there, about 1708, a house, in which Peter Emons then lived; and another, occupied by Peter Bennett, who at that time owned a tract of four hundred acres opposite Milk Island. In the other direction, he had Benjamin Hoppin for a neighbor in 1703; and William Woobury, in 1705. These two, in those years respectively, settled at Gallop's Folly, and are the first who appear as residents in that part of the town. Curiosity may prompt inquiry concerning the name given to the last-named locality; but no further satisfaction can be gained than that afforded by the tradition of the place, that a man named Gallop once carelessly ran a vessel into the cove there, and lost her, mistaking it for the entrance to another haven; and that, to perpetuate the memory of his fault, it received the name by which it has ever since been known. It might be supposed that the unfortunate man was Benjamin Gallop of Boston, whose sloop was cast away near Pigeon Cove in 1712; but the name was given many years before: and a last resort for conjecture as to its origin may be found in the possibility that it came from John Gallop of Boston, an early pilot, who may have had charge of the "great shallop," which, in 1635, was cast upon the rocks, coming out of Annisquam Harbor.

CHAPTER VIII.

SHIP-BUILDING.—FIRST SCHOONER.—NEW SETTLERS.

"OF all fabricks," says the famous captain who first coasted along the shores of "the fair headland Tragabigzanda," "a ship is the most excellent." If he could revisit the desolate waters which, less than two centuries and a half ago, he navigated in a small boat with eight men, and contrast the rude and clumsy barks of his own time with the stately and magnificent ships which now leave these waters to traverse the most distant seas, and carry the blessings of civilization to the remotest ends of the earth, what would he say of the present excellence of this "fabrick"? In his enthusiastic admiration of New England, he did not overlook its materials for progress in the noble art which so attracted his admiration: and, if he had lived to the full age of man, he might have seen several specimens of the first colonial attempts in it; while the lapse of a hundred years from his discovery of Cape Ann would have shown him the product of a kindred though inferior genius, which, in 1713, was launched from its shores, and was the first of the neat and graceful craft which now, by the name of "schooner," are known to all the maritime nations of the earth.

In 1642, no less than five ships were built in the Massachusetts Colony.* Soon after that date, the business was commenced in Gloucester, as already noticed in a preceding chapter; the cause or result, probably, of the settlement of an eminent shipwright in the town. But there is no reason to believe that it continued for any considerable length of time one of the leading

* Young's Chronicles of Massachusetts, p. 185.

branches of industry here; nor does it appear that any vessel larger than a shallop or a sloop was owned in the place before the eighteenth century. In 1698, a ship was built in the town, for Boston merchants;* and the notice of this occurrence is the first sign of the activity in that employment in which our people soon afterwards engaged on their own account. In the revival of this business in Gloucester, Thomas and Nathaniel Sanders appear conspicuous. They each built a sloop in 1702;† and, in 1704, the former built two brigantines, one of eighty, and one of a hundred tons. Eight vessels of the last-named description, and one ship, were built here in the three years immediately following 1703; and, from that date to 1712, upwards of thirty sloops were built of timber furnished by the town's common land. Most of these sloops were open; and, of this class, a few measured about fifty tons in burthen. Some of them were sold out of town; but the larger portion were owned here, and were, without doubt, employed in the business of the place. No means exist for gaining information concerning the vessels built

---

* "Liberty is given to the gentlemen of Boston that is concerned in building a Ship heare in the towne of Gloucester to get what timber is needful upon the town's common land, provided they employ such men of the town as are capable of working upon the ship" (Town-records, October, 1698).

"Sold by y[e] Selectmen, by order of ye towne, to Mr. Timothy Thornton, so much timber as may be needful for ye building of ye Ship, at one and nine pens per ton" (*ib.*, February, 1699). Timothy Thornton, Esq., son of the Rev. Thomas Thornton of Yarmouth, was a merchant of Boston, and one of the largest ship-owners and most noted ship-builders of that period. He also took an active part in public affairs as commissioner, selectman, and representative. Besides the transaction above mentioned, he had other business connections with our people. He died Sept. 19, 1726, aged seventy-nine years. To one of his descendants (J. Wingate Thornton, Esq., of Boston, author of the "Landing at Cape Anne") I take pleasure in acknowledging my indebtedness for many favors in the preparation of this work.

† "Jany. 28, 1702.—then sold to Nathanill Sanders twealff tres for one pound ten shillings; to be oak trees for his youse about y[e] Sloop he is going to build" (Town-records).

"December, the 28th day, 1702.—then receaved of James Parsons, Jephery Parsons, John Parsons, and Nathanaell Parsons, a bond for to pay to the towne the sume of three shillings pr. tunn, if they do sell or dispose of the Sloop out of the towne which Thomas Sanders is a building for the above said Parsonses; and the said Parsonses is to pay to the towne three shillings pr tunn in case the s[d] Sloop be sold or disposed of out of town before six years be expired after the Launching of the said sloop" (*ib.*). A similar bond was required from all the grantees who, about this time, had timber from the Town's Common for building vessels to use in the town.

in the town for many years subsequent to the first decade of the last century; nor does it appear, at any period of our later history, that the business of ship-building has been the employment of a considerable portion of the people. For more than half a century, few of the vessels employed in the foreign commerce of the town have been built in it; and nearly all those engaged in the fisheries have been built in a neighboring place.

There is no subject connected with the first century of the history of New England about which so little is known as of the small vessels employed in navigating its waters. Specimens of the habitations, furniture, and dress of our ancestors have come down to our times; but of the small craft employed in their coasting, fishing, and trading voyages, our information is hardly sufficient even to enable the imagination to represent satisfactorily their form and appearance when under sail. We know that they had shallops, sloops, pinnaces, barks, and ketches; but, concerning the masts, spars, rigging, and sails of these vessels, it may be said that we know nothing.

The ship-carpenter who came over to the Plymouth people in 1624 soon died, but not till he had built them two shallops; one of which they employed in the fall of the next year to carry a load of corn on a trading voyage up the Kennebec River. She had "a little deck over her midships to keepe ye corne drie; but ye men were faine to stand it out all weathers, without shelter." The next year, they "tooke one of ye biggest of ther shalops, and sawed her in ye midle, and so lengthened her some 5 or 6 foote; and strengthened her with timbers, and so builte her up, and laid a deck on her; and so made her a conveniente and wholsome vessell, very fitt & comfortable for their use, which did them servise 7 years after; and they gott her finished, and fitted with sayles & anchors ye insuing year." Such were the first vessels of the Pilgrims. In the Massachusetts Colony, we find Gov. Winthrop, the year after his arrival, building the "bark" "Blessing of the Bay," of thirty tons; which was valued five years afterward at one hundred and sixty pounds. During the subsequent seventy or eighty years, frequent mention is made in the histories and records of the time of small vessels of the different kinds before named, used mostly in the Colony; but we are not favored in any case with a description of the hull, spars, sails, and rigging.

The ketch was then probably what she was before and afterwards, — a vessel with two masts, having the principal one placed so far aft as to be nearly midships; and the other, a short one, almost close to the stern. In the early days of navigation, these masts carried lateen-sails; but, in the last century, the larger mast had the yards and sails of the foremast of a ship, and the smaller was rigged like the mizzen-mast of a bark of the present day. This vessel seems to have been a favorite with our New-England ancestors. One of only sixteen tons burthen cleared from Boston for Virginia in 1661. In 1670, the shipping of a distinguished Boston merchant consisted almost entirely of vessels of this class;* and, a few years later, the fishing vessels of Salem are called "catches." It were useless to conjecture about the rig of the other small craft that have been mentioned; for it is hardly a matter of much interest, except with reference to a question to be presently considered. The conclusion to which all inquiry on the subject will lead is, that little is known about the vessels used on the coast of New England before 1713; when Capt. Andrew Robinson of Gloucester gave a new name to our marine vocabulary, and a new rig to the commerce of the world.

A current tradition of the town relates the origin of the "schooner;" and abundant testimony, of both a positive and negative kind, confirms the story so strongly, that it is unnecessary to take further notice here of the verbal account. Dr. Moses Prince, brother of the annalist, writing in this town,

* In searching the Suffolk Probate Records for information on the subject of this chapter, my eye rested on the following, in the inventory of the estate of Capt. Peter Oliver; and it seemed to me worth copying: —

Catch called ye Sarah	£50	1-8 of a Catch Society	£60
old shallop & apurtenance	8	5-32 of a Catch Hopewell	50
3-16 of a catch Endeavour	80	2-3 of a Catch Roebuck	40
3-16 of a Ship Supply	150	1-3 of a Catch Mary Ann	40
3-8 of Catch Expedition	60	1-2 of a Catch Exchange	20
1-16 of Ship Content	30	2 shallops and furniture	30

This gentleman was "an eminent merchant in Boston." He was grandfather of Andrew Oliver and Peter Oliver; names famous in the History of Massachusetts.

Sept. 25, 1721, says, "Went to see Capt. Robinson's lady, &c. This gentleman was the first contriver of schooners, and built the first of the sort about eight years since; and the use that is now made of them, being so much known, has convinced the world of their conveniency beyond other vessels, and shows how mankind is obliged to this gentleman for this knowledge." Nearly seventy years afterwards, another visitor gives some further particulars of this interesting fact. Cotton Tufts, Esq., connected with us by marriage, being in Gloucester, Sept. 8, 1790, writes: "I was informed (and committed the same to writing) that the kind of vessels called 'schooners' derived their name from this circumstance; viz., Mr. Andrew Robinson of that place, having constructed a vessel which he masted and rigged in the same manner as schooners are at this day, on her going off the stocks and passing into the water, a bystander cried out, '*Oh, how she scoons!*'* Robinson instantly replied, '*A scooner let her be!*' From which time, vessels thus masted and rigged have gone by the name of 'schooners;' before which, vessels of this description were not known in Europe nor America. This account was confirmed to me by a great number of persons in Gloucester."† The strongest negative evidence corroborates these statements. No marine dictionary, no commercial record, no merchant's inventory, of a date prior to 1713, containing the

---

* "*To scon*, v. a. To make flat stones, &c., skip along the surface of the water." *Clydes.*

"*To scon*, v. n. To skip in the manner described above; applied to flat bodies. *Ibid.* Isl. skunda, skynda, festinare." — *Jamieson's Etymological Dictionary of the Scottish Language, Supplement*, 1825.

† The schooner, in the marine language of France, is *la Goëlette:* "Navire qui, dit-on, servit d'abord exclusivement sur les côtes d'Amérique, et qui, depuis, est devenu assez commun en Europe . . . La Goëlette n'est nommée ni dans l'Hydrographie du P. Fournier, ni dans le Dict. de Desroches (1687), ni dans celui d'Aubin (1702). On trouve, dans le Dict. de Saverien (1781), les orthographes Goualette et Gouelette. On y lit aussi, sous la rubrique Goulette, la définition d'un petit navire qui ne doit être autre que la Goëlette. L'Encyclopédie Méthodique (1786) mentionne la Goëlette en ces termes: 'Petit bâtiment fort usité parmi les Anglais, surtout ceux d'Amérique, et dans nos Colonies d'Amérique.' Les mots, *fort usité*, nous autorisent à croire que, déjà assez longtemps avant l'année 1786, le navire dont il s'agit était en usage dans les parages Américains; mais nous ne saurions fixer l'époque de sa première construction, qui nous paraît ne pas remonter plus haut que le XVIIIe siècle." — *Glossaire Nautique.*

word "schooner," has yet been discovered;* and it may, therefore, be received as an historical fact, that the first vessel of this class had her origin in Gloucester, as stated by the respectable authorities above cited.

One can imagine the eagerness with which the active and inventive mind of Robinson seized upon the strange word applied to the peculiar motion of his vessel as she glided from the stocks, and the delight with which he exclaimed, as, according to the custom of the time, he dashed a bottle of rum against her bow, "A scooner let her be!" Tradition points to a spot on the wharf of Messrs. Samuel Wonson and Sons, then owned by Capt. Robinson, as the place where this vessel was built. The name given to her was meant at first, probably, to be her own particular appellation; but after she was "masted and rigged" in a peculiar manner, which was soon adopted by others, she became the type of a class, and the designation passed from a proprietary to a common use. That she was so "masted and rigged," is evident from the fact that she became the type of a class: and mariners, at least, will be interested in a few sugges-

* The result of my explorations in these fields may interest some readers. Let us begin at home. In the ten years immediately preceding 1713, more than thirty sloops were built in the town, but no schooner. The first mention of a vessel of this class in our records occurs in 1716, when a new *scooner* belonging to the town was cast away at the Isle of Sables. In the inventory of the estate of John Parsons, who carried on the fishing business, we have, in 1714, "1-3 of a fishing vessel, £19; 1-2 of a shallop, £15; 1-2 of an open sloop, £20:" but among the effects of Nathaniel Parsons, deceased, in 1722, are given "Scooner 'Prudent Abigail,' £180; scooner 'Sea Flower,' £83; and scooner 'Willing Mind,' £50." The notes of my examination of the Essex Probate Records show, from the inventory of Capt. Beamsley Perkins of Ipswich, 1721, "a skooner, £200; small ditto, £22;" the first mention of the name I could find there. In the next year appears, in the inventory of Capt. John Stacy, late of Marblehead, "a skooner called 'Indian King,' £250." A day's examination of several volumes of the Suffolk Probate Records ended at 1714 with the desired result. No schooner was found. In that year was entered the inventory of John Wilson, shopkeeper, of Boston, from which I copied as follows: "A sloop lying at Cape Anne (1-4), £45; a quarter of another sloop at Cape Anne, £45; 1 quarter of the sloop 'Society,' £40; the Sloop 'Sea Flower,' £20; one half of a sloop, £75; 1-8 part of a sloop, £25." The early Boston newspapers do not always mention in their marine intelligence the class to which a vessel reported belongs. In looking over imperfect files of these papers, the first schooner I found was the "Return," outward bound (June, 1718) for Great Britain; the next (March, 1720), the "Hope," for Virginia; and the "Phœnix," for Terceira. In 1722 were the schooner "Hope," for Virginia; a schooner of about fifty tons, taken by pirates at the eastward; the schooner "Mary" and schooner "Samuel," taken by Capt. Edward Low, a pirate, near Cape Sable; and the schooner "Milton" and schooner "Rebeckah."

tions concerning this peculiarity; though, from want of information about the small vessels of the preceding period, absolute certainty cannot be attained.

The vessels of the early period of English navigation are represented with lateen-sails; and, of these, each mast carried one. In the sixteenth century, these sails had given place, on two of the masts, to others, similar in form to the lower-sails and top-sails now in use for large vessels. On the mizzen-mast, the lateen-sail was still retained, and was the only sail carried on it. In the progress of improvement, this sail was reduced in size, and a top-sail was placed above it: and, at the close of the seventeenth century, the sails of a ship were nearly the same as they are now; with this singular exception, however, that the lateen-sail still kept its place on the mizzen-mast. But, in the course of a few years, this was reduced by taking away the part of the sail that projected forward of the mast; and it then became the modern spanker. The next step in the slow march of improvement was to shorten the lateen-yard by removing its superfluous part, and thus to convert it to the same use now served by the gaff; that is, to support a *fore-and-aft* sail, made in the form of a trapezium or trapezoid.* This sail, so sup-

* A, B, antenne qui portait l'Artimon latin, et qu'on appela *l'ourse*; B, E, F, partie de l'Artimon, qui disparut au XVIII. siècle: B, F, partie inférieure de l'antenne qu'on fit disparaître ensuite; F, C, partie supérieure qui est devenue la Corne d'Artimon, façonnée en croissant au point F; F, C, D, E, Artimon dans sa forme actuelle; A, A, orses qui manœuvraient l'antenne d'Artimon latin. — *Glossaire Nautique.*

ported, seems to have originated as here described; and Capt. Robinson, even on the watch for improvement, soon learned of this, and probably adopted it for his new vessel. It is nearly certain, that, before this time, no vessel was known to carry two trapeziform sails, suspended by gaffs, and stretched out below by booms: and, unless his "scooner" was the first to display them, it is uncertain when they came into use; and no effort to ascertain the peculiarity that characterized her will be likely to be crowned with success.

The tide of immigration continued to set towards the town, bearing many who became permanent settlers. First in the order of time since those last noticed comes JONATHAN SPRINGER, blacksmith, who in 1704, then of Scituate, bought land in Gloucester; and, about the same time, moved into the town. He had, in 1708, a grant of land and flats on which to erect a wharf and warehouse. He owned the house at the corner of Front and Pleasant Streets, still standing, though in a condition somewhat changed from its original appearance. This house, with other property, he sold, in 1710, to Philemon Warner. His wife Elizabeth died Nov. 16, 1713; and his own death followed on the 25th of the next May. Besides Jonathan, Elizabeth, and Lydia, — his children born in Gloucester, — his will mentions Abigail, Samuel, and Mary.

SAMUEL DAVIS married Ann Robinson, Feb. 23, 1704; and had nine children. He is probably the person of the same name, son of Isaac Davis of Falmouth, Me., who, with his brother John, is mentioned as living here in 1733. One of his children was drowned in the Mill Pond; near which, in the vicinity of Poles, he appears to have lived. In 1725, he had a grant of land adjoining his own at the Cape; and had then, perhaps, moved to that part of the town where John also then resided.

In 1706, WILLIAM SAMPSON and his wife Christian were in town. In that year, their son William was born. He was probably the aged citizen who is remembered by some of our elderly people as living about the close of the last century. But the name is rendered most remarkable in Gloucester by John Sampson, who, in 1708, came hither from Newbury, and took up his residence with Moses Durin, sen., and died Jan. 27, 1712, at the extraordinary age of one hundred and three years. When he came to this town, he had a wife Sarah, son Jonathan, and grandson John, not twenty-one years old.

PETER LURVEY removed from Ipswich to Gloucester in 1707. In 1710, he married Rachel Elwell, by whom he had eight sons. He was probably the ancestor of the families now in town bearing that name.

WILLIAM WOODBURY came from Beverly about 1705; when he bought, for £35, four of the Cape lots situated at Gallop's Folly. By his wife Judith he had a son Nicholas, born in 1707, who died the same year; and a daughter Judith, born in 1710. He died Jan. 17, 1713. Caleb Woodbury, who married Hepzibah Lane in 1718, and had several children, may have been his son. He resided at Gallop's Folly, where descendants are still living.

The following-named persons also appear in Gloucester about this time: THOMAS WISE, by whose wife Elizabeth a daughter Dorcas was born, June 15, 1705. DAVID DOWNING: he had a wife Susannah, by whom a daughter Lucy was born in 1706. He died in 1723, aged forty-six. JOHN MARINER, Jun., in 1706, had liberty to set up a house at Fresh-water Cove. He married Sarah Sawyer, and had several children. A John Mariner died Dec. 21, 1717, aged seventy-three; and Rachel Mariner, widow, Oct. 14, 1723, aged seventy-six, — father and mother, probably, of the preceding. JEFFREY MASSEY moved into town from Salem about 1707; became a commoner; and died in 1716, aged about fifty, leaving his wife a town-pauper. She died in 1718, aged sixty-two. JOSIAH TAINER married Rebekah, daughter of Richard Dike. He first appears here in 1707; when, and in two subsequent years, he had children born to him. JOHN COY and his wife Sarah moved into town from Manchester in 1706, and settled at Kettle Cove. He had two daughters born here, — Mary in 1708, and Hannah in 1712. A John Coy, "only surviving son and sole heir to Richard Coy, formerly of Salisbury," was of Wenham in 1706. HENRY MAINS and wife Abigail, from Boston, settled here in 1707, and had a daughter Abigail born the next year. He died before 1726. SAMUEL STOCKBRIDGE and Mary Villars were married here in 1708, and had the births of five children recorded. A family of SANFORDS moved into town, probably from Falmouth, about 1707; when Robert Sanford had a grant of land near Benjamin Hoppins's house. He died May 15, 1709. Bethiah Sanford, aged twenty-eight, died Feb. 20, 1720. A Widow Sanford died July 6, 1721, aged seventy-two. Josiah Sanford married Hannah Day of Manchester in 1719, and had three sons born here before 1725; when, it is supposed, he returned to Falmouth. JOHN MINZEE, or MINSEY, was warned out of town in 1708. He had a wife Edee, by whom his daughter Elizabeth was born in 1710. JOSEPH PRIDE, or PRYDE, settled in town about 1710, when his daughter Amy was borne by Elizabeth his wife; who died May 8, 1716, aged thirty. He married again, and had other children.

PAUL DOLLIVER and PETER DOLLIVER came to town about this period. It is not known how they were connected, if at all, with each other, or with the first family of the name in town. Paul Dolliver settled at Fresh-water Cove, near Richard. He married Mary Wallis, Feb. 11, 1713; and died about 1749, leaving a son Paul, who became a sea-captain, and died of small-pox on his passage from the West Indies, Aug. 17, 1760, aged thirty-two. Peter Dolliver, in 1708, bought land, which, from the description, is supposed to be the lot on Spring Street now owned by one of his descendants. The name does not again appear till the marriage of Peter Dolliver and Abigail Sanders, Jan. 25, 1722. He died of small-pox in February, 1764, leaving sons William and Peter, each of whom had a son William, — the fathers, respectively, of two of the few citizens in town bearing the name of Dolliver.

SAMUEL LANE (brother, it is supposed, of John, the first settler of the name here) removed into town about 1707. In 1708, he had a grant of land; and probably fixed his residence near that of his brother, on the north part of the Cape. A daughter Rachel, who died in childhood, was born to him the same year by his wife Rachel. Nothing more is known of him, except that he was a blacksmith by trade, and that he died Dec. 30, 1724, aged above sixty. Samuel Lane (his son, without doubt) married Mary Emmons, Oct. 23, 1722, and had several children; two of whom (Samuel and Zebulon) settled in the Harbor Parish about 1750. They both had families. The former was father of Stephen, who perished by shipwreck at Scituate, Dec. 28, 1774; leaving a son Jonathan, the father of our distinguished marine painter, Fitz H. Lane. Mr. Lane was born Dec. 18, 1804. At the age of eighteen months, while playing in the yard or garden of his father, he ate some of the seeds of the apple-peru; and was so unfortunate as to lose the use of his lower limbs in consequence, owing to late and unskilful medical treatment. He showed in boyhood a talent for drawing and painting; but received no instruction in the rules till he went to Boston, at the age of twenty-eight, to work in Pendleton's lithographic establishment. From that time, his taste and ability were rapidly developed; and, after a residence of several years in Boston, he came back to Gloucester with a reputation fully established. Since his return to his native town, he has painted many pictures, all of which have been much admired. He has often contributed a production of his pencil for the promotion of a benevolent enterprise; and, with characteristic kindness, he furnished the sketches for the engravings in this work.

Philemon Warner came from Ipswich in 1710, and bought Jonathan Springer's estate. He was a blacksmith, and some of his descendants were brought up in the same trade. By his wife Abigail he had two daughters, born here. He died about 1740, leaving a son Philemon, who married Mary Prince in 1726, and had eleven children. He became an elder of the First Church; and died April 14, 1778, aged eighty-one. His son Daniel was captain of one of the companies stationed here in 1775, and afterwards a colonel in the militia. He died in May, 1810, aged seventy-nine. Nathaniel, another son, commanded one of the Gloucester companies at the battle of Bunker Hill, and continued in service till the retreat from Long Island the next year; when, not advancing in rank by promotion as he expected, he left the army, and returned to Gloucester. He was a very brave officer; and might have attained distinction, if he had not allowed his anger to overcome his patriotism. Capt. Warner was never married. He died in February, 1812, aged sixty-eight. Elias Elwell, youngest son of Elder Warner, became a merchant of Boston; and died May 27, 1781, aged thirty-one. Two of the daughters of Elder Warner were wives of distinguished men, — Mary, of Hon. Samuel Holten of Danvers; and Susanna, of Hon. Cotton Tufts, M.D., of Weymouth, — an eminent physician. Capt. William Warner, son of Daniel, a venerable citizen of eighty-seven years, is the only representative of this family, in the male line, now living in Gloucester. Capt. William Warner of Boston, perhaps a son of our first Philemon, commanded a company raised by himself in the expedition to Cape Breton in 1745; and died on his passage home, Nov. 5 of that year, aged forty-five, and was buried in our ancient graveyard. He left a wife and four children.*

* An account of all the persons known to have settled in town before 1711 has now been given. As the population begins at this time to increase by immigration more rapidly than heretofore, I shall confine my notices of new-comers to such as became founders of existing families, or were otherwise prominent. I subjoin, however, a list of settlers from 1701 to 1750 inclusive, which contains all new-comers who are known to have been heads of families during that period: —

Nehemiah Adams.
Isaac Annis.
John Andrews.
William Andrews.
Benjamin Averill.
James Averill.
Stephen Ayres.
Thomas Ayres.
Jabez Baker.
Daniel Barber.
Rowland Battin.
Abraham Battin.
John Ball.
Philip Bayley.
Nathaniel Bayley.
Benjamin Bickner.
James Birch.
Thomas Bishop.
Francis Bloyd.
William Botheam.
Joseph Bond.
Benjamin Boynton.
Enoch Boynton.
Thomas Boffee.
Ebenezer Bowman.
Thomas Bryant.
Edward Bragg.
James Broom.
John Brewer.
James Brady.
William Bryant.
John Brock.
Josiah Bradbury.
John Burrill.
Abraham Burrill.
Valentine Butler.
Stephen Butler.
John Butler.
Stephen Burns.
William Burns.
Jacob Burnham.
Stephen Burnham.
Jacob Carter.
John Carter.
Joseph Carlisle.
William Carlisle.
Thomas Canneby.
Ebenezer Cass.
John Choate.
Josiah Choate.
Thomas Chubbs.
Stephen Cleigh.
Samuel Clark.
Ebenezer Cleaves.
Joseph Clough.
John Coy.
Thomas Cotton.
John Coombs.
Anthony Coombs.
James Condis.
Joseph Coward.
William Coas.
John Couillard,
Elias Cook.
Josiah Cook.
James Croxford.
John Curtis.
John Cumings.
Samuel Currier.
John Davis.
Samuel Davis.
Sylvanus Davis.
John Dane.
William Deal.
George Dennison.
David Downing.
Paul Dolliver.
Peter Dolliver.
Elisha Donham.
Jonathan Downing.
Felix Doyl.
Solomon Driver.
Thomas Dresser.
Moses Durin.

Nathaniel Durin.
Joseph Eaton.
Thomas Edes.
Samuel Elliot.
Cooly Emons.
Daniel Emons.
Edward Emons.
John Eulin.
Hugh Evans.
Joseph Everdean.
William Fears.
Jonathan Fellows.
Thomas Finson.
John Flin.
Samuel Fleming.
Nathan Fletcher.
Thomas Foster.
Richard Fowler.
Daniel Fuller.
Edward Gearing.
John Gilbert.
Daniel Gibbs.
Charles Glover.
Samuel Gott.
James Godfrey.
John Goodridge.
Thomas Goss.
Richard Goss.
Joseph Greley.
James Grant.
Josiah Grover.
Edmund Grover.
John Grover.
Andrew Grimes.
Stephen Greenleaf.
Samuel Griffin.
Daniel Gutridge.
Philip Gullison.
Daniel Gordon.
John Harris.
James Hardy.
Isaac Hall.
Isaac Hawes.
John Hale.
Robert Herring.
Joseph Herrick.
William Hilton.
Daniel Hill.
Joseph Hibberd.
Jacob Hibbard.
Timothy Higgins.
Samuel Hidden.
Benjamin Hoppin.
John Howard.
Solomon Howard.
Robert Honnors.
Richard Holland.
Jabez Hunter.
James Huse.
John Huse.
William Jackson.
Rev. Richard Jaques.
William Jefford.
Thomas Jenkins.
Josiah Jewett.
Edward Jumper.
Joshua Kendall.
John Kelsey.
Joseph Killam.
Benjamin Kinnicum.
John King.
Michael Kingsbury.
Nathaniel Kinsman.
John Knight.
Nicholas Kuetville.
Samuel Laighton.
Richard Langsford.
Samuel Lee.
Joseph Littlehale.
Nathaniel Low.
Peter Lurvey.
James Macoy.
Neal Macfederic.
John McClinch.
Daniel McAfee.
Henry Mains.
Jabez Marchant.
Ebenezer Marchant.
William Manning.
John Mariner.
Isaiah Marsh.
James Marsh.
John Matchet.
James Mattocks.
Jeffrey Massey.
Thomas Messervey.
John Minzee.
James Millens.
William Milbury.
John Mogridge.
Luke Morgan.
William Moore.
Robert Nason.
John Newman.
William Newman.
William Nelson.
Henry Newcomb.
John Noble.
Thomas Oakes.
Richard Palfrey.
William Parslee.
Benjamin Pattee.
James Paterson.
William Paine.
John Pearce.
Samuel Pearce.
James Pearson.
Benjamin Perkins.
Thomas Penill.
Richard Peters.
William Peters.
James Phipps.
Thomas Phipps.
Dr. David Plummer.
Moses Platts.
James Poland.
John Pollard.
John Powell.
Digory Preston.
Joseph Pride.
Thomas Rand.
Isaac Randal.
Robert Randal.
Jacob Randal.
William Rawlings.
Caleb Ray.
John Redding.
Benjamin Redding.
John Rigel.
Nathaniel Rust.
William Samson.
John Sampson.
Nathaniel Sanders.
Thomas Sanders.
Robert Sanford.
John Sadler.
Gregory Savery.
Thomas Saville.
Thomas Sheath.
Ephraim Shelton.
William Simerton.
Daniel Smith.
Richard Smith.
Eliakim Smith.
Jonathan Springer.
John Stacy.
Rufus Stacy.
Robert Stewart.
William Steele.
John Stenchfield.
Daniel Stanley.
John Stone.
Nathaniel Stone.
Hugh Stone.
David Stone.
Samuel Stockbridge.
David Stockwell.
Josiah Tainer.
Richard Tandy.
George Tappan.
Ebenezer Tarbox.
John Tarbox.
Philip Tewksbury.
John Thomas.
Samuel Thomas.
Joseph Thurston.
Rev. Samuel Tompson
Dr. Edward Tompson.
Jonathan Trask.
Nathaniel Travis.
Richard True.
John Tyler.
Peter Uran.
Richard Varrell.
Thomas Varrell.
Samuel Varrell.
Richard Vaughn.
John Walklate.
Philemon Warner.
William Webb.
Dr. Nicholas Webster.
James Webster.
John Wells.
Zaccheus Welcome.
William Westway.
Joseph Whiston.
Jethro Wheeler.
Rev. John White.
John White.
James White.
William White.
John Whiting.
George Williams.
John Williams.

Thomas Williams.
Evan Williams.
Joseph Winslow.
William Wilson.
Benjamin Winter.
John Wise.
Thomas Wise.
Joseph Wise.
Benjamin Wise.
John Winnery.
John Wonson.
Josiah Wood.
William Woodbury.
Ezekiel Woodward.
John Wotton.
Thomas Worley.
Ichabod Young.
William Young.
William Younger.

Stephen Burns was drowned at the eastward, November, 1718. Josiah Choate died Aug. 26, 1798, aged eighty-three. Samuel Fleming was drowned on the Banks, fishing, 1730. Daniel Fuller was lost at sea, on a fishing voyage, 1755. Capt. Robert Honnors lived at Kettle Cove; and died in September, 1763. John Knight and wife Lydia were of Manchester, Oct. 30, 1708; but were then, with two children, baptized by Rev. John White of our church. Another child (Benjamin) was baptized in 1709; and was probably the same who married Grace Tucker in 1735, and had a son Job, who was lost, with all his crew, on the Grand Bank, about 1790, leaving a son Stephen, who was a shipmaster, and was lost at sea about 1810. Joseph Killam died in the Second Parish, March 12, 1806, aged a hundred years, eleven months, and twelve days. Samuel Lee was severely wounded in the expedition against Port Royal in 1707. He died June 8, 1721, aged thirty-three. Nathaniel Low was from Ipswich. He sailed on a voyage from that place in 1742; was taken, and carried a prisoner to France. After his release, he went to England, and died in the city of Salisbury. William Nelson's wife Elizabeth was drowned from a canoe in the Harbor, Nov. 8, 1718. A William Parslee died April 18, 1725, aged seventy-four; and a Widow Parslee died in 1741. Thomas Penill was son of Philip Penill of Trinity Parish, Island of Jersey; and died before 1726. Dickri or Digery Preston had a son Joseph, who appears to have grown to manhood. It may have been a Beverly family; for William Presson of that town died about 1718, leaving young children. One of these, perhaps, was the father of William, who came from Beverly, and settled on the Chebacco Road. He was a tailor, and died Dec. 22, 1814, aged seventy-seven, leaving descendants of the name still living in Gloucester. John Reading died Nov. 17, 1716, aged fifty-six. John Stone, and probably the others of that name, were from Beverly. Robert Stewart was a native of England. He died before 1764, leaving a son Robert, who settled at Fresh-water Cove. Richard Varrell was from Ipswich; whence the other Varrells also probably came. John White was from Salem, and returned thither before 1732. He had a son John born here in 1722; the same, perhaps, who was a merchant of Salem, and died in October, 1792, aged seventy.

CHAPTER IX.

SECOND PARISH. — REV. SAMUEL TOMPSON: HIS MINISTRY AND DEATH. — SECOND PARISH MEETING-HOUSE. — SAMUEL PEARCE AND THE MERCHANTS. — DAVID PEARCE AND WILLIAM PEARCE. — LOSSES AT SEA. — NEW SETTLERS.

THE inhabitants of the town, residing on the westerly side of Annisquam River, had for sixty years been put to great inconvenience in attending public worship. Most of them were compelled to travel from three to five miles for this purpose; and, in the severe season of the year, few probably would be willing to encounter the difficulties attending bad roads and the passage over the ferry. They accordingly petitioned the town in March, 1710, for land on which to set a meeting-house. The petition was referred to a committee of five to consider and report what was best to be done concerning it. They did not report in favor of the petitioners; but they made a recommendation, which was agreed to by the town, that the selectmen, in engaging a schoolmaster for the people of that section of the town, should endeavor to procure a man, who, in the judgment of their reverend pastor, was suitably qualified to preach to them on the Lord's Day, for about three or four months in the winter season, in some convenient place to be designated by the inhabitants. The town voted to pay the schoolmaster out of the town-treasury, and to continue the arrangement three years.

In pursuance of the vote of the town, the selectmen agreed with Mr. Samuel Tompson, December, 1712, for twelve pounds, to keep a school there three months, and to perform the work of a minister during that time. At the expiration of three years, a further agreement was concluded, by which he was to have forty pounds for a year's teaching and four months' ministerial labor. But the people, wishing to settle and maintain a minister among them, petitioned, in March, 1716, to be set off as a separate precinct; and the town immediately complied with their request, by voting their consent, "that the inhabitants that live on the north-west and westerly side of this line — viz., beginning at the mouth of Annisquam River, the river to be the line unto the mouth of Little River, then Little River to be the line unto the head of said river; from thence on a straight line to the sea, on the easterly side of Kettle Cove — be set off as a precinct, in order to the settling and maintaining a gospel minister amongst them." Peter Coffin, Daniel Ring, Abraham Sawyer, James Dyke, and Joseph Lufkin, belonging to the section thus set off, entered their dissent.

The parish was incorporated by the General Court, June 12, 1716. At their first meeting, they set apart the 6th of September following to be observed as a fast preparatory to the calling of a minister. On the 5th of October, Mr. Samuel Tompson, with whose qualities as a preacher and a man they had become well acquainted, received a unanimous invitation to settle with them. They voted him a salary of sixty pounds per annum, so long as he could live comfortably by it; a condition of settlement which only his early death, perhaps, prevented from becoming a source of disagreement and discord. They also voted him, according to a prevalent custom of the time, a "settlement" of one hundred pounds. His ordination took place Nov. 28, 1716. Rev. Messrs. Wise and Fitch of Ipswich, and Cheever of Manchester, officiated on the occasion.

Mr. Tompson was a son of Rev. Edward Tompson of Marshfield, and was born at Newbury, — where his father instructed a school a few years, — Sept. 1, 1691. He graduated at Harvard College in 1710.

The records of the church, commencing with Mr. Tompson's ministry, are preserved; but they contain nothing of general interest. All the baptisms in the parish, during his own and the succeeding ministries, appear to have been recorded; and these give the records a value which should secure their preservation.

No memorials of Mr. Tompson's life and character, no incidents of his pastoral career, have been handed down to the generation now living in the place of his ministry. He died Dec. 8, 1724, aged thirty-three. The announcement of his death, in a newspaper of the time, is accompanied by the following remarks: "He was of a pleasant aspect and mien; of a sweet temper; inoffensive in his whole behaviour; pious and peaceable in his conversation; his ministerial gifts superior, and his fidelity, diligence, and success answerable; orthodox in his faith, and a fast friend to the constitution of these churches. And, as he preached, so he lived and died in the faith."

Mr. Tompson married, Nov. 21, 1716, Hannah Norwood. Their children were — Mary, born in 1719; Samuel, 1721; Edward, 1722; Abigail, 1724; and Samuel, 1725. The house in which he resided is still standing, and is situated a few rods north-west of the spot occupied by his meeting-house. His final resting-place in the old burying-ground of his parish is marked by a stone bearing the following inscription: —

HERE LYES BURIED
Y[e] BODY OF Y[e] REV[d]
M[r] SAMUEL TOMPSON
PASTOUR OF Y[e] 2[d]
CHURCH OF CHRIST IN
GLOSESTER AGED 33
YEARS DEC DECEMBER
Y[e] 8 1724.

The inventory of his estate amounted to £416. 2s., of which his books were appraised at £22. 7s. 6d. The parish paid Mrs. Tompson her husband's salary to the close of his year, and generously voted £30 in bills of credit to pay his debts. She probably soon removed from town with her family, as none of them are again mentioned here.

Joseph Haskell and Benjamin Haskell, members of the Second Parish, were deacons of Mr. White's church when the new church was formed, and were immediately elected to the same office in that. At their decease, their places were filled by other members of the same family, which kept this prominence in the church almost to the end of its existence.

The parish had already erected their meeting-house when

they chose Mr. Tompson as their minister. It stood on an elevated plateau, and commanded fine views both inland and seaward. The timbers of the frame were of oak, and very large. On three sides of the interior, it had a gallery, of such dimensions that it struck a modern beholder as out of all proportion to the size of the area upon which it was erected. That part of it assigned to the males of the congregation had on its front a row of long wooden pins, upon which they hung their hats. The floor and gallery were at first filled with long seats; but those on the floor soon began to give way to pews, and, in course of time, were all removed for the same purpose. The first privilege to build a pew was sold, for twenty shillings, to Benjamin Haskell, jun., Mark Haskell, and William Haskell, 3d, who were to have the two back seats going in at the west door, at the left hand of the meeting-house, "to build a pew for them and their wives, and to be seated nowhere else." This sale gave dissatisfaction to some; as it appears, by the record, that the parish was called upon, and agreed "to stand by the committee" who sold the privilege. Our fathers displayed considerable interest in the arrangement of their religious assemblies. They had a committee to "seat" the people in the meeting-house; and sometimes, by vote of the parish, designated the place which particular persons should occupy. Their proceedings in this last respect strike us as both amusing and ludicrous. For instance, in 1742, the Second Parish votes "that Capt. William Haskell should sit in the fore seat, where Capt. Eveleth sits; and that Joseph Haskell should sit in the side fore seat;" and, in 1757, "that Mr. Joseph Hibbard's wife move out of the long fore seat into the short fore seat."

The Second-Parish Meeting-house lasted through four generations, and outlived even the parish organization itself. It was taken down in 1846, when its frame still had its original strength, and only needed a new covering to secure it for another century or more against the assaults of the elements and of time. It was then probably the oldest church in New England standing in the shape in which it was originally built. Its venerable appearance and beautiful location made it an object of especial attraction to strangers; and to the people of the parish, though they had long ceased to use it for worship, it was dear, and consecrated to their hearts by its association with the joys and sorrows of their ancestors for more than a hundred years. Loath to see it demolished, they appealed to the public for money to repair it; but no sufficient response was made, and the ancient edifice was razed to the ground. In anticipation of that event, a drawing was made of its appearance at the time, and is correctly copied in the following engraving: —

The year 1713 deserves notice in our annals for the first mention of Samuel Pearce, the Gloucester ancestor of a family, which, by its wealth and influence, occupied a commanding position in the town for more than half a century. He had a brother John; perhaps the person of the same name who was here in 1712, and, in 1735, had a grant of land at Squam, where he had a shop. Samuel Pearce came from Duxbury. His grandfather Abraham Pearce, or Pierce, was in Plymouth as early as 1623; and removed thence to Duxbury, where he died before 1673. His father, also named Abraham, was born in Plymouth in 1638, and died in Duxbury in 1718. The son (Samuel) was married to Mary Saunders in Duxbury, Jan. 18, 1703. She died before 1728, when he married Abigail Pool.

His children born in Gloucester were — David, Jonathan, and Joseph, besides others who died in infancy. He was a shipwright, and had his residence on Eastern Point; to which place he was probably attracted by the demand at that locality for persons of his craft. The date of his death is not known. His son David, born in 1713, married Susanna Stevens in 1736; and died about 1759, leaving several daughters and three sons, — David, Joseph, and William. The sea then, as it has ever since, afforded the chief means of subsistence to our population; and David Pearce, the eldest of these sons, embarked upon it in his boyhood, well furnished by nature with the qualities which usually command success. He was enterprising, industrious, temperate, and frugal; and consequently, in early manhood, accumulated sufficient means to become the owner of two vessels engaged in the Labrador fishing, of one of which he himself was master. Continued success soon enabled him to increase this, and engage in other branches of business, and to attain, finally, for wealth, and extent of trade, the first rank among the merchants of the town. He shared with others the losses which resulted to our fishery and commerce from the disputes with the mother-country; and the commencement of the Revolutionary War found him considerably reduced in property. But he still had sufficient, with the help of partners, to build and fit out a large ship for privateering; which business he pursued to the end of the struggle, and was so much enriched by it as to be able to engage again extensively in his old maritime adventures of commerce and the fishery. Upon the establishment of peace, the country entered upon a career of great commercial prosperity, in which Mr. Pearce was a large participant. During a period of twenty years, his enterprise was crowned with such eminent success as to entitle him to a place among the wealthiest merchants of his time.* He owned several ships, some of which were built for his own use. One of them, of a burthen then

* The amount of Mr. Pearce's property was once estimated by himself at three hundred thousand dollars; but his brother, the late Col. William Pearce, never considered him worth more than two hundred thousand. If that was its value, it must have been the largest estate ever accumulated in Gloucester.

unusual, was employed in the whale-fishery; and the rest were kept in the European and India trade. With a class of smaller vessels, he carried on the West-India trade and the fisheries. With scarcely a single exception, the course of this active merchant was one of constant prosperity from youth to old age; when, at threescore and ten, as if to mark the instability of all worldly success, a series of misfortunes reduced him at once from affluence to bankruptcy. His most serious losses resulted from disasters to his ships; one of which, his last and best, with a valuable freight, was lost on the passage home from India. Against this loss he supposed himself protected by insurance: but his contract was vitiated by deviation; and the misfortune was so ruinous as to close his commercial career.

Mr. Pearce had devoted himself exclusively to business; and, having accumulated a large fortune, he was undoubtedly little accustomed to apprehend entire ruin from any hazards of the sea, or casualties of trade. The great and sudden change in his circumstances might therefore be expected, considering the frality of human nature and the usual weakness of age, to cast a shadow over his future peace and happiness; but it is said that he bore the trial with resignation, and did not allow the loss of his property to tinge the evening of his life with the hues of sadness and discontent. Some of our elderly people remember him in the days of his prosperity; and they speak of him as a man honest in all his dealings, and no less respected when wealth had departed than in the time of his greatest affluence. The venerable merchant passed from his high position to a state of dependence, in which he lived about ten years. He died of hernia, about the middle of March, 1818, aged eighty-two. His place of business was the wharf now known as Central Wharf. There he had a distillery, oil-works, and stores for merchandise. At the head of the wharf, on Front Street, he built a large house, in which he resided till his failure, when he removed to a smaller one on Middle Street.

Mr. Pearce married three times: first, Bethiah Ingersol of this town, who died of cancer in 1792, aged fifty-two; next, Mary, a sister of his first wife; and, last, Mrs. Elizabeth Gilbert of Brookfield. He had several children by his first wife; one of whom (David), born Jan. 18, 1766, graduated at Harvard College, 1786, and became a merchant in Boston. He married, in 1793, Rebecca, daughter of Dr. Charles Russell of Boston; and died in 1807, leaving several children.* Abigail, one of the daughters of our merchant, married Benjamin P. Homer, Esq., a wealthy merchant of Boston; and died in 1811, aged thirty-seven.†

Another distinguished citizen of this family was William, brother of the preceding, born in 1751. Left an orphan at an early age, he was provided for in the family of a maternal uncle; with whom he remained, receiving only such advantages of education as were common at that time, till he was old enough to commence a seafaring life. Good traits of character were early developed in him; and such were his habits of enterprise, sagacity, and prudence, that, when quite young, he was employed by his brother in the management of his extensive business operations. At about the age of twenty-one, he was placed in command of a vessel in the West-India trade; which he pursued with success, and in a few years acquired sufficient property to be able to establish himself as a merchant. During the Revolutionary War, he participated in the risks and profits of privateering; and, when peace took place, engaged in extensive commercial pursuits, which increased his property largely, and elevated him in the principal business marts of the world to rank with the most eminent merchants of New England. He continued in active business about fifty years; sharing, during the latter portion of the time, the labors and profits of it with

---

* These were two sons and three daughters: namely, Charles Russell, who became a merchant in Baltimore, Md.; David, who died unmarried; Catharine Russell, who married Commodore Geisinger of the United-States Navy; Harriet Rebecca, wife of Redmond Lawrence, Esq., of Bucks County, Penn.; and Helen, who married a Mr. Ostrander of New York.

† Mrs. Homer had nine children; one of whom (Mary B.) married Thomas Dixon, Esq., a gentleman of considerable distinction, and, for many years, Consul of the Netherlands for four of the New-England States; having his residence in Boston. To his son, B. H. Dixon, Esq., I gratefully acknowledge indebtedness for information and for interest in this work.

the members of his family, who, together with himself, constituted the well-known firm of William Pearce and Sons.

The life of this prominent citizen was one which claims much eulogy. He had a nice sense of commercial honor, and his business was conducted with an honesty that never suffered a stain. His wealth and character raised him to a position of great influence in his native town, which he retained many years, and never used in any manner that lessened the respect and esteem of his fellow-citizens. His daily life was irreproachable. His habits were all regulated by such a regard to temperance, that he could never be induced by convivial acquaintances to indulge in the dissipation and folly to which many of them were addicted. In public spirit, he was always among the foremost: but he had no ambition for the distinction of public office; having never, but on two occasions, been elected to such places. One of these was the command of a regiment of militia; and the other, that of delegate to the Convention for revising the State Constitution in 1820. Apart from his business, the sphere of his usefulness was private life.

The best characteristics of this good man were brought out, as usual, by severe trial. He had outlived the common limit of human life, and had long withdrawn from the cares and anxieties of business, — having secured, as he supposed, an abundant competency for his declining years, — when the commercial house of which he was the founder, and in which his name and property had always been used, was suddenly obliged to yield to the pressure of pecuniary embarrassment.

The shock came upon him as a tempest from a cloudless sky. Sudden descent from affluence to poverty is an ill not often borne with cheerfulness, or even resignation; but it was the crowning excellence of this venerable townsman, that he sustained the trial with Christian fortitude. He had long been a professor of religion; and he now gave proof, that, in laboring for the meat which perisheth, he had also provided for himself that which endureth for ever. He did not mourn the loss of property; no repining escaped his lips, but, instead thereof, the beautiful accents of resignation and content; illustrating the apostolic paradox, — "having nothing, yet possessing all things." His later years were years of rare felicity. Tender domestic attentions; freedom from the usual attendants of advanced years, — loss of faculties, pain and helplessness; exalted contemplations in view of the life beyond the grave, — all united to present in him the perfect picture of a happy old age. With patriarchal mien and feeble step, he moved about in almost daily visits; till at last, in his ninety-fourth year, a calm and peaceful death closed his well-spent life. He died Feb. 3, 1845.

Col. Pearce was twice married, and had several children. His oldest son William, born in 1777, spent a few years in a seafaring life, and then was admitted a partner in his father's business, from which he retired upon his appointment to the office of Collector of the Customs. He retained that place several years, and was removed from it by President Jackson in 1829. He was a representative to the General Court in 1806 and 1807. He died Dec. 14, 1841; then holding the office of President of the Gloucester Bank. George W., another son of Col. Pearce, has also been Collector of the Port, and was a representative to the General Court in 1841. One of the daughters of Col. Pearce married William W. Parrott of Portsmouth, who removed to Gloucester, and became a partner in the firm. He was for many years one of the leading citizens of the town, and its single representative seven years; after which he was a senator. He died Sept. 24, 1858, aged eighty-one. Edward H., a grandson of Col. Pearce, was a representative in 1856 and 1858.

Joseph Pearce, son of the first David, was an early settler of New Gloucester, Me.; and died there in 1837, about ninety years of age.

The early part of the eighteenth century has been noticed, in a previous chapter, as a period of great enterprise on the part of our citizens in the building of vessels. It is known that some of them were employed in the transportation of wood to Boston, and that others were used in fishing. That period undoubtedly marks the beginning of the maritime business of the town; but no incidents of its history have come down to us of an earlier date than 1716, — a year memorable in our annals for the first sad and sweeping calamity by shipwreck. Often since, by the same cause, has the town been shrouded in mourning; but, considering the scanty resources both of population and property upon which this misfortune fell, it stands almost without a parallel in all the subsequent disasters to be noticed in our history. Five vessels — upon a reasonable supposition, comprising not less than one-tenth part of the entire tonnage of the town — were wholly lost in that year on a fishing voyage to Cape Sable; and about twenty men — a fifteenth part, probably, of all the male citizens of the place — perished by the catastrophe.*

This loss of population was soon made up by immigration; and, among the families which came into town about this time, the names of some occur which are supposed to be represented by persons now living here, — Young, Rust, Langsford, Grover, Merchant, Williams, and Wonson.

The first YOUNG who appears in town was Ichabod, who, in 1716, married Abigail Elwell, and was drowned at sea, October, 1723. In 1719, he had sixty poles of land on the north-east side of the way going to the head of the Harbor. Another person of this name (William) married here, in 1725, Sarah York. He was, without doubt, the Gloucester ancestor of all the persons

---

* The excellent town-clerk of that day made a particular record of this sad loss, which I here transcribe: —

"About the middle of August, 1716, Daniel Stanley, master of a new scooner, was on a fishing voyage, near the Isle of Sables, with several other fishing vessels. There arose a very violent storm; wherein, as 'tis thought, said scooner was cast away upon the norther barr of said Isle of Sables. There was, in said scooner, said Stanley, æ. 23; Thomas Day, 40; George Denning, 30; William Botheam, 25; Francis Perkins, 17; and Abraham Thurrell of Newbury."

"On the 14th day of October (being Sabbath day), a number ('tis said about 14 sail) of fishermen were coming from Cape Sables, some of them within 30 or 40 leagues of our Cape, 7 of said vessels belonging to our town. There arose on said day a very Extraordinary storm, which lasted all that day and a great part of the night following. A few days after, four of our vessels arrived, some of them much broken, like wrecks; and four more are not yet heard of: viz., a sloop, Jeremiah Butman, æ. 26, master; with him, Andrew Sargent, 25; Richard Emons, 20; Morris Somes, 24; Peter Allen, 23. Another sloop, John Davis, æ. 26, master: with him, Joshua Giddings, æ. 38; and two men more. A third sloop, Stephen Ayres, master, æ. 26: with him, John Wise, 25; and two men more. A fourth sloop, James Elwell, æ. 25, master; and with him, Jeremiah Allen, æ. 18; Benjamin Josslyn, æ. 21; John Huchs, 25; and Jas. Farnham of Boston. This fourth sloop was seen near Cape-Sable shore in said storm; and none of the abovesaid vessels or men have been heard of since."

on the north side of the Cape bearing this name; and of Samuel L., who graduated at Bowdoin College in 1840, and, after spending a few years in trade at Lane's Cove, studied medicine, and settled as a physician in Marblehead.

NATHANIEL RUST had an acre of land, near the head of Little River, in 1729; but his marriage to Miriam Andrews of Ipswich is recorded here in 1717. He had a large family; and from him and from Samuel Rust, who married Anna Proctor in 1738, it is probable that all of the name in town have descended.

RICHARD LANGSFORD and Mary Row were married in 1719, and were the parents of five sons and four daughters. In 1726, he had a house and land on the north of Pigeon Hill; where, or in that vicinity, his descendants have lived to the present time.

The first GROVERS in town were Abigail and her child, from Beverly; who were warned out of town, according to a law of that time, in 1705. In 1719, the marriage of Josiah and Hannah Dolliver is recorded; and about that time, or soon after, Edmund Grover, with his family, came from Beverly, and settled at Sandy Bay. These two Grovers were brothers, sons of Nehemiah of Beverly, who married Ruth Haskell. The father of Nehemiah was Edmund; the same, perhaps, who was of Salem in 1637, and died in 1683, aged eighty-two. Josiah Grover had four sons; by one of whom only (Joseph), the name has been perpetuated. Joseph lived at Fresh-water Cove, where he had three children born before 1764, when he removed to Haverhill. His son Josiah was born in that year; and died in Atkinson, N.H., in 1856, aged ninety-two. On the organization of the church at Sandy Bay, Edmund Grover was chosen a ruling elder. His wife Mary died in 1757, aged seventy-eight; and he took the next year a bride of fourscore, who survived the marriage but a few months. He died Feb. 5, 1761, at an advanced age.

EBENEZER MARCHANT of Yarmouth married here in 1719, and has the birth of one child recorded. It is not known how, if at all, he was connected with Jabez, who appears in town soon after that date. The latter married Mary Babson in 1721, and had several children. She was probably the widow of John Babson, and daughter of John Butman, who lived at the head of Lobster Cove; where, in 1723, Jabez Merchant had a grant of half an acre of land. She died in 1778: the date of his death is not known. They had several children; the oldest of which was Daniel, who married Hannah Woodbury in 1744. His son Jabez was a soldier of the Revolution; and died in January, 1829, aged eighty. Another son (William) was the father of Epes, who settled at the head of the Harbor Cove soon after 1800; carried on the fishing business extensively for many years; and died April 10, 1859, aged seventy-eight.

The name of Williams is first found here in the records of the First Church, which show the baptisms of Elizabeth in 1707, and Mary in 1709, daughters of JOHN WILLIAMS. It is first mentioned in the town-records on the marriage of John Williams and Jane Robinson in 1720. Seven children are recorded as the fruit of this marriage; among whom was Abraham, probably the one who was lost on a fishing voyage in 1766. Also, in 1720, George Williams, a seaman, appears to have taken up his abode in town; and, in 1722, Thomas Williams; both of whom had children.

JOHN WONSON settled at Sandy Bay; where, in 1726, he had a house. He married, in 1720, Honor Wise, who was a widow; her husband, John Wise, having been lost at sea in 1717. The second husband must also have left her a widow in a few years; as, in 1730, she married Isaac Prince. The last child of four borne by her to Wonson was Samuel, the father of Samuel, who settled at Eastern Point, and died in 1829, about eighty years of age, leaving descendants, who are now among the most active and enterprising business-men of the town. One of the family (John) was a representative three years, and died Dec. 31, 1857, aged seventy-seven.

CHAPTER X.

FIRST PHYSICIANS. — DR. NICHOLAS WEBSTER. — DR. EDWARD TOMPSON. — DR. DAVID PLUMMER. — WORKHOUSE. — PROVINCE LOAN. — NEW SETTLERS. — SLOOP TAKEN BY PIRATES.

BESIDES the formation of a new church, another indication of the increasing population, at this period, is the settlement of a physician in the town. The early ministers of New England studied both physic and divinity: and it is supposed that Mr. Emerson thus qualified himself to minister to the bodily diseases as well as the spiritual wants of his flock; but the only evidence that he served them in this double office appears in the settlement of Hugh Row's estate, in which he receipts for twelve shillings and two glass bottles, "being all that was due to him for physic." About the time of Mr. Emerson's death, and for several years later than that, cases are mentioned of resorting abroad for medical help. In 1699, the selectmen had power from the town to send Ralph Andrews to the Lynn doctor, James Kibber, to be cured of his lameness, "if the said Kibber doth think he can cure him." In 1715, Robert Elwell died in Ipswich "under the doctor's hands. Female practitioners of the healing art were also occasionally resorted to; * a few instances

* 1700: Ann Millet was paid by the town £2. 6s. for what she did to the curing of Elinor Gooding. 1712: The town voted "that the requist made by Capt. John Harraden and Nathaniel Parsons concerning Elizabeth Hoping, about Enys Herrick cureing of her sore brist, her husband being not able; and these two men before mentioned ingaged to see her paid five pounds, if she did cure the woman's brist; and, if she could not cure it, she would have three pounds, or else the said Herrick would not medle with it. And it is left to the selectmen to consider the cure or no; that is, whether the woman's brist was cured by the said Mrs. Herrick." 1713, March 2: The selectmen paid Mr. Nathaniel Parsons £2. 10s. "for money which he payd for the cure of or parte of ye cure of Benj. Hoppin's wife." 1722: Mrs. Mary Ellery was paid £3. 18s. "for cureing Ebenezer Lurvey and his Diat." 1725, March 5: Elizabeth Gardner receives £1. 10s.; "it being for what she did to the cureing of the widow Peny's brest."

of which occurred, even after the settlement of a professional doctor in the town.

The first physician in Gloucester was NICHOLAS WEBSTER, unless John Newman be entitled to that distinction. The latter is called physician in 1712; but his name is usually given without the professional title. Dr. Webster, in March, 1717, bought a house of Thomas Sargent. The only allusions to this person in connection with Gloucester are as "physician" and "doctor;" but he had previously filled the clerical office, if, as is supposed, he is identical with Rev. Nicholas Webster of Manchester. He was born in Newbury in 1673; graduated at Harvard College, 1695, and died here after a few months' residence, Dec. 22, 1717, aged forty-three.

About three years after the death of Dr. Webster, Dr. EDWARD TOMPSON appears as a resident of the town. He is supposed to have been a brother of the minister of the Second Church. His intention of marriage with Ann Peker of Haverhill is in our town-records, and the births of his two children (Ann and Abigail) are there given. In 1721, he was engaged for one term to teach the school for £9. In 1725, he had land "on the town-neck, on the way leading from town to Squam;" and, in that and the following year, he was one of the selectmen. With the end of his duties in that office, his connection with the town appears to have closed. It is probable that he removed to Haverhill, where a Dr. Edward Tompson died about 1750.

The departure of Dr. Tompson did not leave the town without a physician. Dr. DAVID PLUMMER (probably son of Joshua of Newbury, born in 1696) married here, in 1723, Ann Newman; and, from that date, was a permanent resident in town. He lived in the Town Parish, which was still the chief seat of the population; probably on or near the homestead of Rev. John Emerson, the grandfather of his wife. The public records furnish all the information we have concerning this physician. His wife Ann died about 1736, having given birth to one son (Samuel) and five daughters. He next married, in 1737, Anna Barber, a widow; by whom he had two sons (David and Daniel), and several daughters. She survived her last husband; and the mention of her widow's dower, April, 1748, gives the only notice of the probable date of Dr. Plummer's death. SAMUEL, born in 1725, was educated in his father's profession, and succeeded to his practice. An unusual share of domestic trouble fell to the lot of this citizen. His first wife (Mary Low) died in 1749; his second (Hannah, daughter of Rev. Joseph Moody of York), in 1752; and his third (Elizabeth, daughter of Rev. Joshua Gee of Boston), in 1762. His fourth wife was Widow Anna Sanders. Dr. Plummer died Jan. 30, 1778, aged fifty-three. No further incidents of his life, deserving permanent record, have come down to us. His career was strictly a professional one; and his character, as sketched by one of his contemporaries,* was adorned with the highest virtues. By his several wives he had eleven children, — six sons and five daughters. The tragic elements of life enter largely into the history of the sons, and throw around one of them a veil of impenetrable mystery. Samuel, the oldest, born in 1752, graduated at Harvard College in 1771. He returned to his father's house, and engaged in the study of his profession; and, while thus employed, public suspicion rested upon him so strongly, as the author of a crime of the blackest dye, as to compel him to take an abrupt departure from the town. A female negro slave, belonging to his father, had been discovered to be in a state of pregnancy; and not returning one night from the Poles pasture, to which she had gone for the cows, a diligent search for her revealed the horrible fact that she had been murdered. A sword, with which the deed was done, was found in a crevice in a large rock. It was known to belong to Dr. Plummer; and

---

* Rev. Obadiah Parsons, in the following words: "A gentleman in whom were united the tender husband, the affectionate parent; and in whom the town has lost a distinguished and celebrated physician, a most important member of society; and his country, a warm, steady, and firm friend; the church of which he was a member, one who had the Redeemer's interest nearly at heart. He was one who pursued the direction the apostle gave to the Romans, xiv. 8. Without flattery, no man in this town, and among his numerous connections, was more universally beloved while living, nor whose death was more universally lamented. He lived in the Fourth Parish in this town, and died of a violent fever. In his last sickness, he exhibited a truly Christian patience and resignation; till, as I trust, he fell asleep in Jesus. Help, Lord; for the righteous fail."

the name of his son was immediately associated with this act of double wickedness. As no legal measures were taken to investigate the case, he did not leave home immediately; but the increasing mutterings of the people at length aroused apprehension of arrest, and he was obliged to flee to escape the possible consequences of the awful deed which had been committed. He left the town by the way of Squam Ferry and the Ipswich Road, and never again but once returned to it. Thirty years afterwards, on a Sunday morning, he made his appearance in his native place once more, and stopped at a tavern at the Harbor. His stay was short, extending only to the next day. No disguise was necessary, of course, after this lapse of time, to make him seem to others, as he must have felt himself, a stranger. It is not known that he avoided recognition, or that he sought to exchange greetings with the friends and acquaintances of his youth whom death had still spared. In company with a cousin, to whom he made himself known, he visited the spot of his birth and the haunts of his early years. Around these scenes he lingered several hours: but no visible emotion disclosed the state of feeling which they awakened; and he took his departure from them and from his companion, without leaving any information of himself by which his previous or subsequent career can be traced. Joshua, brother of the preceding, born in 1756, graduated at Harvard College in 1773, and also adopted his father's profession. He settled in the Harbor Parish of his native town; but, after a few years' practice here, removed to Salem, where he died in August, 1791. His wife was Olive Lyman of York, Me.; who, with seven young children, survived her husband. One of these children (Caroline), who died in Salem a few years since, by her will endowed a professorship in Harvard College, and also left a large sum to a literary institution in Salem. Dr. Plummer, though still a young man at the time of his death, had acquired considerable celebrity as a physician and surgeon. Of the other sons of Dr. Samuel Plummer, two came to their death by drowning: David, by shipwreck on Plum Island; and John, by being knocked overboard, just outside of Eastern Point, by the boom of a yacht which he was taking to the West Indies for sale. Another son (Joseph) settled in Weymouth. DAVID, son of Dr. David Plummer, born in 1738, became a merchant, and had a store at the corner of Hancock and Front Streets. He was a prominent citizen many years, though without official distinction. In the early days of the Revolution, his political affinities were not entirely agreeable to his townsmen; and, in order to shield himself from the suspicion of cherishing Tory principles, he was obliged to make a public declaration of his sympathy with the popular cause. His religious sentiments, too, found no favor with a large portion of his contemporaries; but they gained him the posthumous fame of being handed down, on the marble which marks his grave, as "one of the most distinguished members of the Universal Church in this town." He died in July, 1801. DANIEL PLUMMER was the father of Aaron, an aged citizen still living, who was representative in 1831 and 1832.

In 1719, the town built its first work-house. It had not for many years been without paupers; but the number was so small, that separate provision was made for each by the selectmen. The accommodations provided do not indicate a large number of this unfortunate class: for the house which the town ordered the selectmen to build was to be "24 or 26 foot long and 12 foot wide, and 6 foot stud between joynts." It was built in a few weeks, at a cost of twenty pounds; and immediately had for an occupant Ruth Miller. It was set upon land on the south-easterly side of Governor's Hill, reserved by the commoners for that purpose. By a vote of the town in 1732, an enlargement was provided for; but another vote in the next year, directing the selectmen to let it, authorizes an inference that it then had no occupants. This building was sometimes called Ruth Miller's house. She was a pauper several years, during a few of which she was probably the sole occupant of the tenement. The custom of providing for that class in private families, which had existed from the beginning, still prevailed, and continued long after the period of which we now write: but it might sometimes have been difficult to contract for the maintenance of a pauper; and in some cases, perhaps, the need of public help could be satisfied by furnishing a place of abode. One or both of these causes probably led to the erection of the first work-house.

Dependence upon public charity for subsistence has always been one of the last necessities to which the race that peopled New England would yield; and therefore, in every period of the history of our town, the class of paupers has comprised few who were not utterly helpless and friendless. The ratio of this class to the whole population was no greater in early times than it is now. Few then were very poor, and none were rich. For more than fifty years after the settlement of the town, it does not appear that any person in it was worth a hundred pounds, exclusive of real estate and farming stock; and, of that, not more than two or three had enough to relieve them from the necessity of daily toil.

Though a mint was in operation in the Colony as early as 1652, our ancestors had little to do with gold or silver coin. They not only did not accumulate it, but, such was its scarcity in their time, they rarely handled it. By early laws of the Colony, wampum and bullets passed currently in the payment of small sums; and the support of the government and the ministry could be paid in the products of the earth and the sea. In 1690 commenced the era of paper money, with the issue, by the Colony Government, of bills of credit. The first of these issues, made in the form of a loan to the towns, was in 1721; when, of £50,000 issued, Gloucester received £600. 10s., which was placed in the hands of Samuel Stevens, Ensign William Haskell, and Lieut. John Davis, as trustees, with directions to let the same on good and sufficient security, in sums not less than £10, at six per cent per annum, to any person dwelling in the town. This kind of currency continued in use more than half a century; and the people of Gloucester, without doubt, experienced their full share of all the inconveniences and loss with which it was attended. In 1726, this money was called in to be repaid to the Province treasury. Of another loan, in 1728, of the same kind, Gloucester let out its proportion as before; but had not succeeded, in 1739, in calling it all in.

The population of the town was still increasing by immigration;

but the new settlers deserving particular notice are few. The following, however, should be mentioned: —

William Fears first appears here at his marriage, July 24, 1721, to Naomi Stanwood; by whom he had sons William and John and two daughters. The date of his death is not known; but it appears that he was alive in 1755. His son William married Ann Bray, Nov. 27, 1746; who bore him, Aug. 26, 1747, twin-sons (William and John), and six other children in subsequent years. William married, in 1774, Widow Patience Williams; who died Nov. 25, 1842, at the advanced age of ninety-four.

James Broom, born in England, came to Gloucester about 1721; when he married Mary Tricker, by whom he had three sons and six daughters. Of the former, nothing is known beyond the period of infancy. They did not perpetuate the name here, and the blood only exists in descendants of the female line. Broom kept a tavern and barber's shop in the old house still standing on the south side of Middle Street, the second east from Hancock. His daughter Rebecca became expert as a barber, and carried on the business many years in the house at the corner of Pleasant Street and Middle Street. Her shop was long a place of resort for all the wits and genteel idlers of the town. Her husband was Andrew Ingersol, by whom she had a daughter Rebecca, who inherited her mother's peculiar faculty, and succeeded to her business. She was intelligent and lively; and through her intercourse from childhood with all classes of people, seamen and landmen, acquired a fund of information which made her a very agreeable talker. She last occupied an old house which stood on a lane leading from Front Street to the water-side; and many of our middle-aged people remember the attractions of pictures, birds, and anecdotes, which made the shop of "Aunt Becky" a place of the highest enjoyment in their youthful days. One of James Broom's daughters (Esther) married Sargent Ingersol, settled in Maine, and lived to be about a hundred years old.

Nehemiah Adams had a half-acre lot in 1725; but he was here in 1721, when he married Hannah Riggs. He had several children; but the only sons who married and settled in town were Nehemiah and Andrew.

Jonathan Trask came to Gloucester, about 1722, from Salem; where in the previous year, by his wife Hannah Gage, his son John was born. Seven sons were born to him in Gloucester. This name appears early in the Massachusetts Colony. William Trask was with Conant at Salem in 1628; and was, perhaps, one of his company at Cape Ann. He was a citizen of distinction, and died in 1666, at an advanced age. Osmand Trask of Beverly died about 1676, leaving several children, among whom was a Jonathan. Besides the sons above mentioned, Jonathan of Gloucester had a daughter Hannah, who, with her brother Jonathan, made oath to the inventory of her father's estate in 1745. He left a son Jonathan, who married Abigail, daughter of Capt. Charles Byles. This second Jonathan served as a soldier in the French War with his father-in-law; was at the taking of Quebec; and, at the commencement of the Revolution, enlisted as lieutenant in a company which was stationed on Winter Hill, near Boston, and afterwards in Cambridge. He went to Long Island with his company, and was in the engagements with the enemy there; but soon returned home in consequence of severe illness brought on by exposure and fatigue. He was confined to his house two years, and retained a broken constitution till his death, about 1800, at the age of seventy-seven years. His wife died in 1827, at the advanced age of ninety-seven. John and Isaac, sons of the last-named Jonathan, were both lost at sea. The former went to England just before the Revolution, and remained in that country. Soon after the peace, he had command of a ship which came to Newfoundland to load with dry fish for the Mediterranean; and, while there, wrote to his friends in Gloucester, — the last tidings ever received from him. Isaac Trask was in the army in the early part of the war; but, after about two years' service, he left it, and engaged in privateering. While in that employment, he was taken prisoner, and compelled to serve on board an enemy's ship. He was obliged to fight against his country, in the engagement with the fleet of Count de Grasse, as an attendant upon a gunner to hand cartridges and balls; many of which he contrived to slip overboard, while the gunner supposed they were going into the guns. He made many attempts to escape, and was severely whipped for one of them; but he did not get clear till the war was over. He perished on the Grand Bank, about 1790, in a violent gale, in which several fishing vessels foundered. Israel, another son of Jonathan, born in 1765, went to the camp with his father in 1775, and remained with him till the evacuation of Boston by the British the next year, when he returned to Gloucester. Only one employment then remained open here for an active youth; and upon it this lad soon entered. He made several cruises' privateering, and experienced the varied fortune by which that employment was attended. In 1779, he embarked, in the ship "Black Prince," in the unfortunate expedition to the Penobscot; and remained on board till she was blown up at the head of navigation on that river. He then returned home on foot; travelling, the first part of the journey, through a dense wilderness. After a short stay at home, he again engaged in privateering, and was twice taken, and confined on board a prison-ship. From the last one, at Halifax, he escaped, in a foggy night, in a boat which two of his fellow-prisoners had just taken from a ship under the ears of a sentinel, after swimming two hours to get it. The party that escaped in her, after they had been out at sea ten days, were picked up by a privateer, and brought to the United States. Peace soon followed, and fair prospects of success invited attention to maritime pursuits. The subject of this notice, still a youth, with a scanty stock of school education, but an abundance of energy and self-reliance to supply the defect, then entered upon a seafaring life as his chosen calling. In due time, he rose to the command of a vessel, and finally to a participation in the business and profits of ownership. He acquired a competency long before old age came on; and, with an occasional adventure in commerce, spent the latter part of his life in the care of his estate, amid the enjoyments of home. He took a deep interest in public affairs, and was twice elected senator from Essex County. By temperance and exercise, he preserved the advantages of a good hereditary constitution, and retained in a wonderful degree, to the end of his life, all the mental and physical faculties with which nature had endowed him. It was only a few days before his death that his erect form and agile step were missed from our streets. He gave much attention to intellectual cultivation, and could speak several foreign languages with fluency; but he is best remembered by his townsmen as a man of pure morals, of benevolent heart, and very courteous manners. He died Oct. 4, 1854, aged ninety; leaving several daughters, and one son who is settled in Illinois. His youngest son Olwyn died in Texas of a wound received in the battle of San Jacinto.

THOMAS SAVILLE is said by his descendants to have come to this town from Malden. Families of this name were early in Massachusetts; but it is not known to which our settler belonged. He was a cooper, and took up his abode in Squam, where he lived to the age of eighty-four years. He married, in 1722, Mary Haraden; by whom he had a son John, who married here, but did not perpetuate the name in town; and a son Jesse, by whose descendants the name is still borne here. He also had a son Thomas, of whom nothing is known; and other children, who died young. Jesse Saville was an officer of the customs in 1770, when such employment was held only at the expense of much unpopularity and considerable personal danger. The strict performance of what he considered his duty made him odious to his townsmen, and for it he suffered severely in his person and property. It also subjected him to annoyance in later days, as the hostile feelings engendered by his official acts long survived the events which called them forth. He lived a useful but retired life; and died March 11, 1823, at an advanced age. Mr. Saville had several sons. John went to sea at the age of fourteen; was taken by a British frigate, and carried to England, whence he never returned. Oliver died of small-pox on a voyage to India; and David was lost at sea with the whole company of the ship "Winthrop and Mary." Besides these sons, there were Thomas, James, and William, who married and left children. The first of these was father of David, representative in 1835 and 1836; and the last was the well-known citizen, who died Jan. 12, 1853, aged eighty-three. He was a schoolmaster in early life; next, a trader; and finally, for about twenty years, town-clerk.

William Coas, a seaman, born in England, came to Gloucester about 1723, when he married Mary Gardner of this town. He had, in 1725, a grant of land on the south side of the way leading to Eastern Point; and died about the 1st of January, 1764. Five children are recorded to him; one of whom (William), born in 1725, commanded one of the first privateers sent from Gloucester in the Revolutionary War. His first cruise was attended with great success, as will appear in another chapter; but his last was disastrous, and, for himself, had a fatal termination. On that cruise, he was captain of the ship "Starks." When only a few days out from home, the ship was taken, and he was carried a prisoner to Halifax; where he was kept some time in confinement, and then put on board a cartel bound for Boston. On the night after she sailed, a violent storm arose; in which it is supposed the ship went down, as no tidings of her fate were ever received. He was a man of great enterprise, daring, and bravery; not without some of the faults of the privateers-man, nor destitute of the best qualities of a true-hearted sailor. The name is still borne here by descendants.

Charles Glover. — This name came before us in the first years of our history; and now re-appears, though no connection is traced between the two persons who bore it. The last one was married here, in 1723, to Hannah Butman. He was employed here in 1727 and 1728 in teaching school; but, after that, his life appears to have been one of poverty and sickness. In 1730, the town allowed Epes Sargent, Esq., for money paid to "ship of Charles Glover." In subsequent years, he was relieved by the town; and, in 1737, the expenses of his last sickness and burial were defrayed at the public charge. He left a son Charles, who died of small-pox, Jan. 22, 1764, aged thirty-one.

John Stacy, the first of the name in Gloucester, appears in town in 1723; when he was appointed an innholder, on the condition that he should sell no mixed drink on the sabbath-day.

He was a son of Thomas Stacy of Salem, who died in 1690, leaving a farm in Ipswich, where John subsequently settled. He is called a miller in Ipswich, and a millwright in Gloucester. His wife Mary died Sept. 6, 1720; and it appears by the Ipswich records, that, within two months afterwards, he was again intending marriage. The name of the intended wife was Elizabeth Littlehale. Nothing further is known of him than that he died Feb. 22, 1732, aged sixty-seven. He was probably the father of Nymphas, who married Hannah Littlehale in 1724. Nymphas was a shoemaker, and many years a deacon of the First Church. He died Nov. 14, 1774, aged seventy-five, leaving several children. The oldest (Nymphas) pursued his father's business, and succeeded to his office in the church. He was married six times (if he married twice according to his published intentions), and died a widower, at an advanced age, in Wiscasset, Me. He removed to that place, late in life, to reside with a son who had settled there. Another son of the first Nymphas was Benjamin, two of whose grandsons (Eben H. and Eli F.) have been collectors of the customs for the district of Gloucester. Eben H. was a delegate to the Constitutional Convention of 1853. Philemon, a brother of Benjamin, graduated at Harvard College in 1765. He was employed for several subsequent years in teaching school; but he abandoned that occupation in 1779, and cast his lot with the unfortunate company of the privateer ship "Gloucester," whose melancholy fate will be noticed in another place. He married Mary Rand in 1772, who survived her husband fifty years, and died in Boston in 1829. A Rufus Stacy settled here about 1731, and had a wife and children. Concerning him, Rev. John Rogers makes the following entry in an interleaved almanac of 1758, against the date of July 13: "News comes of Capt. Samuel Day and Rufus Stacy being taken by the Indians this day week in their fishing boat;" and again, the 15th: "The above news confirmed by the arrival of Nathan Patch, who liked to have shared the same fate."

In the month of April, 1724, the sloop "Squirrel," owned at Annisquam, arrived at that place, from which she had sailed a short time before on a fishing voyage, under the command of

Capt. Andrew Haraden. This vessel had been taken, on the 14th of April, by John Phillips, a noted pirate, who the next day, with all his company, abandoned his own vessel, and went on board the "Squirrel," which was a fine new vessel, then on her first voyage. On the 17th, Haraden, with John Philmore and six other prisoners forcibly detained by Phillips, devised a plan for delivering themselves from this piratical crew, which they executed the next day in the following manner: The sloop being new, and not entirely finished, the captain had been provided with the tools necessary to complete the unfinished work; and, after the capture, the pirate employed Haraden about it. On the 18th, at twelve o'clock, the appointed hour, the tools being on deck ready for work, and the vessel making good way through the water, Edward Cheeseman, one of the men who planned the recapture, seized John Nott, the master of the pirates, while he was walking on deck, and threw him overboard. Haraden immediately struck down Phillips with an adze; another man despatched Burrell, the boatswain, with a broad-axe; and the others fell upon James Sparks, the gunner, whom they also threw overboard. The rest of the pirates then surrendered themselves prisoners. Capt. Haraden brought in the heads of Phillips and Burrell; and tradition affirms that the head of Phillips was hanging at the sloop's mast-head when she arrived at Annisquam. One of the number engaged in the recapture was a French doctor, who was killed on board the sloop, just as they arrived in the harbor, by the premature discharge of a gun which he was about to fire. On the 25th, Thomas Haraden, Israel Tricker, and William Mills, made oath before Epes Sargent, Esq., justice of the peace, to the particulars of the capture; and the sloop proceeded to Boston with the prisoners and forced men, who were arraigned before the Admiralty Court on the 11th of May. Cheeseman, Philmore, Henry Giles, Charles Ivernay, John Coombs, John Baptist, Henry Payne, Peter Taffery, Isaac Lassen, John Butman, and three negroes, were acquitted as forced men. John Rose Archer and William White were found guilty of piracy, and sentenced to be hung on the 2d of June. Two others (William Phillips and William Taylor) were also found guilty, and were sentenced to death; but were reprieved for a year and a day, to be recommended to the king's mercy. Archer and White were executed at Charlestown Ferry, under their own black flag, June 2, 1724. White's body was afterwards hung in irons on Bird Island. On the sabbath before their execution, Rev. Dr. Sewall preached to them from Matt. xviii. 11. They both appeared penitent at the gallows. Hangman's Island, in Annisquam River, received its name from some connection with this event. Tradition reports that some of the pirates were hung there. This, we have seen, is not true with respect to any who were brought in alive. It is not improbable that the dead bodies of Phillips and Burrell were suspended from a mock gallows or a tree on that islet.

Haraden, Cheeseman, Philmore, Giles, Ivernay, Butman, and Lassen petitioned the General Court to be rewarded for taking this piratical crew. The court, considering the service performed to be of great importance, granted them £32 each, and an additional ten pounds each to Haraden, Cheeseman, and Philmore,* who particularly distinguished themselves in the action. They also granted £20 to Capt. Haraden to pay the expense incurred in bringing the sloop and pirates from Gloucester to Boston.

This gang of pirates had taken, between the 29th of August, 1723, and the date of Haraden's capture, thirty-four vessels; taking from them what they liked, and killing or beating and abusing the crews. One of these vessels was a schooner belonging to this town, commanded by Mark Haskell. Philmore was one of the crew of this schooner, and was taken by the pirate, who kept him on board of his vessel several months. Nothing is known of their conduct towards Haskell and the rest of his crew. Philmore made a statement of the proceedings of the pirates while he was kept among them; from which it appears that Phillips killed two of his gang for attempting to leave him

---

* John Filmore of Wenham died about 1723, leaving a son John, who was undoubtedly the one taken by Phillips, and the same who was intending marriage with Mary Spillar of Ipswich, Nov. 28, 1724. He had a son Nathaniel, who became a resident of Bennington, Vt.; and died there in 1814, leaving a son Nathaniel, who was father of Millard Fillmore, late President of the United States.

and head a piratical expedition themselves, in a snow he had taken bound from New York to Barbadoes. Philmore also states that he contrived the plan for retaking the "Squirrel."

Phillips was known to be cruising about Cape Sables before he took Haraden's sloop. He had taken the schooner "Good-will," of Marblehead, on the 4th of April, and had used the crew very ill; and it was upon information of this, or some other piratical act at the same time, that Lieut.-Gov. Dummer despatched the ship "Sea Horse" in pursuit of him.

Our waters had been infested by pirates several years before the depredations of Phillips. Of Quelch's gang, an account has been given in a preceding chapter. Hutchinson relates that a pirate-ship, carrying twenty-three guns and one hundred and thirty men, commanded by Samuel Bellamy, appeared off Cape Cod in 1717, and took several vessels; one of which, with seven of his crew, was retaken. His ship was soon after cast ashore on Cape Cod in a storm, and the whole company except two were drowned. Six of the company, who were probably in the vessel recaptured, were taken to Boston; where they were tried, found guilty, and hung. It seems that more than two of Bellamy's crew must have saved their lives when the ship was wrecked, or that some left her before that event; for the Massachusetts Records state that John Pearce and Richard Martin were taken in a sloop, of which Daniel Collins was master, in 1717, by a sloop with pirates, who had escaped from the ship wrecked at Cape Cod. It is not stated that the vessel taken belonged to this town; but two of the men bore Gloucester names.

CHAPTER XI.

SECOND PARISH. — REV. RICHARD JAQUES: HIS MINISTRY, SICKNESS, AND DEATH. — THIRD PARISH. — REV. BENJAMIN BRADSTREET: HIS MINISTRY, SICKNESS, AND DEATH.

IMMEDIATELY upon the death of Mr. Tompson, the Second Church took steps to fill its vacant pastorate. Mr. William Tompson,* brother of the late pastor, was sent for; and the choice of the people wavered for a time between him and a Mr. Denis, but finally settled unanimously upon Mr. Richard Jaques, to whom they offered one hundred pounds settlement, and one hundred pounds yearly salary, "so long as he should perform and carry on the whole work of the ministry." He accepted these terms, and was ordained Nov. 3, 1725.

Mr. Jaques was born in Newbury, April 12, 1700; and graduated at Harvard College in 1720. Nothing appears to show that the harmony of the parish was disturbed during the first years of his ministry; but, during the latter part of it, a controversy respecting his salary was carried on, which probably grew out of the original terms of settlement. He was to receive his salary in public bills of credit, which were to be increased or diminished in amount according as the bills should fluctuate in value. The lowest sum it reached in lawful currency was forty-four pounds. The last year of his public labors, it was fifty-three.

In the spring of 1764, Mr. Jaques was rendered unable to perform his ministerial duties by an attack of paralysis, from which he never fully recovered. The terms of his settlement

* He was settled over the church in Scarborough, Me., in 1728; and died there in 1759.

were such, that his salary now ceased; but the parish made him a small allowance from year to year during the latter part of his life. The relations between pastor and people were no longer of an harmonious character. He considered himself ill used by his people (with reference, probably, to their unwillingness to make any permanent provision for his support); and, on one occasion, was so angry with them as to refuse to deliver the church-records to a committee which had been sent to get them. In this unhappy condition of affairs, they set apart the 30th of October, 1766, for a fast; in the religious exercises of which they were assisted by Rev. John Rogers of the Fourth Church, and Rev. Benjamin Tappan of Manchester. These clergymen called on Mr. Jaques, and found him "much discomposed." They advised the people "to make him easy;" as, if they did not, they would not easily find a young man to come and settle with them. A few days after the fast, the parish sent a committee to Mr. Jaques to inquire the reason why he was "troubled with his people;" but the result of their interview was not recorded. Repeated attempts were made during the two following years to settle a colleague with him: but no effort succeeded till 1769, when Mr. Daniel Fuller was obtained; the parish having, in March of that year, made their aged and infirm pastor easy by voting him an allowance of twenty shillings per month.

Mr. Jaques died April 12, 1777, — the day on which he completed his seventy-seventh year; having been confined to his house, and most of the time to his bed, for the long space of thirteen years. He was so helpless at the time he sold his house to Mr. Fuller, about 1770, that it was necessary to carry him to his new abode on a litter. Mr. Jaques preached a thanksgiving sermon for the success of the expedition to Cape Breton, July 18, 1745, from Heb. xi. 33, 34; but it is not known that any of his writings were printed. His wife was Judith, daughter of Col. Thomas Noyes of Newbury. She died about 1789, aged eighty-nine. Their only son Thomas married Sarah Haskell of this town, and resided here till a few years before his death; when he removed to Newbury, where he died about

1805, upwards of eighty years of age. His youngest daughter married a Bray of this town, and has descendants living here.

The people of the northerly part of the Cape began now to discuss the expediency of organizing themselves into a separate church and precinct. For fifty years after the incorporation of the town, this section of its territory does not seem to have attracted more than two or three families. A portion of it, between Lobster Cove and the sea, is designated in our early records as Planters' Neck, and is shown to have been laid out into lots, and granted to some of the first settlers; but there is nothing to indicate the erection of any dwelling upon it for many years. The whole section, including even Planters' Neck, has very little cultivable land; and therefore presented inducements for settling to no other class than fishermen. It is known that Robert Dutch had "a house upon the stage-neck with the stage and all belonging to it, and thirty acres of land, bounded with the river, and upon a line from Lobster Cove to the sea." This property, in 1656, came into possession of Edward Haraden; who, from the best information now attainable, settled upon it, and became the first permanent settler in Annisquam. Before the end of the century, it is probable that Norwood, Davis, Day, Sargent, York, Lane, and the Butman families, had taken up their residence there; and, in the next twenty-five years, sufficient additions had been made to these to induce the people to seek a parish organization and settle a minister in their own locality. About forty of them petitioned the town, Nov. 11, 1726, for liberty to set up a meeting-house in a convenient place upon some of the unappropriated land. Their petition was debated at some length: but their wish was not granted till Jan. 24, 1728; when the town consented "that the inhabitants of Annisquam, and those that live on the northerly side of the Cape, so far southerly as the southerly side of Pigeon Hill pasture, and from thence westerly on a line to the bridge that is over the brook on the southwesterly side of John Tucker, jun.'s house, and thence by said brook as it leadeth into the cove called Goose Cove, and thence by said cove to Annisquam River, should be set off as a precinct by themselves, to maintain a gospel minister among them." These inhabitants next petitioned the General Court for a confirmation of the doings by which they were thus set off; stating, that, having hitherto been under great inconvenience in attendance upon the public worship of God, they had built a meeting-house, and agreed with a minister to settle among them. This petition was granted; and they were incorporated as a separate precinct, June 11, 1728.

The new parish proceeded immediately to settle a pastor, and, on the 29th of July, voted that Mr. Benjamin Bradstreet should be ordained as their minister. They agreed to give him one hundred and twenty-five pounds the first year, one hundred and thirty the second, and one hundred and thirty-five pounds yearly afterwards. They also voted him a settlement of one hundred pounds and a wood-lot. In 1732, an addition of ten pounds was made to his salary for preaching nine lectures during the summer months. During the last few years of his life, his salary was eighty-two pounds per annum.

Mr. Bradstreet was born in Newbury, and received his education at Harvard College, where he graduated in 1725. His ordination at Squam took place Sept. 18, 1728. The sermon on that occasion was preached by Rev. John Tufts of Newbury, from Col. iv. 17. It was published, with a preface by Rev. John White of the First Parish. The church was soon organized; and a covenant, couched in the usual language of such instruments, was adopted, and signed by the following male members: —

Benjamin Bradstreet.
Edward Haraden, sen.
Anthony Bennett.
Benjamin Davis.
Samuel Lane.
Joseph Thurston.
John Lane.
Samuel Gott.
James Lane.
Jethro Wheeler.
Daniel Collins.

The original book of church-records is missing; but its loss is well supplied by a fair and excellent transcript in an existing book, made by one of Mr. Bradstreet's successors. The copy contains the names of all persons who were admitted into full communion with the church, of those who owned the covenant, and those who were baptized, during Mr. Bradstreet's ministry.

In 1738, the parish, wanting help to maintain their minister, voted to petition the First Parish to set off to them additional territory, so as to include the settlement at Sandy Bay. They had voted a few years before, that, in case the people in that remote section would join with them, they would agree to make and maintain a convenient way through the woods to Mr. John Pool's at that place.

In the absence of all knowledge to the contrary, it may be presumed that Mr. Bradstreet's ministry was a quiet and successful one. It continued nearly thirty-four years, and terminated with his death. His health began to fail in the fall of 1761, and the parish took measures to supply the pulpit. The next spring, they voted to give Mr. Cleaveland of the Fifth Church forty-five pounds to preach to them one-half the time. At the same time, Mr. Bradstreet went away on a journey for the benefit of his health; and while returning home in May, 1762, suddenly became very ill at Danvers, and died there on the 31st of that month. He was buried on the 3d of June. The following ministers attended the funeral as bearers: Mr. Jewett, Mr. Walley, Mr. Parsons, Mr. Rogers, Mr. Cleaveland, and Mr. Chandler. Mr. Jewett prayed and Mr. Chandler spoke at the grave.

No printed or written notice of Mr. Bradstreet's life and character has come down to us; but tradition reports that he was a good man and an acceptable preacher. His wife was Sarah Greenleaf of Newbury; and his children were — Sarah, Thomasine, Humphrey, Martha, Elizabeth, Mary, Benjamin, and a second Sarah. It is not known that either of the sons lived to mature years. One of the daughters is said to have died while in the act of putting on her outer clothing to go to meeting. Elizabeth married James Day, and died in 1821, aged eighty. Mary was twice married; first to Timothy Haraden, and next to William Fuller.

Some disagreement existed among the people of the new parish, with reference to the best location for their meeting-house;

which, by the decision of the majority, was erected at the head of Lobster Cove. It was a plain building, and, in outward appearance, much like that of the Second Parish, but considerably larger. It was struck by lightning in October, 1755; and, in 1830, gave place to a new one.

CHAPTER XII.

EMIGRATION TO FALMOUTH, ME. — NEW SETTLERS. — GRAMMAR SCHOOL. NEW GLOUCESTER, ME. — BATTERY.

QUITE a remarkable occurrence in the history of the town, which took place about this time, was the emigration of a considerable number of families and a few single individuals to the town of Falmouth, now the city of Portland, Me. Though nearly a hundred years had elapsed since the first settlement of that place, it did not contain, in 1726, more than sixty families. Its isolated situation exposed it in time of war to the attacks of the Indian enemy, who had twice destroyed it entirely, and had, on each occasion, killed many of the inhabitants. Of those who escaped from these scenes of slaughter and fire, or fled at other times in alarm for their lives, several found refuge in Gloucester, and became permanent residents of the town. An interesting historical connection between the two places had existed, indeed, from the early settlement of both; for among the early inhabitants of Falmouth were six of our own pioneers, of whom two became victims of savage cruelty on the first destruction of the place by the Indians, as elsewhere related in this work. On the final resettlement of the town, this connection was strengthened by the emigration above mentioned. In 1727 and 1728, a large number of Gloucester men were admitted inhabitants there; of whom it seems quite certain that the following twenty-five removed to the place: —

Richard Babson.
John Brown.
Anthony Coombs.
John Coy.
John Curtis.
John Dolliver.
William Davis.
William Elwell.

Ephraim Foster.
Thomas Haskell.
Benjamin Ingersol.
Thomas Millet.
John Millet.
Joseph Pride.
Thomas Redding.
Jeremiah Riggs.
Ebenezer Roberts.
John Sawyer.
Isaac Sawyer.
Job Sawyer.
Jacob Sawyer.
Jonathan Stanwood.
John White.
William White.
Benjamin York.*

The names of seven other persons belonging to this town are borne on the list of admissions; but it is not certain that they all went to Falmouth, though it is probable that some of them did. They are, —

John Haskell.
Philip Hodgkins.
Jedidiah Hodgkins.
Robert Nason.
Thomas Sargent.
William Stevens.
James Stanwood.†

* Some of these names are noticed in other parts of this work; but they are brought together here in order to give the whole matter of the emigration under one view, as an interesting event in our history. The list of persons admitted inhabitants of Falmouth in the years stated is contained in Mr. Willis's History of Portland. Mention is also made of several of them in the journal of Rev. Thomas Smith, the first settled minister there, edited with valuable notes by Mr. Willis. To both of these works, as well as to information otherwise derived from Mr. Willis, I acknowledge the indebtedness of this History. The list does not give any names as belonging to Gloucester; but I presume there can be no doubt with regard to all that I have given. Mr. Smith calls Dolliver, "Skipper Doliver." Under 1726, he says, "This summer, there came from Cape Ann one Davis, — a pretty troublesome spark, — with his family; also one of his wife's brothers, no better than he; also one Haskell, a sober sort of a man, with his family." William Davis's wife was Patience Foster; and she had a brother Ephraim. The sober Haskell was, of course, Thomas. Thomas Redding was, I suppose, son of Richard Babson's second wife. John Brown was probably son of our settler of the same name. William Elwell was, I suppose, brother of his wife. Anthony Coombs married Mercy Hodgkins in 1722. She and Philip and Jedidiah Hodgkins may have been children of Samuel, elsewhere mentioned; though Philip is said to have been of Newbury in 1728, when he purchased land in Falmouth.

† John Haskell may have been a brother of Thomas. Robert Nason and Rebecca Day were married here in 1720, and had a daughter Mary, born in 1729. He fell overboard from a fishing vessel, and was drowned, in 1734. Thomas Sargent, a grandson of our early settler William, married Elizabeth Haskell in 1710, and had several children. It is a common name, and he may not be the one mentioned in the list. I have no evidence, however, that he resided here after 1729. Our records notice the birth at Falmouth, May 4, 1723, of William, son of William Stevens, by Margaret his wife. It does not appear that the father was of our early family of that name. James Stanwood and Jonathan Stanwood were brothers; and grandsons, I suppose, of our early settler, Philip. Both were married, and had children.

Other names of Gloucester persons appear on the list: but they might have been intended to designate individuals of some other town; or they might have been those of some of our inhabitants who designed to remove, but afterwards changed their minds.* The descendants of a few of this Falmouth emigration are yet numerous in Portland and its vicinity.

To compensate for the large loss of population which has just been noticed, the town was constantly receiving accessions from abroad. Within the ten years following the commencement of the emigration to Falmouth, it is probable that more than one hundred new residents were added to our number; but, so fleeting is the impression that mere numbers make upon history, a single page will suffice for a notice of all those in whom the present generation will feel interested. Among the settlers of this period, represented by families still existing in town, were Joseph Herrick, George Dennison, and William Steel.

JOSEPH HERRICK — descended probably from Henry, an early settler of Salem — came to Gloucester with his wife Mary about 1725. His children, born here, were — Eunice, Mary, Joseph, and Israel. He resided, it is supposed, in the Second Parish; where he died Jan. 12, 1771, aged eighty-one. One of this family (Theophilus) has been four years a representative.

GEORGE DENNISON first appears here on occasion of his marriage to Abigail Haraden, Jan. 14, 1725. He had several children; and died March 14, 1748, aged forty-eight. His son Isaac died April 2, 1811, aged seventy-nine; leaving a son Isaac, who was a soldier in the Revolutionary War, and died June 21, 1841, aged eighty.

WILLIAM STEELE and his wife Anne have recorded in our town-records, between 1732 and 1742, the births of five sons, — William, James, Jonathan, John, and Joseph; from one of which, the families of the name now living here have probably descended. A William Steele perished, with the whole crew of one of our privateers, in the Revolutionary War.

---

* These names were John Lane, James Davis, Samuel Davis, John Gilbert, John Roberts, Michael Webber, and Robert Randall. I am quite sure that most of these persons lived here long after the emigration to Falmouth.

The names of two other settlers of the same period should be mentioned, — DANIEL GIBBS and SAMUEL ELLIOT. The former came here about 1727, when he married Mary, daughter of Thomas Sanders. Traditionary accounts represent him to have been a merchant of high standing; and the journal of Rev. Jacob Bailey, who taught the grammar school here in 1758, gives a favorable impression of his personal qualities. He is said to have erected and occupied the house recently standing on the corner of Middle and Pleasant Streets, on the spot where the Baptist Meeting-house now stands. Having no children, he adopted one of his wife's kindred, — Thomas Sanders, — whose history and melancholy end are given in another place. From Mr. Bailey's notices of Mr. Gibbs, it appears that he was attached to the Episcopal form of religious worship. He died March 21, 1762, aged sixty-two: Mrs. Gibbs died in 1769, at the age of sixty.

SAMUEL ELLIOT came from Beverly; and was, without doubt, a descendant of Andrew Elliot, an early settler there, who died in 1704, aged seventy-six. He was a shoemaker by trade. In January, 1733, he sold his house and land in Beverly; and March 20, in the same year, married Hannah Hodgkins of this town. His residence was near Poles; but how long he lived there, or when and where he died, no one now knows. He had a large family of children. His son Andrew lived on or near his father's homestead, and died in 1821, aged eighty-one; leaving a wife, who, it is said, was a Virginia woman. She died in the work-house in 1825, aged eighty-eight. James, another son, born in 1748, married Martha Day, and died, while still a young man, of small-pox; leaving a wife and three sons — James, Samuel, and William — in low circumstances. Not long after her husband's death, she removed with her three boys to New Salem, Mass. James, by his own exertions, obtained a good education; became a lawyer, and settled in Brattleborough, Vt. He was a representative in Congress from that State four years, and held other offices of distinction. He died at the age of sixty-four. Samuel was also a self-made man, and a lawyer in Brattleborough forty years. William was in trade in Boston for a number of years, but died in Brattleborough in 1839. Descendants of these brothers, of the same name, are living; but the family has long been extinct in Gloucester.

Another settler who came to town about this time was JOHN HEWS, or HUSE. According to his own account, he was born in Wales in 1685. At the age of seventeen, he was draughted to go on board a ship-of-war; and was a sailor in the expedition of Sir George Rooke against Cadiz, and in the capture of the Spanish galleons at Vigo. Some time after this, he was transported to Virginia for crime; and, when his time expired, got passage on board of a schooner then on a trading voyage from Gloucester, and came to this place. Here he had his home till his death. He was in the expedition to Louisburg in 1745, and in that of 1758; at the latter date, a veteran soldier of seventy-three. Of his history from this time, little is known. His last place of residence was in a house on the corner of a lane leading to the old Ferry; and there, in August, 1793, he died at the extraordinary age of one hundred and eight years. He was a very profane man, even to the end of his protracted existence. He long wished for death, and would sometimes cry like a child, for fear, as he used to express himself, that God had forgotten him. About three years before he died, he attempted to cut his throat with a razor; but the dulness of the instrument and the toughness of his skin prevented him from succeeding. At last, utterly despairing of a release from life in a natural way, he resolved on starvation; and refusing all nourishment, and admitting nothing but cold water to his lips, in thirty days he ended the life of which he had become so weary. He was twice married, — first to Hannah Bray in 1735, and next to Eunice Allen in 1763. The last bride was thirty-six years old, the bridegroom being seventy-eight. Her mother forbade the banns, but afterwards consented. No children by either marriage are recorded; but a son John was a fruit of the last one. He served a short time in the army, in the Revolutionary War; and spent several years in a seafaring life. His last years were passed in the work-house; where he died May 13, 1849.

The public grammar school continued to be kept in the central part of the town, without change of place, for about thirty years; though it is evident that a considerable portion of the children must have been deprived of its benefits by the distance which separated them from the schoolhouse. Private schools for small children were undoubtedly kept in the most thickly settled of the distant parts of the town; and it was probably for their accommodation that the commoners granted land in 1725 to the people at the head of the Cape, and in 1726 to those at the head of the Harbor, for schoolhouse-lots.

The last master of the grammar school, of whom notice has been taken, was Joshua Moody. He was succeeded by Samuel Tompson, who kept it till 1715; when Joseph Parsons was appointed to the place, and continued in it six years. During the following fourteen years, eleven different teachers were employed, of whom all but two appear to have been graduates of Harvard College. In 1734, the town voted to petition the General Court for a grant of a township of land to help maintain the school: but no public aid was given; and the people, relying upon themselves alone, then proceeded to make it (what it continued to be for many years) a "circulating" school. The "town," as the seat of the early settlement was still distinctively called, was fast losing its importance. Wealth, and consequently power, had been for some time radiating from the centre to the circumference; and, within twenty years from the period of which we now write, so reduced in its proportion of property had the old "town" become, that the parochial limits containing it contributed less than one-sixth to the support of the public burthen. It is not strange, therefore, that some dissatisfaction was manifested at the monopoly of the school by the inhabitants of the section where it was located. The first note of discontent came from the people of Squam, who commenced an action against the town for not giving them their proportion of the school according to agreement; and finally succeeded in bringing about an arrangement that satisfied all parts of the town. In a town-meeting, October, 1735, a plan was adopted by which the territory was divided into districts, conforming to the parish lines afterwards established; with the exception, that three school districts were formed from the section now known as the First Parish. The number of districts was seven; and the school was apportioned to each, according as its proportion of the town-rate was to the whole tax. Each district was to provide a convenient schoolhouse; and, in case of neglect to do so, was to lose its turn for three years, — the time employed in the circuit. To conform to the old Colony law, the school was, of course, wherever kept, to be free for all the inhabitants of the town. This arrangement continued many years, gave the people no further trouble than to vote triennially that the school "circulate" as heretofore.*

The agricultural portion of the population could now find no further room for expansion within our own territory, and its surplus labor must seek distant fields. All the arable land in the town was under cultivation; and the youth who had been brought up to husbandry must turn to the sea for support, or make a home on the wild lands in Maine, which were to Gloucester, in the last century, what the "West" is to Europe now. They chose to emigrate, and their names or progeny are now scattered all over the flourishing State which they helped to found. On one spot they perpetuated the name of the home they had left; and New Gloucester, after the lapse of nearly a century, still

---

* Two of the triennal apportionments are preserved, and are interesting as showing the relative wealth of the districts at their respective dates: —

"Dec. 3, 1751. — The Town scool was proporscioned For three years.

The Harbour Ward's proporsion	9 mos.
Eastern Point & ye head of ye harbour	4½ "
The western side of ye cut	3 "
The Cape	1½ "
The Westerly Ward	7 "
The Town, or 4th Parish	5½ "
Squam Ward	5½ "
	36 mos."

"Dec. 29, 1757. — The Selectmen proportioned the School to the several parishes according to the town rate in 1754, for two masters each three years; equal to one master 6 years.

The Harbor Parish	33 months.	
The Cape	8 "	19 days.
The Town Parish	10 "	16 "
Squam Parish	11 "	4 "
The West Parish	18 "	27 "
	72 "	6 days."

contains many families who feel an affectionate interest in "old Cape Ann."

That town had its origin in a grant by the General Court, in 1736, to a number of our inhabitants. The first meeting of the proprietors was held here April 27 in that year. Joseph Allen, Esq., was chosen moderator; and Ezekiel Day, clerk. An assessment of three pounds was ordered, and a committee was chosen to look out a good place for the new township. They made a selection of about three thousand and forty acres lying on the back of North Yarmouth; which was the next year surveyed, and laid out into lots. Three of the lots were set apart for public purposes; and the remaining, sixty in number, were, in February, 1738, divided among the proprietors,* who proceeded at once to the work of settlement, first giving the place the name of New Gloucester. The soil of the new town had enough of the characteristics of that of the old to remind the emigrants of the home they had left. The surface is hilly, and, in some places, very rocky; but considerable of it is fine interval, and offered to the early settlers many favorable spots for good farms. The top of Harris Hill, around which the first clearings were made, affords a fine and extensive view of the surrounding country, including a high elevation of land in the distance, called Streaked Mountain; and, from another hill in the town, the

---

* The following are the names of the original proprietors: —

Joseph Allen.
Joseph Allen, jun.
Thomas Allen.
John Allen.
Rev. Benjamin Bradstreet.
Thomas Bray.
Nathaniel Bray, jun.
John Bray.
Moses Bray.
Aaron Bray.
James Broom.
Lieut. James Davis.
James Davis.
Jedidiah Davis.
Ezekiel Day.
Eliphalet Day.
Timothy Day.
Pelatiah Day.
George Dennison.
Isaac Eveleth.
Andrew Elwell.
Lieut. William Haskell.
William Haskell, 3d.
Henry Haskell.
Josiah Haskell.
Thomas Herrick.
Samuel Hodgkins, jun.
Josiah Ingersol.
Nicholas Kidvell.
David Plummer.
John Millet.
William Parsons.
Ebenezer Parsons.
John Parsons.
Samuel Pearce.
William Ring.
William Ring, jun.
John Roberts.
Benjamin Roberts.
Stephen Robinson.
Nathaniel Rust.
John Sargent.
Joseph Sargent, jun.
Nathaniel Sanders.
Nymphas Stacy.
John Smith.
Samuel Stevens.
Samuel Stevens, jun.
John Stevens.
David Stanwood.
Benjamin Tarbox.
John Tyler.
Philemon Warner.
Philemon Warner, jun.
Michael Webber.
Rev. John White.
Thomas White.
Adam Wellman.
Thomas Witham.
Humphrey Woodbury.

John Low appears as a partner of Stephen Robinson in the fifty-eighth lot.

White Mountains in New Hampshire are distinctly visible, about fifty miles off, in a direct line.

The settlement was begun in the spring of 1739; and, in 1742, such progress had been made, that the proprietors say they had made a good road twelve miles long; cleared twenty acres of land, some of which was under cultivation; had built bridges, a sawmill, and several houses, — all at an expense of about £500. Encouragement was held out to settlers: the proprietors conveyed them to North Yarmouth by water, voted to build a meeting-house, and seemed to be going on prosperously in their enterprise; when, in 1744, the settlement was broken up on account of the danger to which it would be exposed in the war with the French and Indians which commenced in that year. On the restoration of peace, it was found that their houses and mill had been destroyed; that a bridge had been carried away by a freshet; that their road was out of repair; and that, in fact, most of the pioneer work of settlement must be commenced anew. Among the first measures for resettling the place was the erection of a block-house. Workmen were sent down to build it in 1753; and, in 1754, it was furnished with arms and ammunition. In 1756, about twenty men,* some of whom had families and cattle, had taken up their abode there; and the permanent settlement of the town may be dated from that time. Their situation was still a perilous one, however, on account of the hostility of the Indians; and, on petition of the proprietors, the General Court, to give them some relief, made their block-house a provincial garrison. This building stood about one hundred rods south-west of the present Meeting-house, not far from the Burying-ground; and, besides being a protection for the settlers, it served also for a place of public worship till they built one specially devoted to that purpose.

The settlement continued a languid existence till the peace of 1763 put it out of the power of the French to add stimulus to the cruelty of the Indians on the eastern frontier. It then began to increase; and, in less than two years afterwards, contained

* Of these persons, I can give the names of three only, — Benjamin Roberts, Nathaniel Eveleth, and William Goodrich.

about forty families. The last meeting of the proprietors in the parent town was held at James Broom's tavern, Oct. 12, 1763; and the first at New Gloucester, at the Block-house, Nov. 22 following. The officers of the latter were — Samuel Merrill, moderator; and Isaac Parsons, clerk. The next year, they voted to build a schoolhouse and hire a schoolmaster; and, soon afterwards, a church was organized and a minister settled. Of the several preachers who had officiated at the garrison, the choice of one for pastor fell upon Rev. Samuel Foxcroft, who graduated at Harvard College in 1754. He was ordained at New Gloucester, Jan. 16, 1765. All the proceedings at a New-England ordination of the last century are supposed to have been characterized by a good deal of seriousness: but this occasion was not of a solemn cast throughout; for an honest-hearted minister who was present lets us behind the scenes a little, and says that they had a "jolly ordination, and lost sight of decorum." Mr. Foxcroft died March 2, 1807, in his seventy-third year. His wife was Lucy Ellery of this town. He left a son (Joseph Ellery Foxcroft), who became a prominent citizen of New Gloucester; and died about 1853, at an advanced age. Of the families which removed into the new township from its resettlement to 1774, the date of its incorporation, the largest proportion emigrated from this town.* For about half a century, a constant

* A proper effort now might secure a perfect, or nearly perfect, list of all the early settlers. I find in the proprietors' records a list of the subscribers to the Meeting-house in 1770, which I here give in alphabetical arrangement: —

David Barker.
Robert Bailey.
Nathaniel Bennet.
Jonathan Bennet.
Peleg Chandler.
Ebenezer Collins.
Adam Cotton.
Daniel Dunham.
Nathaniel Eveleth.
Perkins Eveleth.
John Graffam.
Peter Graffam.
Ezekiel Glass.
Job Haskell.
Israel Haskell.
Jacob Haskell.
Jacob Haskell, jun.
John Haskell.
Nathaniel Haskell.
William Harris.
Henry Hackett.
Ezekiel Hackett.
Daniel Lane.
Ebenezer Lane.
Benjamin Lane.
Ebenezer Mason.
John Magguire.
Moses Merrill.
Joseph Merrill.
Moses Merrill, jun.
Benjamin Merrill.
Imlah Merrill.
David Millet.
Hugh Nevens.
Simon Noyes.
Isaac Parsons.
Samuel Parsons.
David Parsons.
Edward Parsons.
John Prince.
Jonathan Row.
Zebulon Rowe.
William Rowe.
Josiah Smith.
Moses Stevens.
John Stenchfield.
John Stenchfield, jun.
Roger Stenchfield.
James Stenchfield.
William Stenchfield.
John Tyler.
Jeremiah Thoyts.
Samuel Tarbox.
John Tufts.
Barnabas Tufts.
William Warner.
William Blay West.
Barnabas Winslow.
Joshua Winship.
Davis Woodward.
John Woodman.

intercourse was kept up between the parent town and its eastern offshoot; but the bonds of close relationship and strong affection have become weakened by time, and the strongest tie that now connects them is that which binds all men to the homes and graves of their ancestors.

The account of our historical connection with New Gloucester may properly be closed with its incorporation; though it may be stated, that it continued to receive accessions from the old town during the Revolutionary War and a few subsequent years.

As early as 1703, the town, in a petition to the General Court, earnestly called the attention of that body to its defenceless state in case of hostile invasion; and asked to have a fortification erected on the "small island, or neck of land, out into the harbor." The insignificant maritime trade of the place, and the sparse population of the Harbor section, at that time, might have justified the refusal of the petition; but, in thirty years, a change had taken place, and the danger had not diminished. A considerable fleet of vessels was now owned in town; the trade of other ports on the coast was increasing; and their vessels often sought shelter in this harbor, the shores of which had become so thickly settled as to expose it to the danger which an

---

All the Bennets, Collins, Eveleths, Haskells, Millet, Parsonses, Prince, Rowes, Stenchfields, Warner, and Woodward, were, I suppose, from our town. Perhaps some of the others had also resided here. Col. William Allen was one of the early settlers; but I know not whether he went before or after the date of this subscription. Of all the first settlers from Gloucester, Isaac Parsons became the most prominent citizen of the new town; and lived, I think, to be the last. He died Oct. 9, 1825, aged eighty-five. He was a deacon of the church, a representative and senator; and held other important offices. He buried four wives, and a fifth survived him. Nathaniel Eveleth was town-clerk over forty years, and died Nov. 23, 1824, aged eighty-eight; leaving a son Nathaniel, who died in 1849, at the age of eighty-five. Other settlers, who died in old age, were — in 1815, Abraham Sawyer, aged seventy-eight; Mary, his wife, eighty. In 1824, William Harris, ninety-three; Jonathan Somes, seventy-one. In 1825, Jonathan Bennet, seventy-nine. In 1827, Enoch Fogg, eighty-two; Richard Tobie, eighty-seven. In 1828, John Haskell, eighty-four. In 1832, Moses Bennet, seventy-nine. In 1833, Eliphalet Haskell, eighty. In 1834, Nathaniel Ingersol, eighty-two; Hannah Haskell, eighty-five. In 1835, Thomas Wharf, eighty-seven. In 1837, William White, eighty-five; Joseph Pearce, ninety-two. In 1838, Nathan Haskell, eighty-seven; Joseph Brown, eighty. In 1839, Mary Haskell, eighty-four. In 1841, Jemima Parsons, ninety-four. In 1842, Stephen Rollins, ninety-four; Martha Pearce, eighty-seven. In 1843, Zebulon Row, ninety-four; Joseph Eveleth, seventy-five; Isaac Eveleth, eighty-three; Solomon Atwood, ninety-three; Sarah Stenchfield, eighty-eight. In 1846, Judith Haskell, ninety-four.

important maritime town has always to fear in a war with a naval power. In 1734, the Provincial Government was again reminded by the town, that, in case of war, it would be "naked to the enemy:" but nothing for its protection appears to have been done till 1743; when, under grants of the General Court in the two years immediately preceding, appropriating money* for the erection of a suitable breastwork and platform, and for eight mounted twelve-pounders, with all necessary warlike stores, our fathers found themselves prepared to meet a hostile demonstration upon their own waters.

The Harbor Cove of Gloucester is formed by a short sand beach, which projects from the shore, and has at its end a small rock-bound hill, that seems to stand as a sentinel to overlook the waters by which it is almost surrounded, and watch every movement upon their surface. Upon the south side of this hill, about midway between its summit and the shore, was erected the battery, which, in case of attack, was to protect the shipping and homes of our ancestors. It is not known that they ever fired a single shot from it at an enemy; and though, for several years, it might have presented an appearance somewhat imposing to the mariners who sailed along under its eight twelve-pounders, nothing of the original work now remains but a few mounds, such as are often seen on the site of a long-abandoned breastwork.

The erection of this fort was probably hastened by the threatening aspect of affairs at that time between the mother-country and her ancient and constant enemy,—France. Though, in the war which followed, none of our people met the enemy in defence of their homes, many of them were called to face the frowning walls of Louisburg, and had the fortune to share in the renown which resulted to the victors on the reduction of that strong fortress.

The sand-beach and hill just alluded to as forming the inner harbor, now the seat of an active business and a considerable number of dwellings, had, at the time the battery was erected,

* £400 in 1741, and £126. 18s. 4d. in 1742.

but recently begun to attract the attention of the business-men of the town. This locality was then variously called "Stage Neck," "Neck Beach," and "Watch-house Neck;" and the point where the battery was placed, "Watch-house Point," from the watch-house which was probably set up there thirty or forty years before. In 1720, Ensign Joseph Allen, Samuel Stevens, jun., and Thomas Allen, had a grant of "eighty feet front of ground at high-water mark, on ye neck of land called 'Stage Neck,' at ye north-easterly side," on condition that they should build a wharf on it within three years. This seems to have been the first grant, and it was not followed by any other till 1730; when several additional ones were made, and a considerable portion of the beach was let for fifteen years, at twelvepence per year. Three years afterwards, one hundred and thirty feet front were laid out for a graving-place for public use; and a committee was chosen to repair the beach, that the sea might not break over it "& spoyl the harbour." Subsequently, the following persons had wharf privileges on the beach or neck,— Capt. Gibbs, Philemon Warner, jun., Ezekiel Woodward, jun., Eben and Jacob Parsons, William Parsons and Stephen Parsons: and finally, in 1749, a committee of the commoners was chosen "to bound out the neck beach, and to give records to Messrs. Nathaniel Sargent, William Parsons, Capt. Nathaniel Ellery, John Stevens, and Nathaniel Allen;" they paying one thousand and ten pounds, old tenor,* for the same.

* The name of a depreciated paper currency. The sum mentioned was equivalent to about three hundred and fifty dollars in silver money.

CHAPTER XIII.

FOURTH PARISH. — REV. JOHN ROGERS: HIS MINISTRY, DEATH, AND FAMILY. — TAVERNS. — EXPEDITION TO LOUISBURG. — PEG WESSON. — PEOPLE ALARMED. — NEW SETTLERS.

IN the early part of the eighteenth century, the population at the Harbor began to increase more rapidly than that of the other parts of the town. The fishery began to be more extensively prosecuted; some foreign commerce was carried on; and men of business, wealth, and influence were multiplied. Attendance on the public worship of God was, in those days, neglected by none whose absence could not be justified on the plea of necessity; and a community somewhat compact and numerous, as that in the Harbor had become in 1733, would be likely, at the first favorable moment, to shorten the inconvenient distance which separated it from the Meeting-house. The First Parish voted, in that year, to build a new meeting-house in this part of the town; and meetings were held to carry forward the project: but no vote could be obtained for a rate to build it on account of the parish. Strong feelings were enlisted on both sides. The people of the northerly part of the parish resisted what they foresaw would terminate in the dismemberment of the parish; but to no purpose. A number of the members residing in the southerly part erected a large and commodious meeting-house on Middle Street in the Harbor, and offered it to the parish on conditions which were accepted; and on the 12th September, 1738, at a parish-meeting, they carried a vote, that a lecture should be held in it on the 28th, and that the public worship of God should be continued there for the future as it used to be in the old one. Upon this, the northerly portion of the parish immediately called a parish-meeting to endeavor to get set off as a separate precinct; but, when it assembled, this proposition was voted down by one hundred and seven nays to seventy-seven yeas. Further progress in the matter, at this time, was interrupted; and, in the midst of confusion and excitement, the moderator declared the meeting adjourned. The minority now applied to the General Court for relief. Their petition was signed by Nathaniel Coit and eighty-four others. In it they say, —

"Whereas eight inhabitants of said parish have lately built a new meeting-house in the Harbor, about a mile southward of the old one, without any leave or vote of said parish, although the parish, by vote, laid out a convenient place to set one on when wanted (that place is between the old meeting-house and the new one); and since the proprietors of the new meeting-house have made an offer of it to the parish on these terms (reserving all the pews and considerable part of the room in the gallery to procure the cost of building it), and the parish, by vote, accepted said house for the public worship of God; by reason of which, the northerly part of the parish, who are your humble petitioners, labor under great discouragements and inconveniences in attending public worship, by reason many of them live two or three miles from the new meeting-house (many of them are seafaring men, and have no conveniences for going to meeting but on foot; which is very uncomfortable for elderly people, women, and children), — near about ninety families must go by the old meeting-house to go to the new one. Most of your petitioners could go home at noon from the old meeting-house; but, if obliged to go to the new one, cannot: which renders your petitioners' case to be very difficult. Also the bigger part of the body of the new meeting-house is built into pews, to the number of eighty or ninety; and the major part of your petitioners are unable to purchase them. These, with many other reasons, moved us to desire the church to consent that we might have preaching in the old meeting-house at our own cost the winter following; but could have no favor shown us there. Then we applied to the parish to set off all who live nearer the old meeting-house than the new, in order to call and settle an orthodox minister; but were still denied. The second and third parish have taken this opportunity to enlarge their own district, the southerly part of the first parish joining with them, in order to hinder us from a settlement. Therefore we humbly pray the court would take our difficult circumstances under their wise consideration, and set off to the old meeting-house all these parishioners that are nearer that than to the new meeting-house, with their estates, into a distinct precinct." — In concluding, they request, that, if the court should not grant their petition, they would send a committee to view the parish, and consider the case at the cost of the petitioners. Daniel Witham, Ebenezer Parsons, and Eliezer Parsons, were chosen by the parish to draw up a remonstrance, and give the reasons why this petition should not be granted; and Capt. Andrew Robinson was chosen to appear for the parish before the Governor and Court. The subject was referred to a committee to report at the next session; but no final action was taken till Aug. 4, 1741, when the court ordered, "That if the non-petitioners in the parish do not, within twelve months from the end of that session, remove the new meeting-house to the place agreed on by the precinct, or the precinct erect there another house convenient for public worship; that, in such case, the petitioners be erected into a separate precinct, agreeably to their petition, unless the inhabitants of the first precinct shall, within the term aforesaid, agree to have the public worship of God carried on in both houses at the same time, and so settle another learned and orthodox minister there to assist the Rev. Mr. White in the ministry; the two ministers to preach in the old and new meeting-houses by turns, or otherwise as they shall agree."

The disaffected portion of the parish again presented a long memorial to the General Court, Sept. 2, 1742, showing that the court order of the previous year had not been complied with; that no agreement had been made between the two parties; and hoping, "if they could be by themselves," to enjoy a long and lasting peace, they prayed to be set off into a separate precinct. The separation was agreed to in parish-meeting by a vote of fifty yeas to thirty-five nays; and the General Court ordered, Dec. 15, "that the first precinct in Gloucester be divided into two precincts, as follows: the dividing line to begin at the north-easterly end of Squam precinct line, by Sandy Bay, and to run as the said line does to Squam River, to Goose Cove, and land which has Capt. Allen's warehouse on the north-easterly side, and land late Mr. Nathaniel Sawyer's on the southerly side; and so to run on the northerly side of said Sawyer's land to the highway, and in the said highway to Mr. Nymphas Stacy's corner; and then northerly on said way to Mr. James Wallis's house and land, including the same to the northward, and in the highway that leads to Sandy Bay to the Parting Path so called; and in that way to another Parting Path, near Witham's house; and thence on the way to the beach on the seashore, and by the same, round the Cape, Pigeon Cove, and Sandy Bay, unto Squam line aforesaid: all the land, estates, houses, and inhabitants, included in the northerly and westerly side of said lines, way, and sea, or so many of the inhabitants that have not petitioned, that are thus included, as shall manifest their willingness herefor by a subscription, and present it to this court at the next session, to be incorporated into one distinct precinct; and that the southerly part, whereof the Rev. Mr. John White is the present pastor, be accounted the first precinct in said town of Gloucester."

Being the weaker party, the seceders, though occupying the very spot where most of the first settlers were located, were obliged to submit to a degradation of numerical rank, and thenceforward to be known as the Fourth Parish. The first steps were now to be taken in the formation of a church and in the organization of the parish. The church was organized Oct. 27, 1743. A covenant was signed by seventeen males; and, in March and April following, seventy-six females were received by dismission from the First Church. According to the custom of the time, the church first made choice of a minister, and then the parish acted upon the proceedings of the church. Rev. John Rogers of Kittery, Me., was chosen by the new church; and the parish, on the 12th December, 1743, concurred by a vote of thirty-nine to eleven, and agreed to give him £250 old tenor per annum salary, and £400 in the same currency for settlement; the latter to be paid in four equal annual payments.

Mr. Rogers was a son of Rev. John Rogers of Kittery, and was born there in August, 1719. He graduated at Harvard College in 1739. His ordination over the Fourth Church took place Feb. 1, 1744. On this occasion, the introductory prayer was offered by his uncle, Rev. Nathaniel Rogers of Ipswich; sermon by his father; charge by Rev. John White of the First Church, Gloucester; right hand of fellowship by Rev. Richard Jaques of the Second Church; and concluding prayer by Rev. B. Bradstreet of the Third Church.

Mr. Rogers's ministry continued for a period of thirty-eight years. It is not known that any thing occurred during the course of it to disturb the harmony of the parish; and it may therefore be inferred that the relations between pastor and people were characterized by none other than Christian feelings and conduct. His people were mostly engaged in maritime pursuits; and the total ruin of their business by the Revolutionary War, and the general distress that prevailed at that time, cast a deep gloom over the parish. The people could derive no support from their accustomed employments, and most of them enlisted in the army or engaged in privateering. Some died in captivity, and many perished at sea, leaving families in the lowest state of destitution and misery. Never were the services of a faithful, sympathetic minister more useful than in that dark hour; and Mr. Rogers proved himself a messenger of heavenly peace and consolation, carrying to wounded and aching hearts the balm to heal and the hope to cheer. The pecuniary condition of the parish was so low, that his salary was only paid in part during this troubled period; and he was obliged to eke out a sufficient maintenance by supplying destitute parishes in neighboring places. He died considerably in debt to some of his parishioners; but the parish owed him a large sum, which was the subject of negotiation with his administrator during many years after his death.

Having thus shared in the sufferings of war, Mr. Rogers was not permitted to greet the return of peace. He did not live to see the independence of the country fully established, though hostilities had ceased when he came to his sudden end. His death took place Oct. 4, 1782; and the manner of it was in striking accordance with an ejaculatory prayer which he uttered while recalling to mind the sufferings of one of his people, — a female, whose groans in the agonies of death had deeply affected him: "Lord, grant me an easy passage through the valley of the shadow of death." This was his prayer; and the answer came while on a visit at the house of a friend and parishioner, where he had dined. He rose from the dinner-table, complaining of a pain in his breast; seated himself in an arm-chair; and was observed to place both of his hands on the top of his cane, and lean his head forward to rest upon them. Having remained in this position long enough to excite alarm, his friends gathered around him; and it was found that he had passed the dread vale, without a struggle or a groan. He seemed to have had some presentiment of the near approach of death; for, conversing with a friend and fellow-laborer in the ministry a few days before that event, he said, "I have done my work; I shall never preach more; and the distinguishing doctrines of the gospel never appeared so interesting and important as now. And, as I have lived, so I mean to die, bearing my testimony to the truth and importance of those doctrines I have always made capital through the course of my ministry."

Towards the close of his life, he was frequently ill. He was troubled with many bodily diseases, chiefly of the nervous and peripneumonic kind, which somewhat obstructed his usefulness.

Mr. Rogers was a man of large frame and robust appearance. He was an earnest preacher, and attracted the attention of his hearers by the constant and violent gestures with which it was his habit to enforce his arguments and exhortations. It is not known that any of his compositions appeared in print. He was accounted a good scholar and an excellent preacher, and was esteemed and approved in his day as an evangelical, pious, and faithful minister of Jesus Christ. He belonged to a family which claims the distinction of descent from "the martyr," "the first of that blessed company who suffered in the reign of Mary;" and which is really entitled to the renown of having furnished to the New-England churches, through five generations, some of their most able, faithful, and godly ministers.

Mr. Rogers was thrice married. His first wife was Susanna Allen, to whom he was married Oct. 16, 1744. The birth of her first child in April, 1746, which lived but a short time, was soon followed by her own death. Mr. Rogers next married, Jan. 28, 1748, Mary, daughter of Nathaniel Ellery, who died in 1766, aged forty-three. He took, for his third wife, Mrs. Abigail Woodward, April 2, 1770; who survived her husband many years, and died March 12, 1819, aged eighty years. His children were — John born in 1748; Mary, 1753; Anna, 1754; Susanna and Catherine, 1756; William, 1758; Daniel, 1771; and Sally. John was prepared for college — partly by his father and partly by his grandfather — at Kittery, and graduated at Cambridge in 1767. He was designed by his father for the ministry; but, having doubts of his spiritual qualification, he entered another field of labor. Soon after he graduated, he commenced teaching a school in Manchester; and afterwards, in his native town, engaged in the same employment, and continued in it more than forty years. In 1782, he was elected town-clerk; and, in each successive year till his death, was chosen to the same office. Even in times of bitter political strife, no one thought of displacing him; a fact that sufficiently attests the ability and faithfulness with which he discharged the duties that devolved upon him. He died Nov. 24, 1827, aged seventy-nine; having made, about a year before his death, a public profession of religion. Mary, the oldest daughter of Rev. John Rogers, was twice married, — first to James Riggs in 1775, and next to Elias Haskell. Anna married William Babson in 1777, and died in June, 1826. Susanna married John Babson in 1775; and died, after a lingering and painful illness of twenty-two years, at Mount Desert, September, 1828. Catherine died unmarried. William, the second son, was for a short time in the army of the Revolution. In the early part of his career, he engaged in maritime pursuits; but was chiefly employed during his life in teaching school, and in performing the duties of an office in the Custom House, which he held many years. He died Dec. 18, 1832, aged seventy-four; leaving a son Isaac, who settled in the ministry at Farmington, Me.; and another (John L.), who was a shipmaster many years, and was appointed, by President Taylor, Collector of Gloucester in 1849. He died in September of that year, greatly lamented as a man of high moral and religious worth. Daniel, youngest son of Rev. John Rogers, became a sea-captain; and died in Gloucester, April 20, 1824. Sally married Capt. Theodore Stanwood; and died June 25, 1825, aged fifty-two. Mr. Rogers was the only settled minister that this parish ever had. The parish kept up its organization till 1839 for the purpose of taking care of its meeting-house; though it also had, for many years, the management of the public school kept within its limits, which was supported by money raised by the town.

The Fourth Parish worshipped in the old church on the Meeting-house Green till 1752; when they erected a new one on the south-east corner of the green, a few rods from the site of the old one. It was a large building, with a door on the south side, and one on the east and one on the west end. A belfry with a tall spire rose from the roof at the west end. A gallery was built around three sides of the interior; and the floor was filled with pews, excepting a space in front of the pulpit, which had long seats. The building was kept in very good repair nearly to the time when it was taken down. Religious worship was occasionally held in it in its last years, principally by clergymen of the Methodist persuasion, one of whom (Rev. L. B. Griffing) was announced to preach the last sermon in it, June 14, 1840. On that occasion, the concourse assembled was so great, that it was not deemed prudent to test the strength of the old building; and the services were held on the Green. The sermon was from 1 Kings viii. 57: "The Lord our God be with us as he was with our fathers: let him not leave us nor forsake us." The meeting-house was taken down in the same year. The spire had been removed several years before to the top of Poles Ledge, where it stood some time. The bell had long been cracked, and its last doleful tones were in melancholy unison with the closing existence of the parish and the departed glory of its abandoned and decaying temple.

For the first hundred years of our municipal existence, it does not appear that the selectmen received any fixed compensation for their services; but each, at the end of his official term, was paid according to the work he had done for the town. For the year 1744, these officers (five in number) received about five dollars each; and the charge to the town the same year for their expenses, at two taverns where they held their meetings, was nearly thirty pounds, old tenor (about seventeen dollars). Whether these bills were unsatisfactory to the town or not, we do not know; but, from some cause, a vote was passed at the town-meeting in March, 1745, that the selectmen should be allowed for the ensuing year a salary of five pounds, old tenor, "for doing the town's business and finding themselves." This expression may be considered as somewhat significant that the tavern-bill, at least, was a cause of dissatisfaction: but, whatever might have been the public feeling in regard to it, no permanent change was effected; for, in 1749, the expenses of the fathers of the town at Capt. Ellery's tavern ran up as high as seventy-eight pounds, old tenor.

It had long been the custom for the selectmen to meet at a tavern for the transaction of their business. These meetings were not frequent; but, when they did take place, they probably continued a whole day: and the meals and drink for the Board, at the end of the year, were brought as a charge against the town. We have the cost of a single meeting on one occasion, which was when the town-officers were sworn in in 1740, when the "expense for the Selectmen and Licker at the house of Mr. James Stevens" was £3. 18s. 2d. Stevens's Tavern was the old Ellery House, still standing, "up in town." It was not only the first tavern, the location of which is known; but it is probably one of the oldest houses in town now standing in its original shape.* Its venerable appearance turns our thoughts at once back to the past; and only a slight exercise of the imagination is necessary to revivify the scene of 1740, with its solemn assumption of municipal duties, and the simultaneous discussion of town-affairs and the quality of the dinner and the "licker." The worthy citizens inducted into office as selectmen, on this occasion, were Capt. James Davis, Abraham Davis, Nathaniel Ellery, Timothy Day, and Jabez Baker.

Not much can now be ascertained concerning the ancient taverns of Gloucester. That of "landlady Judkins" has been already mentioned. After her, George Harvey enjoyed the patronage of the town-officers. In 1717, and a few previous years, John Day, sen., entertained the selectmen. Next Thomas Millet and John Stacy appear as innholders. These were all

* See engraving of it, p. 280.

predecessors of James Stevens, who was himself succeeded by Capt. William Ellery. Probably all these kept in the ancient centre of the town, near the Meeting-house; but, during most of this time, the Harbor also had its taverns. The petitioners for a license for Mrs. Mary Perkins, in 1749, state that two had been kept in this part of the town the greater part of the time for thirty years; that two were then wanted much more than in times past; and that the Harbor could not "any way be conveniently without two." These taverns were James Broom's on Middle Street, and Jonathan Ingersol's. Ingersol's house was patronized by the committee of the First Parish in 1743 and 1744; but his death about that time made an opening for a new tavern, and Mrs. Perkins obtained a license to keep one. Her husband (Benjamin Perkins) had recently died at sea, leaving her the care of a large family. She was one of the eight daughters of Andrew Robinson; but, of her qualities as a hostess, no account has come down to the present generation. Her house (a very large one) stood on Front Street, on the spot now occupied by Burnham's public-house. Mrs. Perkins became blind, and died in 1759.

The year 1745 is memorable in the annals of New England for the expedition against Louisburg, a strongly fortified town of the French, in the Island of Cape Breton. The fortification of the place had been many years in building, and had cost the French Government several millions of livres. The town had also a large business; having, it is said, employed six hundred vessels in its trade and fisheries, and exported five hundred thousand quintals of cod annually. In a war with France, the fishery of New England lay, of course, at the mercy of this stronghold of the enemy; and the reduction of the place was, therefore, a matter of the highest importance to the people of Gloucester, who now yearly sent several vessels to the Banks of Newfoundland. "Some," said Rev. John White,* "have not

* In a sermon preached by him after the departure of the expedition to Louisburg. His text was Ps. lxxiv. 21: "Oh! let not the oppressed return ashamed: let the poor and needy praise thy name." It was an earnest appeal to his hearers to pray for the success of the expedition, and shows the venerable preacher to have been filled with

unfitly called Cape Breton a hornet's nest. 'Tis not safe, in a time of war, to go near them. They will sting all that come near them. We have already, ever since the war commenced, been great sufferers by them. They harbor our enemies that come to lay waste our infant eastern settlements; they molest and break in upon our fisheries, and break them to pieces; they lie near the roadway of our European merchandise, and they can sally out and take our corn-vessels: and therefore our oppressions from thence, so long as it remains in the hands of the enemy, are like to be intolerable. We must remove these our enemies, or they will destroy us. There is a plain necessity of it; and woe to us if it be not reduced!"

The kings of England and France mutually declared war in March, 1744; and, before the news reached Boston, the Governor of Cape Breton sent a large force, which surprised and took the English garrison at Canso. It is quite probable, too, that cruisers from Louisburg made some captures among the New-England fishing vessels, which must have put to sea before the war was known here. Mr. White's language authorizes such an inference. Louisburg was deemed impregnable; but there was seen to be a necessity for its reduction, and the Governor of Massachusetts made application to the British ministry for aid in attempting it. In the mean time, the men taken at Canso, who had been carried prisoners to Louisburg, arrived in Boston on parole, and gave the Governor such accounts of the condition of that fortress as made him resolve on an enterprise for its reduction, without waiting for an answer from England. The attempt was considered one of no small degree of temerity, and all the circumstances of the expedition fairly belong to the romance of history. The Governor's proposal to the Legislature for undertaking it was adopted by a majority of one vote; and, in the short space of two months, about four thousand troops, principally belonging to Massachusetts, were collected at Boston, and embarked under William Pepperrell, as commander, on the

---

an enthusiastic interest in it. The discourse was not published; but, coming into my hands in the original manuscript, in June, 1845, I had it printed in the "Gloucester Telegraph."

24th of March, 1745. At Canso, they were joined by a naval force ordered thither by the British Government. On the 16th of June, the city and fortress surrendered; and the Colonial troops, instead of returning "ashamed," came home to diffuse joy and gladness through every part of New England.

It would be gratifying to know the number and the names of the Gloucester men engaged in the expedition to Louisburg; but that information cannot now be obtained. It can scarcely be doubted, that nearly all the fishermen of the town eagerly seized the opportunity to break up the "hornet's nest," which prevented their approach to the places which furnished them with the means of subsistence. The Massachusetts archives show that a Capt. Byles, and his company of forty-one men, were at the siege of Louisburg, and were on pay from Feb. 16 to Sept. 30. The Capt. Byles here mentioned was undoubtedly Capt. CHARLES BYLES of this town; who, according to the statement of an aged descendant recently deceased, commanded a company at Louisburg, and also in the next French War.

The services of Capt. Thomas Sanders in the expedition have been already mentioned. Several letters and notes addressed to him while in command of the transports in Chapeau-Rouge Bay, by Admiral Warren and General Pepperrell, are yet preserved by one of his descendants.

Job Stanwood received from the General Court, in 1747, £12. 10s., in consideration of his services and sufferings in the expedition; and, in 1749, was granted a pension of £15 per annum for life. He lost his left arm.

David Stanwood was wounded; and, soon after his return from Cape Breton, obtained from the Provincial Legislature a grant of £5. In 1746, he had a further allowance of £8; and was recommended to the Governor to be placed in the garrison at Brunswick, in room of an effective man. He had another grant of £5, in 1747.

A son of Thomas Ayers is said to have been lost in the expedition; and James Parsons and Samuel Goodwin returned home sick, and died, — Parsons on the 11th, and Goodwin on the 18th, of August, 1745.

No account of the part borne by Gloucester in the expedition to Louisburg would be complete without the story of Peg Wesson. The popular belief in witchcraft had not then ceased, and Peg was reputed a witch. She lived in or near an old building on Back Street, called "the Garrison;" and there, just before the departure of the Gloucester soldiers for Cape Breton, she was visited by some of them, who, by their conduct towards her, aroused her indignation to such a pitch, that, on their departure, she threatened them with vengeance at Louisburg. While in camp there, these men had their attention arrested by the singular movements of a crow that kept hovering near them. After many attempts had been made in the usual way to kill the bird, it occurred to one of them that it must be Peg Wesson; and, if so, that no baser metal than silver would bring her to the ground. He accordingly took his silver sleeve-buttons from his wrist, and discharged them at the bird; which fell, wounded in the leg, and was soon killed. Upon their return to Gloucester, they learned, that, at the exact moment when the crow was killed, Peg Wesson fell down near the Garrison House, with a broken leg; and that, when the fractured limb was examined, the identical sleeve-buttons fired at the crow, under the walls of Louisburg, were found, and extracted from the wound! Such is the story of Peg Wesson; and, incredible as it may seem that it was ever received as truth, some now living can testify to the apparent belief in it with which it was related by many persons not more than fifty years ago.

The next year after the fall of Louisburg, a large French fleet appeared at Nova Scotia; and, in all our towns, great apprehensions of an invasion were felt. The selectmen of Gloucester were instructed by the town to petition to the General Court to finish the Battery, and furnish it with ammunition; and the people of this and some other seaports were in such fear, that they sent away their effects. But various accidents combined to render the enemy powerless for harm; and, after a few weeks of anxiety, all cause for alarm ceased to exist.

At the March meeting in 1748, the town voted that the selectmen should take care of the poor, as "they formerly used to do."

This duty had been for a few years previously performed by officers chosen specially for it, who were only required to agree with individuals for the maintenance of the paupers, as no work-house was yet established. The amount paid for the support of the poor, — seven in number, — this year, was £281. 16s., old tenor; or about one hundred and forty dollars, lawful money.

The maritime business of the town had been steadily increasing for several years, notwithstanding the interruptions by war; and was constantly attracting new settlers. Only a few of them, however, left descendants in town to perpetuate their names here, or were themselves prominent while they lived in it. Of these, all who came to Gloucester between 1735 and 1750 will be here mentioned.

JAMES PEARSON, a sea-captain, is said by descendants to have come to this town from Bristol, England. He married Hannah, daughter of Capt. Andrew Robinson, Jan. 6, 1738; and settled at Eastern Point. He married a second wife (Mary Edgar), Feb. 3, 1749; and died March 24, 1789, in his seventy-seventh year, leaving several children. WILLIAM, his oldest son, engaged in maritime employments, and accumulated considerable property by privateering in the Revolutionary War. He was a representative several years; and, for a short time, President of the Bank. His death took place Dec. 5, 1826, at the age of eighty-five. He had children, but survived all of them. One of them (William) was educated a physician, and commenced the practice of medicine with great promise in his native town; but his career was early ended by a sickness which resulted from a fall from his horse, as he was one night descending the hill near Farm Ledge, on a visit to a patient. The fall caused a hemorrhage, by which he was so much reduced as to be obliged to seek a mild climate in winter; and, while on a second visit to the West Indies, he died at St. Eustatius, Feb. 9, 1795, aged twenty-six. He was buried, by the Concordia Lodge of that place, with Masonic solemnities. Edmund, brother of the preceding, was lost at sea on a voyage to France. William Bonaparte, another son of Capt. William Pearson, died in 1825, aged twenty-eight, leaving two sons; one of whom (William) is a graduate of Yale College, now residing in California. JAMES, the second son of Capt. James Pearson, was bred to a maritime life; and during the Revolutionary War, though then in early manhood, he commanded the large privateer-ship "Starks." After the peace, he settled in mercantile business; and died in October, 1793, aged forty-one. He was captain of the artillery company, and was interred on the 18th with military honors. A printed notice of his death says that he was "a benevolent citizen and fervent patriot; in war, an undaunted soldier; in peace, an industrious merchant; but, more than all, a man of great native integrity. He bore his sickness with fortitude; and, in the firm belief of a blissful immortality, resigned his life with calmness to the God who gave it." He left daughters, and a son James, who was lost at sea.

JONATHAN FELLOWS is supposed to have come from Ipswich about 1740. He settled in Squam. His only public service known to us was that rendered as captain of a company against the French in the campaign of 1755; and, of that service, no particulars can now be ascertained. He died June 20, 1759. By his wife Elizabeth,* he had sons Nathaniel and Caleb, and two daughters, born here. Cornelius Fellows, who was chosen one of the selectmen in 1774, and moved out of town that year, may have been another son. He and Nathaniel and Gustavus Fellows are said to have removed from Gloucester to Boston, and to have become distinguished merchants. A Samuel Fellows was ensign in the company of Capt. Jonathan Fellows in 1755. He is the same, probably, who, as an officer of the customs, or in some other equally unpopular capacity, made himself so odious to the people here in 1768, that a mob of about seventy persons, headed by several respectable citizens, suspecting that he was concealed in the house of Jesse Saville, proceeded thither one night in September of that year, and thoroughly searched the building in pursuit of him; making use of a good deal of violence in their behavior, and showing a determination to deal severely with

* I suppose she was the daughter of Caleb Norwood and his wife Alice. The latter, becoming a widow, married Rev. John White; and left, with other children by her previous husband, a daughter, — Elizabeth Fellows.

the object of their animosity if they could find him. He sought safety, it is likely, in flight; as his name does not appear in our subsequent history.*

JOHN DANE came, in 1743, from Ipswich; where his ancestor, John Dane, was an early settler. He was a shoemaker, and had his shop and dwelling on Front Street. He married Abigail, daughter of John Pool, Jan. 27, 1743, and had several children; but the name was not perpetuated here in the male line beyond the second generation. He died July 21, 1793, in his seventy-fourth year. His son William was a shopkeeper on Front Street, and acquired some property. He was a representative in 1812; and died in December, 1820, aged seventy-four. Another son (Joshua), who kept a little shop, and was a man of quiet but peculiar habits, died April 21, 1845, aged eighty-one; leaving an only son (John), a merchant in Boston, since deceased.

EBENEZER CLEVES came from Beverly, and married Anna Stevens, March 4, 1744. Six sons and two daughters are recorded as the fruit of this marriage. The name is not borne by descendants in Gloucester; but the Rockport Family of the same name are probably from this settler.

JOHN HALE, son of Samuel Hale of Newbury, where he was born in 1722, was a shoemaker, and came to Squam Parish about 1746; when, by his wife Elinor, his son Samuel was born. Besides two daughters, he had three other sons, only one of whom (Benjamin) settled in Gloucester. SAMUEL graduated at Harvard College in 1766, and was for some time the teacher in an academy near Portsmouth, N.H. He afterwards engaged in the practice of law in that town; but at the opening of the Revolution, having enrolled himself on the royal side, he felt obliged to leave the country, and go to England. Of his subsequent career, nothing is known. He died in England about 1787. George D. Hale, a son of Benjamin Hale, has been Collector of the Customs for the District of Gloucester.

JOSEPH CLOUGH married Susanna Tarbox in 1748, and a

* In 1769, he was captain of one of the king's armed cutters, and was complained of for disorderly conduct in delivering from the sheriff's hands a man named Merrill, who was under arrest for debt.

second and a third wife within the next fourteen years. In 1750, he had a grant of a small piece of land, near the Windmill, to set a house upon; for which he was to pay ten shillings. Besides several daughters, he had sons Joseph and William, and Benjamin and John, twins.

JOSEPH EVERDEAN first appears here in 1748, when he married Anna Broom. He died suddenly in a boat, coming from Cape Cod, March, 1764; leaving, besides other children, a son Joseph, who settled in town, and died in May, 1837, aged eighty-six.

CHAPTER XIV.

FIRST PARISH. — REV. SAMUEL CHANDLER. — HIS MINISTRY, SICKNESS, AND DEATH. — HIS FAMILY.

IT has already been mentioned, that the failing health of Rev. John White of the First Church made it necessary, in 1750, to provide him help in the work of the ministry. Mr. Samuel Moody of York, grandson of the pastor, who had preached here several months, was the choice of a majority of the church as a colleague to Mr. White; but several opposed, and he declined a call to settle here. The committee who waited upon him at York then made arrangements with Rev. Samuel Chandler of that place to preach here a few sabbaths. He arrived in town, Saturday, Feb. 23, 1751, and preached the next day. His forenoon sermon was from Isa. lv. 1. Mr. Chandler received an invitation to settle, though some made objections, and spoke to him in a discouraging manner: but finally, on the 30th of September, a committee of the church waited upon him to propose certain questions, to which satisfactory answers were given; and the 13th of November following was fixed upon for the installation. The second, third, and fourth churches in Gloucester, the first in Manchester, the second in Rowley, and the second in Andover, were invited to assist by delegates in the services on that occasion. It was nearly fifty years since this church had engaged in a similar ceremony; and the present one undoubtedly drew together, from the Gloucester churches and those in the neighboring town, a congregation sufficient to fill the capacious meeting-house in which it took place. Nothing more is known of the religious services of the occasion, than that the sermon was preached by Rev. Samuel Phillips of Andover (grandson of Rev. John Emerson,* and the pastor under whose ministry Mr. Chandler was brought up) from Luke xiv. 21. But into the social festivities of the day we are permitted to take a look by the colleague himself, who informs us that "Deacon William Parsons entertained the council at his own charge; Mr. William Stevens, the Schollars and Gentlemen, at his own charge; and Mr. John Stevens entertained the Council in the morning with Plumb Cake."†

Mr. Chandler was a son of Josiah Chandler of Andover, where he was born in 1713. He graduated at Harvard College in 1735; and, in 1742, was ordained minister of the church in York, Me.; where he remained, occasionally teaching school in addition to his ministerial duties, till his removal to Gloucester. The parish agreed to pay him a salary of eighty pounds per annum, and to let him have the use of the parish land. They also voted to provide him a suitable house, barn, and garden, in a convenient place.‡ No event of any interest in parish or church affairs occurred till 1753; when the inhabitants of Sandy Bay were set off into a separate precinct, and took rank, of course, as the Fifth Parish. In 1755, Mr. Chandler, with the unanimous consent of his church, went as chaplain in Col. Plaisted's regiment in the expedition against Crown Point. He was engaged in the service from Sept. 8 to Dec. 28. The next spring, Col. Plaisted came to Gloucester on purpose to procure his services for the campaign of that year; but the parish would not consent to his going.

The church-records give no account of any deacons, after those mentioned at the commencement of Mr. White's ministry, till 1756; when Deacon John Parsons and Deacon Philemon

---

* He was a son of Samuel Phillips of Salem, who married Mary, daughter of Rev. John Emerson. He was minister of the Second Church in Andover sixty years, till his death, in 1771, at the age of eighty. He published several sermons, one of which was that delivered at the installation of Mr. Chandler.

† A few little volumes of a journal kept by Mr. Chandler have been preserved, from one of which the account of the "entertainments" given at his installation is extracted.

‡ Mr. Chandler owned and occupied, at the time of his death, the gambrel-roofed house, still standing, on the south side of Middle Street, about midway between Short Street and Centre Street.

Warner were elected ruling elders. At the same time, Eliezer Grover, Jeremiah Parsons, and Ezekiel Woodward, were chosen deacons. These were succeeded by Nathaniel Kinsman, Hubbard Haskell, and Nymphas Stacy, jun., who were all chosen, in 1772, to fill the vacancies then existing. In the mean time, Nymphas Stacy, sen., and Isaac Parsons, had also been deacons.

The condition of political affairs in 1768 was threatening; and the church, according to the usage then prevailing, sought the divine aid and protection through fasting and prayer. Thursday, Oct. 6, was set apart for these exercises: and the special subjects of prayer were, the critical state of things in the mother-country; the precarious situation of the rights and liberties of the Colonies, in consequence of the oppression and impositions laid upon them; and the difficult circumstances of the Province, arising from the dissolution of the General Court, and the apprehension of the fearful calamity of a military government. Mr. Chandler passed through all the anxieties of that troubled period; but he did not live to hear of the first blood shed in the war which followed. His ministry and life were drawing to a close in the fall of 1774. His health failed, and his parish made an appropriation to provide him assistance in his duties, — such as an occasional supply of his pulpit.

The declining days of Mr. Chandler were rendered painful and wearisome by long sickness and suffering; but no bodily infirmity or distress could move him to sorrow or repine, while his soul was filled with the deepest anxiety and alarm on account of the danger of fearful magnitude that threatened the eternal welfare of his beloved flock. A new teacher had come to his people, and, with plausible arguments and captivating eloquence, was "wresting and torturing the word of God," and, in opposition to the venerable authority of ancient interpretation and universal belief, was proclaiming the final salvation of the human race as a doctrine of the Holy Scriptures. The sick pastor could not send forth from the pulpit a voice of warning against the dangerous heresy; but he called to his brethren * in the ministry to

* One of these was Rev. Dr. Stillman of Boston, concerning one of whose visits the following anecdote is told. On the occasion alluded to, he took for his text John xii.

come and sound the alarm; and then, as a last effort of his concern for the people of his charge, sent to his pulpit to be read, a few weeks before his death, a short address; in which he admonished them, as one drawing near the eternal world, to take heed lest they should be led away with error, and to beware of the false prophet, who, if it were possible, would deceive the very elect.

Mr. Chandler died on the 16th of March, 1775, aged sixty-two. We have a brief sketch of his character from a young brother* in the ministry, who had from childhood attended upon his religious instructions: —

"He was a gentleman of clear apprehension, solid judgment, firm, and of a thoughtful, inquisitive temper of mind. These, sanctified and improved, fitted him for the high and honorable office he sustained, and which he discharged with fidelity. As a preacher, he delivered the truth as it is in Jesus; showing in his doctrines uncorruptness, gravity, and sound speech, that could not be condemned; exhibiting a bright example of the same in the course and tenor of his life. He was blessed with a great degree of wisdom and prudence, the happy effects of which hath been evident in a variety of instances. The welfare of his people and of the church of God lay near his heart. He was a warm friend to his country. In every relation, he maintained the character of a sincere disciple of his Lord and Master, the Lord Jesus Christ. Many and various were his trials on his passage through life, under which his patience was conspicuous. Under the hand of God, in the consumption which closed the scene of life, he discovered great sub-

32, "And I, if I be lifted from the earth, will draw all men unto me," and announced to his hearers that it would be his purpose to show that Christ did not mean by this language to declare that he would draw all men unto him to a state of endless happiness. One of the congregation was Josiah Cheever, who had kept a small shop on Front Street; a man whose intellect had been somewhat disordered, in consequence of disappointment in a love-affair: for his father, Rev. Amos Cheever of Manchester, had supplanted him in the affections of a fair daughter of Deacon James Davis of Squam. Having listened attentively to the doctor, he rose at the conclusion of his discourse and said, "Dr. Stillman, it is quite enough for you to try to prove John Murray a liar, without attempting to make Jesus Christ one." The condition of his mind was generally known, so that no notice was taken of the interruption. Soon after this time, Cheever's mind became still more unsettled; and, becoming a town-pauper, he died in our work-house, Jan. 31, 1806, aged seventy-four.

* Rev. Obadiah Parsons of the Third Church.

mission and resignation to His holy will, who was his staff through the valley of the shadow of death, and now is (as I trust) his portion for ever."

Tradition confirms all that is here said of Mr. Chandler. His domestic life was one of singular infelicity; and the reports concerning it, not yet passed into oblivion, render it probable that all the gentleness, patience, and resignation that marked his character were schooled to a severe exercise in his conjugal and parental relations. His wife, to whom he was married in 1738, was Anna Pecker of Haverhill, who had either a disordered intellect or a perverse heart. She annoyed and troubled her husband in unusual ways; and, in the judgment of charity, it may be allowed that reason rather than conscience was deficient. Mr. Chandler had a son John, who was a seafaring man, and is said to have caused his father much anxiety and trouble; but of his history and end no particulars are preserved. He also had a daughter Anna, whose conduct was the source of less happiness than sorrow; but her frailties were buried with her in an early grave. She died Feb. 19, 1765, of consumption, aged twenty-two. Another daughter (Sarah) married William Haynes in 1769. He was a sojourner in town then; but it is not supposed that he remained here many months. He was a sea-captain, and was never heard from after he sailed on his last voyage. Mrs. Haynes died in Providence, R.I., while on a visit, Feb. 28, 1813, aged sixty-six. Mrs. Chandler, after her husband's death, opened a small shop in the house where she had long resided, in Middle Street; and, after keeping it a short time, removed out of town. These three children came to Gloucester with their father. He had one (Samuel) born here June 20, 1753. He graduated at Harvard College in 1775, and then went one voyage or more, privateering, from Newburyport; after which he taught a mathematical school in that town till within a few weeks of his death, which occurred in May, 1787. His wife, whom he married in Newburyport, survived him; and married, for her second husband, John Mycall. She also outlived him, and died at an advanced age.

CHAPTER XV.

SANDY BAY. — FIRST SETTLERS THERE. — FIFTH PARISH. — REV. EBENEZER CLEAVELAND. — HIS MINISTRY AND DEATH. — HIS FAMILY.

THE formation of a new parish at the Cape completed the parochial divisions of the town. The progress of settlement there at the beginning of the last century has been mentioned in a preceding chapter; and, before proceeding to notice the organization of the church, — which, of course, took rank as the fifth in town, — it is proper to give some account of the increase of population in that remote section during the fifty years that followed.

The indentation of the coast between Andrews's Point and Straitsmouth Point, at the head of the Cape, began to be called Sandy Bay about the time that the first settlement was made there. The first separate grant of land in that locality was that made to John Babson in 1695, at Straitsmouth, "to sett up fishing upon." It is not known that Babson had his home there; though a cellar upon his land still marks the spot where he, or some of his successors in the fishery there, once had a house. He sold his land at Straitsmouth in 1721 to Jefford Cogswell, Jacob Perkins, and James Smith of Ipswich. These were probably the Chebacco fishermen, concerning whose visits to the Cape tradition yet preserves remembrance; though it is said that fishermen from that place were accustomed, at an earlier date, to frequent the shores of the Cape for the purpose of landing and drying their fish. One circumstance keeps alive the memory of Babson and the Chebacco fishermen. The former, or some member of the family, was attacked one day by a bear; and, after a terrible struggle with his antagonist, succeeded in slaying him with a knife. He then flayed the animal, and spread out his skin to dry upon the rocks near the sea, at the end of a neck of land, where it was seen by the fishermen, who gave the place the name of Bearskin Neck.

In 1697, Richard Tarr had a house at Sandy Bay, on land granted to him by the town, on the south side of Davison's Run. Perhaps he settled there a few years before that date; as it is certain that he was a resident of the town in 1693, and probable that he was here as early as 1690. Tradition states that Tarr was induced to settle there by the coasters, who, on their visits to the shore to take away wood, occasionally needed help from land. Whatever the inducements, he is distinguished in our history as the first permanent settler at the end of the Cape. His descendants are numerous, and some of them still occupy a portion of the land upon which he found a lonely home a century and a half ago.

The next settler at Sandy Bay was John Pool. The extensive tract of land which he bought there of John Emerson, jun., in 1700, was situated on the north side of Davison's Run. On this land a house had been built; whose occupant, if it had one before Pool, is not known. It was probably a mere hovel, and not the substantial tenement which Pool himself occupied several years before his death. Tarr and Pool were, therefore, near neighbors. Their land was good for planting; the primeval forest sheltered them from the wintry blasts, and afforded the means of diffusing a cheerful warmth in their dwellings; and the broad Atlantic came to their doors with its various offerings for use and enjoyment. Such was the beginning of the flourishing town which now occupies the north-easterly extremity of our Commonwealth.

Several years elapsed before any new settlers were attracted to the spot where the two pioneers at the Cape were located. Between 1700 and 1712, a few persons settled on the north-easterly end of the Cape. In 1708, Peter Emons was on the south-east end; and, within five or six years after that time, Peter Bennet was also there. Neither of these two became permanent settlers; and the old cellars over which their houses once stood afford the only evidence to show where they lived while there. Bennet bought a large number of the lots laid out to the commoners in 1708, between Long Cove and Starknaught Harbor; and he made his home there, probably, for the purpose of cutting down his wood, and hauling it to the landings on the seashore. Emons, it is likely, was also employed in the same kind of work. At the end of the first quarter of the eighteenth century, nearly all the land at the head of the Cape had passed into the possession of individual proprietors; and there can be no doubt, that, during all this time, an active business was carried on in exporting the wood with which it was covered. That business gave employment to the large number of vessels built in the town in those years, and was the chief inducement to the settlement of the easterly shores of Cape Ann.

It is not easy to ascertain who was the first to join Tarr and Pool at Sandy Bay. In 1715, a John Davis, with his wife and family, from Ipswich, moved into town. He may have been the person of the same name, son of Isaac Davis of Falmouth, who, in 1734, was living in Gloucester, about seventy-four years old; and the "old Mr. John Davis" of Sandy Bay, who in 1748, and for several preceding years, received assistance from the town. The latter had a son Samuel, who married Deborah Harris in 1723; became a captain, and an elder of the church; and died Aug. 25, 1770, aged sixty-seven. He had several children; four of whom (sons) were lost at sea. Ebenezer Davis, who had a brother Samuel (probably the preceding), married Elizabeth, daughter of Richard Tarr, in 1715. It does not appear that he lived at Sandy Bay; but it seems quite certain that the other Davises here mentioned became residents there between 1715 and 1723.

In 1719, Jabez Baker, weaver, son of Cornelius Baker of Salem, removed to Sandy Bay from Beverly, and settled near Richard Tarr. He had a wife Rachel, by whom three daughters — Mary, Bethiah, and Abigail — were born here. She died June 5, 1731, aged forty-seven. Jabez Baker became an elder of the church; and died Aug. 24, 1758, leaving a wife Jane.

With him came a son Jabez, who, in 1733, married Anna Smith of Beverly, and had several children. The only one of his sons known to have married here was Joseph, who married Mary Norwood in 1770, settled in Squam, and died at an advanced age, leaving no descendants. Jabez Baker, jun., was a sea-captain; and died about 1753, leaving a vessel and a farm. His wife survived him almost half a century; and died March 3, 1800, at the age of eighty-seven.

The next settler at Sandy Bay is supposed to have been John Wonson, of whom some account has already been given. He married a daughter of Richard Tarr in 1720; and had a house, the site of which is still pointed out by the elderly people who live near it.

Edmund Grover, who has also been before mentioned, was dismissed from Beverly Church, and recommended to a church in Gloucester, in July, 1722. He located himself near Loblolly Cove, at a considerable distance from the other settlers in Sandy Bay. Nehemiah Grover and Ebenezer Grover, his sons, settled near him. The former died Jan. 13, 1761, a few days before his father; and the latter, Oct. 25 in the same year. Each of these sons had several children. Two other sons — Edmund and Eliezer — settled in the First Parish, at the head of the Harbor; to which place Eliezer removed from Sandy Bay after 1740. He died Dec. 25, 1795, aged eighty-five. Edmund became a seafaring man; and, being master of a schooner to Virginia, was drowned there, Feb. 8, 1742, aged about thirty-six. It does not appear that he left sons; but the name is still borne in Gloucester by descendants of Eliezer.

Another person, who, about the same time, settled in Sandy Bay, was Samuel Clark, who, in 1726, had a grant of half an acre of land north-westerly from John Wonson's house. He was son-in-law of "old Mr. John Davis;" and was probably the person of the same name who had, by his wife Elizabeth, a daughter Abigail born in 1728, and a son Henry in 1734.* A

---

* These are recorded in the town-records. The records of the First Church show the following baptisms of children of Samuel Clark: Samuel, 1722; Ann, 1723; Susanna, 1725; Elizabeth, 1727; Joseph, 1728; Hannah, 1736; and Nathaniel, 1739.

Samuel Clark, jun., supposed to be a son of this settler, married Widow Elizabeth Tarr in 1747.

Joshua Kendall married Mary Tarr in 1730, and is supposed to have settled in Sandy Bay about that time.

Henry Witham, son of Thomas Witham, married Rachel Parsons (a widowed daughter, it is supposed, of Jabez Baker) in 1733, and settled in Sandy Bay, near the Grovers, at the south-easterly end of the Cape. He had a large family of children; became an elder of the church there; and died March 18, 1777, aged eighty-two.

Thomas Dresser, whose origin is not known, first appears at Sandy Bay on his marriage to Sarah Tarr, Jan. 6, 1733. He was living there in 1754; but nothing further is known of him, except that he had several children. His house was near the Corner.

John Row, son of Stephen Row, married, in 1736, Mary Baker (who was probably the first child of Jabez born in Sandy Bay), and joined the settlers, who now constituted a small village in the vicinity of his father-in-law. He kept a tavern in the house, still standing, on the hill opposite a road leading to the Burying-ground. John Row, his son and his grandson, were distinguished for military services, which have already been related.

Elias Cook came from Marblehead, and had, in 1738, a grant of sixteen rods of land, where his dwelling stood, joining land of Samuel Davis and Caleb Tarr. He may have been in Sandy Bay as early as 1731; when, by his wife Sarah, his daughter Sarah was born. Besides her, he had Francis, Benjamin, Samuel, and William.

In 1738, a malignant throat-distemper, which prevailed with extraordinary fatality throughout New England, for about two years, began its ravages at Sandy Bay, and took from the settlers, as they say in a memorial to the General Court, "thirty-one of their pleasant children by death." There were then in the place twenty-seven families, containing more than one hundred and forty persons. Several of these families are mentioned in the preceding account of the settlers. Some of them were of the second generation, of which were five Pools, and three or four Tarrs.*

Of the settlers at Sandy Bay between 1738 and 1754, we know the names, but not the date of settlement there. Stephen Butler married Widow Elizabeth Gott in 1752, and had his residence in Sandy Bay in 1754.

Thomas Goss, a fisherman, son of Thomas Goss of Squam, who came from Marblehead, married Mary Tarr in 1751, and settled in Sandy Bay. In his advanced years, it is said that he and part of his family removed to Maine.†

John Hobson, jun., from Rowley, married Widow Martha Pool in 1753; and, after a short residence at Sandy Bay, returned to Rowley.

Eliezer Lurvey, son of Peter of this town, married Sarah Pool in 1742; and died in June, 1790, aged seventy-three.

Job Lane, son of John, the first of the name in town, married Mary Ashby in 1734. He had a second wife, Abigail Parsons, and was living at Sandy Bay in 1754.

About 1740, Joshua Norwood bought of the Chebacco fishermen their land at Straitsmouth, and settled there with his son Joshua. He had previously lived in a house between Pigeon Hill and Halibut Point, erected, according to tradition, by two men belonging to Salem, to conceal their mother, who was accused in the witchcraft fury of 1692. This house, with various additions and recent repairs, is still standing, and arrests the attention of

* The following-named persons are supposed to be the heads of families alluded to: —

Jabez Baker.	Ebenezer Grover.	Ebenezer Pool.
Jabez Baker, jun.	Eliezer Grover.	Caleb Pool.
Samuel Clark.	Thomas Harris.	Jonathan Pool.
Elias Cook.	Thomas Harris, jun.	John Row.
John Davis.	Samuel Harris.	William Tarr.
Samuel Davis.	Edward Jumper.	Caleb Tarr.
Thomas Dresser.	Joshua Kendall.	Benjamin Tarr.
Edmund Grover.	John Pool.	Samuel Tarr.
Nehemiah Grover.	Joshua Pool.	Henry Witham.

† Thomas Goss had a wonderful dog. Being out one day in his boat, fishing and gunning, accompanied by his dog, he was blown off the coast, and picked up by a vessel bound to Chesapeake Bay. Soon after his arrival there, he missed his valued animal, and supposed him to be lost; but, to his great surprise, he found, on reaching home some days afterwards, that the dog had arrived, in a weak and emaciated condition, a short time before.

every passer. For several years it was occupied for a summer boarding-house, and its delightful situation and fine advantages attracted many men eminent for taste and culture. Of Joshua Norwood's marriage and family, some account has already been given. His son Joshua had a house near the south part of Gap Cove; but his last days were spent alone in an old house on Pigeon Hill. He died about 1785.

James Parsons, a grandson of Jeffrey who settled at the Farms, married Abigail Tarr in 1744, and fixed his residence at Sandy Bay. He died in January, 1789, aged sixty-seven, leaving a large number of descendants.

Thomas Finson, son of Thomas who was killed by Indians in 1724, was born in 1720, and was living at Sandy Bay in 1754. He was drowned at Plum Cove, May 13, 1762.

Joseph Thurston, the first of the name in town, resided several years at Pigeon Hill. He married the widow of Thomas Finson, and had several children, one of whom (Joseph) had settled in Sandy Bay in 1754. At a later date, the father removed thither; and died there May 29, 1780. Joseph Thurston, jun., died June 8, 1801. His wife was Agnes Davis, daughter of Capt. Samuel Davis.

Two Sheltons (Ephraim and Israel) appear in Sandy Bay about 1750. The latter, in the record of his marriage to Widow Susanna Oakes in 1753, is said to be from Carolina. He removed to Woolwich, Me., and died there at an advanced age. Ephraim married Martha Langsford in 1749, and Abigail Pool in 1754. He had a son Ephraim, who settled in Newcastle, Me.

Daniel Williams, from Beverly, was residing at Sandy Bay in 1753, when he married Hannah Clark. It is not known how long he resided there. He left no sons at that place.

In 1741, James Hardy owned a house at Sandy Bay; but nothing further is known of him than that he is said to have removed to Maine.

Thomas Oakes was living in Sandy Bay in 1748. He married Jane Somes in 1730. She died in 1745; and he next married Susanna Clark, who became a widow, and married

Israel Shelton. Thomas Oakes had a son Thomas born in 1733.

The Harrises had, in 1754, removed from Pigeon Hill to the southerly end of the Cape; and were thus brought within the limits of the Sandy-Bay settlement. Thomas Harris died in 1764. Of the eleven children of Thomas Harris, jun., two were sons, who died on the same day, in the fatal year of 1738. Samuel Harris, according to the records, had but one child, — a daughter; but it is certain that he had, besides, daughters Ann and Judith, and a son Samuel, who settled in Maine.

Another settler at Sandy Bay, about this time, was John Blatchford. He is said to have been born in the west of England, and to have come to New England by the way of Newfoundland. He married Rachel Clark, Jan. 7, 1755; and died about the commencement of this century, at a very advanced age. He always asserted that he was on the Thames when three oxen were roasted whole on the ice on that river, and supposed himself then about fourteen years old. That event took place Jan. 19, 1716. He had four sons and two daughters. Samuel, one of the sons, removed to Eastport, Me.; another (Nathaniel) died in Gloucester, Jan. 11, 1852, aged eighty-five; and Henry, the youngest, died in Rockport in 1853, aged eighty-four. John, one of this family, was representative in 1834 and 1835.

The foregoing account of the early settlers of Sandy Bay comprises all who are known to have resided there to the year 1754, when the whole number of tax-payers at that place was thirty-seven; * of whom probably about one-half got their living

* The map gives the location of all the families at Sandy Bay to 1754, as nearly as can be ascertained. The following is a list of the tax-payers there in that year, not including the estates of Jabez Baker, jun., and Caleb Tarr, deceased: —

Jabez Baker.
Stephen Butler.
Capt. Samuel Davis.
Thomas Dresser.
Samuel Davis, 4th.
Thomas Finson.
Elder Edmund Grover.
Nehemiah Grover.
Nehemiah Grover, jun.
Ebenezer Grover.
Thomas Goss.
Thomas Harris, jun.
Samuel Harris.
John Hobson.
Eliezer Lurvey.
Job Lane.
Joshua Norwood, jun.
Ebenezer Pool.
Francis Pool.
Stephen Pool.
Jonathan Pool.
Caleb Pool.
John Pool.
James Parsons, jun.
John Row.
Ephraim Shelton.
Israel Shelton.
William Tarr.
Joshua Tarr.
Benjamin Tarr.
Benjamin Tarr, jun.
James Tarr.
Jacob Tarr.
Joseph Thurston, jun.
Henry Witham.
Samuel Wonson.
Daniel Williams.

Joshua Norwood, sen., and Thomas Harris, sen., paid no tax of any kind. William

from the sea, and the rest by cultivating the soil. Only two vessels of sufficient value to be taxed were then owned there; and the taxable property of the settlement was about one twenty-fourth part of the whole valuation of the town. The distance of these settlers from the town schoolhouse forced them to rely chiefly upon their own exertions for the education of their children; and their remoteness from the meeting-house deprived a large portion of them of the advantage and enjoyment of public religious worship. They had a schoolhouse soon after 1725, when the commoners granted them land on which to erect one "to keep a good school in for the godly instruction of children, and teaching of them to read and write good English." They also had sometimes preaching in the winter; and, in 1740, obtained from the First Parish remission of one-third of their parish-rates, on condition of supporting religious worship in their own village four months in a year. The parish had once refused them this privilege, and were now apparently only induced to grant it by an act of the General Court compelling them to do so. Rev. Moses Parsons was their minister one winter; but the names of others who were employed in occasional preaching at the Cape are not known to us.

The act for the incorporation of the Fifth or Sandy-Bay Parish received the approval of the Governor, Jan. 1, 1754. The westerly line of the new precinct extended from Cape Hedge to the highway near Beaver Dam, and thence in a northerly direction to the Squam-Parish line.

The meeting-house was erected by the parish about the time of its incorporation. It stood near the head of Long Cove, about forty feet easterly from the Baptist Meeting-house now standing there. It was about thirty-six feet square, two stories high, and unprovided with belfry or steeple. On the south side was a porch, in which was the entrance to the building, and a stairway leading to the gallery. The floor was furnished with

---

Tarr, Elder Grover, and Jabez Baker, in consequence of advanced age probably, were not assessed for a poll-tax. Nineteen persons paid only a poll-tax. The whole assessment for town-tax was £12. 3s. 6d. The three largest taxes were those of Ebenezer Pool, Caleb Pool, and John Pool, who together paid £3. 0s. 3d.

pews, excepting a space, each side of the middle aisle, near the pulpit, where were three long seats. It was taken down in May, 1805, just before the decease of the venerable minister who had been its only occupant as the pastor of the parish.

The new church was organized Feb. 13, 1755. The ministers of the First, Third, and Fourth churches, with delegates, were present to assist in the ceremonies and solemnities of the occasion. The following are the names of the members who were dismissed from the First Church to form the new one: Edmund Grover, Jabez Baker, Nehemiah Grover, Henry Witham, Jonathan Pool, Samuel Davis, John Row, James Parsons, jun., Samuel Clark, jun., and Eliezer Lurvey. They selected, for their minister, Ebenezer Cleaveland, who was ordained in December, 1755, with a salary of sixty pounds per annum. In January following, Edmund Grover and Jabez Baker were chosen ruling elders, and Henry Witham and Samuel Davis were chosen deacons. In forming themselves into a parish, the people of Sandy Bay assumed a pecuniary burthen of no inconsiderable amount; and it is a fact in their history, which their descendants may remember with pleasure as an evidence of their religious character, that the salary paid to their minister in 1755 was more than four times the amount of their town-tax the same year, and more than twice that of their town and province tax the year preceding.

Mr. Cleaveland was a son of Josiah Cleaveland of Canterbury, Conn.; and was born in that town, Jan. 5, 1725. He and his brother John were sent to Yale College, and were both expelled for attending a Separatist meeting while at home during a vacation. They justified themselves on the ground that their father and a majority of the church attended the same meeting. This act of the college government awakened public indignation, and the persecuted brothers were so far restored to favor as to obtain their degrees. John received his for 1748. It is not known how or where he was employed between the close of his college-life and the time of his settlement over the Fifth Parish here. It is said that he was a chaplain in the army sent against Ticonderoga in 1758, in the triumphant campaign to Canada in

1759, and for three months in 1765 at Fort Edward in the same capacity. His church consented, in June of that year, that he should go as chaplain with Col. John Whitcomb. In January, 1762, during the last illness of Mr. Bradstreet, the Squam Church procured the consent of the brethren at Sandy Bay, that their minister should preach to them some part of the winter; and, just before the death of Mr. Bradstreet, they proposed to pay forty-five pounds to secure Mr. Cleaveland's services one-half the time.

In June, 1775, Mr. Cleaveland obtained the consent of his church, that he should join the Revolutionary Army as chaplain. He accordingly joined it; and, in the following winter, was stationed at Dorchester Heights. He served in Rhode Island in 1777, and in other places afterwards. On his return home, he found his parish in a distressed condition. Some of his people had fallen in battle; some had died in prison-ships; many had perished at sea; and nearly all the rest fit for service were absent, fighting for their country's rights. They were deeply in debt to him for his past labors; and the best they could do for his future support was to give him ninety quintals of hake-fish per annum. He was compelled, therefore, to seek his living in another field of labor; and accepted an offer to become Superintendent of Dartmouth-College lands at Llandaff, N.H., preaching also in that and some of the neighboring towns. He remained there till about 1785; when he returned to Sandy Bay, and preached to his former flock, when not otherwise engaged, for such contributions as they could raise for him. After a few years, he again removed, and preached in Amesbury till some time in 1797; when he came back to his old home at the Cape, and finished his days in the house which he built there at the commencement of his ministry. He died July 4, 1805, aged eighty.

The usual language of eulogy employed to describe a sincere and faithful Christian minister may be used in giving the character of Mr. Cleaveland. In all his private relations, he was kind and loving; and his public duties were performed in such a manner as to gain him the respect and affection of his people. His virtues were subjected to severe trials; but they came from the ordeal with increased brightness. Unusual domestic troubles fell to his lot; but he kept his faith, and preserved a patient, serene, and affectionate spirit to the end. He died with Christian resignation; trusting, as he said, "in the same God who had protected him when the bullets were flying about his head on the battle-field," and resting "on the doctrines of free grace his hope of immortal glory."

He lies buried in the Parish Burying-ground in Sandy Bay. His gravestone, besides the usual inscription and a tribute to his worth, has the following lines: —

"Farewell, thou man of God! We saw thy grief;
Nor youth nor hoary days produced relief:
By painful crosses try'd, by sorrows prov'd,
By good men honor'd, and by Jesus lov'd,
Thy many years one hallow'd current ran;
A faithful pastor, and a godly man."

The only production of his pen, known to have been printed, is a sermon, entitled "The Abounding Grace of God towards Notorious Sinners," published in 1774.

Mr. Cleaveland's wife was Abigail Stevens of Canterbury. She died Dec. 25, 1804, aged seventy-seven. When expiring, she repeated the following lines: —

"Mercy, good Lord! mercy I crave;
This is the total sum:
For mercy, Lord, is all my suit.
Lord, let thy mercy come!"

They had twelve children. Filia Nata, an Alice, and William Pitt Amherst, died young. Olive married Isaac Pool, and removed to Bristol, Me., where both died in advanced life. Lydia married Nathan Fletcher, and had a second husband, named Lenox. She removed to Newburyport, and is supposed to have died there. Abigail, born in 1751; married, first, Reuben Brooks, who was taken in the "Yankee Hero" in 1776, and died in Halifax; second, James Henderson, who was lost in the privateer "America" in 1781; third, a Slater, who was drowned at Sandy Bay, just after embarking on a trip to Maine; and, fourth, Oliver Stevens, jun. She died June 3, 1790. Ebenezer, born in 1754, became a captain in the Revolutionary War; afterwards kept school; and was, at one time, engaged in the fishing business, in which he met with no success. He married Lois Pool, and died Nov. 26, 1822, without children. Mary, born in 1759, married Professor John Smith of Dartmouth College. John Vass, born in 1764, married Hannah Hale, daughter of John Hale of Squam. He removed to Amesbury, while his father was living there, to assist him in some business matters; and died there about 1796. His wife died about a year before him. He left a son John, now living in Quincy, Ill.; and two daughters, one of whom married a Fitts of Providence, and is now deceased; and the other is living unmarried in St. Louis. Alice, born in 1766, was deficient in intellect; and died in the Gloucester Alms-house, Sept. 1, 1814. Hephzibah, born in 1769, died unmarried at the age of nineteen. Beulah, born in 1772, married John Burns; and removed to Quincy, Ill., 1834, where she died in March, 1855.

CHAPTER XVI.

EXCISE ACT. — FRENCH WAR. — POPULATION. — TAXES AND TOWN EXPENSES. — SCHOOLS. — SMALL-POX. — STAMP ACT.

IN July, 1754, a town-meeting was held to consider a bill, that had been recently brought before the Legislature of Massachusetts, for granting an excise on wines and distilled spirits; and which, meeting with great opposition there, had been referred to the towns. One section of the bill required persons, consuming any of these articles in their houses, to give an exact account thereof to the collector of the excise, or his deputy, whenever called upon to do so. The town voted this provision to be "highly disagreeable to the inhabitants, and very grievous, as being inconsistent with the natural rights of mankind, and much more with the liberty of Englishmen;" and instructed their representative to act in conformity with these sentiments. The bill, however, was passed; and the town next sought relief "at home," by taking measures to prevent it from obtaining the royal assent.

Another public matter which engaged the attention of our people this year was the union of the English Colonies of North America, proposed by a convention of delegates from several of the Colonies, held at Albany. William Stevens, Esq., representative from Gloucester in the General Court, voted there in the affirmative on the question concerning the union; and he appeared at a town-meeting held early in 1755, to speak on the subject. The meeting heard the plan of union, but took no action thereon.

One object of the proposed union of the Colonies was a combination of the strength of all of them for attack and defence in the war between France and England, which was then seen to be inevitable, and which, after four years of hard fighting, was to free our ancestors, and their descendants for ever, from the fear of French domination in North America. Not many towns had a larger interest at stake in the war than Gloucester. Its Grand-Bank fishery had now become important; but the fishermen were a good deal annoyed by French cruisers, and, in some instances, had been captured. The war was, therefore, to decide for them, whether they should visit the fishing-grounds without fear of molestation or not. We know but little concerning the part borne by our people in the events of that exciting contest. The population of the town furnished one whole company, and several soldiers for other companies, in the first year of the war, and probably contributed as large a force each year till peace was established; but the deeds and sufferings of our townsmen, intrusted mainly to the insecure keeping of tradition, are now almost forgotten.

The Gloucester Company in the first campaign formed part of an expedition against Crown Point. It was commanded by Capt. Jonathan Fellows. John Row was lieutenant; and Samuel Fellows, ensign. Abijah How, one of the soldiers, died on the way home from Albany.*

One of the expeditions of 1755 was that against Nova Scotia; which resulted in the expulsion and dispersion of the French inhabitants of the peninsula, who, though professing neutrality, had actually a large number of men in arms against the English. The decision to remove these people and destroy their settlements was adopted, upon full and mature deliberation; and, whatever necessity for it might have seemed to exist at the time, the act is now universally condemned as one of greater than savage cruelty.† A few of these wretched Acadians found a temporary home in Gloucester. Of those who came first, thir-

* David Riggs, a soldier in a company commanded by Capt. John Whipple of Ipswich, died during this campaign, near Lake George.

† One of our greatest poets has sung in touching strains of the woes of these people; and an eminent historian of our country (Bancroft) says, "I know not if the annals of the human race keep the record of sorrows so wantonly inflicted, so bitter, and so perennial, as fell upon the French inhabitants of Acadia."

teen were ordered by the General Court to be removed to Wenham, and the rest (eleven in number) to Methuen. Others were brought here afterwards, for whose subsistence the selectmen of the town provided at the expense of the Province Treasury. The building in which some of them were kept at the public charge was called the "French Neuter House."

The 18th of November, 1755, was a memorable day throughout New England and many other parts of the country, as that of the "great earthquake." A contemporaneous record of its effects here is preserved on a blank-leaf of an old account-book, and says, "Half-past four in the morning was the most shocking earthquake as ever I knew in this land. It shattered a great many chimneys in this town and in other towns." The occasion was improved by the ministers of the country to make a religious impression upon the minds of the people, and many additions were made to the church. The pastors of this town kept a fast on account of it, in the Fourth Parish, Jan. 1, 1756. Rev. Samuel Chandler preached in the forenoon, from Ezek. xxxiii. 5; and Rev. Benjamin Bradstreet in the afternoon, from Prov. i. 24–29.

The day of the annual public fast, in 1756, was April 29. Rev. Samuel Chandler delivered an address to the soldiers about to join the army for service against the French; which, at their desire, he copied for them. During the services at the Meeting-house, a sudden gust of wind, which many supposed to be an earthquake, created such an alarm in the congregation, that most of the people rushed out; but order was soon restored, and the exercises proceeded. It is significant of the character of the people and of the age, that these soldiers again assembled in the house of public worship on the day of their departure, May 3; when the venerable Mr. White prayed for them, and his colleague gave them a word of exhortation. Of the particular service of these soldiers, no account is preserved. They were undoubtedly a part of the expedition designed to attack Crown Point, but which did not reach that place, as the capture by the French of important English posts on Lake Ontario changed the plan of operations.

The next year of the war was not distinguished by any offensive operations against the French;* but it will always be a memorable one in the annals of the country, for the surrender of Fort William Henry, and the plunder and massacre of the soldiers by the Indians which followed. How many Gloucester men were there, or were elsewhere engaged in the war in 1757, no one knows. On the 22d of March, a very cold and snowy day, the two militia companies of the town were assembled in the First-Parish Meeting-house, and seventeen men were enlisted from them for actual service. According to family traditions, several of our men were attached to the force at Fort William Henry; and one of them (Nathaniel Pulcifer) is said to have been exposed to the massacre, from which he escaped, and lived to be nearly a hundred years old.

The war had been disastrous to the English, so far; and the Colonies were in a gloomy state: but, under the energetic administration of William Pitt, the spirit of the British, both at home and in the Colonies, rose to the necessity of the occasion; and, in 1758, a powerful army was organized for the vigorous prosecution of the contest. In the preparations for the campaign, our own town was the scene of considerable military display. On the 18th of April, a general meeting of officers was held at Col. Allen's, followed by a "genteel entertainment." On the 23d, the transports, with the troops from this and some of the neighboring towns probably, sailed for Halifax to join the large force there assembling for an attack on Louisburg; and, on the 24th of

---

* A large force was collected at Halifax, with the design of attempting the reduction of Louisburg; but the place was so strongly garrisoned and defended, that the project was abandoned. Early in the year, an embargo was laid by the Legislature on all vessels in the several harbors of the Province, restraining them till the 10th of April; the object of which was to prevent the discovery of the intended expedition. In violation of this act, seven fishing vessels proceeded to sea from Gloucester: two of which belonged to Epes Sargent, jun.; and one each to Winthrop Sargent, Thomas Sanders, jun., Daniel Sargent, Daniel Rogers, and Hubbard Haskell. The king's attorney was directed to prosecute these persons. They urged in their defence, that they acted in no contempt of authority, but under a misapprehension of the intention of the act. By subsequent action of the Legislature, fishing vessels were allowed to sail, and to be absent twelve days; but were not permitted to go east beyond Casco Bay, nor south farther than Cape Cod.

May, a large company, commanded by Capt. Andrew Giddings,* marched out of town, "accompanied," says the journalist† who records the fact, "by a great concourse of people." This company consisted of about eighty men, and was in the unsuccessful expedition to Ticonderaga. It is not known how many, if any, of its members fell in battle, or were victims of other casualties of war. Job Ring and Gaspar Clouse died at Lake George; but they were not all, probably, who returned home no more. Louisburg surrendered on the 26th of July; and the receipt of the intelligence here gave rise to great rejoicings. This "hornet's nest," which had long been a source of annoyance to our mariners and fishermen, remained in possession of the English till peace was concluded, when it was conveyed to them by treaty. The fortifications were demolished at an expense of fifty thousand dollars, and the place has ever since been a heap of ruins.

The successes of 1758 inspired the English with sufficient boldness to attempt the next year the reduction of Quebec. It was a daring project; but it was happily accomplished by the brave Wolfe and his gallant army: and, soon afterwards, the long struggle of the French for a controlling power in North America ceased for ever. Several Gloucester men, according to family traditions still current, were in the battle on the Plains of Abraham, near Quebec; but no record is preserved to show the part borne by our people in the successful campaign of 1759. The

---

* A list of this company is in my possession. Its lieutenants were Nathaniel Bayley and Isaac Martin. Samuel Davis was ensign. A memorandum on the same paper says, "Andrew Giddings, ensign in Capt. Bayley's company in the campaign of 1758 to Ticonderoga, and became commander of the company before the storming of Ticonderoga." But Rev. Jacob Bailey calls it "Capt. Giddens's company" at the start. Nathaniel Bayley came from Newbury to this town, and married here Mary Davis, Oct. 1, 1747. He had several children. March 8, 1758, in a petition to the General Court, he represents that he was at great trouble and expense in enlisting men "for the last Crown-Point expedition," in expectation of receiving a captain's commission, but received only a first lieutenant's. He requested an allowance, but did not obtain any. He afterwards commanded a company in Gen. Amherst's army, and was engaged in the reduction of Canada in 1760. His son Nathaniel, a lad of twelve years, was with him in Canada, and there had the small-pox, by which he lost an eye. The father also had the disease, and died of it in December, 1760. The son was "an exemplary professor of religion, and member of the First Church;" and died here Jan. 15, 1828, in his eightieth year.

† Rev. Jacob Bailey.

citizens of the town testified their joy at the great event by an illumination and the firing of cannon, and gladly contemplated the approaching termination of the war. Besides interrupting trade and industry, it had inflicted a heavy pecuniary burthen on the town, well calculated to impress us with a sense of the sacrifices made by our fathers to secure to us the fair heritage we enjoy. Once more turning their attention again exclusively to the pursuits of peace, they advanced steadily in a career of prosperity till called upon to resist the oppressions of the mother-country, and assert and maintain their rights in the struggle which gave them liberty and independence.

An estimate of the population of the town at the commencement of the eighteenth century, in a preceding chapter, gives the number of inhabitants, in 1704, at about seven hundred. Taking the best basis for calculation we can now command, the town had twice doubled its population at the end of half a century from the last-named date; and contained, in 1755, about twenty-eight hundred inhabitants.*

With regard to the increase of property, our information is very scanty; but it is quite certain that no person in the town had yet acquired enough to be accounted rich, according to the standard by which wealth is now measured in mercantile communities. It is not supposed that half a dozen citizens, in 1755, possessed an estate of the value of ten thousand dollars. Nor were there many so poor as to require public aid. The practice

* In 1738, the number of inhabitants to each family in Sandy Bay was a fraction over five. In 1754, there appear to have been thirty-nine families there, containing, according to the same ratio, about two hundred persons. The number of families in the West Parish, in 1755, was one hundred and two. The taxable property in each of the parishes, except Sandy Bay, was probably then very nearly in the same ratio to the whole as the population of each parish to the whole number of inhabitants in the town. Proceeding upon this supposition, and taking the town tax assessed upon each parish in 1755, and allowing five persons to each family, we arrive at the following results: —

	Tax.	Families.	No. of Inhabitants.
First Parish	447.84	255	1275
Second Parish	178.66	102	510
Third Parish	146.27	83	415
Fourth Parish	141.44	79	345
Fifth Parish	44.89	39	200
Total	959.10	558	2745

of "letting out" the poor was still continued; and the whole number of this class in 1757 was nine, — three males and six females, — who were supported at an expense of two hundred and three dollars. Assistance rendered to a few others carried up the total expenditure for the poor in that year to about two hundred and eighty dollars.

The taxes for the payment of town-expenses, a century ago, were very light; but, considering the means upon which they were levied, they were no lighter, perhaps, than the heavy rates of the present time. And yet, if it were so, how heavily must the expenses of the French War have borne upon the people of that day! The town's proportion of the Province-tax, in the first year of the war, was double the amount of the town-tax for the same year; and, in 1758, it was between three and four times the amount raised in that year for the current expenses of the town. But economy was a habit with our fathers; and, so far as it was founded upon moral duty, it gives them a high claim upon our regard. They knew the art of frugal living, and enjoyed all its advantages; but it strikes us with some amazement that they could in 1757, with a population of one-fourth of the present census of the town, have all the benefits of a good town-government at an expense of less than nine hundred dollars per annum. Making all due allowance for the difference in the value of money between their day and ours, we still have proof of great economy in their public expenditures.*

It is gratifying to find that nearly one-half of the expenses

---

* At the May meeting in 1757, the town voted a rate of £300 "for necessary charges, and for purchasing stock of ammunition, arms, &c." The expenditures under this grant, reduced to dollars and cents, were as follows: —

On account of the poor	$281.68
For schools	407.37
Miscellaneous	35.94
Selectmen's pay	86.62
Selectmen's expenses at Capt. Ellery's tavern	48.60
Ammunition, — 5½ bbls. powder, 6 cwt. bullets, 1,000 flints	209.90
	$1070.11

The tax for repair of highways was made in a separate assessment, as down to a recent time; and all who chose to do so, "worked it out." In 1754, the allowance for labor on the highway was three shillings for a man; and twelve shillings for a man, a yoke of oxen, and cart.

of the town at that time was incurred for the support of schools. By an arrangement made in 1758, the grammar school was permanently located at the Harbor, and a circulating school was maintained in the other parishes. No essential change was made from this plan till the adoption of the district system. The first teacher of a permanent public grammar school in the Harbor was Samuel Whittemore. He was succeeded by Rev. Jacob Bailey,* who taught here about a year and a half. After him, Samuel Pierce and Thomas Pierce † taught alternately about two years; next, Thomas Marrett, ‡ a short time; then James Prentice, § who was succeeded by Philemon Stacy in 1767. The latter continued in office till the school was broken up by the Revolutionary War. One of the teachers in the out-parishes, during all the time now under notice, was Ebenezer Bray, a townsman; who, on account of some bodily infirmity, received, in 1760, a grant of seven

---

* Rev. Jacob Bailey taught the grammar school here from April, 1758, to November, 1759, at a salary of £26. 13s. 4d. per annum, exclusive of board. He graduated at Harvard College in 1755. After leaving Gloucester, he became an Episcopal preacher in Maine, and next in Nova Scotia. He died in 1808. During his stay here, he preached for Mr. Chandler, when the latter was ill. The Puritanic strictness of the pastor must have considerably relaxed to allow him to send to his flock a preacher who could countenance by his presence a proscribed form of social enjoyment; as, according to his journal, Mr. Bailey did, once at least. He records, June 26, 1758: "One evening this week, I was invited to a dance at Mr. Comerford's, where I found a number of gentlemen and ladies, the choice of the town; viz., Mrs. Ingersol, Mrs. Elwell, Mrs. Ingersoll, Polly Smith, Nabby Sanders, Betty Davis, Hannah Babson, Molly ——, Mrs. Comerford."

† These persons may have been brothers. Thomas Pierce married Anna Haskell in 1762, and, in the same year, was ordained the minister of Scarborough, Me.; where he died in 1775, aged thirty-seven.

‡ Thomas Marrett was a native of Cambridge, and graduated at Harvard College in 1761. After teaching the grammar school in the Harbor, he settled in Squam, where he also taught occasionally. He was one of the selectmen a few years during the war; and died June 24, 1784, aged forty-three. His chirography in the Squam-Parish Records is remarkably bold and elegant.

§ James Prentice was a native of Cambridge, and graduated at Harvard College in 1761. He taught the grammar school about four years. In 1775, and perhaps before, he kept a tavern at the corner of Middle and Pleasant Streets. Soon after the battle of Bunker Hill, he is said to have taken command of a company, and to have served during most or the whole of the war. He afterwards settled in Boston, where he kept a boarding-house many years for the accommodation of Cape-Ann people. He died there Nov. 26, 1797, aged fifty-six. His wife was Lydia, daughter of Capt. Thomas Sanders. She continued the boarding-house till 1806, when she returned to Gloucester. They had no children.

pounds from the town to aid him to acquire a knowledge of the Latin language. He had already kept school, in his native parish and other parts of the town, three years. Under the arrangement by which the schools were now conducted, each parish, except the fifth, enjoyed several months' public instruction every year. The latter could only have a three months' school in two years.

Among all the calamities to which our people were exposed, for a considerable part of the last century, few caused greater alarm than the small-pox. Inoculating with the virus, which greatly lessened its fatality, came into practice extensively about the middle of the century; and, towards the close of that period, the valuable discovery of Jenner, that inoculation with the cow-pox is nearly an infallible security against the former disease, relieved the public mind of the terror which that malady formerly occasioned.

It does not appear that this grievous calamity ever afflicted the people of Gloucester as it did some other towns; as, for instance, those of Boston in 1752. But it prevailed here in 1764 to such an extent as to cause a very general alarm, and interrupt the usual pursuits of life. In the year of its distressing prevalence and fatality in Boston, our public authorities took precautionary measures to prevent its introduction here by establishing a guard at the Cut and at the Battery; and it is not known that a single case occurred in the town. But, in 1760, the disease was here; though no one is known to have died of it. One family was carried away from town by water. Another death occurred in 1762; but the disease does not seem to have spread. In January, 1764, it broke out in the Harbor Village; and several families moved from their houses. In the first case, it proved fatal; and, several other cases occurring, we find, on the 7th of February, "almost all the Harbor are moving on account of the small-pox: nothing but carting, — all in motion." It prevailed about three months; during which, eight of the inhabitants fell victims to the disease. The whole number that took it cannot be ascertained; but it is known that the charge upon the town-treasury on account of it was nearly three hundred dollars, one item of which was for medical attendance from abroad. Eighteen persons, including several of the most prominent citizens of the town, took the disease by inoculation, of whom only one died. Soon after the distemper made its appearance, a town-meeting was called, which instructed the selectmen to use all possible means to prevent its spreading; and it was undoubtedly owing to great exertions to that end that there were no more deaths. Having happily got rid of the infection, the town was for several years spared a like infliction.*

A darker day was about to dawn, — a day of such misery and gloom, that, if it had not ushered in the blessed years of political independence, would have tinged our history with a hue that none could contemplate without a shudder and a tear. The Stamp Act, that odious measure for taxing the Colonies, had passed the British Parliament, and become a law. It is not necessary here to notice the opposition which it aroused throughout the country; but, to do justice to the memory of our own people for the part they performed on this great occasion, it is proper to place now before their descendants the language in which they uttered their sentiments. The act was to go into operation, Nov. 1, 1765. On the 7th of the preceding month, in a very full town-meeting, the people of Gloucester declared, "*nemine contradicente* and most unanimously, That the Stamp

* For some of these facts, I am indebted to Rev. S. Chandler's journal. The following additional items from the same source may possess interest for some readers. "1764, Feb. 5: The small-pox increasing: five down, sick; and some more expected." "7th: There are four sick of the small-pox at old Mr. Doliver's, — himself, John Warner, James Tyler, and Zebulon Witham, jun., very bad; and two at Tarbox's." — "12th: There was no meeting in the Harbor, on account of the small-pox. Mr. Doliver's house is the hospital. In the evening, visited and prayed at Elder Warner's: his son John supposed to be dying; small-pox." — "March 7: The people are moving home." — "11th: I preached in the Meeting-house, after four sabbaths deprived of it on account of the small-pox." — "15th: This day set apart for religious worship, humiliation, prayer, and thanksgiving, relative to the infectious sickness that has lately been among us. I preached — forenoon — Lam. iii. 40. Afternoon, Mr. Rogers preached. In the evening, I went, at the desire of a number of young people, to Mr. Hub. Haskell's. Expecting only a few, I found the house full. I preached *extempore*, John v. 6: 'Wilt thou be made whole?'" Mr. Chandler gives the names of those who died and of those who were inoculated. The former were Charles Glover, Jacob Randal, Peter Dolliver, Zebulon Witham, jun., John Warner, Jonathan Gardner's wife, Mrs. Cook, and Ebenezer Tarbox. The good pastor was faithful to his flock in this distressing season, and visited freely as usual.

Act (the minutes whereof were read) is disagreeable; that the following instructions be given to Nathaniel Allen, and Thomas Sanders, Esq., the representatives in the Great and General Court, —That they by no means make any concessions, or enter into any measures, whereby our liberties which we have as Englishmen by the Magna Charta, or which we, the inhabitants of this Province, have by our particular charter, may in any manner or degree be infringed, or construed in any sense to be given up or lessened. And, in particular, that they, by all direct and lawful means, endeavor that the Stamp Act (as 'tis called) may never take place among us; as it is apprehended, if it should obtain, it would greatly obstruct, if not (in time) totally ruin, the trade and business of the Province, and lay an insupportable burthen upon all, more especially upon the middle and poorer sort of the people, and take from us (though always allowed to have all the liberties of natural Englishmen) the privilege of a trial by our peers, that is, a jury (vesting that power in a Judge of Admiralty), and the general privilege of taxing ourselves, which appear to be the original rights of all mankind that are not slaves, the unalienable rights of Englishmen, and the rights of the inhabitants of this Province by their particular charter. And, further, that they, our said representatives, by no means suffer any grant of moneys to be made for any other besides the usual, necessary, accustomed charges of this Province."

Such was their reception of this edict of tyranny; and it is our glory in their behalf, that they yielded obedience to that higher law, which forbade them to bow their necks to the yoke of the oppressor.

CHAPTER XVII.

THIRD PARISH. — REV. JOHN WYETH: HIS MINISTRY. — DISSENSIONS IN THE PARISH. — HIS DISMISSION. — DISASTERS BY SEA, AND GREAT LOSS OF LIFE. — TIMOTHY ROGERS. — POLITICAL TROUBLES. — THE PEOPLE PATRIOTIC. — SECOND PARISH. — REV. DANIEL FULLER: HIS MINISTRY, DEATH, AND FAMILY. — THIRD PARISH. — REV. OBADIAH PARSONS: HIS MINISTRY, DISMISSION, AND DEATH.

AFTER the death of Mr. Bradstreet, the Third Parish remained nearly four years without a settled minister; but the pulpit was supplied occasionally by Mr. Cleaveland of the Fifth Parish, and other ministers. Rev. Moses Parsons of Byfield was helpful at this time, as appears by a vote passed by the parish, thanking him for his services in their behalf. At length, in the latter part of the year 1765, an invitation was given to John Wyeth to become their pastor, with a salary of ninety-three pounds per annum and the use of the parsonage. This proposal was accepted; and his ordination took place, Feb. 5, 1766. Rev. Amos Adams of Roxbury delivered the sermon, from 1 Cor. ix. 27. Rev. Mr. Barnard of Salem gave the charge; and Rev. Samuel Chandler presented the right hand of fellowship.

Mr. Wyeth was born in Cambridge, March 1, 1743; and graduated at Harvard College in 1760. His connection with the Third Church was a very unhappy one. Many of the parish were opposed to him at the time of his settlement; and the disaffection then existing soon ripened into open and decided hostility. The church-records are silent respecting the quarrel, and it is not easy now to obtain a satisfactory account of it. It does not appear that any thing was alleged against the moral character of Mr. Wyeth; but much fault was found with his pulpit performances and his general demeanor. The latter is said to have been wanting in that sanctified dignity which was then thought to be indispensable in the deportment of a minister. In the parish-records, the members in opposition to the minister are called "the aggrieved brethren." At a meeting of the parish in April, 1767, a petition and report presented by them was dismissed; but, in October following, a committee was chosen to reconcile differences, and was empowered to unite with the aggrieved brethren in calling a council to settle all matters relating to the settlement, support, and dismission of their minister. The action of the council is not known; but Mr. Wyeth was dismissed May 17, 1768.

The hostile feelings with which the minister was regarded by his opponents had frequently found expression in violent and disgraceful acts.* He was molested in various ways, — even to the firing of musket-balls into his house. Many clandestine enormities were committed, and the parish was obliged to seek help and protection from the town; but the latter took no further measures than to pass a vote condemnatory of the course pursued by the malecontents. They next made an effort to induce the town to unite with them in requesting assistance from the Governor and Council in suppressing the open villany that had from time to time been committed in the parish; but the departure of the unpopular pastor soon brought about a restoration of order and peace.

Their minister turned his back upon them; and, from the top of Squam Hill, shook the dust from his feet, with a determination that they should hear from him again. Accordingly, on his return to Cambridge, he commenced an action against the parish to recover pay for his probationary preaching; and the parish

---

* Tradition has preserved an account of one of the petty annoyances to which he was subjected. He had, on one occasion, arranged an exchange of pulpit services with a clergyman in a neighboring town; and, in fulfilment of his engagement, went on Saturday afternoon to the pasture to get his horse, and saddle him for the journey: but, greatly to his surprise and disappointment, no animal like his own was there. He immediately made a stir in the parish, and several went with him to the hills in quest of the missing horse; which, in a short time, was found in the right pasture; but his color was changed from black to white. He had received a coat of whitewash.

was obliged to send a committee to settle with him on the best terms they could. Matters were also in dispute, growing out of the refusal of the aggrieved brethren to pay their parish-rates; but these were finally settled by award of a council.

Mr. Wyeth left the ministry, and gave his attention to law. He lived on a small farm on the West-Cambridge Road, and cultivated his land. His death took place Feb. 2, 1811, in his sixty-ninth year.

The year 1766 is distinguished in our annals as one of peculiar distress. One of those terrible misfortunes that shocks a whole community, and brings unutterable sorrow to many private bosoms, cast its sad gloom over the town. In March, nineteen fishing vessels sailed for the Grand Bank; and, while on the passage thither, were met by a violent storm, which wrecked and scattered the fleet, and sent many to the bottom. Two were cast away at Nova Scotia; seven foundered at sea, with all on board; and several of the rest were so much disabled, that they could not proceed on their voyage. To add to the pecuniary losses of the year, one of the West-India traders was lost on the Island of Nevis. The loss of property, however, could be quickly repaired or calmly borne; but "past the utterance of grief" was the condition of the forlorn and destitute widow and her helpless children.* The General Court abated the Province-tax assessed upon the town, in 1766, fifty pounds, in consideration of this severe loss.

On the 22d of June, this year (1766), died Timothy Rogers, son of Rev. John Rogers of Kittery, Me.; where he was born in 1721. He was a merchant; but he did not find the pursuit of commerce gainful, as may be inferred from the insolvency of his estate at death. The date of his settlement here is not known. He brought to town a wife Lucy, who died April 28, 1759, aged thirty-three. He next married, July 4, 1765, Mrs. Esther Goldthwaite; by whom he had a son Timothy, who

* The number of men lost by these shipwrecks is not known; probably it was not less than forty. The following are the names of a few of them: James Gardner, Edward Jumper, Timothy Higgins, Joseph Giddings, Job Rowe, Abraham Williams, George Singer, Samuel Morehead, and John Haskell.

entered the English Navy, and died at Lisbon in 1797, a gallant and highly esteemed officer of the fleet of Earl St. Vincent.

The oppressive acts of the British Government, by which the complete subjugation of the Colonies to the arbitrary will of Parliament was attempted, belong to general history; and only such allusion will be made to them here as may be necessary to show the particular occasions of various proceedings of the people of Gloucester in this great crisis of their history. Boston, the metropolis of New England, the seat of the Provincial Government, and the residence of many distinguished men (merchants, mechanics, and divines), all patriots, took the lead in opposition to these acts; and every pulsation of liberty and patriotism there met a responsive beat from the hills and shores of Cape Ann.

The opposition to the Stamp Act had procured its repeal; but the plan of taxation was resumed. An act was passed by Parliament, and approved by the king, in 1767, which imposed a duty on tea and some other articles imported into the Colonies. This act led to a meeting of the people of Boston, by which a vote was passed, designed to favor the products and manufactures of the Province, and discourage the importation of certain articles from the mother-country by abstaining from the use of them. The same vote was adopted by the people of this town, at a meeting held Dec. 14, 1767, and entered at length upon the records.

The next year was one of great excitement. The General Court, adhering to its resolutions in maintenance of the people's rights, had been dissolved by the Governor; and Massachusetts was left without a Legislature. Evasion of the revenue-laws in Boston led to a mobbing of the custom-house officers; and some of the government officials, in fear of the popular fury, fled from the town. Military forces, too, were expected from Halifax, to be quartered upon the town, and overawe its people. In this state of affairs, the people of Boston requested the Governor to convene the General Court; and, upon his refusal to do so, proposed to the several towns in the Colony a Convention at Faneuil Hall on the 22d of September. The town-meeting here to take this into consideration was held on the 19th. The vote of Boston and the letter of its selectmen were read. A motion was then made to choose a committee to attend the Convention: whereupon a debate ensued, which ended with the adoption of the motion; only one person being observed not to vote for it. This one, undoubtedly, was Epes Sargent, Esq.; who, during the debate, had desired the people "to be careful of acting." The persons chosen were Thomas Sanders, jun., and Peter Coffin, Esqs. This important meeting was held in the meeting-house of the Fourth Parish. It was gathered to discuss a measure considered by their oppressors, and perhaps felt by some of themselves, to come within a "hair's breadth of treason;" but that love of liberty, which deems no sacrifice made in its behalf too great, guided them in their course on this occasion, and led them on to the glorious victory, with which, as its champions, they were finally rewarded. The Convention was in session six days; and its chief result was to show that a similar body could, if need be and the people willed it, take the whole power of government into their own hands.

In 1769, at the March meeting, a committee was chosen, at the suggestion of the people of Marblehead, to take such measures as might seem necessary to relieve the fishermen of the payment of hospital money; but their action in the matter nowhere appears. At the same meeting, a plan for raising a fund for the support of the poor was read, but not adopted.

In May, Thomas Sanders, jun., Esq., was chosen representative to the General Court, and was instructed to comply, as far as possible, with the spirit of the instructions given by the town of Boston to their representatives.

In the latter part of this year, two severe storms occasioned several disasters on our coast, two of which were attended with loss of life. A schooner belonging to Wells, Littlefield master, was wrecked near Squam, and two of her crew were drowned. This was in September. In December, a sloop belonging to Haverhill, Bennet master, laden with lumber and bound to Gloucester, in attempting to get into Squam, struck upon the Bar, where she beat in part of her bottom. The owner (Mr. Reddington) and another man perished. The master, the only other person on board, was saved. No lighthouse was yet erected on the Cape, and marine disasters were of frequent occurrence.

The unhappy condition of affairs in the Second Parish, noticed in a preceding chapter, was terminated this year. After several ineffectual attempts to obtain a minister,* Mr. Daniel Fuller was induced to settle over the distracted church.

Rev. Daniel Fuller, the colleague and successor of Mr. Jaques, was born in Middleton, Mass., Sept. 1, 1740. His great-grandfather, Thomas Fuller, who settled there, came to New England in 1638; but not with the intention of becoming a permanent settler, as appears by the following extract from his "Meditations and Experience," preserved in the family: —

"In thirty-eight, I set my foot
Upon New England's shore:
My thoughts were then to stay one year,
And here to stay no more.

But, by the preaching of God's word
By famous Shepard he,
In what a woful state I was
I then began to see."

At the age of fourteen, Daniel Fuller was apprenticed to a carpenter; but, his constitution being weak, he was induced to abandon his trade, and prepare for college. He entered Harvard College in 1760, and graduated in 1764. The two following years, he kept a school in Hampton, N.H., and in Haverhill, Mass. He then studied divinity, and began to preach in the Second Parish in Gloucester, July, 1769. He soon received a call to settle, with an offer of seventy pounds per annum, and the use of the parsonage wood-lot so long as he continued to be the minister of the parish. The discord which had so long existed between the people and their aged minister might have suggested some discouraging apprehensions; but he accepted the call, and, in his letter of acceptance, expressed an earnest prayer

* Among those who preached in the parish at this time was Rev. Thomas Lancaster, who, like a candidate for the vacant pulpit nearly fifty years before, became the minister of Scarborough, Me. He was born in Rowley, Mass.; graduated at Harvard College in 1764; settled at Scarborough in 1776; and died in 1831, aged eighty-nine. T. S. Lancaster, Esq., formerly Postmaster of Gloucester, and, for several years past, Town Treasurer, is his grandson.

that love, peace, and Christian charity, might hallow and bless the union. His ordination took place, Jan. 10, 1770; on which occasion, the ordaining prayer was offered by Rev. Samuel Chandler of the First Parish; sermon by Rev. Mr. Smith of Middleton, from Rom. ii. 13; charge by Rev. Mr. Barnard of Salem; right hand of fellowship by Rev. John Rogers of the Fourth Parish; and concluding prayer by Rev. Mr. Holt of Danvers.

The Revolutionary struggle commenced a few years after the settlement of Mr. Fuller; and the parish became reduced to such a strait, as to find it almost impossible to meet their engagement with him. Families were broken up, many of the people were drawn from home, and great gloom and distress reigned all around. During the whole of this period of calamity, Mr. Fuller proved himself a faithful and generous pastor. Notwithstanding the pressure of the times and the scantiness of his salary, he repeatedly remitted money due to him, and encouraged his flock to look forward with patriotic hopes to peace, plenty, and independence. The struggle at length terminated; and a happier season opened upon them, — the commencement of a long, peaceful, and undisturbed ministry, which continued till the infirmities of age admonished the venerable pastor that his days of usefulness in the active duties of his profession were ended. He preached a sermon on the fiftieth anniversary of his ordination; and soon afterwards his pastoral connection with the parish was dissolved. He then went to reside with one of his sons in Dorchester, but frequently visited the scene of his past labors. On one of these visits, he united a couple in marriage; the bridegroom being a grandson of the first pair he married in the parish. On the same day, he preached a sermon in the East-District Schoolhouse; and, on the next day, walked to the Harbor, though he was then eighty-seven years old. In December, 1828, he visited Gloucester to attend the dedication of the new meeting-house erected by the First Parish; on which occasion, he read a hymn. On his return to Boston, the stage in which he was a passenger was overset; and he received an injury, from which he partially recovered: but the shock to his system was so great, that his end was undoubtedly hastened by the accident. His death took place, May 23, 1829, at the house of his son Samuel, in Boston. His remains were interred in Dorchester on the 25th; and, on the following Sunday, a tribute of respect was offered to his memory by Rev. Dr. Harris, in a sermon from Rev. xiv. 13.

Mr. Fuller was a plain, practical preacher; but his pulpit performances alone could not have won for him the love and esteem of which he was the object. His character was distinguished for simplicity, sincerity, meekness, and the most unbounded liberality of sentiment towards Christians of every name and sect. As a consequence of these traits, wherever he was known, every door was open to receive him, and every heart proffered him a cordial welcome. Towards the close of his life, when age had slightly bent his form, and his benevolent countenance seemed to borrow something from that state of eternal felicity to which he felt himself so near, such was the general feeling with which he was regarded here, that it may be truly said that he had the freedom of the town. On his frequent visits to Gloucester, it was his custom to tarry with different friends; and the longer his stay was extended, the more was his departure regretted.

"His own afflictions and pains he bore without repining; and, with faculties unimpaired and faith strengthened, he looked forward with pleasing anticipations of future blessedness; and, full of years and mature in virtue, he departed in peace."

Mr. Fuller married, Aug. 14, 1770, Hannah, daughter of Rev. Benjamin Bowers of Middle Haddam, Conn. She died Feb. 19, 1810, aged fifty-eight. Their children were as follows: —

Hannah Peters, born in 1771, married, first, Dudley Sargent, by whom she had five children; and, after his decease, Peter Coffin. She died in New York in 1835. Daniel, born in 1773, became a school-teacher. He married Mary Brown of Lynn, and had by her two children. He was knocked overboard by the boom of a sloop, in which he was a passenger on the North River, in 1817, and drowned. Benjamin, born in 1776, settled in Boston as a merchant, but had his residence in Dorchester. He was twice married, — first to Marcia Beals of

Boston, and next to Abba Ingly of Dorchester, — and had by both wives eleven children. He died in 1831. Elijah, born in 1778, learned a mechanical trade, and settled in Salem. He was twice married. By his first wife (Mary Phippin) he had six, and by his second wife three, children. He died in 1852. Archelaus, born in 1780, also became a mechanic, and settled in Salem. By his first wife (Ruth Pope), he had two children; and, by his last (Clarissa Gwynn), five. He died in 1826. Samuel Newell, born in 1782, became a sea-captain. He lived in Boston several years; but his residence, for some time before he died, was in this town, at Squam. His wife was Mrs. Lydia Wise of Boston, by whom he had nine children. He was drowned by the upsetting of a sail-boat in Ipswich Bay, Aug. 16, 1850. Mary, born in 1785, was twice married. Her first husband was Benjamin Haskell of Gloucester; and her second, Daniel Millet of Salem. She has recently deceased. Sarah, born in 1787, married James Appleton, who resided in Gloucester several years, and was, during the last war with Great Britain, colonel of the Gloucester regiment of militia. He was afterwards raised to the rank of general. Engaging in business here as a jeweller, he also, for some time, kept a public-house at the westerly end of Front Street, opposite the present Gloucester House. He was a representative in 1813 and 1814. He removed from Gloucester to Portland, and was a prominent citizen of Maine for many years. He now resides in Ipswich, on the old homestead of his family. Mrs. Appleton is yet alive; and ten children, all that have been born to the venerable couple, are still living.

Mr. Fuller was the last minister of the Second Parish. Religious services, supported by voluntary contributions, were occasionally held in the old Meeting-house for a few years, chiefly by Universalist clergymen; and a new religious society of the ancient faith was organized within the parochial limits not long after the death of the venerable pastor with whose decease the history of the parish is here brought to a close.

In the month of March, 1771, there were two shipwrecks on our shores. One of the vessels wrecked, a sloop, was cast away in a violent snow-storm on the 3d of the month, and all on board perished. She was a wood-coaster, bound to Newburyport, where she belonged. The captain's name was Stickney.

The Third Parish, having subsided into its former state of tranquillity, proceeded to seek a pastor for its vacant pulpit. On the 26th of June, 1772, by concurrent vote with the church, July 2 following was set apart as a day of humiliation, fasting, and prayer, for the forgiveness of their sins, and to seek direction of God preparatory to the choice of a minister. The two bodies also chose a joint-committee to wait on the pastors of the several churches in town, and thank them for all their past ministerial services, and labors of love, for their church and parish, and to request their attendance and assistance on the approaching day of fasting and prayer.

A minister was soon found for the vacant pulpit. The choice fell with entire unanimity upon Mr. Obadiah Parsons. He was a son of Deacon William Parsons of this town, and was born here April 5, 1747. His father died when he was about eight years old, and, in his dying moments, solemnly gave this son up to God, and dedicated him to the work of the gospel ministry; having made special provision in his will that he should receive an education suitable for it. He was committed to the care of his kinsman, — Rev. Moses Parsons of Byfield Parish, Newbury; with whom he probably pursued his preparatory studies for college and for the ministry. He graduated at Harvard College in 1768. He was ordained at Squam, Nov. 11, 1772. The council convened at the house of Mr. Jonathan Norwood, and consisted of six clerical and seventeen lay delegates. The services at the ordination were as follows: Introductory prayer by Rev. Manasseh Cutler of Hamilton; sermon by Rev. Moses Parsons, from 2 Cor. iii. 6; prayer and charge by Rev. Samuel Chandler of the First Church; right hand of fellowship by Rev. John Rogers of the Fourth; and concluding prayer by Rev. Ebenezer Cleaveland of the Fifth Church in Gloucester.

The parish voted Mr. Parsons a salary of £86. 13s. 4d.; and, in case of his inability to preach, one-half that sum was to be paid to him yearly. They also voted him the use of the parsonage, and a free contribution.

The former tranquillity of the parish seemed to be now fully restored; but it was not destined to be of long duration. During the first few years of his ministry, their young pastor was visited by domestic affliction in its severest forms; and, under the pressure of calamity, it may be supposed that his exterior deportment at least afforded no grounds of suspicion that he was an unworthy minister of the gospel. No long time, however, had elapsed, when he was charged with a crime sufficient to degrade him for ever from his sacred office as a teacher of piety and morality. An investigation, by the usual mode in such cases, was ordered; but a proper regard for decency will excuse the omission here of details of this portion of the parish history. It is sufficient to say, that, at the mutual desire of pastor and people, an ecclesiastical council was held at the house of the former on the 3d of November, 1779, to take into consideration all matters of grievance subsisting between them. Rev. John Cleaveland of Chebacco Parish, Ipswich, was chosen moderator; and Rev. Eli Forbes of our First Church, scribe. The council adjourned to the meeting-house for a public hearing at two o'clock, P.M. The occasion attracted many people from a distance, and the place of meeting was crowded to overflowing. After prayer by the moderator, the parish and church were called upon by him to present the matters which they meant to submit to the inspection, examination, and advice of the council. The person who made the charge against Mr. Parsons then came forward, and repeated her accusation or complaint, which was adopted by the church for support. Mr. Parsons made a long and able defence; which had so much influence with the council, that after due consideration of the complaint, with all its attendant circumstances, they passed the following votes: —

"1. That the charge or complaint made against the Rev. Mr. Obadiah Parsons was not supported.

"2. That nevertheless, considering the great alienation of affection, especially on the part of the people of his charge (nearly one-half having left his ministry), and the little prospect there is of further usefulness among them, we think it expedient, and advise as prudent, that the pastoral relation be dissolved."

These votes were accompanied with a report, which was accepted by the pastor and the church. The latter made application for a parish-meeting to be called to act upon the doings of the council; which meeting was held on the 15th of November, and resulted in the refusal of the parish to accept the decision of the council. It was voted at the same time, unanimously, under an article in a warrant for a previous meeting adjourned to the same day, that Mr. Parsons be dismissed from the work of the gospel ministry over them.

After his dismission, Mr. Parsons preached for the Second Parish in Beverly; and, Feb. 4, 1784, was settled over the First Church in Lynn. He left his pastorate and the ministry, July 16, 1792, and returned to his native town. Here he taught a school several years, and held the office of justice of the peace. He died in December, 1801, aged fifty-four years. Mr. Parsons was twice married: first to Elizabeth, daughter of Rev. Samuel Wigglesworth of Ipswich; and next, Jan. 28, 1775, to Sarah, daughter of Peter Coffin, Esq., of this town. She died March 6, 1819. By both wives, he had nine children. His son William, born in 1778, studied medicine with his uncle, Dr. William Coffin; and, at an early age, went out surgeon's mate in the United-States frigate "Constitution." He finally settled in the practice of his profession at North Yarmouth, Me.; where he died in March, 1810. He was a kind and skilful physician, and was polite and gentlemanly in his manners. His wife was Judith, daughter of James Porter: she died Oct. 16, 1857. Another son (Obadiah), born in 1782, a youth of uncommon mental development, was injured in intellect by intense application to study, and is said to have died about the time of his father's decease. The oldest daughter (Elizabeth), born in 1770, married Amos Rhodes of Lynn, and died about 1809. Polly, born in 1784, married Jabez Hitchings of Lynn, and died in 1825. These ladies were both highly esteemed for their amiable and virtuous dispositions. The other children of Mr. Parsons are believed to have died young.

CHAPTER XVIII.

Town's Powder. — Hayscales. — Boat and Men Lost. — Town Expenses. — Political Affairs. — Crisis Approaching. — Patriotic Sentiments of the Town. — Action of Boston about the Landing of the Tea nobly sustained by Gloucester. — Tea thrown Overboard. — Boston Port Bill. — Distress in that Town. — Gloucester sends Relief. — Exposed Condition of the Town. — Women and Children removed. — County Convention. — Provincial Congress. — Shipwreck. — Gloomy Prospect. — Military Preparations.

At the annual town-meeting, March, 1772, a vote was passed, that the town's stock of powder and ammunition should be kept in the "Fort, or Battery House;" and that the same should be fitted for that purpose.

At the same meeting, it was voted, That Samuel Whittemore, Daniel Rogers, and Nehemiah Parsons, should have liberty "to set up an engine to weigh hay before the house that was Deacon Woodward's, where the two ways meet; and receive 16d. for weighing each load." This "engine" was set up in a large frame, with a building attached, at the junction of Middle and Front Streets, just west of the present Town House; and stood there about sixty years, or till it was superseded by the platform-balances now in use.

Some time this month, a fishing-boat belonging to the town was lost at Nahant. Only two persons were on board,—William Boynton and Jonathan Collins,—both of whom perished. The former left a wife and six children: the latter was about eighteen years old.

At the May meeting this year, a committee for examining the state of the town-treasury reported, that, one year with another, the annual expenses had been £450 for some years past; and that, as there was £180 in the treasury and collector's hands, £300 would be a sufficient tax for the current year.

In the political affairs of the Province, the crisis was fast approaching. The Governor, on one side, asserted, and argued for, the unlimited power of the king with regard to the charter; and the people, through their representatives, on the other side, fearlessly maintained the rights and privileges, which, according to their interpretation, that instrument secured to them. It was apparent to all reflecting minds, that the question would never be peaceably settled. The people of Boston, at a town-meeting on the 2d of November, sounded the alarm to all the inhabitants of the Province. They issued a pamphlet containing a statement of the Colonial rights, and pointing out the infringements and violations of them by Parliament; which pamphlet, with an impressive letter accompanying, was sent to all the towns of the Province. These documents were submitted to the people of Gloucester at a town-meeting held at the First-Parish Meeting-house on the 25th of December; and a large committee was chosen to consider the same, and report at an adjourned meeting. At the adjournment on the 28th, resolutions were adopted, setting forth the rights and liberties of the people of the American Colonies; that the innovations in government, and despotic measures, adopted by the British ministry, were subversive of those rights, and tended also to the destruction of the religious liberties of the people; that, where civil rulers betray their trust and abuse their power, they forfeit the submission of the subject, and to oppose and resist, in that case, is not resistance of the ordinances of Heaven; that the town of Boston deserved the thanks of all the English Colonies in America, and that the people of Gloucester were ready to join with them and all others, in every legal way, to oppose tyranny in all its forms, and to remain steadfast in the defence of their rights and liberties, dearer to them than their lives; that a committee, to correspond with Boston and other towns, be chosen; and finally, should all other methods fail of desired relief, that they were "desirous of joining with all others in an appeal to the great Lawgiver and Fountain of all justice, and doubted not of success according to the justice of their cause."

The transactions of the meeting were ordered to be sent to the Boston Committee of Correspondence. The Gloucester Committee of Correspondence chosen at this meeting consisted of Daniel Witham, Samuel Whittemore, Joseph Foster, Solomon Parsons, Jacob Allen, Jacob Parsons, and Peter Coffin. Before the meeting dissolved, a vote was passed, instructing Nathaniel Allen, Esq., the representative, to use all lawful and constitutional measures to obtain a redress of grievances.

During the next year (1773), another advance of the momentous struggle indicated the coming crisis. The British ministry, determined to put the resolution of the colonists to the test, and give them a chance to yield their oft-declared principles, or act up to them and abide the consequences, made an arrangement with the East-India Company, by which several cargoes of tea were sent to America, on which, if landed, the hateful duty must be paid. Three of these cargoes came to Boston. Long before their arrival, the proceedings of the people there left little reason to doubt the issue; and, as soon as the first ship arrived, five thousand of the inhabitants of that and a few adjacent towns resolved that no tea should be landed at that port. The other ships came in; and now, within twenty days from the arrival of the first, no satisfactory arrangement with the government officials and the consignees being possible, the patriotic ardor of Boston must subside into a reluctant submission, or blaze out in bold resistance. To encourage the latter, assurances of sympathy and support were sent in from all quarters. The people of Gloucester took a noble stand by their brethren of the metropolis; and an imperishable record preserves the sentiments by which they were animated at this trying season. On the 15th of December, at a town-meeting, with no dissenting voice, they say, —

"When every effort is exerted, every outrage committed, and every refinement of despotism practised, by a wicked and corrupt administration, to involve a free and loyal people in the ignominious gulf of slavery and servile subjection, this town, animated by that ardor which is ever the companion of virtuous freedom, cannot with tame composure observe this last political manœuvre of the British ministry, in permitting the East-India Company to import their tea into America for the purpose of extorting a revenue from us.

"We, with the greatest satisfaction, see the town of Boston, and other towns in this Province, gloriously opposing this pernicious innovation, notwithstanding the numerous obstacles thrown in their way by the great enemies to the liberties of mankind.

"This town think it an indispensable duty we owe to ourselves, to our countrymen, and to posterity, to declare, and we do declare, —

"That we will use our most strenuous exertions, not only that there shall be no teas landed in this town, subject to a duty payable in America; but that we will have no commerce with any person or persons that have, or shall have, any concern in buying or selling that detestable herb.

"That we are determined to oppose every species of tyranny and usurpation, however dignified by splendid titles, or any character that bears the sacred pride of human virtue.

"That, if we are compelled to make the last appeal to Heaven, we will defend our resolutions and liberties at the expense of all that is dear to us.

"That we will hold ourselves in readiness to join the town of Boston, and all other towns, in all measures to extricate ourselves from tyranny and oppression; and —

"That the thanks of this town be presented to the town of Boston for the vigilance and activity they have always discovered in guarding against the subtle machinations, and in combating the open outrages, of our enemies in Great Britain and in this country; and this town shall always record them the friends of human nature, and guardians of that heavenly palladium, — the liberties of America."

The proceedings of the meeting were sent to Boston, and were also published in the "Essex Gazette."

On the next day, seven thousand people (assembled at the Old South Church) resolved that the tea should not be landed; and in the evening, without unnecessary noise, as a solemn act of duty, the patriots of Boston, represented by a body of men disguised as Indians, threw it into the sea.

At the latter part of this and the first of the next year, apprehensions were felt that the small-pox might appear in the town. At a town-meeting in October, a vote was passed for building a pest-house: and a committee, chosen at this meeting, reported at a subsequent one in favor of buying a place on Eastern Point, to be used for that purpose; but nothing further was done about it at that time. At the March meeting in 1774, Jacob Allen and Joseph Foster were chosen special constables, in case the small-pox should come into town; they having had it.

The destruction of the tea in Boston roused the indignation of the British Parliament, and it retaliated by passing a bill for shutting up the port of Boston. It also passed an act for regulating the government of the Province, which seriously abridged the liberties of the people. These acts advanced the struggle one step nearer to its crisis. Boston received the first in a manner becoming the position it had taken as the foremost defender of American liberty; and the representatives of the Province met the last by choosing delegates to a Continental Congress.* The news of these last measures came in May. At a meeting of the people of this town soon afterwards, Mr. Edward Payne† of Boston, being present, was desired to represent the state of that town by reason of the late act of Parliament for shutting it up. That act was read, and also an agreement among the traders of Newburyport not to trade with Great Britain or the West Indies; whereupon the town voted, unanimously, to adopt the plan of the Newburyport merchants, and chose a large committee, including the principal merchants of the place, to consult with the merchants of other seaports, and agree upon the most proper measures to relieve the Colonies under the act of Parliament for shutting up the port of Boston. At another meeting, held in June, the Boston Port Bill was again read, together with other papers, including a covenant not to trade with the inhabitants of Great Britain. After consideration of these documents, the town expressed a desire that the

* These delegates were James Bowdoin, Thomas Cushing, Samuel Adams, John Adams, and Robert Treat Paine. The House voted £500 for their expenses, of which the proportion for Gloucester was £5. 18s. 7d.

† Mr. Payne had formerly resided in Gloucester several years. He carried on the fishing business here about 1755, and had a flake-yard at Eastern Point, and a store at the Harbor Cove. His intention of marriage with Mrs. Rebekah Amory of Boston, Sept. 25, 1756, is on our records.

covenant should be signed by all the inhabitants, and chose a committee to present it to them for their signatures. It does not appear that any refused to sign, though some desired that a few articles mentioned in it should be stricken out.

The complete prostration of business in Boston, under the operation of the Port Bill, threw a large number of persons out of employment; and, to relieve the distress of the poorer class, contributions were sent in from all quarters. Gloucester sent a hundred and twenty sheep in November, 1774; and raised, in money, £117. 7s. 1d.,* which was forwarded in March, 1775, by the hands of Isaac Smith, Esq.†

On the sixth and seventh days of September, 1774, a County Convention, to consider the late acts of Parliament, was held at Ipswich. At the desire of the people of this town, the selectmen, and Committee of Correspondence, appointed Daniel Witham, Peter Coffin, John Low, Solomon Parsons, and Samuel Whittemore, as delegates from Gloucester. The proceedings of this body were similar to those of other assemblages of patriotic citizens throughout the Province at this time.

---

* Of this sum, £10. 6s. 6d. were contributed by the people of West Parish, and £3. 5s. by those of Squam. Nearly all the rest was subscribed in the Harbor Parish. The largest contributors were — Daniel Sargent, £6; Daniel Rogers, £4; Winthrop Sargent, £3. 6s.; and Joseph Foster, David Pearce, John Low, John Stevens, William Coas, and several others, £2. 8s. each.

† This gentleman was an eminent merchant of Boston, having extensive business transactions with our people; by some of whom he appears to have lost considerable money. Timothy Rogers and William Stevens, both of whom died insolvent, were deeply in debt to him, — the former to the amount of £2,317. Mr. Smith came into possession of the Beach Wharf, and carried on the fishing business there several years; during which, he and his family spent much of their time in town. He fitted out seven schooners here for the Grand Bank in 1774; but soon afterwards the war came on, and put an end to his business operations in Gloucester. He died in Boston in 1787, aged sixty-eight; having sustained through life a high character for honesty, benevolence, and intelligence. John Hancock called him the most reliable man in Boston, and evinced his confidence in him by committing the most valuable portion of his property into his hands for safe keeping. Mr. Smith's grandfather belonged to a family in Exeter, England. His father settled in Charlestown, Mass.; and had, besides the subject of this note, William, the minister of Weymouth, who was the father of a distinguished lady, — Mrs. Abigail Adams, wife of John Adams, President of the United States. Mr. Isaac Smith left two sons, — Isaac, H.C. 1767, sometime minister of Sidmouth, England; and William, H.C. 1775, merchant of Boston, whose son, T. C. Smith, Esq., is a well-known and highly esteemed gentleman of that city.

In pursuance of an act of Parliament, the General Court this year held its session in Salem. Peter Coffin, Esq., was the representative from Gloucester. Delegates were appointed to a Continental Congress, and the other proceedings of the Assembly were filled with the prevalent spirit of liberty. The Governor thereupon determined to dissolve the House, and sent his secretary for that purpose; but that officer, being denied admittance, read on the stairs the proclamation which declared the dissolution. It was the last Provincial General Court of Massachusetts. The Governor issued writs for holding another at Salem in October, but afterwards countermanded the meeting. This, however, did not prevent the assembling of the representatives, who, acting upon advice given by the Essex-County Convention, resolved themselves into a Provincial Congress. Peter Coffin, again representative from this town, was authorized to use his efforts to bring about that result, and to serve as a member of the Congress. Soon after this body assumed its new character, Daniel Witham, Esq., was joined to Mr. Coffin as a delegate from Gloucester. He was now a venerable citizen of seventy-four years, and deserved this mark of the respect and confidence of his townsmen for the fidelity with which he had served them, in various offices, for half a century.

At a town-meeting on the 7th of November, a large committee was chosen to take care that the "Association" proposed by the Continental Congress be complied with, and in no way violated. This "Association" pledged all who joined it to complete commercial non-intercourse with the parent-country and the West Indies, and the non-consumption of tea and British goods. There is no record that any person here was dealt with for refusing to belong to the "Association," or for having violated its injunctions when a member of it. This meeting adjourned to the 14th; when a vote was passed to indemnify the constables, and secure them from a warrant of distress, in case they would pay the Province-tax into the town-treasury. The constables, upon this, paid it to the treasurer of the town; who was directed, at a meeting held soon afterwards, to pay it to the receiver appointed by the Provincial Congress.

The sum handed to him was £136, the amount of the Province-tax for 1774.

A distressing shipwreck was added to the grievous public calamities of the last days of this year. The schooner "Neptune," owned by Daniel Rogers and commanded by Jonathan Dennison, sailed from the Harbor on the 26th of December, bound to the West Indies. Before she got out of the bay, a violent gale arose, by which she was driven in, and cast ashore near Scituate. Eight men were on board; of whom six, including the captain and mate, were lost. On the 21st of the preceding month, loss of life by shipwreck occurred on our own shores. A brig from Newfoundland, Charles Ackworth captain, was cast ashore somewhere on the Cape, and totally lost. The captain and two of his crew perished.

The beginning of 1775 opened to our fathers a prospect of suffering and gloom, beyond which no man could see a bright horizon. Argument and entreaty had been exhausted in vain in defence of their rights, and now must come the appeal to arms. A new Provincial Congress assembled at Cambridge, Feb. 1; to which Peter Coffin and Samuel Whittemore went as delegates from this town. They were instructed not to consent to the assuming of the civil government of the Province without the approbation of the town, nor without the consent of the Continental Congress.

At a town-meeting on the 6th of March, in accordance with a recommendation of the Provincial Congress, it was voted, that the trained bands and alarm-lists in the town should meet at the usual place of parade on the following Thursday afternoon, with arms and ammunition complete; which the officers were desired to view, and report the state thereof to the town. The old Committee of Correspondence were continued in office, and the number of selectmen chosen was increased to seven. A committee was chosen to wait upon those suspected of being Tories, and desire them to attend the adjourned meeting, and give the town satisfaction in that particular. There were few of this class of persons. Epes Sargent, Esq., was the only one who refused the satisfaction demanded by the town; and, on account of his refusal, the people voted, "that no person should have any commerce with him or his abettors." *

The sixth Essex regiment of Massachusetts militia comprised six companies belonging to Gloucester, and one to Manchester. On the 28th of January, 1775, Col. John Stevens having resigned, a meeting was held for the choice of field-officers.† Many of those who were the company-officers at this time, became, when the proper season arrived, the most active in enlisting men for the Continental Army, and themselves received commissions in it. In accordance with the recommendation of the Provincial Congress, active military preparations were commenced in town in April. Musket-balls were procured, cartridges made, and small-arms purchased, — all by direction of the town; and a company of minute-men was organized, and placed under the command of Nathaniel Warner. While the town was busy about these matters, came the news of the fight at Lexington, which filled the people with consternation and alarm. They knew that there was a large British naval force in Boston Harbor; and such were their fears, that the exposed and unprotected situation of the town would tempt an attack, that, on the 24th, many of the inhabitants at the Harbor began to seek safety for the women and children by removing to West Parish and Ipswich. The flight was on the sabbath.

* I believe that Mr. Sargent and one of his half-brothers were the only members of the respectable family to which they belonged, who espoused the royal side in the contest. Some of them were ardent patriots; and two, at least, were Continental officers in the Revolutionary War. On a previous page, a particular account of this family is given.

† The officers now elected were — John Lee, Esq., colonel; Capt. Peter Coffin, first lieutenant-colonel; John Low, Esq., second lieutenant-colonel; Samuel Whittemore, Esq., first major; Dr. Samuel Rogers, second major.

CHAPTER XIX.

BUSINESS OF THE TOWN BEFORE 1775.

English Fishing Voyages to New England. — First Colonial Fishing. — Gloucester not Prominent in the Business for many Years. — Commencement of Maritime Business. — Fishery before the Revolution. — Trade with the Southern Colonies. — Early Foreign Commerce of the Town. — Revenue Laws evaded. — Revenue Officers. — One of them seized and ill treated. — John M'Kean smokes one at the Cut. — Commerce and Fishing interrupted by the War.

The reader of this work has noticed, perhaps, that it has yet given but little information concerning the maritime employments of the people. All the knowledge we have upon this subject, down to this period of our history, consists of a few scattered and fragmentary items, which it has been deemed best to present here in one general summary.

Among the chief inducements to the settlement of New England were the advantages it offered for "the great sea-business of fishing;" and who, that has read the writings of the famous discoverer of Cape Ann, and seen in what glowing colors these advantages were set forth by him, will not wonder that all the fishermen of the Old World did not at once repair to the New? for there, says he, "man, woman, and child, with a small hook and line, by angling, may take divers sorts of excellent fish at their pleasure. And is it not pretty sport to pull up twopence, sixpence, and twelvepence, as fast as you can haul and veer a line?" — "And what sport doth yield a more pleasing content, and less hurt or charge, than angling with a hook, and crossing the sweet air, from isle to isle, over the silent streams of a calm sea?"

These words were written by Capt. Smith in 1616; and, though several years elapsed before any considerable settlement was made on the coast he described, fishermen repaired to it every year in increased numbers, and pursued their business with such good success, that, in 1624, no less than fifty ships came on fishing voyages. These vessels sought the best stations on the coast of Maine, west of Monhegan, for their fishing stages; though a few resorted to the Isle of Shoals, and three certainly fished at Cape Ann. The men went to the fishing grounds in boats, and landed the fish they had taken at their stages, where they were dried for market. The most successful fishery in the year just mentioned was carried on near Saco; within two leagues of which place, according to a writer who then visited it, "more fish were taken than in any other in the land." The ships arrived on the coast early in the spring, and left it about midsummer for home or a foreign market. Some of them were of two hundred tons burthen, and carried fifty men, who received, in lieu of wages, one-third part of the fish and oil.*

No accounts are preserved to show how long English fishing ships continued to make voyages to the coast of New England; but it is natural to conclude, that, as the country became settled, the number annually decreased, on account of the reduced expense with which the business could be carried on by the colonists. In the first settlement of the Massachusetts Colony, at Salem, we find preparations for fishing; for, in 1629, salt, lines, hooks, knives, boots, and barvels † were sent over; and mention is made of fishermen among the settlers. As early as 1634, a

* "Another third part is allowed the owners of the ship for their freight; and the other third part is allowed for the victual, salt, nets, hooks, lines, and other implements for taking and making the fish.

"The charge of victualling (which is usually for nine months), the salt, &c., doth commonly amount to about eight hundred pounds: and for that they have (as I said) one-third part of the fish, — which is near sixty-seven ton; the ship being laden, which will make thirteen hundred and forty quintals (at the market). Sometimes, when they come to a good market, they sell their fish for forty-four rials a quintal; and so to thirty-six rials, which is the least; but say they have forty, one time with another: and, at that rate, one-third of the ship's lading doth yield thirteen hundred and forty pounds, which they have for disbursing of eight hundred pounds, nine months." — *Levett's Voyage*, Mass. Hist. Coll., vol. xxviii. p. 186.

† Misprinted "barrels" in Young's Chronicles of Mass., pp. 184 and 185.

merchant of the country was fishing with eight boats at Marblehead; and, the next year, Portsmouth had belonging to her fishing trade six great shallops; five fishing boats, with sails, anchors, and cables; and thirteen skiffs. About this time, also, our own shore was the abode of a few fishermen; and several settlements were established on the coast of Maine. Of the total product of this branch of industry in any one year, our only information is derived from Gov. Winthrop, who says, that, in 1641, it was followed so well, that three hundred thousand dry fish were sent to market.

The geographical position of our own territory, and its striking inferiority to many other spots, even on the coast, for agricultural purposes, would lead us to expect to find among its settlers few not attracted to it for maritime employments. That it was "peopled with fishermen till the Rev. Mr. Richard Blindman came," and that men of that class have pursued their business on its shores during every period of its subsequent history, there can be no doubt; but there is no evidence that the town enjoyed, for more than sixty years after its incorporation, any prominence as a fishing settlement. An early writer, speaking of our fishing trade, intimates that it needed "men of estates to manage it," — a want which industry and frugality would have soon supplied, if the business had been as remunerative as other employments The truth is, probably, that the forest and the soil afforded, during the whole period before named, more profitable fields of labor than the sea. This conjecture is authorized by such facts as the town and probate records have handed down to us concerning our early settlers.

The first notice connecting our settlers with the fishing business is preserved on a loose scrap of paper, which records the judgment given in a case of litigation between two of them about a piece of a net, and making mention of "the bote and voyg." This was in 1651; about which time, Robert Dutch had a "stage" at Stage Neck in Squam. In 1662, Peter Duncan settled in the town, and carried on a small trade at the Point, in the Harbor, where it is supposed that Mr. Thomson erected a building or a frame for the purposes of his fishery in 1639. He is the only one of our early settlers styled a merchant. At this time, not more than fifteen men are known to have resided in that part of the town. Some of these, probably, were fishermen. One of them, in 1663, agreed to pay a debt of fifty pounds in "good merchantable fish and mackerel." Not long after this period, there is reason to suppose that the business of wood-coasting began to engage the attention of the people; and evidence is not wanting that it continued for many years to be their chief maritime employment. In addition to their lawful business, some of the vessels engaged in it occasionally found employment, it appears, in assisting to evade the acts of trade.* With regard to their number and size, we have no positive information; and, indeed, all our knowledge concerning the shipping of Gloucester, for the last twenty years of the seventeenth century, may be summed up in the statement, that, during this period, mention is made of about a dozen sloops, shallops, and boats belonging to citizens of the town.†

The commencement of an active pursuit of maritime business by the people of this town may be fixed at about the beginning of the eighteenth century. It was then that the building of

---

* In 1680, John Price, a passenger from Piscataqua to Boston, put into Cape Ann for a harbor. He saw here two vessels, — one supposed to be a fly-boat, and the other a pink. On board of the latter, he saw taken out several casks and chests of divers sorts, which were put on board of one William Sargent's boat, of Cape Ann, intending for Boston, whereof one Mr. Best was merchant. He also saw taken out of a ketch, then in the harbor, which the merchant told him came from Ireland, several goods, — as saddlery, casks, and tanned hides, — which were put on board the Piscataqua sloop, and brought to Boston. — *Deposition communicated by J. W. Thornton, Esq.*

Nov. 28, 1700. — The Earl of Bellamont, writing to the Lords of Trade about the unlawful trade of the Colony, says, "If the merchants of Boston be minded to run their goods, there is nothing to hinder them;" and "'tis a common thing, as I have heard, to unload their ships at Cape Ann, and bring their goods to Boston in wood-boats." — *New-York Col. Documents.*

† Further information of this beginning of the commerce of Gloucester may be desired by some. In the inventory of Isaac Eveleth's estate, 1680, I find "one-third of a sloop, £9;" in that of Jacob Davis, same year, "part of a sloop and four canoes, £12. 10s;" in that of Bartholomew Foster, 1690, "sloop, £30." In a tax-list of 1693, the following persons are taxed for this description of property: John Sargent, James Sayward, William Sargent, 2d, William Ellery, and John Tinny, each one sloop; James Stevens, Samuel Stevens, and Thomas Millet, one-third of a sloop each; John Fitch, half a shallop; Thomas Day, a boat; Ezekiel Day, half a boat; and Widow Coit, half a boat. Besides the foregoing, Lieut. William Stevens, who died in 1701, owned a part of three sloops.

vessels here was vigorously commenced; and a previous chapter has shown that it was for several years extensively carried on. The division of the woodland, at that time, enabled the people to cut large quantities of wood for sale; and the transportation of this article to market created a need for many vessels. This business increased so rapidly, that, in 1706, no less than thirty sloops were employed in carrying wood from one section of the town alone;* and the whole number engaged in it was not probably less than fifty. But this trade could continue only a few years; at the end of which, other employment for the vessels must be sought. Fishing was, of course, the only resource; and we find, accordingly, before 1720, several sloops engaged in the distant fisheries. The hostility of the French and Indians along the whole eastern coast, as far as Cape Sable, had for many years rendered the pursuit of this business in that quarter one of great danger. A few vessels, however, visited that coast from Salem† and other places; but Gloucester fishermen do not appear to have repaired thither till about the time of the conquest of Nova Scotia by the English in 1710. That auspicious event did not secure them from molestation; for Rev. John White of our church, writing in 1711, says, "The enemy make fearful depredations upon our poor fishermen at Cape Sable;" and, two years afterwards, three men were taken from two of our sloops that were fishing there. Another hazard attended the fishery, from which no human care can afford certain protection. This was early experienced by our fishermen; and the havoc of their class by storms and seas, which has since so often shrouded the town in mourning, imparts a melancholy interest to nearly every period of our history. The first loss by shipwreck we have recorded is that of a new schooner, while on a fishing voyage at Sable Island, in 1716. In October, the next year, four of a fleet of seven were lost on the passage from the fishing ground; and

* Squam River, as appears from the fact that that number of town-vessels paid, in that year, the annual toll for passing through the Cut. In 1710 and 1711, the number was eighteen in each year.

† Salem was, perhaps, the most important fishing town in the Colony. It had, as early as 1689, "sixty odd fishing catches."

to these was added, in 1722, another at Sable Island; involving, in each case, the loss of all the crew.

The history of our fishery from this time to the Revolutionary War, for want of particular information concerning it, may be briefly related. The vessels with which the business was first carried on were the sloops built in the town. A few schooners were added about 1720; of which class, it is probable that the "old bankers" of recent times were nearly exact representations. Between 1720 and 1730, as many vessels appear to have been fitted out from Squam River as from the Harbor; but, after the last date, the preponderance was certainly with the latter place, where it has ever since remained. An account of those of Nathaniel Parsons has been given on a previous page. His was the largest business of his time of which we have any knowledge. Next to him, and a few years later, we find that Elias Davis was a merchant of the most extensive and successful trade; leaving, at his death in 1734, six schooners, a wharf and fishing-room at Canso, and a large amount of other property. His inventory indicates that he lived in good style, and had advanced in the luxury of silver plate beyond most, if not all, of his townsmen.

In 1741, we learn that above seventy fishing vessels belonged to the town: but the condition of the business here at that time, as reported by Rev. John White, was not such as another authority* states it to have been in the Colony generally; nor does it appear to have been prosperous for any considerable time during the next twenty years. Indeed, it is a matter of wonder that the discouragements of that period did not cause a total

* Hon. L. Sabine, in his Report on the American Fisheries, p. 131. Mr. White's account is contained in a letter to the Governor and Council in relation to a call upon the town for aid to the sufferers by a great fire in Charleston, S.C., as follows: "Almost our whole dependance, under God, is upon our Navigation and Fishery; and our other Navigation, on our Fishery: and that has so far failed by reason of the war with Spain, and ye fears of warr with France, as also by reason of ye smallness of ye price of fish, and ye dearness of Salt, bread, and craft, that, of above Seventy fishing vessels, there are few, if any, above ten in that business. Our people are scattered abroad in the world to get their bread: many pressed; many serving as volunteers in his Majesty's Service; and the cry of many for necessaries is very affecting. And we have had three contributions for ye relief of the poor the last year in our congregation, and other Families are very pressing for relief."

abandonment of the business. But notwithstanding the wars between France and England, and the consequent annoyance and occasional capture of our vessels by the cruisers of the enemy, and the demand for men for the provincial armies and for the naval service, the fishery was still pursued. The truth is, it had now become the basis of a profitable foreign trade, for the maintenance of which the merchants of the town would willingly encounter great risks, and could even afford to bear considerable losses.

The peace of 1763 secured to our fathers unmolested use of the fishing grounds; and, from this time to the Revolution, they carried on the business with energy and success: though a terrible disaster,* which inflicted a heavy blow upon the town, occurred in the mean time, as elsewhere related in this work. We know nothing of the relative importance of the Bank and shore fisheries during this period; but it seems that the latter were almost wholly confined to Sandy Bay and the coves on the outside of the Cape, while the chief seat of the former was at the Harbor. Neither can we ascertain the number of vessels and boats engaged in the business in any year except the last of the term here embraced. That employed in the Bank fishery must have been quite large; for nineteen schooners, as we have seen, sailed at one time in the fatal year of 1766. An "estimate of the number of fishing vessels from Massachusetts" before the war, supposed to have been made by a merchant of the town several years after that event, gives seventy-five as belonging to Gloucester; agreeing nearly with the number stated by our selectmen in 1779 to have been owned here in 1775; which was eighty, of an aggregate burthen of four thousand tons. The average value of these vessels, we learn from another source, was about three hundred pounds. The same estimate says that there were owned at Sandy Bay seventy boats, which landed one hundred and sixty quintals of fish each; but this evidently exaggerates.†

---

* The loss of nine vessels with their crews in 1766.

† Of the fisheries of Massachusetts for any period, from the beginning to the present time, we lack full reliable statistics. The earliest table I have seen is one of the cod-fishery "from the year 1765 to 1775." That gives, in relation to the Gloucester

The business yielded a scanty support to the fishermen; and, as a class, they were poor: though then, as in a more recent period of our history, according to the natural course of things, the merchants who carried it on with most success were men who had themselves served an apprenticeship at the hook and line. No means exist for ascertaining the average annual earnings of these men before the war; but the accounts of a single vessel for 1773 are preserved, and show the product of her two trips to the Banks to have been five hundred and fifty quintals of fish, which sold for £302. After deducting a few small expenses, one-half of this sum belonged to the fishermen.* Supposing their number to have been six, we can see that the amount received by each was but a small sum for the payment of his

---

fisheries, "vessels annually employed, 146; tonnage, 5,530; number of men, 868;" an exaggeration, without doubt, in each case. In a covenant for mutual insurance of the bankers in 1774, forty-five schooners are entered; but those of David Pearce and Winthrop Sargent, two principal merchants of the town, and of others owning one or two vessels each, were not put in: enough, in all, to make up the eighty mentioned as belonging here in 1775. The number of our fishing boats at that time cannot be ascertained; but, on the authority of the selectmen for 1779, I can state, that in "foreign merchantmen, coasters, and fishing boats," we had 1,000 tons. I suppose that about one-half of this tonnage was in fishing boats; averaging, as they did a few years later, twelve tons each, and making the whole number about forty. In that case, we should have the aggregate of 120 fishing vessels belonging to the town in 1775, of the total burthen of 4,500 tons. The schooners probably carried an average number of six men each; and the boats, two: making the whole number of fishermen 560. Nearly all the fishermen who sailed from the town at that time belonged to it; and, when we consider that our list of polls then numbered but 1,053, we see at once that the number of men employed in the fisheries here, given in the table above mentioned, must be exaggerated.

* In these fishing voyages, it was the custom for the men to go, as it was called, "on their own hook." An account was kept of the fish caught by each man; and, at the end of the voyage, the proceeds were distributed accordingly. The following account of a season's work by one crew on the Grand Banks, a hundred years ago, may possess interest for modern fishermen: —

Account of fish taken on board the schooner "Abigail," Capt. Paul Hughes, in three fares to the Grand Banks in 1757. She sailed, on the first fare, May 16; and fished twenty-three days. On the second fare, July 13; and fished twenty days. On the third fare, Sept. 22; and fished twenty-four days. She left the Banks, on the last fare, Nov. 5.

	Paul Hughes.	B. Foster.	Rufus Stacy.	Job Galloway.	Nathl. Day.	Wm. Smith.	Total.
1st Fare,	3501	2890	2000	2209	2020	1705	14,325
2d Fare,	1146	689	758	742	615	609	4559
					Abm. Wharf.		
3d Fare,	1996	1421	1026	1293	1294	1121	8151
	6643	5000	3784	4244	3929	3435	27,035

The largest number taken in one day was 1,886, on the first day of June.

proportion of the provisions for the voyage, and the support of his family at home.

The commerce of Gloucester grew directly out of its fishery; but, as to the time when the foreign and coastwise trade of the town commenced, no particulars are known. The first item in relation to this subject is the seizure here, by the Collector of Salem, of the "Snow Esther," in 1725. As early as 1732, a trade had begun with the Southern Colonies, and was continued to about the beginning of the present century. The voyages were made in the winter season, when there was no employment for vessels or men in fishing; and the business was conducted in a manner now little practised in any part of the world. In most cases, perhaps in all, no wages were paid to master or crew; but, in lieu thereof, the privilege of bringing home a certain quantity of Southern produce was granted to each one; who was also allowed, probably, to take out fish on private adventure; as, in the few invoices preserved, this article does not appear among the shipments by the owners. In these invoices, the principal articles are salt, rum, sugar, and molasses. Then follows a long list of other things, including iron-ware, wooden-ware, hats, caps, patterns of cloth for breeches, handkerchiefs, and stockings; making, in all, a cargo of about two hundred pounds' value. On these voyages, the rivers, creeks, and inlets of Virginia, Maryland, and North Carolina, were visited; and there the cargo was bartered in small quantities for corn, beans, bacon, live hogs, and other products of the country. Tradition reports that the trade was not always reputably conducted; for sometimes exchanges were made with the slaves for stolen property, and often a demand for different kinds of rum was supplied from one cask of the New-England liquor. Such proceedings, combined with complaints from the retail traders whose business was affected by this commerce, occasioned, probably, the legislative enactments which are said to have caused its abandonment.

Before the Revolution, the Virginia voyages appear to have met with no interruption, except such as grew out of the wars between the southern English Colonies and the Spanish settlements. At that time, Spanish privateers ranged along the coast, and the newspapers of the time record the capture of two of our vessels; one of which the enemy released after taking out nearly all her cargo, and placing on board of her the crews of several English vessels they had taken.

The foreign commerce of Gloucester was also, for many years after its origin, carried on with the fishing vessels. Before the war, Winthrop Sargent had the brig "King of Prussia," and Epes Sargent owned the "Snow Charlotte," — the only square-rigged vessels known to have then belonged to the town. Of this commerce, we only know that it was of inconsiderable extent till about 1750; when we find notice of voyages to the West Indies, to Bilbao, and Lisbon. The West-India cargoes consisted of fish and other provisions, for which, sugar, molasses, rum, and coffee were returned; while to Europe little was sent except fish, the proceeds of which came home in salt, fruit, wine, and specie. The acts of Parliament for regulating the trade of the Colonies were disregarded; and smuggling, and fraudulent entries, at which the revenue-officers connived, were common. Gloucester had, as early as 1683, been made one of the lawful ports of the Colony, and annexed to the Salem district; but no officer of the customs is known to have resided here till after the commencement by the mother-country of that series of measures which brought on the Revolutionary War. Among these measures was one for a rigid enforcement of the revenue acts; for which purpose, commissioners of the customs were sent over from England, and steps were taken to put an end to the illicit trade carried on in the Colonies. The first person employed in this business in Gloucester appears to have been Samuel Fellows, who in some manner rendered himself odious to our people, as mentioned in a previous chapter.

In 1770, one Mr. Phillips held the office of "land-waiter, weigher, and gauger;" in whose room the commissioners appointed, January, 1771, Richard Silvester. The officers of the customs took upon themselves a difficult duty, and could not fail, in performing it faithfully, to expose themselves to public indignation, and the danger of personal violence; but it is not known that either of the persons here mentioned received any bodily injury at the hands of our people. Silvester was ordered by the selectmen to leave the town, with his family, in September, 1772; but he took no further notice of the order than to publish in the "Boston News-Letter" an ironical card, in which he "prays leave to acquaint these worthies, that he cannot nor will not comply with their request." The exasperated party that searched the house of Mr. Saville in quest of Fellows in 1768, as heretofore related, would probably have left upon his body some mark of their hatred, if he had fallen into their hands; but he luckily escaped, and the anger of the mob was vented upon Mr. Saville and his family. He was knocked down while defending his home; and a servant was threatened by Dr. Rogers, forceps in hand, with the loss of all his teeth, unless he would tell where Fellows was. One or two of the persons engaged in this affair were tried for their offence, and fined; and one of them was confined in jail several months for non-payment of a fine of five pounds; but was finally released by the Governor, who remitted the fine.

The merchants continued to run their goods; and Mr. Saville, not intimidated by the recent scene at his house, accepted employment in the revenue service, which, if he did his duty, would inevitably bring upon him their vengeance. He unwisely defied the public sentiment in a time of high political excitement, and soon reaped the consequences of his temerity. On the night of the 23d of March, 1770, he was seized in his bed by a party of men disguised as negroes and Indians, and dragged in an inhuman manner, a distance of four miles, to the Harbor, where he was subjected to various indignities till his tormentors chose to let him depart for home. The outrage aroused a good deal of feeling in the town, and the attention of the Governor was called to it. That magistrate made a representation to the General Court concerning it; but it was a grievance that could find little sympathy or redress among the representatives of the people. A mulatto servant of Dr. Plummer, mamed George, was tried and convicted in the following November for aiding and abetting in this assault; and in March, 1772, by way of punishment in part, was placed on the gallows in Salem, with a halter round his neck, and kept there an hour; after which, he was whipped. George would not give any information of the persons concerned with him.

Whether revenue-officers continued to reside in Gloucester through the last years of our Colonial existence, or not, we have no means of knowing; but tradition asserts that the merchants of the town did not cease to smuggle extensively till their commerce was destroyed by the war. A story is told concerning one of these smuggling adventures, which is deserving of remembrance for a clever device of its chief actor. A schooner, belonging to Col. Joseph Foster, came in from a foreign port in the night; and, according to custom, the hatches were immediately opened, and the landing of the cargo was commenced, the owner himself assisting. A considerable part was landed and stored before daybreak; but more than half was still on board, and, early in the morning, a tide-waiter was expected from Salem. The fertile mind of Col. Foster hit at once upon an expedient. On the Cut was a watch-house, where John M'Kean, a stout Irishman, had been employed, in a time of alarm about the small-pox, to stop all strangers entering the town, and subject them to a fumigating process. It is sufficient to say, that his majesty's officer of the customs was on that morning ushered into the watch-house by John M'Kean; that he was kept there all day, and released after dark, purified from all infectious disease, so far as a thorough smoking could do it.

The Revolutionary crisis approached, and the commerce and fishery of the town could be no longer pursued. A great majority of the people — comprising the merchants, mechanics, fishermen, and sailors, who depended upon the maritime business of the place for their livelihood — could find no employment in their regular pursuits; and were the more eager, therefore, to prove the sincerity of their declaration, that they would defend their liberties at the expense of all that was dear to them.

CHAPTER XX.

REVOLUTIONARY WAR.

The Appeal to Arms. — Companies formed. — Two of them Fight on Bunker Hill. — Sloop of War "Falcon," Capt. Lindsay, in Ipswich Bay. — He comes into Gloucester Harbor. — Fires upon the Town. — Attempts to take a Vessel out. — Repulsed. — Defenceless State of the Town. — Forts built. — Privateering commenced. — Manly's Prize. — Poverty of the Town. — The Poor relieved by Donations. — Committee of Safety. — The Yankee Hero. — Supremacy of the People asserted in Official Acts of the Town.

The first blood had been shed in support of American liberty; and every patriotic bosom glowed with the sentiment of "victory, or death." At a town-meeting on the 21st of April, the representatives to the Provincial Congress were authorized to act according to their discretion with respect to assuming the civil government. An express was sent to Cambridge to see if fire-arms could be purchased; and a Committee of Safety, consisting of thirty-one of the most prominent and respectable citizens, was chosen. The minute-men were disbanded, paid off, and thanked for their readiness to serve; and the enlistment of men for actual service was now earnestly begun. The town undertook to provide arms and blankets * for those who could not furnish themselves; and agreed to supply, during their absence, the families of the soldiers depending upon their wages for payment. A large number of men, hitherto engaged in the

* These were supplied by private families, and were paid for by an order on the town-treasury.

commerce and fisheries of the town and the mechanical employments connected therewith, were now without employment; and no difficulty was found in filling up the ranks of several companies. It is not easy to ascertain the whole number that enlisted in Gloucester and repaired to the different encampments around Boston: but it is certain that there were four companies, composed wholly of Gloucester men, with the exception of about six persons; and that another company, commanded by Captain Parker of Ipswich, had about thirty of our men in it.* Besides these, there was another company, commanded by Capt. James Collins, which marched to Cambridge on the 15th of June. No roll of this company has yet come to light; but our town-records furnish a list of twenty-three of its members to whom guns were delivered.†

Two of these companies were in the battle of Bunker Hill. One, enlisted by Capt. Nathaniel Warner in four days, marched to Cambridge in the latter part of May. The morning after the redoubt was thrown up on Bunker Hill, when it was discovered that the enemy was preparing for an attack, this company, with others, had orders to march to the hill to assist in the defence. They made a rapid march to Charlestown: though their order was so much broken by the haste in which they had marched from the camp, and the galling fire kept up from one of the British ships to annoy the troops crossing the Neck, that the men got separated; and, in forming them into company after reaching

---

* The following were the officers of these five companies:—

1. In the seventeenth regiment, Col. Moses Little, Capt. Nathaniel Warner, Lieut. John Burnham, Ensign Daniel Collins.

2. In the same, Capt. Joseph Roby, Lieut. Shubael Gorham, Ensign Enoch Parsons.

3. In the twenty-seventh regiment, Col. Ebenezer Bridge, Capt. John Rowe, Lieut. Mark Pool, Ensign Ebenezer Cleaveland.

4. In the thirty-eighth regiment, Col. Loammi Baldwin, Capt. Barnabas Dodge, Lieut. Matthew Fairfield of Wenham, Ensign Joseph Knight of Manchester.

5. In Col. Little's regiment, Capt. Gideon Parker of Ipswich, Lieut. Joseph Eveleth, Ensign Jonathan Trask.

† We have the authority of the selectmen for 1779 for the assertion, that, during the first campaign of the war, Gloucester "had upwards of two hundred and twenty men in the field, besides numbers who joined the marine department, as more suitable to their former occupation."

the peninsula, it was found that ensign Collins and a few of the soldiers were still in the rear. Warner was impatient; and, leaving the missing men to find their way to the scene of action, ordered his company to march. They went more upon a run than a quick march, and arrived on the ground just as the firing commenced. The captain then asked Gen. Putnam where he should take his post; and was told by him to get to the fort, if he could. At this time, from some cause, the company separated into two divisions. One, with the captain, went on to the redoubt; and the other, under Lieut. Burnham, passed on till they came in view of the left flank of the enemy, and commenced their firing at the outside of the south-west corner of the fort, where they remained during the action. Lieut. Burnham had two men killed in the engagement, and three wounded as the retreat began. At this time, Capt. Warner, with his men, came out of the redoubt, and went towards the rail-fence, where the firing was still kept up. In firing his musket on leaving the fort, the barrel split in his hands, but did him no injury. He soon procured another, and, having loaded it, raised it up to fire; when it was struck by a ball, which split the stock, and glanced off the barrel without wounding him. He soon found another gun, and received another shot from the enemy. A ball struck his breeches-pocket, split the handle of his penknife, glanced off; and again he received no injury. Lieut. Burnham continued on the retreat, supporting his wounded soldiers,* till, overcome with fatigue, they stopped by a stone wall to rest; but here the shot flew about them thickly, and they went on. By this time, the Continental troops were all on the retreat to Ploughed Hill. The two men killed were Daniel Callahan and Benjamin Smith. The latter was standing by the side of Benjamin Webber

* Perhaps one of these wounded soldiers was Nymphas Stacy; concerning whom, the following anecdote is still remembered. Stacy was struck, in the retreat, by a spent ball, in the leg. The limb being paralyzed for a moment, he fell, and was caught up by Burnham, and borne away. After carrying him some distance on his shoulders, Burnham became fatigued, and stopped to rest. He asked his wounded soldier how he felt; and the latter, having recovered the use of his leg, replied, that he was not hurt, and that, as Burnham himself must be a good deal fatigued by the heavy burden he had carried, he might mount on his back, and have a "lift along."

when shot, and fell dead across his feet. Webber himself was shot in the right arm, in the act of raising his gun to fire the last charge he had left. Alexander Parran was wounded in his right arm, and lost the use of it entirely.* Ensign Collins, who was left on the march from Cambridge to bring up the rear, is said to have come in with his men in season for the action; but nothing is known concerning the part they bore in it.†

The other Gloucester company which took part in this memorable battle was one composed of men living at Sandy Bay and the Farms. It is said to have been enlisted by Daniel B. Tarr, its orderly sergeant; who gave the command of it to John Rowe. This company marched from Gloucester on Monday, June 12; going through Wenham on their way to the camp.

---

* The next winter, he was allowed £10. 4s. for the loss of his gun, for board and nursing twelve weeks, and conveyance home. Some time afterwards, Parran went on a cruise in the privateer brig "Fair Play." Off Guadaloupe, the vessel was fired into, and sunk. Some of the crew saved their lives by swimming; but Parran, having no use of his right arm, was drowned. He was son of Samuel Parran of St. Leonard's, Calvert County, Md.; and is said to have been the first that enlisted in Capt. Warner's company.

† The last survivor of this company known to me was Major John Burnham. When asked by Capt. Warner to help enlist his company, and take the rank of lieutenant, he was in a bad state of health, and supposed to be in a consumption. He was in the military service of his country, without a furlough, or leave of absence, for any purpose of his own, throughout the whole Revolutionary War, to the closing scene at Yorktown, in which he actively participated. He was not even then dismissed from the service in which, by a faithful performance of duty, he had gained such honorable distinction; but was continued in commission till the 1st of January, 1784, when his regiment was discharged. He received a captain's commission in 1777, and had the command of a company of light infantry about six years; at the end of which time, he was promoted to the rank of major.

Major Burnham was a native of Gloucester, and here acquired a mechanical trade. After the war, he came home, and resumed the business in which he was brought up. Upon the resignation of Mr. Sargent, the first Collector of the Customs for this district, the place was offered to Major Burnham; but he declined the offer, and soon after moved to Derry, N.H. The first Pension Act for the relief of Revolutionary soldiers did not include him in its benefits: but his claims were strongly enforced; and among the means used for obtaining a pension for the old soldier was a letter to the Secretary of War from Gov. Brooks, containing the most honorable mention of his services. He finally succeeded in obtaining a pension of five hundred dollars per annum; and his passage to the grave, through the infirmities and feebleness of a life protracted to an unusual length, was undisturbed by the feeling of poverty and dependence. He died in Derry, June 8, 1843, aged ninety-four.

On the 16th, they had reached the Mystic River; and, in the afternoon of that day, took up their march from that place. About dark, they halted. In a short time, by the yet lingering twilight, they descried approaching a large number of soldiers, who were soon found to be a detachment from the army at Cambridge. As soon as they came up, Capt. Rowe's company joined them; and the whole body then moved towards Breed's Hill. On its arrival there, they went silently to work with picks and spades to throw up the intrenchment. When the redoubt was finished, and while the enemy were landing, Capt. Rowe, with part of the company, was despatched to carry off the tools. On their return, these men were ordered to the extreme left wing of the Provincial troops, near Mystic River. It thus happened that the company was divided; and it was not again united during the day. Ensign Cleaveland and Sergeant Haskins remained in the redoubt with one part; while Capt. Rowe and Lieut. Pool, with the other, were on the left of the line: some assisting in building the rail-fence, as a protection from the bullets of the enemy; and others, at the end of the line on the bank of the river, building up a small breastwork with stones and dirt. They were thus engaged till the English advanced, about three o'clock, P. M. Major M'Cleary gave them particular directions how to act: they were to load and fire, with one knee resting on the ground; and, after the first fire, not to wait for orders, but to load and fire as fast as possible, taking care not to throw away any shot by firing at too long a distance. The enemy, as is well known, were repulsed twice; but, at the third attack, the ammunition at the redoubt gave out. A retreat was ordered, and the troops at the rail-fence joined in it. They retreated that night to Ploughed Hill. Capt. Rowe had three of his men killed in the battle, and two wounded. Francis Pool and Josiah Brooks were killed at the rail-fence, while in the act of firing. William Parsons was killed at the redoubt. Daniel Doyl was hurt by a ball, which, having passed through the palisade, struck him on the breast, and broke a button off his clothing, but did not enter his body. William Foster was wounded, on the retreat, in the wrist. Sergeant Haskins had two cartridges left when he retreated from the fort; but he fired them away upon the enemy, when he got to the rail-fence.*

Such was the part borne by Gloucester on that great day, — the 17th of June, 1775. The fidelity of its people to their principles was next to be put to the test on their own soil.

The sloop-of-war "Falcon," Capt. Lindsay, one of the ships which had aided the British at the battle of Bunker Hill, on the 5th of August made her appearance in Ipswich Bay, and came nearly to the mouth of Squam Harbor; when Lindsay despatched a barge, with about fifty men, to land on Coffin's Beach, and get a supply of sheep from the adjacent pastures. Major Coffin, with a few men from his farm and its vicinity, — not more than five or six, — suspecting his design, repaired to the beach, and, from behind some sand-knolls, kept up such a brisk firing upon the barge as she approached, that the officer in command, supposing a whole company of soldiers to be lying in ambush, concluded to put back to the ship, without effecting his object. Perhaps a bullet from the major's rifle, which struck the brass plate of his sword-belt and glanced off, influenced his determination. As the barge neared the ship on its return, she was hailed by Lindsay, and sent into Squam Harbor to cut out a deeply laden schooner, supposed by him to be a West Indiaman. Upon boarding the vessel, it was discovered, that, instead of a valuable cargo of West-India products, she had nothing in but sand.

These disappointments did not tend to soften Lindsay's feelings towards the "rebels." He continued cruising about our Cape, and impressed several men from the vessels and boats of this and the neighboring ports. On the 8th of August, he fell in with two schooners from the West Indies, bound to Salem; and, having made a prize of one, chased the other into this harbor. She was run ashore on the flats between Pearce's

* From a return of this company, made after the battle, it appears that it then had forty-four privates; of whom, all but six were fishermen and sailors. Thirty-five were natives of Gloucester. Seventeen were under twenty-one years of age, five only over thirty, and none over forty. The youngest was William Low, a lad of fourteen. John Rowe, jun., a son of the captain, was sixteen. For a roll of each of the Gloucester companies that fought on Bunker Hill, see Appendix V.

Wharf and Five-pound Island; and Lindsay, who had followed her as far as he safely could, came to anchor, and prepared to take possession of her where she lay. Before attempting this, however, he sent in a boat, with a flag; and the Committee of Safety went on board of his ship, where they were detained till they promised to release the schooner. But the citizens would not suffer the schooner to be taken out; and had, in the mean time, strained every effort in preparing to give the British crew a warm reception if they should attempt it.

Our people had no guns mounted, and little ammunition; but they got two old swivels, and, hastily mounting them on carriages, proceeded with these, and all the muskets that could be procured, to protect the schooner. One of the swivels was placed under the direction of Capt. Joseph Foster; and the other, under that of Capt. Bradbury Sanders, — both zealous patriots. Part of our men repaired to the wharf; and the rest, to the hill on the opposite side of Vinson's Cove. By this time, Lindsay had manned two barges with fifteen men each, armed with muskets and swivels, and sent them, under the command of a lieutenant with six privates, in another boat, to seize the schooner, and bring her under the "Falcon's" bow. As soon as they reached the vessel, some of the barge-men boarded her at the cabin-windows: whereupon a smart fire was opened upon them by our people on the shore, which killed three of the enemy, and wounded the lieutenant in the thigh. The latter returned to the ship; and Lindsay then sent in the other schooner, and a cutter he had to attend him, well armed, with orders to the commanding officer to fire on the "damned rebels" wherever he could find them. At the same time, he commenced cannonading the town from the ship, and poured several broadsides into the most thickly settled part of the place. "Now, my boys," said he, "we will aim at the damned Presbyterian Church!" — "One shot more," my brave fellows, "and the house of God will fall before you!" To complete the work of destruction which he had thus commenced, the infuriated captain then sent a boat, with some of his men, to land on Fort Point, and attempt to set the town in flames by kindling a fire among the fish-flakes on the beach; but this purpose was frustrated by a body of our people, who went round to the spot, and made prisoners of all the men.

During all this time, the party at the water-side were performing wonders; and their bravery was at length rewarded by a complete victory. They got possession of both schooners, the cutter and barges; and, with them, took thirty-five men. Several of these were wounded, — one of them so severely, that he died soon after. Twenty-four were sent to the American camp at Cambridge; and the rest, having been impressed from this and the neighboring ports, were sent to their homes. One of the latter was Duncan Piper, a native of England, but a resident of this town. He was standing up in the bow of one of the boats as it drew near the shore; when, perceiving a musket aimed at him by one of the men there, he called his own name loudly two or three times, and thus, perhaps, saved his life.*

The attempt to set the town on fire was a very unfortunate exploit for the enemy: for, in addition to the capture of those who were engaged in it, the boatswain of the ship, in applying fire to the combustible matter prepared, carelessly allowed it to reach the powder-horn he was holding; which caused it to explode, and occasioned the loss of his hand.

The loss of our people by this fight was two men, — Benjamin Rowe, who was killed on the spot; and Peter Lurvey, who was mortally wounded, and died in a short time. One other man was slightly wounded. The broadsides which Lindsay poured into the town did but little damage. Several houses received a shot; and one, which was fired into the Meeting-house,

* One of Lindsay's impressed men was William Moore, a relative of Sir Hamilton Moore. He had resided several years at Fresh-water Cove, where he built a house. In 1757, he taught a public school at the Cape. Being out in a boat with his son Joseph, he was taken by Lindsay, and carried away. He probably died soon after, as he never returned to Gloucester. The son, then a boy of about twelve years, was put ashore near his home, and became a very useful citizen. He possessed a good deal of mathematical talent, was frequently employed as a teacher in our public schools, and was also the teacher in navigation of two generations of our seafaring men. He was a man of simple tastes and habits, and of many excellent traits of character. He died Oct. 28, 1845, aged eighty-two.

is yet preserved. Our fathers were wont to boast, that the only loss of life they caused was that of a hog belonging to Deacon Kinsman, which had nearly the whole of his back-bone taken out by one of the balls. In order to be prepared against a renewed attack by Lindsay, the people of the town procured an old nine-pounder, which they mounted; and they also sent out of town for a supply of powder: but the next day, to the great joy of the inhabitants, the ship was warped out of the harbor, and steered out to sea.*

Public attention was now drawn to the defenceless state of the town; and a detachment of riflemen, under Major Robert Magaw, was sent from the camp at Cambridge for its protection. In October, a company from Ipswich was ordered here to assist the towns-people in fortifying the place. Breastworks were thrown up on an eminence near the Old Battery; one at the Stage, near Fresh-water Cove; one at Duncan's Point; and one on a bank near the Cut.

A company, under Capt. John Lane, had been stationed all summer somewhere on the Cape for the defence of the seacoast: but it does not appear to have been engaged in the affair with Lindsay; and, therefore, was not probably near the scene of action on that day. In September, this company was supplied with wood and barracks by the town. It suffered in some degree from the non-payment of wages; but, in November, was allowed to draw clothing from the public stores.

In the latter part of the summer, the people of Gloucester commenced privateering; but at first only on a small scale, making use of their fishing boats for the purpose. These were prepared for the business by lengthening the hatchway, and stepping four swivels in the combings. They took a few prizes of little value; one of which was a brig from Canada, bound to

---

* Having acquitted themselves so well of their duty, I suppose the wearied actors repaired to James Prentice's tavern for refreshment; as I find his charges against the town that day were — for thirteen buckets toddy, £2. 18s. 4d; five suppers, and two quarts of rum, 6s. 8d. He was also paid 12s. for attendance on wounded men.

The boats taken from Lindsay were got on shore, and hauled up back of the First-Parish Meeting-house, where they remained two years, and were then sold for the benefit of the poor of the town.

Boston, with a deck-load of live stock for the Ministerial troops, and coal and iron in her hold. She was taken to Wheeler's Point in Squam Harbor, and there discharged.*

While these little craft were thus employed, armed schooners, in the public service, were also cruising in the bay to intercept any vessels that might arrive with supplies for the enemy. These vessels frequently put into Gloucester at night, and sailed again the next morning. One of them — the "Lee," Capt. Manly — brought into our harbor, on the 28th of November, a prize of inestimable value. This was the "Nancy," from London, bound to Boston; an ordnance-ship, having on board a great quantity of small-arms and ammunition, besides cannon, and a large brass mortar of a new construction. These articles were all greatly needed by Gen. Washington. They were landed here, and carted to the camp at Cambridge; where they were joyfully received, and where the mortar was pronounced the noblest piece of ordnance ever landed in America, and christened, in consideration of its high value, the "Congress."

A deep feeling of anxiety and gloom pervaded the town as this year was drawing to a close. Probably few towns in New England had a larger proportionate share of families, which depended upon their daily labor for their daily bread, than Gloucester had in the beginning of 1775. As many as three-fourths of the men of the town were fishermen and sailors, and laborers and mechanics depending upon mercantile business. Of the former class, those who had families to support, almost without an exception, seldom saved enough from a summer's work to enable them to keep out of debt through the winter; and many of the latter class, for want of full employment, made no accumulations for a time of need. It is evident, therefore, that when they were debarred from their accustomed labor, and no sufficient work could be procured, a considerable degree of

* Before her ballast was all taken out, she heeled off, and fell into the channel; where, a few years ago, a portion of her bottom could still be seen. The oxen forming part of her deck-load were brought to the Harbor, and sold at auction in front of Prentice's tavern. According to the custom of the Canadian French, these cattle had been worked by the horns; and it is said that the purchasers found it difficult to make them draw with the yoke.

poverty must exist. They were now in that condition. It is true, a large number of the people had enlisted in the army, and would, with their wages, do something for the support of their families; a few found employment in the armed vessels of the Province; and some were earning a little by seizing such of the enemy's small craft as they could catch along the shore: but there still remained a distressingly large proportion of our people, whose productive industry this year could not secure them against dismal forebodings for the coming winter. This subject was considered at a town-meeting in October; but no provision was made to supply the poor with either food or work, as contemplated by some: but, early in January, it was found necessary to take up two schooners, and send them to Virginia for grain.* Before the return of these vessels, however, the town was obliged to authorize the selectmen to buy or borrow two hundred bushels of corn for the use of the people.

The distressed condition of the poor here also excited the sympathy of private individuals at home, and some distant people of benevolence, who contributed to their relief. Among these benefactors of the town were the Friends in Pennsylvania, whose timely donations, together with those from domestic sources, lightened many heavy hearts during this gloomy winter.

At the annual town-meeting in 1776, a new Committee of Safety, consisting of thirteen prominent citizens, was chosen, to whom four more were added at a subsequent meeting;† and a vote was passed to petition for an abatement of the Province-tax for the preceding year.

On the expiration of the time for which they had enlisted in the army, many of our soldiers returned home; and, choosing

---

* One of these vessels belonged to Capt. William Ellery; and the other, to Capt. William Coas. The town voted to get insurance to the amount of £400, not to exceed thirty per cent for the voyage.

† This Committee were — Col. John Stevens, Jacob Allen, Major Whittemore, Capt. Coas, Capt. Winthrop Sargent, Capt. Jacob Parsons, Capt. William Ellery, Dr. Samuel Plummer, Col. John Low, Daniel Thurston, Capt. John Rowe, Mr. John Hale, Col. Peter Coffin, Deacon Nathaniel Haskell, James Porter, Capt. John Smith, and Deacon Hubbard Haskell.

employment better suited to their habits and liking, they shipped on board of the privateers, which, in the spring and summer of that year, were fitted out at this and the neighboring ports of Salem and Newburyport. One of those sent out from the latter port in the summer was captured, under singular circumstances, while on her passage round the Cape to Gloucester, whither she was bound for the purpose of completing her armament and crew. She was called the "Yankee Hero," and was commanded by Capt. John Tracy. She sailed from Newburyport on the 10th of June. On the same day, a large ship appeared off the Cape, which seemed to be clumsily worked, and to have but few men on board. Supposing she could be easily taken, the people of Sandy Bay made preparations to board her. They were urged on by Lieut. Pool, who, on this occasion, showed more valor than discretion. He pursuaded Capt. Rowe, against his own better judgment, to join in the enterprise; for the latter had some suspicions that the vessel was a ship-of-war in disguise. Every mechanic, fisherman, and farmer, that could be found, was enlisted, to the number of about twenty; and, having procured three fishing boats, they proceeded fearlessly to the attack. They had scarcely left their moorings, when the "Yankee Hero" hove in sight, coming round Halibut Point. The boats steered directly for her; and, upon getting alongside, the men were received on board by Capt. Tracy, who eagerly declared his readiness to attack the British ship. The boats were sent back, and the brig made all sail, and stood towards the ship; into which, as soon as she got within cannon-shot, she let off a broadside. The ship immediately opened two tiers of ports, and sent such a broadside in return as satisfied our Cape men of their great mistake. Pool wished to board the ship, and carry her, sword in hand, or die in the attempt; but his advice of this reckless measure was unheeded, and a fight commenced almost under the ship's guns. The brig maintained the contest about an hour; at the end of which, having spent all her ammunition, she struck to the British frigate "Milford," of thirty-six guns. The brig's last gun was filled with pieces of iron, spikes, and a crowbar. The latter, being the only missile left on board, was thrust into the gun by Pool, who, when he went on board of the frigate as a prisoner, discovered this new implement of war sticking through the bits of her windlass. It was called, by the British sailors, the "Yankee belaying-pin."

There is no doubt that our people made a gallant defence after they got into this fight; but the wonder is that they should have got into it at all. In an account of this affair, printed at the time, the number of killed and wounded is greatly exaggerated. The only person killed on board the "Yankee Hero" was Hugh Parkhurst.* Capt. Tracy was shot in the thigh. Reuben Brooks was wounded in the head; and died, in Halifax prison, of the wound and small-pox combined. Ebenezer Rowe lost his hand. These are all who are known to have been killed or wounded in the engagement. The frigate, with the prisoners, went first to Nantasket Roads; thence to Halifax; and thence to New York, where the prisoners were placed on board a prison-ship. Here many of them had the small-pox. Capt. Rowe, Lieut. Pool, and many others, were sent on shore, sick with this disease, to a hospital which the British had prepared on Staten Island. When they recovered, not being called for immediately to return to the ship, they let themselves to a sutler in the British camp, who used in his business a small sloop, on board of which they were employed. Being left with her on one occasion, they took the boat in the night, and escaped to the Jersey shore to the camp of the American Army.

At a town-meeting on the 27th of May this year, Peter Coffin, Samuel Whittemore, Daniel Rogers, John Low, and William Ellery, were chosen representatives to a General Court to be held at Watertown; the condition of the poor was again con-

* Hugh Parkhurst, it is said, left his paternal home, in London, in consequence of a dispute with his father upon American politics; and, in company with a brother, arrived in New England about 1770. He settled in Gloucester that year; and, being well educated, soon found employment as teacher of the public school in Sandy Bay. In the spring of 1775, he taught in the Fourth Parish; and, on the 17th June, fought in Capt. Rowe's company at the battle of Bunker Hill. He married in town, and left an only son, William; who died in Gloucester, Jan. 18, 1858, aged eighty-three, leaving sons extensively engaged in the business of the town.

sidered, and a loan of £100 was authorized to purchase provisions for their relief.

The allegiance of our fathers to the British crown had ceased to be a duty. For many years, the late educated town-clerk had headed every page of his records with "Anno Regni Regis Georgii," &c.; but this was now abandoned, together with the customary official recognition of royal authority in warning town-meetings in his majesty's name. The town-meeting just mentioned was the first that was called in the name of the government and people of the Colony of Massachusetts Bay. One other step remained for them; which the people of Gloucester soon took, by signifying their readiness to renounce all political connection with the land of their ancestors.

CHAPTER XXI.

FIRST PARISH. — REV. ELI FORBES SETTLED. — HIS PREVIOUS CAREER. — HIS MINISTRY IN GLOUCESTER. — HIS DEATH AND CHARACTER. — HIS FAMILY. — HIS PRINTED PRODUCTIONS.

THE First Church appointed the 26th of April, 1775, for a day of fasting and prayer: and it was observed, undoubtedly, with all the solemnity befitting the occasion; for it was one of more than usual importance, both on account of the budding dissensions within the church, and the threatening aspect of political affairs.

For the first time since the first year of this century, the parish was now without a pastor; and no action was taken for several months to supply the vacant pulpit. Temporary preachers were employed; one of whom (Rev. O. Parsons of the Third Church) preached nine sabbaths, between Mr. Chandler's death and the settlement of his successor. In April, 1776, the church had voted to call Rev. Eli Forbes to be their pastor; and, on the 2d of that month, the parish concurred by a vote of about three-fourths of the large number in attendance at the meeting. He had already preached several times for the parish. The dissentient votes were probably cast by Mr. Murray's friends; several of whom, a few days afterwards, addressed Mr. Forbes a note, in which they endeavored to dissuade him from accepting the call, by setting forth the gloomy prospects of the parish in relation to the business concerns of its members, and intimating that his happiness would be best consulted by rejecting the offer that had been made to him. This letter had no other effect than to call forth a brief reply, from which his advisers reaped no satisfaction. Mr. Forbes accepted the offer of the parish; which was, that he should have £80 per annum during the depression of business, and £110 on the revival of trade. He was installed June 5, 1776. On that occasion, Rev. E. Ward of Brookfield opened with prayer, Rev. Ebenezer Parkman of Westborough "*moderated* and preached," Rev. John Rogers gave the charge, and Rev. Daniel Fuller gave the right hand of fellowship.

The new pastor was a native of Westborough, in this State; and was born in October, 1726. He entered Harvard College in 1744. In July of the following year, he was demanded as a soldier, and cheerfully shouldered his musket, and marched more than a hundred miles to oppose the French and Indians. Having been released by the interposition of his friends, he returned to his studies, and graduated in 1751. He was ordained minister of the Second Parish in Brookfield, June 3, 1752. In the year 1759, he was in the service of the Province, from March 31 to Nov. 15, as chaplain in a regiment under Col. Timothy Ruggles; ministering often on the same day at different stations from three to five miles apart. At the close of the campaign, he, with Mr. Brainerd, another chaplain, had four hundred invalids committed to their charge to march with them to Albany, and to serve both as chaplains and officers. For this service, which he represented to the General Court as tedious and expensive, he received an allowance. In 1762, he went as a missionary to the Oneidas, one of the six nations of Indians; and planted the first Christian church at Onaguagie, on the river Susquehannah. Having established in this place a school for children, and another for adults, he returned, bringing with him four Indian children; whom he sent back again in a few years, after providing them with such knowledge as would be useful to them. He also brought with him a white lad, who had become a complete savage; but, being civilized and educated at Dartmouth College, was employed as an agent of Congress during the Revolutionary War, and was very useful. In 1767, Mr. Forbes was empowered by the Provincial Government to get two males and one female from among the children of the Maqua Indians, in order to educate them on the fund given by Sir Peter Warren.

Mr. Forbes continued at Brookfield till March, 1776; when, having fallen under the groundless suspicion of being a Tory, he requested and received a dismission. His settlement here took place at a time when a deep gloom overspread the town. The people were cut off from their ordinary means of livelihood, and reduced to the necessity of enlisting in the army, or engaging in the precarious employment of privateering. The parish, therefore, prudently provided for a contingency which was not unlikely to happen, and annexed a condition to the proposals originally made to Mr. Forbes, that, in case the parish should be broken up, or he should be unable to perform the duties of the ministry, it should not be obliged to pay him his salary.

Another source of difficulty in the parish was the discontent manifested by the friends of Mr. Murray; several of whom, as members of the church, were made the subjects of discipline by that body. They absented themselves from public worship, and were called upon to give their reasons for so doing: but they declined controversy; and, though they did not satisfy their brethren, they contented themselves with assuring them that "they were influenced by reasons of a purely religious nature, which were entirely between God and their own souls; that they trusted to have a good conscience, and were happy in the belief that Jesus only was appointed their Judge." The church addressed several letters afterwards to these absenting members, of which no notice seems to have been taken; and finally sent one suspending them from communing with that body. The persons thus suspended were —

Epes Sargent, Winthrop Sargent, Ebenezer Parsons, David Pearce, Catharine Sargent, Judith Sargent, Rebecca Parsons, Hannah Tucker, Rebecca Smith, Judith Stevens, Anne Babson, Nancy Saunders, Lydia Prentice, Jemima Cook, and Jemima Parsons. Although but four males are included in the list, it contained the names of two of the most prominent members of the parish, — Epes Sargent and Winthrop Sargent. All these persons had embraced the religious sentiments of Rev. John Murray; and, as they could no longer continue on amicable relations with the church, they wisely declined controversy, and quietly submitted to the sentence that had been passed upon them. A few years after this event, a considerable portion of the congregation ceased to attend upon Mr. Forbes's ministry, and resorted to a place of worship in which the character of the Deity and the ultimate destiny of man were set forth by their favorite preacher in a light no less congenial to their feelings than consonant to their views of religious truth. The parish, however, continued to tax them; and, upon their refusal to pay, endeavored to enforce compliance by legal compulsion: but a long and expensive lawsuit resulted in favor of the seceders, and secured to them the reasonable privilege of supporting a Christian minister of their own choice. A warfare of ten years was now brought to a close; and, though the church and parish were the persecuting party, it can scarcely be doubted that they entered upon a state of peace and rest as gladly as those whom they had vainly striven to hold in religious bondage.

During all this contention, Mr. Forbes took the right position, — that of silence and inactivity. The wise pastor was more solicitous to maintain the peace and harmony of society than to gather to the parish coffers a few grudgingly paid dollars; and, while he undoubtedly considered the seceding members to be in a condition of dangerous delusion, the only means by which he tried to win them back was a constant manifestation of kindness and regard, the memory of which has long outlived that of the ill feeling engendered by the occasion that called them forth.

The remainder of Mr. Forbes's ministry was passed in the quiet discharge of the ordinary duties of his office, which he continued to perform till far advanced in life. In 1804, the health of the venerable pastor began to fail; and on the 15th of December of that year, at the age of seventy-eight, his long and useful life was brought to a close. A short time before his death, the degree of Doctor of Divinity was conferred upon him by Harvard College.

As a preacher, Dr. Forbes possessed respectable talents, and his pulpit performances commanded the attention and approbation of his congregation. He had a sufficient command of language to enable him to write with readiness and to speak with fluency; and many of his sermons were so well received at the time of delivery as to be desired in a printed form. In stature, he was slightly above the medium size; and, in manners and address, gentlemanly and engaging. His countenance bespoke the pure and amiable qualities of his mind, and ever beamed with such unbounded good nature, that he was eagerly welcomed in every social circle. In his intercourse with his parishioners, he suffered no irksome restraint to be felt in his presence; but, on all proper occasions, always strove to excite childhood to laughter, youth to mirth, and mature age to cheerfulness. At the time of his call to this place, his fidelity to the Colonial cause was questioned; but no further proof that his sympathies were all with the popular side need be sought, than his settlement in a parish of undoubted attachment to the principles of the Revolution. His political sentiments, however, were strongly conservative; and they led him to denounce with unmeasured horror the successive revolutions in France, as destructive of all the best institutions of society, and opposed to the highest good of the human race. For many years, he annually preached a political sermon, in which his views of the exciting events of the times were freely and fearlessly stated. French Jacobins and their American sympathizers received little mercy at his hands; and, on one occasion, the severity of his language was accompanied by such earnestness in delivery as to give great offence to a Jacobin parishioner, and cause him to leave the meeting-house before the conclusion of the sermon. The gestures of the venerable preacher are said to have been so violent on this occasion as to send his wig from his head, and throw it whirling down into the deacon's seat below.

The wife who accompanied Mr. Forbes to Gloucester was Lucy, daughter of Rev. Ebenezer Parkman of Westborough. She died Jan. 16, 1776; and he next married, in the same year, Mrs. Lucy, widow of Hon. Thomas Sanders, who survived the marriage less than four years, and died June 5, 1780, aged forty-eight. A few months afterwards, he took for his third wife the widow of Capt. Thomas Parsons of Newbury; who died in Boston, of small-pox, at the house of her daughter, Mrs. Gorham

Parsons, Sept. 19, 1792. Her daughter Mary, wife of Ignatius Sargent, died of the same disease, at the same place, fourteen days after her mother. They both took the disease by inoculation; having visited Boston for that purpose. The fourth and last wife of Mr. Forbes was Mrs. Lucy Baldwin of Brookfield, a sister of his first. Each of these two wives died of cancer; the last on the 13th of March, 1804, after several years of feebleness and pain. Mr. Forbes had two children, — a son and a daughter, — both by his first wife. The son (named Eli) is not known to have engaged in any profession or steady employment. It is said that he was a captain in the army in 1798; that he then joined a regiment stationed at Oxford, in this State, when war was threatened with France; and that, after leaving the army, he went to Baltimore, and was for some time teacher of a school. In that city, or its vicinity, he died. The daughter (Polly) married Peter Coffin in 1773, and died May 18, 1795, aged forty. One of her daughters married Henry Phelps; some of whose posterity remain in town, and are the only descendants here of Rev. Dr. Forbes.

Mr. Forbes's printed productions, besides those published during his ministry at Brookfield, were a Family Book of Sermons; Sermon on repairing his Meeting-house, 1792; on the Dedication of the Town Grammar Schoolhouse, 1795; on the Death of Col. Low, 1797; and the Convention Sermon, 1799.

CHAPTER XXII.

DECLARATION OF INDEPENDENCE. — TOWN CONSENTS TO A STATE CONSTITUTION. — LOAN FOR THE POOR. — ENLISTMENT. — THE PRIVATEER "WARREN." — OTHER PRIVATEERS. — STATE ARMED VESSELS. — TOWN-MEETING. — LARGE CLASS OF POOR. — LOSS OF THE PRIVATEER "GLOUCESTER." — DR. SAMUEL ROGERS. — PRIVATEER "SPEEDWELL." — STATE CONSTITUTION REJECTED. — THE TOWN DELINQUENT. — A COMPANY RAISED. — SMALL-POX. — THE PRIVATEER "STARKS." — DISTRESSED CONDITION OF THE TOWN. — DEPRECIATED CURRENCY AND EXORBITANT PRICES. — THIRD CRUISE OF THE "STARKS." — NOTICE OF OTHER PRIVATEERS. — LOSS OF THE "TEMPEST." — TRUE HISTORY OF REVOLUTIONARY PRIVATEERING A SAD ONE.

THE advice and sympathy of the wise and good pastor — the subject of the preceding chapter — were, at this time, of great value. Questions of grave importance were constantly arising, which, together with the distressed condition of many families in the town, called into exercise all the wisdom, courage, and benevolence of our fathers. The war had borne with great severity upon them; but they did not waver for a moment in the support of their principles. On the 24th of June, the great question of a declaration of independence by Congress came before them at a large town-meeting called on purpose to consider it; and they voted unanimously, if that body should resolve upon the measure, to support them in it with their lives and fortunes. In ten days, the Declaration was proclaimed to the world. The immortal document was read from all the pulpits of Gloucester, and copied into the records of the town.

Another subject of great interest at this time was a form of government for Massachusetts, which came before our citizens on the 20th of September; when they voted their consent, that the House of Representatives, together with the Council, should "enact a Constitution, or form of government, for this State, to be made public for the inspection of the inhabitants before ratification by the Assembly."

Winter was approaching, and the town had no supply of money or provisions in the hands of its officers to relieve the pressing wants of its numerous poor. There was but one resource, which was to authorize a loan for this purpose; and that they adopted. A serious inconvenience, not seemingly necessary, was added to the unavoidable burthens of the people. Tradition states that the gristmills of the town were at this time neglected, and not in working order; and a vote of the town concerning them justifies the statement. It is, indeed, but a few years since an aged female died, who had, during the war, walked from her home here to a mill in Ipswich, with a peck of corn on her back, and returned with it in the same way after it was ground. The wives and mothers of the Revolutionary period were, in Gloucester, the greatest sufferers.

At the close of this year and the beginning of 1777, exertions were made by the town to enlist men for the Continental Army. In December, a bounty of £6 was offered to each soldier; and, in March, it was voted to pay the soldiers who had enlisted, or might enlist, to the number of sixty, the sum of £14 in a town-treasurer's note on interest, payable in three months. Enlistment in Gloucester for the land-service now went on slowly.* Privateering was an employment more congenial to a maritime community; though its profits were uncertain, and its risks great.

The first vessel that put to sea from Gloucester on a privateering cruise was a fishing schooner, called the "Britannia." She was purchased by a company, who changed her name for one which they honored more, — "Warren;" and fitted out during the summer of 1776, under the command of Capt. William Coas. She had eight old guns, mounted on new carriages, and such

* The company now enlisted was for three months' service, and was commanded by Mark Pool. It is supposed to have joined the Northern Department of the American Army; but nothing is certainly known in relation to its particular movements.

small-arms as could be procured; on some of which, the locks were tied with rope-yarns. During the month of September, she captured, and sent into Gloucester, three prizes; two of which were very valuable. The first, which arrived on the 14th, was the "Picary," a ship of about four hundred tons. The name of her captain was Brookholt Cleaveland. She came in under the command of Capt. Harris of Ipswich as prize-master.* Two days afterwards, the "Warren's" second prize came in. She was a brig of about a hundred and twenty tons. She had been on the coast of Africa; but, when taken, she was from Tobago, bound to London, in ballast, with some elephants' teeth and gold-dust. The next prize arrived on the 30th. She was a ship of five hundred tons, called the "Sarah and Elizabeth;" and, when taken, was from Jamaica, bound to London. Her captain's name was Foot. She was captured in the night. The captain's wife and a number of ladies were on board, who were greatly terrified, under the apprehension, that, if any resistance was made, they might be murdered by the Yankees, whom they supposed to be Indians; and, by their crying and screaming, induced the captain to surrender without firing a gun. The next morning, when he saw to what an insignificant craft and small force he had surrendered his fine ship, which he could have defended easily and successfully, he became completely unmanned, and gave vent to his mortification and regret in tears. The ship was sent in under charge of John Somes as prize-master; and was sold the next spring, for a small sum, to Capt. Foot, who remained in Gloucester through the winter.†

---

* The "Picary" was from Tobago, bound to London. Her cargo consisted of 325 hhds. sugar; 161 bales cotton; 168 pipes, 29 hhds., and 10 quarter-casks, Madeira-wine; and some indigo. The carpenter of this ship was Robert Watson, who settled in town, and was the ancestor of persons still living here bearing that name.

† The cargo of the "Sarah and Elizabeth" yielded a large amount of money to the captors. It consisted of 394 hhds. sugar, 180 puncheons rum, 20 casks indigo, 70 live tortoise, 6 casks tortoise-shell, 50 bags cotton, some cash and plate, and a quantity of mahogany. One of the men belonging to this ship (Thomas Moore, a ship-carpenter) settled in Gloucester. He was a superior workman, and was employed after the war, by our merchants, in building vessels. He built, near his residence, on the west side of Annisquam River, the brig "Lightfoot" for Winthrop Sargent; and, at the head of the harbor, the brig "Dolphin" for William and James Pearson.

The subsequent cruises of the "Warren" were not so successful. She was commanded on the second cruise by Capt. John Colson, and took but one prize, — a topsail schooner, with a West-India cargo of sugar, coffee, and cotton. On her next cruise, she was under the command of Capt. Silas Howell, and was captured the third day from home, and carried to New York.*

Another fishing schooner, called the "Langdon," was converted into a privateer; but of her fortune and fate nothing is known. If they were foreshadowed by an accident which befell her at the commencement of the voyage, she was not successful; for, in firing a salute on going out of the harbor, one of her guns burst, and wounded four of her men.

Among the first privateers sent out from this town was the sloop "Union," commanded by Capt. Isaac Somes. She captured a ship bound to Lisbon with a cargo of fish, and a brig laden with salt. The latter was purchased by a company, named the "Gen. Mercer," and fitted out on a cruise, under command of James Babson. On the coast of France, in company with a Philadelphia privateer, she captured two or three brigs, which were sent in there, and condemned.

Five small armed vessels, commissioned by the State this year, made Gloucester Harbor their rendezvous. They were commanded by Capts. Manly, Skinner, Waters, Hibbert, and Burke. They cruised during the day in Boston and Ipswich Bays, generally returning to port at night. Manly captured a brig with a cargo of oats, bacon, porter, and other articles. She was chased ashore by the frigate "Milford," on to the rocks at Brace's Cove, where the prize-crew landed. Capt. Joseph Foster, with a company of minute-men, marched over from town to protect the vessel, in case the frigate should send a force to take possession of her. He got out some of the cargo; but, during the night, a boat's crew from the frigate boarded the brig, and set her on fire, by which she was destroyed.

---

* Capt. Howell was prize-master of the first ship brought into Gloucester which was taken at sea. She was called the "Ann," and was captured by a Philadelphia privateer.

At the town-meetings in the early part of 1777, several matters of interest were considered and acted upon. A letter of thanks was voted to Capt. Andrew Giddings, who had recently made a handsome donation of molasses and flour to the town for the use of the poor. The selectmen, and Committee of Safety, were directed to determine the town's quota of soldiers for the present campaign; and the same officers were to do what they could to prevent any West-India goods and provisions belonging to the inhabitants from being carried out of town for a week. The meeting also voted unanimously to comply with the late act of the General Court, rating the prices of goods and provisions. At this time, too, the following officers were chosen for the militia: Major James Collins, colonel; Capt. Daniel Warner, lieutenant-colonel; Capt. John Row, major.

In May, the representatives chosen were Peter Coffin, Esq., and Daniel Rogers, Esq. The latter desiring to be excused, John Low, Esq., was chosen in his place.

During the summer, the small-pox again made its appearance in town; but it did not spread. A pest-house was built this year, near Richard Varrel's, on a back road leading off from the Manchester Road, just west of Bond's Hill.

As winter approached, the condition of the families of our soldiers became a subject of anxious concern and deliberation. Such was the impoverished state of the town, that it was found necessary to send a memorial to the General Court, stating its inability to comply with the resolves of that body respecting supplies to the soldiers' families; for whose relief, the only apparent resource at this time was a subscription for voluntary contributions. But all the means at the command of the benevolent were hardly adequate to give even a meagre support to the whole number of families depending upon public charity; for, in addition to the common calamities of war, the town was now depressed by the unfortunate issue of one of its privateering adventures.

The most important enterprise of this kind in which our people were engaged, this year, was the fitting-out of the brig

"Gloucester." She was a new vessel, owned by David Pearce and others; and was placed under the command of Capt. John Colson. Great pains were taken with her armament and equipment. She mounted eighteen carriage-guns, and had a crew of one hundred and thirty men, including officers. Confident expectations were entertained of a successful cruise; but it was the unfortunate destiny of this vessel to go down at sea, with nearly the whole company that embarked in her. It is believed that she sailed about the 1st of July, 1777. Not long after leaving port, she captured the brig "Two Friends," a valuable prize, with a cargo of wine and salt, and sent her in under charge of John M'Kean. She also took, on the Banks of Newfoundland, a fishing brig, called the "Spark," having on board part of a fare of fish and some salt. This vessel was brought in by Isaac Day as prize-master. No further tidings of the "Gloucester" were ever received. Various conjectures were entertained as to the cause of her loss, — some founded upon the model of the vessel, and some upon other circumstances; but nothing was ever known concerning it. The number and the names of those who were lost in her cannot now be ascertained; but current tradition has always affirmed that sixty wives in Gloucester were made widows by the loss, and that the calamity overwhelmed the town with sadness and gloom. To the mourners, the following winter was one of unutterable grief; which was somewhat aggravated by the tales which superstition bore to their dismal firesides, that the fate of their friends had been indicated by signs from the invisible world. It was currently reported, and believed by many, that one dark night, about the time it was supposed the ship was lost, a ball of light (called, by seamen, a corposant) was seen to move about the town in a mysterious manner, and approach successively the homes of all who were on board of her; remaining a few moments at each one of them, to indicate the melancholy fate that had befallen the ship and her unfortunate crew.

Among the losses by death in 1777 should be mentioned the decease of Dr. Samuel Rogers, Feb. 18, aged thirty-seven. He was son of Col. Samuel Rogers, a prominent citizen of Ipswich;

and cousin of Rev. John Rogers of our Fourth Parish. Nothing is known of his early education. In 1758, he was attached to the forces sent against Ticonderoga; and, though only nineteen, he served in the capacity of surgeon. By a letter to his father, dated Louisburg, June 21, 1759, it appears that he was then stationed there with a regiment, of which he was an assistant surgeon. He had settled in Gloucester, May 4, 1767; when he married Elizabeth Willis. At the opening of the Revolution, he took an active part in the military preparations then going on, became an officer in the militia, and also had command of a company of minute-men. An obituary notice gives him a high character "as a physician, a soldier, a citizen, a patriot, and a friend." Dr. Rogers left a widow and three daughters.*

Another privateer sent out this year was the schooner "Speedwell;" Philemon Haskell, captain. She captured three fishin brigs, — the "George," "Dolphin" and "Phenix," — each with a part of a fare of fish and some salt. The "George" was sent on a voyage to Bilbao; and, on her return, brought to this town John Beach,† a man whose peculiarities will long keep his name in traditional remembrance. The "Dolphin" and "Phenix" were fitted out to the West Indies with cargoes, and both were

* John, brother of Dr. Rogers, also settled in Gloucester. July 6, 1773, the latter was allowed pay by the town for disbursements on account of this relative, then confined by a broken leg.

† John Beach was an Englishman. He bought the Sanders Estate on Middle Street, and added two stories to the house in a fanciful style of architecture. He also built, on his land there, a rope-walk; and carried on the manufactory of cordage for several years. He was principally distinguished for his wild pranks on convivial occasions. In the latter part of his life, he went to Ohio; and died at Chillicothe, in that State, about the beginning of 1819. By his first wife, — who was a daughter of our eminent merchant, David Pearce, — he had several children. Two sons (William and John) survived their father. The former was representative in 1824 and 1825. Having been a prominent and ardent supporter of Gen. Jackson for the Presidency, he was appointed, in 1829, Collector of the Customs for this district, and retained the office till 1839; when he removed to Chillicothe, where he died Nov. 22, 1840, aged fifty-three. He was a popular man; and, for many years, exercised great influence as the leader of the modern Democratic party in this town. Besides filling the offices already mentioned, he also held that of selectman, captain of the Gloucester Artillery, and colonel in the militia. Col. Beach left a son John, who graduated at West Point, and settled in the Western country. John, the other son of Capt. John Beach, died May 16, 1841, aged fifty-nine, leaving no sons. William, brother of Capt. John Beach (a native of Bristol, England), died here May 29, 1797.

taken by the enemy. The salt taken in the fish-vessels came at a time when it was greatly needed, and was sold for a very high price. Indeed, such was the scarcity of this article about that time, that the attention of our people was turned to the erection of salt-works in several places. They were set up at Norman's Woe, at the Cut, and at Squam.

In the early part of the year 1778, the attention of the town was called to a form of government both for the United Colonies and for Massachusetts. In the preceding November, Congress had agreed upon a plan "of confederation and perpetual union between the thirteen United States." This plan was submitted to the Legislature of Massachusetts, and some of the towns expressed an opinion in favor of adopting it. The representatives of Gloucester were instructed, by a vote of the town, to act on this question as they should judge most for the advantage of the Colonies.

The Constitution for the State was prepared by the Legislature of 1777, and submitted to the people early in the next year. The people of this town, when they elected their representatives for that year, expressed an opinion, that it was best for them to do nothing about forming a Constitution; but gave them no instructions. When the instrument came before them at a town-meeting on the 1st of April, a committee of seven was chosen to take it into consideration, and report at another meeting. It was finally disapproved by the unanimous vote of the town; one hundred and nine persons voting against it. At the town-meeting last mentioned, the Committee of Safety were desired to let the lands belonging to refugees and the subjects of Great Britain, and to sell their buildings.*

* I do not know the name of a single "refugee" belonging to Gloucester who owned real estate. There may have been a few of this class of persons, but certainly no prominent citizen. A subject of Great Britain owned a large lot of land on the westerly side of Short Street, extending from Middle Street to Front Street. It had formerly belonged to Nathaniel Allen, Esq., a merchant of the town, who became bankrupt just before the war commenced. Mr. Allen's mansion was on the Front-street end of the lot, and was taken down about ten years ago. It was a large and handsome house in the olden time; but it became a good deal dilapidated during the war, in consequence of having been used as barracks for the troops stationed here to protect the town.

At the May meeting, Col. Coffin and Col. Low were again chosen representatives. A rate of two thousand pounds was voted for town-expenses; an amount which indicates a considerable progress in the depreciation of the paper-currency. The town, having become delinquent during the summer in furnishing its quota of clothing, and liable to prosecution, voted, on the 20th of August, that the selectmen should represent at Court what had been done, and the reasons why it was impossible to procure more. The selectmen were also desired to notify the people of the several parishes, who could do it, to bring in to them shirts, shoes, and stockings for the army; to make up one hundred and thirty-seven pairs of each, — the required number.

The enemy had at that time a large foree at Newport, which created considerable alarm throughout New England; and it was deemed advisable to attempt their expulsion. For this purpose, several volunteer companies were raised to join the Continental troops, comprising the American Army, stationed there. One of these companies was raised in Gloucester by Capt. Mark Pool, and was in the engagement with the British when the latter made their assault upon the fortifications which the Americans had thrown up near the town. The American Army, as is well known, were obliged to retreat from the island.

During the last four months of 1778, great excitement prevailed in the town, on account of the small-pox. The people had taken a firm stand against inoculation; having voted, in the spring, "to have no inoculation in town on any terms:" but, in October, they were obliged to recede, and provide hospitals in different parts of the town to accommodate the inoculated.* The disease seems to have spread all over the town at this time; but we have no knowledge who were its victims, or how many they numbered.

Great exertions were put forth again this year to fit out another large vessel for privateering; and David Pearce and

* Capt. John Fletcher received the thanks of the town at this time for his generous offer of £100 towards inoculating the poor.

others, with the aid of some of Ipswich, succeeded in getting ready for sea the ship "Gen. Starks." She was a new ship of four hundred tons, built for the owners, and mounted eighteen guns. She was chiefly owned by Mr. Pearce, who is said to have embarked a large portion of his capital in the enterprise. She made two short cruises this year, under the command of Capt. William Coas, but met with poor success; taking only a schooner loaded with salt, and a ship called the "Providence;" the latter, it is supposed, without cargo.

The old privateer, the "Speedwell," was again fitted out this year; but nothing further is known of her doings, than that, on one of her cruises, she had been out but a short time when she encountered a severe gale of wind, in which her guns were all thrown overboard, and she was obliged to return to port.

The business of privateering on a small scale was again resorted to about this time. A boat called the "Trial," with twelve men, twelve oars, and twelve guns, was sent out to cruise along shore. She had a small place built up forward to receive the arms and ammunition, and she carried one sail. The crew went ashore every night to encamp and cook. The commander was Thomas Sanders. On one expedition, they took, off Canso, three coasters; two of which were got safely to Gloucester, and the other was retaken.

The fifth year of the war arrived, and brought with it no alleviation of the suffering and misery which hung like a pall over the town; and, let us add with grateful admiration, it brought no abatement of the firm and patriotic determination of our fathers to contend for their principles to the last. Their resources were again taxed, even beyond their ability to pay, for their proportion of the public burdens; and they were obliged to plead to the General Court for an allowance, and ask that an agent from that body should be sent to view the impoverished condition of the town. They continued, however, to do their best to furnish their quota of men and clothing for the army, and in no case failed to come up to the full measure of every demand made upon them within their means to supply.

In addition to the suffering and distress which the war brought upon the people, they were now afflicted with a loathsome disease, which, in the early part of 1779, had spread all over the town, defying every effort to check it. The year is still spoken of, by some very aged persons, as that in which "the small-pox went through the town." The disease was so widely spread, that all were exposed to it; and the prejudice against inoculation, as the safest way of taking it, yielded to necessity, and the citizens submitted to a general inoculation. Several died; but no particulars have been preserved to inform us how many or what proportion of those who took the disease became its victims. Tradition reports, that of one hundred and ten who, in one of the villages of the town, were inoculated, but two died. The expense incurred by the town, in consequence of this sickness, was considerable, and added to the burden of taxation already pressing so heavily upon the people.

All money transactions were at this time attended with a good deal of embarrassment, and often with considerable loss; for the paper-money had depreciated so much as to be worth no more than about three cents on a dollar. With this miserable currency, and exorbitant prices of all the common articles of living, it is not difficult to picture the condition of the people as one of extreme poverty. Efforts were made by Congress, by the State Legislature, and by Conventions, to mitigate the evils of a depreciating currency, and to thwart the designs of monopolists, extortioners, and speculators. At a meeting held in October, Gloucester approved of the doings of a Convention held at Concord, in July, for these purposes, at which prices were affixed to all the products of the country; but the people did not pay any attention to the acts of the Convention, and no permanent benefit resulted from them. It was found, even in that troubled time, that the let-alone system was the best for trade.

On the 5th of April, 1779, the privateer ship "Gen. Starks" sailed on her third cruise. As this was the most important enterprise of the kind, considering the size of the ship, the number of men enlisted, and the general preparations for the cruise, which was undertaken here during the war, a particular account of it may be deemed worthy of record. She had a crew of a hundred and thirty-five men and boys, and mounted eighteen guns. Her officers were —

William Coas, captain.
Thomas Haskell, first lieutenant.
Job Knights, second lieutenant.
Duncan Piper, third lieutenant.
James Pearson, sailing-master.
Hodgkins, sailing-master's mate.
Edward Bowden, boatswain.
James Snoddy, boatswain's mate.
Philip Priestly, boatswain's mate.
William Thomas, gunner.
Samuel Davis, gunner's mate.
M. Parker, captain of marines.
Jabez Farley, steward.
William Fears, steward's mate.
Jerry Row, armorer.
Peter Dowsett, quartermaster.
Josiah Parsons.
John Gwyer.
Samuel Hodgkins.
N. Perkins, carpenter.
Nathaniel Perkins, carpenter's mate.
Joseph Smith, cook.
John Hardy, cook's mate.
Jack Short, drummer.
David Knights, fifer.
Josiah Smith, surgeon.
Benjamin Somes, captain's clerk.

On the tenth day out, she encountered a gale of wind on the Grand Bank; during which, one of the men (William Steele) was lost overboard. She then cruised to the eastward, and fell in with a brig from Limerick, with a cargo of beef, pork, and butter, which she took, and sent into Gloucester; where she arrived safe, and gave great joy to the people, who were much in want of provisions at that time. She continued on her cruise, without seeing any of the enemy's vessels, till she reached the Western Islands, where she made a ship and a brig to windward. The ship hove out an English ensign, and bore down for the "Starks;" the brig following. The "Starks," outsailing the enemy, took in her light sails. As soon as the British vessels came within gunshot, the ship was found to be a vessel mounting twenty-eight guns; and the brig, one of fourteen. They opened a fire upon the "Starks," which returned for it a broadside at long shot. A running fight was kept up some time; when Capt. Coas justly concluded that it would be only wasting ammunition and uselessly exposing his men to continue the action against such superior force, and hauled off. The brig rounded to, to rake the "Starks;" but her shot fell short. The ship threw one shot into the "Starks's" mizen-mast, five through the boat on the booms, and one into her quarter. The "Starks" then cruised to the eastward, and made a sail; which proved to be the British ship "Porcupine," of fourteen guns. She struck to the "Starks" without firing a gun. Capt. Coas took her guns and light sails, gave the captain some provisions, and restored him his ship. Six of the guns taken from the enemy were mounted on the "Starks's" half-deck, and manned with marines to increase her force. She next fell in with an English brig from Bristol, with an assorted cargo; which was taken, and sent in. A few days after, she took a sloop bound to Oporto; and, after taking off her sails, rigging, cables, and anchors, sank her. After cruising a while off Cape Finisterre and down the Bay of Biscay, the "Starks" put into Bilbao to refit for a cruise homeward. Here the ship was entirely stripped, and her armament was taken ashore. At this time, a sickness — brought on board by one of the men taken from the Bristol brig, and pronounced by the surgeon the yellow fever — broke out among the "Starks's" crew; which made it necessary for Capt. Coas to hire a house on shore for a hospital, where thirty of his men were down at once, a number of whom died. As soon as the "Starks" was ready for sea, the authorities at Bilbao offered Capt. Coas a thousand dollars if he would go out in the bay, and take a warlike vessel, — supposed to be an enemy's cruiser. He accordingly sailed; and, in a few days, saw a brig and a lugger, the latter of which kept to the windward, out of his way: but on speaking the brig (which proved to be a Dane), and ascertaining that the lugger was a Guernsey privateer, he endeavored to decoy the latter down to him by hoisting an English ensign. She immediately bore away, and ran down under the lee of the "Starks;" which, on being hailed, gave the name of an English ship from Whitehaven. The crew of the "Starks" were then mustered to their quarters; the English ensign was lowered, and the American flag run up instead. The British vessel was then ordered to strike to the "Gen. Starks." She was then about fifty yards to leeward; and, instead of striking, she luffed, intending to cross the "Starks's" fore-foot, and escape on the wind. But the "Starks" luffed at the same time, and gave the schooner a broadside; upon which she surrendered. The schooner mounted eight guns, and was manned with sixty men, eight of whom were wounded by the broadside from the "Starks." One of these (the steward) had both legs shot off, and died the next day. The prize was a good deal crippled, but was got into Bilbao, and sold for sixteen hundred dollars; to which was added the sum stipulated for taking her. Here Capt. Coas was now joined by a number of Americans, who came from different places to obtain a passage home. They were mostly prize-masters and others who had been retaken, and some of them belonged to Gloucester. The "Starks" sailed for home about the 20th of July. When a few days out, she decoyed an English cutter; but, while the lieutenant and boat's crew were on board the "Starks," her real character was discovered, and the cutter escaped by outsailing her. In about ten days after this, she made a sail under a cloud of canvas, and came up with her after a severe chase of four hours. The enemy, finding he could not escape, hauled up his courses, and prepared for action. After a brave resistance of two hours, he surrendered to the "Starks," having first sunk his mail; for the vessel proved to be an English packet from Jamaica, bound home. When he struck, all three of his topmasts were shot away. He had six men killed and nine wounded. The "Starks" had one boy killed and five men wounded; one of whom was shot in both legs, and in the head by a musket-ball, besides being struck betwen the shoulders by a splinter.* One of the wounded men had his right hand shot off. The prize was put in charge of Duncan Piper, and ordered for Gloucester, where she arrived safe. The next prize taken by the "Starks" was a brig, with a cargo of fish, from Newfoundland, bound to Lisbon. Of fourteen guns which she showed, ten were Quakers (wooden guns); useful sometimes for

* The man thus severely wounded was John Low, whom I give as authority for many of the facts, contained in this work, concerning Gloucester privateering. His father was Stephen Low,—a descendant, probably, of Thomas Low of Ipswich; from which town, or its vicinity, it is supposed that he removed to Gloucester. Stephen Low married Elizabeth Woodbury of Hamilton, and died May 8, 1790, aged seventy: his wife died Nov. 28, 1797, aged seventy-two. In consequence of the loss of one leg,—which was supplied by a wooden one,—John Low abandoned a seafaring life, and established himself in a small shop on Front Street. This shop was a famous resort for the principal men of the town many years. Mr. Low died Oct. 30, 1845, aged eighty-five. He had a brother (Francis) who settled in Manchester, and died there in August, 1837, aged ninety.

intimidation, but availing nothing for purposes of attack or defence. This vessel was also sent to Gloucester, where she arrived safe. Soon after this, two other fish-brigs were taken, and sent in. More of the English fishermen might have been taken; but Capt. Coas prudently suffered them to escape, as his crew had been greatly reduced to man the prizes, and twenty of his men were on the sick-list: besides, he had on board eighty-four prisoners. The "Starks" was, therefore, steered for home; where she arrived on the 15th of September.

The future history and fate of this ship, for want of the dates of her various cruises, will be traced here. During the winter of 1779–80, — which was one of excessive coldness, — she lay frozen up in the harbor from the middle of December to the 20th of March. Her provisions and wood were hauled alongside by teams. The harbor was frozen over from Black Bess to Dolliver's Neck, — a state in which it has not been seen for many years. It it said, that, at this time, a number of persons went on the ice to Ten-pound-Island Ledge, and took the marks and bearings. The two next cruises of the "Starks" were not successful. On the last, she encountered a severe gale of wind; during which, all her guns but five were thrown overboard. With these, however, she engaged an English ship of superior force; but found her too heavy, hauled off, and returned to Gloucester. Her next cruise was attended with better luck. She was commanded, as she had been on the two previous ones, by James Pearson. He sailed directly to the mouth of the St. Lawrence, in order to intercept the Quebec fleet. He was in the fog there several days; but, as soon as it cleared away, he discovered three ships of this fleet, which were captured, and sent to Gloucester. Their names were the "Detroit," "Polly," and "Beaver." Three vessels of this fleet were also taken by the ship "America" of Newburyport, commanded by John Somes of this town; and three by the ship "Brutus" of Salem. The "Starks" returned to Gloucester, having made one of the best cruises ever made in America in so short a time. Having been so fortunate on this cruise, Capt. Coas was induced to take command of her again. He was out but a week, when he was captured by the ship "Chatham," and carried to Halifax. It is said that the "Starks" was converted by the English into the "Antelope Packet," which was wrecked at the Pellew Islands. After remaining some time at Halifax as a prisoner, Capt. Coas went on board a cartel with some of his officers, and sailed for Boston. The same night, a violent storm arose; in which, it is supposed, the cartel foundered, as she was never again heard from.

Another cartel, having on board some of the "Starks's" crew, put into Gloucester. The men were landed at the town-landing, in the Harbor Cove, most of them sick, and some not able to walk. A few of them could only get up the hill by crawling on their hands and knees; but, by the sympathy and kindness of friends, they were soon made comfortable, and restored to health. A few of the "Starks's" crew were on board of a cartel which got embayed in a violent snow-storm in Ipswich Bay. The men were sick, and the captain was a stranger in that place; so that the vessel would probably have been wrecked, if Capt. William Allen of Gloucester — who was then lying sick in his berth — had not offered, if he could be helped to the place, to stand in the companion-way, and pilot her over Squam Bar.

For the history of Gloucester privateering during the remainder of the war, dates are wanting; and it may, therefore, be properly given in this place, arranged under the names of the different vessels with which it was carried on.

Schooner "Wasp." — She was first commanded by Isaac Somes. She took a brig from Ireland, laden with provisions, and sent her into Gloucester. She next sailed on a cruise, under the command of John Somes, and fell in with the privateer "Harlequin" of Salem. While in company, they made a sail, which proved to be a ship from Jamaica, with a cargo of rum. They both gave chase; but the vessel struck to the "Harlequin" before the "Wasp" got up with her. Capt. Somes offered to put some of his men on board the prize to bring her in, and share the proceeds; but the captain of the "Harlequin" would not allow any participation. On the arrival of the "Wasp," her crew claimed a share of the prize-money, in proportion to her men and guns; and, on the refusal of the other crew to pay, they carried their claim into court, where their case was managed by Theophilus Parsons, and resulted in their favor. It is said that Mr. Parsons made a conditional agreement with the claimants, by which he received for his services three hogsheads of the prize-rum.

Brig "Wilkes." — This vessel was built by David Pearce; and, after making a mercantile voyage to the West Indies, was fitted out as a privateer, under command of Job Knights. She was taken, and carried into Newfoundland; but was afterwards retaken by some men belonging to Marblehead, and brought back to Gloucester. Capt. Pearce purchased her, and sent her out again, under command of John Beach. She was taken on this voyage, off the West Indies.

Brig "Success." — This vessel was also built by David Pearce. He sent her to the West Indies as a letter of marque. She was taken on the passage home, and carried into Halifax.

Brig "Friendship." — She was built by William Pearce and others, and was commanded by Isaac Elwell. On a voyage to the West Indies, she captured a small brig of a hundred and thirty tons, with a cargo of rum.

Ship "Gloucester Packet." — This was the Jamaica packet-ship taken by the "Starks." She was purchased by David Pearce, who sent her on a voyage to Cadiz as a letter of marque; John Beach, commander. She captured a brig called the "Mary," with a cargo of flour.

Schooner "Speedwell." — She was owned by William Pearce, and was fitted out as a privateer; but took nothing.

Schooner "Union." — She belonged to William Gee. Daniel Parsons commanded her, and had a crew of thirty men. She took a brig from Ireland, with beef, pork, and clothing.

Shallop "Speedwell." — She was purchased by a company, and decked over, leaving a large hatchway to serve as quarters for the men in action. She had four swivels stepped in the combings of the hatch, and small-arms according to the number of her crew, which consisted of twenty-five men. She was commanded by Thomas Saunders, and sailed for a cruise off Canso to intercept some of the vessels trading between that place and Halifax. She was chased ashore in the Gut by some British cruisers, and lost.

Ship "Tiger." — She was a privateer of sixteen guns; John Tucker, commander. She took one prize, which was retaken, and carried into Halifax. The "Tiger" was soon after taken, and carried into the same port.

Brig "Ruby;" Solomon Babson, commander. — She captured a brig from Ireland, laden with beef, pork, and butter; which was sent to Gloucester.

Brig "Robin Hood." — This was a small brig, mounting nine guns, under the command of Sargent Smith, who performed a notable exploit in the capture of a British packet of greatly superior force. When Capt. Smith fell in with this vessel, he had no expectation of taking her; but, as his brig was a fast sailer, he thought he might venture near enough to give her a few shot in passing. He accordingly brought his guns all on one side; and, when the brig came abreast of the packet, gave her a heavy broadside. The effect of this was such, that another one was given; upon which the ship surrendered. She mounted sixteen guns, and had on board a hundred men, including forty passengers. The prize-crew put on board felt it necessary for their safety to confine the prisoners in the hold of the ship. She was carried into Martinico. The prisoners were sent in a cartel to Antigua, and exchanged for Americans who had been taken in a privateer under charge of Duncan Piper.

The "Civil Usage." — This was a privateer, carrying sixty men, commanded by John Smith, who lost his life in a rash attack upon an English transport-ship having eight hundred persons on board. Capt. Smith fell in with this ship, and, as soon as he got within fighting distance, opened a fire upon her; which was returned from the transport. He continued the fight with great bravery and spirit, till it was made certain that he must haul off or surrender. In the early part of the engagement, he received a wound from a musket-ball, in the throat; and while remaining on deck during the action, as he attempted to swallow some water, he could only prevent the liquid from taking a wrong direction by pinching his wound with his finger and thumb. He died of the wound, and his vessel put into Martinico.

The last two vessels were owned, wholly or in part, in Newburyport; probably by persons formerly belonging to Gloucester, or having business connections with its citizens. Persons of other towns were interested, in a few instances, in vessels hailing from Gloucester.

Ship "Tempest." — This vessel was built by a company, and fitted out for the West Indies as a letter of marque. The day of her sailing is not known; but it is supposed to have been in 1782. Her captain was Isaac Somes. William Oxden was first mate; and Nathaniel Low, second mate. The religious feeling of the people was greatly shocked at the name given to this ship; and, when they saw the appropriate emblems and devices with which her bow and stern were adorned, they indulged the most melancholy forebodings concerning the punishment that might overtake what they deemed a daring defiance of the power of Him who rides upon the whirlwind and directs the storm. And when, not many weeks after she sailed, tidings were received of her foundering at sea, with all on board, in a violent tempest, the sufferers were looked upon as men who had devoted themselves to destruction by embarking on board of a doomed ship, rather than such as had perished in the ordinary providence of God. She sailed from Gloucester in company with the ship "Polly," Capt. Joseph Foster. They kept company till they got into the Gulf Stream, where they encountered a severe gale, attended with the most terrific thunder and lightning. During one brief flash, by which several men on board the "Polly" were stunned, the "Tempest" was seen by Capt. Foster, a short distance off; but, when the next flash enabled him to discern distant objects, she was missed, and never again seen. Capt. Foster supposed that she was taken aback, and went down stern foremost. She had a large crew, of which the greater part probably belonged to Gloucester. It was a singular circumstance, that the builder of the ship was killed by lightning the next year after she was lost.

The history of Gloucester privateering during the Revolutionary War, here brought to a close, is believed to contain some notice of nearly every enterprise of that kind undertaken in town. True, it is, for the most part, but a mere sketch of voyages; but even some account of these may be deemed worthy of preservation, when it is considered what interests, hopes, disappointments, sorrows, and sufferings were connected with them. A true history of our Revolutionary privateering would be a record of individual experience; of widows' broken hearts; of orphans' bitter tears; of the agonies of men struggling with the ocean, in the face of death; of physical suffering in prison-ships; of wanderings in foreign lands, without friends, without money, and without health; and, worst of all, of the demoralizing influences of a practice which every enlightened conscience declares to be at war with the justice of God and the happiness of man.

CHAPTER XXIII.

INDEPENDENT CHRISTIAN SOCIETY.

Distinguishing Sentiments of Universalists. — John Murray, first public Preacher of them in America. — His Early Life. — Comes to America. — Visits Gloucester. — Has his Home here. — House of Worship built for him. — Lawsuit. — He visits England. — Returns, and is ordained in Gloucester. — His Removal to Boston, and his Death. — His Character. — His Wife and Family. — The Society incorporated. — Meeting-House.

The benevolent affections of the human heart rejoice in the paternal character of the Deity as revealed in the New Testament; and they reject with horror the doctrine, that sins committed in time can only be expiated by eternal punishment, — a doctrine which, although accepted for many ages by the popular belief, can be maintained as a part of divine revelation only by false interpretations of Scripture, and which is clearly disproved by the plain declarations that teach the final salvation of the human race. These are the distinguishing sentiments of Universalists, whose first organized body in America was formed in Gloucester, under the name of the Independent Christian Society.

The doctrine of future eternal punishment was denied, in an early age of the church, by one of its brightest ornaments; * one who was among the most eminent of that period for genius and learning, and a just and pure life. It was also opposed by religious teachers in succeeding times; and a few solitary voices had been raised against it in America, prior to the period when

* Origen.

the opposition took the form of a regular religious denomination in this town. About that time also, an author, supposed with good reason to have been a learned doctor of divinity of the popular creed, minister of the First Church in Boston,* after a close and critical study of the Scriptures for several years, came out an anonymous advocate of the doctrine of universal salvation. But the first public preacher of this doctrine, in this country, was JOHN MURRAY; to whom the little company of believers here attached themselves with a constancy and affection that remained unshaken till death.

This preacher — the first minister of the Society of Universalists in Gloucester, which was called into existence by his preaching — was born in the town of Alton, in Hampshire, England, Dec. 10, 1741. He was the oldest of a large family of children. He appears to have possessed from early life keen and sensitive feelings, which rendered him peculiarly susceptible of religious impressions. His parents were both very rigid Calvinists; and so strict was his father in his attention to the concerns of religion, that he was regarded by his friends as a person of eminent sanctity. The parental discipline to which the son was subjected was of the severest kind; and he often passed, he says, "from the terror of the rod to the terrifying apprehensions of future and never-ending misery." At the age of eleven, his family removed to Ireland. Here his father joined the Methodists, whose preacher (Mr. John Wesley) distinguished him in a particular manner. The social worship of this sect excited a powerful influence on the feelings of the son, and he soon became a class-leader and preacher in their connection.

Little is known of his early education. Soon after the establishment of the family in Ireland, an Episcopalian clergyman of the neighborhood, who was strongly attached to the father, and who had charge of an academy of high repute, generously offered to take his son into his own family, prepare him for the university, and procure him admission to it. This offer was declined; and nothing further is known concerning his early opportunities

* Rev. Charles Chauncy, D.D.

for acquiring knowledge. A large portion of his youth was passed in a state of religious excitement, with some intervals of melancholy. Having lost his father by death, he went to reside in the family of a wealthy friend, where he was much caressed; but failed to find sufficient contentment to extinguish the desire that now possessed him, and the resolution he had formed to go to London. His patron reluctantly parted with him; but he generously supplied him with money: and, in a short time, the youth was intoxicated with the pleasures and gayety of a London life. The means of dissipation were soon exhausted. His mind was aroused to the sin and folly of his course, and his heart became affected with deep and sincere repentance. With the aid of friends, he found employment; but he was not designed for business. His former habits of religious devotion returned, and much of his time was given to public worship and private prayer. He became a constant attendant upon the preaching of Whitefield, and visited many other places of public worship; finding among religious people many admirers, some of whom suggested that he should assume the office of a public teacher.

At one of the religious meetings, he met with a young lady named Eliza Neale, with whom he formed an acquaintance that soon ripened successively into intimacy, love, and marriage.

So high an opinion was entertained of his talents, that he was urged by his religious friends to attempt the reclaiming of a young lady of remarkable piety, who had become a convert to the doctrines of Mr. Relly.* Mr. Murray had, on one occasion, seen a number of Relly's followers gathered in an open field for worship, and could hardly restrain his indignation at the thought of the blasphemies to which they had assembled to

* James Relly gathered a society in London, to which he proclaimed the final salvation of mankind. He entered into public life as an associate of Whitefield: but, after a time, renounced his Calvinistic opinions, and "taught that Christ, as a Mediator, was united to mankind; and, by his obedience and sufferings, had as fully restored the whole human race to the divine favor, as if all had obeyed or suffered in their own persons." — "He believed in a resurrection to life and a resurrection to damnation. Believers only, he thought, would enjoy the former; and unbelievers, after death, would dwell in darkness and under wrath till the final restitution of all things." Mr. Relly died about the year 1783, in the full faith of the doctrine he had preached. — *Mod. Hist. of Universalism. Mosheim: Ch. Hist.*

listen, and that the blasphemer was permitted to promulgate his sentiments. His zeal in opposition to the preacher led him to undertake with alacrity the task of bringing the young woman back from her errors. But he found this no easy matter. Her questions perplexed him; he became embarrassed; and the result of the errand was a tacit admission that she had gained the advantage, and a most cordial hatred of the sect she had joined.

A manuscript was shown to him about this time, written by one of his religious friends, with a view to confute the "Union;" a work in which Relly had unfolded his peculiar religious views: but the arguments failed to convince him that Relly was in error, and a perusal of the "Union" itself and the preaching of Relly brought him to the belief, that "the testimony delivered by him was the truth of God."

This led to his expulsion from Mr. Whitefield's society, and the loss of the friendship of his religious associates. Severer troubles soon followed. His wife and infant son were removed by death. He had incurred debts which he was unable to pay; for which he was arrested, and thrown into prison; where he remained till released by the interposition of his wife's brother. By the death of his wife, for whom he felt the strongest love, he was thrown into a state of melancholy and despair; and acting under the incitement of the accounts of America which he heard from a gentleman from this country, whom he met at the house of Mr. Relly, he resolved to enter upon new scenes in a distant land, where a somewhat eventful and unexpected career was to open before him. He embarked on his passage to cross the Atlantic in July, 1770.

It does not appear that he came to America with the purpose of making public proclamation of the doctrine he had embraced; but an acquaintance, commenced under very peculiar circumstances, with a man named Thomas Potter, led him to appear as a public preacher. He made Potter's house his home, but travelled a good deal, preaching in many of the large cities and towns amidst great opposition and heavy persecutions. He found many, however, by whom he was warmly welcomed; and in Portsmouth, N.H., he received an invitation to settle. In November, 1774, being then in Boston, he was visited by Mr. Sargent of this town, and invited to come to Gloucester. In compliance with the invitation, he came down immediately, and was received with much kindness, and hospitably entertained by the Sargent Family. Mr. Chandler, the minister of the parish, being sick, the elders and deacons waited upon Mr. Murray, and conducted him to his house. He obtained permission to preach in his pulpit; and the sentiments he advanced found a ready reception in many hearts. About four years prior to this period, the writings of Mr. Relly had been brought to this town by an Englishman named Gregory; and with such effect had they been perused, that Mr. Murray found here, as he states, "a few persons upon whom the light of the gospel had more than dawned." More than three-quarters of a century have passed away since that memorable visit; and, with this lapse of time, all personal recollections of the excitement it produced, and the deep impression it left, have ceased to exist. Tradition reports that his first sermons were not of a controversial character, but were designed to draw his hearers to the love and service of God by a touching and vivid portrayal of the divine benignity.

After remaining in town nine days, he returned to Boston, where he continued about a month, preaching to large congregations, in face of a strong opposition, and notwithstanding every means was restorted to to prevent his speaking in public. In December, he again visited Gloucester, and was cordially received by his friends. "Here," he writes in his journal, "my God grants me rest from my toils; here I have a taste of heaven. The new song is sung here, and 'WORTHY IS THE LAMB' constantly dwells upon their tongues."

The Parish Meeting-house was now closed against him; and his followers assembled, at stated times, at the house* of Winthrop Sargent, where their religious worship was held. On this visit, he fully stated his views to Mr. Chandler. They met, of

* This house was in the rear of the large three-story house afterwards built by Mr. Sargent on Front Street, at the head of Duncan Street.

course, his decided opposition, and drew from him a warning address to his people; which was read to them, and afterwards printed in the "Essex Gazette."*

Surrounded by a small circle of admiring friends, Mr. Murray now concluded to make Gloucester his home, occasionally visiting other places, as he might be called; but the enemies of his doctrine here now made open demonstration of their hostility, which gave rise to gloomy forebodings as to his prospect of happiness and rest in this place. In May, 1775, he received and accepted an invitation to serve as chaplain in the Rhode-Island brigade, and repaired to the camp at Jamaica Plain. An effort was made by the chaplains of the Continental Army to remove him; but the commander-in-chief would not grant their request. He continued with the army till obliged by sickness to leave, when he returned to Gloucester, and remained until his health was restored. After his recovery, he made a successful appeal to his friends in the army, in favor of that large class of our people who were reduced by the war to the last stages of indigence; and obtained considerable supplies of necessary articles, which were distributed among them. But neither his benevolence, nor the friendship of several of the most respectable families in town, could shield him from the effects of that "exquisite rancor of religious hatred" which had gained possession of the hearts of his enemies, and was expressed in very decided acts of outward hostility. Personal violence was threatened, and a mob was collected; which was only dispersed by the repeating, by one of the elders of the church, of the timely advice addressed by Gamaliel to the persecutors of the first apostles of our religion. The shafts of persecution fell harmless at the feet of their object, while the impotence of their rage only served to redouble the fury of his opposers. They affected to believe him to be a political character in disguise; and, under this pretence, pro-

* This address was also printed in an appendix to a pamphlet published by Rev. John Cleaveland of Chebacco Parish, Ipswich, entitled "An Attempt to nip in the Bud the Unscriptural Doctrine of Universal Salvation, and some other Dangerous Errors connected with it, which a certain Stranger, who calls himself John Murray, has of late been endeavoring to spread in the First Church of Gloucester;" &c.

ceeded against him as a vagrant. On the 27th of February, 1777, he was cited before the Committee of Public Safety (all the members of which, then present, being his inveterate enemies), and subjected to an insulting examination, which he sustained with dignity and Christian forbearance. He was warned to leave the town before the 1st of March following; and the acts of the committee were approved at the next town-meeting, by a vote of fifty-four in their favor, and eight against them. But this ebullition of religious malevolence spent itself in vain. Mr. Murray remained, and his opinions rapidly spread.

On Christmas Day, 1780, Mr. Murray's adherents first assembled for public worship in a small building they had erected for that purpose. About two years before this time (Jan. 1, 1779), they had adopted a covenant, in which they professed themselves an independent church of Christ, and received Mr. Murray as their minister. The State Constitution was adopted the same year; and, as no particular form of association for religious worship was therein prescribed, the friends of Mr. Murray believed that the covenant they had signed constituted them a religious society within the meaning of that instrument. They also believed that this covenant constituted him their ordained minister (as the word "ordain" signifies no more than "to appoint"), and that no public acts or ceremonies were necessary to confer upon him the powers and privileges possessed by those whose ordination had been attended with these circumstances. Holding these opinions, they refused to pay the taxes assessed upon them for the support of the parish minister; and thereupon their property was seized, and sold at auction. An action was instituted for the recovery of this property, and was brought in the name of Mr. Murray, on the ground that a particular clause of the Constitution secured to him all money paid by his supporters for the support of public worship, if they wished it to be so applied.

This lawsuit involved principles affecting the rights of all religious sects, and was prosecuted with all the spirit and determination that a desire for the enjoyment of religious freedom could inspire. Eminent counsel were engaged on both sides. Mr. Rufus King, Mr. Sullivan, and Mr. Tudor, managed the case for the plaintiff. The parish employed Theophilus Parsons and Mr. Bradbury. The case was kept in court three years. Several trials and reviews were had; and at last, in June, 1786, a conclusive verdict was obtained in Mr. Murray's favor. At the last trial, the interpretation of the Constitution by the judge, different from what it had been on previous trials, was altogether in favor of the plaintiff; and his instructions to the jury were clear, and just in conformity with this change of opinion: but so difficult was it for them to yield to the spirit of religious toleration, that, after being out several hours, they returned to court, saying they could not agree. The judge again addressed them, and they retired once more. The foreman (Mr. Tracy of Newburyport) made an earnest appeal for Mr. Murray, urging that his supporters had as good a right to worship God according to the dictates of conscience as others had, and that he was prepared to render a verdict accordingly. He then composed himself to sleep, with the remark, that they might arouse him as soon as they could agree. During the night, they came to an agreement; and, in the morning, went into court with their verdict.*

Mr. Murray usually spent his summers in travelling; and, at the time of the termination of his long-protracted law-case, he was absent in Connecticut. The rejoicing of his friends soon reached his ears, and the occasion of it afforded him much satisfaction. Their trials, however, had not yet reached their end. The enemies of Mr. Murray, seizing the advantage that might be gained by the doubts concerning his legal qualification to perform the marriage ceremony, entered a complaint against him, and obtained a verdict which condemned him to pay a fine of fifty pounds. The Judges of the Supreme Court were of opinion that he was not an ordained minister in the sense of the

---

* Tradition has handed down the following anecdote connected with this trial. Mr. Giddings, a Quaker, was on the stand to testify that Mr. Murray's supporters had a house of worship. It had been objected against them that they had a secret, which, in the state of public affairs at that time, might be dangerous to the liberties of the people. Mr. Giddings, being questioned on this point and pressed rather closely, at length answered, "Yes, they have a secret; and it is this (quoting Ps. xxv. 14): 'The secret of the Lord is with them that fear him, and he will show them his covenant.' They have no other secret, to my knowledge."

law, as the forms of his ordination were not sufficiently notorious. As this decision rendered him liable to prosecution for every marriage he had solemnized, he was advised to leave the country until the interference of the Legislature could be obtained in his behalf. He accordingly embarked for England in January, 1788; and, after a boisterous passage, had the satisfaction of landing on his native shores, and meeting once more his venerable mother. During his absence, his friends made application to the Legislature for his relief. The petition of his congregation here was lengthy and earnest; and an act was obtained, indemnifying him from all pains and penalties for having performed the marriage ceremony under a mistaken conviction that he was qualified so to do. Before the end of the year, he returned to the United States. He was now relieved from the apprehension of persecution through the courts of justice; but his friends, wishing to place the pastoral relation in which he stood to them beyond all cavil or doubt, and to put him on the same footing with other ministers with respect to ordination, appointed Christmas Day, 1788, as the time for carrying their desires into effect. The ceremony of the occasion was simple, but solemn and impressive; and was concluded by a sermon from the newly ordained pastor, from Luke x. 2: "The harvest truly is great, but the laborers are few."

Mr. Murray remained in Gloucester about four years after his last ordination. In 1793, he was induced by the solicitations of his friends in Boston to become their settled minister; and, on the 23d of October, was installed in that place. His connection with the society there was a happy one, and continued till his death; which, preceded by six years of helplessness, took place Sept. 3, 1815. He died at the age of seventy-four. During his long confinement, much of his time was employed in perusing the Scriptures; and his dying words testified that his religious belief remained unchanged to the last.*

* Mr. Murray published "Letters, and Sketches of Sermons," in three volumes. He also wrote an account of his early life, which is contained in a Memoir of him published by his wife. From this Memoir I have derived many of the facts in my narrative of his career.

The last of the early friends and supporters of Mr. Murray have, within a few years, passed away. They dwelt with delight upon the memory of his earnest and effective preaching, and of the joy and gladness diffused by his presence in the social circle. The undecayed freshness of their love and admiration preserved the vividness of their recollection of his person and manners. They described him as a man of medium stature; of intelligent countenance, beaming with good nature and benevolence; and of easy address and gentlemanly deportment. Respecting his character, the sober judgment of age did not reverse the opinion they adopted at a period of life when enthusiasm exercises an influence upon the reason. They admitted that suspicions were entertained as to the purity of his heart; but these, they asserted, were wholly groundless, and only cherished in minds from which religious bigotry had banished every sentiment of justice and charity. They pointed to the fact, that he enjoyed during his long life, and retained to its close, the confidence and love of many, as much distinguished for virtuous conduct, and a high regard for morality, as any of those who assumed to judge him; and, in absence of all proof that their friend was unworthy of their affection, they clung to the memory of his virtues, and cherished and defended it to the end.

As a preacher, Mr. Murray excelled in the power, ease, and grace with which he presented his views in extemporaneous discourse. In this he was highly gifted. He possessed not only facility, but felicity, of diction; for the fluency with which he spoke was always accompanied by language so well chosen as to need no correction, and by such a charm of voice and manner as always left a deep impression upon his hearers. His society increased in number from year to year; and, at the time of his departure, had, through its numerical strength and the virtue and intelligence of its members, attained such a position as to secure it from the persecution with which bigotry and intolerance sought so zealously at first to destroy it.

The bitter persecutors of Mr. Murray were undoubtedly sincere; but scoffers may be so as well as bigots. Happily, no religious oppression can now find justification on the plea of honesty. Time has fully proved the groundless nature of their alarms as to the immoral tendency of the doctrine he advocated; and candor will allow, that the early believers here in the final salvation of all men will as well stand the test of that trial which judges the tree by its fruits as the members of any other religious sect. Many of them lived to extreme old age, and died in faith, declaring their love for the Saviour, whom they had found the strength of their hearts here, and whom they believed they should have as their portion for ever.

After remaining a widower several years, Mr. Murray married, soon after his return to the United States from his visit to England, Mrs. Judith, widow of John Stevens, and daughter of his early and constant friend, Winthrop Sargent. Her former husband had died some months before in St. Eustatia; whither he had fled from creditors, whose just demands the bankrupt condition of his affairs rendered him unable to satisfy. She was born in 1751, and was gifted with uncommon beauty of person, and a superior mind, which was cultivated and enriched by education. In 1798, she published the "Gleaner," in three volumes. The articles contained in these volumes were originally published in the "Massachusetts Magazine." They present the sentiments of the writer on various subjects, but possess the unity of a narrative in the romantic story of "Margaretta." She appeared as an authoress under the name of "Constantia," and with a strong desire for literary fame; but her writings have failed to secure her the posthumous celebrity she craved, and the "Gleaner" has now no readers out of the small circle of literary antiquaries. Mrs. Murray also wrote poetical essays, which were published in the "Boston Weekly Magazine," with the signature of "Honora Martesia." The fruits of her union with Mr. Murray were — a son, who died at birth; and a daughter (Julia Maria), who married A. L. Bingaman, Esq., of Mississippi, and died in the autumn of 1822, leaving a son, who married a Miss Livingston of New York. Mrs. Murray died at Natchez, June 6, 1820, aged sixty-nine.

The society was as yet only an association of individuals. In

1785, they organized themselves under a "compact," containing a few regulations for their future government. This provided for no compulsory payment for the support of public worship, which depended entirely on the voluntary contributions of the members, who, in 1788, found it necessary to sign an obligation to pay their several parts of Mr. Murray's salary according to the proportion of their town-tax. The sum thus raised in that year for their "dear brother in God, and Christian teacher," was one hundred pounds. The "compact" was signed by upwards of eighty males, who were probably all of the supporters of Mr. Murray at that time. It is handsomely written on parchment, and has been carefully preserved. Finding no form of association they had yet tried suited to their wants, they obtained from the Legislature, in 1792, an Act of Incorporation under the name they at first adopted.

The meeting-house erected by Mr. Murray's friends was a small building, without belfry or other architectural ornament. It stood on the westerly corner of Spring and Water Streets, and was taken down about 1805, and removed to the farm of Col. Pearce, where it has ever since been used as a barn.

CHAPTER XXIV.

Loss of Polls. — One-sixth of the People living upon Charity. — Loan to hire Soldiers. — Further Loans. — State Constitution. — Town Delinquent. — Prospect of Peace. — Ship "Harriet" cut out of the Harbor by the Enemy. — Recaptured by our People. — The Town-Treasury. — Peace.

Five years of war had passed, and our fathers had given pretty good proof of their ability to come at last triumphantly out of the struggle; but the prospect immediately before them was gloomy, and their present condition was such as to require the brightest hopes of future good to cheer them on in their contest for independence. One item of the town's loss during those years speaks volumes of suffering and sorrow. The number of its ratable polls had decreased from one thousand and fifty-three in 1775 to six hundred and ninety-six in 1779. Three hundred and fifty-seven of our people had perished at sea, fallen in battle, died in prison-ships, or in some way had become victims of the war. The wail of woe from broken-hearted widows and destitute orphans, bereaved parents, and afflicted friends, is just dying away upon our ears, leaving a sad impression of the depth of misery from which it issued; but all the wretchedness and suffering resulting from this great sacrifice of the youth and the active men of the town can never be described or conceived. The poverty which was one of its unhappy consequences is sufficiently attested by the fact, that seven hundred and fifty, or about one-sixth of the whole population, were at this time living chiefly upon charity. The town did not furnish enough from its soil to support its people two months in the year; its shore-fishery was unproductive for want of a market; its few privateering enterprises had yielded the means of subsistence to a small number only; and its foreign trade was nearly annihilated.* From all these considerations, it may readily be seen that Gloucester had thus far borne a heavy share of the burdens, sacrifices, and sufferings of the war; but, great as these had been, another year of trial was before them.†

Of the State's quota, in 1780, of four thousand men to join the Continental Army for six months, the number to be raised here was thirty-two: which the town voted, June 19, to raise by a tax; and chose a committee for that purpose, with authority to borrow sixty thousand dollars.‡ On the 6th of July, the same committee were authorized to borrow sixty thousand dollars more: and, if they should agree with any soldier who would prefer to take a town-note, the Treasurer was directed to give one payable in six months; such notes to be reckoned as a part of the sum the committee were authorized to borrow. Three men were procured at six thousand dollars each; and the town then agreed to offer that sum for the remainder; and if, upon an average throughout the State, the bounty amounted to more than that, to secure to each soldier the difference.

On the 17th of July, the town voted to raise a tax to procure thirty-eight men as militia, and offered £300 per month to each man who could be procured for three months' service. Authority was also given for another loan of $60,000. On the 7th of August, they voted to raise $51,060 to pay soldiers; and directed that all money and goods furnished by the inhabitants

* About seven hundred tons of our shipping employed in foreign commerce, and several valuable cargoes, were captured by the enemy in 1779.

† It was at this period of great poverty that a large troop of women, in want of the necessaries of life, marched to Col. Foster's store, and made known their determination to supply themselves with provisions and groceries from his stock, in spite of all resistance. Some of the number were prepared to take an exact account of the articles delivered to each person, with reference to payment, if they should ever be able to pay; but, pay or no pay, they would have them, and proceeded to help themselves accordingly. This merchant was one of the most ardent patriots of the town; and it is related of him, that his conduct on this occasion proved him to be one of the most benevolent: for the tale of suffering and destitution that the women had to tell so touched his feelings, that he liberally supplied their wants, and dismissed them with words of the utmost kindness and sympathy.

‡ The paper-money was now depreciated to about one-seventieth of its nominal value.

for the campaign be carried to the several committees, for them to lay before the selectmen in order for payment. In addition to all this heavy expense for raising soldiers, the town's quota of provisions and clothing for the army was to be provided: and, to meet the charge of these items, a tax of £40,000 was levied; and the selectmen were authorized to borrow that sum in anticipation of payment. It would afford gratification to know some particulars concerning the supply of such demands upon the pecuniary resources of the town; but all we can know of the financial operations of our fathers, at this period, is the little that is contained in the votes which they passed in town-meeting. The valuations and tax-lists of the time have not been preserved.

While the people were making these great efforts to secure the independence of their country, the prospect of final success encouraged them to set about the formation of a Constitution for their future government. In February, 1779, the Legislature recommended that a vote should be taken in the several towns of the State in relation to this measure; and, a majority having expressed an opinion in favor of it, a Convention of Delegates assembled in September, at Cambridge, to engage in this important and interesting work. The delegates from Gloucester were Winthrop Sargent, Joseph Foster, Peter Coffin, Samuel Whittemore, and Epes Sargent.

The Convention completed their work in March, 1780; and submitted the Constitution they had agreed upon to the people of the State. A town-meeting to consider it was held here on the 8th of May; when a committee was chosen to report concerning it, at an adjourned meeting to be held on the 22d of the month. On that day, the Constitution was accepted by a vote of forty-eight in its favor. No negative votes are recorded; nor is any thing more known of the debate on the subject than that Capt. Sargent and Col. Foster said that they objected to it.

The first election under the Constitution was held on the 4th of September. The vote of Gloucester was small. Hon. John Hancock had thirty-six votes for Governor, and Hon. James Bowdoin twenty-nine for Lieutenant-Governor. Peter Coffin,

Esq., was the first representative from the town under the new government.

In January, 1781, the town was called upon to raise forty-eight men for the Continental Army; and although it voted a tax of £1,000, in silver money, to pay the bounty authorized by the State (fifty dollars to each man), the committee appointed for raising the men reported in April that they had not procured them. While the town was thus delinquent, the General Court passed resolves inflicting a heavy penalty on those towns that failed to procure the soldiers which they were called upon to furnish. Our people voted to petition for an abatement of the men ordered to be raised, in consideration of their condition, — of the inroads that had lately been made upon them, and the vessels that they had lost: but they continued their efforts to get them; and, in August, it appears that the men had been procured. The town's quota of clothing and provisions for the army this year appears to have been raised without complaint; though the taxation necessary to procure it, with the other assessments made upon them, must have been a grievous burden to the people.

In the early part of 1782, a ministry, supposed to be favorably disposed in regard to a peace with the United States, came into power in Great Britain; and measures were taken on both sides to bring about that desirable event. Besides the first great question, — the acknowledgment of independence, — the people of Gloucester were interested to preserve their ancient privileges on the fishing grounds. The importance of an article to secure these privileges in any treaty of peace that might be made had been considered by the Legislature of the State and by Congress; and this town, at a meeting on the 28th of January, gave its representatives instructions concerning it, declaring that such an article was "of the utmost consequence, not only to this town, but to the State in general."

At the March meeting in 1782, the selectmen were instructed to petition the General Court for a guard to be stationed in the town; but they did not anticipate an event that soon occurred, showing the necessity of such protection. On the night of the

31st, the ship "Harriet," commanded by Capt. John Beach, lying in the harbor, loaded for Curaçoa; and, having but two men on board, was cut out by some men sent in from an English fourteen-gun brig. On the previous day, a black-looking boat, apparently a fishing vessel, was seen to come into the harbor, and anchor outside of Ten-pound Island; but, as only two or three men appeared on deck at a time, she attracted little notice. The "Harriet" belonged to David Pearce; who, on rising from his bed on the morning of April 1, missed his ship from the place of her anchorage, and discovered that she was outside of the harbor, running off in an easterly direction, with a strong, fair wind, and having in company the small vessel seen in the harbor the day before. No time was to be lost in taking measures for her recapture. Accordingly, Mr. Pearce proceeded immediately to the Meeting-house, and rang the bell with violence until a general alarm was given. It then became a matter of inquiry how the ship was to be retaken; and this was soon settled. The ship "Betsey," belonging to the same owner, was then lying across the dock, at the head of his wharf, for the purpose of being graved. She had no ballast, or goods of any kind, on board; and was entirely dismantled, having her top-yards and rigging all down, leaving only her lower masts standing, with the topmasts launched.

It was determined to put this vessel in order, and start in pursuit of the captured ship as soon as the tide (which was now at the lowest ebb) would serve. Volunteers in great numbers attended to the necessary preparations; and, while these were going on, a fine crew of about one hundred men were enlisted for the enterprise. The rigging was replaced, sails were bent, ballast, stores, guns and ammunition were taken on board: and, as soon as there was sufficient water, the ship began to move from the dock; the men all the while at work on the rigging and in bending sails, and receiving articles from gondolas alongside as she was moving into the outer harbor. The wind being light, she was assisted by tow-boats in getting out of the harbor. About one o'clock, these were all cast off, and the ship proceeded on her cruise, under command of Capt. Joseph Foster; the owner of both vessels, Capt. Pearce, being also on board. The direction which the "Harriet" had steered had been observed; and it was supposed to be the captor's intention to take her to the enemy's station, on the eastern coast. Capt. Foster accordingly took an east-north-east course; and, in the mean time, had his ship put in complete order for action. She was pierced for twenty guns; and as her armament was complete, and her crew brave, and animated with the strongest feelings of resentment, success was certain, if they should be so fortunate as to overtake or intercept the enemy.

Great was their joy, therefore, when, at daylight the next morning, the captured ship was seen from deck, in company with the brig and boat. She was soon overtaken, and given up without an effort on the part of the enemy to retain her. The brig, indeed, was glad to escape from the now dangerous company. Capt. Foster gave chase to her; but as she was some distance ahead, and as night was coming on, and they had achieved the object of the enterprise, the pursuit was abandoned, and the course of the two ships changed for home. There were several jolly fellows on board of the "Betsey;" and as provisions, wines, and liquors in abundance had been provided, the night was passed in merriment, and in rejoicing over their success. The prize was put under charge of William Pearce; and both vessels arrived in the harbor the next afternoon, to the great joy of the inhabitants.

The news that the "Harriet" had been cut out was received in the principal towns on the seaboard very early, and preparations were made in several of them to recapture her. The privateer ship "M. de La Fayette" started in pursuit from Salem a little after one o'clock, and returned the next night; an armed vessel was rowed out against the tide from Newburyport for the same purpose; and the new privateer ship "Resolution," belonging to Beverly, sailed from Portsmouth the same afternoon: but they all returned to port without seeing the enemy or his temporary prize.

The sequel of this event revealed the fact, that the brig was sent by Capt. Mowatt from the British station on the Penobscot, under the command of a midshipman, with particular orders to cruise off Cape Ann; to take a fishing boat, and man her well, and, if an opportunity presented, send her into Salem, Beverly, or Marblehead; to cut out any armed vessel that might be fitting away from either place; and, in case of success, to proceed to the English station. The boat was manned with twenty-five men, and came into this port about a fortnight before the "Harriet" was cut out. They found this vessel nearly ready for sea, with a valuable cargo on board; and so reported on their return to the brig. They convinced the commander of the brig that they had been on shore here, by producing a hat and some blocks they had stolen out of a schooner. They said that no military watch was kept in the town, and that the stores might be broken open, or the ship cut out, without danger to themselves. The enterprise was accordingly resolved on; and, but for the zeal and spirit of our people, would have been accomplished. But the worst feature of this transaction remains to be told. Daniel Somes, a native of the town, and having many friends in it, was one of the party on board the boat; and, in all probability, greatly assisted them by his knowledge of the harbor and town. Where he joined the British, and for what reason he traitorously abandoned his home and country, no one knows.

The surrender of the British Army at Yorktown on the 19th of October, 1781, was the last great military event of the Revolutionary War; and Gloucester was thenceforth relieved of one of the heavy burdens the contest had laid upon the town, — the furnishing of its quota of soldiers for the army. It was a welcome relief: for it had at last become so difficult to hire men for this purpose, that the town was obliged to petition the General Court to accept a partial fulfilment of its last requirement of the State for soldiers; and the last act in town-meeting, in relation to this subject, was a vote to apply to the Legislature to be released from the payment of fines which the town had incurred for not raising their quota.

Being happily rid of this external pressure, the town now gave attention to its financial concerns. Into these the depreciation of the paper-money had introduced a good deal of confusion; and the conduct of the Treasurer seems not to have been satisfactory to the town. As some of the assessments, during the last few years, had been laid in specie, and some in the depreciated paper-currency, it may be inferred that the balance at any time in the treasury would be represented by both kinds of money. At the March meeting in 1782, Nehemiah Parsons was chosen Treasurer in place of Jacob Allen. A committee to examine the state of the town-treasury had been chosen several weeks before. Having had two added to their number afterwards, they made a report to the town in May, which was read and accepted. By this report, it appears that the balance in the late Treasurer's hands was upwards of thirty-four thousand dollars; about one-half of which was justly due from him in specie, at the rate of seventy-five dollars in bills for one dollar in specie, and the rest in the Continental money. The report accuses Capt. Allen of some improper transactions with reference to the paper-money: but he declined paying over his balance in any currency but the depreciated paper; whereupon the town ordered the new Treasurer to lay an attachment upon his estate. How the matter was finally settled, is not known. The report of this committee makes no mention of the debts of the town at this time, and nothing appears to show the amount of them; but it was probably considerable, and existed in the form of outstanding town-orders. All persons having these were notified in May, 1784, to bring them to the Treasurer, in order that a list might be made, and a tax raised to pay them off.

In April, 1783, proclamation of a suspension of hostilities between Great Britain and the United States was made by Congress. On the 3d of September, the Definitive Treaty of Peace was signed at Paris; and, on the 22d of October, the joyful intelligence of this fact was received in Gloucester by the arrival here of the ship "Robin Hood," Capt. Smith, from London. We have no account of any public rejoicings on this occasion; but, though many internal difficulties remained to be surmounted, every heart was happy that the war was terminated, and the great blessing of independence secured.

CHAPTER XXV.

VIEW OF THE TOWN AT THE CLOSE OF THE WAR.

THE Revolutionary period is an epoch in the history of Gloucester, on which the mind dwells with mingled emotions of pleasure and pain. The men and women who bore its sufferings and achieved its triumph have all passed away, and the stream of time is fast bearing into oblivion the traditions that tell of their sorrows and their joys. Let us, therefore, before giving them a parting benediction, linger a while around their homes, and gaze upon the dwellings, of which nearly every one had, during the war, been the scene of some severe form of human distress. Many of these abodes are still standing; and, with the aid of a few venerable citizens who were children at the close of the Revolution, we may fill out a picture, and obtain a pretty correct view of the town as it then appeared.

The Meeting-house Green will afford a favorable spot from which we can look abroad upon the original settlement. Just below, stood then, as it stands now, the venerable mansion, built, and occupied many years, by Rev. John White. Looking farther towards the south, might be seen, on the road leading to the Harbor, three more large houses, still standing; the largest of which was also built by Mr. White, and was his home when he died. A few small tenements might also be seen in the same direction, on the left; but on the right, around the burying-ground, and on the edge of the river, where several of the first settlers lived, not a house was now to be seen. East of the Meeting-house, on the opposite side of the road, was the large gambrel-roofed house, still standing, built by Col. William Allen, and then owned and occupied by John Low, jun. Farther east, on the road to the Mill, stood the house built by Joseph Allen about a hundred years before. Near by, on the same road, might have been seen in more ancient times the houses of Rev. John Emerson and Landlady Judkin, and a few other early settlers; but, at the period of the Revolution, these had disappeared. On the road leading over Fox Hill were several small dwellings, the homes of some of our soldiers and seamen. Some of them still remain, now dilapidated and untenanted. On the northerly side of the Meeting-house Green, on opposite sides of the road, were the residences of Col. John Low and Rev. John Rogers; the latter still standing. Farther along, on Ferry Lane, at the Ferry itself, and on the road to Ring's mill, were several small houses; some of which we yet see there. On this road, there stood also, on the farm yet in possession of one of his descendants, the residence of William Pearce,—afterwards a distinguished merchant of the town. A short distance beyond his house, on the opposite side of the road, was the dwelling occupied not long before by Dr. Samuel Plummer. A little farther on, close to the Milldam, on a spot over which the road now passes, was a large gambrel-roofed house, somewhat famous in later years as the place where Methodism was first preached in Gloucester. On the two roads diverging from this spot,—one to the point between the two rivers, and the other to the Squam-Parish line,—and on the by-ways connected with them, may yet be seen a sufficient number of the buildings that stood on them in the Revolutionary time, to give one a pretty correct idea of the appearance of the settlement then.

In another part of the ancient settlement, the scene is wholly changed. Parallel to the highway leading, by the river-side, from the Mill to Squam, and separated from it by elevated land, the visitor to that region sees a short road; from the ends of which, two other roads extend far into the pasture till they come together at a point. For most part of the distance, these roads are still well defined by stone-walls, and may be safely, though not comfortably, travelled in a carriage. Various conjectures have been offered respecting the inducements that led to the peopling of this remote and sterile spot: but it is sufficient to know that the land cost little or nothing; and, barren as it was, would yield vegetables, pasturage, and fuel. At the period of our history of which we are now writing, about forty houses were scattered along the sides of these roads; and the whole district was known by the appellation of Dogtown. At the place where they met, stood a large house, of the gambrel-roof style; the site of which is still indicated by the cellar, around which are yet visible the foundations of out-buildings and a ruined well. In 1814, this building was hardly habitable; and, in that year, its last tenant, Abraham Wharf, sought relief from poverty, and the accumulated sorrows of more than threescore and ten years, by putting an end to his existence, under a rock, where he had crawled for that purpose. Many of the other dwellings were of the same shape as that just noticed, but of smaller dimensions; and a few were low, one-story tenements, with a sharp roof. Most of them had, during the war, been the homes of men who served their country on the battle-field or the ocean; and most of them long afterwards continued to be the abodes of widows of fallen soldiers, or sailors who had gone down at sea. In the parish in which this district was situated, there were living, twenty years after the war, sixty of this unfortunate class; a number not much exceeded, probably, by the married females then residing there. Many of these poor widows resided in the old houses in Dogtown; and the last of them are still remembered, as they were seen bearing to market the berries and herbs which yielded them a scanty support.

> "But now the sounds of population fail;
> No cheerful murmurs fluctuate in the gale;
> No busy steps the grass-grown footway tread;
> But all the bloomy flush of life is fled."

The poor widows have all found rest in the grave; and the old dwellings that scarcely afforded a shelter for their declining years have also disappeared: but the ancient cellars, the grass-grown roads, and the traditions of the place, still impart a melancholy interest to the deserted hamlet.

The portion of the town just described — the seat of the first meeting-house, of the first schoolhouse, and, for many years, of the larger portion of the inhabitants — had, at the commencement of the Revolution, reached the maximum of its growth. It then contained about a ninth of the property; and, probably, about a sixth of the population of the town. In both these respects, it has been losing in rank ever since; though, such is the force of habit, it is still customary to call it Town Parish, and to speak of going "up in town."

Before passing to a view of the settlement at the Harbor as it appeared seventy-seven years ago, some account should be given of the previous growth of that part of the town. Of the first settlers of the town, or those who were here before 1651, twenty-eight became permanent residents; of which number, ten appear to have lived at the Harbor. Six of these had their houses on or near what is now Front Street; two were at Vinson's Cove; one at the point called, in our later history, Duncan's Point; and one lived at the Cut.

One of the first roads in the town, without doubt, was the present road, leading nearly in a straight line, for about a mile, from the north-west part of the Harbor Cove to the Meeting-house Green. Diverging from this, near the foot of Governor's Hill, a path led along over the ridge back of the two coves here mentioned, and joined on what is now called Union Hill, — a shore-path or road, that connected at the Harbor Cove with the one leading to the "Plantation." The former of these paths was the origin of Back Street and Prospect Street. It is not known when or by whom the first house was built upon it; but it does not appear that any person except William Coleman had lived there before 1700. The shore-path was laid out as a public highway, twenty-one feet wide, in 1698; and, in later times, became known according to its present divisions of Front Street and Spring Street. At the commencement of the last century, the growth of the settlement at the Harbor had been so slow, that probably not more than twenty families were then living there. Babsons, Collinses, Elwells, and Princes were still living on the homesteads of their fathers, on Front Street; where, soon after this time, Nathaniel Ellery and Job Eveleth took up their abode. Both of these men were active shipwrights, and each built several small vessels during the period of activity in that business heretofore noticed.

Of those who had moved into town since the first settlement, Card, Duncan, Thomas Sawyer, and James Wallis, fixed their abodes at the Harbor, — Wallis, it is supposed, at the foot of Governor's Hill, near the Swamp; Sawyer, at the Beach; Duncan, at the point which has since borne his name; and Card, on a spot, near the water-side, a few rods south of the eastern end of Front Street, where still stands the house, which, according to tradition, he built and occupied. This venerable dwelling was built, without doubt, before the close of the seventeenth century, and is supposed to be the oldest house in town. In size, form, and internal arrangement, it is a specimen of the best houses of the time of its erection; and as such, and as the only architectural relic of the early period of our history in the part of the town we are now describing, an engraving of it is here presented.

When, soon after 1700, the people of the town actively engaged in the building of vessels and in the maritime employments of fishing and wood-coasting, the Harbor section acquired several new residents, and began to gain that preponderance in wealth and population which it has ever since retained. The margin of the shore at the head of the Harbor became gradually dotted with houses; and Eastern Point, where Robinson and some of the Elwells seem to have been the first to locate, was found, in 1728, to have fifteen families at least. Now also the unoccupied land between the two highways came into use for house-lots. A portion of this unoccupied territory was swampy land; and, in the early period of our history, was covered with water. There were suitable sites for dwellings, however, sufficient for a large increase of population; and a new street, laid out over it in 1737, gave evidence of prosperity and growth. This street was at first called Cornhill Street, but soon exchanged that for the name of Middle, which it has ever since borne. On this street, in the next year, a few wealthy citizens built a large meeting-house, the first at the Harbor: and, finding a majority of the parish to be now living nearer to the Harbor than to the "town," they procured the removal of their minister to the new house of worship; and finally, by the secession of their brethren of the ancient settlement, became themselves the First Parish. In 1755, the new parish had gained so much upon the other parts of the town, that it had attained in wealth and population nearly to an equality with the aggregate of all the other parishes, as has been seen on a previous page: but reverses by war, shipwreck, and the political troubles preceding the Revolution, checked this gain; and, during the next twenty years, its proportionate increase was not so great. It contained, however, in 1775, more than one-half of the property of the town. No census of that period gives the whole number of inhabitants; but, from such data as we have, it may be estimated at nearly five thousand, of which about one-half were living in the Harbor Parish. The larger portion of the people of this parish resided in the central village; and the rest were scattered along the highways in the outskirts, and in the little hamlets at Freshwater Cove, Eastern Point, and the Farms.*

* The number of polls in 1775 was 1,053; and, if the ratio of these to the population was the same then as it is now, it would give, as the whole number of inhabitants at that time, 4,945. Distributing these among the several parishes according to the valua-

In each of the last-named places, some memorials of the Revolutionary period still remain. In the first of them may have stood, at the close of the war, about a dozen houses; two of which, on the south side of the road (the habitations of Dollivers and Babsons), have since fallen to ruin. The places of others have been supplied by new tenements; but the whole number has not been much increased. On Eastern Point, there were, it is said, at that time, but fifteen dwellings. Among those which have since disappeared were the "great house" of Capt. Robinson; the Elwell House, on the side of the way going up the hill, on the spot where the centenarian Robinson had lived; the Hidden House, on the opposite side; and the Tarbox House, at a little distance off, in the pasture. Not far from the "great house," near the water-side, was the residence of Capt. William Coas, who had often filled his house with captured property, but who died poor, though leaving a trunk-full of Continental money. A few of the ante-Revolutionary dwellings are left in this locality; but the march of improvement has obliterated almost every thing that could remind one of that time. At the Farms, it is not so. There were standing there, at the close of the Revolution, fifteen or sixteen houses, mostly of the one-story, gambrel-roof style. Several of these yet remain, and the natural features of the spot have undergone little change. Nearly all the occupants of these abodes were of the old families of Rowe, Parsons, and Witham; and nearly all of them had been severe sufferers by the war. Six sons of one family are reported to have been its victims.

The houses standing in the time of the Revolution, that still remain, are mostly of the gambrel-roof shape; and differ from each other but little in form, though much in size. This style

---

tion of each in 1779, we have the following division of the population in the year first named: —

First, or Harbor Parish	2,565
Second, or West Parish	895
Third, or Town Parish	558
Fourth, or Squam Parish	655
Fifth, or Sandy-Bay Parish	372

These proportions, of course, are only approximate; but they are near enough to give a pretty correct view of the rank of each parish in respect to population.

seems to have prevailed about fifty years, and to have gone out of favor entirely before the end of the last century. In the Harbor Parish, there yet stand about one hundred houses of this class; all but two of which date back beyond the memory of any living citizen. Many of them are scattered along the old streets of the central village, and are associated with interesting persons or events of the Revolutionary time. The three avenues already noticed were still the only streets of the village, at that period; with the exception that an ancient path, connecting the upper and lower streets, had become the residence of a few families. This path is our modern Pleasant Street. The ledges and rocks by which it was formerly disfigured have disappeared; and other changes have been so great, that it is only by two of the five old dwellings still standing on it that it would be recognized by one of its primitive inhabitants. At the close of the war, it had on the westerly side, between Middle Street and Back Street, three houses: one of which was the Gibbs House, on the corner of Middle Street; and another, the residence of Dr. Witham. On the opposite side of the street were five dwellings. One of these, at the lower end of the street, on the spot now occupied by the Custom House, had a large garden attached to it, and was the residence of Epes Sargent. Passing up the street, we find the others occupied, in the order in which they stood, by Nymphas Stacy, Capt. John Babson, John Oakes, and Solomon Ingersol, unless the latter had already moved away. These five houses are still standing, though only three of them remain where originally located.

On the north side of Back Street, and its continuation, Prospect Street, there stood twenty-two houses; which, with the exception of two that were at different times destroyed by fire, yet remain; and nearly all of them are unchanged in outward appearance, save by the addition of paint. On the south side of these streets were but seven or eight houses, five of which may still be seen there, and, as well as most of those on the opposite side, can be readily recognized by the style of their architecture. Though exhibiting a great change and improvement since the Revolutionary period, these two streets preserve, probably, more of their ancient look than any other part of the Harbor. One of them could also show for many years the last relics of a bygone and now-forgotten state of society; for it was on Prospect Street that two venerable old slaves — Gloucester and Bacchus — had their homes as freemen, and died nearly fifty years ago, one about ninety, and the other almost a hundred, years of age.

On Middle Street, there yet stand seventeen dwellings that were built before the war; most of which were erected by merchants and ship-masters, and were in the best style of their time.* Not more than six have, since that date, disappeared; and it is not difficult, therefore, to present a view of the street as it then looked. At the easterly end, on the north side, was the Gibbs House; which at the close of the war, or not long afterwards, was the residence of Thomas Sanders, the schoolmaster. Next to this, on the spot now occupied by the rear end of the Baptist Church, its front standing on a line with the street, was a gambrel-roofed house, where James Prentice kept a tavern. The next houses were those of Capt. John Matchet, Capt. William Dolliver, and Hon. Thomas Sanders; all now standing as they then stood, with the exception of Mr. Sanders's house, the upper part of which has since been altered. Adjoining the lot of the latter, westerly, was that of the First-Parish Meeting-house, whose dark and frowning side rose from the street-line of the lot. West of the Meeting-house, the space was unoccupied as far as the path which afterwards became School Street. This path had been used many years. It had two branches: one leading to a few houses on the south side of Back Street; and the other up by the Windmill, on Windmill Hill, where the Collins Schoolhouse now stands, and onward to the road going "up in town." Next to this path, westerly, on the spot occupied by the Orthodox Meeting-house, was a small house, of a date prior to that of any now standing on the street. It must have been one of the first houses erected on it; and it

* Mr. Chandler's journal shows the date of erection of two of these houses. "1760, June 16: Mr. Whittemore's house raised, in the afternoon." — "1764, July 10: Mr. Sanders's house raised."

was the last to fall, having stood till about 1824. In size and appearance, it was much like the Card House, represented on a previous page. Its occupant for many years was Josiah Haskell, long the sexton and tithing-man of the parish. Adjoining this house, on the west, was a small shop, in which Haskell worked at his trade (that of a tailor) in company with Daniel Witham. Next came in succession, as they now stand, four gambrel-roofed houses; the first of which was occupied by Nehemiah Parsons, afterwards a merchant of Boston; the second, by Madam Rogers, widow of the minister of the Fourth Parish; the third, by William Parsons, who also became a merchant of Boston; and the fourth, by Philemon Haskell as a tavern. This building merits a moment's attention. It was originally of large size for a private residence: but it was necessary to add to its accommodations to make it convenient for a tavern; and, for that purpose, an unsightly projection was set up, covering one-half of its front, and extending on to the street. This unsightly excrescence remained till a few years ago; when the building was restored to its ancient form, and the street was also relieved of its only disfigurement. A new generation watched the progress of the work with interest only in the great improvement going on; but occasionally a veteran of the Revolution would tarry on the spot, and make the old rooms alive again with the life of the olden time. Perhaps Haskell inherited this house, and with it the vocation of host, from his mother, who, a hundred years ago, kept the fashionable boarding-house of the day. Not far from Haskell's tavern, extending nearly to the western end of the street, was a wide, open, swampy space; part of which is now occupied by the Universalist Meeting-house, and the handsome avenue leading to that building. No street connected here with Back Street; but the swamp was crossed by a row of stepping-stones, that led to the lane now known as Pine Street, where two or three houses were already erected. Next to this open space were the two houses still standing at the end of the street, — one occupied by Francis Low, and the other by Rev. Eli Forbes; the latter so much changed in outward appearance, that its original owner (Deacon William Parsons) would not recognize it now as the place of his earthly abode. Continuing from Middle Street to the Cut, we find on the north side of the way a row of eight houses of the old style, two of which date their erection since the war. The first in the row was the residence of Daniel Rogers, and was moved by him to its present position from the land in front over which the street now passes. Returning through Middle Street, the first house on the south side was Mr. Whittemore's, still standing, with the addition of a third story. Next came a large, vacant space; and then the residence of Col. Coffin, yet remaining, at the head of Short Street, which, at that time, was but a foot-path. This house had previously been occupied, and was probably erected, by William Stevens, a merchant and prominent citizen a century ago. Between this house and the lane now known as Centre Street were four dwellings, three of which still remain. The first had been recently erected and was occupied by John Stevens. The land in front of his house, extending down to Front Street, was laid out in terraces, and tastefully arranged as a flower-garden, as befitted the home of the accomplished lady of the mansion.* Next, and near to this house, was one that had been owned and occupied by Rev. Samuel Chandler; but was now, or about this time, the residence of Dr. John Manning. Then came the house of James Hayes, a recent settler, and afterwards a leading citizen. The next house was that of Capt. Andrew Giddings, which stood near the lane, and was taken down forty years ago. Between this lane and that which afterwards became Hancock Street was an unoccupied, open space, upon which were several locust-trees; but the most striking object on this spot, remembered by any aged citizen, was a whipping-post, where the last punishment of this kind in town was inflicted upon a woman for theft, about eighty years ago. On the space between Hancock Street and Pleasant Street we still see three houses of the olden time, the first of which was the residence of one of the most distinguished patriots of the town, — Col. Joseph Foster. The next was famous several years before the war as Broom's tavern; and is said by some to have been occupied by

* Afterwards Mrs. Murray.

Prentice, also, as a public-house. It is probably the oldest building on the street. The last of these three was the one-story, gambrel-roofed house, standing on the corner of Pleasant Street. Before and during the Revolution, the famous barberess (Rebecca Ingersol) and her daughter had their shop in the south-east room of this building; and by professional skill, and lively and intelligent conversation, made it a noted place of resort for the merchants, ship-masters, sailors, and soldiers of those times. Next, and near to Broom's tavern, was standing, at the close of the war, a house that is supposed to have been long occupied, previous to that period, by some of the Ellery Family. Its occupant then was Epes Ellery, a son of the first Nathaniel. This and the Giddings House are the only houses on the south side of the street that have fallen since the Revolution, with the exception of a small tenement that stood near the easterly end of the street, and was the home of a German family named Hoffains.

To complete our view of the Harbor Parish as it appeared at the close of the Revolution, it only remains for us to pass along the ancient shore-path, or highway as it had then become, leading from the Cut to the head of the Harbor. At the Cut, two houses of the three which then stood there yet remain; the other having since yielded to time and decay, after sheltering four generations of the Stevens Family. The house first approached on coming into the village is said to have been occupied during the war as a tavern, with the sign of a pine-tree; and to have been somewhat noted for an annual convivial assemblage of the negroes of the town. On the right of the way passing to Front Street, nearly the whole space, as far as the water-side, was covered with fish-flakes; no memorial of that day now remaining, save a single small house of the style then so popular. At the entrance of Front Street were two houses, now standing, but showing no marks of their venerable age. The one on the right was the residence of Nathaniel Ellery; and that on the left had been long occupied by Col. John Stevens, but had now come into possession of Daniel Rogers, a prominent merchant, and was his home for the rest of his life. Passing along, with the north side of Front Street in view, was first seen, on the spot where the Gloucester House now stands, a small building, occupied as a mechanic's shop, in the rear of which was a small tenement belonging to the early period of our history, and standing down to a recent time. Between these buildings and Short Street, no part of the space was occupied, except that on the corner of the last-named street, where stood the Allen House, heretofore mentioned. On the opposite corner of this street stood the mansion, built, and occupied nearly fifty years, by Dr. William Coffin; one of the first three-story houses erected in the town. Next, and several rods distant, was the house of Capt. James Babson, on the spot which had been the home of his ancestors for several generations. A part of this house still remains; but no traces of its antiquity are preserved. A little farther on stood a building familiarly called Joe Sargent's; where Eldad Prindall did most of the tailoring of the town, and where, at an earlier date, Mrs. Prince kept a house of entertainment, and made, according to tradition, the first coffee drank in Gloucester. Between this building and Centre Street were two, that still stand, owned or occupied by Col. Daniel Warner, who had a blacksmith's shop in or near one of them. On the corner of Centre Street stood a small tenement, where lived a woman then known as "Granny Keeley." Crossing this street to the opposite corner, next appeared Deacon Kinsman's dwelling, yet standing, though considerably changed in outward appearance. Then came the little shop of John Dane; next, the dwelling-house of the latter; and then the house of Capt. Samuel Babson. All but the last of these are still standing, and bear the look they have worn for a hundred years. The one last named was violently shaken by the great earthquake of 1755; about which time, the venerable merchant (Samuel Stevens) who owned it was carried from it to his grave. The next building stood on the corner of Hancock Street, and had been long occupied by Nathaniel Ellery; but was now the residence of David Plummer, who had a shop in the easterly end of it. It was a large, gambrel-roof house at this time; having attained that shape by successive additions to the small dwelling supposed to have been built by Mr. Ellery in the previous century. On the opposite corner of the street, we still see the residence of Deacon Hubbard Haskell; one of the only two houses on Front Street yet occupied by descendants of those who lived in them a hundred years ago. Leaving this, however, we begin to mark again the changes of time; for the two houses next to Deacon Haskell's have disappeared in the march of improvement. The second of these two houses was, during the latter years of the last century, the noted tavern of Benjamin Somes; noted not so much for its entertainment to travellers, as for the jolly and occasionally turbulent demonstrations of our own citizens within it. Between this house and Elder Warner's, on the corner of Pleasant Street, were two or three small buildings; one of which was the blacksmith's shop of Mr. Warner. The house of the latter still stands, — the oldest on the street, without doubt; for it is known to have been erected before 1710. Returning through Front Street, the first house on the south side was Capt. William Pearson's, previously the residence of Dr. Samuel Rogers, and just now changing its ancient appearance. Next came a large house, mentioned in a previous chapter as Mrs. Perkins's tavern; occupied, at the time of which we write, by Capt. Coas Gardiner, who married her daughter. This house has long been down. The next building was the gambrel-roof house, still standing, with one end near the street-line, then owned and occupied by James Porter. Between this house and one built by Abraham Sawyer, about 1760, at the head of David Pearce's (now Central) Wharf, were four or five small buildings, principally used as mechanics' shops. The house last mentioned was occupied by Mr. Pearce during the war; soon after which, he built the house still standing on the opposite corner. Leaving this spot, we come to a wide, unoccupied space, where persons yet living have picked berries on land now the most valuable of any in the town. This vacant territory is said to have extended nearly to that part of the street, opposite the foot of Short Street, where stood a small shop, occupied by Edward Northey, a goldsmith. A few rods from Northey's shop, at the head of what was then called Long Wharf, was another small shop; which, after making several migrations in the street, finally left it for another spot. Between Long Wharf and the end of the street, besides one or two buildings of inferior character, there stood two dwellings of a better style, — the homes of William Murphy and John Logan. Turning into Washington Street, we see changes at almost every step. On the left, a large ledge of rocks rose above the surface, extending to Middle Street, and re-appearing at the opposite corner. At that place stood a small schoolhouse, the only one in the village. It was erected, several years before the war, by private subscription; and is supposed to have been occupied by the Grammar School. A single house on Granite Street, and a cluster of four or five near the junction with High Street, some of which are still standing, were the only other buildings on that side of the street. On the opposite side, with the exception of the houses on the corners of the streets leading into this old highway, but one house could be seen, — a large gambrel-roof one, still remaining.

Let us next pass over that part of the old shore-path which is now Spring Street. Beginning at the corner of Pleasant Street, we find there the house supposed to have been built by Col. Epes Sargent. It was occupied by his descendants of two generations; and stood, with various alterations, till a recent time, on the spot where it was erected. A short distance from the Sargent House was a small dwelling, occupied for some time by Samuel Lane. Next, farther down the street, stood, and still stands, the house of Peter Dolliver; then came the house of William Fuller, now down; and next, at a considerable distance, in the vicinity of Vinson's Spring, three houses, yet remaining there. On the south side of this street, at the termination of Front Street, we still see a large house, built and occupied by Winthrop Sargent; and, at a little distance east of it, another, the residence of Daniel Sargent, — both prominent merchants before the war. Next to the latter stood the meeting-house erected by the friends of Rev. John Murray; and beyond this, elderly persons tell us, no dwelling was standing on that side of the street. But at a short distance from the end of it, on the highway leading along by the head of the

Harbor, was a settlement of about twenty houses, a few of which yet remain. On the right hand, at Rose Bank, we still see the house of Bradbury Sanders; several rods farther on, that of Deacon Eliezer Grover, which no longer preserves its original appearance; and, next, the Leighton House, built and occupied by Edmund Grover, jun., more than a century ago. Passing along, at the turn of the way leading to Eastern Point, we see the home of a family prominent in our history for the greater part of the last century, — that of Thomas Sanders. At a little distance from the latter, on the opposite side of the road, still stands the house of John Sanders, a grandson of Thomas. Between this house and Cap Rock, — a large bowlder, then resting at the corner of Prospect and Jackson Streets, — on the north side of the road, one or two other houses of the olden time yet remain; but, at the close of the war, a row of about eight tenements occupied this space, now covered with modern dwellings.

A large portion of the land in the easterly part of the village was then owned by the Sargent Family. With the exception of a few house-lots, this family held the entire tract embraced between the Harbor, on the south; Pleasant Street and Duncan Street, on the west; Prospect Street, on the north; and Chestnut Street, on the east. On the shore-side of this land, the merchants of this family had their wharves, stores, and fish-flakes; the latter covering almost the entire space between Duncan Street and Vinson's Cove. On this space, at Duncan's Point, rises a small hill; upon which now appears, as the most conspicuous object, the stone house of Mr. Lane, the artist. On that spot, at the close of the Revolution, stood a solitary and venerable oak-tree, twenty-three feet in circumference. It had long been a cherished object, and a favorite resort for the people; and, when the news of peace arrived, the ancient oak was fixed upon as the place at which the joyful event should be celebrated. Its hollow trunk and leafless branches were brilliantly illuminated; and, though no living person could remember the grandeur of its maturity, all agreed that it could not have surpassed the splendor which it now exhibited in its decay.

We have now sketched the appearance of the several streets of the Harbor Village at the close of the Revolutionary War, and have looked upon the homes of some of the actors in that struggle. Besides the houses noticed, there were a few small tenements standing in by-places and along the shore of the Harbor Cove. If, with the aid of the imagination, we restore these, the view, it is believed, will be as correct as it can now be made.

In the Second or West Parish, we still see many memorials of the Revolutionary period, and several of a time yet more remote. The Eveleth House, and that of Byles, of Jacob Davis, of Woodward, and those of some of the Haskells, invariably attract the attention of the passer by their venerable aspect; and several others show their ante-Revolutionary origin. In this agricultural district, the number of ancient houses that have been taken down since the war has been little more than made good by the erection of new ones; and no great change has been made in any part of it to alter the view in any important respect. The greatest change in the landscape is seen by looking at the farm of Col. Coffin, near the entrance of Squam Harbor; where, in place of a wide extent of well-wooded territory, we now see a collection of barren sand-hills. Gone, too, is the large dwelling of the owner, the house for his slaves, and every other mark that the farm was once the most valuable one in town. In another part of the parish, we look in vain for the old Meeting-house: but we see around us the dwellings of all its pastors; and, finding no relic or descendant of any of these, we are impressed with the truth, that the families of men are more evanescent even than the frail works which their hands create.

Leaving the parish at Coffin's Beach, and passing over to Squam Point, we still find ourselves in presence of venerable dwellings of the days of the Revolution. Two of them are of the popular gambrel-roof style, and were both built, it is supposed, by some of the Haraden Family; though one was, at this time, owned and occupied by Capt. William Babson. Another was the house of William Davis; and another was the home of descendants of the early settlers of this spot, — the Haradens. Several small tenements have disappeared, and new ones have been erected; but enough of the old look remains to lead us back to a remote era. One road led thence to the Meeting-house, at the head of Lobster Cove. On the south side of this road, bordering the Cove, were scattered several houses, a few of which have been spared to the present time. Among these, the residence of Rev. Benjamin Bradstreet is yet pointed out. At the head of the Cove, the Meeting-house no longer stands; but, around the one now occupying the same spot, we may still see some of the homes of the Revolutionary times, all easily recognized by their architecture. One of these was that of James Davis, a leading man in the town for many years. Another was once occupied by Rev. John Wyeth; and has in one side the hole of a bullet, shot into it for the purpose of killing or frightening that minister. Not far distant, on a by-road leading into the woods, were a few dwellings; of which those of Jesse Saville and the Dennison Family were remote from the highway, and were in secluded and lonely situations. It was the former of these that was searched by an exasperated mob in September, 1768, as related in a previous chapter.

Continuing on the road around the Cape, a few small houses could be seen at the coves; but it is only at wide intervals of space that an unmistakable relic of the ante-Revolutionary period can be met with now. Entering within the boundary of Rockport, we still see the old homestead of the Wheelers; and farther on, at Pigeon Hill, the residence of a family of soldiers, — that of Capt. John Rowe. Around this spot, and throughout the old parish of Sandy Bay, nearly all is changed and new. On no other part of the Cape have growth and improvement been so marked as here. The population has increased tenfold, and the usual characteristics of a large and flourishing town have obliterated nearly all the memorials of the hamlet. At the close of the war, this parish contained, probably, about eighty houses; most of which were situated on the highway leading into the village from the Harbor, and passing along by the two coves towards Long Beach. Several of them were at these coves, and were small tenements, occupied by the fishermen who pursued their business there. Some of these yet remain, and with a few others scattered along the road in the outskirts of the settlement, to the number of about twenty-five in all, serve to guide a beholder in tracing out the habitations of the last century. These dwellings were the best of that time, and some of them were good farm-houses — the abodes of descendants of the ancient settlers, Tarr and Pool. One is still pointed out as the residence of the patriotic minister of the parish, — Rev. Ebenezer Cleaveland.

To complete this sketch of the town as it appeared at the close of the war, it should be added, that few of the houses were painted, and that many were in a dilapidated and unsightly condition, which bore witness to the general poverty of the people. In another respect, too, the effect of the war was plainly visible. The roads of the town, requiring frequent repairs on account of the uneven surface and rocky soil upon which they are built, had been greatly neglected, and were hardly passable in a carriage, with comfort and safety.* But all these inconveniences could be speedily overcome; and with the blessings of independence and self-government secured, and a wide field for enterprise opened, energy in business, and morality of life, would again bring all the substantial enjoyments of existence.

* The number of pleasure-carriages in town at this time was thirty-one; comprising "chairs, sulkeys, and chaises."

CHAPTER XXVI.

SCHOOLS RE-OPENED. — TOWN GRAMMAR SCHOOLHOUSE. — SCHOOL-DISTRICT SYSTEM ADOPTED. — LOSS OF A DUTCH SHIP-OF-WAR OFF CAPE ANN. — MEN DROWNED NEAR CHEBACCO RIVER. — CAPE POND STOCKED WITH ALEWIVES. — SHAY'S REBELLION. — FEDERAL CONSTITUTION ADOPTED. — GLOUCESTER REGIMENT OF MILITIA, AND GLOUCESTER ARTILLERY. — GENERAL TRAINING. — CUSTOM-HOUSE, POST-OFFICE, CENSUS, AND TONNAGE. — FIRE-ENGINE. — FORT. — FRENCH FROM ST. PETER'S AT SANDY BAY. — SHIP WRECKED AT SALT ISLAND. — WORKHOUSE. — GLOUCESTER BANK. — GLOUCESTER-ROAD LOTTERY. — MARINE DISASTERS. — LIBRARY. — SAILORS ENLIST FOR WAR WITH FRANCE. — FREDERICK GILMAN. — DANIEL ROGERS. — DEATH OF WASHINGTON NOTICED BY THE TOWN.

THE schools of New England fitted our fathers to enjoy and to gain the blessings of civil and religious liberty; and it is upon these institutions that their descendants must depend for the perpetuity of these blessings. In view of their high duty in this respect, the people of Gloucester, as soon as the war was over, took measures to re-establish a grammar school, by authorizing the selectmen to hire a house and procure a teacher. In the several parishes, also, schools were again opened, and generally maintained, from this time during a portion of each year, upon the system in use before the war. These parish-schools were often of an inferior order; but, poor as they were, most of the children acquired the ability to read and write. The grammar school, too, did not meet all the wants of the people of the Harbor, where it was located; and some of them combined to erect a schoolhouse, and carry on a private school. The building erected by them about 1790 is still standing, on School Street; but it has not, for many years, been used for its original purpose.

One of the most earnest friends of the public schools, at this time, was the Rev. Eli Forbes. In behalf of the School Committee, he presented a report to the town, in 1790, concerning the condition of the schools, in which he urged reforms; among which were the better remuneration of teachers, the erection of a building for the grammar school, and provision for the education of females, — "a tender and interesting branch of the community," says he, "that have been neglected in the public schools of this town." These suggestions were not immediately acted upon: but, in 1793, a grant of three hundred pounds was made for a new schoolhouse, which was completed the next year; and on the 5th of March, 1795, was solemnly dedicated, with suitable religious exercises, to the great work of educating the young, so that they should "be accounted unto the Lord for the generation of the righteous." The venerable pastor of the First Church now saw part of the fruition of his labor; and led, with heartfelt gratitude and joy, the interesting ceremonies of the dedication. A procession was formed at the Meeting-house, and proceeded to the new schoolhouse, where Mr. Forbes offered a consecrating prayer; after which, it returned to the house of worship, where he preached a discourse founded upon these words of the Psalmist: "Instead of thy fathers shall be thy children, whom thou mayest make princes in all the earth."

This building stood on what is now Granite Street. It was square, of two stories, and was furnished with a belfry and bell. Besides occasional use as a schoolroom, the upper part served the different boards of town-officers as a place for meeting; and the lower room was often used for elections and other town-purposes. After standing nearly sixty years where it was originally located, it was moved to Beacon Street; and there, after suitable interior alterations, was converted to the use of one of the primary schools of the town. Its outward aspect is somewhat changed; but it still has enough of the old familiar look to remind many of our citizens of the varied experience of good instruction and bad instruction that they acquired within its walls.

The salary of the grammar schoolmaster was fixed, in 1796,

at one hundred and thirty pounds per annum; an increase of forty pounds in three years. The incumbent of the office, at this time, was Obadiah Parsons. He taught it several years, but not without complaint on the part of some of the people; though, on the only occasion when their dissatisfaction came before the town, the public voice seems to have been in favor of the teacher.

No change was made in the system upon which the public schools were conducted, till 1804; when the town availed itself of a law of the Commonwealth, which permitted the division of its territory into school-districts. At first, only eleven districts were established; among which, the school-money, after deducting the salary of the grammar schoolmaster, was divided according to the number of polls in each district. The whole amount raised in 1805 was two thousand dollars.

Resuming the chronological course of our history, the first event of interest to be noticed is a terrible calamity that occurred on the coast in the fall of 1783. A Dutch ship-of-war of fifty guns, having been dismasted in a violent gale in September, and the men reduced to great distress, the captain, one of the lieutenants, and about forty men, left in one of the boats when not far from Cape Ann, and got on board of a brig which they descried in the distance. The ship went down in about three minutes afterwards, carrying with her three hundred and three men. The persons saved were taken from the brig by a sloop sent out from Gloucester for their relief, and were all landed here. The ship was one of a squadron bound to Philadelphia with the Dutch minister.

The next year, Oct. 31, a distressing accident in our own waters deprived the town of some of its useful citizens. By the upsetting of a boat near the mouth of Chebacco River, the following persons were drowned: Capt. Thomas Herrick, aged fifty; Lieut. Ephraim Choate, forty; Benjamin Choate, his oldest son, aged eighteen; Samuel Avery, thirty; John Avery, twenty; William Collins; and John Rider, a stranger. Thomas Jacques was the only person saved; and he is said to have been the only one of the party that could not swim.

A project for stocking Cape Pond with alewives was brought before the town at the May meeting in 1784, and a vote for carrying it into effect was passed: but the object does not seem to have been accomplished at that trial, or at any subsequent one for several years; for, in 1816, we find a committee making a long report about opening the stream, and putting the fish into the pond. The "opening of the stream" is supposed to have reference to the removing or otherwise surmounting the obstacles to the upward course of the fish, occasioned by the dams at the two mills. Whatever was the cause by which the design had been so long in abeyance, the pond about this time received its new inhabitants; and, in the opinion of some of that time, the beginning of an important alewife-fishery was commenced. The privilege of taking the fish for five years was sold by the town in 1827: but the quantity taken was of too little amount to render the business worth attention; and the stream was soon abandoned to the children, who sought its banks "to see the alewives run."

In the fall of 1786, the discontent which had for some time been muttering in the western part of the Commonwealth broke out in open insurrection, and, for the moment, threatened an overthrow of the State Government. Shay's Rebellion found neither advocates nor apologists in the people of Gloucester. On the call for troops, the town responded instantly by voting to raise a company, and appropriating money to pay it. This was done at a town-meeting on the 15th January, 1787. A company was raised on the same day, and placed under the command of a distinguished soldier of the town (John Rowe), with William Kinsman for lieutenant; and William Tuck, ensign. This company was attached to Col. Wade's regiment, and was marched to the scene of disturbance: but the speedy dispersion of the rebels relieved it of the necessity of a long service; and, at the end of forty-five days, it was disbanded.

A more pleasing duty next devolved upon our people, — the consideration of the Constitution of National Government, adopted by the Convention of Delegates from the several States, held at Philadelphia in 1787. On the 18th of December, delegates to the State Convention for "assenting to and ratifying" this Constitution were chosen in this town. The persons to whom this important business was intrusted were Daniel Rogers, John Low, and William Pearson, — wise and prudent men, whose exertions and sacrifices for independence were a sufficient guaranty that they would act wisely in all efforts to establish a government that would secure its blessings. In the Convention, they gave their votes for the ratification of the Constitution; an act so agreeable to their constituents, that, on the evening of their return home (Feb. 7, 1788), "a generous entertainment" was provided for them, at Capt. Somes's tavern, by the principal citizens of the town, "as a testimony of their approbation, and to give a social opportunity to reciprocate their congratulations on the decision which had taken place." *

This Constitution declared that a well-regulated militia was necessary to the security of a free State; and the war from which the people had just come forth victoriously had taught them the importance of keeping up a military organization. The Gloucester companies composed the third Essex regiment. No general muster had taken place here for more than twenty years; when, on the 3d of November, 1788, this regiment was ordered out for exercise and review. Upwards of three

* The occasion was one of great joy to all our people. Even the ladies caught the spirit of rejoicing, and celebrated the event in a creditable manner. "We learn from Gloucester, that, on Thursday last, nearly thirty young ladies, inspired with the love of industry, assembled at the house of Capt. Philemon Haskell for the praiseworthy purpose of a federal spinning-match: when, to their honor, their spirited exertions produced ninety-nine skeins of excellent yarn; practically declaring that they neither labored in vain nor spent their strength for nought. The day thus industriously concluded finished not the harmony of their federalism. In the evening, to crown the pleasure of the day, with additional company, they regaled themselves with an agreeable dance; and, at a modest hour, parted in love and friendship, with hearts convivial as they met, leaving others to admire their female patriotism, and to go and do likewise." — *Salem Mercury*, Oct. 21, 1788.

A spinning-party was not a new thing in town. Twenty years before, on two occasions, several industrious females of the First Parish met at the house of their minister, and passed the day in this employment. On the last, thirty-eight of these "daughters of industry" assembled for the purpose of "laying their hands to the spindle." Their object seems to have been a charitable one, as several furnished both materials and labor. After the toil of the day was over, a sermon was delivered to them by their minister, at the meeting-house, from Exod. xxxv. 25.

hundred and fifty men appeared under arms, well equipped, and went through with their exercises to general satisfaction. In the afternoon, they were reviewed by Col. Pearce, the officers of the Artillery Company, and several gentlemen of the town; and the evening, it is said, "was closed with convivial cheer, good-fellowship, and a seasonable return home, after drinking several patriotic sentiments, with a discharge of a field-piece to each." The Gloucester Artillery had been recently organized, under the command of James Pearson; and had, on the 11th of September, received a "very elegant stand of colors" from Capt. David Pearce. The flag was presented at Mr. Pearce's house, where the company partook of an ample and generous refreshment at his invitation. In 1791, Capt. Pearson had liberty from the town to erect a gun-house, on the spot, at the head of Pleasant Street, from which a building, erected at a later date for the same purpose, has just been removed. The first building was a small one; and, after a few years' use by the company, was removed, and converted into a dwelling.

The annual "general training" was kept up for about forty years from this time; and the day on which it occurred was the greatest holiday of the year, — men, women, and children all mingling in its enjoyments. To the latter, especially, was it a day which has no like for our present generation of juveniles. First came from the field itself, on the evening before the important day, a sound of preparation, in the erection of a single booth, or tent; the precursor of a whole line that were to dispense good-cheer on the morrow. At early dawn came other sounds; and soon the discharge of muskets, or the drum and fife, aroused the young to the pleasures in store for them. Breakfast was hastily despatched, if not altogether neglected; for the ear was impatient to catch the welcome sound announcing the approach of the "Honey-pinks," or some other company from the outskirts of the town. In due time, these all appeared: then followed the forming into line and the march to the field, where the evolutions of the soldiers, the cheering strains of the music, and the general hilarity that prevailed, filled the hours with joy, and left nothing to regret, except that these hours were so short and fleeting. But the signal for departure must at last come; and soon the sound of all the drums and fifes of the regiment, gathered into one band, announces that the whole body of the military is in motion towards the village. There, again formed into line, with "all the pomp and circumstance of glorious war," the officers, by order of the colonel, marched to the centre, and received from him, as he rested upon the proud steed that had borne him through the duties of the day, the thanks to which they themselves and their several companies were entitled.

A vacant space in the rear of Back Street, where the Railroad Buildings now stand, was sometimes used as a training-field: but the Meeting-house Green was generally resorted to on these occasions; and it was there that the middle-aged men of to-day beheld in their boyhood the expiring glory of the militia.

The Federal Government having been organized in 1789, a custom-house was established in Gloucester in the fall of that year; and, soon afterwards, a post-office. In the following year, the first national census showed the number of our inhabitants to be five thousand three hundred and seventeen; an increase, probably, of about eight per cent since 1775. Under the acts of the new National Government, for regulating commerce, upwards of seven thousand tons of shipping were registered and enrolled here; part of which was engaged in the fishery,—which was again successfully pursued,—and the rest in a profitable foreign trade.

In 1793, we first find fire-engines in the town; thirty pounds having been granted at a meeting in that year towards paying for them, to which a sum was probably added by private contributions. A fire-club was organized about the same time, though one had existed many years before.

In May, 1794, the town ceded to the United States the land on Watch-house Neck, where a breastwork had been thrown up in the early part of the Revolutionary War, for the purpose of erecting a fort for the protection of the town. The work was immediately commenced, and there soon arose upon the site of the old layers of turf the fortress that we now see there in ruins. During the last war with Great Britain, a company was stationed there: but, after peace took place, it was occupied for many years by a keeper only; and at last, about 1833, having then no tenant, the wood-work of the house was set on fire by some mischievous boys or men, and consumed. Still further destruction may be anticipated; and therefore a representation of its appearance about that time is presented in the accompanying engraving.

On the 10th of October, 1794, the people of Sandy Bay were surprised by an unexpected arrival. Four shallops, with fifty French persons, — men, women, and children, — came into their cove from St. Peter's; whence they had been driven by the English, who had taken it a few months before. They were on their way to the French consul at Boston; but, the homes at Sandy Bay being opened to them, they went on shore, and had their wants liberally supplied.

A distressing shipwreck at Little-Good-Harbor Beach was the principal event in our history in 1796. Early in January this year, the ship "Industry," Capt. Miles Barnes, belonging to Boston, was lost on that beach, near Salt Island, in a violent snow-storm. By her log-book, which was kept till eight o'clock, it appeared that she sailed from Portsmouth, Eng., Nov. 3, in ballast. All hands perished. The bodies of the captain, mate, and four men, were found, and buried from the First-Parish Church with proper religious solemnities, including an address by Rev. Dr. Forbes. The owner of the ship bore public testimony to the attention and humanity of our citizens on this melancholy occasion.

Some account has been given, in a previous chapter, of the erection by the town of a building which was called a work-house, though it does not appear that it was ever much occupied by paupers. The poor were annually let out to board until 1796, when they were brought together into a house just erected for their accommodation, on what is now Granite Street. The sum granted to build the house was £513. 14s. 5d.; and the building then erected, with various additions, served the town for this use a little more than fifty years.

VIEW OF THE OLD FORT AND HARBOR 1837.

The Gloucester Bank, the first, and, for more than fifty years, the only one in town, was established this year. Most of the merchants, traders, and capitalists of the town were subscribers to its stock; but a few, who were opposed to a paper-currency, would give no encouragement to the project. The sum of forty thousand dollars was subscribed as capital by thirty-five persons; who, on the 22d of April, 1796, signed a "covenant" containing the terms on which their business was to be conducted. The bank went into operation in August. At the expiration of three years, the time named in the "covenant," that instrument was renewed, but was soon made void by an Act of Incorporation obtained from the Legislature. Successive legislative enactments have continued its existence, and increased its capital to three hundred thousand dollars. It has been conducted with eminent success; for it has satisfied the public, and has paid to its stockholders one hundred and twenty-nine dividends, which have averaged nearly seven per cent per annum. It is one of the oldest banks in the United States.*

On the 6th of October, 1796, was drawn the second scheme of the Gloucester-Road lottery, amounting to eighteen thousand dollars, and subject to a deduction of one-third. This lottery was granted by the General Court in answer to a petition of the town, voted at the May meeting in 1795, "to defray the expense of turning the road in Fresh-water Cove." At that time, it was not unusual to obtain money in this manner to carry on a public work; but the benefits thus gained were a poor compensation for the depravation of morals growing out of the lottery system, and it was soon abandoned.

In the spring of this year, the proprietors of the Gloucester

---

* Presidents of the Gloucester Bank: 1796, John Somes; 1816, William Pearson; 1818, John Kittredge; 1822, William W. Parrott; 1834, Benjamin K. Hough; 1837, William Pearce, jun.; 1842, Isaac Somes. Cashiers: 1796, Joseph Allen, jun.; 1829, Henry Smith; 1836, John J. Babson; 1855, Benjamin F. Somes.

The increasing business of the town seemed to many to warrant the establishment of a new bank in 1855; and a charter was therefore obtained for the "Bank of Cape Ann," which went into operation, March 3, 1856, with a capital of one hundred and fifty thousand dollars, and has been so conducted as to secure the confidence and favor of the public. The only president it has had is Gorham P. Low; and the only cashier, Samuel J. Giles.

Social Library had liberty from the town to place their books in the Grammar-schoolhouse Building. This body had been recently organized, and had already made a considerable collection. The number of proprietors was sixty, and the annual assessment was usually two dollars. Only a small amount was, of course, available for the purchase of books; but the society managed to add a number every year, and had accumulated nearly two thousand volumes in 1830, when nearly the whole were destroyed by the great fire of that year. The founders and supporters of this library are mentioned with deep gratitude by many of our present citizens, who found in its rich store of history, biography, and poetry, the only means of intellectual culture accessible to them in their early days.

In 1798, the National Government was involved in a difficulty with France, growing out of the war between the latter country and England. By the encroachments of the French upon American commerce, the Gloucester merchants had suffered considerably; and, when the preparation for hostilities was commenced, our sailors and fishermen were prompt, as usual, to sustain the honor and interest of their country. On board of one vessel (the sloop-of-war "Herald"), it is said that fifty-two of these mariners enlisted. Besides the stimulus of patriotism, they found, perhaps, an additional inducement to service in this ship in the fact, that a townsman (William V. Hutchings) was the first lieutenant.*

In May, 1798, died Major Frederick Gilman. He had been a successful merchant of the town; but, in consequence of reverses, had become bankrupt shortly before his death. He was commander of the artillery, and was buried under arms; and his funeral was also attended by the fire societies, and by the officers of the third regiment in uniform. Major Gilman married Abigail, daughter of Benjamin Somes; who, with four chil-

---

* William Vinson Hutchings was son of William Hutchings, and his wife Rachel Elwell, who was a great-grand-daughter of our early settler, William Vinson. Mr. Hutchings left the navy, and entered the merchant service. While in command of a large ship belonging to Boston, he was engaged at Batavia to proceed to Japan, and is said to have been the first American shipmaster who visited that country. He ultimately became a merchant in Boston; and died there, May 25, 1810, aged forty-seven.

dren, survived him. After her husband's death, she kept a shop a few years on Front Street, and then removed to Salem, having previously placed her son Samuel — a gifted lad — at Atkinson Academy to fit for college. This youth graduated at Cambridge in 1811; and, in after-life, amply fulfilled the promise of his early years. For nearly forty years, he was the minister of a Unitarian society in Charleston, S. C.; where he was highly esteemed as a faithful pastor. Besides a high rank in the ministry, he also had a wide reputation as the author of several literary productions of great merit. He died in Kingston, Mass., Feb. 9, 1858, aged sixty-six.*

In the closing year of the century occurred the death of another prominent citizen, — that of Daniel Rogers, Esq., on the 4th of January, at the age of sixty-six. Mr. Rogers was a son of Rev. John Rogers of Kittery, Me.; and therefore a brother of Rev. John of our Fourth Church; and of Timothy, merchant, of Gloucester; of both of whom, some account has been given in this work. He was placed, when a boy, by his father, in the service of Col. John Stevens of this town, who had a little grand-daughter (Rachel). This child required considerable tending, of which a large share fell to the lot of the new member of the family: but he contrived, by pinching and pricking the little one, to rid himself of this employment; and, having other cause of discontent, soon ran away from his disagreeable home. He was next apprenticed to Nathaniel Allen, another merchant of the town, with whom he served his time. Upon attaining his majority, he commenced business for himself, and pursued it with such enterprise and sagacity, that he soon accumulated wealth, and became one of the leading merchants of the town. His business was broken up by the war: but, upon the establishment of peace, he commenced with renewed ardor; and, for several years, his transactions were extensive, and only exceeded by those of David Pearce. At one time, he had sixteen vessels engaged in the fisheries and foreign commerce. His career was

* For an interesting biographical sketch of Dr. Gilman, see Harvard-College Necrology, in Boston Daily Advertiser, July, 1858.

one of steady prosperity and untarnished reputation; and was attended with such pecuniary success, that he supported the expense of a numerous family, of generous living, and unbounded hospitality; and died possessed of a considerable estate. Mr. Rogers was twice married: first, to Elizabeth Gorham, Nov. 6, 1759, who died March 14, 1769; and next, March 2, 1770, to Rachel Ellery,—the little Rachel whom, when an infant, he had so unwillingly taken to his arms. By these two wives he had twenty-one children. Several of his sons engaged in business in Gloucester; and one of them (Timothy) was, for a few years, a merchant in Boston. Another son (Daniel), graduated at Harvard College in 1798, settled in business in this town, and died Oct. 15, 1819, leaving several children; one of whom is George H., merchant of Gloucester at the present time. One of the daughters of Mr. Rogers (Esther) married John Rowe, Esq., a lawyer, who settled in town about the time of his marriage; and, after a residence here of ten or twelve years, removed to Quincy, where he died in May, 1812.

Mr. Rowe was an honest and virtuous citizen, and his departure was a public loss. The hold he had taken upon the regard of our people is evinced by his election nine times as representative. He was also a senator from Essex County.

While the town was lamenting the loss of the prominent and valuable citizen just noticed, every heart was filled with sadness at the death of the great and good WASHINGTON. Of this mournful event, suitable public notice was taken here, at a town-meeting held Feb. 5, 1800; when a committee of five was chosen to wait on the Rev. Dr. Forbes, and request him to deliver a eulogy and offer public prayer at the First-Parish Meeting-house, on the 22d instant,—the birthday of the departed benefactor. On that occasion, the church was dressed in mourning; and a large audience gathered to engage in the solemn and touching exercises of the day.

CHAPTER XXVII.

INDEPENDENT CHRISTIAN SOCIETY. — REV. THOMAS JONES. — HIS SETTLEMENT, MINISTRY, AND DEATH. — HIS CHARACTER. — HIS FAMILY. — SUCCESSION OF PASTORS TO THE PRESENT TIME. — MEETING-HOUSE. — NEW UNIVERSALIST SOCIETY: ITS MINISTERS, ITS DISSOLUTION, ITS MEETING-HOUSE. — THIRD PARISH. — REV. EZRA LEONARD. — HIS SETTLEMENT. — CONVERSION OF MINISTER AND PARISH TO UNIVERSALISM. — HIS DEATH AND CHARACTER. — HIS FAMILY. — PASTORS WHO HAVE SUCCEEDED HIM. — COL. JOSEPH FOSTER.

MR. MURRAY'S removal to Boston did not dissolve the ties of affection by which he was bound to his early friends in Gloucester; and he often preached here during the long period that the society remained without a pastor. The pulpit was mostly supplied, however, by itinerant preachers; among whom, those who officiated most frequently were Rev. Hosea Ballou and Rev. Thomas Barnes. Each of these remained here several months at a time.

In March, 1804, the society, by a unanimous vote, gave Rev. Thomas Jones, who was then preaching in Philadelphia, a call on probation for six months; and, on the 4th of September following, invited him to become their minister for life, at a salary of six hundred dollars per annum. This was accepted, and he was installed on the 26th of the same month. The clergymen present were Rev. John Murray, who offered the introductory prayer, and delivered the sermon and charge; and Rev. George Richards of Portsmouth, N.H., who made the installing prayer, and gave the right hand of fellowship.

Mr. Jones was born at Narbath, Pembrokeshire, South Wales, April 5, 1763. A serious turn of mind, and a taste for study, led him, at the age of nineteen years, to enter the seminary established by Selina, Countess of Huntingdon, at Trevecca, in Wales, to educate young men to preach the doctrines of the Calvinistic Methodists. After spending three years at this institution, he left in 1785, at the age of twenty-two, and immediately received ordination. He was, till about 1790, an earnest and sincere preacher of the doctrines in which he had been educated. His sentiments then underwent a complete revolution, and he avowed his belief in universal salvation. This was, of course, the signal for his exclusion from the sect whose views of religious truth he had hitherto advocated, but not for his separation from the religious community to which he then ministered.

At that time, he was settled over an Independent Congregational church in Reading, Berkshire County, in England; and those Christian friends, instead of casting him off, severed their connection with Lady Huntingdon's sect, and attended his ministry until 1796. In that year, at the solicitation of Rev. John Murray, he came to America; and, not long after his arrival, took charge of a society in Lombard Street, Philadelphia; where he preached till his removal to Gloucester.

As several members of the society resided in Sandy-Bay Parish, Mr. Jones preached there a certain number of sabbaths in each year, during the early part of his ministry here. At a later period, he taught, for a short time, the Town Grammar School. Excepting this employment, his constant care and undivided attention were bestowed upon the people of his charge for thirty-four years; at the end of which, his advanced age and impaired health rendered it necessary that he should be relieved of a portion of the active duties of the ministry. The society accordingly took the necessary steps to obtain a colleague pastor; and in August, 1838, entered into an engagement with Rev. Daniel D. Smith.

Mr. Jones continued to preach, occasionally, after the settlement of his colleague: but the peace and harmony of the society were ere long broken up in consequence of a division among its members with reference to the conduct and character of the junior pastor; and the venerable senior, although in no way blamable for the deplorable condition to which the society had become reduced, acceded to an arrangement, in 1841, by which his pastoral connection with it was dissolved. Instead of the salary of six hundred dollars per annum, with which he was originally settled for life, he consented to receive the sum of four hundred dollars yearly, on condition that the sum of two hundred dollars per annum should be paid to his wife after his decease, if she should survive him. The society had always dealt generously with him; having voted, in nearly every year of his ministry, an addition to his regular salary; besides which, his friends often gave occasion for the exercise of his gratitude by the bestowment of liberal gifts.

The health of the aged pastor was now gradually failing. He was endowed by nature with a good constitution, which he was careful to preserve by temperance and bodily exercise. But the strongest system must yield to the assaults of time; and his seemed to sink, without any confirmed disease, by slow and gradual decay. He was confined to his house a long time; and, during the last fortnight of his life, he was so low as to take little notice of what was passing around him, and to be understood with difficulty when he spoke. His mental faculties, however, seemed yet to be in vigorous action; and his spirit would occasionally task the agents of its communion with earthly things, and give assurance that his firm and unwavering faith was still, as it had been through many a dark hour, the strength of his heart. About seven o'clock on Thursday evening, Aug. 20, 1846, he called his family and friends to his bedside, and took a solemn and affectionate leave of all; and, soon after, drew his last breath. He died in his eighty-fourth year. He was buried, on the 22d, from the meeting-house in which he had preached more than thirty years. Rev. A. D. Mayo delivered, on the occasion, an appropriate sermon from Ps. xxxvii. 37.

As a preacher, Mr. Jones confined himself within a narrow range of subjects. The Bible was his constant study; and he dwelt much upon doctrinal points, and expositions of Scripture passages. The paternal character of God, and the divine life of Christ, were, however, themes upon which he delighted to dwell; while no occasion was ever lost for laying open the odious nature and the evils of sin. His most earnest prayer was for the "spread of the everlasting gospel;" because he felt, that, wherever this should be received in its purity, its believers would not only rejoice in the liberty wherewith Christ hath made them free, but would abjure every species of tyranny, and assert their claims to civil and religious freedom,—the holy birthright of every child of God. On no subject was he warmed to such a degree of enthusiasm as on this. He valued as highly as any native the high privilege of citizenship of this republic; and, on every suitable public occasion, paid the homage of his admiration to the great men who were its founders. He was no orator; but, in all his pulpit performances, he was earnest and fervent, and sent directly to the heart of every hearer an entire conviction of his sincerity. There was not variety enough in his preaching to attract young and restless minds; but few, who attended his ministry to the period of sober age and of settled convictions of religious truth, failed to reap edification and improvement from it.

The domestic and inner life of this pastor was one of rare beauty and excellence. He was eminently kind, single-minded, and conscientious; and he bore, with the fortitude of a philosopher and the resignation of a saint, the severe and unusual afflictions that fell to his lot. He was not fitted by nature for familiar intercourse with his fellow-beings; and he labored under so much embarrassment in this respect, in complying with the just demands of society from his profession, as sometimes to consider himself thereby disqualified for his office. But the natural reserve of his manners gave place, in the circles of affection and long-tried friendship, to a cordial freedom and easy conversation. It was his inexpressible joy to meet in these circles true and loving friends; and though he followed, one after another, most of his early ones to the grave, he enjoyed the high satisfaction of knowing that they died in faith, rejoicing with him in the hope, that the sweet communion in which they had lived on earth would be renewed in the society of the just made perfect in heaven.

He was much abroad in the open air; for his serene and meditative spirit reaped instruction and joy in contemplating Nature.

He loved her in all her moods and aspects: the raging sea, the shining stars, and budding flowers, each struck in his soul a chord of that music which was constantly celebrating the power, wisdom, and goodness of God.

Mr. Jones's wife, to whom he was married in England, was Sophia Newell. She survived her husband a few years, in a state of bodily and mental infirmity; and died April 17, 1850, aged eighty-four. Their children were Olwyn, Thomas, Sophia, and Mary. The first fell from a wharf in Gloucester Harbor, and was drowned, when about eleven years old. Thomas established himself as a baker in this town, and "passed away in a moment of strange delirium, when man is not accountable for what his hands perform." Sophia is the wife of Capt. Benjamin Atkins of Gloucester. Mary married Loa Richardson of Cambridge, and died a childless widow.

The first measures adopted by the society to obtain a colleague for Mr. Jones were taken in December, 1837; when an invitation to fill that office was given to Rev. M. H. Smith of Haverhill, which was declined. The next attempt resulted in an arrangement by which Rev. Daniel D. Smith, a brother of the preceding, became the junior pastor. He was installed Dec. 20, 1838; on which occasion, the sermon was preached by Rev. O. A. Skinner of Boston.

Mr. Smith's father was Elias Smith, an occasional preacher, first of Free-will Baptist, and then of Universalist sentiments. The early advantages of education enjoyed by the son were of a very limited character; but a quick and retentive memory, and a remarkable command of language, enabled him to meet the demands of a sect whose preachers have not hitherto been generally distinguished for intellectual culture. At the time of his settlement here, he was about thirty years of age. He had been settled over several societies at different times, and left a large and flourishing one at Portland when he entered upon his duties here. He commenced his ministry in this place under the happiest auspices. The society was large, and well disposed in regard to every measure that might be deemed necessary for their improvement on the part of the junior pastor; while his ministerial gifts and social qualities immediately attracted the people strongly towards him. But the domestic relations of the new pastor were soon found to be inharmonious, and a short time only had elapsed when a feeling of dissatisfaction arose against him. Consequently, before the close of his second year, the peace and harmony of the society were destroyed by the conflicting opinions in regard to his character entertained by the members. Many of the society had withdrawn at this time, and several others had ceased to attend his ministry; so that it was deemed expedient by Mr. Smith to send in his resignation. This was in October, 1840. His resignation was accepted; but in consequence of an earnest appeal to the society, setting forth his troubles and injuries, a vote was passed in January, 1841, by which he was engaged to preach till the annual meeting in April. A large portion of the society, believing him to be a faithful minister and a worthy man, were still content to follow him as their religious guide. They adhered to him to the end; and on his departure from town, which took place soon after the termination of his last engagement to preach, they dissolved their connection with the society, and, not long after, formed themselves into a separate congregation.

Mr. Smith next preached to a society in Richmond, Va.: but he had a powerful body of friends in Gloucester, who recalled him after he had made a short stay in that city, and employed him to preach to them, and to minister also to their physical ills; for, during his absence, he had qualified himself to practise medicine, and he returned to town with a medical degree. After continuing a few years here on this second residence, he removed to Boston, and has since devoted himself chiefly to his medical profession.*

The society made an arrangement with Mr. Jones in May, 1841, by which his connection with it as pastor was dissolved: but it did not seek to supply the pulpit with a permanent ministry till December, 1842; when Rev. Frederic F. Thayer of

* Soon after he removed to town, the oldest son of Mr. Smith was lost overboard from a schooner, in which he was a passenger for Philadelphia.

Cambridge, a graduate of Harvard College of 1840, was invited to the vacant pastorate. The invitation was accepted; and his installation took place, March 28, 1843, when Rev. O. A. Skinner of Boston preached the sermon. The society was in a condition of pecuniary embarrassment; and, at the close of the year 1844, he sent in his resignation; which was accepted. The committee of the society, in their letter of acceptance, assured him that no cause of dissatisfaction existed, and bore their testimony to the fidelity with which he had discharged his duties. Mr. Thayer continued but a short time in the profession he had chosen, and finally engaged in trade.

The society now took measures to free itself from debt; and, through the indefatigable exertions of a few of its members, raised by subscription, in a short time, the large sum necessary for that purpose. An effort was also made to induce the seceders to return; but it did not meet with success.

As the society had now thrown off the incubus of its debt, it ventured once more to look after a candidate for settlement; and in June, 1845, contracted with Rev. H. B. Soule to become its pastor, at a salary of seven hundred dollars per annum. Before the expiration of a year, Mr. Soule asked and obtained his dismission; not, however, in consequence of any change in his relations with his people. He next settled in Hartford, Conn.; and is now deceased.

Mr. Soule was succeeded by Rev. Amory D. Mayo. He entered upon his ministry here in July, 1846, at a salary of six hundred dollars; which was subsequently increased to one thousand. Mr. Mayo was born in Warwick, Mass. He went nearly through the course of collegiate instruction at Amherst College, when the state of his health compelled him to leave. In such intervals of ease as he could obtain, he pursued the studies connected with the profession to which his inclination directed him, and had but recently begun to preach when he settled as the pastor of this society. He had not then regained a condition of vigorous health; and, during the continuance of his ministry here, he was often obliged to ask, for a season, for a partial or entire respite from his labors. Notwithstanding such interruptions, he had the satisfaction to see his efforts crowned with success, and the society restored to its former prosperous state. His preaching attracted a large congregation, and made a deep impression upon his hearers. It was with great reluctance, therefore, that the society accepted his resignation, which he tendered Oct. 1, 1854.

Mr. Mayo was married, about the time of his settlement here, to Miss Sarah C. Edgarton of Shirley, Mass.; a lady of uncommon mental endowments, which were improved by self-culture to such a degree as to entitle her to a respectable rank among the literary females of the country. The fine qualities of her heart immediately won the love of those with whom she became connected as a pastor's wife; and when, in a sudden and unlooked-for moment, she was summoned to enter the heaven of which she had thought so much, her departure was mourned as that of a dear and long-loved friend. She died July 9, 1848, at the age of twenty-nine. Her husband has offered an appropriate and tender tribute to her memory in the memoir which he has prefixed to a selection from her writings.

The present pastor of the Independent Christian Society is Rev. W. R. G. Mellen, who was born in Phillipston, Mass., June 29, 1822. He received his classical education at New-Salem Academy, and studied theology in Worcester. He was the pastor, for a few years, of a Universalist society in Cambridge, and also of that in Auburn, N.Y.; from which place he removed to Gloucester. He commenced his labors here in May, 1855. The society pays him a salary of sixteen hundred dollars per annum, and enjoys under his ministry a high degree of prosperity.

In November, 1824, the society held a "jubilee," a semicentennial commemoration of Mr. Murray's first visit to Gloucester. Though much social festivity was indulged in, the chief joy of the occasion was of a religious kind. The most prominent preachers of the sect were present, and several public religious exercises were held.

The meeting-house in which the society now worships, on Middle Street, was erected in 1805, at a cost of about ten thousand dollars, of which Col. Pearce contributed fifteen hundred. Its architect and builder was Col. Jacob Smith.* No effort to ascertain the date of its dedication, or an account of the ceremonies of that occasion, has been successful. The spacious yard in front of the building was originally bordered on each side by a row of Lombardy poplars, which were removed about 1826 to make room for the avenue of noble elms that now contribute so much to the beauty of the street and to the attractions of this house of worship.

The friends of Rev. Daniel D. Smith, after their withdrawal from the Independent Christian Society, proceeded to form themselves into a new religious body, and took the name of the Independent Universalist Society. April 13, 1843, seventy-seven members signed a paper to support preaching. Mr. Smith preached for them during the following summer, while on a visit to the town, and then received an invitation to become their pastor; but his engagements at Richmond were such, that he could not come till the next year. In the mean time, they had religious worship nearly every Sunday, conducted by ministers from abroad.

Mr. Smith preached for this society till the summer of 1848. In 1849, Rev. David H. Plumb became their minister, and remained with them till July, 1852. In April, 1853, they made an engagement with Rev. G. J. Sanger; and had his services till March 2, 1856, when he preached his farewell sermon. The dissolution of the society soon followed; upon which a large portion of the members returned to the parent body, which, by this acquisition and other gains, was restored to its former high rank in the denomination to which it belongs.

The new society held their worship in the Murray Institute Hall at first, and afterwards in the Town Hall till the autumn of 1845; when they began to occupy a small but neat meeting-

* Col. Smith was a native of Ipswich, and was somewhat famous as a master-builder. Besides this meeting-house, he built, about the same time, one in Sandy Bay, and one in Manchester. He died March 18, 1812, aged forty-six. His son Henry was Cashier of the Gloucester Bank, and died Sept. 26, 1836, aged forty-six. Charles Card Smith of Boston, a gentleman of literary taste and culture, and a contributor of critical notices and reviews to the leading periodicals, is a grandson of Col. Smith.

house on Elm Street, which was erected by a subscription of some of the members, at a cost of about three thousand dollars. This building was purchased by the Methodists in 1858, and is now their place of public worship.

The unhappy termination of the ministry of Rev. Obadiah Parsons in the Fourth Parish, together with the troubled state of the people during the Revolutionary War and their impoverished condition long afterwards, discouraged for many years an attempt to fill their vacant pulpit: but the vitality of the parish was preserved by occasional preaching; and at last, in 1802, an earnest effort to settle a minister was commenced. The first one invited (Rev. Mr. Dickenson) declined the call; but the next trial was successful, and resulted in obtaining Rev. Ezra Leonard, who, after having preached some time as a candidate in the year 1804, received and accepted an invitation to become their minister.

Mr. Leonard was a son of Ezra and Elizabeth Leonard of Raynham, Mass.; of which place his family were among the first and most important of the early settlers. He was born in 1775, and graduated at Brown University in 1801. He was ordained over the Squam Parish, Dec. 5, 1804; on which occasion, the sermon was preached by Rev. Perez Fobes, LL.D., of Raynham, with whom he had studied divinity. The terms of support on which he settled were an annual salary of four hundred dollars, and a settlement of like amount to be paid in four yearly instalments.

The only incident in the history of his ministry, deserving notice in this work, is the remarkable conversion of both pastor and people to the doctrine of universal salvation. This took place in 1811; and, though individual change of opinion affords no cause of wonder, it is certainly enough to excite astonishment, that a whole society should turn about in this way, and act upon an important religious question as if it were a mere matter of expediency. It appears to indicate great indifference on the part of the people to what are usually considered fundamental religious truths, or a surprising personal influence on the part of the pastor; but the truth is, a leaven of Universalism had long existed in the parish. Some of the members, who had become believers in it, were familiar with the Scriptures; and, by argument and conversation, led others to think and inquire, and thus prepare themselves for a change. Mr. Leonard himself, before his conversion, was often engaged with his parishioners in discussing the Calvinistic creed; and, as they confided in their pastor as a good and learned man, it is not strange, under all the circumstances, that, when his mind reached the turning-point, they should find themselves drawn along with him. The only action of the parish that followed Mr. Leonard's declaration of the change in his religious opinions, was a vote, passed in December, 1811, that he should continue to preach the gospel as usual till the next March meeting. A few of the members still adhered to the old creed; but they made no serious attempt to create disaffection, and the affairs of the parish went on in a calm and peaceful flow.

Mr. Leonard continued to be the minister of the parish till his death. His connection with it during a long course of years yielded him a large share of happiness, and was productive of a great amount of good to his people. The only interruptions of the regular routine of his duties as a parish minister were caused by his employment a few terms in school-teaching, and by his election one year as a representative to the General Court. He died Sunday morning, April 22, 1832, aged fifty-seven years. His sickness was a severe lung-complaint, which he bore with exemplary fortitude and resignation. The funeral services were held at the meeting-house; on which occasion, an appropriate discourse was delivered by Rev. Thomas Jones. The place of his interment in the Parish Burying-ground is marked by a neat marble monument, erected by his people in 1837.

Mr. Leonard possessed sufficient talents to satisfy the people of his charge during a long ministry; but he preached most effectively in the beauty of a benevolent and holy life. The highest fame as a pulpit orator would hardly have survived the generation that heard him; but the memory of his untiring devotion to his people, and of his kind disposition and overflowing charity, will preserve his name in grateful remembrance till it is supplanted by one who shall surpass him in all the virtues that distinguished his career. His benevolence to the poor, his compassion for every kind of sorrow and trouble, and his words of kind encouragement and consolation, are to be particularly remembered, because they were striking and marked traits of his character. Such was his desire to increase his usefulness, that, towards the latter part of his life, he devoted himself assiduously to the study of medicine; and, while he was a representative, attended a course of medical lectures. In the remote village where he lived, there was no settled physician; and a knowledge of medicine, and the gratuitous dispensing of its benefits, enabled him to add another to the ties of affection which already bound the people to their pastor. His character was also distinguished by simplicity, candor, and good-humor; so much so, that he seemed sometimes to have too little regard for professional dignity. But these traits, in a place where few artificial distinctions in society existed, increased his popularity, and attracted towards him more of the love and admiration of the people than he could have otherwise possessed.

Mr. Leonard married, in 1805, Miss Nancy Woodbury of this town, by whom he had two sons and three daughters. The oldest son (Warren Augustus) died in Philadelphia, June 10, 1825, aged fourteen. Ezra, the other son, married Elizabeth Saville, and is still living. Stella, the oldest daughter, married Capt. William Day, and settled in Portsmouth, N.H.; where she died Aug. 27, 1841. Ann, the next, married David Saville, and now resides in Lexington, Mass. Augusta, the youngest daughter, married Joseph Day, and also settled in Portsmouth; where she died Oct. 8, 1841. Mrs. Leonard died Aug. 23, 1850, aged sixty-four.

The following have been the ministers of this society since Mr. Leonard's death: Abraham Norwood, 1832; Elbridge Trull, 1833; John Harriman, 1834; George C. Leach, 1837; M. B. Newell, 1842; J. A. Bartlett, 1845; B. H. Clark, 1847; E. W. Coffin, 1848; N. Gunnison, 1854; E. Partridge, 1857; Lewis L. Record, 1859.

The meeting-house erected by the Third Parish in 1728 stood till the summer of 1830. The last sermon was preached in by Rev. Ezra Leonard, on Sunday, Aug. 7, in that year, from Acts vii. 49. A new one was immediately erected on the same site, and dedicated Jan. 5, 1831. The sermon on the occasion was preached by Rev. Thomas Whittemore, from Acts xvii. 24.

In the year 1804, a prominent citizen of the town departed this life, — Col. Joseph Foster; who died Dec. 10, aged seventy-four. Col. Foster was a native of Ipswich. He was brought up in humble circumstances, and was indebted solely to his own energy and shrewdness for his advancement in life. He is supposed to have come to this town about 1760, and to have entered immediately upon those mercantile employments, in which, as a ship-master or merchant, he was afterwards engaged to the end of his days. In the Revolutionary crisis, he was a patriot of the most ardent stamp; and was always ready to lend his personal exertions and his pecuniary means to help the town through the struggle. He was a man of rough manners; but he enjoyed the confidence and esteem of his townsmen, and was chosen frequently to various important public offices. He was several times elected representative, and was one of the delegates to the Convention for forming the State Constitution. He built and occupied a house near the easterly end of Front Street, at the head of a lane leading to his wharf; but he had previously resided in a house still standing at the head of Hancock Street. His business had been pursued with such success, that he died possessed of a large estate. He left a son Joseph, who became a sea-captain, and was lost at sea about 1816; having never been heard from after leaving home on a voyage to the West Indies.

CHAPTER XXVIII.

FIRST PARISH. — REV. PEREZ LINCOLN. — REV. LEVI HARTSHORN. — REV. HOSEA HILDRETH. — REV. LUTHER HAMILTON. — REV. JOSIAH K. WAITE. — REV. WILLIAM MOUNTFORD. — REV. ROBERT P. ROGERS. — FIRST-PARISH MEETING-HOUSES. — FIFTH PARISH. — REV. DAVID JEWETT. — REV. WAKEFIELD GALE. — DEATH OF PROMINENT CITIZENS.

WHILE the measures for supplying the religious wants of a portion of our people — related in the preceding chapter — were in progress, another pulpit was about to become vacant. The death of Rev. Dr. Forbes, in the last month of 1804, left the First Church without a pastor; an event that had occurred but once before in more than a hundred years. After the lapse of a few months, the Rev. Perez Lincoln of Hingham accepted a call to settle over the parish; and was ordained Aug. 7, 1805. The sermon at his ordination was preached by Rev. Peter Whitney of Quincy, from Rev. ii. 10, latter clause; and was printed. Mr. Lincoln was son of David Lincoln of Hingham, and was born Jan. 21, 1777. He graduated at Harvard College in 1798, and studied divinity with Rev. Dr. Barnes of Scituate. He entered upon the duties of his office here with zeal and devotion; but death, after a few years, put a period to his ministry. His health began to fail in the fall of 1810, when he ceased to preach. His complaint, which was of a pulmonary nature, made such progress, that he left his parish in April, 1811, on a journey, with some hope of benefit; but his frame rapidly gave way to the encroachments of the disease, and he died at Hingham on the 13th of June following. His last words were, "I die in full hope of a blessed immortality, and in a firm trust in the merits of that Redeemer which I have endeavored faithfully to preach to others." Though his ministry was a short one, it had continued long enough to enable him to secure the respect and love of his parishioners, by the evidences, exhibited in his daily life, that he possessed a pure mind, warm heart, and correct judgment. He is described by a contemporary as a man of conciliatory manners and agreeable deportment. It is also said that he was a good classical scholar, and that his sermons were written with great care, and in a style remarkably neat, chaste, and correct.

Mr. Lincoln's salary was one thousand dollars a year. His church consisted of sixty-six members at the beginning of his ministry; and, during its continuance, thirty-eight were added: the number of baptisms, in the same time, being two hundred and forty-five; of marriages, sixty-five; and of deaths, two hundred and one.

Mr. Lincoln's wife was Sophia, daughter of Thomas Loring, Esq., of Hingham. She remained a widow, and died Oct. 2, 1817, leaving no children.

The pulpit now made vacant by the death of Rev. Perez Lincoln remained without a settled pastor upwards of four years; but preaching was held without interruption, except during two winters. At length, the Rev. Levi Hartshorn, having first preached to the people on the 9th of June, 1815, received and accepted a call to become their minister, at a salary of seven hundred dollars. Mr. Hartshorn was born in Amherst, N.H., in 1789. He graduated at Dartmouth College in 1813, and was ordained over the First Parish here Oct. 18, 1815. The sermon on the occasion was preached by the Rev. Daniel Dana, D.D., of Newburyport, from 1 Cor. i. 23, 24. The right hand of fellowship was given by Rev. David Jewett of the Fifth Parish.

The ministry of this young pastor, like that of his predecessor, was soon cut short by death. He addressed his people, and administered the sacrament to his church, for the last time, Sept. 5, 1819. Leaving soon after on a visit to his father at Amherst, he was there taken sick with typhus-fever, and died under the parental roof, on the 27th of that month, greatly lamented by his church and people.

Mr. Hartshorn's wife, to whom he was married about a month after his settlement here, was Hannah Elliott of Amherst. He left two sons,—Edward and Samuel Elliott; the latter of whom died Dec. 1, 1819. The former still lives, and is a practising physician in Berlin, Mass.; where Mrs. Hartshorn also resides, in the family of her son.

In a sermon preached to the bereaved parish, Feb. 20, 1820, by Rev. Dr. Dana, the character of their deceased minister is fully described. As a preacher, he is represented to have dwelt much upon "those doctrines which illustrate the awful degeneracy and ruin of man, and which ascribe all his salvation to the sovereign grace of God, through the atonement of the divine Redeemer and the renewing energy of the Holy Spirit;" while, as a pastor, the virtues ascribed to him by his friend, and yet held in affectionate remembrance by the few survivors of his flock, show that he had attained the highest degree of excellence of which frail humanity is capable.

Mr. Hartshorn was the last person who died in the office of minister of the First Parish. The divisions with regard to some of the fundamental doctrines of Calvinism, which, about the time of his death, had begun to rend many of the ancient churches of New England, were beginning to separate the members of this parish; and, though some attempts were made to settle a minister, none resulted in success till after a lapse of nearly six years. During this period, the pulpit was supplied by various ministers; of whom Rev. Albert Barnes, Rev. Andrew Bigelow, and Rev. Orville Dewey, each remained several months.

At last, the church and parish united in a call to Hosea Hildreth, who was then, and had been for many years, an instructor in Phillips Academy, Exeter, N.H. He accepted the invitation, and was ordained Aug. 3, 1825. The sermon on the occasion was preached by Rev. Dr. Holmes of Cambridge, from 2 Cor. xii. 19. Mr. Hildreth was born in Chelmsford in 1782, and graduated at Harvard College in 1805. He brought to the performance of his new duties all the qualities necessary to make him useful as a Christian minister, and he entered upon them with the fairest prospects of success; but the seeds of division and decay had taken such root in the ancient parish, that no effort could restore its former strength and vigor. The Baptists and Methodists, proselyting within its limits, drew away many members; and dissatisfaction finally crept into the church, from which seven members withdrew in 1829, — alleging as a reason, that they could not be instructed or edified by the pastor's preaching. Against this, the chief objection was understood to be, that it was not sufficiently doctrinal, and was not marked by an explicit avowal of the pastor's views upon important doctrinal points. He did, indeed, enforce good works more than good belief; and, in his daily life, was constantly active in endeavoring to promote the moral and intellectual improvement of the whole town. His zeal and ability in the cause of temperance, both here and abroad, finally procured him an appointment as a public lecturer and agent; and his connection with the parish was dissolved, at his own request, Dec. 31, 1833. Mr. Hildreth died at Sterling, July 10, 1835, leaving a widow* and several children, of whom three were sons. Richard, the oldest of them, has earned a wide reputation as the author of an excellent "History of the United States." Samuel T., a graduate of Harvard College, and a young man of great promise, died Feb. 11, 1839. Charles H., the only one born in Gloucester, is a physician in his native town.

The next minister of the parish was Rev. Luther Hamilton, a native of Conway, and graduate of Williams College in 1817. He had recently been pastor of a church in Taunton, and came to Gloucester as a decided Unitarian in his religious views. To these views, a majority of the parish were now attached; but a majority of the members of the church still held to the ancient faith. With sentiments irreconcilably opposed, it was not to be expected that these bodies could act harmoniously together; and the parish invited Mr. Hamilton, and fixed the day for his installation, before the concurrence of the church was asked.

---

* Mrs. Hildreth died in Gloucester, at the house of her son-in-law, Mr. James Mansfield, Jan. 22, 1859.

This conduct was deemed by the latter a mark of contempt; and, before the day fixed for Mr. Hamilton's installation arrived, they held a meeting, and voted that all connection between the church and parish should be then dissolved. The organization of the church was kept up till 1837; when, most of its members having joined other churches, this venerable body, after a duration of nearly two hundred years, ceased to exist.

Mr. Hamilton was installed Nov. 12, 1834. The sermon was preached by Rev. Dr. Brazer of Salem, and other Unitarian clergymen also engaged in the services of the occasion. Before the expiration of a year, a majority of his parish were as eager to discharge him as they had been to settle him. It was a time of considerable political excitement; and without any knowledge of his intentions, or even of his political sentiments, on the part of the majority of his parish, who were Whigs, he accepted from the Democratic party a nomination as representative; and was elected to that office in November, 1835. At a parish-meeting held soon afterwards, his political opponents procured a vote to dissolve the connection: but Mr. Hamilton availed himself of the conditions of his settlement, which allowed his ministry to continue three months after notice of dissolution; and continued to preach, though to a very small congregation, during the winter. At the close of his labors here, he left the ministry, and took an office in the Boston Custom House.

At the time of Mr. Hamilton's dismission, the parish had become so reduced, that only about fifty male members belonged to it. The Orthodox portion had withdrawn, and the remaining members constituted a society of decided Unitarians. With entire unanimity, they proceeded, in the spring of 1836, to seek a minister; and soon made an engagement with Rev. Josiah K. Waite, who was installed July 19, 1837. The sermon on this occasion was preached by Rev. Alexander Young of Boston. The ministry of Mr. Waite continued till Sept. 30, 1849, when he resigned his pastoral office. He was a faithful pastor and a kind friend; and his labors in behalf of temperance, and other good works, entitle him to the grateful remembrance of our people.

Mr. Waite's successor was Rev. William Mountford, a native of England, whose reputation as a writer preceded his own arrival in this country. Having preached to the First Parish soon after he came to the United States, his pulpit performances were so satisfactory, that they gave him an invitation to settle as their minister. He began to preach to the parish in 1850, but was not installed till Aug. 3, 1852. Rev. F. D. Huntington of Boston preached the sermon on this occasion. Mr. Mountford resigned his office, May 13, 1853; but continued to supply the pulpit till the next fall.

The present minister of the parish (Rev. Robert P. Rogers) was settled over it, Aug. 30, 1854. His installation afforded an opportunity to a few of the people to greet a friend, who, many years before, had ministered to them in holy things, — Rev. Orville Dewey, D.D., who preached the sermon on that occasion. Mr. Rogers was born in Boston, Aug. 29, 1824. He is a nephew of the late Rev. Dr. Channing; and therefore a descendant of our ancient settler, William Ellery. He was some time a student in Harvard College, of the class of 1844; but, in consequence of ill health, was obliged to leave before his class graduated. He received his theological education at the Cambridge Divinity School, from which he graduated in 1849; and in January, 1850, settled in the ministry at Canton, Mass., — his only pastorate previous to that in which he is now successfully engaged, and with which the history of the First Parish is here brought to a close.

The First-Parish Meeting-house, built by seven members* of the parish in 1738, was erected on a new street, then recently laid out by the name of Cornhill Street, but now known as Middle Street; and was of large dimensions. If the vote of the parish, agreeing to its size, was followed, it was sixty feet wide, seventy-five feet long, and thirty feet stud. It stood parallel to the street, nearly out to a line with its northern side; and, though no drawing of it has been preserved, the accompanying engraving, taken

* These were Epes Sargent, Andrew Robinson, Thomas Sanders, Nathaniel Ellery, William Ellery, Philemon Warren, jun., and William Parsons.

from the memory of aged persons long familiar with its appearance, may be regarded as almost, if not quite, an exact representation of it. Of the original appearance of the interior, no exact description can now be given. The pulpit was on the north side, opposite the front-door; and was entered by a single flight of stairs at the westerly end. These stairs also gave access to two long seats — one for the elders and one for the deacons — in front of the pulpit. A spacious gallery extended round the other three sides, and was reached by a flight of stairs in each corner of the meeting-house. The stairs at the westerly end were removed about 1770, when a flight was built in the tower; but those at the easterly end remained till 1792, when the porch on that end was raised one story to make room for changing the access to the gallery there. For many years, a portion of the floor was occupied by seats, of which those at the eastern end were set apart for the negroes. In course of time, however, these seats gave place to pews; a row of pews was also built along the wall, the whole distance of the gallery; and the arrangement of the interior became such as is remembered by the elderly and middle-aged people of the present time. Those worshippers who were nervous will not soon forget the annoyances by which their devotions in the house of God were disturbed. The pews, which were square, were all built with an open-work top, formed by a rail that rested on round pieces of wood, about a foot long, inserted in the edge of a board beneath. These open spaces in the pews offered to restless urchins a constant temptation to play, and thus occasioned considerable noise in the house. But the greatest clatter came from the hinge-seats, when they were let down by the standing congregation at the close of prayer. This has been not inaptly compared to an irregular discharge of musketry. These noises, however, disturbed only a portion of the worshippers. It was on windy days, when the great building shook upon its foundation and the timbers creaked with startling sounds, that the whole assembly were awed by a feeling of insecurity, even in the temple of the Lord.

The tower of this meeting-house was seventy feet high, and

[illegible] of the p[illegible] [illegible] three [illegible] 17[illegible] [illegible] however, these [illegible] built along [illegible] to p[illegible] B[illegible] were [illegible] with [illegible] were [illegible] a feel[illegible] [illegible]

FIRST PARISH MEETING HOUSE, 1738 – 1828

was surmounted by a spire of equal height. The latter, according to Chandler's journal, "fell by the wind, Oct. 23, 1761, about twelve o'clock at night;" and was not replaced till 1765, when the parish voted to build a new one a third shorter than the old. This one was shaken so violently by the great gale in September, 1815, that its fall was for some time momentarily expected. Though it did not yield to the force of the wind, the effect of another gale was feared; and it was soon afterwards taken down to give place to a shorter and stronger one.

Public worship was held in this house, for the last time, on Sunday afternoon, April 6, 1828; when the pastor of the parish (Rev. H. Hildreth) preached, to about six hundred hearers, a sermon on the duty of supporting the Congregational institutions of the New-England Fathers. The building was soon afterwards removed; and, before the close of the year, the meeting-house now standing on the same spot was erected. This was dedicated Dec. 25, 1828. The sermon was preached by the pastor; and one of the hymns was read by Rev. Daniel Fuller, then in his eighty-ninth year.

There remained, in 1805, another long-vacant pastorate to be filled. The Sandy-Bay Parish had been without a settled minister more than twenty-five years, though the place of one had been partially supplied at different times by Mr. Cleaveland, as heretofore related. The church was desolate, and the people exhibited the usual signs of a want of religious instruction and New-England sabbath influences. The field was therefore an inviting one to a sincere, earnest, and resolute spirit; and such the parish happily found in the Rev. David Jewett, whom they chose to be their pastor. Mr. Jewett was son of Jacob Jewett of Hollis, N.H.; and was born there July 16, 1774. He graduated at Dartmouth College in 1801, and was ordained over the Fifth Parish here Oct. 30, 1805. The sermon on the occasion was preached by Rev. Samuel Worcester of Salem, from Jer. iii. 15. Rev. Perez Lincoln gave the right hand of fellowship; but neither of our other parish ministers took part in the exercises, though both were present.

A considerable number of the people of the parish were Universalists; and, by an agreement with the majority, had control of the pulpit a certain proportion of the time, when they had Rev. Thomas Jones to preach to them. This state of things, as might have been expected, led to a verification of the Scripture maxim relating to the instability of a house divided against itself; and a dispute grew out of it, which finally resulted in a lengthy lawsuit, the result of which was a surrender by the minority of their privilege in the meeting-house.

Mr. Jewett's views of religious truth were those entertained by most of the New-England churches of his time; and he considered it his duty to do all he could to prevent the spread of what he thought a dangerous delusion in his parish. But, though his course was firm and decided, it was not marked by the rancor which is often engendered in a religious warfare; and he forfeited neither the affection of his friends nor the respect of his opponents.

According to the just standard by which the success of a ministry should be measured, that of Mr. Jewett entitles him to a high rank among the ministers of the town. He found a church of ten members, which he increased to two hundred and fifty. He found his people, if not in a low state of morals, yet rapidly tending thitherward; and he arrested their downward progress, and improved and elevated them to such a degree, that the success of his labors was often the theme of remark in places beyond the sphere of his work. It was, therefore, with a happy retrospect that he could resign his office, and cease from labor, which he was compelled by ill health to do, in 1836. He removed from town, and died at the house of his son-in-law, in Waltham, July 14, 1841. The people of his parish desired that his remains should rest in a spot connected by many solemn recollections with the memory of their faithful and beloved pastor; and they were accordingly brought to Rockport in July, 1856, and interred in the Parish Burying-ground, where a handsome granite monument marks the place of their repose. The occasion was one of deep interest. On the 13th of that month, Rev. William R. Jewett, son of the deceased minister, preached a sermon at the meeting-house, and then made an address at the grave; which was responded to, on behalf of the people, by Dr. Benjamin Haskell.

Mr. Jewett's successor was Rev. Wakefield Gale, who is still the minister of the society. Mr. Gale was born in Pembroke, N.H., Jan. 18, 1797. He graduated at Dartmouth College in 1822, and at Andover Theological Seminary in 1825. For the succeeding ten years, he was pastor of a church in Eastport, Me.; which place he left in answer to a call to fill the vacant pastorate in this church. His installation took place, May 4, 1836; when Rev. William M. Rogers of Boston preached the sermon, from Mark xvi. 15. The long continuance of Mr. Gale in the ministry upon which he then entered is the best evidence of the success that has attended his labors. The whole number of persons who have belonged to this church since its formation is seven hundred and thirty-eight, of whom three hundred and thirty-seven have been received under the ministry of the present pastor. One hundred and nine males and one hundred and ninety-four females are now communicants. It also has a large sabbath school. Of all the parish churches of Gloucester, the Fifth (now the First Congregational Church of Rockport) is the only one that has preserved a continued existence and the faith of the early settlers.

The meeting-house now occupied by this society was erected in 1804, and dedicated in October of that year. Rev. Abiel Abbott of Beverly preached the dedicatory sermon. The venerable Cleaveland preached in it one Sunday, soon after its dedication; and baptized nineteen children. In 1840, it was greatly altered and improved, both inside and out, at an expense of eight thousand dollars; so that it is now a very neat and handsome edifice.*

---

* This house of worship was struck by lightning, Sunday, July 3, 1842, and considerably injured. Rev. Mr. Gale has kindly furnished me the following particulars of this event: "Immediately after the benediction in the afternoon, the pastor, observing that the rain poured down in torrents, requested the congregation to be seated for a few moments. Scarcely had they complied with the request, when the whole house was surrounded and filled with the intensest light of which any one can conceive, proceed-

About the period with which the present chapter opens, death deprived the town of a few citizens, who may properly be noticed here.

Mr. Joseph Procter, who is said to have come to Gloucester from Danvers, died Jan. 29, 1805, aged sixty-one. He carried on the fishing business quite extensively, and was for several years one of the selectmen. He left descendants in the town; one of whom (Joseph J.), a citizen of the highest respectability and usefulness, was a representative in 1839, and died Sept. 2, 1848, aged forty-six.

On the 10th of August, 1805, died John Gibaut, Esq., aged thirty-eight. His father (Capt. Edward Gibaut) was born in the Island of Jersey, and was for sixty years a resident of Salem; from which place he removed to this town, and died here Nov. 1, 1803, aged seventy-five. The son was an only child. He was a merchant, or, at least, engaged in mercantile adventures; and had recently arrived from India, when about 1801, in reward for his partiality to Mr. Jefferson, he received the appointment of Collector of Gloucester. He is said to have died a bachelor.

Samuel Whittemore, Esq., died suddenly July 15, 1806, aged seventy-three. He was a native of Cambridge. He graduated at Harvard College in 1751, and commenced teaching in Gloucester the next year; from which time he became a permanent resident. He served the town as a representative, and held many other offices usually conferred upon prominent citizens; in all of which he was esteemed for an honest and faithful discharge of his duties. He was twice married: first to Margaret, daugh-

---

ing from what appeared through the doors and windows large balls of fire falling to the ground. On examination, it was discovered that the lightning had struck the house on the west side of the tower; and, running quite across the house above the doors and windows, passed down the corner post, tearing off or shattering all the covering in its course. At the same moment, a large portion of the electric fluid escaped from the lightning-rod at the opposite end of the house, ploughing the hard ground for a considerable distance, and so rarefying the air, that every pane of glass in the cellar window burst out. Great alarm seized the congregation for a moment: but, happily, no one was injured; though probably some would have been, had they not remained in the house."

ter of Rev. Joshua Gee of Boston; and next to Mrs. Sarah Parsons of Gloucester. One son and three daughters, all by the last wife, still survive. A grandson (George) graduated at Harvard College in 1857, — more than a century after his grandfather.

CHAPTER XXIX.

POLITICAL EXCITEMENT. — FEDERALISTS AND REPUBLICANS. — STORMY TOWN-MEETING. — FEDERALISTS TRIUMPHANT. — EMBARGO. — MARINE DISASTERS. — SLOW INCREASE OF POPULATION. — FIRST BAPTIST SOCIETY: ITS MINISTERS AND ITS MEETING-HOUSE. — WAR WITH ENGLAND. — GLOUCESTER OPPOSES THE WAR. — COUNTY CONVENTION. — MILITARY PREPARATIONS FOR PROTECTION OF THE TOWN. — BRITISH SHIP "NYMPH." — THE ENEMY ATTEMPT TO TAKE A VESSEL AT SANDY BAY. — TAKE VESSELS IN SQUAM HARBOR. — LAND AT SANDY BAY. — ALARM AT GALLOP'S FOLLY. — ENGINE-HOUSE TORN DOWN BY INDIGNANT MILITIA. — COMMERCE UNDER A NEUTRAL FLAG. — SCHOONER "ADOLPH." — GLOUCESTER PRIVATEERING DURING THE WAR. — CASE OF HYDROPHOBIA. — PEACE.

NATIONAL politics had, as yet, occasioned little excitement in the town: but the foreign policy of Mr. Jefferson's administration aroused a strong opposition; and, in 1806, a violent party spirit prevailed. In that year, the ticket for representatives, composed of persons friendly to that policy, — five in number, — was elected by a plurality of sixty-nine, in a vote of five hundred and thirty-five. The Republicans retained their ascendency the next year; but the embargo laid by the President towards its close, by which the chief business pursuits of our people were threatened with destruction, aroused the Federalists to make a strenuous effort to carry the town at the March meeting in 1808. Upon a trial of strength, on the vote for three selectmen, after an animated contest, the Federal ticket was elected; Benjamin K. Hough, a leading member of the party, having two hundred and fifty-five votes, against two hundred and forty-one given for the highest Republican opponent.

The defeated party, confident of success in a full vote, rallied their forces at an adjournment; and after much marching in and out of the meeting-house, by both parties, to ascertain the qualified voters, — for the voting was then by hand-ballot, — they carried a vote to choose four additional selectmen. During all this time, great confusion prevailed, arising from the disputing of votes; and the passions of the people were excited to the highest pitch: but finally the balloting for the four selectmen was finished some time after dark, when it was shown that William Babson, jun., Joseph Procter, and Josiah Choate, each had three hundred and twenty-nine votes; and Solomon Pool, three hundred and twenty-four. These composed the Federal ticket. The two highest on the Republican ticket had three hundred and twenty-eight each. One of these was Daniel Rogers, jun., the moderator of the meeting. There were also three or four scattering votes. By a strange use of arithmetic, the moderator declared three hundred and thirty-two necessary for a choice; and that, accordingly, none were elected. Hereupon a motion was made to adjourn; which was tried, declared, and doubted, again and again. The Parish Committee had forbidden the use of lights in the meeting-house, and the floor of the holy edifice presented a dim scene of wild confusion and discord worthy of Pandemonium itself. At length, at half-past ten, the moderator, upon his own proposition, was permitted to name a committee to fix upon a day of adjournment. The committee agreed upon the next Friday; and to that day the meeting was accordingly adjourned. At the adjournment, after calling the meeting to order, the moderator announced that he had made a mistake in counting the scattering votes at the last meeting; and, upon correcting it, had found that three of the Federal candidates were elected. Each party had its full strength on hand, ready for another struggle; and the equally balanced power of the two sides rendered the contest one of great interest and excitement. The first trial came on the motion to proceed to choose the seventh selectman; which was carried by the Democrats, three hundred and twenty-nine to three hundred and twenty-eight. This victory was followed by another, in the election of Daniel Rogers, jun., their candidate for selectman, by a vote of three hundred and thirty-two, against three hundred and thirty-one; and thus ended the first hard-fought political battle in the town.

These meetings were held in the First-Parish Meeting-house. The leaders of each party residing at the Harbor entertained their friends from the outskirts with unbounded hospitality; and each side had its own place of refreshment for general resort.

A full vote had not yet been obtained, and the two parties went zealously to work to prepare for the State election soon to be held. The Democrats, not unreasonably, expected success. They had the influence of the Pearce Family, of the government officers, of Capt. John Somes, of Capt. William Pearson, and of many other prominent citizens, besides the popular cry of "Free trade and sailors' rights." The Federalists had the advantage, perhaps, in working and talking partisans; and were not without strong leaders; among whom Mr. Hough, well known and popular; James Hayes, Dr. William Coffin, Dr. John Manning of Sandy Bay, Major Kimball of Squam, John Mason, and Lonson Nash, — a young lawyer and ardent politician, just moved into town, — were conspicuous. The day of election came, and ended with a decided victory for the latter; Mr. Gore, their candidate for Governor, receiving four hundred and fourteen votes, against three hundred and sixty-four cast for Mr. Sullivan, the Democratic nominee. At the election for representatives, in May, the Federalists were again successful, by a vote nearly as large as that for Governor; and continued to maintain their ascendency for a period of eight years.

In common with the other seaport towns of New England, Gloucester was suffering severely by the embargo; and the people, at a town-meeting on the 22d of August, 1808, voted to petition the President to "suspend it, or so much of it as operated against the export trade of the country to Spain, Portugal, and their Colonial dependencies." They asked for bread, and received a stone. Instead of relief, came the so-called "Enforcing Act," — pronounced by an historian* of the United

* Hildreth, vol. vi. p. 110.

States "the most arbitrary piece of legislation which our national history exhibits;" and the poor resource of submission and complaint was all that was left to them. The latter they did not fail to utter in resolutions in town-meeting, and in a spirited and eloquent address to the General Court; all of which are preserved in the records of the town. They also gave an emphatic expression of their views of national policy in the vote for Governor in the spring of 1809, when the Federal candidate received more than two-thirds of the votes.

Party lines had now become strictly drawn; and party spirit ran so high, that all social and convivial gatherings exhibited the political affinities of the people as distinctly as the caucus or the polls. The young and the gay had their Federal balls and Republican balls; while the older people had their political suppers, parties, and excursions. Party celebrations of the anniversary of American independence were also in vogue. The Federalists had one in 1808; on which occasion, an oration was delivered by Lonson Nash, Esq.; after which, the great mass of the party partook of a sumptuous dinner at Federal Hall: while the Republicans, on the same day, assembled at a grand party dinner, and gave vent to their patriotism in toasts, songs, and speeches. Inseparable from this state of high party excitement, which continued several years, were frequent personal disputes, that sometimes ended in blows: but, as a party, the Federalists exhibited little of the oppression or insolence of power; and, even in their public rejoicings over a triumph, seldom gave greater cause of offence than occasionally to stop their processions before the house of a prominent opponent, when some jolly tars, in a boat, would pretend to be in shoal water, and make considerable noise with their "Yo, heave ho!" in tacking ship to get out of danger.

During the years over which we have just passed, the town suffered by two marine disasters: by one, a loss in character; and, by the other, a loss of valuable lives. On the 28th of February, 1807, the ship "Howard," Capt. Bray, from Calcutta, with a cargo of India goods, bound to Boston, was cast away in a violent storm, near Grape-vine Cove, on Eastern Point. Soon after the ship struck, she broke in two; and the captain, mate, and two hands, were swept away by a sea, and drowned. The rest of the men got ashore. The cargo was scattered along the shore; and, notwithstanding the best exertions by the owner's agents, and some of our own people, a greal deal of it was pilfered. The other disaster was the loss of three Sandy-Bay fishing-boats, of about twenty tons burthen each, in a severe storm in May or June, 1808, on Cashes Ledge, by which eleven persons — all who were on board — perished.

The third United-States Census, taken in 1810, showed the population of Gloucester to be five thousand nine hundred and forty-three; a gain of about twelve per cent since 1790. This was the smallest percentage of increase in any period of twenty years since 1700; a fact which shows that neither the chief business of the town — the fisheries — nor its foreign commerce had, during the last period, been pursued with any very prosperous results. Of those who emigrated during this period, the coast and forests of Maine received a considerable portion; of whom, and of preceding emigrants, the condition became so poor, during the war that followed, that one of the overseers made a journey to that district in 1813 to attend to such as were supported there at the charge of the town.

In June, 1811, was incorporated the First Baptist Society in Gloucester. This society owes its origin to the labors of Benjamin Hale, jun., a respectable ship-master of Sandy Bay, who, while absent on a foreign voyage about 1804, was converted in a somewhat remarkable manner. Upon his return from this voyage, he opened his house for religious meetings: and through his labors, with occasional assistance, several persons were brought together from different parts of the town; and on the 30th of March, 1808, a church, consisting of eight males* and ten females, was organized. In 1809, Capt. Hale was licensed to preach, and he frequently exercised his gifts for the edification of

* The names of these were Benjamin Hale, John Smith, Ebenezer Pool, Seth Woodbury, William Smith, Nehemiah Grover, Nathan F. Morgan, and Solomon Pool. Capt. Hale removed from Sandy Bay about 1812; but returned, and died there in 1818, aged forty-two.

the church; though, for about three years from this time, Rev. Elisha S. Williams of Beverly often officiated. In 1812, the church had increased to thirty-two members; but, during the next eight years, it had no additions, and only had public worship a few sabbaths in each year, though religious meetings were held at the house of one of the brethren (Ebenezer Pool) every Sunday afternoon. At the end of this time, the society made an effort to settle a minister; and finally succeeded, in December, 1820, in obtaining Rev. James A. Boswell, a young and devoted pastor, under whose ministry the church began to increase and prosper. Mr. Boswell left in February, 1823. The society was poor, and long periods elapsed in which it had no preaching. At last, they procured Rev. Reuben Curtis in the fall of 1827, who remained about three years. He commenced his ministry during the time of a great revival at the Cape, when upwards of two hundred were added to the old church there, and over sixty to the Baptist Church.

The following has been the succession of pastors since Mr. Curtis: Bartlet Pease, 1831; Otis Wing, 1834; Gibbon Williams, an Englishman, 1837; Benjamin Knight, 1838; Otis Wing, 1840; L. B. Hathaway, 1843, died in his ministry; Benjamin N. Harris, 1844; Samuel C. Gilbert, 1846; Thomas Driver, 1849; George Lyle, 1850; Thomas Driver, 1852; Allen E. Battel, 1855; Joseph M. Driver, 1856 to the present time.

The Baptists of Sandy Bay held their meetings for public worship in a hall for about two years after the settlement of Mr. Boswell. In 1822, they erected their present house of worship, and occupied it that year, though no pews were built in it till 1828. It was not dedicated with the usual formalities; but an appropriate discourse was delivered by Mr. Boswell when it was first opened for religious worship.

The political troubles in which the country had long been involved with Great Britain were now to be settled by the arbitrament of battle. In June, 1812, the Congress of the United States declared war against that nation; a measure deemed by a majority of the people of Gloucester, as of the whole Northern section of the Union, unwise, impolitic, and unjust. The business interests of the town were almost wholly commercial, and the people had long suffered from what they felt to be the hostility of the government to the maritime prosperity of the country. "Our home," they said, "is on the ocean; our wealth we draw from the deep; and by dangers and sufferings, which from repetition have become familiar, we support ourselves, our wives, and our children." Depending thus upon a free use of the sea for their maintenance, they gave expression to earnest denunciations of the war that drove them from their customary pursuits, and omitted no occasion to declare their sentiments by their votes. A strong war-party, however, existed in the town, and made in the spring of this year a vigorous struggle for the ascendency; throwing four hundred and one votes for Dr. John Kittredge for moderator of the March meeting, against four hundred and ninety-four cast for Mr. Hough. This was a full vote, and therefore a full expression of the political views of the people.

A few days after the declaration of war, a town-meeting was held, at which an address to the citizens of the Commonwealth, on "the portentous crisis of our national affairs," was adopted with but two dissenting voices; and, on the 13th of July, the town, in its corporate capacity, chose delegates to a County Convention for the purpose of consulting upon the "awful and alarming situation of the country." The delegates were William Dane, Robert Elwell, 3d, John Mason, Lonson Nash, and Daniel Rogers. The convention assembled at Ipswich, July 21, and adopted a "declaration" embodying the views upon national affairs held by the Federal party, and expressing in strong language their opinions and feelings in opposition to the war.

The anticipated effects of the war upon the prosperity of the town were fully realized. The fisheries were interrupted; its commerce was nearly destroyed, though some was carried on under cover of a false neutrality; and many of its citizens were made captives at sea, and confined in English prisons. It was not till the second year of the war, however, that the enemy began to annoy our people at home, and create alarm for the safety of the town. The militia and the artillery company of the town were as yet its sole means of defence, with the exception of a subaltern's guard, having four cannon, stationed at the fort commanding the entrance of the inner harbor. This force was now increased; more large guns were supplied; the old fort at the Stage was repaired, and barracks were built there; and two companies of State militia — one under command of Capt. Benjamin Haskell, and the other under that of Capt. Widger of Ipswich — were raised by draught, and stationed here for the protection of the place. Another company was draughted by authority of the United States, and stationed at the Government Fort, under command of Abraham Williams of Newburyport.

The necessity for these preparations was soon apparent. In August, 1813, the British ship "Nymph," then cruising off the coast, commenced depredations upon the fishermen and coasters, and occasioned considerable alarm among the inhabitants. She made several captures: but her captain released his prizes upon the payment of a ransom; for the purpose of raising which, the masters of three coasters and six fishing-boats were ashore at one time. The amount then required was two hundred dollars for each vessel. Resistance in all these cases was, of course, useless; but in one, in which the force of the enemy was less formidable, our people defended their property successfully. Some time in August, one of the enemy's cruisers, of about sixty tons, called the "Commodore Broke," stood into Sandy Bay, with the intention of taking one or more loaded coasters then lying at anchor there. Having neared the shore, and wishing, perhaps, first to try the courage of the people, she fired several large and grape shot into the village; upon which the men of the place assembled on the Neck, and from the north-easterly part of the old wharf, where they had a small cannon, began to fire upon the enemy with that, and also with their small-arms. At this time, the captain of the cruiser had commenced sweeping out of the bay: but the Cape men did not let him escape without showing him a token of their spirit and skill; for the first cannon-ball they fired at him entered the schooner under her transom, and, passing under deck, came out near her stem, above water. The firing upon the vessel was kept up from Bearskin Neck, and the men at Pigeon Cove gave her several musket-shot as she passed their shore: but she got off without further damage; and our people, by their bravery, preserved a considerable amount of property. In the next year (1814), the enemy had several large ships on our coast, and the summer was one of constant alarms; so much so, that many families moved their most valuable effects into some of the neighboring villages. On the 6th of June, an English frigate came into Ipswich Bay, and sent two barges, well manned, into Squam Harbor, to take or destroy a few vessels then lying there. One of these — a sloop laden with lime, belonging to Boston — was burnt; another sloop was sunk; and two small schooners, laden with fish, were carried off. While committing these depredations, the enemy showed some forbearance in sparing, at the entreaties of Oakes and Millet, a sloop belonging to them, and in leaving another unharmed on account of her name, — the "Federalist." About the same time, a Portsmouth schooner, laden with flour, was chased by one of the enemy's cruisers into Gloucester Harbor, and run ashore somewhere on Eastern Point. Some men were sent from the cruiser in a boat to take possession of the schooner; but Col. Appleton, then commanding the Gloucester regiment of militia, had by this time arrived at the spot with the artillery company, who used their guns with such effect, that the enemy were driven off, and the schooner was saved.

In this or the preceding year, another schooner, being chased by an English frigate, was run ashore at Norman's Woe. The artillery hastened to her relief; but the barges of the frigate, under protection of her guns, succeeded in getting her off and taking her away.

A more important affair occurred in September at Sandy Bay. The people of that place had, in the spring of this year, erected at their own expense a fort on the point of Bearskin Neck, and procured for it three carriage-guns, which were placed in charge of a corporal, with a detachment from one of the companies at the Harbor. On the 8th of September, the British frigate "Nymph" took one of the fishing-boats belonging to the place;

and her skipper (Capt. David Elwell) was compelled to act as pilot for two barges, full of men, which the captain of the frigate determined to send in to get possession of the fort. These barges started from the frigate about midnight, and, hidden from sight by a dense fog, were rowed with muffled oars towards the Neck; and, having reached it, one of the barges proceeded into Long Cove, and landed her men at what is called "the Eastern Gutter." The enemy then marched to the fort; took the sentinel by surprise; made prisoners of the soldiers, fourteen in number; and spiked the guns, which they threw out of the fort. The other barge went into the old dock on the western side of the Neck; where her men soon encountered some of the people of the village, who had been roused by an alarm given by a sentinel stationed on the Neck, not far from the houses. It was now daybreak, and a clear morning. Several musket-balls were fired at this barge by three of the Cape men, who got in return cannon and grape-shot, but received no injury from them. To silence the alarm-bell, which was now ringing, several shot were fired at the belfry of the Meeting-house, one of which struck one of the posts of the steeple. But this attempt had a disastrous and nearly fatal termination for the enemy; for the firing of their large gun caused a butt to start in the bow of the barge, which soon began to fill with water, and finally sunk just as the men got her in near the rocks back of the pier. The officer in command, and a few of his men, ran across the Neck; and, seizing a boat, made their escape. The rest, a dozen or more, were made prisoners. In the mean time, the men who took the fort had, with all their prisoners, or a part of them, got into their barge, and were on their way back to the frigate.

The alarm created by this affair soon spread all over the Cape; and the military forces of the town, under Col. Appleton, started for Sandy Bay; though, upon news that they were not needed, only a part proceeded to the place. An exchange of prisoners was proposed; but Col. Appleton, not feeling authorized to make one, detached a platoon, under Lieut. Charles Tarr, to take charge of those in possession of our people till they could be sent to the depot in Salem. On the night following, a number of men in disguise rescued the prisoners from Tarr, and effected an exchange; by which the men who had been carried away in the barge, and some belonging to other places, previously taken (about twenty in all), were released. It is difficult to conceive any other design in this landing than a wanton destruction of life and property: and yet the English captain, in the conclusion of the affair, promised the Cape people unmolested use of their fishing-grounds during the rest of the fall; and he kept his word.*

A few days after the affair just related, the people of the town were again alarmed, by a reported attempt of the enemy to land near Gallop's Folly. One of their frigates had chased a boat ashore at that place, and sent in a flag, with a demand that an officer of the ship should be allowed to search her. Whether this was a ruse to cover a design to help themselves to some of the cattle grazing near the shore, as some supposed, or not, no one can tell; but, whatever the purpose was, the presence of Col. Appleton with the whole military force of the town, numbering about four hundred men, soon caused the withdrawal of the enemy, and relieved all apprehensions of harm for the moment. While marching and countermarching in sight of the enemy's

---

* A contemporary newspaper account of this affair differs so much from that which I have given, derived from actors in it, that I here insert it: —

"Thursday, Sept. 9, 1814. — About daybreak, three barges full of men, from three frigates and a seventy-four, landed at Sandy Bay, and took possession of the fort, in which were four guns and fourteen men. The men were made prisoners. They then turned the guns upon the town, and fired upon the Meeting-house, where the alarm-bell was ringing. The artillery and militia companies, and soldiers from the fort, were immediately on the march (the artillery in thirty minutes from the alarm). A skirmish took place, in which several were killed and wounded on each side; the number not known. Our troops finally succeeded in driving off the enemy after they had spiked the guns at the fort and thrown them overboard, and succeeded in taking thirteen prisoners by one of their barges upsetting. Great credit is due to the militia and regulars of Gloucester for their activity. It is said they turned out to a man in a very few minutes. Great consternation prevailed at the first alarm at Gloucester; as it was represented the enemy had landed three thousand troops, and were marching directly into the harbor. Four of the fourteen prisoners escaped from one of the barges by swimming, and one was drowned." No life was lost; but it was supposed for a time that a missing man was drowned. The gun taken from the barge is still preserved at Rockport.

ship, Col. Appleton received a message from the Committee of Safety at the Harbor to return thither as soon as possible, as there were strong indications that the enemy were intending to land there. He therefore hastened back, but found the alarm subsided.

It was on this occasion that a memorable outrage was committed by some of our own soldiers on their return from the Cape. While the East-Ward Company was on its march down, one or two engine-men — a class exempted from military duty — assailed the soldiers with some jeering remarks, by which their anger was greatly excited. A day of hard duty did not tend to mollify them: and, as soon as they were dismissed after their return, some of the most furious rushed immediately to the engine-house, which was just in the rear of the company's place of rendezvous, near the First-Parish Meeting-house, and, in a few seconds, levelled it to the ground; not, without entreaty, sparing even the engine from destruction. A few suggested the propriety of seeking and punishing the offenders; but it was thought best by the majority to forgive the offence as a sudden ebullition of patriotic indignation.

It has been already stated, that, during the war, some commerce was carried on by our people in vessels disguised as neutrals. But this was not pursued to any great extent; for, though the profits were large, the risk and expenses were also great. Adventurers belonging to other places also made use of our port with one vessel, at least, under a neutral flag. In the latter part of 1813, a vessel, purporting to be the Swedish schooner "Adolph," came into the harbor, ostensibly from St. Bartholomew, but really from Halifax, N.S.; furnished, of course, with forged papers, to carry out the deception. She was laden with sugar; but also brought many valuable goods of the prohibited British manufacture, which, by various ingenious devices, were smuggled ashore. In a few days, she was cleared, with a cargo of flour, for St. Bartholomew; but her port of destination was Halifax. After an absence of fourteen days, she was again at anchor in Gloucester Harbor. A fortnight for a voyage to the West Indies and back was rather too barefaced an imposition to succeed at the Custom House; and the collector seized the vessel, stripped off her sails, and placed an inspector on board. Before all this was done, however, several contraband articles were landed; and some were sunk under the vessel, to be recovered at a favorable time. The crowning act of recklessness and daring remains to be told. One night in January, during a violent snow-storm (the master and crew being on board), the agents on shore, with the help of several men, took the sails from the place where the collector had deposited them, and carried them on board the schooner; which, in a few hours, they made ready for sea. During all this time, they kept the custom-house officer locked in the cabin; but, when the vessel was about to leave her anchorage to put out of the harbor, he was forced into the revenue-boat, and left, with a bottle of liquor and some bread and meat, to pass the rest of the night there as pleasantly as he could. The schooner got safely out of the bay; and, as may be supposed, did not again return. When the storm cleared away in the morning, the report was soon spread abroad, that the Swedish schooner had sunk at her anchors; but the poor sufferer in the custom-house boat had a different tale to tell.

The people of Gloucester did not engage in privateering to any great extent during the war. The only vessels of considerable size that were fitted out from the town were the schooners "Swordfish," "Thrasher," and "Orlando." The two former were taken by the enemy on their second cruise. The "Orlando," after making two cruises, in which she took no valuable prize, was lengthened thirty feet, and rigged into a ship. She was then fitted out again as a privateer, under command of Capt. Joseph Babson, who had previously commanded her one cruise as a schooner. She was no more fortunate, however, in her new rig than in the old one. The most daring performance of either of these vessels was the capture, by the "Thrasher," of an English East-Indiaman of twenty guns, manned with upwards of a hundred men. The "Thrasher" was of about one hundred and fifty tons burthen, and carried fourteen guns and ninety men. When she fell in with the ship, a large fleet of English merchantmen, under convoy of ships-of-war, was in sight. The captain of the "Thrasher" (Robert Evans) made up his mind to attempt the capture of the Indiaman by boarding; and accordingly ran boldly alongside of her. The boarders, to the number of twenty-seven, immediately sprang upon the deck of the ship, and, almost without resistance, secured instant possession of her. The English captain was ignorant of the existence of war between the two nations, and was therefore, in some degree, taken by surprise; though the audacity of the attack was sufficient to overpower a commander of ordinary self-possession and bravery. The ship was one of the most valuable prizes ever captured; but the victors, for want of common prudence, soon lost her, and became prisoners themselves. The prize-master, instead of keeping her on her course while daylight lasted, so that he could avail himself of the night to effect his escape from the fleet, foolishly steered off in another direction, and thus attracted attention from the English ships-of-war; one of which immediately gave chase, and soon again placed her in possession of her captain and his crew. The "Thrasher" herself, not long afterwards, was captured by an English frigate, and sent into Gibraltar.

Besides these vessels, three or four fishing-boats were fitted out from the town on privateering cruises. The largest and most successful of these was the "Madison," of twenty-eight tons. She carried twenty-eight men; and, in one short cruise, took a ship of four hundred tons, laden with timber and naval stores, and a brig of three hundred tons, bound to Halifax, with a valuable cargo. Both of these prizes were sent into Gloucester, and are said to have yielded to the captors about nine hundred dollars a share.

A bold achievement in the merchant service, at this time, is worthy of notice. The brig "Pickering" of this town, of two hundred and fifty tons, Elias Davis captain, was taken, while on her passage from Gibraltar home, by the British frigate "Belvidere." After taking from the brig all her crew except the captain, and his son, who was first mate, the British captain placed her in charge of a prize-crew, and ordered her to Halifax. The captain of the brig, loath to lose a fine new vessel of which he himself was part owner, devised a plan of recapture; and, with the aid of his son, again got command of her, and brought her safely to Gloucester.

In the fall of 1813, a few small vessels belonging to the town went out on coasting voyages to Southern ports, where they were detained by the Embargo Act of the following winter. Several of the masters left their vessels; and, embarking at Elizabeth City, N.C., in an open boat, arrived home in April, 1814, after a passage of thirty-four days, during which they had hauled their boat fifty miles across capes and headlands.

Before passing along in this period of our history, some account should be given of the only case of hydrophobia ever known to have occurred in the town. On the 8th of November, 1813, a young girl named Mina Dowsett, aged fifteen, died of this dreadful disease. In the month of March preceding, she was bitten by a dog on entering a dwelling where the animal belonged; but, as no effects of the virus were manifested till three days before she died, all apprehensions of injury had subsided. The case was attended with all the usual characteristics of the disease, till death relieved her from its tortures.

It was by restrictions on trade that Gloucester was the greatest sufferer in the war of 1812: for, though many of its men engaged in privateering and the naval service, nearly all of them returned to home and friends; and, though many of the people were deprived of accustomed gratifications, there was none of that want of the necessaries of life, which, in the Revolutionary struggle, was so severe and distressing. And yet peace was now welcomed with extravagant demonstrations of joy, strangely contrasting with the apparent indifference with which that of 1783 was received. The emotions of the people were, however, in both cases, properly expressed: in the latter, they were too deep for jubilant celebration.

However wide apart the views of our people had been with regard to the justice and necessity of the war, there was no difference in the feelings with which, in February, 1815, they received the news of peace. On the evening of its reception, the large meeting-house of the First Parish was brilliantly illuminated; and, for the first time, its venerable walls resounded patriotic songs, mingled with shouts of merriment and joy. There was also an illumination at Sandy Bay. Shortly afterwards, the event was celebrated by a grand ball; and soon a revival of trade and the regular pursuits and rewards of industry added their testimonial to the advantages and blessings of peace.*

* The following fractions represent the proportion of the property of the town in each parish at the close of the war: —

First Parish	210-360
Second Parish	87-360
Third Parish	42-360
Fourth Parish	15-360
Fifth Parish	56-360

CHAPTER XXX.

THE FEDERALISTS LOSE ASCENDENCY. — THE SEA-SERPENT. — BOYS DROWNED. — UNIVERSAL BENEVOLENT SOCIETY, AND ITS MINISTERS. — JOHN KITTREDGE. — SHIPWRECK OF BRIG "REBECCA ANN." — DR. EPHRAIM DAVIS. — FIRST PREACHING OF METHODISM IN TOWN, AND METHODIST SOCIETIES. — FIRST PRINTING-PRESS. — "GLOUCESTER TELEGRAPH." — ABORTIVE EFFORTS TO ESTABLISH RELIGIOUS JOURNALS. — SHIPWRECK OF THE "PERSIA." — EVANGELICAL CHURCH AND SOCIETY, AND ITS MINISTERS. — NORTH ORTHODOX CONGREGATIONAL CHURCH, AND ITS MINISTERS. — SECOND BAPTIST SOCIETY, AND ITS MINISTERS. — GREAT FIRE. — POLITICAL EXCITEMENT. — DEMOCRATS AND WHIGS. THE "GLOUCESTER DEMOCRAT." — REVIVAL OF REGULAR PUBLIC WORSHIP IN THE SECOND PARISH. — DR. EBENEZER DALE. — DR. HENRY PRENTISS. — GREAT STORM. — MANY VESSELS WRECKED, AND SEVERAL LIVES LOST.

IT has already been stated, that the Federalists maintained their ascendency in the town for eight years. Political excitement subsided in some degree after the peace of 1815, but did not wholly die away till after the Republicans obtained the control of the town. This event took place at the March meeting in 1816; when their ticket for selectmen prevailed by a plurality of twelve, in a vote of six hundred and fifty-four. The Federalists were peculiarly sensitive, perhaps, on this occasion, and complained loudly of some of the acts of the moderator, — Dr. Kittredge. But the mission of their party was accomplished. They were beaten again on the vote for Governor in April, and again at the representative election in May, when Capt. Parrott was chosen over Mr. Hough. Some embers of the old fire were kept alive, and blazed out once more in the attempt, in 1823, to elect Mr. Otis Governor: but, soon after that time, the old party lines became entirely obliterated; and, for a period of about ten years, no questions of national politics created excitement in the town.

In August, 1817, Gloucester became a centre of public interest on account of the visit of the famous sea-serpent to its waters. The particulars relating to the appearance of this creature in our harbor were gathered by the New-England Linnæan Society, and were given on oath before Hon. Lonson Nash, then and still a magistrate of the town.

Mr. Nash himself saw the serpent at the distance of about two hundred and fifty yards. It was so long, that the two extremes were not visible at one view with a telescope; and he therefore judged it to be from seventy to a hundred feet in length. He perceived eight distinct portions, or bunches, apparently caused by the vertical motion of the animal, which he conjectured to be straight. In this vertical motion all the testimonials agree, as well as in the apparent bunches. The track made in the water was visible for half a mile; and the progress of the animal, when on the surface, a mile in four minutes: but, when immersed, he appeared, by the motion of the water, which could be often traced, to move a mile in two minutes, or three at the most. His body was of the size of a half-barrel, apparently rough, and of a very dark color: in which latter particular, all the accounts coincide.

A ship-master and two of his men approached this monster within the short distance of thirty feet. In their description of its head, they say it darted out its tongue, the extremity of which resembled a harpoon, to the extent of two feet, raising it perpendicularly, and again letting it fall. They also describe its motion as at the rate of twelve or fourteen miles an hour.

Another ship-master, who saw the serpent three times at the distance of about one hundred and fifty yards, twenty or thirty persons being present, thought its length eighty or ninety feet, and its size that of a half-barrel. In turning short and quick, the first part of the curve it made resembled the link of a chain; but, when the head came parallel with the tail, they appeared near together. When on the surface of the water, its motion was slow; the animal at times playing about in circles, and at others moving nearly straight onward. In disappearing, it apparently sank directly down.

Ten depositions were given in, all of them agreeing as to the size, shape, and motion of this wonderful creature, as well as in less important particulars. On the 14th of August, he was approached within thirty feet; and, his head appearing above water, was greeted with a ball from the gun of an experienced sportsman belonging to the town. A moment's anxious suspense followed, during which the men in the boat expected to pay dearly for their temerity; for the creature turned immediately towards them, as if to approach. But he sank down, and went directly under the boat, again making his appearance at about one hundred yards' distance. He did not turn down like a fish, but appeared to settle directly down like a rock.

The sea-serpent was seen in Long-Island Sound on the 5th of October, 1817, by several persons, and in many other places within a few subsequent years. He came into our vicinity again in 1819; when he was seen by a person at Marblehead, who thought he could perceive as many as twenty protuberances. But this gentleman was a little "fluttered;" and his testimony is less reliable, as well as less minute, than that of another gentleman, who saw him, about the same time, at or near Nahant. In a letter to Col. T. H. Perkins, who, it seems, had seen the serpent in our harbor in 1817, he describes his appearance, and states that he saw him at a distance of about one hundred and fifty yards, and examined him attentively four or five minutes. His description of the monster does not vary in any material respect from that of the persons who saw him here.

The capture of the young sea-serpent, about four weeks after the depositions in relation to the large one were given by some of our citizens, was not the least remarkable event connected with this affair. This creature was killed by a farmer, near Good-Harbor Beach, with a pitchfork, and was exhibited for a few days at the house of Capt. John Beach; after which, it was carried to Boston, and examined by a committee of the Linnæan Society, who pronounced it to belong to the same species as the great serpent.

Another circumstance should not be omitted. This was the capture, during the period of the excitement, of a monstrous fish, reported extensively to be the sea-serpent itself, but finally ascertained to be nothing of greater strangeness than a very large horse-mackerel.

The existence of an enormous marine animal of the serpent kind had been affirmed long before this time. One had been seen in our own waters even as early as 1639; when a visitor* to New England was told "of a sea-serpent, or snake, that lay quoiled up like a cable upon a rock at Cape Ann. A boat passing by with English aboard, and two Indians, they would have shot the serpent; but the Indians dissuaded them, saying, that, if he were not killed outright, they would be all in danger of their lives." The existence of such an animal had been avouched by Pontopiddan, Bishop of Bergen; by Rev. Donald M'Lean of Scotland; and, in our own country, by a man in Plymouth in 1815; and by Rev. W. Cummings, who saw a sea-monster in Penobscot Bay in 1809, judged by him to be sixty feet long, and reported by the inhabitants of some of the islands there to have been frequently seen by them. In view of all this testimony, and particularly of that of so many intelligent and respectable citizens of Gloucester, what shall we say? — that this monster was indeed a visitor from that "gloomy and pathless obscure," the home of —

> "Salamander, snake, dragon, — vast reptiles that dwell
> In the deep"? —

or that all the relations concerning him must take their place in the history of popular delusions?

In the chronological course of events, we next come to a melancholy disaster that occurred in the Harbor Cove, Sunday, April 11, 1819. On the afternoon of that day, five boys, who had gone out in a boat for fishing and diversion, were thrown overboard by the upsetting of their boat near Sargent's Wharf. They were all supposed to be drowned; but, the bodies having

---

* Josselyn: Massachusetts Historical Collections, vol. xxiii. p. 228.

been soon recovered, great exertions were made to resuscitate them, and one was restored to life. The four corpses were buried from the First-Parish Meeting-house.*

A new society of Universalists was organized in the town (at Sandy Bay) on the 7th of February, 1821, under the name of the Universal Benevolent Society. The constitution was signed by twenty-three persons, many of whom had formerly been for some years members of the society at the Harbor. The Universalists of Sandy Bay united with those of the opposite faith in erecting a meeting-house there in 1804, on condition that they should have the use of it two-fifths of the time; and, for a considerable period, they had religious services in it, on their allotted sabbaths, by Rev. Thomas Jones and other preachers. Difficulties in relation to this partnership finally arose, and terminated in a lawsuit; the result of which was, that they were obliged to give up the right in the house for which they had originally stipulated.

The new society carried on religious worship a few Sundays in every year, for several years, in the schoolhouse near the Beach, opposite the Burying-ground. The ministers who officiated for them most frequently were Revs. Lafayette Mace, J. H. Bugbee, J. Gilman, J. P. Atkinson, and H. Ballou. In 1829, they built the house of worship they now occupy; having laid the corner-stone, June 24 of that year, with Masonic ceremonies. It was dedicated Oct. 8, when Rev. Thomas Jones delivered the dedicatory sermon.

Rev. Lafayette Mace was the first minister of the society who preached in the meeting-house. The succession of ministers to the present time has been as follows: 1830, Lucius R. Paige; 1832, B. B. Murray; 1835, A. C. L. Arnold; 1837, Charles Spear; 1839, Gibson Smith; 1841, John Allen; 1844, H. C. Leonard; 1846, E. Locke; 1849, S. C. Hewitt; 1850, H. van Campen; 1853, A. C. L. Arnold; 1856, William Hooper; May, 1858, J. H. Farnsworth, who is the minister at this time. He

---

* The names of these lads were William Turner, aged eighteen; William Smith, sixteen; James Smith, fourteen; and Benjamin Butler. The boy resuscitated was named Daniel Sargent.

was born in Hartford, Conn., in 1822; and was educated in the public schools, in which he has also been a teacher. His ministry, previous to his removal to Rockport, was at Belfast, Me. His labors for the society have advanced it to a higher degree of prosperity than it has ever before enjoyed.

Passing along to 1822, we come to notice the death, Aug. 31, of John Kittredge, Esq., at the age of forty-five. He was a son of Hon. Thomas Kittredge, an eminent physician and earnest republican of Andover. He graduated at Harvard College in 1795, and studied medicine; but left the practice in 1805 to take the office of collector of the customs here. Dr. Kittredge was a prominent and useful citizen, and his death was a public calamity. His only son (Thomas), born Nov. 17, 1811, graduated at Dartmouth College in 1833, and received a diploma as a practitioner of medicine at Jefferson College, Pa.; but never entered upon the public practice of his profession. He died in Milton, July 27, 1845.

In the year 1823, our shore was again the scene of a distressing shipwreck. On Sunday evening, March 30, the brig "Rebecca Ann," Capt. Timothy Walker, putting in for a harbor at the commencement of a violent snow-storm, went ashore at Norman's Woe. All on board — ten in number — were immediately swept from the deck by the violence of the sea; and, with the exception of one man, were all drowned. This man (named Dix) was saved by gaining a rock, over which the sea did not break. Among the sufferers were two passengers, — Capt. John Whitten of Kennebunk, and Robert Patten of Eastport. The bodies were all found, and buried, with suitable religious solemnities, from the First-Parish Meeting-house, on the following Wednesday. The brig was bound to Porto Rico; but, having sprung a leak when three days out, was returning to port when driven into our harbor by the storm.

On the 11th of December, 1825, died Dr. Ephraim Davis. He is said to have been born in Connecticut, and to have studied medicine with Dr. Holmes of Canterbury. He came to Massachusetts when a young man, and practised successively in Essex, Manchester, and Sandy Bay, before settling in the Harbor Parish; where he ended his days at the advanced age of eighty-five, leaving a son of his own name.

About this time, efforts began to be made to form a Methodist society in the town, — efforts which, here as in every other part of the country, have tended, in a marked degree, to promote the cause of religion, morality, and education. The first preacher of this sect who visited the town was Rev. George Pickering, presiding elder of the Boston District. This was in 1806. Just before that year, John Edney, an English Wesleyan, moved into town, and occupied a house then standing on the westerly edge of the Mill Pond, in Town Parish. It was probably at Edney's desire that Mr. Pickering came here to preach; for the first meetings were held at his house. Their religious exercises were marked by the peculiarities usual to the sect at that time; and great crowds flocked to Edney's house, out of curiosity, to know something about the new kind of worship introduced into the town. Upon this, some of the citizens became alarmed for the peace and good-order of society; and, having made formal application to the selectmen to interfere, that body called upon the minister, and requested him to leave the town. But there was no fear that the hateful spirit of religious persecution could be again aroused in Gloucester; and the preacher calmly assured the officers of the town, that he knew what he was about, and that he should remain and preach just as long as there was a prospect of doing good. A few converts were the fruits of these early labors: but the field appears to have been almost entirely abandoned from this time till 1821; when, and during the four following years, Mr. Pickering, as a missionary of the New-England Conference, frequently visited the town, and preached either in a private house, or in the old meeting-house "up in town." On these visits, "class-meetings" for religious inquiry and conversation were held; and then were laid the foundations of a permanent ministry.

A society, consisting of about twenty persons, was organized in 1826; in which year, Rev. Aaron Wait was appointed to the new station, which embraced the whole Cape. His Sunday labors were usually performed in the old meeting-house, before mentioned, till the fall of 1828; when he began to preach in a new one erected on Prospect Street, in the Harbor Parish. This building was dedicated Oct. 22 of this year. Rev. John Lindsey, presiding elder, preached the sermon on that occasion. Mr. Wait and the following succeeding ministers — William R. Stone, Aaron Lummus, Aaron Josselyn, John Bailey, and Leonard B. Griffing — labored both in the Harbor and Town parishes, occasionally preaching at Sandy Bay, till 1838; when a meeting-house was erected for the Methodists of Town Parish, at a cost of about twenty-five hundred dollars, on a lot given for the purpose by Samuel Curtis. It was dedicated Nov. 16, 1838. The sermon on the occasion was preached by Rev. Moses L. Scudder of Boston. The society worshipping in it has enjoyed constant preaching down to the present time, and is now in a flourishing condition. It has upwards of eighty communicants, and a sabbath school of one hundred and fifteen scholars.*

The Methodists at the Harbor also had constant preaching, in their first house of worship, till 1858; when they purchased the meeting-house on Elm Street, erected a few years ago by seceders from the Independent Christian Society, which they now occupy.†

The Methodists of Sandy Bay erected a small house of worship in 1838, which was dedicated by Rev. L. B. Griffing in the same year. The first minister stationed there was Rev. Israel Washburn, in 1839. In 1843, this society seceded from the Conference, and became a Wesleyan Church; but returned in 1858, and formed a part of the Lynn District. They enlarged their chapel in 1844. Their church has fifty members; and their

* The succession of ministers has been as follows: 1838, L. B. Griffing; 1840, Benjamin F. Lambord; 1841, Ziba B. C. Dunham; 1842, Zachariah A. Mudge; 1843, Thomas C. Pearce; 1844, C. R. Foster; 1845, Daniel Richards; 1847, John Paulson; 1848, John G. Cary; 1850, Jarvis Wilson; 1851, Augustus F. Bailey; 1853, William F. La Count; 1855, Z. B. C. Dunham; 1856, Horace F. Morse; 1858, Samuel A. Cushing.

† The following ministers have preached to this society since 1838: E. M. Beebe, Stephen Hiler, H. P. Hall, Joel Steele, Mr. Burrows, H. M. Bridge, W. C. Clark, John Collum, J. Wilson, Linus Fish, H. R. Parmenter, and N. Soule. Three of them (Messrs. Burrows, Clark, and Collum) were local preachers, who had lay-occupations.

sabbath school, sixty-four, and a library of two hundred volumes.*

Another event of this period, worthy of notice in our annals, was the establishment of the first newspaper in the town. On Monday morning, Jan. 1, 1827, was issued the first number of the "GLOUCESTER TELEGRAPH;" afterwards, and ever since, published on Saturday. It was a sheet of five columns, of about the usual size; two of which were devoted to advertisements. Of these, one was a list of letters remaining in the post-office, — nearly eighty in number. Another announced the departure of the stage for Boston every morning at eight o'clock; and for Sandy Bay three times a week, at five, P.M. Only five tradesmen advertised their goods. Its editor, proprietor, and printer was William E. P. Rogers, a native of the town. He continued to publish it till 1833; when, upon taking charge of a newspaper in Bangor, he sold the "Telegraph" to Gamaliel Marchant, who himself removed to Bangor in 1835, when the paper passed into the hands of Henry Tilden and Edgar Marchant. The two Marchants were brothers, and had served apprenticeship in the office. Mr. Tilden soon became sole proprietor of the paper, and published it till 1843; when it was purchased by its present editor and proprietor, John S. E. Rogers, who also served his time in the office. The "Telegraph" was commenced as a neutral paper in politics; and it remained "open to all parties, influenced by none," till 1834; when, upon the commencement of a vigorous political warfare between the friends and opponents of President Jackson's administration, under the name of Democrats and Whigs respectively, it became a strenuous advocate of the principles of the latter. The present publisher made it again a neutral paper, but soon devoted it once more to the interests of the Whig party; which it continued to maintain till the party ceased to exist. In common with most of the political journals of the North, it now advo-

* The ministers have been, — in 1840, Thomas G. Brown; 1841, John P. Bradley; 1842, Daniel Richards; 1843, Charles O. Towne; 1845, William Davenport; 1846, David Mason; 1848, George Waugh; 1850, William C. Clark; 1852, David Mason; 1854, Alonzo Gibson; 1856, L. P. Atwood; 1858, Elijah Mason.

cates the principles of the new Republican party. The "Telegraph" has been published semiweekly since 1834. Its value as a repository of materials for the future historian of the town has been greatly increased by its present conductor.

The establishment of a printing-press in the town induced an effort the same year for the publication of a religious journal. The first number of this paper, with the title of "Christian Neighbor," was issued Nov. 7, 1827, from the office of the "Telegraph." Its editor was Samuel Worcester. It did not profess to be a controversial paper; but its sectarian bias in favor of what are commonly called "evangelical doctrines" was manifested in its principal editorial article: a "Review" of three printed sermons by three ministers of the town, — Rev. H. Hildreth, Rev. Thomas Jones, and Rev. E. Leonard. A sufficient number of subscribers did not answer to the appeal for its support, and no second number was published.

A more successful result might have been anticipated from an attempt made afterwards to establish a paper in support of Universalism: but this was also a futile effort; for it began and ended with the first number of the "Liberal Companion," issued also from the office of the "Telegraph," and edited by Rev. B. B. Murray, minister of the Universalist Society of Sandy Bay.*

On Thursday night, March 5, 1829, our coast was again the scene of a melancholy shipwreck. On that night, in a violent snow-storm, the brig "Persia," from Trieste, bound to Salem, was cast ashore on the back side of Eastern Point, near Brace's Rock; and all on board were lost. The hull of the vessel was broken into fragments, and, with the cargo, — consisting chiefly of rags, — was strewed along the coast. No knowledge of the disaster was obtained till Saturday; when, and on the following day, nine bodies were found on the shore. Four of these were delivered to their friends, and the remainder were

* My efforts for several years have not succeeded in procuring a copy of this paper, or in learning its date. Of the "Christian Neighbor," the only copy known by me to be in existence is in my possession. It is a small sheet, having four pages of four columns each.

buried from the Universalist Church. The whole number lost was supposed to be thirteen.

The rupture in the First Church, noticed on a preceding page, was soon followed by the organization of a new religious society. The seceders were organized into a new church by an ecclesiastical council convened for that purpose, Nov. 17, 1829; when Rev. Dr. Beecher of Boston preached a sermon, in the evening, at the Methodist Meeting-house. The society was formed at a meeting of persons held March 13, 1830, at the house of Andrew Parker, by warrant from a justice, on the call of Nathaniel Babson and twelve others; and called the Evangelical Society.* They voted to raise money by subscription for preaching and other expenses; and, in a few months, took measures for building a house of worship; which was erected the next year, and dedicated on the 8th of September. On the 14th of January, 1832, the society met at the meeting-house, and adopted rules, to which forty-two persons affixed their names; and, on the 12th of June following, they voted a unanimous concurrence with the church in inviting Mr. Charles S. Porter to become their pastor. He accepted the call, and was ordained Aug. 1, 1832, in the Universalist Meeting-house, which was granted for the occasion, at the request of the new society, whose own house was not thought large enough to accommodate the audience that would be likely to assemble. Rev. Charles S. Porter was born in Ashfield in 1804, and graduated at Amherst College in 1827. His connection with the society was dissolved May 4, 1835; when he generously gave up a debt of a considerable amount that it then owed him. During Mr. Porter's ministry, the settlement of a decided Unitarian in the First Parish produced another breach in that ancient body; the result of which was, that several of its members joined the Evangelical Society. Mr. Porter was succeeded by Rev. Christopher M. Nickels, who was installed in September, 1835. He con-

* The two persons here named were the founders of this society. Deacon Nathaniel Babson was a son of Capt. William Babson of Squam. He died suddenly, of disease of the heart, Feb. 1, 1836, aged fifty-two.

tinued in the ministry here about twelve years, and was held in high esteem as a faithful and devoted pastor and a useful citizen. His successor was Rev. James Aiken, who was settled in 1848. The next minister was Rev. J. L. Hatch, from 1853 to 1856. The present pastor is Rev. Lysander Dickerman, who was born in North Bridgewater, Mass., in 1826; and graduated at Brown University in 1851. He was ordained over this society, April 29, 1858.*

The meeting-house erected by this society in 1831, at the corner of School and Middle Streets, was sold, and removed from that spot, in 1854. In the same year, a new and beautiful one was built on the same site, and dedicated to the worship of God, March 22, 1855. The dedication-sermon was preached by the pastor (Rev. J. L. Hatch), from Isa. iv. 5.

In 1830 was also gathered the North Orthodox Congregational Church at Lane's Cove. At an ecclesiastical council convened Aug. 25, three males and ten females were, with suitable religious exercises, organized into a body with this name; and on the 2d of March, 1831, Rev. Moses Sawyer was installed as their minister. Mr. Sawyer was born in Salisbury, N.H., in 1776; and graduated at Dartmouth College in 1799. His connection with this church lasted till March, 1836; after which, the society remained without a settled pastor till Aug. 12, 1840. On that day, Rev. David Tilton was installed as their minister; and continued in that office till March, 1850.

From July, 1850, to August, 1854, Rev. Edwin Seabury preached to the society. He was succeeded by Rev. N. Richardson, who was its minister from December, 1854, to April 1, 1857. The present pastor is Rev. Francis N. Peloubet. He was born in New-York City, Dec. 2, 1831; graduated at Williams College in 1853, and at Bangor Theological Seminary in 1857. His ordination over this church took place, Dec. 2, 1857. Rev. Jacob Ide, D.D., of Medway, preached the ordination sermon. The number of communicants belonging to this church is fifty-two. The sabbath school has two hundred and ten

* His connection with the society has been recently dissolved.

registered scholars. This new society erected a small house of worship in 1828, which was repaired and enlarged in 1853.

Another of the churches of the town (the Second Baptist) also dates its existence from this year. One of the males — composing the First Church of this sect, organized at Sandy Bay in 1808 — was John Smith,* of the Harbor Parish. He had been a member of the First Church, but withdrew from it in 1806 to join the Baptist Church in Beverly. He, and a few earnest persons who joined with him, held their meetings at first in private houses; but soon attracted so many to their worship as to be obliged to seek other accommodations, which they found in one of the schoolrooms of the village. At these meetings, and at their public baptisms, they were sometimes disturbed by the noise and disorderly conduct of persons drawn by that idle curiosity which every thing new serves to arouse; but no serious persecution was attempted. One of their early preachers was Rev. James A. Boswell, who removed to the Harbor from Sandy Bay in 1823. They increased so slowly, however, that several years elapsed before they formed themselves into a church-organization. This event took place, Dec. 29, 1830; when twenty persons were constituted the Second Baptist Church of Gloucester. The religious exercises of the occasion were conducted by Rev. E. P. Grosvenor of Salem. Their first minister was Rev. Samuel Adlam, a native of Bristol, Eng., who was installed March 24, 1831; when Rev. Mr. Aldridge of Beverly preached the sermon of installation. Mr. Adlam resigned in 1834. Since that time, the succession of pastors has been as follows: Rev. William Lamson, June, 1837, to Oct. 1, 1839; Rev. J. A. B. Stone, Nov. 13, 1839, to Oct. 1, 1841; Rev. William Lamson, Nov. 10, 1841, to July 28, 1848; Rev. Joseph R. Manton, Feb. 14, 1849, to Sept. 2, 1850; Rev. Miles Sanford, March 19, 1850, to July 10, 1853. Rev. Sam-

* John Smith was a carpenter, a native of Ipswich. He was one of an unbroken succession of John Smiths, which has continued through several generations in the same family. His memory is cherished, not only as a principal founder of the Baptist Church, but as a man of strict piety and integrity. He died Oct. 29, 1828, aged sixty-eight.

uel E. Pierce, the present pastor, was ordained Sept. 27, 1853. The sermon on that occasion was preached by Rev. Arthur S. Train of Haverhill. Mr. Pierce was born in 1827, in New-York City; and received his collegiate and theological education at Princeton, N.J. His ministerial career as a settled pastor commenced with this society, which is now one of the largest and most prosperous religious organizations on the Cape.

The first meeting-house erected by this society stood on Pleasant Street, and was used as their place of worship about twenty years. In 1850, they built the large and handsome one they now occupy, at the corner of Pleasant and Middle Streets, at an expense of fourteen thousand dollars. It was dedicated March 19, 1851. The sermon was preached by the pastor, Rev. M. Sanford.

Before 1830, the town never suffered severely by fire. The few single buildings that had been burned, have, with one exception, been mentioned in this work. The one excepted was a building used as a store and sail-loft, and was consumed on the night of March 16, 1766. A more serious calamity of this kind distinguishes the year 1830 in our annals, as that of the "great fire." On the 16th of September, at about four o'clock in the morning, this conflagration commenced in the rear part of a large building owned by Samuel Gilbert, and occupied by him as a dwelling-house and a store, near the westerly end of Front Street. The next building, on the west, was a three-story one, recently purchased by Mr. Gilbert, and fitted for a store. It had in former times, for many years, been the principal tavern of the town; and had in its rear a large stable, adjoining the Town Landing. The fire was soon communicated to these, and to a two-story house, having a shop in front, on the east side of Mr. Gilbert's house, and very near to it. Thence, crossing a lane leading to the wharf of James Mansfield, it swept away his store and dwelling-house adjoining. The next building attacked by the flames was a two-story one, belonging to Cyrus Stevens, having its end towards the street, with a lane leading to the old "Long Wharf," on the west, and another lane on the east, separating it from a three-story building owned by Zachariah Stevens, and occupied by him as a dwelling, and by Samuel Stevens as a store. A few feet distant from this was another large house, with a shop in front, occupied by S. and G. W. Dexter. All these rapidly disappeared before the devouring element; but, as the flames had not yet crossed the street, no great fear was entertained that the village would be wholly destroyed. At this point, however, the house of Dr. Prentiss (formerly the residence of Dr. Coffin), on the opposite side, at the foot of Short Street, caught; and, with two other dwellings on the easterly side of Short Street, were soon destroyed. It was now supposed that the conflagration would be general, and the people living on Middle Street began to move their effects: but, timely assistance coming in from the neighboring villages and towns, the flames were soon subdued on the north side of Front Street; but not till they had consumed, in addition to the buildings already named, a long two-story block, and a three-story building near to it, both occupied for stores and dwellings. The buildings next to the one last mentioned were two small one-story shops, which were burned or demolished. Back of these shops was the dwelling-house of Mrs. Hannah Dane, of which the third or upper story only was destroyed; the flames having been stayed at this spot. Continuing their ravages on the other side of the street, the fire next burned a small two-story house belonging to Mrs. Sally Allen. A large three-story house, a few feet distant from the latter, went next. Crossing the head of Smith's Wharf, a block of six two-story buildings was next destroyed. Between this block and the house of Mr. Eli Stacy, a large garden, with several trees in it, intervened; and here, by great exertions, the progress of the flames was arrested. Only the course of the fire on the street has been described. In the rear of the buildings, on the south side of the street, were many storehouses and workshops, forming a compact mass of combustible matter, over which the flames spread with such rapidity, that many of the buildings on the street were first attacked by the fire burning behind them. The spreading of the flames was stopped about noon. The only building left standing upon the space between the Town Landing and Central Wharf was the house of Mr. Stacy, at the head of the lane leading to the wharf.

Among the circumstances that combined to render this fire so destructive, the chief to be mentioned are the absence of an unusual number of our men, an inefficient fire-department, and a fresh wind that rose soon after the flames broke out. Twenty dwelling-houses and forty stores and out-buildings were consumed; and the estimated amount of all the property destroyed was one hundred and fifty thousand dollars. It was not so customary then to seek protection by insurance as it now is, and many of the sufferers were reduced to poverty. Of this class, the greater number were assisted from the money liberally contributed in Boston and other places for their relief. As soon as the news of the fire spread abroad, public sympathy was aroused, and donations* began to come in. Among the first to manifest a kindly feeling was the Hon. Josiah Quincy, who sent a handsome sum of money in grateful testimony of his interest in the town, on account of the attention shown by its people to his dying father in 1775, and of the respect with which the remains of the patriot were here consigned to a temporary burial.

This great fire did not materially retard the prosperity of the town: that had been greatly accelerated for a few previous years by the success of the mackerel fishery, and its continuance seemed now to rest upon a firm basis. The census of this year showed gratifying evidence of this recent prosperity, in a larger increase of the population since 1820 than in any preceding decennial period.

The progress of events brings us to another period of violent political agitation in the town. At the presidential election in 1828, Gen. Jackson had received but seventy-seven votes of five hundred and thirty, — the whole number cast. No great efforts were made to increase his party till he became a candidate for re-election in 1832; when he obtained a small majority of the votes cast, and an entire Jackson ticket for representatives was for the first time elected. The measures of the National Ad-

* The contributions acknowledged by the selectmen amounted to $14,284.

ministration the next year aroused a strong opposition throughout the country, and led to the union of all its opponents, under the name of "Whigs;" the supporters of the President at the same time assuming that of "Democrats." In one or the other of these two parties, all the voters of the town enlisted themselves in 1834; when the interest in the contest became so general, that few were neutral, and none indifferent. The Whigs were stimulated to extraordinary exertions by the course of the Democrats; for that party, having been unsuccessful in an attempt to bring the "Gloucester Telegraph" to their aid, established a new paper in the town, which, with Robert Rantoul, jun., as the chief writer for its columns, could not fail to exercise great influence. The "Telegraph" had previously espoused the Whig side; and the two newspapers, with their respective supporters, entered upon an earnest and somewhat bitter political warfare.

Mr. Rantoul had settled in the town, in the previous year, in the practice of law. He was not then known as a politician, and was supposed to have no affinity with the party which he here joined, and of which, though not active in electioneering, he became the chief man. He made here a brilliant start in politics; and, but for the overwhelming preponderance of the Whig party in the Commonwealth, would have soon won his way to places of the highest distinction. As it was, he was obliged to content himself for some years with a seat in the General Court; where, from 1835 to 1838 inclusive, his talents secured him a wide renown as the able, bold, and independent representative from Gloucester.*

---

* Mr. Rantoul removed from Gloucester to Beverly, his native town, in 1839. He became Collector of Boston in 1843; United-States District Attorney in 1845; senator in Congress for a few days in 1851; and in the same year, by the united votes of the Democratic and Free-soil parties, representative in Congress from his native district. From this sphere — in which, without doubt, he would have become distinguished — he was removed by death, Aug. 7, 1852, aged forty-six years. As a lawyer, Mr. Rantoul's connection with Gloucester affords no matter for history, beyond the mention of his residence here.

It is quite a remarkable fact, that few gentlemen of the legal profession have lived in the town, and that no one has ever died in it. The lawyers now in business here are Hon. Lonson Nash, and Charles P. Thompson, A. Tullar, and B. H. Smith, Esqs. Mr. Nash was one of the representatives of the town as long ago as 1809, and afterwards a senator.

The first trial of strength between the Whigs and Democrats at the polls took place at the November election in 1834, when nearly every voter of the town, then at home, deposited his ballot. The Democrats achieved a decided victory,* and maintained their ascendency, electing members of their party to all the principal town-offices, till the election for State officers in 1838. They had then become divided in consequence of the nomination of Mr. Rantoul for Congress instead of Mr. Cabot, the old candidate; and the result of the election was, that a portion of the Whig ticket for representatives to the General Court were elected. Smarting under this defeat, the friends of Mr. Rantoul, comprising more than two-thirds of the party, called for another representative election; and, as most of the fishermen absent at the previous election had now arrived, they felt confident that both divisions of the Democratic party could at least prevent the success of the Whigs. The contest was very spirited and exciting; but the bitterness usually engendered on such occasions was all confined to the two divisions of the hitherto dominant party. The full strength of all the parties was brought to the field, and again the Whigs became the victors.†

Having healed its feuds, the Democratic party regained its ascendency in 1839, but only retained it till the next year; when, by the incorporation of Sandy Bay as a new town, it was thrown into a minority. At the presidential election in 1840, it was beaten by a large majority:‡ but it again prevailed, through the

* The vote now polled was one thousand four hundred and thirty-two; the largest by several hundred that had ever been cast in the town. Of these, the Democrats had seven hundred and seventy-one; and the Whigs, six hundred and sixty-one. The whole number of legal voters in the town was one thousand six hundred and thirty-four, distributed as follows:—

First Parish	668
Second Parish	123
Third Parish	341
Fourth Parish	74
Fifth Parish	428

† The number of votes thrown was one thousand five hundred and twenty. The highest Whig candidate received seven hundred and sixty-three; the Rantoul ticket had six hundred and twelve; and that supported by Mr. Cabot's friends, one hundred and forty-five.

‡ The vote of Gloucester at this election was — Harrison, six hundred and ninety-one; Van Buren, four hundred and forty-nine. That of Rockport — Harrison, two hundred and fifty-one; Van Buren, three hundred and four.

distractions of the Whig party, in 1842 and 1843; after which, it won no victory in the town. Nor did its old opponents again become firmly established in power; having never but once afterwards (in 1849) elected their candidates for representatives.

Since 1840, political questions have occasioned no considerable degree of excitement in the town. In 1843, the Native-American sentiment found earnest supporters; who, for a short time, carried the elections. Again, in 1854, under a new organization, it commanded the support of a great majority of the people, and kept its predominance till it was superseded by the slavery question.

The political paper established in the town at the commencement of the memorable contest between the Whigs and Democrats in 1834 was called the "Gloucester Democrat." It was a small sheet, having five columns on a page. The first number was issued on Tuesday, Aug. 18; and it continued to be issued on Tuesdays and Fridays till Feb. 16, 1838, when it was merged in the "Salem Advertiser." Charles W. Woodbury appears in the imprint as its editor and proprietor; but its most important political articles were understood to be from the pen of his brother-in-law, Mr. Rantoul. In September, 1837, the paper passed into the hands of F. L. Rogers and G. W. Parsons; by whom it was published till it was discontinued.

Another Democratic paper, called the "Jeffersonian Republican," was started by the friends of Mr. Rantoul to aid his election to Congress in October, 1838; but its publication ceased with the defeat of the party at the representative election in November.*

About this period, measures began to be taken for a revival of public religious worship in the Second Parish. For many years after the close of Mr. Fuller's ministry, no regular religious exercises were held, though there was occasional preaching in the old meeting-house. The people of the parish were divided in opinion

* Besides the newspapers that have been already noticed, the only others that have been published in the town, except a few ephemeral sheets, are the "Gloucester News" and the "Cape-Ann Advertiser." The former was edited by John J. Piper, and published semiweekly from Oct. 11, 1848, to the last of December, 1851. The "Advertiser" was first issued Dec. 19, 1857, by Procter Brothers; and was published on alternate Saturdays nearly a year. It was next made a weekly paper, and has been continued as such to the present time.

on doctrinal points; and no unanimity in the settlement of a minister could, therefore, be expected: consequently, those of them who were attached to the faith of their ancestors took steps for the re-organization of the church and the erection of a new house of worship. This building, which is the small meeting-house standing on the main road to Essex, was dedicated Jan. 1, 1834. Rev. John P. Cleaveland of Salem preached the sermon on that occasion. No permanent ministry was established over this church till Nov. 11, 1840; when Rev. Isaac Brown was ordained. He was taken sick, not long afterwards; and died at his mother's house in Hamilton, Sept. 13, 1841. The next minister was Rev. Henry C. Jewett, a native of Rowley, who was settled in August, 1842; and died suddenly of scarlet fever, Nov. 4, 1846, aged forty-four. His successor was Rev. Charles A. Williams, who preached to the society from November, 1846, to October, 1848. Rev. Levi Wheaton was the next minister: he was ordained Jan. 23, 1850, and was dismissed May 11, 1858. The present pastor (Rev. C. B. Smith) commenced his labors in June, 1858. Mr. Smith was born in Litchfield, Me.; received his theological education at Bangor, in that State; and was ordained at Levant in October, 1849.

On the 29th of June, 1834, died Dr. Ebenezer Dale, aged fifty-one. Dr. Dale was born in Danvers, and was brought up at a mechanical trade. Being of a studious turn of mind, he applied himself assiduously to intellectual culture; and, after having acquired the necessary preliminary education, devoted himself to the study of medicine with Dr. Kittredge of Andover. He settled in Gloucester in 1810; having been induced to do so chiefly by the desire of some of the leading Republicans of the town, to whom the two principal regular practitioners (Dr. Coffin and Dr. Manning) had made themselves obnoxious by their ardent support of Federal politics. He soon found a competent patronage; and, through a long course of practice, was distinguished for the kindness and attention with which he discharged his professional duties. He also secured the respect and esteem of the people by the zeal which he manifested for the public good, particularly in the cause of education, and in all efforts for the relief of the poor. He was afflicted for many years with a pulmonary complaint: but he bravely contended with the disease, and did not yield till the last moment; having, only the day before his death, though then very ill, made the usual round of visits to his patients. The death of this good man, as might have been expected, was one of Christian composure and resignation.

Dr. Dale's wife was Miss Serena P. Johnson of Andover, who, with ten children, survived her husband. Of these children, three sons and a daughter have died unmarried. Frank, a shipmaster, with his wife and son, perished off Cape Horn in 1859. The survivors are Ebenezer and Theron J., merchants of Boston: William J., who graduated at Harvard College in 1837, and is a physician of Boston; Martha, who married Dr. J. A. Swett of New York; and Serena, wife of Mr. John A. Appleton, of the eminent publishing-house of Appleton and Company, New York.

Dr. Henry Prentiss, another physician of the town, died Oct. 13, 1839. He was a son of Rev. Thomas Prentiss, D.D., of Medfield; and was born in 1798. He graduated at Harvard College in 1817; and, soon after completing his medical studies, commenced practice in Gloucester. Upon the death of Dr. Coffin in 1827, he entered upon the enjoyment of an extensive practice, which even failings in his later years did not seriously diminish. He was highly esteemed by his friends as a skilful physician, and a man of warm and benevolent heart. His wife was Caroline H. Staniford of Boston; who, with her children, removed from town soon after her husband's decease.*

One of the most distressing events of our history occurred on Sunday, 15th of December, 1839. The preceding day was one of uncommon mildness, and was perfectly clear. Many vessels,

---

* This work has given some account of every physician of the town who had his residence here when he died. The only temporary practitioners of the last century, known to me, were Dr. Caleb Rea, who appears to have lived in town from 1748 to 1756; and Dr. Thomas Babbit, who married Polly Jackson Babson, May 10, 1787, and, after a short residence here, removed from town. About 1800, it is said, he was a surgeon in the United-States Navy. His only child, whose birth is recorded in Gloucester, was Fitz Henry, who was born Oct. 10, 1789; became lieutenant in the navy, and was killed in battle on board the frigate "President." William and Edward, other sons of

in consequence, left Eastern ports for a Southern destination: but they had proceeded no farther than Cape Ann, when the wind changed to south-east, with signs of a heavy blow; upon which most of them sought refuge in Gloucester Harbor, where, in the course of Sunday forenoon, they arrived, and found an anchorage. In the afternoon, the wind increased to a terrific gale, bringing rain and snow, and a sea such as had rarely been witnessed on our shores by the oldest people. The scene in the harbor was now watched with intense interest and anxiety by the spectators on the land, who saw the fate of the hapless mariners in the terrible breakers of the lee-shore; and many of them hastened round to afford help, if human help could avail. One after another, the vessels were seen to strike adrift, and apparently hasten to destruction. The fearful end of many, however, was arrested by cutting away the masts; while some, with little less good fortune for their crews, were thrown upon a sandy beach, where, with assistance from the shore, most of the lives were saved. But it was the sad fate of a few to be carried upon the rocks, and dashed to atoms in a moment. From these, several men were lost. As one of the vessels approached the breakers, two men, in the vain hope to escape the death that threatened them, took to their boat; but had scarcely loosed from the vessel, when a merciless sea swept them into eternity. About twenty wrecks were strewed along the shore on the westerly side of the harbor, when night closed over the scene, and added darkness to the horror of the howling wind and raging sea. The gale abated during the night; but the morning presented the astonishing spectacle of thirty dismasted vessels riding at their anchors in the harbor. From these, the crews were taken off

---

Dr. Babbit, entered the navy, and served in it many years, —William as a surgeon; and Edward in various ranks, till he finally attained that of captain. Both of these brothers are deceased. Physicians of the present century, who removed from town after many years' practice in it, are Joseph Reynolds and Amasa D. Bacon. The former practised in Sandy Bay from 1838 till about 1840, and then came to Gloucester; whence, in 1853, he removed to Concord. Dr. Bacon settled in Squam in 1837, and removed thence to Sharon in 1851. The physicians of the town at the present time are here given, with the date of commencing practice here: Isaac P. Smith, 1831; Joseph S. Barber, 1832; Herman E. Davidson, 1842; Joseph Garland, 1849; J. F. Dyer, 1851; Charles H. Hildreth, 1852; A. B. Hoyt, 1858.

by a few brave men who ventured out for that purpose; while to the shipwrecked mariners every relief was extended that humanity could dictate. The exact loss of life on our shores by this dreadful gale was never ascertained. Including the persons who perished by the wreck of a schooner at or near Pigeon Cove, twenty are known to have been lost. The bodies of some were taken away by their friends, and the rest were buried from the First-Parish Meeting-house on the following Sunday, when an appropriate discourse was delivered by Rev. J. K. Waite from Exod. xv. 10: "Thou didst blow with thy wind, the sea covered them: they sank as lead in the mighty waters."

This severe storm occurred at a season of rest from the labors of the fishery, and the lives and property of our own people were not exposed to its ravages; a fortunate circumstance for the town, as its chief business was at that time in a state of great depression. Into this, however, it had only temporarily fallen. The census* of the next year indicated recent prosperity; and the lapse of four or five years brought a revival of "good times," and the commencement of a successful prosecution of the fisheries, which has continued to the present day.

* By the State Census of 1840, the population of Cape Ann is shown to have been distributed as follows: —

Gloucester, First Parish	4,112	
Second Parish	657	
Third Parish	1,163	
Fourth Parish	462	
		6,394
Rockport		2,728
Total		9,122

The population of Cape Ann, at different periods, is here given: —

1704	by estimate		700
1755	by estimate		2,745
1765	by Colonial Census		3,763
1775	by estimate		4,945
1790	by United-States Census		5,317
1800	by " "		5,313
1810	by " "		5,943
1820	by " "		6,384
1830	by " "		7,510
1840	by " " Gloucester	6,350	
	" " Rockport	2,650	
			9,000
1850	by " " Gloucester	7,786	
	" " Rockport	3,274	
			11,060
1855	by State Census, Gloucester	8,935	
	Rockport	3,498	
			12,433

CHAPTER XXXI.

THE TOWN OF ROCKPORT.

Growth of Sandy Bay. — Early Fishery. — Pier built. — Isinglass Factory. — Stone Business commenced. — Soil improved. — Government Breakwater. — Separation from Gloucester attempted. — Separation accomplished. — Incorporation. — Territory of the New Town. — Dr. John Manning. — Dr. James Goss. — Business. — Centennial Celebration. — New Church. — Grog-Shops attacked, and Liquor destroyed. — Growth and Improvement of the New Town.

It is a striking fact in the history of the town, that the head of the Cape — the latest settled portion of its territory — had, up to 1840, outstripped all the older localities in a proportionate increase of population. Sandy Bay did, in fact, gain largely and steadily in numbers for a long period, while the rest of the town was either stationary or retrograding. Its population at the close of the Revolution is estimated to have been four hundred; and, in 1792, seven hundred. In a little less than fifty years from the last-named date, it had quadrupled; while that of the Harbor had not even doubled in the same time. This growth is attributed to the success of the shore-fishing for most of this period, to persevering industry in agriculture, and the quarrying of stone; to all of which, the economy and other good habits of the people have been important auxiliaries.

The proximity of these people to the ocean gave easy access to the ledges off the coast, and invited early attention to shore-fishing; but they could only pursue this business in small boats, on account of the want of a harbor, or even a place of refuge in case of a storm. As early as 1743, Ebenezer Pool, John

Pool, and Benjamin Tarr, with such others as should join with them, had "liberty to build a wharf at the Whirlpool, so called; and also so much of the Neck called Bearskin Neck as is sufficient to set a warehouse on:" but it was not till 1811 that the people felt themselves sufficiently able to construct an artificial harbor. In that year, they erected the breakwater on the northwest side of the Neck; and, in 1819, a wharf opposite: the two structures forming a small but safe haven, and gaining for the people, considering the means at their command, an honorable testimonial of their efforts to supply the only convenience that Nature had denied them.

With better accommodations for business, they now procured vessels of a larger class for their fishery; and, in the course of a few years, engaged in the coastwise trade.

In 1822, a small establishment was set up in the village, for the manufacture of isinglass from hake-sounds; the only one for this purpose in the country. The business has yielded profit; but it is of no material importance, on account of the limited demand for the article.

To another branch of business, — the quarrying and exportation of stone, — commenced two years subsequently, the people of the Cape are indebted in no small degree for their advancement in wealth and their present prosperity.

But the most gratifying results of labor are displayed on their soil. By that ceaseless industry which always accomplishes wonders when well directed, these people have here, as well as at the border of the sea, contended with formidable natural obstacles; and thrifty orchards and fruitful fields now greet the eye, where once barren and rocky plains alone were presented to the view.

Other circumstances, marking and contributing to the prosperity of Sandy Bay, were the establishment of a post-office, with a triweekly mail, in 1825; the formation of a mutual marine insurance company in 1827; and the building of a breakwater at Long Cove by the United-States Government. This great work was commenced in 1836, and was in progress till 1840; when the appropriation for it was exhausted, leaving the structure still incomplete. The end projecting into the sea was greatly damaged by the furious seas that beat against it during a severe gale in October, 1841 ; but, though incomplete and damaged, the work is useful in rendering the Cove a safer place of anchorage, and in protecting from the violence of an easterly gale the vessels lying at the piers since erected within it.

The interest and convenience of the people at the head of the Cape seemed to demand that they should be set off as a town long before the final separation took place. They did, indeed, make an attempt to that end in 1818,* when the subject was brought into town-meeting, and a committee was chosen to consider it ; but, wanting unanimity among themselves, no further action was taken till 1827. In that year, the matter was again agitated, and brought formally before the town ; but ended as before. In neither case was the project opposed by the people of the Harbor ; for the interests and sentiments of the two sections frequently clashed, and sometimes the citizens of the former had even proved influential enough in town-meeting to procure an adjournment to their own parish. When, therefore, the Cape people ceased to disagree among themselves, they found no obstacle to a peaceful and equitable separation, and the organization of one of those popular New-England democracies, — an independent town-government.

The act for the incorporation of Rockport passed the two legislative branches, and received the approval of the Governor on the same day, — Feb. 27, 1840. The first town-meeting was held on the 9th of March following, when all the usual town-officers were chosen.

The portion of the old town set off as the new contained about two-sevenths of the property of the whole ; and it was upon this basis that the settlement in relation to the division of debts, liabilities, and property, was made.

The territory of Rockport includes all of the Fifth Parish of Gloucester, and a portion of the Third adjoining it, situated on

* Sandy Bay, including only the Fifth Parish, then possessed three hundred and eighteen polls, — just one-fourth of the whole number in the town ; and had a valuation of $192,732, — that of the whole town being $1,127,566.

the north-east end of the Cape. The principal settlement of the latter section is at Pigeon Cove, now called the North Village of Rockport. A few settlers were scattered around this Cove and in its vicinity before the Revolutionary War; and, in 1792, thirteen boats fished from it: but the place has risen in importance within the last thirty years, chiefly in consequence of the quarrying carried on there, and the erection of a breakwater and a pier, which have afforded increased accommodations for carrying on the fishery. This breakwater was built in 1831; and, though apparently a sufficient barrier against any sea, it yielded in the great storm of 1841, when the breakers knocked a portion of it away, and swept into the Cove as of old, causing considerable destruction of property. The break, however, was soon repaired; and, the whole work being strengthened, it contributes materially to the prosperity of this thriving village.

The matters worthy of historical record since the incorporation of Rockport, not already noticed, are few. The death of an old physician of the place may properly be noticed as the first.

On the 5th of November, 1841, died Dr. John Manning, aged eighty. His father was Dr. John Manning of Ipswich, whose father was Dr. Joseph Manning of the same town; both of whom lived to advanced age. At the age of seventeen, he joined the American Army, in Rhode Island, as surgeon's mate. Afterwards he practised four years in Chester, N.H.; and removed thence to Gloucester about 1786. Here he lived in the Harbor Parish till 1798, when he removed to Sandy Bay, — his home for the rest of his life. His attention to pursuits out of his profession was given, first to commerce, and afterwards to agriculture; but the ample estate he acquired came principally from his medical practice, in which he was distinguished for skill and success. In politics, he was an ardent Federalist; and was frequently elected a representative by his party. In religion, he belonged to the Universalist sect; but made no professions. He was a man of considerable eccentricity of character, which was manifested even in the closing hours of life, and rendered it difficult to ascertain the real emotions of his heart at that solemn period.

Dr. Manning's wife was Miss Hannah Goodhue of Ipswich. Her death, the first in her household for forty-one years, occurred Jan. 22, 1840.

Four sons of Dr. Manning survived their father, — Joseph B., John, and Charles B., who graduated at Harvard College respectively in 1808, 1810, and 1819; and James. Joseph B. studied law, but never engaged in active practice. With the exception of occasional journeys to the South for the benefit of his health, his life was spent in the home of his childhood. There he employed his time chiefly in philological studies, the fruits of which he gave to the world in two remarkable books.* He died a bachelor at Ipswich, while on a visit, May 22, 1854, aged sixty-seven. John commenced practice as a physician in Waldoborough, Me., in 1813. He made one cruise as surgeon of a privateer in 1815; after which he returned to Waldoborough, and remained there till 1842; when he removed to Rockport, and practised there till his death. He died Feb. 7, 1852, aged sixty-two, leaving four sons. One of these (William H.) has been Collector of the Customs in Gloucester, and another (Joseph) has settled in the practice of medicine in Rockport. Charles B. was a physician in his native place; and died there Dec. 16, 1843, aged forty-four. James, the only survivor of these brothers, is a trader in Rockport.

Another aged physician of Rockport died Nov. 29, 1842. This was Dr. James Goss, at the age of seventy-nine. He was a native of Billerica, and settled in his profession at Sandy Bay about 1792. Besides attending to the duties of his medical practice, he was often employed in writing deeds and other instruments; and, by his various services, secured the respect of society, and the reputation of a useful man. He was one of the representatives in 1832.

* The first of these is an octavo pamphlet of forty-eight pages, entitled "Epeögraphy; or, Notations of Orthoëpy. To which is prefixed Lektography; an Improvement in Alphabetical Writing for representing Sounds of Words, as described in Letters-Patent of the United States." The second is entitled "The Voice of Letters: Ancient Proprieties of Latin and Greek; the Standard of English Letter-Customs, their Inherent System, and preferred Orthography."

Dr. Goss was twice married, — first to Polly Jaquith of Wilmington, and next to Hannah Smith of Ipswich. Sylvester and George, two sons by the first wife, became printers; married, and settled away from home; and are both dead. Eliza, the only child by the second wife, married William Caldwell.*

For the first few years after the incorporation of the new town, the fishing business was in a depressed condition; and, like the parent town, it remained nearly stationary in population; the State census of 1845 showing a slight loss to each. It was but a temporary shock, however; for the fishery again became successful, and, with other branches of industry, — some of which were new, — placed the town upon a footing of steady and increasing prosperity.

During the period of depression, the enterprise of the people was turned to manufacturing; the result of which was the establishment, in 1848, of a mill for making cotton duck. One of the signs of thrift in the new town was the incorporation of the Rockport Bank. This institution went into operation in 1851; and, by prudent and successful management, has acquired a good reputation.†

On the 2d of January, 1854, the people of Rockport celebrated the one hundredth anniversary of their incorporation as a parish, in accordance with a vote of the town passed several months previously. The principal feature of this occasion was the delivery by Dr. Lemuel Gott of an historical discourse, at the Congregational Church, in the afternoon and evening of that day. A recent snow-storm, of unusual severity, prevented the attendance of people from abroad; but the church was entirely filled by the inhabitants of the town, who listened with great interest as the orator of the day recounted the most prominent events in the history of Sandy Bay.‡

---

* The physicians of Rockport, at the present time, are Benjamin Haskell, Oscar D. Abbott, and Joseph Manning.

† The officers of the Bank are Ezra Eames, President; and Jabez R. Gott, Cashier; who have held their respective offices ever since the bank was established.

‡ The people of Rockport should take the necessary steps for the printing of this discourse; and of another, delivered by Dr. Gott at the dedication of a schoolhouse, giving an account of the schools at Sandy Bay in past times.

This commemoration was not only an occasion of interest to the people as a town, but it was one of peculiar joy to the parish as a religious body; for its members could look back upon half a century of remarkable growth and prosperity, and forward to the time when another church, of like faith, — a scion from their own stock, — should be planted at their side.

The Second Orthodox Congregational Church of Rockport was organized March 15, 1855; and now has sixty-one members. Its pastor is the Rev. David Bremner. He was born in Keith, Scotland, Jan. 25, 1828; and after a preparatory course at Gilmanton Academy, N.H., entered Dartmouth College, where he graduated in 1850. He completed his theological studies at Andover in 1853, and was ordained over the new church in Rockport, May 2, 1855. The sermon on that occasion was preached by Rev. Prof. E. A. Park, D.D., of Andover. This society erected a chapel for public worship in 1856.

One other event — the most memorable in the history of Rockport — remains to be noticed. On the 8th of July, 1856, at nine o'clock in the morning, a regularly organized band of women, led by a man bearing an American ensign, appeared in the principal street of the town, for the purpose of making a demonstration against the grog-shops of the place. They did not stop to consider their legal right to abate these nuisances: for, as mothers, wives, sisters, and daughters, they were suffering under the terrible evils they inflict; and they needed no stronger inducement than the law of self-protection. Animated by this purpose, they proceeded successively to thirteen places where ardent spirits were unlawfully kept for sale; and, seizing casks, demijohns, and decanters, containing the bane of their happiness, poured their contents into the street, occasionally breaking a vessel in order to hasten the flow of the hated fluid to the ground. Having finished their work at about three o'clock, P.M., they repaired to the "Square," and exchanged congratulations upon the performance of the good deed they had done; after which they separated, and went to their respective homes.

This proceeding of the Rockport women has been the subject of legal investigation; but, whatever may be the decision of the courts in relation to it, it will still find defenders, — as it has hitherto found them, — on the ground that the sufferers by an intolerable public evil may proceed in their own way to correct it, when no legal remedy can be had. But this is dangerous doctrine, and should immediately suggest the thought, that, in seeking in this way a cure for present ills, we may flee to others that we know not of.

By the census of 1855, the population of Rockport is shown to have increased about thirty per cent since its incorporation. Its increase in wealth in the same time has been steady, and large enough to be beneficial. Mindful of the higher interests of life, the people of the new town have repaired and beautified their churches; erected commodious and handsome schoolhouses; and, in general, given much attention to all that concerns religious, moral, and intellectual culture. They have thus taken the best means to secure a continuance of their prosperity, and the perpetuity of those virtues which have made them hitherto a happy community.

CHAPTER XXXII.

Post-Office established. — Stage to Boston. — Public Schools. — College Graduates. — Most Distinguished Educated Men. — Gloucester Lyceum. — Death of aged and of prominent Citizens. — Catholic Church.

Among the most important events in the history of Gloucester, that remain to be noticed, are the establishment of railroad connection with Boston, and a change in the system of conducting the public schools.

The chief means of intercourse with the metropolis, enjoyed by the people of the town during the first century after its settlement, were those afforded by the fishing shallops and wood-coasters; but, as soon as the maritime business of the place rose to be important, one or two small vessels found regular employment in running between the two ports.

Before the establishment of a post-office in the town, the people received their letters by a messenger who went twice a week to Beverly to get them. They were probably brought by mail to Salem, and thence sent across the ferry to Beverly with the letters for that place. How long this arrangement continued, it is not easy to ascertain. The only person known to have been employed as a messenger is John Oakes. The place for the reception and delivery of letters was, it is said, at Philemon Haskell's tavern. A post-office was established in town soon after the adoption of the Constitution; and was at first, and for several years, kept in the shop of the postmaster, Henry Phelps, in the building standing on Front Street, opposite the head of Central Wharf. Its location was afterwards changed from time to time, as the convenience of the successive postmasters required, till its permanent establishment in the building erected by the government for a custom-house and post-office.

The first regular communication between Gloucester and Boston, by land, was established in 1788 by Jonathan Lowe.* On the 25th of April in that year, he commenced running a two-horse open carriage between the two places; leaving Gloucester twice a week, in the morning, and returning the next day. The route was through Salem, Danvers, Lynn, and Malden, to Winnisimet Ferry, by which the coach usually entered Boston; though it sometimes went round through Medford. Nearly a whole day was occupied in making the journey. Although this period is within the memory of living persons, it was in the early days of stage-coaching; for, besides the Gloucester coach, only four stages ran into Boston at that time, — one from Salem, one from Portsmouth, one from Providence, and one from New York. Tradition reports that the first arrival of this vehicle in town created a great sensation, and that several of the principal citizens were treated to a ride in it before it was used for public travel.

The first change in these accommodations was that by which the stage was made a triweekly one; which continued till about 1805, when a daily line was established. Four-horse coaches were soon substituted for the old vehicles, and continued to afford communication once a day for many years. At last, another daily stage was added; and passengers were enabled to visit Boston, and return the same day.

The completion of the Eastern Railroad aroused a strong desire for a line from Gloucester to connect with it; but the project was supposed to be impracticable till 1844. On the 14th of September in that year, a meeting of citizens was held to take the subject into consideration. As a consequence of this meet-

---

* Jonathan Lowe belonged, probably, to the Ipswich Family of Lows. He had his stage-office in a tavern, which he kept for many years, at the corner of Front Street, near the Town Landing. He died Feb. 22, 1815, aged fifty-six. Two of his children survive, — a daughter, the wife of Hon. Lonson Nash; and a son, Hon. John W. Lowe, who was one of the representatives in 1830, and a senator in 1847 and 1848.

ing, the route was surveyed, and the Eastern-Railroad Company was induced to undertake the enterprise.

The cars commenced running regular trips on the Gloucester branch on the 2d of November, 1847; having on the previous day carried a party of citizens, by invitation of the company, on a pleasure excursion to Salem. This road has proved to be a profitable investment to the company that built it, and has contributed largely to the recent prosperity of the town.*

The history of the public schools of Gloucester has been traced to 1804, when the town was divided into eleven school-districts. Each of these districts received its proportion of the money raised by the town for district-schools, and expended it under the direction of a Prudential Committee of the district.

The Town Grammar School was still continued in compliance with the law of the Commonwealth, and was kept in the Harbor Parish. The permanent location of the school there gave great dissatisfaction to the people of the other parishes, who complained that they were excluded by distance from its benefits; and who finally succeeded, in 1826, in making it a circulating school. Tired at last of dissensions about it, the town practically abolished the school, by voting yearly that the money appropriated for its support should be divided among the several districts.

A Town Grammar School was not opened again till 1839. Its re-establishment was due to the efforts of Robert Rantoul, jun. That distinguished citizen was not afraid to revive an unpopular subject, and to tell the people that it was not "consistent with the obligation of good citizens to obey the laws, or even with the first principles of common honesty, any longer grossly to violate or cunningly to evade the wholesome provisions of the statute" requiring such a school. Its renewed existence was not of long duration. It was again discontinued in 1845, and was never but

* A steamboat has occasionally, during the summer months, within the last twenty years, made trips between Boston and Gloucester; but the first one put on the route by the people of the town was the steamer "Mystic," chartered for that purpose, and run in 1859, and since purchased by a company in the town to be continued in the business.

once afterwards (in 1849) revived upon the old plan and with its ancient name.*

One of the evils of the district system was a constant tendency to the division of sparsely settled territory into small districts. The number of these bodies increased from eleven in 1804 to twenty-three in 1840. The separation of Sandy Bay from the town took off seven districts; but new ones were afterwards formed in the old town, and a still further division was in contemplation, when the people were aroused to the necessity of a thorough reform in the system upon which the schools were then conducted, or an immediate resort to a better one.

The School Committee for 1849 addressed themselves to this work; and, in their annual report, showed that the principal obstacles to the success of the public schools, as then conducted, were unsuitable schoolhouses, inequality of school advantages, and poor teachers: of all of which, the district system was, in

---

* The following is a list of the teachers of the Town Grammar School:—

Name	Year
Thomas Riggs	1699
John Newman	1703
John Ring	1705
Joshua Gardner	1707
Joshua Moody	1709
Samuel Tompson	1711
Joseph Parsons	1715
Edward Tompson	1721
William Osgood	1722
Edmund March	1723
Isaac Abbott	1724
Daniel Witham	1726
Joseph Manning	1727
Charles Glover	1727
Daniel Witham	1728
Nathaniel Walter	1730
Walter Hastings	1732
Mather Withington	1733
Parker Morse	1734
Aaron Smith	1735
Benjamin White	1739
Samuel White	1742
Nehemiah Porter	1746
Thomas Jaques	1747
Jonathan Pierpont	1748
Samuel White	1749
Thomas Rand	1752
Thomas Jaques	1773
Samuel Whittemore	1753
Jacob Bailey	1758
Thomas Pierce	1760
Samuel Pierce	1761
Thomas Marrett	1762
James Prentice	1763
Philemon Stacy	1767 to 1776
Thomas Sanders	1784
Obadiah Parsons	1794
John Ewins	1802
Ezra Leonard	1804
Eli Forbes	1804
Nathan Parks	1805
Joseph B. Felt	1812
John Manning, jun.	1812
John Whipple	1812
Nathan D. Appleton	1814
Isaac W. Mulliken	1816
Paul Ferson	1817
Ezra Leonard	1818
Daniel W. Rogers	1820
Thomas Jones	1820
Daniel W. Rogers	1821
Thomas Cochran	1821
James Boswell	1822
Ezra Leonard	1822
Daniel W. Rogers	1823
Charles Smith, 3d	1823
Lonson Nash	1824
William Whipple	1826
Richard Gardner	1839
Thomas Baker	1849

High-School.

Name	Year
Moses Patten	1850
C. J. Adams	1852
J. S. Chamberline	1856
L. Z. Ferris	1858
Peter Ripley	1859

their opinion, the chief cause, and ought, therefore, to be abolished, leaving the sole management of the schools to the town in its corporate capacity. Their plan for a re-organization was brought before the people at one of the most numerously attended town-meetings ever held, and adopted, after full discussion, with scarcely a dissenting vote. It was the noblest act ever performed by the town; and the extraordinary and almost enthusiastic unanimity with which it was carried — involving as it did the necessity for a large increase of taxation — may be contemplated with the highest satisfaction, as the beginning of a creditable state of public feeling in regard to the cause of education, which has never since ceased to exist.

The whole number of public schools of all grades, now kept in town, is twenty-four in summer, and twenty-nine in winter, attended by nearly two thousand scholars. A uniform course of instruction and equal school-privileges have been established for all the children. Two high-schools, one for each sex, are open to the youth of the whole town, who may be admitted upon reaching a certain standard of qualification, and may there pursue advanced studies; while the primary and grammar schools, located in different parts of the town, enable all, who attend the course of study therein prescribed, to acquire sufficient knowledge of the common branches of education for any of the ordinary duties or business of life. These schools possess the confidence of the people, and are believed to be equal to those of any town in the State, supported at no greater expense.* But there yet remains a wide gap between their actual and their possible condition. When this shall be bridged, and the schools shall become effectual for the highest moral, spiritual, and intel-

* The total expense of these schools, for the year 1858, was as follows: —

For teachers' wages	$9,277.11
„ fuel	613.58
„ pay of committee	1,000.00
„ miscellaneous items, and repairs	648.56
„ care of schoolhouses	533 16
	$12,072.41

The committees' pay goes to one member, who is created, by the Board, Superintendent of the Schools. This office was filled by Thomas Baker from 1850 to 1856. Since 1857, its duties have been performed by Henry Cummings.

lectual culture of our children, they will indeed be fountains of virtue and intelligence to fertilize and bless the town.

Though the town has long been generous in its support of public schools, the people have ever been backward, except at one period, in bestowing upon their sons the advantages of a college education. Up to 1765, only eight of them have this distinction; but, between that date and the commencement of the Revolution, thirteen received a college degree, — a number greater than that of all the graduates belonging to the town for the next fifty years, or the last twenty.* The general pecuniary

---

* Natives and residents who have graduated at College. Those marked *R.* were of Rockport.

Harvard.	
John Emerson	1689
John Eveleth	1689
Daniel Witham	1718
Moses Parsons	1736
Benjamin White	1738
Jeremiah Allen; died an undergraduate.	
John Newman	1740
Samuel White	1741
Thomas Sanders	1748
Philemon Stacy	1765
Epes Sargent	1766
Samuel Hale	1766
John Rogers	1767
Peter Coffin	1769
Winthrop Sargent	1771
Samuel Plummer	1771
Thomas Sanders	1772
Nathaniel Ellery	1772
John Low	1773
Joshua Plummer	1778
Joseph Allen	1774
Samuel Chandler	1775
David Pearce	1786
Daniel Rogers	1798
Seth Low	1804
Joseph Bolles Manning	1808
John Manning	1810
Joseph L. Stevens	1810
Samuel Gilman	1811
Charles B. Manning	1819
George Augustus Meredith	1827
John Osborn Sargent	1830
Noah Worcester	1832
William J. Dale	1887
Samuel T. Hildreth	1837
Samuel D. Dexter	1843
William M'Kenzie	1855
William Parsons	1856
Robert E. Babson	1856
George Whittemore	1857

Dartmouth.	
Francis Norwood	1818
Thomas Kittredge	1833

Amherst.	
William R. Jewett	1831
Benjamin Haskell	1832
Nathaniel Richardson	1835
James Challis Parsons	1855
Joseph B. Reynolds	1855

Brown University.	
Jabez Tarr	1883
Nathaniel Pool, *R.*	1853
Benjamin H. Smith, jun., *R.*	1857
Charles R. Sewall, *R.*	1857
Reuben B. Pool, *R.*	1857

Bowdoin.	
David S. Rowe	1838
Samuel L. Young	1840

Yale.	
William Pearson	1841

Union.	
Benjamin Pool, *R.*	1844

Nearly all these graduates have been mentioned in the course of this work. Of those who have not, the following should be noticed:—

Seth Low, H.C. 1804, was a son of David Low, a sojourner in town, who married Hannah, daughter of Deacon Nathaniel Haskell. His father was a sea-captain, and resided a few years in the Second Parish, where Seth was born March 19, 1782. He left college in his third year, on account of an affliction of the eyes; but received a de-

prosperity indispensable to a high degree of intellectual culture has not been, till recent times, enjoyed to such an extent as to afford the means of pursuing it; but, now that this is no longer wanting, the wise and thoughtful will be likely to recognize the fact, that the true greatness of a town does not consist in its accumulations of wealth, but in the number of its learned, serious, honest, and well-educated citizens.

Of all the educated men and scholars who have been born in Gloucester, the two best known and most distinguished are Epes Sargent and Edwin P. Whipple. The former has been mentioned on a preceding page. His spirited song, "A Life on the Ocean Wave," has carried his name into every house in the land; and various other products of his active literary career have gained him an honorable fame.

Mr. Whipple was born here March 8, 1819. The accident of his birth is all that connects him with our history; for his father (Matthew Whipple) had then recently come into town, and died soon afterwards, leaving a widow and children, who removed to Salem while Edwin was still a child. He there enjoyed the

---

gree in 1849. He had chosen the ministry for his profession; but, upon leaving college, he changed his plans, and went into a drug-store in Salem. He removed thence to Brooklyn, N.Y., in 1828; and died in that city, June 19, 1858. His funeral sermon, preached by Rev. Dr. Farley, has been published.

George Augustus Meredith, H.C. 1827. The true name of this graduate was Israel Elwell. He was a natural son of Gorham Parsons, deceased; and, when he was old enough to fit for college, he was placed by his father in a school at Jamaica Plain, with the assumed name. His career at college was marked by extravagance and dissipation, and finished with a confirmed habit of intemperance. After graduating, he studied law, and practised a short time in Northampton. There his true name was discovered: whereupon he left the place, and visited his native town. He next went to New York; where, for an act of petty larceny, he was put in prison, from which he was released by the good offices of President Kirkland. He then went to New Orleans, and there met some college friends, by whose influence he obtained employment as a teacher: but he soon forfeited their confidence; and, to escape further annoyance, they procured him a passage in a steamboat for St. Louis. This must have been about 1833; since which time, nothing is known of him.

Noah Worcester, H.C. 1832, was a son of David Worcester, who resided in Gloucester when his son entered college. The latter became a physician and professor in the Western-Reserve College, Ohio. He died in Ohio in 1847.

Samuel D. Dexter, H.C. 1843, was a son of Samuel Dexter. He entered the ministry, and was settled over an Orthodox society in Exeter, N.H. He died in 1850.

Jabez Tarr, Brown University 1833, was a son of Jabez Tarr of Sandy Bay. He had chosen the ministry for his profession; but was taken away by death, April 11, 1834.

benefit of good schools till the age of fifteen, when he entered upon a business employment in Salem; whence, in a few years, he removed to Boston. In that city, so rich in literary advantages, he found means for the cultivation of the uncommon intellectual faculties with which nature had endowed him; and, soon after he reached manhood, began to attract attention as a writer and lecturer. In the latter vocation, few men have instructed and delighted a larger number of the people of the United States than he.

Considering the little attention that has been given in the town to literary culture, it is not surprising that much remains to be done for the improvement of the people in useful knowledge. The only literary institution on the Cape, of any importance, is the Gloucester-Lyceum Library. The Lyceum was established in 1830, with the chief design of developing the talents of its members in lectures, essays, and debates. To this end of its formation, the labors of that wise and earnest friend of education, Rev. Hosea Hildreth, constantly tended; but it soon lost the character of a school which he wished to give it, and became only a vehicle for the entertainment of its members through the medium of popular public lectures. The institution no longer retains even this feature, and preserves only its corporate existence as the custodian of an excellent library, which, by the efforts of public-spirited citizens of the town, acting under the immediate stimulus of a generous offer by a native * residing in Boston, was formed, and placed in its care, in 1854. This library contains about two thousand volumes; and, when a suitable increase and a free use of its contents shall be provided for, the full extent of the value of such a blessing will be realized.

The memory of a few citizens who have died in the later years of our history, and have not yet been noticed, should be preserved here.

On the 26th of January, 1840, died William Pew, aged one hundred and seven, as reported; but he had not, probably,

---

* Samuel E. Sawyer.

quite reached that extraordinary age. He had, however, without doubt, attained the age of one hundred years, if not more; for he was a soldier in Braddock's defeat. He was born in Virginia, but came to Gloucester when a young man, and settled near Fresh-water Cove. His chief employment was that of fishing, in which he was noted for industry and success. His great age attests the strength of his constitution, which was also one of great power of endurance, and was not much shattered till near the end of life. He left descendants bearing the name, some of whom are among the principal business-men of the town of the present day.

Oct. 24, 1842, died James Mansfield, aged seventy-seven. He was born in Salem; and, in early life, was a mechanic. He came to Gloucester when young, and married a daughter of William Murphy, whose estate on Front Street, at the head of Long Wharf, came into his possession. He there kept a shop, and engaged in the fisheries; adventuring occasionally, also, in foreign commerce. He pursued his business with honesty, industry, and success, till old age; and was succeeded in it by his sons. Mr. Mansfield avoided official employment, with the exception of that of a bank-director, which he held for a long course of years.

Jan. 20, 1847, died Mrs. Joanna Andrews. She was born in Chebacco Parish, Ipswich, Oct. 11, 1744 (O.S.); and was, consequently, more than one hundred and two years old. Her maiden name was Burnham. Her mother died at the age of ninety-two, and a sister was living at ninety-four. At the age of one hundred, this remarkable woman was able to keep a separate domestic establishment in the house of her grandson, and to attend to her own wants. From that time, her decay was as gradual, and marked in retrogressive order by the same stages, as an infant's growth.

July 15, 1849, died Richard Friend, aged eighty-three. He was a son of Richard Friend of Wenham, and was brought up to the trade of his father (that of a carpenter), at which he worked some time after his removal to Gloucester. He finally engaged in the fishing business, at the head of the Harbor; and carried it on several years with success. His integrity procured him repeated election to the office of a bank-director, while the kindness that marked his character gained him universal esteem. The progeny of this valuable citizen is so numerous, that the town will not, it is likely, be without Friends for many generations to come. One of his sons (Joseph) was representative in 1849. Samuel Friend, a distant relative of the preceding, and a respected and useful citizen, together with his wife, were two of thirteen victims of small-pox in the spring of 1850. He died May 22, at the age of sixty-eight.

March 10, 1850, died Samuel Giles, aged sixty-two, a native of Salem, and, till middle life, a ship-master; in which employment he acquired wealth. His wife was a daughter of Samuel Wonson of Eastern Point; at which place, after quitting the sea, he was induced to employ his capital with his family connections in the fishing business. He was a prominent member of the Baptist Church, and was esteemed as an honest and useful citizen. Capt. Giles avoided public office, but served one year as representative. Having no children, he adopted a sister of his wife, — now the wife of Rev. William Lamson, D.D., formerly minister of our Baptist Church.

Feb. 15, 1852, died Henry Phelps, aged eighty-six. He was born in Salem; of which place his father was a ship-master, and was lost at sea in 1786. The son graduated at Harvard College in 1788. A club-foot and an imperfect development of the right arm and hand offered discouragements; but he chose the profession of medicine, and, after studying with Dr. Plummer of Salem, was established by him as a physician and apothecary in Gloucester in 1790. He acquired some practice as a doctor, but soon abandoned that branch of his business. He was many years postmaster and principal acting magistrate in town, and was often employed as a scrivener. He continued to keep a shop on Front Street till about the age of eighty; when, becoming dependent upon filial support, he went to reside with a daughter in the outskirts of the town; and there, without much pain and suffering, in the midst of kind attention, he sank quietly and gradually to his rest. Mr. Phelps was thrice married, and had several children; of whom one son and one daughter settled in town.

June 6, 1852, died John Mason, aged eighty-three. He was a native of Cambridge, and was descended from Hugh Mason, an early settler. He was a carpenter, and worked at his trade on first coming to Gloucester; but abandoned it soon, and was for some time employed as master of the workhouse. He next engaged in tavern-keeping; which was his chief business till old age. Possessing considerable mathematical talent, his services were often sought as a surveyor; but his most important work in this line was a correct map of the town, which he published. He also made himself useful by his general knowledge of municipal affairs. A strong will and great independence were striking traits of his character. He had three sons. Alphonso, first a mechanic and then a bank-officer in Cambridge, and next a partner in business with his father, and United-States' surveyor in Gloucester, perished by the burning of the steamer "Lexington" on Long-Island Sound, Jan. 13, 1840; having, during the ten years of his manhood spent in his native town, won the warmest esteem of all who knew him. Sidney went in early life to St. John's, P.R.; and, as the result of his own exertions, became a prominent and successful merchant there: whence he removed to New York, where he now resides. John was also a merchant in St. John's, but has for several years been established in Philadelphia.

Dec. 6, 1853, died William Ferson, aged seventy-nine. He was born in New Boston, N.H.; to which State his great-grandfather (Paul M'Pherson) emigrated from Ireland in 1718. To that country the family had removed, with other emigrants, from Argyleshire, Scotland, in the early part of the seventeenth century. He graduated at Dartmouth College in 1797; and, during most of the next year, was teacher of the Academy in Amherst, N.H. He next went through a course of medical study, and then established himself in practice at Sandy Bay; from which place he removed to the Harbor Parish in 1805 to take an office in the custom-house, for which he gave up his medical profession, except during a few years which he spent in

Ohio, whither his father and other members of his family emigrated. He continued in office till the general dismissal of government officials by President Jackson in 1829. On his retirement from the custom-house, he offered his services to the public as an agent for the transaction of any business in which he could make himself useful; and spent the remainder of his life in active employment in a great variety of offices, public and private. He filled nearly all the most important town-offices; was a bank-director, treasurer of the Savings Bank, three years a member of the Executive Council of Massachusetts, and one year a senator. It was the testimony of all who knew him, that, in all these offices, his conduct was marked by kindness, integrity, and perfect fidelity. He encountered sorrows and trials; but a strong religious faith bore him triumphantly through them all, and finally crowned its perfect work by illuminating the dark valley of the shadow of death with all the brightness of celestial day. Dr. Ferson left but one son, who married, — William G., a merchant in Michigan.

March 10, 1855, died Benjamin K. Hough, a native of Chelsea, aged eighty-nine. Genealogical research might connect him with our early settler, William Hough. By the death of his father, he was left in his boyhood to the care of friends, some of whom belonged to the Sargent Family; and was placed by them in the store of David Plummer of this town. After a short service there, he went into the counting-room of Winthrop Sargent, where he remained till he entered into business for himself; after which, his life, till his retirement in old age, was spent in various branches of trade and commerce. In the first political divisions that agitated the country, he took a deep interest, and became a warm advocate of the doctrines and measures of the Federal party; with whose leaders in Massachusetts he was brought into intimate connection as a member of the State Government, and was held by them in high esteem. It is not, however, for any political prominence that he best deserves to be remembered, but for the high qualities he displayed in the various walks of life. In public intercourse with his fellow-beings, he was a true Christian gentleman; and, in private relations, a friend of rare sympathy, kindness, and benevolence. Of no man who has lived among us can it more truthfully be said, —

> "He had a tear for pity, and a hand
> Open as day for melting charity."

Mr. Hough was twice married; but his only surviving child is a son, who bears and perpetuates his name.

Among all the changes in the town which these venerable citizens had witnessed, none were so striking as that which was shown by the recent increase of population. Before 1840, there were few persons of foreign birth or parentage residing in Gloucester. A single Irish family, or, at most, two or three, were all of that origin then living here; but, within a few years after that time, a rapid growth of business commenced, and created a demand for labor, which only could be supplied from a foreign source. Consequently, a large portion of the late additions to the population is Irish; though the success of the fisheries for the last fifteen years has attracted many fishermen from the British Provinces, and several Portuguese from the Azores to engage in them. The foreign population of Gloucester and Rockport combined, in 1855, was fifteen hundred and seven.

The Irish and Portuguese are of course, with scarcely an exception, attached to the Catholic faith, and to the religious rites and worship which that enjoins. The first Mass in Gloucester was celebrated on the 1st of January, 1849, in a room of a Catholic family. The officiating priest was Rev. John McCabe of Salem. After that time, it was celebrated several Sundays in each year in the Town Hall till 1855; when, through the exertions of Rev. Thomas Shahan of Salem, the meeting-house first erected by the Baptists was purchased, removed to Park Street, and converted to a Catholic chapel. It was dedicated Sept. 30, 1855; when the sermon of the occasion was preached by Rev. S. O'Brien of Boston. By the labors of the former priest, a small chapel was also opened in Rockport in 1857.

The priest now ministering to the Catholics of the two towns (the first one settled on Cape Ann) is Rev. Luigi Acquarone.

The Catholic population of the Cape at the present time, according to an estimate of Dr. Acquarone, is twenty-five hundred. This estimate is not probably much too large, considering that the number of infants of this population baptized in two years and seven months, ending in September, 1859, was three hundred. Some of these infants are born to an inheritance of vice and ignorance; and, to be faithful, the historian must not fail to warn those who are beholding this with indifference, that it will require all the good influences of churches and schools, and the best exertions of wise and philanthropic citizens, to make them men and women whom the town will be happy to own as her sons and daughters.

CHAPTER XXXIII.

MODERN BUSINESS OF THE TOWN.

NATURE has denied to Cape Ann a fertile soil; but she has given it a harbor of such excellence as will make it the seat of an active population, so long as men shall pursue that "great sea-business of fishing" which first attracted people of the English race to its shores. This business must, in the future as in the past, constitute the chief employment of those who dwell upon its rocky territory; for, though its safe and commodious harbor can well accommodate a large foreign and coastwise trade, its proximity to a great commercial metropolis will ever discourage the growth of any other than a local business. This assertion is warranted by the fact, that its registered tonnage was less in 1855 than in 1790.*

The foreign commerce of Gloucester (which, before the Revolutionary War, was of no great extent) rose, after the peace, to be of considerable importance. In 1790, upwards of forty ships, brigs, schooners, and sloops were employed in it: and, during the twenty years succeeding, vessels belonging to the town visited most of the principal ports in Europe and the West Indies; and a few made voyages beyond the Cape of Good Hope. One of

* From the latter part of 1789 to the close of 1790, the amount of tonnage registered under the acts of the Federal Government, regulating commerce, was four thousand and eighteen tons: namely, four ships, seven hundred and seventy-one tons; nine brigs, a thousand one hundred and eleven tons; twenty-three schooners, a thousand six hundred and five tons; and seven sloops, five hundred and thirty-one tons. The amount of registered tonnage of the District of Gloucester, at quinquennial periods from 1825 to 1855 inclusive, was as follows: 1825, three thousand three hundred and eighty-nine tons; 1830, two thousand and ninety-eight tons; 1835, three thousand six hundred and four tons; 1840, two thousand three hundred and two tons; 1845, two thousand three hundred and eighty tons; 1850, two thousand eight hundred and seventy-three tons; 1855, three thousand nine hundred and thirty-one tons.

those engaged in the latter (the "Winthrop and Mary") was owned by an association of merchants* called the India Company. She was of about one hundred tons' burthen, originally a schooner; but was altered to a ship, and properly manned and armed to suit the dignity of the India trade. Having made two voyages safely to Calcutta, she was next sent to Sumatra; but was never heard from after leaving that island on her homeward passage. This occurred about 1800.

The Bilbao trade was also resumed by our merchants after the war. The first vessel that ever left Massachusetts Bay with a cargo of fish for a European market, was the ship, belonging to the Dorchester Company, which sailed from Cape-Ann Harbor for Spain in 1623, as stated in a previous chapter of this work; but, of the great trade in that article of which that voyage was the commencement, we know little more than the beginning and the end. In 1767, there were sent to Bilbao from the ports of Essex County as many as fifty-one thousand quintals of fish; of which quantity, Gloucester, without doubt, furnished a considerable portion. The merchants of the town finally abandoned the trade soon after the beginning of the present century; chiefly, it is said, in consequence of discriminating duties at that port in favor of the fish of other countries.

The interruption of the business of France, occasioned by the revolution in that nation, opened, for a short season, a profitable market for American fish; of which some of the Gloucester merchants took advantage. One schooner, fitted out from the town in 1793, went to the Grand Bank, and took twenty-one thousand fish, with which she sailed for Nantes; but, upon arriving on the coast, was ordered to Belle Isle, where the fish were sold in a green state at a half-crown apiece, producing over ten thousand crowns. This was a rare case, of course; and, as might be expected, the business was soon overdone, and finally, upon the resumption of the French fisheries, abandoned altogether.

* These were Ignatius Sargent, William Pearson, John Somes, David Plummer, James Hayes, Joseph Foster, jun., Fitz W. Sargent, Aaron Parsons, Thomas Parsons and Nehemiah Parsons.

The peace of 1783 also enabled the merchants of Gloucester to pursue the West-India trade again for several years without interruption. A considerable portion of this trade — that carried on with the French islands — finally ceased to be profitable, in consequence of the large bounty by which the importation of French fish was encouraged; and, before 1830, was totally abandoned by the merchants of the town. About the same time, the unimportant commerce carried on with some of the other islands was also given up; and Gloucester turned attention to the home market, which began then to be opened, and which it has ever since found to afford the best customers for its staple products. If a particular account of our West-India trade should ever be written, one incident of it, possessing interest in these days of huge ships and a vast commerce, will command the attention of the historian. This was the fitting-out, during the embargo preceding the last war with Great Britain, of several of the small fishing-boats of the town on voyages to the West Indies. One of these boats was of thirteen tons' burthen, and the largest was not more than twenty. The act was unlawful; and they departed, of course, by stealth. The fish which they carried were sold at high prices, and the boats were disposed of without great loss; though the master of one ventured home with a cargo of coffee, which he landed at Squam in the night, and, before morning, was again out to sea to set his boat adrift in Massachusetts Bay, where she was finally picked up.

The only branch of foreign commerce which has been steadily pursued by merchants of Gloucester, for a long course of years, is that carried on with Paramaribo, or, as it is usually called here, Surinam, the capital of Dutch Guiana. Boston vessels traded to Surinam as early as 1713; for two arrived at the former port from that place in one week of that year: but it is not known that any Gloucester vessel engaged in the trade till about 1790, when, it is said, Col. Pearce sent a vessel there. The chief article of export is hake, supplied in part by Maine fishermen; though other provisions (as beef, pork, lard, hams, and flour) are sent in large quantities. The return cargoes consist almost wholly of molasses and sugar; but some coffee and cocoa are also brought. Under the stimulus of the very high prices of sugar and molasses in 1857, the trade of Gloucester with Surinam for that year probably exceeded in amount that of the whole foreign commerce of the town in any previous year of its history.

The commerce of Gloucester began with the shipment of wood to Boston; a business which, in course of time, compelled the people of the town to seek their own supply abroad. This, according to the lapse of years, they obtained from places more and more remote, till at last they came to depend on Nova Scotia for this essential article. The wood-coasters of that Province began to come to Gloucester about twenty years ago. The vessels were then of no greater average burthen than forty tons; but the size has increased with the growth of the business, and has now reached an average of seventy-five. The number of arrivals of foreign vessels, nearly all of which were these wood-coasters, was, in 1859, one hundred and forty-two. Before the Reciprocity Treaty with Great Britain, these vessels generally took home specie; but, since that happy event, they have carried provisions and other articles from the well-supplied stores of the town.

Considering the conveniences of the harbor, and the fact that the town had a large body of men bred to the sea, it might have been expected that the enterprising and wealthy merchant (David Pearce) who fitted out one or more vessels on whaling voyages would have given that business such a start in the town, as to have led to its continued and successful prosecution; but, after he ceased to carry it on, no one appears to have engaged in it till 1832, when two companies were formed for the purpose of re-commencing the business. Two ships were fitted out; but an unprofitable result of their voyages caused an abandonment of the enterprise, and a general consent on the part of the people that destiny seemed to direct them to a pursuit of other inhabitants of the deep, as that upon which the town must depend for its prosperity. In that pursuit they were already extensively engaged, with such industry and success as to leave them no occasion to seek other means of living.

Standing on the spot* where Mr. Thomson set up the frame for his fishery, the beholder finds himself in the centre of a seat of the fishing business, which, for activity, enterprise, and extent, has no equal on this continent, and perhaps is not surpassed by any in the world. It is proper, therefore, that this concluding chapter of the history of the town should trace the growth of this business, and the principal changes in it, since the Revolution; to which period, some account has been given of it in a previous chapter.

At the commencement of the Revolutionary War, eighty schooners and a large number of Chebacco boats were engaged in the fisheries of Gloucester. The schooners were employed on distant grounds; and were therefore, during the war, useless for the business in which they had been engaged. Several were converted into privateers, a few rotted at the wharves, and some were preserved till peace again made it safe to resort to the "Banks." One of them, of fifty-five tons, survived every accident, to be registered in 1790, at the venerable age of twenty-two, in the foreign commerce of the town. No means exist for ascertaining how many vessels engaged in the Bank fishery immediately upon the return of peace. One statement says that sixty were employed in it in 1788, and fifty in 1789. Another, in giving an account of fish caught by vessels from the town in the fall of the last-named year, shows that forty-four vessels took four hundred and twenty-six thousand seven hundred fish, and that fifteen of these vessels belonged to Eben Parsons and Daniel Sargent, two merchants of Boston. Seven more belonged to each of the two principal merchants of Gloucester, — David Pearce and Daniel Rogers. Concerning this revival of the fishery, it may be further stated, that the Custom-House Records

* This spot, it seems, must have been Duncan's Point. It was granted to William Southmeade; and went, with his widow, to William Ash, who sold it in 1651 to John Jackson; from whom it passed, in 1662, to Peter Duncan. Peter Mud's Neck, "lying over against John Jackson's two or three acres," was granted to John Briars in 1658. This Neck was certainly on the Eastern-Point side, and must have been our modern Rocky Neck, the eastern end of which is opposite Duncan's Point. The only answer I can give to inquiry about Peter Mud is, that, May 31, 1651, a man by that name gave a deposition, somewhere, about John White, master of ship "William and John."

show the enrolment, between Oct. 2, 1789, and Sept. 10, 1790, of one brig, sixteen sloops, and forty schooners, of an aggregate burthen of three thousand one hundred and eight tons. Some of the "Bankers" made three trips in a season, and, if remarkably fortunate, landed from all, together, as many as forty thousand fish; but all the traditions of the business report that the average earnings of the fishermen were so small, that they were kept in a condition of poverty. It is not surprising, therefore, that the number of vessels engaged in it decreased from year to year till 1804, when we find that only eight, of more than thirty tons' burthen, were engaged in the Gloucester fisheries. This small number had probably dwindled to less in 1819, when an effort was made to put new vigor into the business by the establishment of a corporation to carry it on. In that year, the Gloucester Fishing Company, with an authorized capital of fifty thousand dollars, went into operation. They built six schooners; and with visions, perhaps, of a renewal of the ante-Revolutionary prosperity of the town, commenced by giving their vessels names having initial letters in alphabetical order. The "Amity," "Borneo," "Crescent," and "Diligent" were of the old model, deemed best for the Grand-Bank fishery, and were employed in that; while the "Economy" and "Favorite" were built according to a modern style, and sent in pursuit of cod and mackerel on our own coast. The Bounty Act passed by Congress in 1819 (the same now in force), or the anticipation of that act, may have added stimulus to this project: but a business which private capital avoided could hardly be expected to yield profit, even to the best corporation management; and accordingly, in the third year, this enterprise came to an end, with a loss of all the interest on the capital, and a portion of the capital itself. Since this period, it is probable a year, in which no vessel has gone to the Grand Bank from Gloucester, has sometimes passed; and not even the high price of cod in recent years has tempted many of our people to send their vessels to that fishing ground.

The shore-fishery of Gloucester had risen to some importance before the Revolution; and, upon the return of peace, the enterprise of the people was again directed to this pursuit, to which some encouragement was given by early acts of the General Government. In 1792, one hundred and thirty-three Chebacco boats,* measuring in the aggregate fifteen hundred and forty-nine tons, were engaged in it. These boats resorted to the ledges and shoal grounds near the coast, where they found, at different seasons, cod, hake, and pollock; and pursued their fishery with such success, that, in twelve years from the last-named date, the number of boats engaged in it had increased to about two hundred, while the tonnage had nearly doubled. At this time, the boat-fishing was chiefly carried on at Sandy Bay and the other coves on the outside of the Cape; but the advantage of a good harbor for their larger boats drew a few of the people away from these localities, to settle on Eastern Point, soon after 1800. The business, however, was not profitable enough, even with additional encouragement from the General Government, to attract many new adventurers, or even to stimulate much the enterprise of the old ones; and it had a slow growth for the next quarter of a century, — the annual average increase of tonnage during that time having been only about one hundred and twenty-five tons. At the end of this period (in 1828), the whole number of vessels upwards of twenty tons, engaged in the Gloucester fisheries, was one hundred and fifty-four, measuring five thousand eight hundred and ninety-nine tons; to which are to be added about forty boats, of an average burthen of fifteen tons. The total annual product of the cod-fishery of the town at this time is said to have been about sixty thousand quintals. But another fishery had now begun to attract the attention of the fishermen; and the shore-fishing for cod, except that carried on in winter, declined from this time, till it came to be, as at the present day, of insignificant account in the business of the town.

Gov. Winthrop, standing "to and again" within sight of Cape

* These boats were of a peculiar construction; and were, without doubt, first used at Sandy Bay. A tradition is current there, that the first one was built in a garret at Chebacco (now Essex); which place has supplied nearly all the fishing schooners that have been used in Gloucester for many years. In the view of the harbor, accompanying this work, the artist has represented one of the Chebacco boats and one of the old "Bankers," — vessels which have now almost entirely disappeared from our waters.

Ann all of one day in June, 1630, "took many mackerels." In 1653, the exportation of this fish from Boston had commenced; and there can scarcely be a doubt, that it has continued without interruption to the present day. Early regulations concerning this fishery were made by both the Plymouth and Massachusetts Colonies; but the interest in it seems to have been confined to the south side of the bay, from the ports of which several schooners were employed in it before the Revolutionary War. Scituate is said to have had thirty vessels so engaged in 1770; but Gloucester fishermen do not seem to have given much attention to it till about 1820. At that time, the size of the Chebacco boats was increased; and it began to be common to furnish them with a bowsprit, and call them "jiggers." The boats had before this day occasionally caught a few mackerel, which they sold fresh in Boston, when they could be disposed of in that condition; but the market was sometimes overstocked, and then they were brought home to be salted, and inspected according to the inspection laws of the State, under which an inspector was appointed in Gloucester in 1808, who, for several years, packed all the mackerel that were landed in the town, amounting in all to a trifling quantity. The remarkable abundance of these fish in Massachusetts Bay about 1820 induced the fishermen of the town to make preparations for mackerel-catching on a large scale. They built "jiggers" of forty tons' burthen or more, and made regular trips in pursuit of mackerel only; sometimes finding them so plenty as to fill up in a few days, when they would start for Boston to pack out and sell. In this stage of the business, it was customary for the fishermen to go to Boston for this purpose: but, as it increased, they were soon made aware of the advantage of packing out at home; and, since about 1826, the business has been kept wholly in the town. The first "great year" of the mackerel fishery in Gloucester was 1825; in which year, a single jigger, carrying eight men, took over thirteen hundred barrels. More vessels now engaged in it. The fish came almost to our own doors; and were in such abundance in the autumn of 1830 and 1831, that, for several days together, the fishermen were employed all day in catching, and all night in splitting and salting. In the former of these years, more than fifty-one thousand barrels were packed in Gloucester; giving the town a prominence in the business, which it has ever since retained. The mackerel is a capricious fish, and its habits are not understood even by the most experienced fishermen. Not long after the years of plenty just mentioned, they began to be scarce in Massachusetts Bay, and finally to avoid the coast; so that, since 1850, hook-fishing for mackerel in our own waters has proved a total failure. The enterprise of the fishermen, however, has pursued them into their distant retreats in the Bay Chaleur. The first vessel sent there from Gloucester on a mackerel voyage, went, it is said, in 1832. In five years from this time, a large number resorted thither from the town; and later, upon the failure of the fishery on the New-England coast, nearly all the vessels of the town engaged in it, and it became the only source from which the demand for this fish could be supplied.

The fishery for halibut and cod on George's Bank is an enterprise of recent times. About 1830, it is said, a Gloucester schooner first resorted to that shoal for fishing. It was not, however, till several years after this time, that any considerable number of vessels engaged in the business. The opening of railroad communication with all the cities and principal towns in the country, and the use of ice, enabled even the most distant inhabitants to supply themselves with these excellent articles of food in a fresh condition and at a low price. The Boston market, in which hitherto one or two thousand pounds of halibut would have sufficed for a daily supply, now furnished purchasers for all that could be brought till the weather became too warm for transportation; and, when that season arrived, the fishermen could sell at home, to be smoked and dried, all that should find no sale in the former place. This fishery had risen to such importance in 1847, that the Gloucester vessels took in that year considerably more than three millions of pounds, which sold for something over seventy thousand dollars. In fact, this fish has been so abundant, and such enormous quantities of them have sometimes been brought in, that the poorer qualities have been thrown overboard in our harbor. On the opening of railroad connection with Boston, it seemed expedient and practicable to bring the Boston and other dealers in halibut to Gloucester to purchase; and, to carry out this design, a company was organized to buy the fish of the fishermen, and await purchasers from abroad. But the enterprise was a failure. The amount purchased was nearly two millions of pounds, for which about forty-four thousand dollars were paid.

The George's fishery for cod is also quite a remarkable feature in the modern business of the town. The great abundance in which this fish is sometimes found on that Bank recalls to mind the "pestering" of Gosnold's ship with them off Cape Cod, and the "strange fish-pond," where Capt. Smith found them so plenty, near Monhegan. It is only within a few years that the fishermen have gone to George's in winter in pursuit of cod. The inducement to engage in this employment was the importation of fresh herring from Newfoundland; a business in which several schooners belonging to the town are now engaged every winter. The schooners engaged in the George's fishery are generally from eighty to ninety tons' burthen. The fishermen begin about the 1st of January to get them ready for the hard and dangerous work in which they are to be employed; and, by the middle of the month, are waiting only for bait, which the arrival of the herring vessels usually supplies about that time. The success of the trip depends mainly upon wind and weather. Sometimes the whole fleet return to port with the loss of cables and anchors, and without any fish to compensate. Often better luck attends them; and occasionally three or four favorable trips in succession yield a generous but still hardly adequate reward for the risk, labor, and suffering of the employment. Such trips were the commencement and a part of the work of one crew in 1859, — the best year's work ever made by any one in Gloucester. The skipper and owner of the vessel in which these trips were performed was Mr. Peter Sinclair,* who

* Mr. Sinclair is an Orkney Islander; but has been for several years a resident, and one of the most successful fishermen in Gloucester. He once brought in from George's Bank, after an absence of just one week, three hundred and fifty quintals of cod, and three thousand pounds of halibut.

took, in the winter and spring last year, cod to the amount of twenty-six hundred dollars; one hundred thousand pounds of halibut, which sold for three thousand dollars; and, in two trips to Bay Chaleur, five hundred and sixty-five barrels of mackerel, which produced six thousand four hundred dollars; making a total of twelve thousand dollars. Many of the vessels engaged in the George's fishery make great voyages; but at what a fearful expense of human life is the business carried on! and how little is it to be wondered at that none but the stoutest hearts will brave the perils and hardships of the employment! Twenty-five men in three schooners, in the last spring alone, found in it a watery grave, and also an unknown end; for no tidings ever come from the missing George's fishermen. After they have been out three or four weeks, friends begin to inquire anxiously of returning mariners for husband, son, brother, or father, and watch from the hills in agonizing suspense; but nothing comes save the moan of the sea, which sounds their requiem.*

One more branch of the Cape-Ann fisheries remains to be mentioned, — the winter shore-fishing carried on at the coves on the outside of the Cape. Before the use of railroads, this business was of little account in the industrial enterprise of Gloucester; though, long before that time, it was customary for the country people, who came in with their produce, to take away loads of frozen fish, many of which were carried into Vermont and Canada. The price, however, was often so low, that the fishermen received only a miserable pittance for a day of hard labor; but as soon as the railroads opened a wider market, and created, consequently, a greater demand for fish, many vessels, boats, and men engaged in it, and, in favorable weather, found constant and profitable employment in the business. It has always been a wherry-fishing, each wherry carrying but one man, who started in the morning, and rowed or sailed out to the fishing ground, five or six miles distant; but a new custom has been introduced of late, according to which the wherries are towed out and back by fishing boats and schooners, that receive

* See Appendix, VI.

a certain share of the fish for this service. About seven-eighths of this fishery are probably carried on within the limits of Rockport; and nearly all the rest at Lane's Cove, where a breakwater, erected by a company chartered in 1828, affords the fishermen a snug and safe haven. The fish are usually sold at night, as soon as landed, and immediately carted to the railroad station. The exact statistics of this fishery cannot be given: but a reliable estimate shows that the average number of men engaged in it for a few winters past has been nearly three hundred; and the average quantity of fish taken, about eight hundred and fifty tons, producing about twenty-one thousand dollars. The wherries can go out, of course, only when the state of the ocean and the wind permits; but often, when, to a landsman, these seem to threaten suffering and peril, the brave and industrious fisherman may be seen in his skiff in the coldest days of winter, alternately dancing on the top of a wave, and disappearing in the hollow of the sea.*

Such is the modern business of Cape Ann, resulting from its geographical position. Another important branch of industry on the Cape has grown out of its geological structure, and is of modern origin; though our ancestors, in a small way, made the granite ledges serve their necessity and convenience. Early in the last century, the people at Sandy Bay and the other coves on the outside of the Cape employed Joshua Norwood to cut flat blocks of this stone for moorings for their boats. These blocks were about six feet square, and from ten to fifteen inches thick. In the centre, a hole about fifteen inches in diameter was cut, into which an oak butt, twenty feet in length, having part of the roots attached, was inserted. The stone was then dropped at a proper distance from the shore, and afforded a safe mooring for a fishing-boat at all times, except during the prevalence of a heavy easterly gale. Norwood also cut out millstones for sale; and it seems therefore, from these employments, that a humble beginning in stone-cutting may be traced back to him.

An extensive business in the quarrying of granite was com-

---

* See Appendix, VII.

menced in 1824, when Mr. Bates of Quincy came to Sandy Bay, and leased a ledge for that purpose. Another stone contractor engaged in it there in the following year, and employed in it two persons, who have since been prominent in the business. Quarries were afterwards opened in different places on the northerly side of the Cape; and, during one period, a considerable quantity of granite was got out at Squam. The quarries still most extensively worked are situated in Rockport, though some are located in Gloucester. The whole number of men employed in quarrying and cutting, in teaming and in blacksmith's work, is about three hundred and fifty; while about one hundred and fifty are employed in twenty-five sloops constantly engaged in carrying the stone to market. The granite is also shipped to many places in brigs and schooners. The gross amount of sales annually is between two hundred and fifty and three hundred thousand dollars. Much of the granite is cut into paving blocks, and shipped to Cuba and the principal American cities; and a great deal of it is used for building purposes, — the coarser qualities for foundations, and the finer for fronts of stores, such as have been erected of late in Franklin Street, Boston. The Cape-Ann quarries have also furnished great quantities to the principal navy-yards, and for the erection of light-houses, and other public works of the United-States Government.

The prosperity of Gloucester depends entirely on its fisheries; for it has no other industrial pursuit to which, on a failure of this, it can turn. A failure, however, it is not the part of enterprise to fear, or of industry to anticipate. Both of these have, for a period of several years, been rewarded with generous returns; and, in bringing this work to a close, the historian of the town has the satisfaction of presenting it in a condition of present thrift, and of cherishing a well-grounded belief, that the future is full of encouraging prospects.

APPENDIX.

APPENDIX.

I. — Page 33.

THE CHARTER.

This Indenture made the ffirst day of January Anno Dni 1623, And in the Yeares of the Raigne of o^r Soveraigne Lord James by the grace of God King of England ffrance and Ireland Defender of the ffaith &c the One and Twentyth And of Scotland the Seaven and ffyftyth Betweene the right honorable Edmond Lord Sheffeild Knight of the most noble Order of the Garter on thone part And Robert Cushman and Edward Winslowe for themselves, and theire Associats and Planters at Plymouth in New England in America on thother part. Wytnesseth that the said Lord Sheffeild (As well in consideracon that the said Robert and Edward and divers of theire Associats haue already adventured themselves in person, and have likewise at theire owne proper Costs and Charges transported dyvers persons into New England aforesaid And for that the said Robert and Edward and their Associats also intend as well to transport more persons as also further to plant at Plymouth aforesaid, and in other places in New England aforesaid As for the better Advancement and furtherance of the said Planters, and encouragement of the said Vndertakers) Hath Gyven, graunted, assigned, allotted, and appointed And by these pnts doth Gyve, graunt, assigne, allott, and appoint vnto and for the said Robert and Edward and their Associats As well a certaine Tract of Ground in New England aforesaid lying in fforty-three Degrees or thereabout of Northerly latitude and in a knowne place there comonly called Cape Anne, Together with the free vse and benefitt as well of the Bay comonly called the Bay of Cape Anne, as also of the Islands within the said Bay And free liberty, to ffish, fowle, hawke, and hunt, truck, and trade in the Lands thereabout, and in all other places in New England aforesaid; whereof the said Lord Sheffeild is, or hath byn possessed, or which haue byn allotted to him the said Lord Sheffeild, or within his Jurisdiccon (not nowe being inhabited, or hereafter to be inhabited by any English) Together also with ffyve hundred Acres of free Land adioyning to the said Bay to be ymployed for publig vses, as for the building of a Towne, Scholes, Churches, Hospitalls, and for the mayntenance of such Ministers, Officers, and Magistrats, as by the said vndertakers and theire Associats are there already appointed, or which hereafter shall (with theire good liking, reside, and inhabitt there And also Thirty Acres of Land, over and beside the ffyve hundred Acres of Land, before menconed To be allotted, and appointed for every perticuler person, Young, or old (being the Associats, or servants of the said vndertakers or their successo^{rs} that shall come, and dwell at the aforesaid Cape Anne within Seaven yeares next after the Date hereof, which Thirty Acres of Lande soe appointed to every person as aforesaid, shall be taken as the same doth lye together vpon the said Bay in one entire place, and not stragling in dyvers, or remote parcells not exceeding an English Mile, and a halfe in length on the Waters side of the said Bay Yelding and Paying for ever yearely vnto the said Lord Sheffeild, his heires, successo^{rs}, Rent gatherer, or assignes for every Thirty Acres soe to be obteyned, and possessed by the said Robert & Edward theire heires, successo^{rs}, or Associats Twelve Pence of lawfull English money At the ffeast of St. Michaell Tharchaungell only (if it be lawfully demaunded) The first payment thereof To begynne ymediatly from and after thend and expiracon of the first Seaven yeares next after the date hereof And the said Lord Sheffeild for himself his heires, successo^{rs}, and assignes doth Covenant, promise, and graunt to and with the said Robert Cushman, and Edward Winslow their heires, associats, and assignes That they the said Robert, and Edward, and such other persons as shall plant, and contract with them, shall freely and quyetly, haue, hold, possesse, and enioy All such profitts, rights, previlidges, benefits, Comodities, advantages, and preheminences, as shall hereafter by the labo^{r}, search, and diligence of the said Vndertakers their Associats, servants, or Assignes be obteyned, found out, or made within the said Tract of Ground soe graunted vnto them as aforesaid; Reserving vnto the said Lord Sheffeild his heirs, successors, and assignes The one Moyety of all such Mynes as shall be discovered, or found out at any tyme by the said Vndertakers, or any their heires, successo^{rs}, or assignes vpon the Grounds aforesaid And further That it shall and may be lawfull to and for the said Robert Cushman, and Edward Winslowe their heires, associats, and assignes from tyme to tyme, and at all tymes hereafter soe soone or they or their

Assignes haue taken possession, or entred into any of the said Lands To forbyd, repell, repulse and resist by force of Armes All and every such persons as shall build, plant, or inhabitt, or which shall offer, or make shew to build, plant, or inhabitt within the Lands soe as aforesaid graunted, without the leave, and licence of the said Robert, and Edward or theire assignes AND THE SAID Lord Sheffeild doth further Covenant, and graunt That vpon a lawfull survey hadd, and taken of the aforesaid Lands, and good informacon gyven to the said Lord Sheffeild his heires, or assignes, of the Meats, Bounds, and quantity of Lands which the said Robert, and Edward their heires, associates, or assignes shall take in and be by them their Associats, Servants, or Assigns inhabited as aforesaid; he the said Lord Sheffeild his heires, or assigns, at and vpon the reasonable request of the said Vndertakers, or theire Associats, shall and will by good and sufficient Assurance in the Lawe Graunt, enfeoffe, confirm and allott vnto the said Robert Cushman and Edward Winslowe theire Associats, and Assigns All and every the said Lands soe to be taken in within the space of Seaven yeares next after the Date hereof in as larg, ample, and beneficiall manner, as the said Lord Sheffeild his heires, or assignes nowe haue, or hereafter shall have the same Lands, or any of them graunted unto him, or them; for such rent, and vnder such Covenants, and Provisoes as herein are conteyned (*mutatis mutandis*) AND shall and will also at all tymes hereafter vpon reasonable request made to him the said Lord Sheffeild his heires, or assignes by the said Edward and Robert their heires, associats, or assignes, or any of them graunt, procure, and make good, lawfull, and sufficient Letters, or other Graunts of Incorporacon whereby the said Vndertakers, and their Associats shall haue liberty and lawfull authority from tyme to tyme to make and establish Lawes, Ordynnces, and Constitucons for the ruling, ordering, and governing of such persons as now are resident, or which hereafter shalbe planted, and inhabitt there And in the meane tyme vntill such Graunt be made It shalbe lawfull for the said Robert, and Edward theire heires, associats and Assignes by consent of the greater part of them to Establish such Laws, Provisions and Ordynnces as are or shalbe by them thought most fitt, and convenient for the governement of the said plantacon which shall be from tyme to tyme executed, and administred by such Officer, or Officers, as the said Vndertakers, or their Associats or the most part of them shall elect, and make choice of PROVYDED allwaies That the said Lawes, Provisions, and Ordynnces which are, or shall be agreed on, be not repugnant to the Lawes of England, or to the Orders, and Constitucons of the President and Councell of New England PROVYDED further That the said Vndertakers theire heires, and successo[rs] shall fore[r] acknowledg the said Lord Sheffeild his heires and successo[rs], to be theire Chiefe Lord, and to answeare and doe service vnto his Lo[pp] or his Successo[rs], at his, or theire Court when upon his, or theire owne Plantacon The same shalbe established, and kept IN WYTNES whereof the said parties to these present Indentures Interchaungeably have putt their Hands and Seals The day and yeares first aboue written.

SHEFFEYLD.

[SEAL *pendent.*]

II.—PAGE 187.

SELECTMEN, TOWN-CLERKS, AND TOWN-TREASURERS.

Selectmen.

1642.
Mr. Stevens.
Mr. Addes.
Mr. Milward.
Mr. Sadler.
Obadiah Bruen.
George Norton.
Mr. Ffryer.
Walter Tybbot.

1644.
Mr. Stevens.
George Norton.
Walter Tybbot.
Hugh Calkin.
Obadiah Bruen.

1645.
Charles Glover.
Walter Tybbot.
Hugh Calkin.
William Brown.
Obadiah Bruen.

1646.
Hugh Pritchard.
Walter Tybbot.
Charles Glover.
Hugh Calkin.
Obadiah Bruen.

1647.
Thomas Wakley.
Hugh Calkin.
William Vinson.
John Collins.
Christopher Avery.

1648.
Hugh Calkin.
Silvester Eveleth.
William Evans.
William Meades.
William Brown.

1649.
Hugh Calkin.
Robert Elwell.
John Collins.
William Evans.
John Coit, sen.

1650.
Walter Tybbot.
Robert Elwell.
Obadiah Bruen.
Osman Dutch.
George Blake.

1651.
Walter Tybbot.
Robert Elwell.
William Hough.
Silvester Eveleth.
William Vinson.

1652.
William Stevens.
Robert Tucker.
Robert Elwell.
Christopher Avery.
George Ingersol.

1654.
Christopher Avery.
John Hardin.
Robert Elwell.
Richard Window.
Samuel Dolliver.

1657.
William Stevens.
Robert Elwell.
Phineas Rider.
John Collins.
Philip Stanwood.

1659.
William Stevens.
Robert Elwell.
Thomas Wakley.
Stephen Glover.

1660.
Robert Elwell.
William Vinson.
Philip Stanwood.
Samuel Dolliver.

1668.
Robert Elwell.
Henry Walker.
Thomas Millet, sen.
Samuel Dolliver.
Stephen Glover.

1669.
Robert Elwell.
John Collins, sen.
Stephen Glover.
William Sargent.
Thomas Riggs.

1670.
Robert Elwell.
John Collins, sen.
Philip Stanwood.
Stephen Glover.
Thomas Riggs.

1671.
Robert Elwell.
John Davis.

Philip Stanwood, sen.
Stephen Glover.
Thomas Riggs.

1672.
Robert Elwell.
William Haskell.
Stephen Glover.
James Davis.
Thomas Riggs.

1673.
Henry Walker.
William Haskell.
Thomas Millet, jun.
Stephen Glover.
Thomas Riggs.

1674.
Robert Elwell.
William Vinson, sen.
James Stevens.
Stephen Glover.
Thomas Riggs.

1675.
Same.

1676.
Henry Walker.
James Stevens.
William Sargent.
Stephen Glover.
Thomas Riggs.

1677.
Same.

1678.
William Haskell, sen.
James Stevens.
Jeffrey Parsons.
Stephen Glover.
Thomas Riggs.

1679.
Same.

1680.
Same.

1681.
Henry Walker.
James Stevens.
Jeffrey Parsons.
Stephen Glover.
Thomas Riggs.

1682.
James Stevens.
Jeffrey Parsons.
Stephen Glover.
James Davis, sen.
Thomas Riggs.

1683.
Same.

1684.
Same.

1685.
William Haskell.
James Stevens.
Stephen Glover.
Jeffrey Parsons, sen.
Jacob Davis, sen.

1686.
William Haskell, sen.
James Davis, sen.
James Stevens, sen.
Stephen Glover.
Thomas Riggs, sen.

1687.
William Haskell.
William Stevens.
Jeffrey Parsons, sen.
Thomas Millet.
Thomas Riggs.

1688.
James Stevens.
Thomas Riggs, sen.
Joseph Allen.
Joseph Haskell.

1689.
James Stevens.
Jeffrey Parsons, sen.
William Grigs.
William Ellery.
Thomas Riggs.

1690.
John Fitch.
William Ellery.
Joseph Haskell.
Joseph Allen.
James Parsons.

1691.
Capt. James Davis.
Lieut. James Stevens.
Ensign Thomas Millet.
John Fitch.
John Sargent.

1692.
Capt. Davis.
Sergeant Ellery.
Joseph Allen.
John Sargent.
John Davis.

1693.
Capt. James Davis.
William Ellery.
Joseph Allen.
William Stevens.
Thomas Riggs, sen.

1694.
James Stevens.
John Fitch.
John Hadley.
Jacob Davis.
James Davis.

1695.
John Hadley.
Benjamin Haskell.
Timothy Somes, sen.
Samuel Sargent.
Thomas Riggs, sen.

1696.
John Hadley.
Benjamin Haskell.
William Stevens.
Samuel Sargent.
John Parsons.

1697.
Joseph Haskell, sen.
Thomas Bray.
Nathaniel Coit.
John Parsons.
Thomas Riggs, sen.

1698.
James Davis.
James Sawyer.
William Stevens.
Ezekiel Collins.
John Ring.

1699.
Samuel Sargent.
John Parsons.
John Sargent.
William Stevens.
James Davis, jun.

1700.
John Sargent.
Ensign Joseph Allen.
Benjamin Haskell.
Samuel Sargent.
Thomas Riggs, sen.

1701.
William Stevens.
Nathaniel Coit.
James Sayward.
Samuel Sargent.
Thomas Riggs, sen.

1702.
Joseph Allen.
Nathaniel Coit.
John Sargent.
James Davis, sen.
Thomas Riggs, sen.

1703.
William Sargent, 2d.
Nathaniel Coit.
Samuel Sargent.
John Parsons.
Thomas Riggs, sen.

1704.
John Newman.

Nathaniel Coit.
James Davis.
John Ring.
Thomas Riggs, sen.

1705.
Benjamin Haskell, sen.
John Haraden.
Samuel Stevens.
Thomas Riggs, sen.

1706.
Nathaniel Coit.
Lieut. John Davis.
Lieut. James Davis.
Benjamin Haskell.
John Ring.

1707.
John Newman, Esq.
Nathaniel Coit.
Jeffrey Parsons.
Lieut. James Davis.
John Ring.

1708.
John Newman.
Joseph Allen.
Jeffrey Parsons.
Lieut. James Davis.
John Ring.

1709.
John Davis.
Jeffrey Parsons.
Ezekiel Collins.
Samuel Sargent.
John Parsons.

1710.
Benjamin Haskell.
Jeffrey Parsons.
Thomas Bray, sen.
John Davis.
Sergeant Isaac Eveleth.

1711.
Capt. Joseph Allen.
Jeffrey Parsons.
Lieut. John Davis.
Lieut. James Davis.
Thomas Witham.

1712.
Benjamin Haskell, sen.
Thomas Bray, sen.
Jeffrey Parsons.
Ezekiel Collins.
George Giddings.

1713.
Ensign William Haskell.
Thomas Bray, sen.
Edward Haraden, sen.
Jeffrey Parsons.
Thomas Witham.

1714.
Thomas Bray, sen.
Joseph York.
Joseph Haraden.
Ensign William Haskell.
Stephen Row.

1715.
Thomas Bray, sen.
Nathaniel Sargent.
John Ring.
Lieut. James Davis.
Joseph Allen, jun.

1716.
John Newman.
Thomas Bray.
John Ring.
Nathaniel Sargent.
Abraham Sawyer.

1717.
John Newman.
Thomas Bray.
John Ring.
Samuel Sargent.
Isaac Eveleth.

1718.
Benjamin Haskell.
Nathaniel Sargent.
Ensign William Haskell.
Ensign Joseph Allen.
Ebenezer Davis.

1719.
Isaac Eveleth.
Ensign Joseph Allen.
Ebenezer Davis.
Deacon Nathaniel Parsons.
Thomas Bray, jun.

1720.
Lieut. James Davis.
Samuel Sargent.
Elder James Sayward.
Ebenezer Davis.
Thomas Bray, jun.

1721.
James Sayward.
William Haskell.
Nathaniel Sargent.
Thomas Bray.
Nathaniel Ellery.

1722.
Samuel Sargent.
Ezekiel Collins.
James Sayward.
Abraham Sawyer.
Thomas Bray, jun.

1723.
Ebenezer Davis.
Thomas Witham.
Abraham Sawyer.
John Bennet.
William Haskell.

1724.
Daniel Ring.
Thomas Bray, jun.
John Bennet.
Thomas Witham.
Ebenezer Parsons.

1725.
Ebenezer Parsons.
Thomas Bray.
Ebenezer Davis.
Joseph Allen.
Dr. Edward Tompson.

1726.
Nathaniel Ellery.
William Haskell.
Edward Tompson.
James Lane.
Ensign Joseph Allen.

1727.
Ensign Allen.
Nathaniel Ellery.
Samuel Herrick.
Samuel Stevens.
James Lane.

1728.
Samuel Herrick.
Samuel Sargent.
Elder Sayward.
Capt. Robinson.
Thomas Witham.

1729.
Samuel Herrick.
Epes Sargent.
Capt. Joseph Allen.
John Haraden.
Ebenezer Davis.

1730.
Thomas Witham.
Ebenezer Parsons.
John Roberts.
James Lane.
Ebenezer Davis.

1731.
Thomas Witham.
John Roberts.
Ebenezer Parsons.
James Lane.
Ebenezer Davis.

1732.
Daniel Witham.
Ebenezer Parsons.
John Roberts.
James Lane.
Ebenezer Davis.

1733.
William Haskell.
James Lane.
Daniel Witham.

Elias Davis.
Ebenezer Parsons.

1734.

Daniel Witham.
Elias Davis.
William Haskell.
James Lane.
Joseph Allen.

1735.

Edmund Grover.
Ebenezer Parsons.
James Lane.
John Roberts.
Daniel Witham.

1736.

Daniel Witham.
Joseph Allen.
Edmund Grover.
John Roberts.
James Davis, jun.

1737.

Edmund Grover.
John Sargent.
Daniel Witham.
John Roberts.
James Davis, jun.

1738.

Daniel Witham.
Ebenezer Parsons.
David Plummer.
William Haskell.
James Davis, jun.

1739.

Daniel Witham.
Ebenezer Parsons.
Abraham Davis.
William Haskell.
Capt. James Davis.

1740.

Jabez Baker.
Nathaniel Ellery.
Abraham Davis.
Timothy Day.
Capt. James Davis.

1741.

Daniel Witham.
Philemon Warner, jun.
David Stanwood.
Mark Haskell.
Capt. James Davis.

1742.

Daniel Witham.
Nathaniel Ellery.
Abraham Davis.
Capt. William Haskell.
Capt. James Davis.

1743.

Same.

1744.

Nathaniel Ellery.
William Ellery.
Daniel Witham.
William Haskell.
James Davis.

1745.

William Parsons.
Daniel Witham.
William Ellery.
William Haskell.
James Davis.

1746.

John Parsons.
Daniel Witham.
William Ellery.
William Haskell.
Capt. James Davis.

1747.

Daniel Witham.
John Parsons.
William Haskell.
William Allen.
Capt. James Davis.

1748.

Same.

1749.

John Parsons.
Samuel Stevens, jun.
William Allen.
James Davis.
William Haskell.

1750.

Daniel Witham.
John Parsons.
William Haskell.
William Allen.
Capt. James Davis.

1751.

Daniel Witham.
Samuel Stevens, jun.
William Haskell.
Samuel Griffin, jun.
William Allen.

1752.

Daniel Witham.
Samuel Stevens, jun.
William Haskell.
Capt. James Davis.
Capt. William Allen.

1753.

Daniel Witham.
Capt. William Stevens.
Mr. Peter Coffin.
Capt. James Davis.
Capt. William Allen.

1754.

Samuel Stevens, jun.
Peter Coffin.
Capt. James Davis.
John Parsons.
Capt. William Allen.

1755.

Daniel Witham.
Samuel Stevens, jun.
Peter Coffin.
James Davis, Esq.
William Allen.

1756.

Daniel Witham.
Ebenezer Pool.
Peter Coffin.
Jonathan Fellows.
John Low, jun.

1757.

Daniel Witham.
Samuel Stevens.
Nathaniel Haskell.
James Davis, Esq.
John Low, jun.

1758.

Philemon Warner.
Isaac Parsons.
Peter Coffin.
Samuel Griffin, jun.
David Allen.

1759.

Daniel Witham.
Philemon Warner.
Peter Coffin.
Samuel Griffin.
John Low, jun.

1760.

Daniel Witham.
Philemon Warner.
Epes Sargent, jun.
Peter Coffin.
Samuel Griffin, jun.
John Low, jun.
Ebenezer Pool.

1761.

Daniel Witham.
Thomas Sanders, jun.
John Low, jun.
Peter Coffin.
William Norwood.

1762.

Daniel Witham.
William Stevens.
Peter Coffin.
Samuel Griffin.
John Low.

1763.

Daniel Witham.
William Stevens.

Samuel Griffin.
John Low.
Josiah Choate.

1764.
Thomas Sanders, jun.
Timothy Rogers.
Peter Coffin.
Samuel Griffin.
John Low.

1765.
Daniel Witham.
Samuel Whittemore.
Peter Coffin.
Samuel Griffin.
John Low.

1766.
Same.

1767.
Same.

1768.
Daniel Witham.
Samuel Whittemore.
Daniel Sargent.
Peter Coffin.
John Low.
Samuel Griffin.
Francis Pool.

1769.
Daniel Witham.
Samuel Whittemore.
Peter Coffin.
Samuel Griffin.
John Low.

1770.
Same.

1771.
Daniel Witham.
John Smith.
Peter Coffin.
Samuel Griffin.
David Plummer.

1772.
Samuel Whittemore.
Daniel Witham.
Peter Coffin.
Samuel Griffin.
John Low.

1773.
Daniel Witham.
Jacob Parsons.
Peter Coffin.
John Low.
Cornelius Fellows.

1774.
Peter Coffin.
John Low.
Samuel Griffin.
Epes Sargent, jun.
Joseph Foster.

1775.
Jacob Allen.
James Porter.
Samuel Rogers.
Peter Coffin.
Samuel Griffin.
John Low.
Francis Pool.

1776.
David Pearce.
John Smith.
William Ellery.
Peter Coffin.
Thomas Marrett.
John Low.
Francis Pool.

1777.
James Porter.
John Smith.
Thomas Marrett.
Samuel Plummer.
Stephen Pool.

1778.
John Smith.
James Porter.
Daniel Warner.
Daniel Rogers.
Thomas Marrett.
John Low.
John Row.

1779.
Thomas Marrett.
William Pearson.
Nehemiah Parsons.
Joseph Eveleth.
Barnett Harkin.
David Pearce.

1780.
William Ellery.
Barnett Harkin.
William Gee.
Stephen Haskell.
Mark Pool.
Winthrop Sargent.
Daniel Warner.

1781.
Capt. John Smith.
Samuel Leighton.
Daniel Rogers.
Col. John Low.
Barnabas Dodge.
Jacob Allen.
Mark Pool.

1782.
Capt. William Ellery.
Barnett Harkin.
Joseph Allen.
Stephen Haskell.
Barnabas Dodge.
Col. John Low.
Ebenezer Cleaveland.

1783.
John Low.
Barnett Harkin.
Joseph Allen.
Stephen Haskell.
James Hayes.

1784.
Joseph Allen.
James Pearson, jun.
James Hayes.
John Low.
William Babson.
Stephen Haskell.
Mark Pool.

1785.
John Somes.
Joseph Procter.
James Pearson, jun.
Stephen Haskell.
James Day.
John Low.
Caleb Pool.

1786.
Same.

1787.
Same.

1788.
John Somes.
Joseph Procter.
James Pearson, jun.
Stephen Haskell.
James Day.
John Low.
Mark Pool.

1789.
James Pearson, jun.
John Somes.
Joseph Procter.
Stephen Haskell.
James Day.
John Low.
Caleb Pool.

1790.
John Somes.
James Pearson.
Daniel Warner.
Stephen Haskell.
James Day.
John Low.
Caleb Pool.

1791.
Same.

1792.
Same.

1793.
Same.

1794.
Capt. John Somes.
Col. Daniel Warner.
Capt. Isaac Elwell.
Stephen Haskell.
James Day.
John Low.
Caleb Pool.

1795.
John Somes.
Daniel Warner.
Isaac Elwell.
Isaac Eveleth.
James Day.
John Low.
Caleb Pool.

1796.
Eliphalet Davis.
Joseph Allen.
Isaac Eveleth.
James Day.
Ebenezer Pool, jun.
Nathaniel Warner.
John Low.

1797.
Joseph Allen.
Nathaniel Warner.
Isaac Eveleth.
James Day.
David Low.
Ignatius Sargent.
Benjamin Tarr, jun.

1798.
Joseph Allen.
Isaac Eveleth.
James Day.
David Low.
James Goss.
Benjamin Webber.
Joseph Foster, jun.

1799.
Eliphalet Davis.
James Day.
Thomas Parsons.

1800.
James Day.
Thomas Parsons.
Isaac Elwell.

1801.
James Day.
Isaac Elwell.
B. K. Hough.

1802.
James Day.
Isaac Elwell.
William Dane.

1803.
James Day.
Isaac Elwell.
William Dane.

1804.
James Day.
Isaac Elwell.
Joseph Foster, jun.

1805.
William Dane.
Isaac Elwell.
Joseph Foster.
James Dennison.
John Manning.

1806.
Isaac Elwell.
Joseph Foster.
Ebenezer Oakes.

1807.
Isaac Elwell.
Joseph Foster.
Caleb Norwood.

1808.
James Hayes.
William Dane.
Benjamin K. Hough.
William Babson, jun.
Joseph Procter.
Josiah Choate.
Daniel Rogers, jun.

1809.
William Dane.
James Hayes.
Joseph Procter.
William Babson, jun.
Caleb Norwood, jun.

1810.
William Dane.
James Hayes.
Francis Norwood.
William Babson, jun.
John Somes, jun.

1811.
John Somes, jun.
Charles Smith.
James Hayes.
Francis Norwood.
Jonathan Kimball.

1812.
John Somes, jun.
Charles Smith.
James Hayes.
Francis Norwood.
James Dennison.

1813.
James Hayes.
Charles Smith.
John Mason.
James Dennison.
Ebenezer Oakes.

1814.
Charles Smith.
John Somes, jun.
Lonson Nash.
Daniel Haskell.
Ebenezer Oakes.

1815.
Charles Smith.
John Somes, jun.
John Mason.
Ebenezer Oakes.
Jonathan Kimball.

1816.
William Pearce, jun.
Samuel Calder.
Israel Trask.

1817.
Same.

1818.
Isaac Elwell.
Benjamin Stacy.
Charles L. Roberts.

1819.
Benjamin Stacy.
Charles L. Roberts.
Samuel Pearce.

1820.
William Pearce, jun.
Benjamin Stacy.
William Beach.

1821.
Benjamin Stacy.
William Ferson.
Charles Sawyer.

1822.
Benjamin Stacy.
Samuel Pearce.
William Beach.

1823.
Daniel W. Rogers.
Capt. William Pearce.
Samuel Stevens.

1824.
Charles L. Roberts.
Daniel W. Rogers.
Samuel Stevens.

1825.
Daniel W. Rogers.
Samuel Lane.
Winthrop Pool.
William Beach.

1826.
Daniel W. Rogers.

Elias Davison.
Abraham Haskell.
Elisha Brown.
Aaron Giddings.

1827.
Elias Davison.
Daniel W. Rogers.
Aaron Giddings.
William Stevens.
Ignatius Sargent.

1828.
Daniel W. Rogers.
Elias Davison.
William Stevens.

1829.
Same.

1830.
Daniel W. Rogers.
William Stevens.
William Ferson.
George D. Hale.
Gideon Lane, jun.

1831.
William Ferson.
William Stevens.
William Collins.
George D. Hale.
Gideon Lane, jun.

1832.
William Beach.
Elias Davison.
William Collins.
Gideon Lane, jun.
George D. Hale.

1833.
Addison Gilbert.
William Beach.
George D. Hale.
William Collins.
Gideon Lane, jun.

1834.
George D. Hale.
Addison Gilbert.
Alphonso Mason.
Samuel Lane.
John Webber.

1835.
Alphonso Mason.
George D. Hale.
John Webber.
Henry Haskell.
Ignatius Sargent.

1836.
John Webber.
Ignatius Sargent.
John W. Marshall.
Joseph Stacy.
Theophilus Herrick.

1837.
Alphonso Mason.
Epes Ellery.
John W. Marshall.
John Webber.
Ignatius Sargent.

1838.
John Webber.
George D. Hale.
Epes Ellery.
Ignatius Sargent.
John W. Marshall.

1839.
William Ferson.
George H. Rogers.
Benjamin K. Hough, jun.
James Haskell.
John N. Davis.

1840.
William Ferson.
Joseph J. Procter.
Alfred Presson.
John N. Davis.
Frederic Haskell.

1841.
William Ferson.
Alfred Presson.
John N. Davis.

1842.
John Webber.
William Ferson.
Frederic Haskell.

1843.
William Ferson.
John Webber.
Epes Young.

1844.
John Woodbury.
Alfred Presson.
William Ferson.

1845.
William Ferson.
Alfred Presson.
Aaron Fitz.

1846.
William P. Dolliver.
Samuel W. Brown.
Alexander P. Davis.

1847.
George Saville.
Nathaniel Babson.
George Norwood.

1848.
Nathaniel Babson.
John L. Rogers.
George Norwood.

1849.
William Ferson.
Henry Haskell.
John L. Rogers.

1850.
William Ferson.
Nathaniel Babson.
George Norwood.

1851.
William Ferson.
Henry Haskell.
Joseph Friend.

1852.
Alfred Presson.
Gideon Lane.
Eben H. Stacy.

1853.
Alfred Presson.
Gideon Lane.
Eben H. Stacy.

1854.
Gorham P. Low.
Charles E. Grover.
George Saville.

1855.
Charles E. Grover.
Joseph Friend.
James S. Jewett.

1856.
Frederic Haskell.
John S. Webber.
Samuel P. Fears.
Jeremiah R. Cook.
Charles C. Pettingell.

1857.
Alfred Presson.
James Davis.
William P. Dolliver.

1858.
William P. Dolliver.
Aaron D. Wells.
James Davis.

1859.
William P. Dolliver.
John S. Webber.
John J. Babson.

Until recent times, it seems to have been the practice of the selectmen to charge according to the services rendered. The office, however, has never been worth seeking for its emoluments. This Board has also performed the duties of assessors till within three or four years past, when the town adopted the present practice of choosing three persons to each board, with a salary of one hundred dollars to each officer.

Town-Clerks.

Obadiah Bruen	1642	Daniel Witham	1734
William Perkins	1651	James Porter	1776
William Stevens	1651	Samuel Whittemore	1779
Robert Tucker	1652	John Rogers	1782
Edmund Clark	1656	William Saville	1827
Thomas Riggs	1665	Joshua P. Trask	1849
James Parsons	1716	Alfred Presson	1854
Ebenezer Davis	1727	George L. Ford	1855
Joseph Allen	1732	Cyrus Story, jun.	1856

Town-Treasurers.

James Parsons	1697	Eliphalet Davis	1804
John Parsons	1709	William Pearson	1804
James Parsons	1715	James Hayes	1805
John Ring	1716	William Pearson	1807
Lieut. James Davis	1722	William Saville	1809
Nathaniel Ellery	1732	John Smith	1812
Joseph Allen	1734	Ignatius Webber	1813
Daniel Witham	1739	James Hayes	1815
Joseph Allen	1740	Ignatius Webber	1816
Daniel Witham	1741	Zachariah Stevens	1819
William Allen	1749	Samuel Pearce	1820
William Stevens	1763	William Ferson	1822
Thomas Sanders, jun.	1767	Zachariah Stevens	1830
Samuel Whittemore	1774	Daniel W. Rogers	1831
Samuel Plummer	1777	Alphonso Mason	1832
John Low	1778	John Johnston	1839
Jacob Allen	1780	Samuel Stevens	1840
Nehemiah Parsons	1782	T. Sewall Lancaster	1847
James Hayes	1797		

The selectmen performed the duties of treasurer till 1697. No regular salary was paid for many years, though the duties were never gratuitously performed. In 1798, the pay was fixed at $33.33 per annum; but has for several years past been seventy-five dollars.

SELECTMEN, TOWN-TREASURERS, AND TOWN-CLERK OF ROCKPORT.

Selectmen.

1840.
David Babson, jun.
James Haskell.
Thomas O. Marshall.

1841.
David Babson, jun.
James Haskell.
William H. Bradley.

1842.
David Babson, jun.
William H. Bradley.
William P. Burns.

1843.
Same.

1844.
Same.

1845.
David Babson, jun.
William P. Burns.
George D. Hale.

1846.
Same.

1847.
David Babson, jun.

Benjamin Tarr.
John Pool.

1848.
Same.

1849.
David Babson, jun.
William Boynton.
William P. Burns.

1850.
David Babson, jun.
William Boynton.
George Gott, jun.

1851.
David Babson, jun.
William Boynton.
James Manning.

1852.
James Manning.
William H. Bradley.
Thomas Hale.

1853.
Thomas Hale.
John W. Marshall.
Dudley Choate.

1854.
John W. Marshall.
Dudley Choate.
Amos Story.

1855.
James Manning.
William H. Bradley.
Benjamin Atwood.

1856.
John W. Marshall.
Washington Tarr.
Daniel Wheeler.

1857.
John W. Marshall.
Washington Tarr.
Austin W. Story.

1858.
Austin W. Story.
John Manning.
Alfred Parsons.

Town-Treasurers.

1840. John Gott. — 1848. Addison Gott. — 1853. James Manning.
1855. — George Gott, jun. — 1857. Henry Clark.

Town-Clerk.

1840. William Pool.

III. — Page 187.

HIGHWAYS.

The ancient roads of Gloucester were used for public travel many years before they were formally laid out as highways. The date of laying out the most important ones, connecting different sections of the town, is here given: —

1646. May 20. — A common highway out of the woods, lying east of Mill River.
In grants to Zebulon Hill (without date), mention is made of a highway that goes along the head of all the Harbor lots. This must be the High Street of the present time.
1656. Mar. 4. — Highway between Gloucester and Ipswich.
1695. Nov. 15. — Highway across Biskie Island, and from the island to the main.
1698. May 9. — Highway through the Harbor to Vinson's Cove, twenty-one feet wide, and from the "town down to the seaside."
1704. Mar. 20. — Highway from the head of the Harbor to Cripple Cove; and so along to the pasture of William Stevens, deceased (on Eastern Point).
,, July 10. — Highway from Starknaught Harbor to the head of the Harbor, and from thence to the south end of the lane called Ketles Lane.
1707. April 9. — Highway where it had been used and improved for fifty years past, from the gravel-pit at the east end of the gristmill by Lieut. James Davis's dwelling-house and so to the house of Ezekiel Day.

1707. June 2. — Highway from the Meeting-house Green over to Sandy-bay Cove, "where it is now, and hath been for many years, made use of."
" Oct. 21. — Highway round the Cape, from Mr. Samuel Gott's to the gravel-pit by the gristmill.
1708. June 22. — Highway from Sandy Bay to Starknaught Harbor.
1716. Mar. 19. — Highway on the back side of the Cape, from near Folly Cove, to Sandy-bay Brook.
1717. Oct. 30. — Highway from the way that leads to the Mills to Squam.
1719. Mar. 30. — Highway in the West Precinct, called Long-Cove Way.
" " Highway from the Cut Road towards Ipswich to the highway leading from the Meeting-house (in said precinct) to the Ferry.
1721. Mar. 10. — Highway from Mr. Warner's fence to Vinson's Cove, forty feet wide.
1722. April 2. — Highway from Mr. Coffin's farm to Long-Cove Way.
1724. May 26. — Highway from head of Little River to Kettle Cove.
1726. May 11. — Highway from Salem road to Fresh-water Cove.
1730. July 6. — Highway from Thomas Witham's towards Sandy Bay.
1732. Mar. 7. — Highway from the Cut into the Harbor.

IV. — Page 192.

REPRESENTATIVES TO GENERAL COURT.

1642. Geo. Norton, Sept. 8.
1643. Same.
1644. Same, March.
Wm. Stevens, May.
1645. Hugh Prichard.
1646. Not represented.
1647. Obadiah Bruen.
1648. Same.
1649. Same.
1650. Hugh Calkin.
1651. Hugh Calkin.
1652. Robert Tucker.
1653. William Stevens.
1654 to 1665. None.
1665. William Stevens.
1666. William Stevens.
1667 to 1671. None.
1671. William Sargent.
1672. William Haskell.
1673. Silves. Eveleth, May.
Jas. Stevens, Sept.
1674 and 1675. None.
1676. James Stevens.
1677, 1678, and 1679. None.
1680. William Haskell.
James Stevens, Feb.
Jas. Stevens, May.
1681. Wm. Stevens, Jan.
Wm. Haskell, May.
1682. William Haskell.
1683. John Haskell, May.
James Stevens, Nov.
1684. James Stevens.
1685. William Haskell.
1686. James Stevens.
1687. None.
1688. None.
1689. William Ellery.
James Stevens.
1690. James Stevens.
William Sargent.
1691. William Sargent.
1692. William Haskell.
Wm. Stevens, June.
1693. James Stevens.
1694. Same.
1695 to 1699 inclusive,
James Davis.
1700. Thomas Riggs.
1701 to 1703. James Davis.
1704. Nathaniel Coit.
1705. Joseph Allen.
1706. Benjamin Haskell.
1707. Same.
1708. James Davis.
1709. Same.
1710. James Parsons.
1711. Same.
1712. Same.
1713. Same.
1714. Same.
1715. John Newman.
1716. Same.
1717. Same.
1718. Nathaniel Coit.
1719. Same.
1720. James Sayward.
1721. Samuel Stevens.
1722. Same.
1723. James Sayward.
1724. Same.
1725. Samuel Stevens.
1726. James Sayward.
1727. Same.
1728. Same.
1729. Samuel Sargent.
1730. Samuel Stevens.
1731. Same.
1732. Same.
1733. James Sayward.
1734. Joseph Allen.
1735. Same.
1736. William Haskell.
1737. Joseph Allen.
1738. Andrew Robinson.
1739. Same.
1740. Epes Sargent.
1741. James Davis.
1742. Same.
1743. Same.
1744. William Parsons.
1745. Same.
1746. Same.
1747. Same.
1748. James Davis.
1749. Joseph Allen.
1750. James Davis.
1751. William Parsons.
1752. James Davis.
1753. William Stevens.
1754. Same.
1755. William Parsons.
James Davis.
1756. William Stevens.
1757. Same.
1758. Same.
1759. Same.
1760. Same.
1761. Thos. Sanders, jun.
1762. Same.
1763. Same.

1764. Same.
1765. Thos. Sanders, jun.
Nathaniel Allen.
1766. Thos. Sanders, jun.
Nathaniel Allen.
1767. Thos. Sanders, jun.
1768. Same.
1769. Same.
1770. Same.
1771. Nathaniel Allen.
1772. Same.
1773. Same.
1774. Peter Coffin.
1775. Joseph Foster.
1776. Peter Coffin.
Samuel Whittemore.
William Ellery.
Daniel Rogers.
John Low.
1777. Peter Coffin.
John Low.
1778. Peter Coffin.
John Low.
1779. None.
1780. Peter Coffin.
1781. Peter Coffin.
John Low.
1782. Peter Coffin.
1783. Peter Coffin.
Samuel Whittemore.
1784. Joseph Foster.
1785. Joseph Foster.
1786. Joseph Foster.
1787. William Pearson.
1788. John Low.
William Pearson.
Winthrop Sargent.
Joseph Foster.
1789. William Pearson.
1790. William Pearson.
1791. William Pearson.
1792. William Pearson.
Peter Coffin.
1793. William Pearson.
1794. John Low.
1795. John Low.
1796. John Low.
John Rowe.
1797. John Rowe.
1798. Same.
1799. Same.
1800. Same.
1801. Same.
1802. Same.
1803. Daniel Rogers, jun.
1804. John Rowe.
1805. John Rowe.
1806. John Somes.
William Pearson.
Daniel Rogers, jun.
Caleb Norwood, jun.
Wm. Pearce, jun.
1807. Same.
1808. Benj. K. Hough.
Thomas Parsons.
Benjamin Webber.
John Somes, jun.
James Tappan.*
1809. Benj. K. Hough.
Lonson Nash.
John Manning.
John Somes, jun.
John Tucker.
Thomas Parsons.
1810. John Tucker.
Thomas Parsons.
John Manning.
James Tappan.
Robert Elwell, 3d.
John Johnston.†
1811. Same.
1812. John Tucker.
John Manning.
Robert Elwell, jun.
John Johnston.
William Dane.
Ebed Lincoln.‡
1813. John Tucker.
John Manning.
Benjamin Webber.
Jona. Kimball.§
James Appleton.
Daniel Rogers.
1814. John Tucker.
John Manning.
Jonathan Kimball.
Benjamin Webber.
James Appleton.
James Odell.‖
1815. John Tucker.
James Odell.
John Manning.
Benjamin Webber
James Hayes.¶
1816. Wm. W. Parrott.
1817. Same.
1818. Same.
1819. Same.
1820. Same.
1821. Same.
1822. Same.
1823. Winthrop Sargent.
1824. William Beach.
1825. William Beach.
1826. Elias Davison.**
Zach. Stevens.††
1827. Elias Davison.
Samuel Stevens.
1828. Elias Davison.
Samuel Lane.
1829. Same.
1830. Elias Davison.
Samuel Lane.
John Gott.
John W. Lowe.
Aaron Giddings.
1831. Elias Davison.
Samuel Giles.
John Gott.
John Johnston.
Ezra Leonard.
Solomon Pool.

---

* He was a native of New Hampshire, where in early life he taught a school, and had Daniel Webster for a pupil. He came to Gloucester when a young man, and engaged in teaching; but soon went into trade, and finally became a farmer. He died Feb. 6, 1853, aged eighty-five.

† He was born in Newburyport; came to Gloucester, and established himself as a baker. He died June 5, 1857, aged eighty.

‡ Mr. Lincoln was a mechanic, and died here about 1817.

§ Mr. Kimball was born in Ipswich. He came to Gloucester when a young man, and settled at Squam, where he died in July, 1820.

‖ The father of James Odell (also named James) came to Gloucester from Kittery, Me., about 1767. The son became a ship-master, and died in New Orleans.

¶ James Hayes was born in Waterford, Ireland. He came to Gloucester in early manhood, and engaged in mercantile pursuits. He was a prominent citizen many years. In old age, he removed to Charlestown, N.H.; where he died June 8, 1834, aged eighty-five.

** He belonged to a family of Davisons in Hampton, N.H.; but was born in Ipswich, Mass. He was a ship-master of Gloucester many years, and next a merchant in Charlestown, Mass., where he died May 7, 1842, aged sixty-seven.

†† Mr. Stevens was a native of Andover, but became a citizen of Gloucester in early life. It is said that he did not take his seat in the House. He died Aug. 29, 1847, aged eighty-four. His son (Joseph L.) graduated at Harvard College in 1810, and has been for many years a physician in Castine, Me. Samuel, another son, was representative in 1827. Joseph L., son of Dr. Joseph L. of Castine, was one of the delegates from Gloucester to the Constitutional Convention of 1853.

Aaron Plummer.
Wm. Procter, jun.
1832. James Goss.
Nehe. Knowlton.
Samuel Giles.
Samuel Lane.
Gorham Babson.
George Haskell.
Aaron Plummer.
Samuel Gilbert.
1833. John Wonson.
Aaron Plummer.
George Lane.
Josiah Griffin.
Theophilus Herrick.
Gideon Lane, jun.
Gorham Babson.
Aaron Day.
1834. John Wonson.
Aaron Day.
Gideon Lane, jun.
Theophilus Herrick.
Gorham Babson.
Josiah Griffin.
Jonathan Cutler.
John Blatchford.
1835. John Wonson.
John Blatchford.
Aaron Day.
David Saville.
Theophilus Herrick.
Jonathan Cutler.
James Harris.
Robert Rantoul, jun.
Timothy R. Davis.
1836. Timothy R. Davis.
John Davis.
James Harris.
Thomas Haskell.
Luther Hamilton.
Robert Rantoul, jun.
David Saville.
Addison Gilbert.
David White.
1837. Epes Ellery.
John Davis.
Robert Rantoul, jun.
Eleazar Boynton.
David White.
Theophilus Herrick.
Addison Gilbert.
Oliver W. Sargent.
David Donnahew.
1838. Robert Rantoul, jun.
David White.
Oliver W. Sargent.
Eleazar Boynton.
Wm. B. Haskins.
Silas Bray.
1839. Samuel L. Andrews.
R. G. Stanwood, jun.
Joseph J. Procter.
Chris. G. Sargent.
Alexander P. Davis.
1840. Daniel D. Hartley.
Simeon Burnham.
Henry Sanders.
Daniel Robinson.
Wm. B. Haskins.
1841. Wm. Parsons, jun.
George W. Pearce.
William Davis.
1842. Wm. Parsons, jun.
1843. Simeon Burnham.
Henry Sanders.
Elbridge Day.
1844. Jona. Burnham, jun.
Elbridge Day.
Silas Bray.
1845. No choice.
1846. Bartholomew Ring.
George Perkins.
Moses Gilbert.
1847. Bartholomew Ring.
1848. No choice.
1849. Joseph Friend.
Simon P. Burnham.
David Chard.
Bartholomew Ring.
1850. William Babson.
David Chard.
1851. Jeremiah R. Cook.
Wm. H. Haskell.
1852. Jeremiah R. Cook.
Jacob Bacon.
1853. David H. Plumb.
John W. Haskell.
1854. No choice.
1855. Chas. C. Pettingell.
John S. Webber.
1856. Jeremiah R. Cook.
Edward H. Pearce.
1857. John S. Webber.
George Norwood.
1858. Edward H. Pearce.
Fitz. J. Babson.
1859. Jeremiah R. Cook.
John J. Babson.
1860. Fitz. J. Babson.
John J. Babson.

REPRESENTATIVES FROM ROCKPORT.

1841. James P. Tarr.
1842. None.
1843. Thos. O. Marshall.
1844. William Grover.
1845. William Grover.
1846 to 1850 inclusive, none.
1851. Addison Gott.
1852. Newell Burnham.
1853 and 1854. None.
1855. Benj. Parsons, jun.
1856. Samuel York.
1857. Thomas Hale.
1858. Wm. W. Marshall.
1859. Henry T. Lowe.
1860. John D. Sanborn.

DELEGATES TO STATE CONVENTIONS.

1779. — *To Convention for forming State Constitution.*

Winthrop Sargent. Joseph Foster. Peter Coffin. Samuel Whittemore. Epes Sargent.

1788. — *To Convention for ratifying the Federal Constitution.*

Daniel Rogers. John Low. William Pearson.

1820. — *To Convention for revising State Constitution.*

William Pearce. John Kittredge. William W. Parrott. Nehemiah Knowlton.* William Beach. Elias Davison.

1853. — *Convention for revising State Constitution.*

Eben H. Stacy. Joseph L. Stevens, jun.

* He was born in Hamilton; was for many years a resident of Sandy Bay, and took an active part in town-affairs. He was a representative in 1831; and died Nov. 25, 1847, aged seventy-two.

V. — Page 393.

ROLLS OF GLOUCESTER COMPANIES AT THE BATTLE OF BUNKER HILL.

Capt. Warner's Company.

Nathaniel Warner, captain.
John Burnham, lieutenant.
Daniel Collins, ensign.
Jona. Woodman, sergeant.
William Kinsman, „
Alex. Parran, „
Jarus Lincoln, „
Richard Simson, corporal.
Nathan Glover, „
Jonathan Butler, „
Nymphas Stacy, „
John Warner, fifer.
Jonathan Somes.
Andrew Kelcy.
Nathaniel Bennett.
Moses Ring.
Daniel Callahan.
Benjamin Clark.
Andrew Bray.
Josiah Brown.
Levi Lane.
Moses Bennett.
James Preastly.
Josiah Burk.
Benjamin Smith.
Vinson Elwell.
William Averill.
Robert Callaghan.
Thomas Ayres.
David Row.
Benjamin Webber.
Samuel Marshall.
Josiah Ingersol.
Joshua Day.
Joshua Polen.
Zerubbabel Allen.
Isaac Bray.
Larrey Trejay.
Solomon Parsons.
John Andress.
William Segurs.
William Grimes.
Aaron Stevens.
Peter Seavery.
Jeremiah Burnham.
John Chaplen.
William Grover.
Thomas Millett.
Joseph Somes.
Ezekiel Woodward.
Eliphalet Wharf.
Ebenezer Tarbox.
Jonathan Pike.
Ebenezer Goslen.*
William Johnson.
Nathan Brown.
Joseph Howard.
Lemuel Collins.

Capt. Rowe's Company.

John Row, captain.
Mark Pool, lieutenant.
Eben. Cleaveland, ensign.
Danl. Barber Tarr, sergt.
William Haskins, „
William Davison,† „
William Foster, „
Jonathan Row, corporal.
Thomas Finson, „
John Gott, „
William Low, „
Benj. Davis, drummer.
Isaac Haskell, fifer.
Jacob Allen.
Obadiah Atkins.
David Averill.
Eleazer Butman.
Daniel Butler.
David Crage.
Henry Clark.
Daniel Doyl.
Dominicus Davis.
Samuel Clark.
Joseph Dresser.
Richard Dresser.
Thomas Dresser.
Caleb Elwell.
James Phips.
Ebenezer Gott.
Joshua Gore.
Bennet Haskins.
William Jumper.
John Clark.
Joseph Lane.
James Lurvey.
Francis Lane.
Samuel Low.
Henry Morgan.
Henry Parsons.
Hugh Parkhurst.
Joseph Parsons.
Jeffrey Parsons.
John Row, jun.
Joshua Row.
Peter Richardson.
William Row.
Daniel Somes.
John Smith.
Ephraim Sheldren.
John Tarr.
John Tarr, jun.
Jabez Tarr.
James Tarr.
William Woodbury.
Ebenezer Witham.
Spencer Thomas.
Jonathan Parsons.
Peter Emmons.
Thomas Edes.
John Youlin.
John Parrot.
Joseph Low.
Aaron Riggs.
Francis Pool.
Josiah Brooks.
William Parsons.

---

* Ebenezer Joslyn is the true name, without doubt.

† So in a roll at the State House. In a return of the company, in my possession, the name of this sergeant is William Aquart; the same as given to me by Jabez Tarr, the last survivor of the company.

VI. — Page 575.

LIST OF VESSELS BELONGING TO THE TOWN,

Lost since January, 1829, in which a portion or the whole of the crew have perished. It is taken from a list of marine disasters, carefully prepared by the editor of the "Gloucester Telegraph," and published in his paper, June 1, 1859: —

Vessel's Name.	Master's Name.	When Lost.	How or where Lost.	Men Lost.
Lucinda.	Hammond.	1829.	Lobos Islands.	1
Olive.	Doyle.	Aug. 1830.	Fishing.	7
Essex.	Underwood.	" 1834.	N.Y. to Pt. Cabello.	
Vesta.	Fears.	Apr. 1837.	Fishing.	7
B. Franklin.	Norwood.	" "	"	7
Fair American.	Wonson.	" "	"	7
Martha.	Boyd.	Dec. 1838.	Mass. Bay.	4
Sevo.	Barter.	" 1839.	Run down.	4
Ida.	Rowe.	Mar. 1840.	Fishing.	6
Forest.	Rich.	Oct. 1841.	Cape Cod.	8
Byron.	Watson.	Aug. 1843.	Fishing.	10
Confidence.	Wonson.	Feb. 1844.	"	7
Paris.	Parkhurst.	Mar. 1845.	"	8
Gen. Scott.	Bowdoin.	Nov. 1846.	"	8
Canton.	Norwood.	" "	"	7
L. Woodbury.	Fears.	Oct. 1849.	"	10
Wm. Wallace.	Griffin.	Feb. 1850.	"	8
Tuscany.	Pew.	Mar. "	"	8
Walter Scott.	Hibbert.	April, "	"	8
Specie.	Tarr.	April, "	"	7
Flirt.	Stubbs.	Oct. 1851.	Bay St. Lawrence.	14
Princeton.	Guard.	" "	Fishing.	10
Ocean Queen.	Spinney.	Nov. "	"	8
Golden Fleece.	Rust.	Mar. 1852.	"	9
C. E. Parkhurst.	Turner.	" "	"	8
B. Parsons.	Tibbetts.	April, "	"	7
Napoleon.	Parsons.	April, "	"	8
H. A. Holbrook.	Remby.	Nov. "	"	8
Flight.	Willis.	Feb. 1854.	"	12
L. Pulcifer.	M'Donald.	Mar. "	"	9
Gold-Hunter.	M'Intire.	Feb. "	Freighting.	5
Reporter.	Bearse.	Mar. 1855.	Fishing.	8
A. L. Colby.	Brown.	" "	"	8
Bessie Neal.	Herrick.	1855.	From P.E. Island.	5
Kossuth.		Aug. 1856.		2
Oolong.	Kendall.	Feb. 1857.	Fishing.	9
Alexandria.	Miller.	Feb. 1858.	From Newfoundld.	6
J. Franklin.	M'Donald.	Dec. "	From P.E. Island.	6*
Village Belle.	Harvey.	Nov. "	Passage from Bay.	10*
Queen of Clippers.	Stoddard.	Jan. 1859.	To Newfoundland.	6
Young America.	Lord.	Mar. "	Fishing.	8
G. T. Powers.	Powers.	April, "	"	8
C. E. Grover.	Gould.	" "	"	9

* On board of these vessels, there were also passengers; making the whole number of persons lost three hundred and thirty-six. To this sad list, five vessels have already been added in the present year.

VII. — Page 576.

STATISTICS RELATING TO THE FISHERIES.

Statement of the mackerel packed in Gloucester in each year, from 1808 to 1829 inclusive: —

Year	Barrels	Year	Barrels	Year	Barrels
1808	238	1816	123	1824	6,303
1809	46	1817	115	1825	9,359
1810	none	1818	154	1826	11,668
1811	6	1819	109	1827	16,288
1812	none	1820	217	1828	34,203
1813	91	1821	2,176	1829	37,688
1814	none	1822	2,804		
1815	72	1823	3,590		

Statement showing the amount of enrolled and licensed tonnage of the district of Gloucester, the number of barrels of mackerel packed in town and the price of the different numbers, and the price of codfish, in the first week of September in each year, from 1830 to 1859 inclusive: —

	Tonnage.	No. bbls. Mackerel packed.	Price of Mackerel per Barrel.			Price of Codfish per Quintal.
			No. 1.	No. 2.	No. 3.	
1830	9,643	51,618	5.00	4.50	2.62	2.12
1831	10,076	69,759	5.75	4.75	2.62	2.50
1832	9,960	40,674	5.00	4.00	2.75	2.58
1833	11,247	45,529	5.72	4.72	2.85	2.46
1834	11,943	61,319	5.72	4.72	3.35	2.00
1835	13,540	48,539	7.00	6.00	4.00	2.63
1836	14,729	43,987	9.00	8.00	5.00	3.00
1837	16,876	33,274	7.75	6.50	4.12	2.67
1838	16,265	24,232	11.00	9.25	5.50	3.25
1839	15,458	10,241	12.50	10.50	7.00	3.50
1840	14,770	8,870	12.75	10.50	5.50	2.25
1841	14,393	8,559	12.00	10.00	6.00	2.37
1842	13,029	15,335	9.00	6.00	4.00	2.37
1843	12,799	16,328	10.12	8.12	6.00	2.75
1844	13,162	17,455	9.50	7.50	5.50	2.17
1845	14,749	48,711	13.00	10.50	6.87	2.25
1846	15,927	41,513	9.12	6.25	3.87	2.56
1847	16,532	40,006	12.75	8.25	4.25	3.12
1848	18,825	53,500	9.00	6.00	3.37	2.25
1849	18,164	45,579	12.00	7.00	3.50	2.12
1850	19,601	49,993	10.12	8.12	5.00	2.37
1851	21,610	81,627	10.00	6.50	5.12	2.75
1852	23,941	48,012	9.00	7.00	5.75	3.25
1853	27,689	36,196	11.50	9.50	7.50	3.00
1854	29,765	43,201	15.00	12.25	5.00	3.50
1855	30,304	73,102	19.00	11.00	6.25	3.25
1856	25,950	66,529	13.00	8.00	6.00	3.50
1857	26,171	67,311	15.00	12.50	8.50	3.75
1858	30,426	56,489	15.50	12.50	8.50	3.50
1859	32,359	59,664	14.50	12.50	8.50	3.75

Statement of the fisheries of the district of Gloucester for the year 1847, collected by Mr. Addison Winter, and kindly furnished by him for publication in this work. This is, without doubt, the most complete and reliable account of this business, for a single year, which has ever been published. It does not, however, include the winter wherry-fishing.

Whole number of vessels, two hundred and eighty-seven, of an aggregate tonnage of twelve thousand three hundred and fifty-four tons, employing one thousand six hundred and eighty-one men and one hundred and eighty-six boys, and producing as follows: —

7,088,876 lbs. of codfish, of the value of	$181,703
3,879,776 lbs. of halibut, of the value of	70,761
735,506 lbs. of hake, of the value of	12,174
919,188 lbs. of pollock, of the value of	16,556
46,779 bbls. of mackerel, of the value of	290,055
337½ bbls. of tongues and sounds	1,873
39,520 gallons of oil	16,232
	$589,354

Classification of the Vessels according to Tonnage.

Under 10 tons.	10 tons to 20 tons.	20 tons to 30 tons.	30 tons to 40 tons.	40 tons to 50 tons.	50 tons to 60 tons.	60 tons to 70 tons.	70 tons and upwards.	Total.
28	27	29	42	26	49	73	13	287

STATEMENT OF THE GLOUCESTER FISHERIES FOR THE YEAR 1859.

The whole number of schooners, twenty tons and upwards, belonging to Gloucester Harbor in July, 1859, was three hundred and twenty-two; measuring in the aggregate twenty-three thousand eight hundred and eighty-two tons. Of this number, three hundred and one, manned by three thousand four hundred and thirty-four men and one hundred and thirty-four boys, were employed in fishing. So much we learn from a statement published in the "Gloucester Telegraph." The product of the fishery for that year, as nearly as can be ascertained, is here given: —

59,664⅝ bbls. mackerel	$705,833
114,047 quintals codfish	416,271
4,500,000 lbs. halibut	135,000
1,400 bbls. oil	19,600
	$1,276,704

If to this aggregate we add the product of the herring voyages to Newfoundland, and that of the business carried on at Squam and Lane's Cove, not included in the above items, we shall find the total product of the fisheries of Gloucester for 1859 not less than one million four hundred thousand dollars.

The quantity of halibut given is an estimate founded upon information obtained from persons in the business, and is believed to be under rather than over estimated. The number of pounds of this fish sold in town last year to be dried and smoked is known to have been about a million and a half.

VIII.

COLLECTORS OF THE CUSTOMS FOR THE DISTRICT OF GLOUCESTER.

Epes Sargent	1789	George W. Pearce	1841
William Tuck	1796	Eben H. Stacy.	1843
John Gibaut	1802	Eli F. Stacy	1844
John Kittredge	1805	John L. Rogers	1849
William Pearce, jun.	1822	Frederick G. Low	1849
William Beach	1829	William H. Manning	1853
George D. Hale	1839	Gorham Babson	1858

POSTMASTERS OF GLOUCESTER.

Henry Phelps, probably appointed in 1792.
Isaac Elwell, appointed March 8, 1809.
William Stevens, Aug. 2, 1820.
Leonard J. Presson, Nov. 22, 1834.
Gorham Parsons, Feb. 20, 1839.
T. S. Lancaster, June 22, 1849.
O. A. Merrill, May 23, 1853.
Gorham Parsons, Aug. 17, 1853.
John W. Wonson, June 14, 1858.

INDEX.

INDEX.

D.

E.

F.

G.

H.

ERRATA.

Page 11, line 16, for "Thatcher's" read "Thacher's."
" 11, " 36, for "Petter" read "Peter."
" 15, " 37, note, for "Well's" read "Wells."
" 19, note, for xxi. read xxxi.
" 53, line 9, for "Rouse" read "Rowse."
" 54, " 17, for "Thomas" read "John."
" 64, " 11, for "1858" read "1658."
" 79, " 27, for "John Joseph" read "Joseph."
" 235, " 31 and 33, for "Starknought" read "Starknaught."
" 488, " 6, for "Fourth" read "Third."

On page 54, Richard Tarr's name should be added to the list of settlers.

On page 114, Col. John Low is erroneously stated, on the authority of Rev. Eli Forbes's sermon, preached at his funeral, to have been "a delegate to the Convention for forming the State Constitution." Col. Low was a representative in 1777; and, as such, probably helped to make the State Constitution mentioned on page 415.